Florida's Frontiers

A History of the Trans-Appalachian Frontier

Walter Nugent and Malcolm Rohrbough, general editors

Andrew L. Cayton. *Frontier Indiana*

R. Douglas Hurt. *The Ohio Frontier:
Crucible of the Old Northwest, 1720–1830*

Mark Wyman. *The Wisconsin Frontier*

James E. Davis. *Frontier Illinois*

John R. Finger. *Tennessee Frontiers*

Florida's Frontiers

PAUL E. HOFFMAN

INDIANA UNIVERSITY PRESS   BLOOMINGTON & INDIANAPOLIS

This book is a publication of
Indiana University Press
601 North Morton Street
Bloomington, Indiana 47404-3797 USA

http://iupress.indiana.edu
Telephone orders   800-842-6796
Fax orders   812-855-7931
Orders by e-mail   iuporder@indiana.edu

The paper used in this publication meets the minimum
requirements of American National Standard for Information
Sciences—Permanence of Paper for Printed Library
Materials, ANSI Z39.48-1984.

Manufactured in the United States of America

Library of Congress Cataloging-in-Publication Data

Hoffman, Paul E., date
    Florida's frontiers / Paul E. Hoffman.
        p. cm. — (A history of the trans-appalachian frontier)
Includes bibliographical references and index.
    ISBN 0-253-34019-5
    1. Florida—History—To 1821. 2. Florida—History—1821–1865.
3. Florida—Ethnic relations. 4. Frontier and pioneer life—Florida.
5. Human geography—Florida.   I. Title. II. Series.
    F314 .H75 2002
    975.9—dc21
                                                            2001002831

1   2   3   4   5   07   06   05   04   03   02

Contents

⊱ Figures

⮞ Tables

Foreword

For most Americans "the West" refers to the western half of the nation. From the Great Plains across the Rockies and the intermontane plateaus to the Pacific Ocean, "the American West" conjures up a flood of popular images: trappers, cowboys, miners, and homesteading families; the Marlboro man and country-western music. This has been the West since the California Gold Rush and the migration of '49ers propelled the region into the national consciousness.

But it was not always so. There was an earlier American West, no less vivid and no less dramatic. Here the fabled figures were not John Charles Frémont and Geronimo, but Daniel Boone and Tecumseh; not Calamity Jane and "Buffalo Bill" Cody, but Rachel Jackson and Davy Crockett. Geographically, this earlier West extended from the crest of the Appalachian Mountains to the Mississippi River, from the border with Canada to the Gulf of Mexico. It was the West of Euro-American expansion from before the American Revolution until the middle of the nineteenth century, when the line of frontier settlement moved through the first West toward that new, farther West.

Initially the story of the first American West involved two sets of characters: first, the white people of European origin, and south of the Ohio River, African-American slaves, who were spreading relentlessly westward; second, the original settlers, the Native Americans, who retreated grudgingly before the flood. The first Europeans, French and Spanish, appeared on this landscape in the 1600s and early 1700s, and their interactions with the original native peoples involved both cooperation and conflict. The English arrived a half-century later. The Europeans were almost always a minority in number, so they and the Indians sought neither conquest nor annihilation, but mutual accommodation, joint occupation of the land and joint use of its resources. The system of contact allowed both sides to survive and even to bene-fit from one another's presence. Trade developed and intermar-riage followed, and so did misunderstandings and violence. Still, a delicate balance supported by mutual interests often character-ized relations among Europeans and native peoples.

When Anglo-Americans began moving through the Cumber-land Gap from Virginia into what hunters called the Kentucky country in the 1750s, they soon tilted the balance between the two cultures, occupying large portions of Kentucky and pressing against native groups from Ohio south to Georgia. By 1780, the Anglo-Americans had also occupied the former French settle-ments of Cahokia in Illinois and Vincennes in Indiana. Despite strong resistance by several native groups, the seemingly unend-ing reinforcements of white families made the Euro-Americans' gradual occupation of the trans-Appalachian frontier inevitable.

In the 1780s the infant American government issued ordi-nances spelling out how the land between the Great Lakes and the Ohio River was to be acquired from the native peoples, sub-divided, and sold to the citizens of the new republic. The new residents of that region could establish a form of government or-ganization that would lead to statehood and equal membership in the union. A parallel process was soon set up for Kentucky, Tennessee, and the lands south to the Gulf.

In the 1830s and the 1840s, the remaining native groups east of the Mississippi were removed to the West. The expansion of settlement into the trans-Appalachian frontier could now con-tinue unchecked into Illinois, Wisconsin, Michigan, and the great cotton lands and hill country of Alabama, Mississippi, and Flor-ida. The frontier period had been completed—as early as the 1820s in Kentucky, and within the next twenty years throughout much of the Old Northwest and Old Southwest.

In brief terms, this is the story of the trans-Appalachian fron-tier. Over scarcely three generations, the trickle of settler families across the mountains had become a flood; four million people, both white and black, had settled in the frontier regions. Begin-ning with Kentucky in 1792 and running through Florida in 1845 and Wisconsin in 1848, a dozen new states had entered the American union. Each territory and state had its own story, and it is appropriate that each will have a separate volume in this series. The variations are broad. Florida's first European arrived in 1513, and this future state was a frontier for Spain and the United States for over 350 years. Missouri had a long French and Spanish history before the arrival of American settlers, but Kentucky and Ohio did not; Americans in large numbers came quickly to the latter states through the Cumberland Gap.

The opening and closing of the settlement frontier is the subject of these volumes. Each begins with the world that existed when Europeans first made contact with native peoples. Each describes and analyzes the themes associated with the special circumstances of the individual territory or state. And each concludes with the closing of the frontier.

The editors of the series have selected authors who have strong reputations as scholars and interpreters of their individual territories and states. We believe that you will find this history informative and lively, and we are confident that you will enjoy this and other volumes in the trans-Appalachian frontier series.

Paul Hoffman's history of early Florida properly speaks of Florida's *frontiers*, in the plural, because in reality the state had several frontiers. First explored and colonized by Spain, it was part of the Spanish colonial empire from 1513 to 1763. The British, from nearby South Carolina, threatened it for decades; finally they managed to capture it. Florida then reverted to Spain from 1783 to 1810–1813 (West Florida, now the Panhandle), and 1819 (East Florida, the peninsula), for yet another frontier period. The United States acquired it in three pieces (by occupation in 1810 and 1813 and by treaty in 1819). From that point on, its true American frontier period revealed itself. Most of Florida's history prior to statehood in 1845 therefore happened under Spanish auspices, and most of that is unfamiliar to American readers. The author, who is well known for his many writings on Spanish colonial Florida, therefore devotes several chapters to the pre-British, pre-American phase of Florida's history. But as you will discover, he explains the later phases equally well.

Since the Appalachians do not reach Florida, and since it is therefore not precisely part of Trans-Appalachia, you may ask why this series includes a volume on what is now the Sunshine State. One reason is timing. The processes of settlement and development taking place in the early nineteenth century from Kentucky, Tennessee, and Ohio to the future states bordering the Mississippi were also happening in Florida, though with its own peculiar past and amidst its own subtropical climate. Another reason is inclusiveness. The editors believe that although geographical precision excludes it from Trans-Appalachia, the present and future importance of Florida requires that it be included in this series on the early national period in our history. It simply cannot be left out.

Paul Hoffman's book will enlighten and entertain you. All the players are here—the Native Americans, several groups of them; the first Spanish under Ponce de Leon (who treated the Indians worse here, perhaps, than almost anywhere); missionaries, soldiers, and settlers, men and women, during the Spanish period; the British; the American military, preeminently under Andrew Jackson, and the diplomats, including John Quincy Adams, who sealed the deal with Spain; the "maroons," or self-emancipated slaves from Georgia who migrated to Florida's freedom; and many others. Florida had a long and eventful history before statehood was ever dreamt of. That history will unfold before you in the following pages.

WALTER NUGENT
University of Notre Dame

MALCOLM ROHRBOUGH
University of Iowa

Preface

Florida has had many frontiers. Imagination, greed, missionary zeal, disease, war, and diplomacy have shaped its historical
boundaries. Bodies of water, soils and their associated floral and
faunal ecology, the patterns of Native American occupation, and
ways of colonizing have defined where the various Old and New
World peoples who have invaded Florida since 1500 settled. These
same factors influenced the degree to which each group pros-
pered as each successively built its own frontier or frontiers, often upon the remains of its predecessors' efforts. This book seeks
to tell the story of those multiple frontiers and how they were
shaped by natural facts and human actors during the nearly
three centuries from 1565 to 1860.

A work of this scope is necessarily built upon the labors of
others, although part of it reflects original research in Spanish
archival documents. Some readers will not find their favorite authors cited in the notes, but I hope that I have found and used
the essential secondary literature. I know too well that there are
many more articles and even a few other books than those I cite.
Limited time and resources have kept me from examining that
literature or the even more compelling archival materials for the
post-1700 period. Thus I ask my readers to accept this work as a
beginning and overview, one that I hope will suggest avenues of
research that others will follow.

I owe many debts. The scholars whose works I cite herein head
the list. Without their labors, much of this work could not have
been written. Walter Nugent and Malcolm Rohrbough and the
good folks at Indiana University Press have been patient with a
project that took far longer than any of us expected and have
provided encouragement and good editing. The staff of the P. K.

Yonge Library of Florida History at the University of Florida, and particularly Bruce Chappel, opened their rich collection to me in the fall of 1994. The Interlibrary Borrowing staff at Louisiana State University Libraries did their usual excellent job in bringing materials to my desk when the duties of academic life prevented travel to distant libraries. Jeannine Cook, William "Bill" Davidson, G. Douglas Inglis, and Elaine Smyth helped me to acquire some of the illustrations. Drs. David W. Stahle and Malcolm K. Cleaveland of the Tree-Ring Laboratory of the University of Arkansas generously shared their rainfall data for North and South Carolina and Georgia. Drs. Amy Turner Bushnell, Rebecca Saunders, and Jane Landers read parts of the work and made helpful suggestions, but bear no responsibility for what I did, or did not do, with them. LSU's Council on Research supported my sabbatical in Gainesville in the fall of 1994. To each I give my thanks, but especially to Barbara and "Taz," my feline "muse" and desk companion. This book is dedicated to Lyle N. "MAC" McAlister in thanks for his being such an excellent teacher, friend, and example of the scholar.

Abbreviations

AGI   Archivo General de Indias, Seville
        CD   Contaduría
        CT   Contratación
        EC   Escribanía de Cámera
        IG   Indiferente General
        JU   Justicia
        MEX   Mexico
        PAT   Patronato
        SD   Santo Domingo
FHQ   *Florida Historical Quarterly*
SLGF   *Spanish Land Grants in Florida.* Prepared by the Historical
        Records Survey, Division of Professional and Service Proj-
        ects, Work Projects Administration. Tallahassee, FL:
        State Library Board, 1940. 5 vols.
        Data Base   Confirmed Land Grants, organized by year of
        original grant, collection of the author.
Lockey   Joseph B. Lockey Collection, the Library of Congress.
JTC#   Library of Congress, Jeannette Thurber Connor Papers, Mi-
        crofilm. Reel Numbers.
NASP   *New American State Papers.* Wilmington, DE: Scholarly Re-
        sources, 1972.
SM   Su Magestad (Your Majesty). i.e., the King of Spain.
Stetson   John B. Stetson collection of photostats.

Florida's Frontiers

I.

THE SECRETS OF THE LAND

Florida has experienced five frontiers since 1492. The first, a tidewater frontier that embraced the Atlantic coast of much of the Southeast, was created when Pedro Menéndez de Avilés founded St. Augustine in 1565, two generations after Licenciado Lucas Vázquez de Ayllón's pioneering colony had failed in 1526. The last, the American frontier that opened in 1821 when the United States annexed the area of the present state of Florida, closed in 1860 when the federal range and township surveys reached the edges of the Everglades. To be sure, frontier conditions continued to exist after 1860 in isolated areas, but in the main the peninsula had been brought under the various forms of control that nineteenth-century Americans defined as "civilization." The Native Americans who had populated and then repopulated the peninsula were gone, save for a few small remnants living deep in the region of the Everglades. Euro-Americans, along with their Black slaves, their livestock, and their crops, dominated the land.

Some of the survivors of Ayllón's colony anticipated such an outcome, if under different auspices and in a different part of the vast area that the Spaniards called *La Florida*. According to the Spanish historian Gonzalo Fernández de Oviedo, "with all that they had suffered, some praised the nature of the region that they had seen, and said that taking the form that is required for settling in that part [of the world], and enough food until the land is discovered and understood, could not fail to be a good thing because the nature of it is more appropriate for Spaniards [than the Caribbean's tropical areas]."[1]

Discovering and understanding the secrets of the land and its Native American inhabitants proved to be the work of many generations of Spaniards and Anglo-Americans. In the end, they, like the Native Americans, were constrained by a geography that limited the better soils and floral and faunal resources to a few places. We begin with a consideration of these resources and of the Native American presence in that part of the Southeast that the Spaniards called *La Florida*.

Physical Geography

Pedro Menéndez de Avilés and the royal cosmographer Juan López de Velasco had no doubts during the last decades of the sixteenth century that the province of La Florida encompassed the eastern half of North America from the cod fisheries of Nova Scotia in the northeast to the Mexican mines at Santa Barbara in the southwest. A royal decree of 1573 temporarily fixed that southwestern boundary at the Río de las Palmas, the modern Soto la Marina River. The province's northwestern boundary was the arm of the Pacific Ocean that Menéndez de Avilés, in common with some other men of his time, imagined ran across the continent north of New Mexico to within 250 miles or so of the Atlantic coast. La Florida's western limit was New Mexico.[2]

This definition of the province of La Florida was more theoretical than factual. In practice, the sixteenth-century Spanish definition of La Florida roughly encompassed the coastal and piedmont zones of the modern states of Virginia, North and South Carolina and Georgia; the Appalachian Mountains in North Carolina and southeastern Tennessee; parts of eastern Alabama; and Florida east of the Apalachicola River. The first two Florida frontiers were developed on that stage from 1565 to approximately the year 1680. Yet well before Spain recognized the

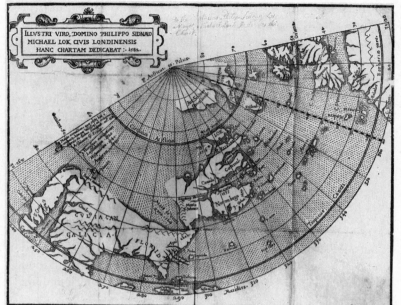

Figure 1.1. Michael Lok, North America, Printed, 1582.
COURTESY OF THE JOHN CARTER BROWN LIBRARY AT BROWN
UNIVERSITY.

English possession of Virginia and most of the Carolinas in the
Treaty of Madrid of 1670, La Florida had come to mean only the
coastal plain south of the Edisto River in South Carolina, Florida
east of the Apalachicola River and, less certainly, the Chattahoochee and Flint river valleys. By 1714, the term meant only the
area of the current state of the same name and sometimes only
northeast Florida. On that much reduced stage, the Spaniards
and then the British and later the Anglo-Americans developed
yet other frontiers.

Understanding, then, that the Florida of our title has varied
in size over time, we can see that initially it embraced most of the
eastern portions of the Southeast. As some of Ayllón's survivors
envisioned, the discovery and understanding of the area's natural
and human resources were the prerequisites if the Spaniards (or
any other old-world peoples) were to settle the land.

To untutored eyes, such as those of the Spanish and French

mariners who first viewed these shores, the Southeast appeared to be an almost unbroken sea of trees from Chesapeake Bay to eastern Texas. From the ocean's shore to a point well inland, the forest appeared to consist almost entirely of pine trees (slash and some long-leaf), although hardwood species were present along streams and rivers. Further inland, the great stands of long-leaf pine trees marked the edge of the piedmont in Georgia and the Carolinas and the northern highlands in Florida. As the traveler Basil Hall, who visited the South in 1827–1828, wrote:

> For five hundred miles, at least, we traveled in different paths of the South, over a countryside of this description, almost everywhere consisting of sand, feebly held together by a short wiry grass, shaded by the endless forest. . . . millions upon millions of tall and slender columns, growing up in solitude, not crowded upon one another, but gradually appearing to come closer and closer, until they formed a compact mass, beyond which nothing was to be seen.[3]

These expanses of pines eventually gave way to the oak-pine-hickory forests covering the piedmont, which in turn yielded to the oak-chestnut-hickory-elm hardwoods on some slopes of the Appalachian mountains.[4]

This seeming uniformity was and is an illusion. Each band of forest is actually composed of many floristic communities, as the early spring flowering and leafing out of deciduous species makes clear. Within communities are mosaics of stands of trees and other plants of varying ages and species. Soils, drainage, temperatures, and rainfall create this diversity. In addition, changes are produced by lightning and its resulting fires, pine bark beetles, and cycles in weather patterns. Human manipulation of the forest alters the environment through the acts of clearing and burning.[5] Moreover, this diversity is dynamic, changing over time in response to the factors just noted. Associated with this floral diversity is a faunal diversity, although most of the species are too small to have food value for humans.

The diversity of soils under this floral exuberance arises from the area's geologic history.[6] Geologists have identified at least a dozen step-like "terraces" on the lower (or outer), middle, and upper (or inner) sections of the coastal plain (from sea level to

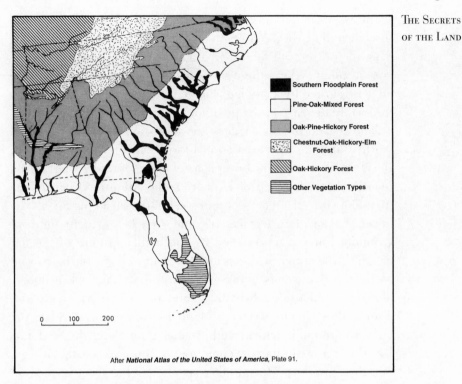

Southern Floodplain Forest

Pine-Oak-Mixed Forest

Oak-Pine-Hickory Forest

Chestnut-Oak-Hickory-Elm
Forest

Oak-Hickory Forest

Other Vegetation Types

0   100   200

After *National Atlas of the United States of America*, Plate 91.

Figure 1.2. Major southern forests. BASED ON *The National Atlas of the United States of America* (1966), PLATE 91, A. W. KÜCHLER, "POTENTIAL NATURAL VEGETATION."

about one hundred meters). Each terrace seems to be associated with a change in the level of the Atlantic Ocean and the warping of the North American plate. Each was once a back barrier marsh surface, bay bottom, or area of alluvial deposition, now often overlaid by other deposits. Inland swamps, marshes, and low areas that flood during the rainy season reflect this history, as do the soils on the terraces. Terrace soils, though highly variable, are mostly acidic, sandy soils of generally low fertility and high moisture content, at least during the rainy season. On the lower coastal plain they are white and yellow, on the middle red-yellow, and on the upper plain red-yellow or grey-brown in color.[7] Terrace edges are sometimes marked by low sand hills which are the remnants of sand dunes, spits, and other coastal features. Although most such bands of sandhills are narrow and discontinuous, they can reach a width of up to ten miles, as for example on the fall line in Georgia, at the western edge of the coastal plain. Where these sandhills are not present, the terrace edge is marked by a sudden change in elevation or scarp. This is uniformly the case in the piedmont.[8]

The coastal plain's terraces are most obvious in Virginia and North Carolina, and least so in Florida. In Florida only five of the eight terraces of the lower coastal plain tentatively have been identified for the strip of land from the Atlantic Ocean to the fifty-foot (fifteen-meter) contour west of the St. Johns River. The lower coastal plain terraces become even less evident south of Orlando, but are represented by the higher ground of the flat woods of the upper St. Johns and Kissimmee River basins as well as by the flat woods between Sebring and Lake Okeechobee, along the Caloosahatchee River, and between Fort Myers and Tampa Bay. On the western side of Florida's central ridge, the terraces are more evident and broader than along the St. Johns River, but are still narrow compared to those of coastal Georgia and the Carolinas. The middle coastal plain has three terraces in Virginia and North Carolina, four in South Carolina and Florida (east of the Haines City Ridge in central Florida and west of the Trail Ridge feature of northern Florida and southern Georgia), but only two in Georgia in a small area near the Savannah River. The upper coastal plain is found mostly in Virginia and the Carolinas, although some of the highest elevations of Florida's central ridge seem to be related to it.[9]

The natural climax forest of the coastal plain varies. On the lower coastal plain it is thought to be an oak-hickory forest on higher ground with pines on the dry sandhills. However, until recently, frequent fires maintained a pine subclimax over much of the area but with hardwood forests in the riverine and swamp bottomlands. At the higher elevations of the upper coastal plain, the predominately pine forests give way to the oak-pine forest of the piedmont. Along the coasts and on the barrier islands, and in southern Florida on higher ground (called hammocks), live oaks (*Quercus virginiana*) are the dominant trees. North of Flor-

Figure 1.3. Physiographic map of La Florida. A SECTION
OF ERWIN RAISZ, "MAP OF THE LANDFORMS OF THE UNITED STATES,"
© 1957. REPRINTED BY PERMISSION OF RAISZ LANDFORM MAPS,
BROOKLINE, MA. 1-800-227-0047.

ida, on bluff and ravine slopes along rivers, beech and magnolia trees dominate in mixed hardwood forests.[10]

The pine forests of the lower and middle coastal plain seem to have supported limited faunal life before modern times. Where the tree canopy is not too dense, the predominately slash pine flatwoods have understories of berry-bearing scrubs (especially of the Ilex family), cane, and saw palmettos (*Serenoa repens*) that provide a little browse for deer, turkeys, and some other species as well as habitat for reptiles. In slightly higher and drier areas, mostly long-leaf pine savannahs were marked by wire grass or bluestem or other grasses and forbes (according to soil, rainfall, and fire conditions) that provided poor, mostly spring browse. The dry, scrub-oak and long-leaf pine forests on the sandhills that mark many of the scarps on the coastal plain were similarly unproductive. Yet within the coastal flatwoods could be found areas of slightly higher ground—hammocks—where oaks (including white oaks), magnolias, pignut hickories, American holly, spruce pines (*Pinus glabra*) and associated plants like saw palmetto, blueberries (in Georgia), and other edible plants flourish and attract some game. Some low areas also form marshes and swamps with all of their biological diversity. The forests bordering the rivers that flow across the pine barrens also abound in edible plants and game.[11] Scattered potsherds and an occasional lithic artifact found on hammocks from the Carolinas to the Everglades attest to their use by Native Americans, but little is known about their roles in annual subsistence or food cycles.[12] For the most part, the pine barrens of the lower and middle coastal plains displayed little floral or faunal diversity and constituted a sort of green desert separating the coastal zone, the fall line, and the piedmont.[13]

The piedmont ranges from less than one hundred meters to six hundred meters (1,969 feet) in elevation. It consists of rolling hills arranged in as many as six terraces, all heavily covered with soils called saprolites. These red-yellow and grey-brown soils developed due to the weathering of the underlying metamorphic and igneous crystalline rocks, and are more fertile than the soils of the coastal plain.[14] The natural climax forest varies from the oak-hickory hardwood forest on the red-yellow soils, especially in Virginia and northeastern Georgia, to a mixed pine and oak-hickory forest on the grey-brown soils, especially on the watersheds of the Chattahoochee River in west central Georgia. In the Carolinas, the piedmont climax forests are banded into eastern and western pine dominant belts and a central oak-hickory dominant belt, the belts reflecting underlying soils. At least five species of oak—including the edible acorn-bearing white oak—and several species of hickories are found in the piedmont's forests. On bluffs and ravine slopes, beech trees dominate the same type of mixed hardwood forests as were noted for the coastal plain.[15]

The Appalachian Mountains rise from 600 to 2,037 meters (1,969 to 6,684 feet)—Mt. Mitchell is the highest peak—in complex patterns of northeast–southwest ridges reflecting their ancient geologic history. Erosion has created numerous deep valleys of varying lengths and compass orientations. Within the Appalachians, the grey-brown soils of the valley floors are deep, well watered and drained; they tend to be fertile, even if often of small areal extent. Soils on the slopes and mountain tops are thin and erode easily if trees and other plant cover are removed.[16] Prior to the introduction of a fungal chestnut blight in the early twentieth century, the dominant forest of the southern Appalachians was the oak-chestnut type. Moist coves, especially with northern exposures, contain mixed hardwood forests of six to eight locally dominant species, each grouping a subset of the thirty species of trees found in the coves taken as a whole. The inter-mountain plateaus and valleys, such as the Ashville Basin, were covered with the oak and oak-pine forests of the adjacent piedmont. The white oak was not common. Pines and other conifers were present, but not abundant except at the border with the oak-pine forest of the piedmont. On the highest mountains, spruce or northern beech-maple forests dominate. The mountains have been described as "a refugium where many plants . . . persisted" during the periods of geologic and climatic change since the Tertiary period, creating an "area of greatest diversity of vegetation."[17]

Peninsular Florida, the particular concern of much of this study, has some additional geological–ecological features that played a role in the story to be told here. In northern Florida and adjacent parts of southwestern Georgia ("the southern or Tifton uplands"), the Tallahassee and Mariana Red Hills and the Madison Hills form a complex heavily cut by stream and river action, often with moderate slopes (10–25 percent grades) into the stream valleys. The general tilt of the hills is to the south and southeast. The soils are red-yellow colored sands overlaying clayey subsoils in the Tallahassee and Mariana area and gray-brown sandy loams in the Madison Hills area.[18] Both types have moderate to good fertility. Although there is some dispute among foresters on the point, the natural climax forest on the tops of the hills seems to have been the longleaf pine and wire grass type, maintained by a high number of lightning-caused fires as well as human activity. However, extensive areas of white oaks, beech, and other deciduous trees, up to thirty-five species per acre, were found on the slopes and in more moist environments, including hilltops. All students of this ecology agree that it is one of the more diverse to be found in the Southeast.[19]

Equally notable are the central ridge and its outlying hills to the east and south. Generally covered with grey-brown sandy soils of varying slope, the middle of the ridge is crossed in a north-to-south pattern by an area of red-yellow sandy loams known as the Arredondo-Kendrick-Millhopper Association.[20] Both soil types are moist to well drained and can be of moderate fertility. The natural climax forest varies with moisture but is generally pines with scrub oaks (on drier soils), although areas of oak and hickory hardwoods occur on the Arredondo-Kendrick-Millhopper Association soils and on the more moist slopes.

Most of the rest of peninsular Florida, north of a line from Fort Myers to Fort Pierce Inlet, has superficially grey, very acidic, infertile soils (over yellow or grey-white fine sands) that flood seasonally because of high water tables and underlying hardpans or limestones.[21] These flat woods soils grow pine and palmetto forests, although they can be used for pasture and, with modern drainage, for growing orange trees and some other crops. Where drainage does not occur, swamps are common. South of a line from Fort Myers to Fort Pierce Inlet, the soils are all of wet types.[22] Prior to the development of modern clearing and drain-

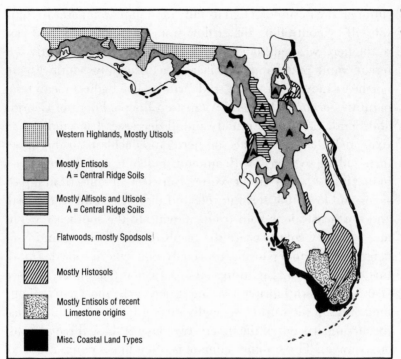

Western Highlands, Mostly Utisols

Mostly Entisols
A = Central Ridge Soils

Mostly Alfisols and Utisols
A = Central Ridge Soils

Flatwoods, mostly Spodsols

Mostly Histosols

Mostly Entisols of recent
Limestone origins

Misc. Coastal Land Types

Figure 1.4. Florida soils. BASED ON *Atlas of Florida* (GAINES-
VILLE: UNIVERSITY PRESSES OF FLORIDA, 1992), "SOIL TYPES OF
FLORIDA." BY PERMISSION OF EDWARD FERNALD, EDITOR, *Atlas of
Florida.*

age methods, this area was covered with wet pine savannahs with
marshes (along the northern edge), cypress swamps, and saw-
grass and other marshes. Tropical hardwoods grow where hammocks rise above this wet environment.[23] Archaeological research
indicates that the line from Fort Myers to Fort Pierce marks the
apparent southern limit, about 1500, of maize cultivation on naturally higher, drained soils and on man-made ridges.[24]

The climate of the Southeast is mild and wet. Frost-free days
range from 210 on the upper piedmont to more than 300 in central Florida, with an average over the piedmont and some parts
of the upper coastal plain of 210 to 240 days. On the middle and
lower coastal plain, the average ranges from 240 to 270 days. In

summer, the Bermuda High usually modulates temperatures and rainfall by controlling the airflow from the south and southeast to the northwest, although peninsular Florida has a slightly different wind pattern that reflects the generally southwest-to-northeast movement of the trade winds. The highest mean temperatures occur in July and August on the piedmont of Georgia and South Carolina. Annual rainfall decreases from more than sixty inches a year in the southern Appalachians to the upper forties along the coast, with amounts reaching into the low fifties in northern Florida. In the winter, rain accompanies frontal passages and lows that form in the Gulf of Mexico and work north and northeast along cold fronts moving to the southeast. Summer rains, by contrast, are the result of daily heating and condensation. Thunderstorms, especially in northern Florida, mark this development. Lightning strikes as many as ninety days a year in northern Florida, making it one of the most active lightning areas in the world, especially during June, July, and August (occurring fifty out of the ninety-two days of these three months, on average). The summer climate is often like a damp rag, cool in the dawn and oppressively hot by mid afternoon. Only along the coast does the land breeze–sea breeze effect moderate temperatures and humidities.[25]

Native Americans and the Land

Within this subtly diverse landscape, Native Americans influenced by the Mississippian cultural tradition devised subsistence strategies that, by 1500, involved the cultivation of maize, beans, and squashes and perhaps other plants on the moister, more friable soils of river flood plains (especially in the piedmont), of lake shores, and of some upland areas.[26] While access to such soils may have been a primary factor in the siting of settlements, also important were access to fresh water and ecotones, the transition zones between the mesic or wetter river and stream valleys and lake shores and the more xeric or dry uplands. Biologically more diverse but smaller in area than the zones up or down slope from them, ecotones provided seasonal berries, nuts and fruits, and a host of other useful plants and animals such as deer, rab-

bits, and tortoises. The upland forests provided mostly nuts, turkeys, deer, and bears, although berries grew where fire or humans opened clearings.

Areas in which all of these environmental qualities could be
found were and are limited; they occur mostly along the western
margin of the inner coastal plain, especially at the fall line, in the
piedmont river basins, in mountain valleys, and in places along
the lower courses of rivers where the ground is high enough not
to flood regularly and adjacent uplands are near at hand.[27] In
Florida, the western side of the central ridge and some of its outlying hills (north of Interstate 4), with their lakes, springs, and
rivers, provide a local variant of this pattern, as do the Tallahassee, Mariana and Madison hills.[28]

As has been noted, the pine forests of the coastal terraces
mostly lacked fertile soils and ecotones. Their contribution to
Native American subsistence seems to have been limited to deer,
turkey, turtles and a few other species, and to the variable floral
resources of the occasional hammock or swamp.

A variation of the environment that Native Americans were
exploiting elsewhere around the year 1500 was present in Georgia, South Carolina, and to a lesser degree on Florida's east coast.
Pleistocene barrier islands like St. Catherines Island, the shallow
bays between these islands and the mainland, and the immediate
shore of the mainland and the mouths of rivers entering the bays
(such as the Satilla and Altamaha Rivers) are cases in point. Live
oak maritime forests growing on the landward side of the islands
and on the mainland and river shores yielded turkeys, raccoons,
deer, turtles, and migratory birds. The oaks grow on soils capable of supporting maize, beans, squash, and a few other edible
plants. But it was the marsh and its fish, shellfish (especially
oysters), migratory and wading birds, fish trapped in tidal creeks
within the marsh, and plants with tuberous roots that offered the
most abundant food.[29]

Florida's coastal zones are similar to those further north, but
are less uniform. The barrier islands are much narrower along
the east coast and generally lack soils suitable for agriculture
south of the St. Johns River. Too, the lagoons south of Daytona
Beach are generally deeper and less filled with marshes than the

bays in Georgia and the Carolinas. These dissimilarities produce different kinds and amounts of fish and shellfish. On the west coast, the barrier island–bay complex exists only from Estero Bay to New Port Richey and from Apalachee Bay westward. There is little marsh, although mangroves serve some of the same ecological functions where they grow. The adjacent mainland is generally high, with live oaks and pine flatwoods. Southern Florida offered an altogether different mix of resources. The wide shallow bays of the west coast (Charlotte Harbor especially) support abundant mollusks (especially the conch) and shellfish as well as shrimp and numerous fish species. Further south, the mangrove coast (Ten Thousand Islands area) is a rich maritime nursery with only an occasional area of high ground.[30]

The annual subsistence or food cycles of Native American peoples varied with the resources in their environments. Maize, beans and squash, where cultivated, set the basic annual pattern for growing and gathering foods. To these dietary basics, local ecosystems often allowed various additions. A by no means comprehensive list of such additions would include acorn meal (preferably from the white oak), seasonal berries and fruits such as plums, persimmons, black cherries, red and white mulberries, raspberries, and muscadine grapes, and nuts such as chinquapins, walnuts, chestnuts, and hickories. The fruits were eaten fresh and were dried for winter consumption. The nuts yielded both meats and oils. Various roots also provided supplementary carbohydrates. Except for arrowroot (in southern Florida) and smilax, we do not know what they were. Deer, bear, raccoons, opossums, rabbits, squirrels, domesticated dogs, birds of all sorts (especially turkeys and ducks), turtles and terrapins, reptiles such as snakes, and fish and shellfish (according to location) rounded out the generally available resources considered to be food by the Indians.[31] Many of these natural plant and animal and maritime resources are highly seasonal and not all are or were found immediately around Indian village sites.

An unresolved question is the degree to which the Indians followed a seasonal round, deserting their villages (the maize-growing sites in most cases) to gather the natural harvest. In the

1560s, European accounts of the Indians of coastal Georgia and South Carolina, and to a lesser degree northern Florida along the coast and the St. Johns River, suggest a prolonged seasonal migration that left villages empty. If these sources are correct, the coastal Indians might have been absent from their villages for six months or more of the year (but not continuously), especially during the fall, winter, and early spring. At least two respected archaeologists have taken this evidence at face value and constructed models of the supposed annual cycle. However, recent research suggests that the coastal Indians were far less mobile across the landscape than was once thought. Indeed, they and the Indians of the interior probably followed a similar annual pattern in which there were heavy summer and fall collections of readily available fruits, berries, and nuts, with storage for the winter, and hunting and fishing year round according to the availability of faunal, avian, or (for the coast) maritime resources. Presumably there were no long periods when villages were totally deserted. Scholars now think that European demands and drought in the early years of colonization depleted stored foods, causing the observed prolonged seasonal flight of coastal peoples from their villages to hunt and gather in the forests. Flight was also a form of resistance to early missionary activity.[32] As will be noted in later chapters, during the height of the Spanish colonial period coastal peoples made additional plantings of maize and beans that supported not only a largely sedentary native population but also its new, voracious European neighbors.

The case for the year-round occupation of the villages rests in part on a better understanding of Native American agriculture. So far as we know, most Native Americans grew maize using swidden or "slash and burn" land-clearing techniques and hill cultivation on plots of 8 to 80 hectares. The burning of the trees and brush to clear sites added nutrients to the soil. In some coastal areas, the Indians added shells (a source of calcium carbonate) to counteract the natural acidity of the soils. Fertility was maintained by burning off stubble, weeds, and leaves in late winter and by interplanting beans which added nitrogen, squash which provided mulch, amaranths whose deep roots brought minerals to the surface when pulled up, and even fruit trees (such as mulberries and plums) and nut trees whose leaves and fruit provided nutrients upon decay. Birds and animals attracted to this feast added their droppings to some human wastes, providing limited additional sources of nutrients. Such plots might produce for up to ten years,[33] and only as fertility declined would a new plot be cleared nearby. The plots seem to have rotated around the village site over a period of a generation or so unless suitable land was so restricted that village sites had to be abandoned when soil fertility declined.

In short, Native Americans were not uniformly settled across the landscape, but rather were concentrated in certain areas where the ecology was suitable for their culturally determined subsistence patterns.[34] Thanks to archaeological work since the 1950s, we know a great deal about both those subsistence patterns and where the Native Americans lived (Figure 1.5).

Although the picture is not entirely clear, the best current archaeological as well as historical evidence suggests that the densest populations of Native Americans in the Southeast resided, circa 1540, in the extensive, favorable ecological resource areas of the piedmont. Numerically significant but smaller outlying areas of population were on the northern Florida hills and the western side of the central ridge, the Altamaha and Satilla deltas, and in the valleys of the St. Johns and Suwannee Rivers. The coastal areas, which provided limited carbohydrate resources, were more thinly populated than the piedmont, and even that settlement was patterned in apparent response to environmental and pre-contact historical factors about which we can only guess.[35] The extensive wetlands of the upper St. Johns River valley, the Kissimmee River valley, and south of the Fort Myers–Fort Pierce line also seem to have had small precontact populations.[36]

In 1540, this settlement pattern was undergoing its own dynamic changes, ones initiated well before Europeans appeared. Studies by Mark Williams, Chester DePratter, and David G. Anderson, built on observations originally made at Etowah and Moundville, have shown that the great Mississippian paramount chiefdoms of the twelfth to fifteenth centuries A.D. were being

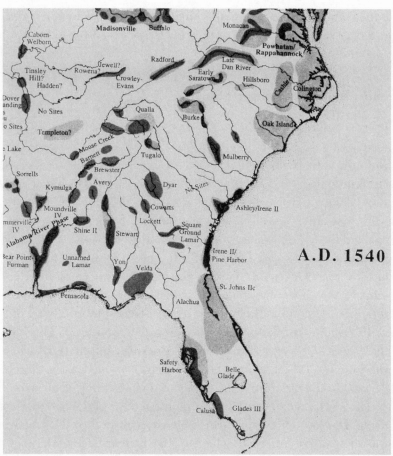

Figure 1.5. Southeastern portion, "Early Historic Phases
in the Eastern Woodlands, A.D. 1540." FROM DAVID G.
ANDERSON, "EXAMINING PREHISTORIC SETTLEMENT DISTRIBUTION IN
EASTERN NORTH AMERICA," *Archaeology of Eastern North
America* 19 (1991), FIGURE 5. BY PERMISSION OF EASTERN STATES
ARCHAEOLOGICAL FEDERATION.

replaced by other, smaller entities through little understood processes that led to the rearrangement of populations, polities, and
even subsistence strategies.[37] It is not known if these changes involved demographic losses. If there were such losses, they were
not as catastrophic as those that followed permanent European
settlement, especially in the seventeenth century. Other societies

either continued to be simple chiefdoms or even loosely organized (segmented) tribes, or they cycled between those forms of
sociopolitical organization.

Native American Demography

It is unlikely that the populations of the chiefdoms in 1500
were as dense as the "high counters" would have us believe.[38]
Not only is there no archaeological evidence of pandemics before
Hernando De Soto (1539–1543), but recent studies have also
shown that at least as early as A.D. 1450 the chiefdoms of the
piedmont and coastal plain were separated by rather wide uninhabited buffer zones across which only the occasional raiding or
trading party ventured. De Soto's famous crossing of a wilderness between Ocute (in Georgia) and Cofitachequi (in South Carolina) is a well-known example.[39] Such buffers would have made
the transmission of Old World crowd diseases like smallpox difficult beyond the boundaries of the major polities.[40] The idea
that there were very dense Native American populations when
De Soto and his army marched through the Southeast is largely
derived from Garcilaso de la Vega and the boastings of survivors.
As David Henige has insisted, applying a dash of deconstruction
to the De Soto chronicles brings us closer to reality. The reality
was that Native American villages typically consisted of only several hundred persons (on average 200–300; 700 at most), as a
few recent archaeological studies have shown on the basis of
settlement site size. However, generalization is difficult because
peoples in the late Mississippian tradition lived not only in villages and towns but also in farmsteads and very small satellite
villages that were spread out around a central place, or up and
down river from it where geography dictated such a settlement
pattern. Chiefdoms, even paramount ones, embraced only a few
thousand persons (a few ten thousands at most) often spread out
for considerable distances along major rivers.[41]

A population of several thousand living on good agricultural
land was exactly the sort of human resource that the Spaniards
had gone after elsewhere in the New World. The question is, why

did they *not* make more of an effort to gain control of the great
piedmont chiefdoms of the Southeast? To answer that question
requires an examination of the Spanish discovery of the Southeast. As we do that, we will look at particular societies they encountered and, in some cases, came to control.

2.

DISCOVERING THE SECRETS

The European "discovery" of southeastern North America and the Native American "encounter" with these strange human invaders and their biological associates, ranging from diseases to cattle, created a drawn-out process stretching well into the eighteenth century. Much of that story falls into the history of Anglo-America, and is well outside the geographic scope of this study. Our story of discovery is largely confined to the sixteenth century and the Spaniards and Frenchmen whose rivalry did so much to shape the history of the region in that period. It is a story that overlaps into the period when the Spaniards were establishing their first frontier in La Florida.

Explorations before 1520

We do not know why the Spaniards failed to explore north and northwest of the Antilles until the second decade of the 1500s.[1] An imperfect explanation is that the inertia of Spanish activity in the New World resulted from Columbus's notion that South America was either a peninsula of Asia or, as he said after 1498, a large but circumnavigable land mass off its southeastern coast. Thus the macro project of Spanish exploration until the return of the Magellan–El Cano expedition from its circumnavigation of the world (1519–1522) focused on getting *around* the "new world," by going south to reach Asia and the Indian Ocean.[2] The discovery of gold on the Isthmus of Panama and the widely held idea that gold was found in the tropics closer to the sun added momentum to Spanish exploration projects. The micro interests of conquistadors (and the Crown, which got a 10 to 20 percent share) in looting known or rumored Isthmanian and Central American societies of their gold, pearls, and labor only slightly modified this inertia prior to 1517.

By 1517, the various southern versions of the Columbian geography that had diverted Spanish attention from areas north of the Antilles were subject to scrutiny. Exploration of the Atlantic face of South America had progressed to the Río de la Plata, a point so far south that sailors could anticipate difficult sailing in rounding the continent, should it be found to have a southern end. By then, too, Balboa in Panama (1513) had confirmed the existence of the "southern sea" (the Pacific Ocean) and Martin Waldseemüller's world map (1507) had shown the Americas to be remote from Asia. In an apparent effort to find out the truth of these matters, Bishop Juan Rodríguez de Fonseca, who supervised the Spanish Empire in America for Ferdinand the Catholic, set in motion the voyages of Magellan (Fernão Magalhaes) and Gil González Dávila. Magellan was to sail southwest until he rounded South America or could find a way through it; and González Dávila was to cross the Isthmus of Panama, take ships Balboa had built on the Pacific side, and sail west.[3] In due course, Magellan's voyage settled the issue of the Americas' relationship to Asia. González Dávila's explorations of Nicaragua in 1519–1520 became part of a reorientation of Spanish activity in the Caribbean away from its primordial Antilles–Panama axis.

By 1517, at least four unrelated events were pointing to the areas north and northwest of the existing conquests as places into which Spanish expansion might flow. Pedro Árias de Ávila's (Pedrárias) regime on the Isthmus of Panama had largely exhausted local gold and population reserves and was poised to seek new conquests further north along the Pacific side of Central America. Governor Diego Velazquez de Cuellar and his associates in Cuba had exhausted the easily exploited gold placers and the local labor to work them.[4] Juan Ponce de León's voyage of 1513 to what he named "La Florida" had revealed what slavers may have known for a decade before: that there was a large "island" north of Cuba inhabited by numerous, hostile natives. But his plans for conquest were postponed while he attacked Carib Indians in the lesser Antilles and defended his claims to Puerto Rico.[5] Captain Pedro de Salazar's slave raid along the Atlantic coast of North America, around 1516, although not widely known, hinted that more than just a large island lay to the west and northwest of the Bahamas.[6] Yet such developments by themselves could not produce a major reorientation in Spanish activity. That required major discoveries of new riches.

The discoveries by Francisco Hernández de Córdoba and Juan de Grijalva of heavily populated cities constructed of stone on the shores of Yucatán and central Mexico in 1517–1518, and the initial richness of Nicaragua, diverted Spanish expansion away from its southern and southwestward thrusts, but also focused it again on areas where looting was easy. Exploration of the shores of southeastern North America might have languished yet longer had latecomers not wanted to get a share of the Mexican riches and had two slavers, Francisco Gordillo and Pedro de Quejo, not needed to obtain human cargoes when none could be had in the Bahamas.

Francisco de Garay was the first would-be jumper of Hernán Cortés's Mexican claims. Appointed governor of Jamaica and steward of the Crown's properties there in 1514, Garay may have intended to engage in a new discovery or conquest as soon as he reached his post. However, only in late 1518 after a conversation with Antón de Alaminos, one of the pilots on the Cuban voyages to Yucatán and Mexico, did he obtain royal permission to search the sea west of Ponce de León's discovery and north of the Cuban ones, ostensibly for a strait that would lead to Asia. Evidently his instructions to the commander of his fleet were to see if Florida indeed was an island, as Ponce de León had thought, and then go to Mexico.

Alonso Alvarez de Pineda commanded Garay's 270-man, four-ship expedition when it sailed from Jamaica in March 1519. The

fleet's initial landfall was on the northern shore of the Gulf of
Mexico, possibly at Apalachee Bay. It then ran south and southeast along the coast to Cape Sable, then back north and west
along the coast past the Mississippi River, which Alvarez de
Pineda named the Río de Flores. If Alonso de Chaves's rutter
contains a navigational record of this voyage, as seems likely, this
leg of the voyage involved exploration of the major bays on the
west coast of Florida. A record of contact with the Native Americans does not exist. Past the Mississippi River, the track may
have been as far west as Vermillion Bay, Louisiana, and then
southwest to the Mexican coast, perhaps to the Pánuco River,
and then south to anchor off Cortés's recently founded town of
Villa Rica de Veracruz. Cortés, who had just begun what became
the conquest of Mexico, captured six men from the Garay fleet—
enough to learn some of the details of the voyage. Alvarez de
Pineda, having escaped Cortés, then apparently worked his way
north along the Mexican coast to the mouth of the Río del Es-
pírito Santo (River of the Holy Spirit: the Sabine River) before
turning for Jamaica. Robert Weddle thinks that along the way he
may have left a colony on the Pánuco River, undoubtedly the
"very large, deep river" mentioned in Garay's contract of 1521.[7]

Once back in Jamaica, Alvarez de Pineda and his pilots drew
up a rough map of the Gulf of Mexico and delivered a rutter
of their voyage. Garay forwarded these items to Spain, along
with a request for permission to colonize "Amichel," a land well
peopled and with "fine gold" in its rivers, lying north of Mexico.
Garay summarized the rest of the coast that Alvarez de Pineda
had explored as "a low, sterile land." He was awarded a contract
for the occupation of Amichel on 4 June 1521.[8]

Garay's subsequent misfortunes—he died as a prisoner of
Cortés in Tenochtitlan—need not concern us. For present purposes, his significance lies in his sponsorship of the mapping of
the shores of the Gulf of Mexico, particularly the west coast of
Florida, and in providing the information that Alvarez de Pineda
had found the Florida Gulf coast a "low, sterile land."[9] To that
could be added Ponce de León's finding of 1513, reinforced by
his fatal wounding and the forced withdrawal of his conquering
expedition of 1521 from Calusa territory, that the residents of

Florida were numerous, well-armed and hostile, and apparently did not cultivate maize.

In sum, the west coast of Florida must have seemed unlikely to provide a quick profit for an entrepreneurial conquistador. Nor did the two Indian societies Ponce de León had seen on the east coast offer better prospects. They were smaller if otherwise apparently culturally similar to the Calusa of the west coast.[10]

Ayllón, Chicora, and the Interior

A very different report about the land and its inhabitants came from the slaving voyage of Francisco Gordillo and Pedro de Quejo, which entered the South Santee River on the Atlantic coast on 24 June 1521, twenty days after Charles V signed Garay's contract. They had sailed independently from Hispaniola to the Bahamas in search of slaves. Finding only each other, they agreed to a company in which Quejo put up a supply of ship biscuit and Gordillo the knowledge that a captain (Francisco de Salazar) sailing for his employer, the Licenciado Lucas Vázquez de Ayllón, had taken a load of slaves from land that lay about five days sail northwest of the Bahamas. They made landfall at the Santee River. After an initial contact with a Native American fishing camp, they moved the ships into Winyah Bay, just to the north. There on 30 June 1521 first Quejo and then Gordillo took possession of the land in the name of the king of Spain and their respective employers. On 15 July, they lured some sixty "Chicora" Indians aboard their ships and sailed. Early in August, they landed their human cargo at Santo Domingo.[11]

The report that Ayllón, a judge of the appeals court (*Audiencia*) at Santo Domingo, spread in Spain in 1522–1523, portrayed the new land of "Chicora" as like Andalucia but with abundant forest resources, pearls and, inland in the province of Xapira, "other terrestrial gems." A fair-skinned, blond king of unusual height named Datha ruled numerous provinces (collectively called *Du-a-e*) from a "stone palace" in the interior.[12] In his petition for a contract to effect a conquest of the new discovery, Ayllón listed twenty-one "provinces," most of which seem to have been chiefdoms and at least one of which, Orista, was clearly not

under Datha's control. Peter Martyr, the contemporary chronicler, recorded that Ayllón and a Native American known to him
as Francisco El Chicorano also said that the Indians kept flocks
of birds; herded tame deer for their milk; grew maize, *xathi* (am-
aranth?), and tubers; stretched the bones of the children who
were to become their rulers; buried their dead in temples; and
celebrated planting and harvesting with elaborate ceremonies.
To this, Ayllón added the claim that these Indians lived "politically"—that is, as civilized persons who followed Natural Law.
In support of this claim, he told stories about the tax system and
the administration of justice. He also claimed that the Indians
believed in the immortality of the soul and a sort of heaven.[13] In
short, this was a land worth conquering because it held easily
exploited wealth as well as peoples who were used to being ruled.
Ayllón's reports were also the first information Spaniards received that pointed to the interior of North America as the location of mineral wealth and large populations.

A few of these tales were true, but Ayllón was lying about the
location (and the tame deer!). The Gordillo-Quejo discovery had
been at 33 degrees 30 minutes North, not the 35 to 37 degrees
Ayllón claimed in written memorials to the Crown, nor the 36–38
degrees his tale of a new Andalucia implied. He probably resorted to this falsehood to raise money for his colonizing venture
and because he intended to explore further north before selecting
a site for his initial colony.[14]

On 12 June 1523, Charles V granted Ayllón a contract to explore the Atlantic coast, select sites, and then found two Spanish
towns. Influenced by the Dominican demand that Spaniards respect Native Americans' natural law rights (life, liberty, and
property, as John Locke would later list them), Charles decreed
that Ayllón's and his colonists' relationships with the natives
would be by trade and the peaceful preaching of the Gospel. The
Spaniards might assume control of native society only if the inhabitants freely agreed to accept Charles as king.[15]

Because of official business in the Antilles, Ayllón did not send
Pedro de Quejo to explore the southeastern coast of North
America until 1525. Quejo's voyage seems to have taken him from
approximately Cumberland Island, Georgia, to very near the en-

trance to the Delaware Bay. Along the way he not only examined potential harbors and gained additional information about the natural resources of the coastal strand but also secured, by undisclosed methods, Indians from the four language groups who lived along that part of the southeastern coast. From the vicinity of Cumberland Island he secured Timucuan speakers; from the Georgia coast, Muskogean-speaking Guale; from the Winyah Bay area, more Siouian-speaking "Chicorans"; and from the North Carolina or Virginia coasts, Algonkian speakers.[16]

The fruits of this exploration were represented in Juan Vespucci's map of 1526 and in Ayllón's decisions about where to land his colony in August of that year. Quejo's report directed Ayllón away from the more northern latitudes he had claimed in his contract and propaganda to the area of the original discovery. Quejo seems to have found that the barrier islands were lightly inhabited and that the natural resources at the higher latitudes, those closer to the ones of the Spanish Andalucia, were not much different from those further south. Indeed, except for a decrease in the sizes of marshes behind the barrier islands and of the frequency of palm trees in the live oak maritime forest as one goes north, there is little difference in the general ecology of the coastal zone along that entire stretch. None of the Indians picked up were understood to report native societies like Datha's kingdom, nor mineral resources like the pearls and "terrestrial gems" of his realm. Only "Chicora" offered access to these things. So it was to Chicora—the South Santee River and/or Winyah Bay—that Ayllón directed his expedition.

The colony of 1526 did not stay long at "Chicora." As the six ships of the fleet, carrying some 600 persons, approached the coast in early August, the flagship ran aground, taking many of

Figure 2.1. The Spanish Southeast, ca. 1526. BASED ON PAUL E. HOFFMAN, *A New Andalucia and a Way to the Orient: The American Southeast in the Sixteenth Century* (BATON ROUGE: LOUISIANA STATE UNIVERSITY PRESS, 1990), MAP 4. BY PERMISSION OF LOUISIANA STATE UNIVERSITY PRESS AND THE AUTHOR.

THE SPANISH
SOUTHEAST
ca. 1526

Name after 1526

Name from 1525 Voyage
(From Juan Vespucci, World Map, 1526)
Modern Name

Cabo de Arenas
Cabo de Santa María?
Ocean City

Cabo de San Juan
Shown but Not Named
Cape Charles

Bahía de Santa María
Shown But Not Named
Closed, Musketo Inlet, 1585

Bahía de Santa María
Shown But Not Named
Closed, Trinity Harbor, 1585.

Cabo de Trafalgar
Cabo de Trafalgar
Cape Hatteras

Río del Príncipe
Shown But Not Named
Closed, Open in 1585

Río de Bajos
Río de Atarazanas
New River Inlet?

Río de Canoas
Río de Arecifes
Cape Fear River

Cabo de San Román
Cabo de San Nicolás
Winyah Bay Entrance

Río Jordán
Río Jordán
South Santee River

Shown But Not Named
Shown But Not Named
St. Helena Sound

Cabo de Santa Elena
Río de la Cruz
Tybee Island

Cabo Grueso
Cabo de Santa Elena
Jekyll Island

0   50   100
Nautical Miles

the expedition's supplies with it to a watery grave. Once ashore, the Spaniards discovered that no Indians were in the area nor any of the good grasses their livestock needed nor many other resources to keep body and soul together, much less make a quick profit. Francisco El Chicorano, counted upon to lead the Spaniards to Datha's riches, deserted them. Another place or a way into the interior would have to be found. Accordingly, scouting parties were sent south by sea and inland to try to find Indian communities near which the Spaniards might lodge during their first winter in the new land. While waiting for those reports, Ayllón had a ship built to replace the lost flagship. When the scouts returned, they reported Indian settlement only to the south, at an area that can be identified as the St. Catherines Island–Sapelo Sound area. The women, children, ill, and livestock were loaded on the ships and sent south, while Ayllón and a largely mounted party of men went inland and then south, evidently using either Indian trails or the open pine barrens for a road. Somehow, the parties reunited at Sapelo Sound.

The city of San Miguel de Gualdape was founded at Sapelo Sound no later than 28 September 1526, the festival of St. Michael the Archangel (the San Miguel of the name). By the end of October it was gone. Although fish were abundant in the tidal creeks, dysentery diseases, short supplies of carbohydrates, Ayllón's death on 18 October (St. Luke's festival) and Indian hostility provoked by one or more parties of foraging Spaniards undermined morale and led to a rebellion. After that was put down, the leaders of the colony decided to remove its survivors. Only about a quarter of the original 600 persons reached the Antilles.[17]

The survivors took with them two contrasting reports of the new land. The one, quoted at the beginning of chapter one, tempered Ayllón's propaganda with the realism of persons who had experienced the difficulties of the land at first hand but who saw its possibilities for Spaniards who would arrive with enough supplies to survive until they understood its "secrets." The other report was wholly negative. This report was incorporated into the official Spanish understanding of the Atlantic coast of North America. As Alonso de Santa Cruz reported in a manuscript composed in the 1540s, from the River of Deer (the Penobscot) on south, "many islands are found, all deserted and of little profit."[18] Oviedo's description of Gualdape says only that it is a flat region, with marshes, a "powerful" river, lots of fish and pine trees, and cold weather.[19] Except for their hostility, the Guale Indians do not figure in the surviving documentation.

Having tested the secrets of the land, the majority of the Spaniards with first-hand experience with North America found it worthless, both on the Gulf Coast (Alvarez de Pineda and Garay's "low, sterile land") and on the Atlantic coast. Whatever the truth about the kingdom of Du-a-e, it lay in the interior, separated from an inhospitable coast by trackless pine forests.

For another dozen years, only one Spanish expedition landed in La Florida, and then quite by accident. There was no one willing to gamble capital on trying to set up a coastal base camp from which to move rapidly inland in the hope of discovering and gaining control of enough riches to refill empty purses and attract other Spaniards. But from the one accidental exploration came knowledge of the larger, maize-growing populations of the interior of the Florida peninsula.

Narváez, De Soto, Luna and the Interior

Pánfilo de Narváez, not unlike Garay seven years earlier, apparently intended to grab part of New Spain, newly removed from Cortés's to royal control. His contract called for him to explore and colonize the upper Gulf Coast, including Garay's Amichel, the back door into Mexico.

Narváez landed in Florida in the vicinity of modern Johns Pass (northwest of modern St. Petersburg) quite by accident. His fleet left its winter ports in southeastern Cuba in the spring of 1528 with only enough water and supplies for a journey to Havana. Off western Cuba a storm struck and blew the fleet northward into the Gulf of Mexico, forcing a landing to replenish water casks. Believing his pilots that "Bahía Honda"—Tampa Bay— lay to the north, Narváez sent the ships on ahead and marched his men north along the coast in the expectation of coming upon that bay, where the ships were to be at anchor. After a hungry

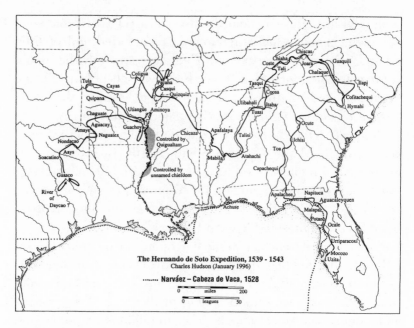

Figure 2.2. Routes of Pánfilo de Narváez and Hernando
de Soto. BASED ON CHARLES HUDSON, "THE HERNANDO DE SOTO
EXPEDITION, 1539–1543." COURTESY OF DR. CHARLES HUDSON.
NARVÁEZ ROUTE ADDED.

march through oak-pine scrub and flat woods, the party reached
the Withlacoochee River and Indians who grew maize. But there
was no evidence of a bay. Stubbornly, Narváez decided to push
on in the general direction of New Spain.[20]

Guided by Indians, and very hungry, the Spaniards turned inland from the Withlacoochee River to follow a track that seems
to have been similar to the one De Soto followed a decade later.
This took them up the western side of the central ridge, although
not, perhaps, through all the main villages of the Ocala, Potano,
and Utina peoples. According to Cabeza de Vaca, the maize fields
(i.e., the villages) were more than a day's march from each other
and there were few Indians. At the Suwannee, they were met by
Chief Dulchanchellin, evidently the paramount chief who ruled
the Suwannee River peoples known to De Soto as the subjects of
Aguacalecuen and Uzachile and to the mission period as the
Utina and Yustaga. Dulchanchellin was escorted by flute players,

as Uzachile would be when he met De Soto eleven years later. After an initially peaceful first encounter and the crossing of the Suwannee River, the Spaniards and Indians fell into hostilities. Captives forced into guide service misled the expedition into thick woods and swamps. Nonetheless, the expedition reached a town of the Apalachee people, although evidently not the main settlements.

Revived to a degree by the foods obtained among the Apalachee, Narváez and his men pressed on toward New Spain. They went southwest to Aute where food was reported to be abundant, but was not. This march brought them back to the Gulf of Mexico and suggested an avenue of escape. Six bargelike boats were built and loaded. The passage along the Gulf coast is one of the epics of discovery literature, which was followed by the even more epochal journey of Cabeza de Vaca and his three companions across Texas and northern Mexico.[21]

While Cabeza de Vaca and his companions were wandering, Hernando de Soto rose from being one of the more successful participants in the conquest of Nicaragua to becoming a leader in the conquest of Peru. He then sought royal favor at the Spanish court. In various petitions, he requested the right to conquer southern Chile, or to be made governor of Ecuador or Guatemala. Each request was denied. In the end, La Florida was offered, and accepted.[22] Why La Florida was proposed and accepted is one of the unsolved mysteries of De Soto's biography.

Apparently De Soto learned a good deal about the earlier expeditions, but judging from the extant documentation, relatively little of that knowledge came from written reports from the expeditions of Ponce de León, Alvarez de Pineda-Garay, Ayllón, and Narváez. Maps and perhaps the manuscript rutter of Alonso de Chaves would have told him about basic geography. But for most of his knowledge of La Florida, he seems to have been indebted to the oral reports of survivors of earlier expeditions, in particular Cabeza de Vaca and mariners. These verbal reports allowed him to construct a plan.[23] For example, we can infer that De Soto knew that supplying a base on the east coast of La Florida from the Antilles would be riskier (because of the Gulf Stream and wind patterns around the Bahama Islands) than sailing back and forth from Havana to the west coast of the peninsula. He also recognized that political control of Cuba, his chosen base, was necessary to guarantee the provisioning of his forces. And we can infer that whatever he knew, he understood how little he knew about La Florida. This uncertainty accounts for the provision in his contract that allowed him to explore for four years before selecting the two hundred leagues of coast that would delimit his governorship.[24]

De Soto did not make the mistake of his predecessors Ponce de León, Ayllón, and Narváez. Each, except Narváez after a time, had clung to the coast, which offered inadequate food supplies for a large force. Instead De Soto took the lesson of his hungry youth in Panama to heart[25] and, using Cabeza de Vaca's report of maize-growing peoples in the interior of the peninsula, moved his army rapidly inland in search of the nearest important chiefdom. Over the four years of the expedition, it moved relentlessly through the maize fields of the Southeast, following a pattern of capturing chiefs, extorting food and labor as ransoms when they were not offered voluntarily or in sufficient quantity, and then moving on to the next chiefdom.[26] This strategy for living off the land meant that the army's course was along the western side of Florida's central ridge, through Apalachee (winter 1539–1540), northward across the Dougherty Plain (and the Flint River, evidently crossed twice), the Ocmulgee River and the Louisville Plateau to the upper Oconee River basin, thence northeast across the lower piedmont (and/or upper coastal plain) in Georgia and South Carolina to Cofitachequi on the Wateree River (near modern Camden, South Carolina) and then up it and the Catawba River into the piedmont. Once across the Appalachian Mountains and out of the Great Valley west of them, the track continued through the piedmont and upper coastal plain to the Mississippi River, which was reached in early May 1541. Across the Mississippi River, the path through modern Arkansas followed river valleys. In only a few areas, notably the deserted Savannah River valley that took ten days to cross, did forest buffers of more than two days' march threaten the army with hunger.[27] (See Figure 2.2. for this journey.)

The track just sketched took De Soto and his men and animals through the territories of some of the largest polities in the region. Apalachee (perhaps), Ocute, Cofitachequi, and Coosa (perhaps) were populous paramount chiefdoms. Except for Apalachee, each controlled much of the piedmont part of a major river basin, the uplands around it, and some of the upper coastal plain just below the fall line. Each contained clusters of villages around multiple administrative–religious centers. Except for Apalachee, which lacked them in 1540, the physical sign of such a center was its temple and residential mounds.[28]

Thanks to comparative ethnography, we think we know how these societies constructed the authority of the paramounts and their subordinate chiefs. Each center, and its subordinate villages, was ruled by a chief whose authority probably arose from his position in the system of ranked lineages and clans, perhaps reinforced by his role as a limited distributor of tributary and luxury goods to other members of the elite, and, on rare occasions, to the commoners. In such societies, the members of lineages helped one another; marriage was outside of the lineage; descent was reckoned through the mother (matrilineage); successions were thus from uncle to nephew, or less commonly aunt to niece; and various forms of male residence rules and modifications of the matrilineal descent rules were used in attempts to maintain the position of males from the highest-ranking lineages and clans. Although there are mission-period and eighteenth-century statements suggesting that the chiefs had the power of life and death over their people, the use of physical force to support their authority is not proven. The paramount's authority was similarly constructed, but also rested on coercion (power) exercised in the form of conquest and the repression of rebellions by chiefs and peoples whose lineage links to the paramount had not existed before conquest, were weak after it in spite of marriage alliances, or had weakened because of individual ambitions and accidents of birth and death that compromised the ranking system of the societies in question.[29] De Soto encountered hints of the instability of such socio-political systems in Ocute, Cofitachequi, and Chiaha where second-level chiefs (or perhaps third-level village chiefs) and principal men were disputing the authority of their superiors, most commonly to collect tribute.[30]

While observing some of the features of this system, notably the uncle–nephew relationship, on the whole De Soto's Spaniards interpreted these societies in terms of their own status system, which rewarded the conquest of "provinces" and "great lords." Thus local leaders—all known as "caciques" to the Spaniards—became the rulers of "provinces" rather than the districts or even villages that they in fact led.

These paramount chiefdoms of the piedmont made lasting, favorable impressions on the Spaniards. The chronicler Rodrigo Rangel characteristically was impressed by the food (maize, spring onions, mulberries, turkeys, and venison) available in the four main centers of Ocute. The gentleman of Elvas recalled that "[Ocute], from [the territory] of the first peaceful cacique to the province of Patofa—a distance of fifty leagues [over 100 miles, an exaggeration?]—is a rich land, beautiful, fertile, well watered, and with fine fields along the rivers."[31] Culturally oriented to towns, none of De Soto's men noticed that a majority of the inhabitants of Ocute (and possibly other chiefdoms as well) lived on farmsteads spread over the uplands near streams that fed into the Oconee River.[32] Cofitachequi (to a lesser degree) and Coosa similarly impressed these writers with their foods and generally promising landscape. Elvas recorded of Cofitachequi that "all the men were of the opinion that they should settle in that . . . excellent region" but De Soto "had no wish to content himself with good land or with pearls."[33] In any case, Luis Hernández de Viedma tells us, the Spaniards and their horses had rapidly exhausted the food resources of Cofitachequi, which Elvas has De Soto evaluating as sufficient for only a month.[34] After passing through the mountains along the Catawba River–French Broad River route where only Xuala had much food, the expedition reached Chiaha, the first of Coosa's seven subordinate chiefdoms. Rangel recalled that "[Coosa] is a great cacique with much land, and one of the best and most abundant [provinces] that they found in Florida." Elvas noted that "in the *barbacoas* [elevated granaries] and fields there was a great quantity of maize and beans. The land was very populous and had many large towns and planted fields which reached from one town to the other. It was a charming and fertile land, with good cultivated fields stretching along the rivers."[35] Both men commented on the plums and large grapes growing in the area.

In Ocute's various towns and at Cofitachequi and Coosa, the Spaniards came across temple and house mounds, some of which were no longer in use. At Cofitachequi in particular, they noted "large uninhabited towns, choked with vegetation, which looked as though no people had inhabited them for some time." Elvas understood from the Indians that a plague had occurred two years earlier (in 1538), causing the former residents of those abandoned places to move to other towns. Archaeological evidence, however, suggests that these sites had been abandoned up to a century prior to the arrival of the Spaniards. Warfare and a generational alternation of the residences of important chiefs because of exogamous marriages between the lineages of dominant towns seem to explain these changes. The case of Cofitachequi's neighbors was by no means unique.[36]

De Soto's track across the lower piedmont in South Carolina and up the Wateree and Catawba Rivers took him through the territory that should have been Datha's "kingdom" of Du-a-e and through the province of Xapira with its "terrestrial gems." None of the chroniclers recorded any attempt to find Datha, but De Soto did keep an eye open for evidence of mineral wealth. His men noted both the fresh water pearls and the fine furs they found at Cofitachequi. Probably because of Native American reticence and his concerns about keeping his force together and fed, De Soto missed the quartz crystal deposits along the Catawba River in North Carolina and the gold placers around Dahlonega, Georgia, in each case by fifty miles or less.[37] The Indians did tell him about the copper they obtained from the Chisca, a people living in the mountains to the north. Men sent to visit the Chisca turned back before finding either them or the sources of the copper that the Chisca traded in the Southeast. They also reported that the route north traversed difficult, mountainous terrain where little maize could be found.[38] De Soto therefore continued on his way to Coosa.

In contrast to their extensive, descriptive reports on these populous, agriculturally rich piedmont chiefdoms, the chroniclers' picture of the Florida chiefdoms other than Apalachee and Aguacalecuen is sketchy, and did not encourage other Spaniards to seek out these areas. Even the accounts of populous Aguacalecuen and Apalachee, especially Apalachee, are brief. Viedma, in particular, makes it clear that the peoples of the peninsula were less interesting than those of the piedmont. There is no record of anyone in the army suggesting settlement because of the population and agricultural potential of the land.

What is said about Florida and its inhabitants is this. Rangel (or perhaps Oviedo, who incorporated Rangel's materials into the manuscript of his *General History*) echoed Garay when he recalled that the area around the initial headquarters town of Ucita, evidently on Tampa Bay, "seemed sterile, as in truth that coast is reputed to be."[39] (This judgment was made in ignorance of the eighteen or more temple mound–centered villages around Tampa Bay and other Safety Harbor phase villages inland as far as the Withlacoochee River.)[40] The route from Ucita to Ocale was through a number of small towns and across swamps and otherwise difficult terrain. The reportedly richer inland provinces of Irriparacoxi ("War Leader") and Ocale (both located on the higher ground of the southern extension of the central ridge) proved to be disappointments, although the army found enough maize, beans, and little dogs at Ocale to sustain it for a few weeks.[41] Itara, Potano, Mocharra (Utinama), Mala Paz, and Cholupaha, the other towns along the route, are hardly described. Elvas suggests that De Soto and his advance party looted them of food as they passed through because the main body of the army found none when it marched north. Rangel notes the "small chestnuts" [i.e., chinquapins?] at Mala Paz, and Elvas says that Cholupaha had "maize in abundance."[42] Evidently these were small populations under independent chiefs.

Aguacalecuen, a day or two north of the Santa Fe River and probably just east of the Ichetucknee River, was the first of the four eastern towns (centers) of the people who created the so-called Suwannee Valley archaeological complex. Although the chief of Aguacalecuen figures prominently in Elvas's and Rangel's accounts, Uzachile, a chief who lived west of the river, was in fact the paramount of these peoples.[43] The advance party found Aguacalecuen deserted, but captured Indians revealed stores of maize. De Soto then called the main body of the army from Ocale. The subsequent capture of the chief led to hostilities, notably at Napituca, as the army marched north and then west through the large towns of Uriutina ("War Chief"), "Many Waters," and Napituca. Food was abundant since it was early September, after the maize harvest.[44] Even though the Indians hid from the Spaniards, the explorers nonetheless guessed that the area was more populous than those from which they had come.

Crossing the Suwannee River (the "River of Deer"), De Soto's army entered paramount chief Uzachile's home grounds but never saw him. Viedma, Rangel, and Elvas say little about this area, but took note of abandoned towns along the line of march (the Indians had fled), the capture of a few Indians, and the river crossings. Archaeological research shows there were at least three clusters of villages.[45]

Elvas describes Apalache province, where the army wintered at Anhaica (modern Tallahassee), as containing many towns within a league and a half of Anhaica. He mentions their abundant stores of maize, pumpkins, beans, dried plums, and nuts. Viedma simply states "there are many towns, and it is a land of plentiful food."[46] Mostly the accounts speak of finding Narváez's shipbuilding camp on the coast and of arrangements made to bring the men who had remained at Ucita (Tampa Bay) to join the army. In fact, Apalachee seems to have had the largest, most centrally governed population in all of the peninsula. The chroniclers' cryptic comments hardly do it justice; perhaps they were influenced by the constant hostility of the Apalachee during the sometimes cold and wet winter months that the Spaniards spent camped in Anhaica.

In sum, the "secrets of the land" that the De Soto expedition's survivors wrote down and those they told orally confirmed earlier negative impressions of peninsular Florida but emphasized the economic and conquest potential of the chiefdoms of the piedmont. Peninsular Florida and its coasts did not contain resources or peoples that Spaniards might profitably exploit in the established ways; they were a source of slaves to be sold elsewhere in the Caribbean. Elvas's summary claimed it to be "a lean land, and most of it covered with rough pine groves, low and very swampy and in places having lofty dense forests, where the hostile Indians wandered so that no one could find them."[47] By contrast, the piedmont polities of Ocute, Cofitachequi, and Coosa had been revealed to be populous and generally friendly. These polities possessed soils potentially excellent for Spanish agriculture. Mineral wealth had eluded the Spaniards, but they had gotten reports of copper and another metal, likely gold, at Chisca. And there were fresh water pearls and fine furs around Cofitachequi. The Spaniards had not sorted out the political and social systems of their unwilling hosts, but thought that they knew which chiefs were the more powerful on the basis of how their fellow Indians treated them and the extent of the lands they governed. And De Soto's men had noticed differences among the Indians such as clothing materials, house types, and palisaded and unpalisaded towns. Overall, the written accounts, and we may assume the oral ones as well, give a good general picture that, at least partially, has been validated by archaeology.

The chronicler Francisco López de Gómara tells us that although many men had lost their fortunes and some had lost their lives in De Soto's reconnaissance, the return of the expedition to Mexico aroused enthusiasm for a conquest. Julián de Samano and Pedro de Ahumada, brothers of Juan de Samano who was the secretary of the Council of the Indies, petitioned for the privilege. Evidently they planned to go to the River of Santa Elena, ascend it to Cofitachequi and there exploit its pearls and fine furs while seeking metals in the mountains. But in the end, no expeditions sailed. The Dominican defenders of Native American natural law rights apparently insisted that La Florida be reserved as a mission field where they could try their peaceful approach to conversion and establishing Spanish sovereignty.[48] The martyrdom of Fray Luis Cancer on a west coast beach in 1549 wrote the end to that.[49]

Spanish interest in La Florida revived in the 1550s. From Mexico came urgent appeals that missionaries be sent north from Pánuco province to convert the Indians who had avenged themselves for Spanish mistreatment during visits to Pánuco by massacring the survivors of the 1554 Padre Island shipwrecks. In Mexico too, the tales of some of the De Soto survivors continued to provoke interest, which grew as the viceroy realized that a generation of young men was coming of age that would not be able to claim incomes from Indian tribute nor find the sorts of economic opportunities in New Spain that had made their fathers and uncles the colony's elite.[50] In Europe, the publication of Francisco López de Gómara's *General History* in 1552 put Ayllón's adventures into print. It also located Ayllón's Chicora at the "Point of Santa Elena" at 32 degrees north (Tybee Island, at the mouth of the Savannah River). Apparently less well known was the gentleman of Elvas's account of the De Soto expedition, published at Evora, Portugal, in 1557. At the same time, the French claim that Giovanni da Verrazzano had discovered the Southeast's coast for France in 1524 was receiving publicity in Giovanni Bautista Ramusio's collection of voyages published at Venice in 1556. Other evidence shows that the French were planning a colonial venture on La Florida's coast.[51]

The Council of the Indies fabricated from these origins a composite plan that responded to secular and state interests rather than the missionary ones that were the original impetus for again thinking about trying to occupy La Florida. As approved on 29 December 1557, the plan called for a large force to be prepared in Mexico, landed on the Gulf of Mexico coast at Ochuse (Pensacola Bay), and then sent inland to Coosa and eventually to the Point of Santa Elena. By stages, the colonists would build a chain of Spanish towns along a road that would connect the Gulf of Mexico and the Atlantic. Indians would be evangelized and might be assigned in encomiendas.[52] Everyone expected the piedmont to become a source for wine and olive oil.[53] The Ochuse colony would also serve as a coast guard station for the benefit of storm-tossed and shipwrecked sailors.

The result, the expedition of Tristan de Luna y Arellana, was a disaster. Sailing in June 1559 from San Juan de Ulloa (modern Veracruz), the fleet landed horses at Mobile Bay in late July and colonists at Pensacola Bay on 15 August. They called their camp Polanza. About half of the supplies had been landed at Pensacola when, on 19 September, a tropical storm drove many of the ships ashore, destroying the supplies they carried and damaging many already ashore. For the next nineteen months, the colonists were usually desperate for food, although some supplies were sent from Mexico.

To relieve their hunger, Luna sent an advance party inland in the fall of 1559, finding Nanipacana, an Indian town and district probably on the Alabama River. By the time Luna moved most of his main force there in the spring of 1560, the Indians had managed to hide what remained of their stored food, harvest the first maize crop, and flee, leaving the Spaniards with a largely uninhabited district.[54] By then, too, the number of persons in the expedition had decreased because many of the sick and useless had been allowed to return to Mexico on supply ships.

Luna next, in May 1560, sent fifty cavalrymen, one hundred foot soldiers, and perhaps fifty servants to seek Coosa, whose alleged agricultural bounty he hoped to tap to support his hungry colonists and their animals. This party moved north, apparently parallel to a river, but whether it was the Coosa or Tallapoosa is unclear. The party passed through three inhabited districts (Talpa, Ynicula, and Atache) and crossed a forest buffer zone broken only by one small area ("six leagues long") of more open land (savannahs) to reach Onachiqui, the first town of the paramount chiefdom of Coosa. Moving more slowly and pausing at Apica to send letters and a party of horsemen back to Nanipacana (they actually left from Coosa), the exploring party seems to have taken a month to move the fifteen or so leagues from Onachiqui to Coosa's main town. As they moved along, the Indians traded food for trade goods that the Spaniards had brought for that purpose. The Spaniards were careful to camp away from the villages and maize fields so as to avoid surprise attack, quarrels with their hosts, and damaging Indian plantings.[55]

The reports sent from Apica and Coosa presented a mixed picture of the country. None of the inhabited districts between Nanipacana and Coosa were as large as Nanipacana. All were being cultivated but had been deserted by the Indians as the Spaniards advanced. None had a town with 150 houses and most towns contained under 50 houses; all were surrounded by heavy pine-oak forests that would have to be cleared before the Spaniards could farm or run cattle. Given these facts and the small extent of cultivated area and open forest around each, the friars—but not Ma-

teo del Sanz, who was the commander of the exploring party—
judged the three districts unsuitable for Spanish settlement even
if the Indians were to be displaced, which would have been forbidden by Luna's orders. Coosa, on the other hand, consisted of
more extensive fields and savannahs and many towns. The visitors could not ascertain the population because the Indians had
removed their families from the towns, leaving just the paramount chief in residence with many of his men and a few serving women.[56]

By the time the search party found Coosa (in July 1560), events
were underway that ended the effort to colonize Coosa. Five
ships filled with supplies were on the Gulf of Mexico bound for
Pensacola Bay. When these supplies arrived, the colonists at
Nanipacana returned to that bay, leaving a message for the men
at Coosa. The arrival of the messengers from Coosa then caused
Luna to decide to take a party there so that he could see the
ground for himself and decide whether to attempt a settlement
at Coosa or any of the intermediate points. Luna's decision led,
in turn, to a rebellion by officers and men, the result of which
was the dispatch by the expedition's officers of a mounted party
to Coosa to report on "the insufficiency of the country" and to
withdraw the men already there until the Viceroy of Mexico
could order what should be done in light of the King's order,
newly received, that the Point of Santa Elena be occupied. Meanwhile, the men at Coosa lived fairly well, exchanging trade goods
and their military skills—used against a rebellious province at
the behest of the paramount chief of Coosa—for food.[57]

The Atlantic Coast Once Again

The final phase of the Luna expedition involved two failed
attempts to obey the preemptory royal order of 18 December 1559
to settle the Point of Santa Elena *first*. The royal order evidently
was motivated by fear that the Scots and French, allied because
of the April 1558 marriage of Mary Stuart to Francis II of France
(who ruled as king from 10 July 1559 to 6 December 1560), might
seize the harbor said to be there. Although somewhat to the north
of the mouth of the Bahama Channel, the Point had come to

have strategic and symbolic importance as the military key to the safety of Spanish shipping sailing north through the Bahama Channel and as the locus of Spain's claim to North America as well as Ayllón's new Andalucia.[58] The ships that Luna sent out in late July or early August 1560 were scattered by a storm in the Gulf of Mexico. Two reached Havana and one sailed to Mexico. A fourth was unaccounted for. The second attempt was made by Angel de Villafañe, Luna's replacement as commander of the colony. Sailing from Mexico in March 1561, his assignment was to reduce the colony at Pensacola to about seventy men and take the rest (230 soldiers) to the Point of Santa Elena by way of Havana. At Havana he allowed the unwilling to go where they wished; many returned to Mexico. Then, with four small ships and about one hundred men, Villafañe sailed north. The voyage, from April to July 1561, reached the Point of Santa Elena and explored northward to perhaps Cape Hatteras (Cabo de Trafalgar on Spanish maps), but did not leave a garrison. Some additional description of the coast resulted, but no finds of precious metals or numerous Indian populations. Two storms scattered the ships. The second one sank the two smaller ones. Villafañe ordered a return to the Antilles and eventually withdrew the men at Pensacola as well.[59]

Shortly after Villafañe left Havana, Antonio Velázquez, the new royal factor for the Florida colony, followed him northward with a shipload of supplies. Not finding Villafañe and experiencing a storm, Velázquez apparently entered Chesapeake Bay, where he picked up two Powhatan Indians. One of them was Paquiquineo, later baptized Don Luis de Velasco in honor of the viceroy of Mexico. Velázquez then sailed to Spain. His arrival at Seville in September caused Lucas Vázquez de Ayllón, the Younger, son of the judge who had tried to colonize Guale in 1526, to claim his long-ignored right as his father's heir to colonize North America. Although no known documents say where he intended to set up a colony under the contract signed with Philip II on 28 February 1562, the evidence we have points to Chesapeake Bay. D. Luis and his companion and some Dominican friars were to return there in the summer of 1562. Had they done so, the mission so established would have been good preparation for a small Spanish agricultural and trading colony.[60]

Meanwhile on 9 July 1561, at Monte Cristi, Hispaniola, and later in Havana, Villafañe and his men swore depositions describing their voyage and claiming, falsely, that there were no ports and no land suitable for settlement at the Point of Santa Elena. Circumstantial evidence suggests that Villafañe and his men had no interest in an Atlantic coast colony and so shaped their reports to excuse themselves for not trying to found one. Their report also suggested that there was no need for concern about a French colony along that coast. On 3 March 1562, at Mexico City, they affirmed their negative judgment in response to the inquiry of Philip II dated 23 September 1561, as to whether that was, in fact, their report.[61]

And so it came to be that the principal legacies of the 200,000 pesos that the Crown spent and the unknown number of lives that the Luna expedition cost were the reorientation of Spanish interest to the Atlantic face of La Florida and the spreading of misinformation about the peoples and resources of the Southeast, especially those of the piedmont paramount chiefdom of Coosa. The colonists at Pensacola confirmed the essentially correct views of Alvarez de Pineda and the De Soto survivors that the Gulf Coast was "a low sterile land." Villafañe and his men similarly denigrated the coast of the Carolinas, declaring that the Southeast was a poor land that would not profit anyone (including the French) and that the alleged port at the Point of Santa Elena had "no entrance" (a lie).[62] The colonists who returned to Mexico—especially the friars and the men who had rebelled at Polanza in August 1560 rather than go inland with Luna to examine Coosa—fabricated the story that Coosa was a small, poor place that "looked so much worse to the Spaniards for having been depicted so grandly. . . . [and that] those they had brought along as guides, being people who had been there before, declared that they must have been bewitched when this country seemed to them so rich and populated as they had stated."[63] In fact, the firsthand reports of the men who had gone to Coosa show that it likely was as populous as in De Soto's time and just as rich in agricultural produce.[64] Only the land between Nanipacana and Coosa was poorly inhabited, with perhaps three small chiefdoms set within the larger buffering forests. But a larger truth was contained in these statements: that the Mexicans were no longer interested in La Florida. As Villafañe and his captains declared in 1562, if exploration were to continue, it should be done from Spain, not Mexico, and north of 35 degrees North, where there were ports said to reach up to four leagues (about twelve and three quarters nautical miles) into the land.[65] And that, as it happened, was where the colony of Ayllón the Younger was to be.

The Spanish discovery of the secrets of La Florida should have moved the explorers on at this point to visit the North Carolina and Virginia coasts and attempt to found a colony on the shores of Chesapeake Bay, where D. Luis and his Dominican missionary escorts were to begin the process of converting his people. However, events in 1562–1563 shifted Spanish attention away from the unexplored promise of Chesapeake Bay to points further south. From that, in turn, came detailed knowledge of the coasts and their peoples, a new exploration of the interior of the Carolinas, and the first Spanish frontier in La Florida.

What happened was that the French began to take an interest in the Point of Santa Elena and that Spanish plans failed. Early in 1562, the Spanish ambassador to France reported Jean Ribault's preparations and departure for some point on the Atlantic coast of North America, eventually confirmed as the Point of Santa Elena, the alleged location of Ayllón the elder's Chicora.[66] Meanwhile, D. Luis and his companion fell dangerously ill upon landing in Mexico and remained there convalescing long after the departure of the dispatch boat that was to take them to Chesapeake Bay on its way to Spain with news of the 1562 convoy. No other shipping could be found and the question of how to provide for the proposed mission was remitted to Madrid.[67] Ayllón the Younger, whose two settlements theoretically would have secured Spain's title to La Florida against the French, delayed his departure from Spain until the fall of 1563, claiming difficulties raising funds and settlers. In the end, he got no further than Santo Domingo. Desertions and financial difficulties caused him to flee to New Granada, where he died in 1565.[68] The collapse of his expedition became known in Spain in the fall of 1564.

By the time that Ayllón the Younger's failure was reported in Spain, Philip II knew that the French did indeed intend to settle at the Point of Santa Elena. A search party sent from Cuba in the spring of 1564 met the Guale and Orista peoples and learned that the men Ribault had left at Port Royal Sound had fled, leaving only a boy, Guillaume Rouffi, a marble column, and the remains of their fort as evidence of their presence.[69] At the same time, news from diplomats and officials in the Caribbean told of a French plan to reinforce a colony at the Point of Santa Elena and to use it as a base against Spanish shipping and the Antilles. This was a report of René de Laudonnière's expedition, which sailed from France 22 April 1564. But rather than going to the Point of Santa Elena, it set up camp (at Fort Caroline) on the south bank of the River of May, the modern St. Johns River. The Saturiwa Indians of that area were friendly and seemed to have plenty of maize and other foods, in contrast to the scant stores that the Ribault garrison had found at Port Royal. The Indians also had a little silver and gold traded from southern Florida.[70]

This French post on the St. Johns River, even more than a base at the Point of Santa Elena, was a threat to the empire's commercial lifeline. Unaware of this new development, in February 1565, Philip II turned to his able naval commander Pedro Menéndez de Avilés with an order to summarize what was known about La Florida and French plans to occupy part of it and to suggest what could be done to prevent such a usurpation of Spain's claim to own it all. Menéndez's memo stressed the strategic threat to Spanish commerce using the Bahama Channel and to the Antilles, whose slave populations might be freed by the French. The land the French were interested in could grow sugar cane, he had heard, as well as cattle. His solution was to place five hundred men in as many as three settlements between the Point of Santa Elena and Newfoundland, after the coast had been carefully scouted for the best ports. This might cost 80,000 ducats.[71] In short, he combined the Ptolemaic notion of similar climates at the same latitudes (the meaning of his mention of sugar cane, which grew in the Canaries and Andalucia); the known location of Ribault's colony; Philip II's evident fixation on the Point of Santa Elena; and the Mexican conclusion of 1562 that exploration should be north of Cape Hatteras. To these four factors, he added a passing reference to the supposed arm of the

Pacific Ocean that reached across North America to near the Atlantic, an idea derived from the Verrazzano voyage of 1524 (see Figure 1.1).[72] Pointedly, he did not suggest establishing a settlement south of the Point of Santa Elena. The document also does not indicate any knowledge of the interior, but Menéndez seems to have had some, including Fr. Sebastián de Cañete's report from the De Soto expedition, because his contract called for a marquisate in the interior.[73]

Anxious to obtain the king's favor and to search for his only son, Juan, who was thought to have wrecked on the Florida coast in 1564 when returning from the Caribbean, Menéndez de Avilés agreed to lead a colony to La Florida to establish Spain's claim by effective occupation and to expel any other Europeans he found there. Then came news of the existence of Fort Caroline and of Ribault's preparations of a reinforcement for Laudonnière's colony. Philip II provided Menéndez with five hundred soldiers and 15,000 ducats in incentive money so that the expedition might beat French reinforcements to Fort Caroline.[74]

Menéndez's force put to sea from San Lucar de Barameda on 29 June. He arrived on the coast of Florida just south of St. Augustine Inlet on 28 August, St. Augustine's festival, but without all of the men and ships because a storm had scattered them. Jean Ribault, commanding the French reinforcements, dropped anchor that same day, but off the mouth of the River of May.[75]

Over the next two and a half months in a series of two battles and two surrenders of shipwrecked Frenchmen (that turned into massacres because the Spaniards considered the French pirates), Pedro Menéndez de Avilés destroyed the French forces except for a few Catholics, musicians, and one group of shipwrecked men who did not surrender. A few persons escaped from Fort Caroline and lived to reach France and tell the story. Fort Caroline, seized in the second battle, was converted into a Spanish fort, San Mateo. The Frenchmen who had refused to surrender were rounded up in November and then left as prisoners among the Ais Indians and then at a small Spanish fort at Jupiter Inlet. They and most of their guards died of hunger and Indian hostility.[76]

And while all of this was going on, the Spaniards built the first St. Augustine. The Spanish Tidewater Frontier was underway.

3.

The Spanish Tidewater Frontier, First Phase, 1562–1586

Except for a few months in 1564, Europeans have been present continuously on the Southeast's coast since early June 1562 when Jean Ribault established Charlesfort on Parris Island, South Carolina. By 1608, the Spanish successors of Ribault's Frenchmen apparently had mastered three of the four great problems of creating a frontier in La Florida. First, they had worked out methods for obtaining enough food and other goods. Second, they had reached an accommodation with the leaders of the coastal Indians that involved their acceptance of Spanish rule. And third, they had found local resources to exploit, although the benefits were confined to an elite group and were insufficient to support sustained economic expansion or to attract civilian settlers. However, they had not succeeded in transforming the European presence from that of an occupying army into a self-sustaining or even expanding settlement of families, even though there were Hispanic families in La Florida. Mixed in with the events that brought about mastery of these problems were the waxings and wanings of the French and Spanish presences along the coasts and up the rivers that flowed to them, presences generally within the distances of tidal flows.

The history of French and Spanish attempts to establish a

frontier on the Atlantic face of the American Southeast during these years is complex and divisible into at least six subperiods. The French attempt of 1562–1565 is the first. The Spanish effort divides into five subperiods: 1565–1570, which may be described as the rise and fall of their most expansive version of a frontier in La Florida; 1571–1586, the rise and abrupt end of a more limited Atlantic tidewater frontier with its center at Santa Elena and a secondary focus at St. Augustine; 1586–1597, a period of consolidation and renewed expansion that ended with the Guale Rebellion of 1597; 1597–1601, a period when Spaniards and Indians came to new agreements about lordship and tribute; and 1600–1608, when it appeared that the Spaniards had finally, and definitively, solved two of the four great problems of colonization and had made some progress on a third. Too, during the first eight years of the seventeenth century, new threats to the continued existence of the colony were turned aside. The new century thus marked the beginning of a sort of heyday for the tidewater frontier, an all too brief period before major epidemics destroyed its demographic basis among the Indians and before the establishment of permanent missions in the interior created the inland frontier with a consequent diversion of Spanish interest and resources. This chapter will carry the story to 1586. The next chapter will complete it to 1608.

The French

The basic story of renewed French interest in North America, 1562–1565, was sketched in the last chapter. What concerns us here is how their experiences at Charlesfort (1562–1563) and Fort Caroline (1564–1565) revealed possible solutions to the first of the four problems (feeding themselves) of colonists on the Atlantic coastal strand.

The thirty men Jean Ribault left at Charlesfort in 1562 apparently experienced little tension with their Native American neighbors but soon had difficulty getting enough food. Soldiers and seamen who were used to being fed or buying their food rather than raising it, they had arrived so late in the summer that they would have had trouble—had they wished to, which they did

☙ 49

THE SPANISH
TIDEWATER
FRONTIER,
FIRST PHASE,
1562–1586

not—growing maize and other foods in the quantities needed to carry them through to the next spring's harvest. The men soon exhausted the supplies Ribault had left and then discovered that the stored surpluses of their Indian neighbors were quite limited. Simply put, the coastal Indians were not commercial producers of basic foods, whatever may have been their trade with other Indians in specialty foods such as bear grease. Moreover, studies of climate using tree rings have shown that the southeastern coast was in the midst of a period of lower than normal rainfall and drought, causing less abundant Indian maize harvests.[1] Even trading as far as Guale, some sixty-five miles to the south, did little to relieve French shortages, which grew more desperate as the winter progressed. In the end, the survivors chose to chance an Atlantic crossing in an open boat rather than stay any longer on a coast where they could not obtain enough to eat.[2]

This sad story was known to René de Laudonnière and the captains of his expedition before they left France and shaped their decision about where to camp for their first winter on the coast. The expedition carried some food and expected to receive supplies in October and March but also expected to obtain food in La Florida. Arriving off the La Florida coast on 22 June 1564, and finding that the Timucuan-speaking Saturiwa Indians[3] of the River of May (the modern St. Johns River) apparently had both abundant food and some silver, the expedition's officers rather quickly agreed with Laudonnière that that was where the expedition should build its fort. As for Port Royal, Laudonnière declared "although the harbor there was one of the finest in the West Indies, the issue was not so much a question of the beauty of the location but more a question of the availability of things necessary to sustain daily life. In our first year, it would be much more important to live in a place with an abundant food supply than to be in a commodious and beautiful port."[4]

The Fort Caroline colony soon replayed the experience of Charlesfort, with locally imposed variations. European food, barely extended by a supply ship in early October 1564, soon ran low. French trade for Indian fall surpluses fairly quickly satisfied the Saturiwa's initial desires for European goods and exhausted the surpluses that they were willing to trade. The colonists then went further afield to seek food, paying higher prices in European manufactured goods as the winter advanced. Maize, edible acorns (probably white oak), and cassena leaves were secured from Cacique Hioacaia (i.e., Ufera, on the Satilla River), who ruled an area about twelve French leagues north of the St. Johns that was said to be the "most productive in maize of any along the coast."[5] Desertions in the late fall reduced French numbers but provided little relief from scarcity. In January 1565, Cacique Orista, the friend and former neighbor of Charlesfort, gave them some maize and a promise of more when the crop matured in the spring. But by May, the French were reduced to capturing a chief and ransoming him for small amounts of food. They obtained some relief from the Indians' early summer harvest in June, but by then their once friendly relations with Saturiwa, the local great chief, were so poor that little of that bounty was made available to them.[6] Like their compatriots of two years before, the French at Fort Caroline could think of nothing except escaping by ship. They would have done so had Jean Ribault not appeared off the St. Johns on 28 August with seven ships, six hundred men, and supplies. The rest of that story was told in the last chapter. On the subsistence question, the French had discovered that nowhere along the southeastern coast could Europeans expect to live year-round by trading for (or stealing) agricultural surpluses produced by Indians. Food would have to be imported or grown.

While thus engaged in a losing struggle to find enough to eat in an unfamiliar environment, the French also explored the St. Johns River Valley and the interior. What they discovered was of more importance to the Spaniards than proof once again that La Florida's Atlantic coast was a difficult place to set up a European community. The Spaniards knew *that* from their own previous experiences there.

French explorations indicated the rudiments of the geopolitical and human geography of northern Florida. About sixty miles up the St. Johns, and about ten miles inland to the west (perhaps near Georges Lake, northwest Putnam County) was the seat of a chief known to them as Outina, a name that meant "chief" in Timucuan. He was Saturiwa's enemy.[7] The chiefdom of Potano

☙ 51

THE SPANISH
TIDEWATER
FRONTIER,
FIRST PHASE,
1562–1586

was west of Outina and at war with it. The (apparently) paramount chiefdom of Aguacalecuen[8] had territories immediately to the west of the lower St. Johns River coastal terraces and extending to (and across) the Suwannee River. Apalachee and the mountains to the north also figured in their knowledge, although vaguely since no Frenchmen visited them. And not least, the French discovered that the silver and gold they found among the north Florida natives were obtained by trade from Indians well to the south.[9]

The Spaniards' Expansive Frontier, 1565–1570

If, as seems likely, Pedro Menéndez de Avilés learned most of what the French knew about La Florida's geography by interviewing prisoners and combining what they reported with Goncalo Gayón's knowledge of the Guale and Orista (gained while pilot for the Spanish search for Charlesfort in 1564), this would explain the details of his plan for an expansive tidewater frontier mentioned in his letters of late 1565 and early 1566. That frontier was to reach from Bahía de Juan Ponce (Calos) on the lower west coast of Florida to the Bahía de Santa María (Chesapeake Bay) on the north. There were to be four foci: garrisons of mostly royal troops at St. Augustine/San Mateo and the Chesapeake, and garrisons, and later towns, composed mostly of his own followers at the Point of Santa Elena and the Bahía de Juan Ponce. St. Augustine/San Mateo and the Chesapeake were sites of potential conflict with France. Santa Elena and the Bahía de Juan Ponce offered potential profits because the Calusa Indians at the Bahía de Juan Ponce were known to have gold and silver salvaged from Spanish wrecks. Santa Elena was the supposed key to the riches of Ayllón's Chicora and the interior. Menéndez believed, as well, that there might be an all-water route across Florida whose terminal points would be San Mateo and the Bahía de Juan Ponce. But, he reminded Philip II, this ambitious plan could not be implemented without royal help, especially because many of Menéndez's own supplies had not arrived in Florida.[10]

With characteristic energy, Menéndez de Avilés set about establishing the posts he projected and solving the supply problem.

His first trip was to Havana via a stop to round up the last of Ribault's men south of Cape Canaveral. He put them and Spanish guards into a fort at Ais, a place where there were coco plums, palmettos, and fish. After arranging for food supplies at Havana, he went to the Bahía de Juan Ponce and thence to St. Augustine (October–March 1566). He established a marriage alliance of sorts with the Calusa paramount chief, "Carlos," at Bahía de Juan Ponce. From St. Augustine the adelantado went to Guale and Port Royal, establishing peace among the Indians and a Spanish fort on Parris Island. On each occasion when he met with caciques, he offered gifts such as knives, mirrors, brass bells, and Spanish foods.[11] The sources do not indicate what they gave him in return. We may infer that the Indians understood these gifts in terms of their own systems of reciprocity.

Sailing again to Havana to arrange for supplies, Menéndez returned to St. Augustine on 10 July 1566 to find twelve hundred men and nine women (eight were married), who had been brought by Sancho de Archiniega as reinforcements to bolster the La Florida garrisons and the major ports of the Antilles against an expected French attack that summer. After a quick trip up the St. Johns River to check on part of the rumored cross-Florida route, Menéndez escorted many of these men to their duty stations in the Antilles (October 1566–February 1567). Others, led by Captain Juan Pardo on expeditions in 1566–1567 and 1567–1568, ventured across the coastal plain of South Carolina, into the piedmont, and across the Appalachian Mountains into the Tennessee Valley. Giving gifts of iron wedges and tools (mostly), Pardo secured what his notary recorded as the voluntary submission of the caciques and cacicas (female chiefs) to Spanish rule, tributes in maize to be held in local granaries, and detailed information about the agricultural, forest, and building-material resources of the interior. Like the exploration up the St. Johns River, Pardo's exploration was supposed to have been preliminary to further expansion.[12]

Menéndez ended his Antilles voyage in Havana where the supply ship, *Pantecras*, provided him and his agents with goods to sell and barter (at a profit, of course) to obtain foods for Florida. Philip II had sent the goods to support the royal soldiers in

᠁ 53

THE SPANISH
TIDEWATER
FRONTIER,
FIRST PHASE,
1562–1586

Florida, but food was more important than shoes. Also on the *Pantecras* were several Jesuits, whom Menéndez placed at Bahía de Juan Ponce and Tequesta (Miami) when he visited both locations in the spring of 1567 on his way back to St. Augustine before returning to Spain to seek additional royal help. Small garrisons were left and additional men ordered to them from St. Augustine. On this trip, Menéndez de Avilés also visited Tocobaga (on Old Tampa Bay), where he arranged a peace between the Tocobaga and the Calusa. Thirty caciques of the Tocobaga attended. A Spanish garrison of thirty soldiers was established as well.[13] Carlos's hostility and reports at Tocobaga that other hostile Indians lay between there and Macoya (on the upper St. Johns) frustrated the adelantado's hope to explore the western end of the supposed all-water route across Florida.[14]

The supply and population situations remained critical. Menéndez de Avilés had exhausted his personal credit (and that of his associates); royal support for the troops was slow to materialize; and, as will be seen, relations with the Indians were covertly and often overtly hostile. Men lost to mutinies and deaths in 1565–1566 had been replaced thanks to the Archiniega reinforcements, but Menéndez had not yet brought out any of the three hundred settlers he was supposed to place in, and initially support in, La Florida. The number of troops and other Spaniards in the colony had fallen somewhat from its early high of nine hundred in 1567.[15]

By 1567, the expansive tidewater frontier included troops stationed (in most cases temporarily) at Chiaha, Cavehi, Joara, Guatari, Canos, Orista, Santa Elena, Guale, San Mateo (formerly Fort Caroline), St. Augustine, Ais and then Jupiter Inlet, Tequesta (Miami), San Antonio de Padua (Carlos), and Tocobaga (Old Tampa Bay) (see Table 3.1). Except for the posts inland from Santa Elena, most of the additions to Menéndez's original list arose as he attempted to extend a sort of *pax hispanica* among the Indians, for example by resolving the wars between Carlos and Tocobaga and Guale and Orista. Officially, the soldiers were there to begin teaching Christianity. Unofficially, these additional posts allowed some of the men partially to live off the country during a period when supplies were critically short. Pardo had formalized this policy by having caciques agree to stock and maintain granaries of maize as a form of tribute. In the winter of 1568 he actually drew some of that maize to help feed Santa Elena.

Only a few of these posts survived for very long. The three (St. Augustine, Santa Elena, and San Mateo) that did had perhaps two hundred persons among them by 1570. Food, or rather its lack, was the undoing of most. Short supplies provoked Spanish abuses and Indian hostility when food and trade goods ran low (e.g., Tocobaga, Tequesta, and probably Pardo's forts). Where Indians did not destroy the garrisons, mutinies by starving soldiers did (e.g., Ais).[16] The collapse came first in south Florida, but the north soon followed. Pedro Menéndez Marqués, the adelantado's nephew, picked up the besieged survivors of the Carlos and Tequesta garrisons in the early months of 1568, after discovering that the men at Tocobaga had been killed.[17] Pardo's inland forts were destroyed by Indian attacks in the spring of 1568, within months of their establishment. Outnumbered and poorly supplied, the Spaniards at Santa Elena welcomed the survivors and their Indian women (slaves and concubines) but did nothing to retaliate.[18] The Jesuits, who had gathered at Santa Elena in the fall of 1568 to renew their missionary activity, found the Orista and Guale unreceptive, although they continued their mission work into 1570.

Along La Florida's east coast, the posts that survived into 1570 also had lost population after 1566. Hunger and death from natural causes and Indian attacks (see below) claimed some men. Others jumped ship in the Antilles if they were lucky enough to be assigned to a ship's crew. The largest losses were the men from the Archiniega expedition. Most returned to Spain in the summer of 1568, when their terms of enlistment ended. The arrival of 200 farmer settlers in the fall of that year somewhat offset their departure, but the result was still a loss of Spaniards.

The economic foundation of the garrisons improved slightly in 1568 but remained precarious. When Philip II renewed the contract for the settlement of La Florida, he sent a shipment of supplies and gave Menéndez extensive rewards and new, financially valuable privileges. For example, Philip II agreed that the

TABLE 3.1 Temporary Florida Garrisons and Missions, 1565–1574

Place	Date Established	Size of Party at Founding	Date Abandoned
San Mateo	September 20, 1565	Unknown	April 25, 1568
Ais	November 2 or 3, 1565	200 Spaniards and 50 Frenchmen	December, 1565
Santa Lucía / Jupiter Inlet	December 13, 1565	More than 100 men	March 18 (?), 1566
"Carlos" (San Antonio de Padua)	After October 15, 1566	23 men and friars; 50 men added in March 1567	June 15, 1569
Tocobaga (Old Tampa Bay)	March, 1567	30 soldiers	January, 1568
Tequesta (Miami)	April, 1567	30 soldiers and 1 Jesuit	Late March, 1568
San Pedro de Tacatacuru (Cumberland Island)	January (?), 1569	50 soldiers in August, 1570	December 1570 (?)
Guale	August 17, 1566	20 men	November 18 (?), 1566
Santa Elena (Parris Island)	April 15 (?), 1566	Unknown	August 16, 1587
Inland from Santa Elena			
Orista	After September 1, 1567	Unknown	By August, 1568
Canos	After September 1, 1567	Unknown	By August, 1568
Guatari	After September 1, 1567	Unknown	By August, 1568
Joara (Juada)	After September 1, 1567	18 soldiers	By August, 1568
Cavchi (Cawchi)	After September 1, 1567	31 soldiers	By August, 1568
Chiaha	January 1, 1567 (?)	39 soldiers	By August, 1568

Source: Paul E. Hoffman, *The Spanish Crown and the Defense of the Caribbean, 1535–585: Precedent, Patrimonialism, and Royal Parsimony* (Baton Rouge: Louisiana State University Press, 1980), 142–43; reproduced by permission of Louisiana State University Press.

newly created royal naval squadron that had begun to patrol the Caribbean under the command of Menéndez in the spring of 1568 would pay the salaries and rations for 150 soldiers in La Florida. Menéndez's share of prize money from the squadron also promised resources for his enterprise in La Florida. And, not least, Menéndez (like Hernando de Soto before him) was named governor of Cuba and thus gained privileged access to the Cuban economy.[19] However, this latter arrangement proved unsatisfactory, in part because Menéndez and his business associates could not control Cuba for their own profit. Meanwhile, the populations of the garrisons suffered . . . and declined.[20]

A final reduction in the number of Spanish soldiers came in 1570. Again in financial difficulties and wanting to force the Crown to create a separate *situado* or payroll for La Florida, in January Menéndez ordered the reduction of the garrisons to fifty men each at St. Augustine, Fort San Pedro (on Cumberland Island, where the garrison replaced San Mateo but was withdrawn to St. Augustine in early 1571), and Santa Elena.[21] In effect, he refused to pay any soldiers from his own funds. The surviving settlers fared no better. And, unable to achieve conversions and complaining of a general lack of support for their work, the Jesuits withdrew from La Florida that fall, remaining only for their brief, failed mission to Bahía de Santa María.

Notably absent from the list of garrisons established in 1565–1567 is the Bahía de Santa María. Menéndez's early letters discuss it enthusiastically as a key to controlling the fisheries off Canada and as a possible route to China (based on Verrazzano's idea of an isthmus, by then thought to be several hundred miles wide, at about 35–40 degrees north), but it rapidly dropped from his concerns in the spring of 1566 after he learned that Father Andrés de Urdaneta, the Spanish expert on the Pacific, did not believe the French geographic ideas upon which Menéndez had based his project for that part of North America. Having already summoned the Powhatan Indian D. Luis de Velasco (Paquiquineo) from Mexico during his earlier enthusiasm for Bahía de Santa María, Menéndez had to allow Dominicans from Mexico and D. Luis to sail to the bay in the fall of 1566. The documentary record suggests Menéndez was unhappy about their voyage.

🔖 **57**

THE SPANISH
TIDEWATER
FRONTIER,
FIRST PHASE,
1562–1586

Perhaps by prearrangement, the crew failed to find the entrance to Chesapeake Bay and sailed on to Spain.[22] Undiscouraged, D. Luis sought out the Jesuits and persuaded them that their mission would prosper in his homeland, far from the bad example and abusive behavior of the Spanish soldiers at Santa Elena. Menéndez tried to discourage Jesuit interest in the bay in 1570 but could not prevent their establishing a mission there. Over the winter of 1570–1571, D. Luis led the Powhatans in destroying it.[23] Meanwhile, as we have seen, the already much reduced remnants of Menéndez de Avilés's expansive tidewater frontier were contracting into the garrisons of Santa Elena and St. Augustine.

In short, by the summer of 1571, the expansive Spanish tidewater frontier had collapsed into two garrison towns containing approximately 150 soldiers on the royal payroll and perhaps fifty other persons. The Spaniards were on the ground, but were far from having reliable sources of food (and other supplies) and lacked truly subjugated Indian populations near their towns. Solutions to those problems, and the building of a self-sustaining Hispanic population, were still to come.

Not evident in the bare bones of Table 3.1 or the narrative just presented was the other major development of this period: the military conquest of the Timucuan towns on the lower St. Johns River and the coast northward to St. Simons Sound, an area known as Mocama. Crown policy and Menéndez de Avilés's initial intention were to establish a *pax hispanica* among and with the Native Americans of La Florida. As, in effect, the new paramount chief of the region, the adelantado intended to use Spanish governmental and judicial processes—the rule of law—to replace clan vengeance and war—the *lex talionis* based in the kinship system—for the resolution of disputes between the chiefdoms and between Indian and Spaniard. Christianity would teach the desired values of obedience and proper moral behavior. Spanish military might would provide the necessary sanctions. But such goals flew in the face of Indian culture and the goals of other Spaniards.

Abusive, often deliberately abusive, behavior by soldiers toward the people of the chiefdoms of Seloy and Saturiwa provoked hostilities within weeks of the Spanish victory over the French. The clashes started first at San Mateo, where soldiers hoped to force their own withdrawal. The Spaniards also sometimes did not meet Indian expectations of gifts when chiefs visited the Spanish camps, thereby further suggesting to the Indians that the Spaniards were hostile.[24] The early stages of war were marked by ambushes of individual Spaniards or of small groups, and Spanish counterraids; the fire arrow attack on the stores buildings at St. Augustine (built in Seloy's village in May 1566); and probably a general refusal to sell food. Too, Seloy may have moved away from the Spaniards, perhaps during the winter of 1565–1566. Although the Spaniards captured a few Indians and may have killed others, most of their attempts to engage the Indians in formal battles failed. After a final, failed attempt to negotiate peace with Cacique Saturiwa in May 1567, the Spaniards, beginning in July, resorted to scorched-earth tactics intended to starve the Indians of "Seloy and Saturiwa" into submission. We have record of such raids for July–August 1567 and again in May–July 1568. According to Gonzalo Solís de Merás, the first raid killed thirty Indians, with three Spanish deaths. Saturiwa responded with the destruction of Spanish livestock and continued ambushes. He also joined the French under Dominigue de Gourgues when they attacked the Spanish blockhouses at the mouth of the St. Johns and Fort San Mateo on 25 April 1568.[25]

Once begun on the lower St. Johns River, the war spread to the rest of Mocama. Saturiwa and his allies ambushed Spanish boats traveling between St. Augustine and Santa Elena on the waterway that passed behind the barrier islands north of the St. Johns River. In retaliation in January 1569, Esteban de las Alas led one hundred fifty soldiers in a raid on Tacatacuru (Cumberland Island) and the island of Cajón (unidentified but either Jekyll or St. Simon's Island). The raid concluded with the building of Fort San Pedro de Tacatacuru. San Pedro replaced San Mateo as the guardian of the inland waterway and the St. Johns River.[26] This fort was abandoned in early 1571 when the garrison was consolidated with its counterpart at St. Augustine. The raid and the fort demonstrated Spanish power but did not effect the sort of conquest that occurred in the lower St. Johns Valley.[27]

☙ 59

The Spanish
Tidewater
Frontier,
First Phase,
1562–1586

Scanty Spanish records indicate that the war in Mocama with Saturiwa and his allies continued into 1571. In that year, St. Augustine was reported to be under Indian siege. After that the war petered out because nothing is said about it, even by critics of Menéndez de Avilés's regime.[28] Probably the several years of drought (hinted at in documents and in the dendroclimatological record) and the repeated destruction of Indian maize fields around St. Augustine and along the lower St. Johns River broke armed resistance to the Spaniards.[29]

The war against Saturiwa and his allies caused the Spaniards to fall into alliances with his traditional enemies. In the summer of 1567 the Spaniards almost brought the Guale into the war to help them retaliate against the Tacatacuru, whom they accused of attacking Esteban de las Alas and two sloops of Spaniards sailing up the inland waterway toward Santa Elena.[30]

More significant was an alliance with Outina, whose hostility to Saturiwa had been known to and used by the French. When Menéndez de Avilés explored the St. Johns in 1566, Outina at first was unwilling to meet the Spaniards, informing Menéndez that they could have peaceful relations only so long as "the cacique was in his land and the adelantado in his." Although he did meet the adelantado when he came back down the St. Johns, the relationship seems to have been what Solís records: that Outina took Menéndez as his "elder brother" and accepted and reciprocated his gifts without accepting the Spanish idea that that made him their subject.[31] Nonetheless, this was the beginning of the incorporation of Outina's "Freshwater" (*Aguadulce*) Indians into the Spanish tidewater frontier.[32]

This incorporation continued and led to an alliance against Saturiwa in 1568. Fragmentary records show gifts of Spanish cloth and iron digging tools to the eleven caciques of Río Dulce, 1565–1569. More importantly, in Spanish minds at least, was the Spanish agreement to send Captain Pedro de Andrada and eighty-five soldiers to join Outina in a war on Potano. This raid in August 1567 resulted in fourteen Spanish deaths. Outina seems to have repaid the obligation thus created when his warriors joined a fifty-man Spanish party under Captain Vascocabal in attacks on the Saturiwa in the spring of 1568.[33]

In contrast to these hostilities at the southern focus of the Tidewater Frontier, Spanish–Indian relations in the immediate vicinity of the northern focus, Santa Elena, were relatively harmonious from 1566 into the early 1570s. This state of affairs arose because the twenty-man Spanish garrison lodged at Guale in August 1566 had left within a month and was not replaced even though Menéndez de Avilés had noted the agricultural potential of the area. Instead, gift-giving, trade and, in 1569–1570, Jesuit missionaries constituted the principal ongoing contacts with the Spaniards. Except for the missionaries, who had barely learned the language before the Order abandoned work in 1570 in the face of growing Guale hostility to the fathers' demands for food (for which they may not have offered anything material in return), these sorts of contact were readily accommodated within what seems to have been the Guales' traditions.[34] Cacique Orista and other caciques from the coastal plain villages north and west of Santa Elena, on the other hand, encountered neighbors who could not be kept at arm's length and had to be accommodated.

The Pardo documents indicate that by 1568 the Spaniards were very familiar with the resources and peoples in the forty leagues (about 100 miles) to the northwest of Santa Elena, the area where the Cusabo lived in small villages alongside streams that crossed the coastal plain. And, as with the Indians in the immediate vicinity of St. Augustine, the documents say little about Spanish relations with the Cusabo. Orista himself seems to have calculated that the advantage of preferential access to trade goods that came from being close to and allied with the Spaniards outweighed the abuse his people suffered at the hands of the soldiers and his people's need to disperse during the winter to gather food to replace stores sold to (or confiscated by?) the Spaniards. Caution probably also entered his calculations. In 1567, the Spaniards captured Ahoya Orata, cacique of a town further upstream on the Edisto River, because he had killed a Spanish corporal. We do not know how they punished him, but out of fear the town's residents burnt it and fled.[35]

In contrast to this situation on the coast, violence attended the end of the Spanish presence in the Piedmont, as has been noted. Lost was not only a presence in territory with potential for Span-

🎺 **61**

THE SPANISH
TIDEWATER
FRONTIER,
FIRST PHASE,
1562–1586

ish farming and prospecting[36] but also a source of food for the hungry garrison at Santa Elena. We have no evidence that the piedmont Indians regularly kept up contact with Santa Elena after the destruction of the Spanish forts in their midst.

The first effort to establish Spanish-style agriculture in the two Spanish towns coincided with the collapse of Menéndez de Avilés's expansive tidewater frontier, the war in Mocama, and the early accommodations between the Spaniards and their neighbors around Santa Elena. Spanish vegetables were introduced very early and were a success. A report from 1567 notes gardens with squash, turnips, and radishes. Archaeological evidence from Santa Elena indicates that watermelons (*sandías*) were also grown. But the effort to introduce domesticated animals was less successful. Menéndez arranged to have horses, hogs, goats, sheep, calves, and chickens sent to the colony in 1566 and 1567.[37] A good many died of natural causes or were eaten by hungry Spaniards, Florida panthers, and bears. Most that survived fell victim to Indian hostility during the Mocama war. Even so, their numbers increased, largely due to continued imports. In 1570 there were fifteen to sixteen mares and ten to twelve cows at St. Augustine; by 1574 when the town had been relocated to its present site, fifty head of cattle and fifty pigs were on an island away from the town (probably Anastasia Island, the site of the town between 1566 and 1572). Lack of fresh water as well as wild animal attacks kept the domesticated animal population size down.[38]

By contrast, we have little information on Spanish agriculture at Santa Elena. As of 1572, the Spaniards there were growing maize and Spanish vegetables although quantities cannot be determined. Experiments with wheat and viticulture may have been underway, especially at Santa Elena, where most of the farmers were taken in 1568. They may have had some domesticated animals. Menéndez's assurances that sugar could be produced were untested, although he at one point sent for a man skilled in sugarmaking. Indeed, except for trade in lumber engaged in by Esteban de las Alas, the potential of the colony for forest products was untapped as well.[39]

This scant success with Spanish agriculture promised but did not deliver an end to the garrisons' dependence on imports from the Antilles and Spain, the royal payroll, and Menéndez de Avilés's own funds.[40] Nonetheless, the Spaniards had begun to grow some of their own food. Although they may not have appreciated it, the long period of below average spring rains that had begun in 1559 came to an end in 1571, removing a climatological restraint on agricultural development.

In sum, when Menéndez de Avilés, his wife, her ladies, his daughter María and her husband D. Diego de Velasco landed at Santa Elena in mid-July 1571, the expansive tidewater frontier was no more, but in its place was a foundation for renewed expansion. That foundation consisted of two towns (St. Augustine and Santa Elena), a sound fiscal basis (the royal payroll) in theory if not yet in practice, an almost completed conquest of the Mocama Timucuans, and a small but committed Hispanic population that was beginning to produce some of its own food and a few babies. Too, the colonists had discovered some exploitable products of the land and, especially for the leaders, several techniques for exploiting the *situado*. However, the colony still clung to the coast's "worthless land and swamps" and was justified on military grounds.[41] Except in Mocama and among the Cusabo near Santa Elena, Native Americans had avoided prolonged contact with the Spaniards and had shaped the few contacts they had had to conform to Indian norms of reciprocal gift giving between leaders. Too, they, like the Spaniards, had undoubtedly observed that they were dealing with a society in which status was of great importance and was signified by ownership of exotic or at least uncommon goods. For both societies, that recognition offered a basis for accommodation within the Spaniards' claim of hegemony.

Establishing the Tidewater Frontier, 1571–1586

Spanish construction of control over the Atlantic coastal zones between and around their settlements at St. Augustine and Santa Elena in the years 1571–1586 began so slowly that little progress had been made by the time they provoked an uprising of the Guale, Cusabo, and perhaps even some of the Mocama Timucuans in 1576. The suppression of that "rebellion," as the Spaniards interpreted it, paved the way for more extensive control and mis-

☙ 63

THE SPANISH
TIDEWATER
FRONTIER,
FIRST PHASE,
1562–1586

sion work aimed at permanently integrating Mocama and Guale into the Spanish imperium. During the same period, Spanish farming took hold on a small scale at both settlements. Discovery and exploitation of local resources continued. A few families of as many as four children were created. In short, the solution of the four great problems of settlement seemed to be underway. These developments had hardly begun, however, when Sir Francis Drake raided St. Augustine (1586) and set the stage for the abandonment of Santa Elena and thus once again for a realignment of the Spanish frontier in La Florida.

The years 1571–1576 are not well represented in the standard governmental paperwork preserved in the Archive of the Indies, although some details have been found in investigations made after the disastrous events of 1576. What we know suggests that Menéndez's family and agents systematically exploited every economic opportunity the colony offered, whether Spanish, Indian, or natural. The profit was large enough that Menéndez's successor and son-in-law, Hernando de Miranda, immediately tried to seize control of this exploitive system, even going to Havana within months of his arrival in Florida to get his hands directly into the business.[42]

Eugene Lyon has shown how Menéndez, Velasco, and Pedro Menéndez the Younger, the adelantado's nephew and the royal treasurer and the central figure in the business, used soldier-merchants such as Captain Alonso de Solís, Juan de Soto, and Diego Ruiz to sell goods to the soldiers. The goods were usually purchased with funds from the *situado* and sold for high prices paid with IOUs that the merchants also may have heavily discounted against the nominal value of the goods. Menéndez de Avilés's merchant creditors brought still other goods to the Spanish towns for sale. The profit for the family and its merchant associates came when the IOUs were redeemed at full value. After the *situado* was repaid (when it had provided the working capital), the balance was profit, in silver. A variation of the scheme was to give gifts to the Indians on the royal account but keep for private profit the gifts (e.g., deerskins) given in reciprocation, according to their custom.[43] Whatever the frauds and abuses, the towns were supplied, if barely.

The Spanish farmers whom Menéndez de Avilés brought to

the colonies in 1568 and 1571 did not escape the ruling family's avarice.[44] They complained in 1576 that the adelantado had not provided them with the livestock he had promised. Like everyone else in the colonies, they had to buy European and Mexican goods from Menéndez's agents and associates at high prices. On the other hand, the farmers may have had freedom in selling their produce. Direct sales to the royal treasury are recorded in 1572 and 1575. However, agents of the ruling family made other purchases of maize for feeding the soldiers.[45] What seems clear is that as of 1576 Santa Elena's twenty farmers (and its Indian neighbors?) produced a lot of maize, some of which was sent to St. Augustine. There, most of the maize fields were said to belong to the governor, who used soldiers to work them. The thirteen married settlers at St. Augustine—presumably some were Menéndez's farmers—cultivated gardens using hoes. They were said to have grown various vegetables and to have sown between twelve and twenty pounds of maize seed (yearly?). They could not cultivate more ground because grinding maize by hand could take up to half of every day. They also could not depend on livestock because the governor controlled this resource at St. Augustine, and thus the ruling family likely owned all of it.[46] But again, the point is that progress was made in solving the problems of feeding the Spaniards.

Spanish hegemony over the Indians did not advance very far during these years, although a kind of reciprocity was established. Spanish gift exchanges with caciques who came to visit likely continued from the earlier period. Fragmentary records suggest that some of the caciques of the Cusabo villages near Santa Elena, and possibly also of Guale province, entered into what they likely understood to be ongoing (annual?) reciprocity arrangements with Velasco, who governed Santa Elena from 1571 to early 1576. He provided the caciques with gifts of tools, clothing, and other goods considered to be exotic by the Indians, goods drawn from the royal stores as well as Velasco's and other Spaniards' private resources. The caciques seem to have supplied the Spaniards with laborers for farm and domestic work and with some sarsaparilla roots, deerskins, furs, and pearls.[47] Velasco's gift giving may also explain why the caciques of Guale province allowed two Franciscan missionaries into their villages in 1573.

The presence of the missionaries and claims that Velasco exacted tribute in maize from the Indians (rather than buying it) signify that this reciprocity may have been unbalanced in favor of the Spaniards. An unbalance could indicate tacit Indian acknowledgement of the paramount status of the Spaniards.[48] Claims that Velasco exacted a tribute in maize (among other things) from the Indians were made in 1577 by some Spanish witnesses against him in an investigation of his rule. The eight hundred arrobas (about ten tons!) of shelled maize that inspectors confiscated from the royal treasurer's widow in 1576 may be additional evidence for such tribute.[49] That quantity of maize almost certainly came from Indian as well as Spanish sources. Pardo, it will be recalled, had levied a maize tribute (by villages) in 1566–1567. We have no information about how many villages among the coastal plain Cusabo and (less likely) Guale paid this tribute or whether the Spaniards gave gifts that the Indians understood to be reciprocation or even tribute to them. What seems certain is that Spanish influence dropped off rapidly with distance from Santa Elena.

The effect of Spanish gifts on native society was illustrated in Franciscan missionary work among the Guale. In the fall of 1573, Fathers Diego Moreno and Juan Cordero, and lay brother Juan, went to Tolomato and Guale town. Sometime later, the cacique of Guale town, who was a nephew and possible heir of the Tolomato cacique (who was the *mico mayor* or quasi paramount of the Guale nation), accepted baptism for himself (as Diego de Valdés) and his wife (as María Menéndez). Velasco and his wife served as godparents. Gifts were showered on the new converts in the hope of moving others to also accept baptism. However no additional baptisms took place before the friars learned of Menéndez de Avilés's death and abandoned their work in the summer of 1575. They seem to have died in a shipwreck en route to New Spain.[50]

The cacique of Guale town and his wife may well have calculated that their baptism would please the Spaniards and so give them better access to Spanish goods and support for his succession to the office of mico mayor when his uncle died. Instead, however, cacique Guale discovered that one of his subordinates showed him disrespect. When Guale went to the man's village, the man's nephew killed Guale with an arrow.[51] The widow then demanded and got Spanish vengeance. Two versions of the story differ as to whether this was done by Spanish soldiers carrying out two (or more) executions in Guale itself and/or by the garroting of the assassin at Santa Elena. The versions agree that Spanish intervention angered the Guale nation.[52] Hernando de Miranda had authorized the killings, apparently with the offhand remark that the deaths of one or two Indians were of no importance to him.[53] But what he had done was to create a blood feud between the clans of the victims and the Spaniards. The intervention apparently alarmed all the coastal Indians, who may have recognized in it both the Spaniards' assumption that they could do what they wished to the Indians and the Spaniards' rather different concept of the rule of law as compared to Indian notions of clan vengeance. Coming after a decade of affronts and abuses, this latest outrage was too much. In concert with the Cusabo and Escamacu, the Guale planned a war on the Spaniards.

The first blow of the Guale uprising fell on Treasurer Menéndez de Avilés, El Mozo, and other treasury officials. Carrying the payroll for the soldiers as they sailed north in early June 1576 along the inland waterway from St. Augustine, they were killed near Sapelo Island. The rebels burned alive two interpreters for the Guale language who were with them, to prevent word from reaching Santa Elena. Shortly afterwards, a Spanish patrol searching for Indian laborers who had fled from Santa Elena after stealing Spanish clothing seized the evening meal from Indians at Escamacu. The Indians, in turn, killed the Spaniards while they slept, leaving only one man, who had been attending to nature's call outside of the village, to escape to warn Santa Elena. Five other Spaniards who had been in Guale seizing maize, and whom an Indian woman had warned of the rebellion, were killed by Escamacu south of Santa Elena. Another patrol that was sent to scout the northern end of Santa Elena Island was ambushed, with only badly wounded war dogs and one Hispanicized Indian escaping with their lives. The Spaniards aban-

☙ 67

THE SPANISH
TIDEWATER
FRONTIER,
FIRST PHASE,
1562–1586

doned their houses and retired to the fort. Gutierre de Miranda, who had come from Havana with the supply ships to take his wife back to Havana, counseled his brother to improve his defenses and go on the attack. Instead, Hernando de Miranda allowed the women of the town to carry him to the ships as part of a general flight. The Indians looted and burned the town as the Spaniards sailed away.[54]

The refugees from Santa Elena stopped at St. Augustine, where the soldiers were forced to land. Farmers and other civilians, and no doubt a favored few from among the soldiers, continued on to Havana, whence some went to Mexico and others to the Antilles. Hernando de Miranda sailed for Spain. Gutierre de Miranda was left in command at St. Augustine. But supplies were soon short and Indian raiding parties occasionally appeared.

The response of Philip II to the news of the rebellion of "his" Indian subjects in Florida was unusually decisive and quick. Pedro Menéndez Marqués was named governor and hastened to La Florida with fifty soldiers and supplies. When he arrived at St. Augustine, he found the inspector Baltasar del Castillo busily investigating the events of the previous summer. Also awaiting him were fields around St. Augustine that had been planted in maize by Gutierre de Miranda's order, and a report that the French were in Guale inciting Indians to attack St. Augustine.[55] The French were the crew of *Le Principe*, wrecked while trading and scouting for a possible new French colony at Port Royal.

Although personally against reestablishing Santa Elena, Menéndez Marqués followed orders and sent Gutierre de Miranda, a hand-picked force, and enough precut timber for a fort to put the new garrison under cover from the Indians. As anticipated, the sudden reappearance of a Spanish fort disheartened the Indians. Menéndez Marqués inspected it in October 1577.

Perhaps during the winter and spring of 1577–1578, but certainly following the arrival in 1578 of the first of the additional 150 soldiers the Crown had ordered to Florida at Marqués's suggestion, the new governor set to work reestablishing Spanish hegemony at St. Augustine as well as in Guale and around Santa Elena. We do not know what was accomplished around St. Augustine. In the north, the Spaniards swept through Guale in the spring of 1579, burning nineteen towns and their maize fields and seizing some of the Frenchmen living there. A second sweep in August into Santa Elena's hinterland produced the defeat of a large Indian force and the deaths of forty Frenchmen at Cosapue. By the late fall, the French threat appeared to be gone. However, a Spanish battle with a French ship in the mouth of the St. Johns River in July 1580 showed that French interest in the Mocama–Guale coast had not ended. Indeed, French sarsaparilla collectors continued to frequent the coast, with Guale and Timucuan assistance.[56] Fragmentary evidence shows that the Spaniards also shipped sarsaparilla from La Florida during these years.[57]

Menéndez Marqués's violent retaliation against the rebels of 1576 produced the desired results in the short term. The caciques of Cosapue (on 14 October 1579) and Orista (on 14 February 1580) swore allegiance to the Spaniards and surrendered the French who remained in their villages. The caciques of Guale province soon fell into line, beginning with the caciques from Guale town (22 January 1580) and Tupique (6 February) and Tupique's heir from Guano (25 February).[58] Likely these lineages were the parties in the murder that had led to Spanish intervention and then the rebellion. Once they had made peace, the mico mayor of Tolomato, the acknowledged paramount of the Guale people, appeared on 7 March 1580 to make obeisance, ratify the peace agreement with Guale, Tupique, and Guano, and agree to pay an unspecified tribute. Over the next five months, with what appears to have been an interruption for maize planting in April and May, the Guale caciques of Aluste, Asopo, Talapo, Ospo, Yagoa [Yoa?], Fasque, Sapala, and Lulopalaque [Otopalo? or Olatapotaque?] all went to Santa Elena and submitted to Spanish rule and the tribute that Tolomato had agreed to pay.[59] Spanish treasury officials later said that the tribute consisted in providing for Spaniards when they passed through the villages. We may infer that each cacique agreed to fill and maintain a granary with the products of communally worked fields. If that was the system, it did not guarantee the Spaniards any given quantity of grain beyond what the harvest yielded.

Peace around the northern focus of the tidewater frontier did not last. Whether because the obeisances of 1579–1580 were

☙ 69

THE SPANISH
TIDEWATER
FRONTIER,
FIRST PHASE,
1562–1586

based on Indian expectations of Spanish gifts that were not met in 1580 or whether there were new abuses by the Spaniards (or yet another reason), in the fall of 1580 Guale again attacked Santa Elena. Peace may have been restored for most of 1581, but Indian raids resumed that winter. The Spaniards killed or captured fifty Indians. These attacks in 1581 may have been in reaction to deaths from the "pestilence" at Santa Elena during the winter of 1581–1582 and to continued Spanish demands, or it may have been clan vengeance for deaths not recorded in Spanish sources.[60]

Peace was reestablished in 1582. To reinforce it, in 1583 Menéndez Marqués held a general Indian conference at Santa Elena. Caciques from the interior and the seacoast gathered to render obeisance and receive gifts, including clothing. In his report, Menéndez Marqués observed that gifts were the only means for attracting the Indians so that the Gospel could be proclaimed to them. He also attempted to get them to believe that a drought, which had broken that summer at St. Augustine, was God's punishment because the northern Indians were not Christians, unlike those around St. Augustine. Many accepted this thesis and were seeking baptism, he claimed, but the Franciscan Francisco del Castillo, Santa Elena's chaplain, was only granting baptism to individuals who knew the prayers. Missionaries were needed. Father Alonso de Reinoso, who was present at the conference, carried that request to the Franciscan houses in Spain.[61]

In contrast to the prolonged rebellion of the Guale, the Indians around St. Augustine seem to have settled back into peaceful relationships almost as soon as Menéndez Marqués arrived. By late 1583, he reported baptisms, at least eighty Indians attending Sunday religious instruction, the establishment of two Indian villages within half a league and another three leagues off, and yet others being laid out as the Aguadulce and groups of the Mocama Timucuans gathered around the Spanish town. Fray Alonso Cavezas, chaplain of the fort at St. Augustine and one of two Franciscans in La Florida since perhaps 1577, was responsible for religious instruction.[62] To the pull of Spanish gifts, trade, and (perhaps) Christianity, the years 1580–1584 added the push of fear of raids by the Potano. Gutierre de Miranda, thirty-three

Spanish soldiers, and Indian bearers from Nombre de Dios and the combined town San Sebástian–Tocoy attacked the Potanos' principal village in 1584, killing twenty of them. Afterwards, the cacique of Potano build a new town further west and left the Indians of the St. Johns River Valley alone.[63]

While the Spaniards were thus reestablishing hegemony over the coastal Indians, they were also making major strides in building up their own population and providing themselves with food. As has been noted, in 1578 the king authorized 150 additional soldiers for La Florida's garrisons, with some increase in the *situado*. Some 25 of the first 150 were drowned off St. Augustine bar when their ship sank, resulting in garrisons of 186 (up from 94 on 28 November 1576) at St. Augustine and 78 (up from 53 on 12 October 1577) at Santa Elena.[64] An additional 44 men were sent in 1580 with Gutierre de Miranda. Accompanying them were their wives and the wives of a number of other soldiers and officers in the colony. These women joined the few Spanish women who had remained from among the adelantado's farmers and the Indian women married to soldiers. As many as four African slave girls accompanied Doña María de Solís, the governor's wife, and Rodrigo de Junco's wife when they moved to St. Augustine.[65] Thirty other Africans, royal slaves from the fort construction at Havana, arrived in St. Augustine in January 1582. They were to relieve the soldiers of carrying timber for the constant rebuilding of the forts and, later, cleared forests for fields. Some slaves then farmed the new fields and were hired by private persons.[66] As well, in the fall of 1584, three Franciscan priests and one lay brother arrived in Florida. They began working among the Indians in the spring of 1585.[67]

Although no reports state the total populations of the two Spanish towns during the early 1580s, we know that in late 1583 the garrisons contained 275 men of an authorized strength of 300, that there were farmers and married men with as many as six young children, and that some of the vacant positions were being used to help these families.[68] Judging from later counts, the non-garrison population may have been another 200 or so, with the larger part concentrated at St. Augustine, where Menéndez Marqués had established his headquarters.

Information on agricultural production at the Spanish settle-

🐚 71

THE SPANISH
TIDEWATER
FRONTIER,
FIRST PHASE,
1562–1586

ments is scanty. Following up on Gutierre de Miranda's work in 1577, Menéndez Marqués continued to employ soldiers to cultivate maize fields around St. Augustine. He claimed they harvested 1,000 fanegas (about 1,600 bushels) in 1578. In addition, he bragged that figs, pomegranates, oranges, grapes, kidney beans (*frijoles*), broad beans (*habas*), melons, squashes, lettuce, artichokes, onions, garlic, and various Spanish greens were growing well in St. Augustine's gardens. To this list he might have added the peach and certain native nuts, fruits, and commensal plants. He had plans to bring in livestock and horses from the Antilles.[69] At Santa Elena at least thirty-three residents had houses and tended thirty-five "gardens."[70] The plants they grew probably were similar to those reported for St. Augustine.

Zooarchaeological data show that the Spaniards consumed pigs, cows, chickens and possibly goats, as well as deer, turtles, opossums, rabbits, squirrels, and even raccoons. They also ate large quantities of mostly non-seasonal fish such as mullet, and migratory and non-migratory birds.[71] We know little about the raising of domestic animals aside from the fact that from 1580 onward the Crown began to include grants of pasturage in the privileges it gave new officials. Too, Gutierre de Miranda made probably exaggerated claims about the income from his Santa Elena hog farm and livestock (possibly cows).[72] Foods, especially wine, salted meat, flour, sweets, and spices, as well as ceramics, clothing, and metal goods continued to be imported, providing a profitable trade for merchants favored by the governor and for the men sent to collect the *situado*.[73]

All of this progress in gaining Indian obedience and requests for missionaries, in Spanish population growth, and in agriculture took place against a backdrop of continuing criticism of the colony and the news, in 1585, that an English colony had been planted on the coast well to the north of Santa Elena. Thus in 1578 and 1580, a fort in the Keys was suggested, to aid shipwrecked mariners. In 1584, patrol boats were advocated as supplements to the forts.[74] Misleading news of Sir Richard Grenville's Roanoke colony project reached Spain from spies and the Spanish ambassador in Paris in the spring of 1585, but Caribbean authorities learned more directly of Grenville's purposes as he passed through the Antilles, gathering livestock and plant samples.

Pedro Menéndez Marqués, who was in Havana preparatory to sailing to Spain when this Caribbean news arrived, decided to visit St. Augustine on his way to Spain, in case the English had settled in La Florida. When he did, the officers persuaded him to remain to replace Gutierre de Miranda, who was an unpopular acting governor. The only news of the English was that Indians had seen their sails north of Santa Elena.[75] For the moment, the threat of an English settlement in or attack on La Florida seemed remote.

That changed on 17 June 1586 when the soldiers of Sir Francis Drake's expeditionary force took, looted, and burned St. Augustine. The Spaniards had had warning of his activities in the Caribbean since January of that year and had built a new artillery platform and fort—San Juan de Pinillo—opposite the end of the channel into the bay. The soldiers, outnumbered and concerned for the safety of their families, who had been removed to the forests west of town when the English appeared off St. Augustine bar, put up a perfunctory resistance, spiked the guns, and decamped to the woods. Drake's men burned not only the town; they also cut down fruit trees and tore up gardens and took building hardware. After the English left, Indians hostile to the Spaniards picked over the ruins for salvageable goods. Sailing north, Drake's pilots failed to find the entrance into Port Royal Sound, thus sparing Santa Elena. Drake sailed on to the Outer Banks, where he found Grenville's Roanoke colony ready to return to England. The building hardware gathered from the ashes of St. Augustine went with them.[76] At St. Augustine, he may have left a minor epidemic among the Indians.[77] Almost overnight, many of the Spaniards' hard-won gains of the previous fifteen years disappeared.

4·

The Tidewater Frontier, Second Phase, 1586–1608

As the smoke cleared over the burned ruins of St. Augustine, the Spaniards set about rebuilding their homes and consolidating their position in La Florida against what Drake had warned would be a return visit. His raid had also emboldened the Icaste and Casacolo Indians south of the town; they talked about capturing St. Augustine's women. Consolidation thus meant both gathering Spanish military resources and strengthening Spanish control of the Indians in the vicinity of St. Augustine.[1]

Once the immediate danger of Indian or English attack had disappeared and the Spaniards had rebuilt their town, they resumed their interrupted efforts to control the Guale and again began to cast their eyes on the human and natural resources of the fall line ecotone west of Guale and of the mountains beyond. But, as had happened with their attempt to establish the tidewater frontier between 1571 and 1586, this renewal suffered a temporary reverse caused by the Juanillo Revolt of 1597 that swept the missions out of Guale. The Spaniards repressed that revolt and accepted the Guale's "voluntary" (but compensated) labor at St. Augustine as part of a general accommodation of the caciques to Spanish rule. This labor supply and the opening of new fields at St. Augustine helped the Spaniards solve their food-supply problems. The accommodation also opened the door to the intensive missionary activity that followed. That, in turn, was barely underway when the continued existence of the colony, or at least its location at St. Augustine, was challenged. In the end, the Franciscan claim of 14,000 converts saved a Spanish military presence in La Florida. Shortly after, preliminary mission work among the Timucuans of north central Florida and renewed interest in the interior of Georgia prepared the way for the shift to the inland frontier after the devastating epidemics of 1613–1617 destroyed half or more of the population of the tidewater missions.

Renewal of the Tidewater Frontier, 1586–1597

The rebuilding and replanting of St. Augustine proceeded steadily between 1586 and 1594 thanks to tools and supplies that officials in Cuba and Spain hastened to the stricken city. The burden, however, fell on the residents and their Indian neighbors. For some Spaniards, starting over was too much. Over the next decade, some family men who had endured life in La Florida for a dozen or more years and men who felt themselves too old to rebuild homes and livelihoods left St. Augustine.[2] Still others left in 1593 because of their roles in overthrowing governor Gutierre de Miranda, one of five men named to that office during these years.[3] The unmarried soldiers, too, seem to have been largely replaced by new recruits. Still, a core of married men and members of the ruling families remained.

Father Andrés de San Miguel's description shows that by 1595, St. Augustine had been restored physically to its pre-Drake condition, with improvements. The houses of the wealthy were constructed of boards (perhaps backed by wattle and daub for insulation), with wooden roofs, an improvement over the palm thatch of earlier periods (Figure 4.1). The mess groups of bachelor soldiers, on the other hand, continued to live in houses of wattle and daub with thatched roofs. Framed by setting posts into the ground, both types of structures required continual upkeep. The town's gardens again produced pears, figs, melons, watermelons, squash, and onions. A few cattle roamed a small

Figure 4.1. St. Augustine, 1595. (SPAIN) MINISTERIO DE
EDUCACIÓN, CULTURA, Y DEPORTE, ARCHIVO GENERAL DE INDIAS,
SEVILLE, MAPAS Y PLANOS, FLORIDA Y LUISIANA, 3. BY PERMISSION.

island near the town (probably "A" on the figure). San Miguel
does not mention maize production but some was grown.[4] By
1600, the town could boast a hospital, a formal market on the
plaza, a fishhouse, a slaughterhouse, and an animal-powered
mill to grind maize (*atahona*). And all that despite the fire of
14 March 1599 that burned the Franciscan convent, the royal
granary, and fourteen houses; and despite the tidal surge of the
hurricane of 22 September 1599 that flooded the town.[5]

Two estimates of St. Augustine's population for the late 1590s
exist. A report from 1598 says that 300 persons were on the payroll and another 400 were dependents, not counting African
slaves and Indian servants. There were sixty married couples.[6] A
more detailed estimate from the year 1600 places St. Augustine's
population at approximately 500, of whom 60 were wives, 110 or
so were children (22 percent of the total), and not more than 30

were African slaves. About one in five of the 275–280 soldiers, sailors, and officers was married. Of the soldiers' and sailors' wives, over half were Indians, judging from later evidence. Officers and officials all had Spanish wives, a social detail that reinforced their higher status in the community.[7] A few widows and orphans of meritorious individuals enjoyed soldier's billets, as did the Franciscans. But whether the population totaled 500 or 700 persons, the numbers do not indicate as strong a demographic base as would have existed had Drake's raid not sown discouragement. Lacking enough women, this population could not replace itself by natural means. The Hispanic population continued to resemble an occupying army, one increasingly made up of men born in the town. These men often had Spanish fathers and Indian mothers.

Consolidation of Spanish military resources came in 1587. Never convinced of the value of Santa Elena, Menéndez Marqués and his associates used the threat of Drake's return to argue for the consolidation of the garrisons at St. Augustine. That suggestion, in turn, opened the door for reconsideration of where the Spaniards ought to have their fort, given the strategic importance of the Florida Straits and the need to aid shipwreck victims. The Council of the Indies suggested that the consolidated garrison be moved to Key Largo. However, Alonso Suarez de Toledo wrote from Havana to suggest abandoning La Florida. He claimed that Spain, with all of its nearby colonies, had not been able to keep the garrison fully supplied. An enemy, lacking access to those resources, would find that "the land itself would wage war upon [him]" and that the claim (which Governor Menéndez Marqués made in his letters) that an enemy base at St. Augustine was a danger to the convoys was "idle talk" because the Florida coast was so dangerous. The money, he felt, should be used to fortify Havana instead. Suarez concluded: "That is what is needed, and plain speaking."[8] But Philip II was unwilling to make a decision with such strategic implications on the basis of the information available at Madrid. Instead, he ordered Major General (Maestre de Campo) Juan de Tejeda (who was in the Caribbean strengthening defenses) to consult with officials from La Florida and Cuba and then decide. When he did so, the arguments of Menéndez Marqués prevailed. On 16 August 1587, Menéndez Marqués landed at Santa Elena with Tejeda's order to abandon the place. When Gutierre de Miranda objected, Menéndez Marqués noted for the record that, among other reasons for leaving, there were no Christian Indians in the area.[9] The dismantling of Santa Elena was finished by early fall. The men, weapons, and supplies were relocated to St. Augustine. In July and unknown to the Spaniards, the third Roanoke Island colony (the "lost colony") had been established.

Tightening Spanish control over the Indians around St. Augustine began in that same fall of 1587. Father Reinoso and the dozen Franciscans he had recruited to serve in Guale and around Santa Elena in response to the Indian conference of 1583 finally arrived in October. Menéndez Marqués and he assigned them in pairs to St. Augustine (La Imaculada Concepción), Nombre de Dios, San Sebástian-Tocoy, San Juan del Puerto, San Pedro de Mocamo (Cumberland Island), and San Antonio (Aguadulce). From these towns they visited subordinate villages.[10] But this intensive effort soon faded as friars departed for Havana. It ended definitively in 1590, when the Franciscan Commissary General ordered that only five Franciscans remain in La Florida even though the new Governor, Gutierre de Miranda, had ordered six of Reinoso's latest recruit class to the province. Reinoso, who evidently protested his superior's order, was replaced as *custodio* of the La Florida missionaries by Fr. Francisco Marrón. These conflicting orders to the friars were the opening round in a century-long struggle between the governors of La Florida, who claimed power over the friars under the *Patronato Real*, and the Franciscans, asserting their autonomy because of Papal decrees. In this instance, the Franciscans had their way. In 1592, only fathers Pedro de Corpa, Antonio de Badajoz, and Baltasar López and lay brother Juan de San Nicolás were in Mocama.[11]

The Indian population the Franciscans were working with did not fare well during these years. In 1588 the spring rains failed and there was no maize harvest. Possibly below average rains and harvests in 1589 and 1591 may have further weakened a population subject to Spanish labor demands. With the ground thus prepared, an epidemic swept the Mocama Timucuans in

1591. We do not know how many died. Evidently the disease did not harm the Spaniards even though they too were under nutritional stress.[12]

The Spaniards' nutritional difficulties during these years were not due solely to the weather. Their limited farming at St. Augustine did suffer from the drought, but the main causes of their problems were man-made. Drake's destruction of fruit trees and gardens was one cause. Another was disruption of the transatlantic trade because of the "Invincible Armada" against England (1588). This disruption meant that the treasury at Veracruz, which paid the Florida *situado* from tax revenues on trade, had insufficient funds for La Florida in 1589 (made up in 1591), 1592 (made up in 1594), and 1596 (made up in 1598). But some of the shortage resulted from Gutierre de Miranda's alteration of the supply system for his personal benefit. He granted a monopoly to a merchant rather than following the custom of using a treasury official to go to New Spain to collect the *situado* and buy goods while allowing other individuals (connected with the officials, of course) to bring goods to La Florida for sale against salaries.[13] This change and the resulting scarcities and high prices, along with Miranda's strict discipline, were the causes of his overthrow in 1593. But that event did not provide immediate physical relief. The Spanish population of La Florida continued to suffer inadequate nutrition and to quarrel over who was to blame.

The arrival at St. Augustine of Governor Domingo Martínez de Avendaño in May 1594 brought an end to this time of troubles and began an expansion of the Spanish sphere back into Guale. Avendaño acted vigorously to restore discipline, to entertain and give gifts to caciques who came to render homage, to do what he could to address the colony's needs, and (in August 1595) to improve its defenses against possible English attack.[14] Finding a new group of Franciscans on hand (they had arrived in 1593), Avendaño encouraged three of them and two of the veterans (Corpa and Badajoz) to go to Guale to begin mission work at Asao, Ospo[que], Tolomato, Tupiqui, and Asopo. Shortly, one of the friars induced the town of Guale to move to St. Catherines Island, evidently causing the first shift of the native population to the barrier islands.[15] The other members of the 1593 cohort, and many of the dozen Franciscans who arrived in September 1595 were distributed to missions in Mocama and Aguadulce to reinforce Spanish hegemony and to provide for the spiritual needs of converts already present in both areas. The rest of the 1595 group were sent to Guale.[16] The governor decided to accompany some of them to their mission assignments and to use the occasion to inspect the missions and establish his authority by receiving homage from the Indians.

Avendaño's inspection tour of October 1595 had important consequences. As he moved north from St. Augustine through Nombre de Dios, San Pedro, Tolomato, and Guale town, he conducted a census. This revealed some 1,400 baptized Indians in Nombre de Dios and San Pedro jurisdictions, in addition to some 1,500 who, it was claimed, had accepted the sacrament at St. Augustine.[17] No figures are given for Tolomato or Guale town, although the latter likely had some baptized Indians.

Aside from informing the Crown what its alms to the Franciscans had obtained in the way of conversions, Avendaño's inspection tour and census had another objective: the imposition of an annual tribute of one arroba (about 25 pounds) of shelled maize on each married man. Avendaño's tribute was a revolution in Spanish–Indian relations. It was also one of Avendaño's answers to the shortage of food at St. Augustine of which he complained in letters of 1594 and early 1595 and which he had partially solved by buying maize from the Indians. Levying a tribute was not new; Menéndez de Avilés, Juan Pardo, and Menéndez Marqués had all followed this practice. But those tributes had required each cacique to maintain a granary under the cacique's control from which to feed soldiers passing through his villages, or, as in Pardo's case, from which maize occasionally could be shipped to Santa Elena. Probably the grain had been raised communally.[18] Indian customs had thus been respected and the cacique's authority and status reinforced. Avendaño's tribute, while still holding the cacique responsible for producing the grain, sharply increased the potential amount and imposed a notion of individual responsibility that, so far as we know, was at variance with Indian customs for supporting elites and tributes to hegemonic figures. The cacica of Nombre de Dios, and the caciques of San Pedro, Tolomato, and Guale were each given a total to collect. Not surprisingly given the revolutionary nature of this levy, collections did not meet the expected totals in the first year. Nombre de Dios paid 48 arrobas and San Pedro and Guale paid 447 arrobas in 1595; the three paid 530 arrobas in 1596, which was probably close to the full amount expected.[19] Tolomato, however, did not pay.

The results of Avendaño's tribute assessment likely did not meet all of the food requirements for St. Augustine, but it did provide a buffer against poor harvests in the fields around the town and against problems with the supply system such as those experienced during the regime of Gutierre de Miranda. It also effected the complete incorporation of the baptized Indians into the Spanish world, at least in Spanish eyes.

Another important aspect of Avendaño's inspection tour concerned how he treated the Franciscans. At each town he inspected, he installed the missionaries with great ceremony, including going down on his knees and kissing their hands.[20] This gesture, designed to impress the Indians with the status of the friars, fit nicely with the latter's notion of their position in Spanish as well as Indian society. Because Avendaño died (24 November 1595) before he had any conflicts with the missionaries, he was used by them thereafter as an example of a governor who gave them the respect they deserved. Fr. Juan Baptista de Capilla may well have had Avendaño in mind when he wrote to the Crown in 1609 that the friars wanted a governor "who with Christian zeal and a right intention will govern, aid and favor us . . . one who esteems priests and who treats them with the respect due to their sacerdotal state. . . . "[21]

This public acknowledgement of their high status seems to have been particularly important to the newly arrived friars. According to the chronicler Torquemada, this 1595 group of friars was from the "New Conversion" Franciscan province of Castile and "boiled with the Spirit and devotion."[22] That is, they were zealots. Avendaño's rendering homage to them seems to have increased their zealotry and emboldened them to think that they could interfere in the internal affairs of the Guale villages in ways that were without precedent. These men also belonged to the school that said that fear of punishment was a necessary and proper tool to use with the Indians. The consequences of these behaviors were first felt in 1597.

The apparent successes of the Spaniards in consolidating their position at St. Augustine, in obtaining the obedience and conversion of at least some of the Mocama Timucuans and the Guale, and in providing themselves with locally produced maize as tribute were attested in the summer of 1597 when at least twenty-five caciques and cacicas visited St. Augustine to render homage to the new governor, Gonzalo Mendez de Canzo, or to seek alliance, and to receive gifts from him. These men and women ruled the Mocama towns of Nombre de Dios, San Sebástian, San Pablo, Antonico (San Antonio?), Ibi (Aybe), San Pedro, Poturiba (Puturiba), and Tocohaya; the Guale towns of Asao, Aspoache (Ospoque or Espogache?), Aluste, Aobi, Tolomato, Tupiqui, Guale, Yoa, and Chacalayte (Chucalate); Tulufina (up the Altamaha); the southern Florida Mayaca and the Mosquitos (groups south of St. Augustine); and the central Florida Timucuan chiefdoms of Timucua/Utina (Aguacalecuen), Potano, and Acuera. Veca/Beca and Becao/Vecao are listed but cannot be identified as to linguistic affiliation or geographic location.[23]

The appearance at St. Augustine of some of these caciques seemed to promise a marked widening of Spanish influence. Ibi, Timucua, Potano, Tulufina, Mayaca, and Mosquitos had had limited contact with the Spaniards and previously had not sought alliance. Nor were they baptized. Each of the non-baptized chiefs is recorded as having sought peace, gifts and missionaries, both of which were evidently understood as twin symbols of alliance. The gifts given to them included hatchets, iron hoes (*azadas*), blankets, and shirts as well as flour for their trips home. Because of his importance, cacique Utina's brother and the nineteen other leading men who accompanied him were given eight complete Spanish suits of clothing, shoes, cloth, hats, and thread.[24]

Following up on these visits, Fr. Baltasar López, operating from his base at San Pedro, visited Ibi, Timucua, and Potano. But he withdrew to San Pedro when he learned of the Juanillo revolt that fall (1597).[25]

In addition, Fathers Pedro Fernández de Chozas and Francisco de Verascola went inland from Tolomato (with D. Juan, heir to that chiefdom) to La Tama, the name then given to the peoples of De Soto's Altamaha, Ocute, and Cofaqui chiefdoms. Warned of hostile peoples further to the west, the Spaniards turned back but reported La Tama (i.e., the piedmont) to be heavily populated.[26]

In sum, the Spanish frontier seemed poised to incorporate the dozen or so villages of the western Timucuans, more of the Mocama on the mainland west of San Pedro, and possibly the Indians of La Tama as well!

Rebellion and Negotiations, 1597–1602

The Juanillo revolt of 1597 was a major jolt to the Spaniards because it seemed to wipe out many of the gains that had been made during the previous five years. It brought to the fore a number of unresolved conflicts that had arisen because of Spanish intrusion into the Indians' world.

The uprising began at Tolomato on 13 September 1597 and quickly spread. D. Juan had organized a group of young men there and in other towns, including a few baptized Indians. That they were likely members of his clan is shown by the participation in the rebellion of D. Francisco, D. Juan's uncle and the friars' choice to be mico mayor. Moving systematically, the rebels killed Fr. Corpa at Tolomato, Fr. Blas de Montes at Tupiqui, Fr. Miguel Añón and Fr. Badajoz at Asopo (Sapelo?), and Fr. Verascola at Asao. Fr. Dávila, at Ospo, was wounded and then enslaved. An attack on San Pedro was beaten off by its residents, led by their cacique, Fr. Baltasar López, and some Spaniards who happened to have been there after bringing supplies.[27]

The friars quickly blamed D. Juan's revolt on the Devil, on the governor (for not backing them up), and on the unwillingness of the Indians to abandon their pagan ways, including polygamy. Treasury officials thought the rebellion was timed to avoid payment of the tribute. The Bishop of Cuba blamed the revolt on a friar who had publicly punished an Indian simply to show his own power, rather than correcting the Indian in private. Analysis of all of the sources reveals that the friars provoked the rebellion by interfering with the status system at Tolomato, and perhaps elsewhere, and by trying to restrict the movement of Indians among the towns.[28]

The specific instances of the friars' interference in the native status system were as follows: They supported D. Francisco, an older man who was more compliant with their orders, for the office of mico mayor rather than D. Juan (derisively called "Juanillo," a diminutive form of Juan) even though the latter had accompanied the friars and a party of thirty Christian and pagan Indians on their trip to La Tama in the summer of 1597. That service must have made him expect support from the friars for his claim. The friars also (publicly?) told D. Juan he could not have more than one wife; but multiple wives were a native marker of high status.[29] Fr. Miguel Añón's use of a gag (*mordaza*) on an Indian of supposedly low status who had blasphemed, and Fr. Blas Rodriguez's threats to whip certain caciques also may have threatened native status systems.[30]

Whatever the causes, the Spanish reaction to the Juanillo revolt was swift, brutal, prolonged, and effective in restoring Spanish control in Guale. Governor Mendez de Canzo rose from a sickbed to lead the first punitive expedition (October 1597), which burned the rebels' towns and food stores but failed to capture the rebels because they had been forewarned and had fled into the woods. D. Juan and his fellows shortly moved to the interior town of Tulufina, where Fr. Dávila's life was spared because a powerful woman had a son in the governor's control at St. Augustine.[31] The effort to obtain Dávila's release in the spring of 1598 involved scouting by the Escamacu and Cayagua (from near modern Charleston, South Carolina), sending a Guale chief to the rebels to arrange terms, exchanging the boy hostages and various iron tools for Dávila (in June), capturing seven of the Indians who had escorted him to the coast, and having the Escamacu and Cayagua kill seven other Indians in La Tama. Once Dávila was safe, the Spaniards, aided by some of their Indian associates, again raided the rebel villages after that year's meager harvest had been stored (in November). That action convinced the Indians under the cacique of Asao to seek peace in January 1599. After some negotiation, Mendez de Canzo went to Guale to receive homage (in June). In September, Espogache, "cacique of Guale" (a title implying he was mico mayor), visited St. Augustine to discuss a general return to peace, and no doubt to forestall another destruction of Indian maize stores that fall.[32]

Peace was restored fully in the spring of 1600. In January, the caciques of Escamacu, Talapo, Talaje, Ufuro (Ufera), and San Pedro visited Mendez de Canzo. To test their sincerity, he sent Spanish soldiers to "sleep in their [the Indian] villages." They did so without incident. In April, more emissaries came from Guale province. Finally, on 10–14 May, Mendez de Canzo hosted a general conference at which Espogache and Ytuçhuco (cacique of the Salchiches of Tulufina) and a number of their principal men made peace in the names of the caciques of Asao, Guale, Tupiqui, Aluste, Ufalaque, Utalapo, Talox, Ospo, Tulufina, Yfulo, and Olatapotoque. Stating that they were "wild men and of little understanding" the assembled Indians asked pardon for the killing of the Franciscans. Mendez de Canzo granted the pardon and told them that in future they should inform him if they were offended by the friars. He also seems to have instructed the caciques to build chapels in their villages in anticipation of receiving missionaries.[33] Only D. Juan and his kinsmen remained at war with the Spaniards.

Finding no other means to bring D. Juan and company to justice, in the spring of 1601 Mendez de Canzo bargained with the Cacique of Asao, evidently the prospective mico mayor of the Guale, to bring him D. Juan, D. Francisco, and any other rebels, alive or dead. When the Spaniards delivered the necessary presents for Asao, his allies, and the caciques of La Tama (whose cooperation was essential) that fall, Asao organized a war party that eventually numbered five hundred men. They laid siege to Yfusinique, the fortified village where D. Juan had taken refuge, and took it on a second try. D. Juan and his heir and "all of his kin" (to the number of twenty-four) were killed.The attacking force suffered eight dead and fifty-six wounded. The scalps of the rebels were sent to St. Augustine.[34]

In making peace after the Juanillo rebellion, the caciques and Mendez de Canzo changed the terms of the Indian–Spanish relationship. The governor had already suspended Avendaño's maize tribute as a reward for the loyalty of the Mocama Timucuans and had suggested permanently reducing it to a symbolic six ears per married man per year for baptized Indians, a proposal subsequently approved by the Crown.[35] At the same time, he tried to clear and plant enough land at St. Augustine to assure the town of a year's supply of maize for use in case the *situado* failed to arrive. Perhaps observing that Indian laborers from the Mocama villages were employed for this task (along with the king's slaves and soldiers), or perhaps at the suggestion of Sergeant Major Alonso Díaz de Badajoz during his spring 1600 visit to Guale (to test the peaceful intentions of the villages), or, less likely, resorting to an Indian custom for dealing with a powerful lord, the cacique of Espogache brought laborers with him in April 1600 when he visited St. Augustine preliminary to the peace conference of May. Although Mendez de Canzo does not say so, he must have been pleased with this voluntary (as he reported it) action. At the peace conference, the governor and the caciques agreed that in future the latter would supply laborers to work the king's fields. (In fact, laborers were made available to all landowners.) Mendez de Canzo in turn, and in accordance with imperial law, agreed to pay for this labor by giving cloth and other items to the caciques, who would, presumably, distribute them to the laborers as payment for their services.[36] The following spring, the cacique of Asao appeared with forty laborers; men from other Guale province cacicazgos also did turns in the fields of St. Augustine.[37] Thus established, labor service in lieu of a per capita tribute was to last until the 1680s.

This shift from per-capita tribute to labor service was at the heart of the new Spanish–Indian accommodation within their superordinate–subordinate colonial relationship. The caciques shifted the risks of crop failure and diminishing soil fertility implicit in a per-capita tribute from their own people to the Spaniards.[38] Moreover, because the labor was compensated, the caciques guaranteed themselves annual supplies of Spanish goods, to be used to reinforce their status among the villagers through display and distribution. And should the Spanish crop fail or fall short, the caciques could sell any surpluses they controlled, earning even more goods for their status system. Indian commoners also gained from the arrangement because it sheltered them from the risks of the harvest, maintained traditions of communal farming, and preserved the autonomy of the villages under their native leaders. The caciques faced only two problems: the friars and their propensity to interfere with native status systems and sometimes to engage in abusive behavior, and the long-term risk that Indians sent to St. Augustine might remain, thereby diminishing the work force for spring planting in Guale (where it occurred slightly later than in St. Augustine), or might die from Old World diseases, hunger, or exposure. For Indian commoners, the two greatest long-term risks were the threats of premature death and insufficient laborers to raise the crops needed to maintain the nutritional well-being of the villages. In 1600, the friars were not a problem in Guale province because none were available to be stationed there. Hence the caciques could be nominally Christian, thereby pleasing the Spaniards, but avoid significant changes in lifestyle. And once friars did become available, they could be expected to work with the caciques to reinforce chiefly power as a means of asserting their own authority over the commoners, as they had done before 1597.[39]

From the Spanish point of view, they had not only secured the symbolically important subservience of draft labor (albeit for small amounts of trade goods) and the agreement of the caciques to become obedient Christian subjects of Philip III, but also the important practical objective of being better able to feed themselves. Spanish documents do not reflect any awareness that the caciques had turned the colonial relationship to their own advantage.

Success and New Threats, 1600–1608

Thanks to this new relationship, the opening of new fields, and three years of average to above average rainfall, Mendez de Canzo was close to obtaining his goal of self-sufficiency in food by 1602. Records of the tithe provide an indication of maize production. Rigorous collection produced high returns of 10,420 arrobas in 1600 and 12,000 in 1602. The latter figure was at least 43 percent of the estimated 27,650 arrobas needed by the town's eight hundred or so residents.[40] After 1599, yields rose and fell more or less with the rainfall but on a descending trend, as might be expected because of declining soil fertility, although many other factors also may have been involved (Table 4.1).

The regular collection of the *situado* during these years complemented local production so well that complaints about a lack of food at St. Augustine are not found in the documents. However, Accountant Bartolomé de Argüelles, a consistent critic of the governor, complained that Mendez de Canzo tried to monopolize the market by favoring his nephew, Juan García de Navía y Castrillón, thereby causing other private traders to stop visiting St. Augustine. But as we have seen, such arrangements were common practice. García does not seem to have had a complete monopoly, unlike Gutierre de Miranda's associate.[41]

One more piece remained to be put into place to complete the consolidation of Spanish control over the tidewater frontier. That was paramountcy over and peace with the Indians along the coast south of St. Augustine. Here, too, Mendez de Canzo seemed to achieve the requisite success. Mendez de Canzo had visited the coastal villages on his way north from Havana in 1596, giving gifts to the caciques and trying to arrange good treatment for shipwrecked Spaniards. A mark of his apparent success was Cacique Ais's request for a translator to instruct his people in Christianity. However, when Juan Ramírez de Contreras, an appropriate translator, was sent with a quantity of gifts, he and the two Indians with him were killed by the Surruque and Ais. The Spaniards retaliated with a night raid that killed some sixty Surruque and captured fifty-four women and children. When the cacique of Surruque went to St. Augustine to try to redeem them, Mendez de Canzo told him to fetch the cacique of Ais as the ransom. When Surruque returned with the *mandador* ("capitanillo") of Ais, both, and twenty-two men with them, were made prisoners, supposedly because the Ais and Surruque held four shipwrecked Spaniards prisoner. The Indian women and children were given to married soldiers as servants; the men were put to work in the fields and as servants to bachelors. In the end, on 31 January 1600, the prisoners were set free because of a royal order forbidding their enslavement.[42] Meanwhile, Mendez de

TABLE 4.1   Maize Tithe at St. Augustine, 1597–1616

Year	Auction Value in Maravedis	Total in Arrobas	Estimated Harvest [at 10%] (at 2.5%)	Georgia Spring Rain (mm)	Notes
1597	23,188	[>170]ᵃ	[>1,700] (6,800)	435 (N)	SD 224, fols 376–83.
1598	52,360	830	[8,300] (33,200)	291 (VL)	ibid.
1599	119,816	[705]ᵇ	[7,050] (28,200)	333 (L)	ibid.
1600	177,140	[1,042]ᵇ	[10,420] (41,680)	603 (H)	ibid.
1601		572	[5,720] (22,880)	506 (H)	
1602		[1,200?]	[12,000]	498 (N+)	Canzo, 1602
1603				484 (N+)	
1604	[62,560]	368ᵇ	[3,680] (14,720)	352 (N)	CD 955, Alas, Cargos
1605				780 (VH)	
1606	[85,085]	500.5ᵇ	[5,000?] (20,020)	422 (N)	(incomplete data)
1607		>161		372 (N)	
1608	[193,800]	1,140ᵇ	[11,400] (45,600)	356 (N)	ibid.
1609	[60,350]	>355ᵇ	[>3,550] (14,200)	393 (N)	ibid.
1610	[112,030]	>659ᵇ	[>6,590] (26,360)	338 (N-)	ibid.
1611	113,917	c. 600ᵇ	[>6,000?] (24,000)	281 (VL)	CD 955, Olivera
1612		>232.5	[>2,325] (9,300)	422 (N)	(incomplete data)
1613		430	[4,300] (17,200)	608 (VH)	ibid.
1614		444	[4,440] (17,760)	393 (N)	CD 958, Soto
1615		740	[7,400] (29,600)	459 (N+)	ibid.
1616		373	[3,730] (14,920)	325 (L)	ibid.

Notes: ᵃEstimated price of 4 reales per arroba.
ᵇEstimated price of 5 reales per arroba.
  Rainfall: Normal = 415 mm ± 86 mm (1 standard deviation); VL = very low; L = below 1 standard deviation; N = normal; H = above 1 standard deviation; VH = very high.
  I have assumed the standard 10% tithe; cf. Worth, *Timucuan Chiefdoms*, 1:188, Table 13–1, using different sources and assuming a tithe of 2.5% on the basis of a 1685 declaration. Estimated production at a 2.5% tithe is shown in ( ). I find most of these 2.5% harvest numbers too high given the soils around St. Augustine. Until the rate of the tithe is documented for these years, all harvest estimates are questionable.

Canzo, like the friars, professed himself satisfied that only fear of punishment, not gift giving, would maintain the peace with the Indians, especially those south of St. Augustine.[43] For a time, this pacification by terror seems to have worked.

Other caciques continued to visit the governor, and were entertained and sent away with gifts. In March 1598 the caciques of Antonico, Mayaca, and Potano and Potano's heir visited St. Augustine. Potano or his heir returned in May 1599, August 1600, and March 1601. Doña Ana, the new cacica of San Pedro, visited in the summer of 1600. Two caciques from "Timucua," i.e., Aguacalecuen/Utina, came in June 1601.[44]

Doña Ana's visit and Potano's heir's last visit revealed that the Indians expected the governor, as paramount, to settle disputed successions to office. Antonio López, the cacique of Poturiba, the cacica of San Antonio, and the caciques of Napoyca, Chicafaya, Cascanque, and Ufera accompanied Doña Ana and sought confirmation of Doña Ana's succession as their paramount and the resolution of various unreported "affairs of their land [the jurisdiction of San Pedro]."[45] Potano's teenaged heir came seeking to solidify his succession to the chieftainship by obtaining Spanish permission to rebuilt his principal town at the site of the one the Spaniards had destroyed in 1584. This would, he said, place him closer to St. Augustine and so enable him better to respond to Spanish requests.[46] The symbolic importance of such a rebuilding is obvious. In each case, Mendez de Canzo acceded to the request.

In sum, by early 1602, the Spaniards had solved two of the four problems whose solution was necessary for a successful colony. They had established their authority over the coastal Indians from the Ais to northern Georgia, although they still lacked enough missionaries to give that authority a continuous physical expression outside of the limited area from St. Augustine to San Pedro. They had established a relatively secure food supply. Unresolved were a self-reproducing population and the development of economic activities that would attract settlers and merchants.

Unable to do much about the population problem, Mendez de Canzo turned to securing the economic future of the colony. Such a future could be assured through continued exploitation of known local resources and by finding new ones. The known local resources besides foods included sarsaparilla roots, ambergris, and tobacco. Documents provide only scant information about the trade in sarsaparilla roots. Evidently they were a major product of San Pedro and Guale provinces, sought by the French as well as the Spaniards, to judge from records of French activity along the coast in 1605 and earlier periods.[47] The Indians south of St. Augustine collected ambergris and traded it to Spaniards who had been sent to visit them for other reasons, thereby pushing the costs of such expeditions onto the Crown while the profits went to the governor and those he favored. In addition, small amounts of local tobacco were harvested, mostly for sale to the treasury. The volume and value of these trades cannot be determined, nor is it known exactly how the governor and his associates, led by his nephew Juan García, profited.[48] But profit they evidently did. Unfortunately, such elite monopolization and the largely extractive nature of the goods meant that these known local economic resources did not serve to attract settlers or even merchants outside of the governors' and treasury officials' circles. That is, they did not prove to be engines of either economic or demographic growth.

To search for new resources, Mendez de Canzo took up the projects of the Adelantado Pedro Menéndez de Avilés: exploitation of the interior and finding a cross-Florida waterway. The latter, assayed in 1601, got no further than Lake George on the upper St. Johns River.[49] The former, which depended on getting more men and supplies, produced only detailed, if in part exaggerated, depositions in 1600 and a new visit to the Georgia back country in 1602. The depositions described La Tama, the area around Joara (the piedmont in North Carolina), and what the English had learned about the piedmont during the period of the first Roanoke colony. All three areas were said to have mineral resources (diamonds at Joara, gold upriver from Roanoke), good soils, excellent supplies of food, and large, civilized Indian populations. The visit, carried out in July and August 1602, yielded confirming information about the agricultural potential of the piedmont and samples of supposed minerals. A report that white men had been in the area could not be confirmed.[50] Proclaiming a willingness to follow up on these reports, Mendez de Canzo asked at first for three hundred additional men and then for a thousand, with supplies for at least a year, so that he could set up a second Spanish town and explore the road to New Mexico. Bartolomé de Argüelles, the king's accountant (*contador*) and an agent for the Franciscans, suggested small-scale exploration first and used the occasion to suggest again that St. Augustine be abandoned in favor of forts at the head of the Keys and in Guale.[51]

Argüelles's criticism and Mendez de Canzo's plans for further expansion (if the Crown would but provide the resources) arrived in Spain as the Council of the Indies was gathering a file in preparation for considering whether to abandon the colony or move its garrison. The Council had gone through a similar exercise in 1593 in response to a comparable suggestion by Argüelles. At the time, Menéndez Marqués and others interested in St. Augustine had argued successfully for continuation. The Council's renewed interest in the question arose from Franciscan suggestions made in the wake of the Juanillo revolt that the garrison be moved to Guale.[52] By November 1600, the Council's file also contained a copy of a report by D. Luis Fajardo systematically rejecting all the arguments for keeping the garrison in La Florida. Souls were not being saved (although martyrs were being created), nothing of value was to be extracted, and there was no deep water port to be kept out of enemy hands (and in any case it was too far from Europe for an enemy to hold, as the English abandonment of Puerto Rico in 1595 had shown). Rather, he said, spend the money on and place the men in Havana, Cartagena, or Puerto Rico.[53] Following established routines, on 5 November 1600 the Council sent orders to the Viceroy of Mexico, the Audiencia of Santo Domingo, and the governors of La Florida and Cuba to give their opinions about moving the garrison or abandoning La Florida altogether.[54]

The Council's challenge to La Florida arrived in St. Augustine in late August 1602 with Fernando de Valdés, who was the son of the governor of Cuba, Pedro de Valdés. Proceeding rapidly, he took depositions from a number of officers and soldiers, who almost uniformly supported keeping things as they were while pointing to the piedmont as the solution to the colony's economic woes and costs to the Crown. The Franciscans whom he interviewed argued for moving the garrison to Guale so that it could better support them when they renewed their work there. Both sides were united in opposing the abandonment of La Florida and in looking to the piedmont and mountains as areas for future growth. Documents in hand, Valdés returned to Havana and forwarded his report. His father and others began to write their own views of La Florida, shaping their opinions in part to fit whatever they knew or could guess about the discussions at court.[55]

Our knowledge of the advice received and the Council's deliberations between 1602 and 1607 is incomplete. It is evident, however, that the discussion of abandoning La Florida was part of a larger discussion of saving money by abandoning it and New Mexico and of depopulating the northwestern coasts of Hispaniola. But that anticipates our story.

With Valdés gone, Mendez de Canzo decided to follow up on a promise made to the Guale chiefs in 1601 that he would visit their towns and inspect the chapels they had promised to build. Leaving St. Augustine on 26 January 1603, he visited San Pedro, Talaje, Tupiqui, and Guale Island (St. Catherines Island). On each occasion he received the homage of the chiefs, had mass celebrated in the newly built chapel, and, probably, gave gifts. At San Pedro on the way home, he presided over the dedication of a new church (on March 10) built in part with funds he had contributed. He then visited the missions at San Antonio and San Juan del Puerto. At the latter, he resolved disputes between the Cacica María and her subordinates.[56]

Mendez de Canzo's successor, Pedro de Ibarra, arrived at St. Augustine on 20 October 1603 and quickly took up the same lines of policy: tightening paramountcy over the Guale and attempting to do so over the coastal Indians south of St. Augustine; expressing interest in exploring the interior for its alleged riches; and, as a new note, taking more vigorous actions against French and English intruders. Like his predecessors, Ibarra's initially correct relationship with the friars quickly became acrimonious because of their claim to not be subject to his authority as the administrator of the *Patronato Real* while themselves exercising temporal as well as spiritual control in the Indian villages. At the height of the dispute, Ibarra claimed that he had told the Indians, "I am your governor, they [the friars] are not!"[57] The visit of the Bishop of Cuba, Juan de las Cavezas, during the year 1606 interrupted but did not end this dispute.

Within two months of Ibarra's arrival, some forty caciques had visited him to render homage and to receive gifts that cemented a personal relationship with him as the new paramount. Not content with that, in November and December 1604 Ibarra visited the subject towns. He delivered iron tools (gifts from Philip III), settled disputes, and reinforced the hierarchy of caciques. He made sure that the Indians received religious instruction and were deferential to the friars where they were in residence. He asked about any abuses by Spaniards passing through the villages, and reminded the Indians not to trade with non-Spaniards. Moving through San Juan del Puerto, Olatayco, San Pedro, Asao, and Espogache to Guale Island (St. Catherines), Ibarra met some fifty caciques, including men from the "Pinales" or mainland subject to San Pedro, and a number of pagan chiefs from the Altamaha River drainage. Several of the pagans asked for missionaries, but Ibarra had none to give (there were only four Franciscans in La Florida at the time); however, he did make a record of their requests and asked the Crown for a dozen friars.[58]

Ibarra's relations with the Indians south of St. Augustine involved the same mixing of gift giving and coercion that his predecessors had used, with equally uncertain results. Thus in 1604, Alferez Juan Rodríguez de Cartaya (who had been along the coast collecting ambergris) took the "Little Captain" of Ais to St. Augustine by force. There he was given gifts and made to promise to bring the other caciques back to St. Augustine to meet with the governor. In May 1605 and again in September, the "Little Captain" and the caciques of Sorruque and Oribia, with varying numbers of their warriors and leading men, visited St. Augustine and received gifts. On the latter occasion, the "Great Captain" (perhaps the cacique) of the Ais was also present and agreed that the "Little Captain" and two youths should remain for religious instruction. In a parallel move, Ibarra sent a translator with hoes and maize seed to teach the Ais how to cultivate that crop. They had previously lived by gathering and fishing. The upshot was enough peace so that when a new contingent of Franciscans landed at Mosquito Inlet, they were welcomed and escorted to St. Augustine.[59] Relations remained good into 1607. During Holy Week of that year, Ibarra entertained the caciques of Yega, Santa Lucía, the "Little Captain" of Ais (now baptized as D. Luis), and various other rulers of groups as far south as the Keys. All were sent home with Spanish clothing and all, Ibarra claimed, had asked for missionaries. This was important because he proposed to build a fort at the Bocas de Miguel Mora (Boca Raton?) in order to control Carlos Bay (Florida Bay) and the lower coast and to guard the entrance to the Miami River, which he had recently had sounded and explored as a way to "Lake Miami" (Lake Okeechobee). All he needed were men and supplies![60] The Crown never provided them.

Far from exploring and exploiting the back country, Ibarra only repeated the tales of mines and requested more men. The Crown did approve his proposed exploration, but did not send the hundred soldiers he requested. Bishop Cavezas's endorsement made no difference either. Having only 150 able-bodied soldiers, Ibarra could not spare any for the interior.[61]

Foreign intrusion was more of a concern to Ibarra than to his predecessor. Reacting to reports from Indians, in the fall of 1603 he and the governor of Cuba both sent parties to check a report of European captives, or a foreign colony, among the Calusa of southwest Florida. Neither found any evidence. But there was substance to the news that an Anglo-French ship and two escorts were spotted along the Guale coast. The Guale Indians captured four crewmen. Francisco Fernández de Ecija captured the ship and twenty-one of its crew in the Savannah River. A further three Frenchmen survived the wreck of one of the escorts at the Jordan River (Santee River). Fernández de Ecija's follow-up voyage of 2 August to 21 September 1605 showed that the coast south of Cape Fear was free of European intruders, for the moment.[62]

The party of Franciscans noted above were the order's and the Crown's response to Ibarra's request of January 1604. Their arrival in November 1605 began a renewal of full Spanish hegemony over the tidewater frontier. While the friars rested from their

difficult voyage from Havana, Gaspar de Salas visited the caciques of Guale province who had expressed a desire for missionaries to see that churches and housing for the friars had been
prepared. Vainly, Ibarra expressed the hope that once the friars
were on station they would restrict themselves to preaching and
leave governmental matters to him.[63]

Once Salas reported that preparations had been made, four
friars were assigned to the north. Five others, and two lay brothers, were assigned to the existing missions in Mocama, once again
reinforcing Spanish dominance over their nearest Native American neighbors. When Bishop Cabezas visited La Florida in 1606,
he found missions at Nombre de Dios, San Juan del Puerto,
among the Aguadulce (San Antonio and [San Sebástian–] Tocoy,
apparently with an unmanned mission [*visita*] at Potano, all on
the upper St. Johns River), at San Pedro, Talaxe, Espogache, and
Guale Island. Each seems to have been in a head town of a chiefdom except for the Aguadulce mission, which served the small
towns of several caciques. In all, the bishop confirmed 2,074 Indians and 370 Europeans.[64]

The friars in Mocama and Guale province built on the work
of their predecessors, the accommodation that the caciques and
Mendez de Canzo had reached, and some shrewd tactics whose
general tenor was to support the authority of the caciques. One
of the first things the friars did was to accept, after initially protesting, the changes in spouses that had happened during the
1597–1606 period. Indian women, including some who had been
baptized, had left their husbands for others and the men had,
in turn, taken new wives. The friars stopped short, however, of
accepting Cacique Guale's sororal polygamy, which ended when
God, according to the friars, caused both sisters to die. To solve
this and many other problems in the long term, the friars carefully began to train the children of village elites to be obedient
servants of the clergy.[65] Supporting the authority of the caciques
fit the friars' own authoritarian tendencies and seems to have
made the caciques willing allies, as the friars "slipped laterally"
into native social hierarchies just below the caciques.[66]

The friars support of the power of the caciques (and their
own) involved a number of methods. In some situations, a ca-

cique held the crucifix while the missionary led the people in kneeling and venerating it—and so, indirectly, the cacique was worshiped! Another way was to tell the Crown that the governors' failure to support the absolute power that the caciques supposedly had in the pre-contact period (a power that extended to life and death) was producing breakdowns in the social order of Indian towns. On its face, this claim was less a support for chiefly power than an excuse for the friars to exercise civil authority by such means as using their *aguaciles* (sheriffs) to punish Indians who went from town to town without permission from the chiefs.[67] But it might also have been the case that some caciques were using the friars' desire to exercise civil authority ("discipline") as a way to exercise, without seeming to do so, power that Indian tradition denied to them.

Also supportive of chiefly power, although not of the friars' making—but likely supported by them as a necessary part of the conversion process—was the practice of distributing clothing (and other gifts) to Christian as well as pagan caciques. This custom seems to have quickly evolved along with the annual visits of the caciques to St. Augustine with their work parties. According to Father Escobedo (a friar who served in La Florida in the 1590s), when some of the baptized caciques were asked why they had returned to their pagan ways after 1597, they replied that they had become Christian for the sake of the clothing, and "forgot" that religion when the clothing grew torn and tattered.[68] Escobedo seems to have found this behavior curious, but it is consistent with the caciques' use of clothing and other European goods to reinforce their statuses, as has been suggested above.

This renewal of the missionary activity in Mocama and Guale led to renewed Franciscan interest in the Timucuan speakers of north central Florida, just as in 1595–1597. Many historians of the missions have accepted Franciscan claims that Fray Martín Prieto's visits to Potano and Utina/Aguacalecuen in 1606 and 1607 mark the beginning of permanent missions in what will hereafter be called the inland frontier. But Oré's account, the source from which all later writers draw, describes Prieto's and his companion's activities as just *visiting* three of the four Potano towns—San Francisco, San Miguel, and San Buenaventura— during these years. The companion was stationed at San Fran-

cisco for a brief time, but fled in the face of Indian hostility, first
to San Miguel and finally to St. Augustine. At Santa Ana, the
fourth town, an old cacique, who remembered bitterly the way
that De Soto had mistreated the people, resisted the missionaries
until a storm flattened all of the village except for the chapel!
Indians did accept baptism at San Buenaventura, the town rebuilt at the site destroyed in 1584, and later at San Miguel and
San Francisco.[69] However, no friars were resident for more than
a few months at a time before 1609, except possibly at San Buenaventura, which in any case had had contact with the Aguadulce
mission station since the 1590s.

As far as concerned Utina/Aguacalecuen, or Timucua as it
now begins to be called, Oré states that Prieto visited the chief a
number of times and got him to visit St. Augustine early in 1608,
apparently not long after the cacique of Ivitachucho (in Apalachee) visited. Both apparently rendered homage, received gifts,
and, in Timucua's case, asked for a friar. But no progress was
made with baptisms until after June 1608, when Prieto brokered
a peace with the Apalachee led by the cacique of Ivitachucho.
Apparently the cacique of Timucua demanded peace because he
thought that Christian Indians would not fight.[70] Although the
claim is made that Cacique Timucua was baptized in 1608,
in fact he was baptized at St. Augustine on Easter Sunday,
29 March 1609, amidst much pomp and with liberal gift giving.[71]

These developments, which set the stage for the inland frontier, took place against a backdrop of a new threat to the continued existence of Spanish Florida. Evidently, the results of the
Valdés inquiry had not stopped consideration of whether to keep
the colony. Too, Mendez de Canzo made it his business after he
returned to Spain to discuss (in 1605) the testimony of the Valdés
inquiry and to recommend that rather than abandon the Christian natives around St. Augustine, the garrison should be reduced to 150 men, without artillery. By October 1606, rumor at
St. Augustine had it as "certain news" that the King *had ordered*
the abandonment of St. Augustine.[72] However, the decree of 13
February 1607 only ordered destruction of the fort and offered
to help Christian Indians relocate to Hispaniola. It thus pointed
toward a Spanish withdrawal from La Florida without actually
ordering one. The reasons given were those that had been ad-

vanced by Luis Fajardo a decade earlier: that there were few conversions (four thousand are mentioned) and most Indians remained hostile, that there were no precious metals or other
riches, that there were no ports suitable for ships of the convoys
or naval forces, that there was no passage to any other place (a
reference to the cross-Florida route and the alleged portage to
Verrazzano's false sea), and that the province would not be useful to any of Spain's enemies.[73]

When the order of 13 February 1607 to dismantle the fort
reached St. Augustine in October, it provoked replies from the
Franciscans and from Ibarra. The replies were united in informing the king that the Christian Indians would be in danger
of losing their lives to their pagan enemies if the Spaniards were
fewer in number. There were over six thousand converts, and
Apalachee was a vast new field with over thirty thousand souls
awaiting the Gospel. And there was, in fact, a danger to the convoys if the French were to become established on the coast.
Ibarra added that an eighty-man coast guard station at the Bocas
de Miguel Mora (near Miami) would provide aid to shipwrecks,
one of the abiding concerns of the Council of the Indies. He also
denied that there were no sources of wealth and no good harbors.[74] The Franciscans informed the king that "it is a fine thing
that the Devil in ministering to those who wish to be of account
in the world [causes them to] give Your Majesty documents to the
effect that such a holy work not go forward, causing the people to
decrease [in number] so that timid souls, of Spaniards as well as
of priests, become frightened and wish to turn back."[75]

As if to prove the dire predictions of the friars, in the summer
of 1608 five subordinate caciques in Guale refused to obey "their
lord" (the mico mayor?). Spanish soldiers were sent to bring
them back into line.[76] It is unclear if the decree of 1607 played a
role in this disturbance.

Faced with this evidence of new conversions and reacting as
well to the news of the establishment of Jamestown in 1607, the
Crown relented. By a decree of 16 August 1608, it allowed the
fort, its artillery, and its garrison of 300 places to remain. In addition, 120 replacements were ordered to fill vacancies and to replace the unfit. This was followed by an order to Governor Ibarra

to send Captain Francisco Fernández de Ecija or another agent to spy out Jamestown as a first step toward a Spanish effort to expel the English.[77] The tidewater frontier was secure from Spanish abolition for the foreseeable future.

Besides granting La Florida a continued lease on life, in 1608 the Crown also made it clear that the garrison's soldiers could not be used to support mission work. As the king informed Ibarra, "my will is to spread the Gospel without arms or soldiers [and only] by means of ministers and preachers of it."[78] He might have added that trade, gift giving, and Spanish intervention in Indian politics were also important adjuncts to the mission effort.

The year 1608, then, proved to be fateful. The Spanish presence in La Florida was continued, the method of further expansion was decreed, and the Franciscans were poised to begin mission work along the inland frontier among the peoples of Florida's central ridge. By then, enough land had been cleared around St. Augustine to provide most of its requirements for maize. Indian labor for those fields and many other uses was being supplied under the arrangement made in 1600 with the Guale (and earlier with the Mocama Timucuans). The supply of European foods and products was supported by theoretically regular payments from Mexico's treasury and controlled for the benefit of the governor and other influential persons through mechanisms worked out and perfected during the previous forty years. Sources of at least limited wealth, also monopolized by the elite, had been found on the land (sarsaparilla, ambergris). Only a Spanish population capable of reproducing itself was lacking for a successful colony. Incorporation of the Indians in the tidewater areas from the Florida Keys to Port Royal Sound into the Spanish ecumene was underway, with degrees of success that varied with distance from St. Augustine and past efforts.

And yet for all of this apparent success, the Spaniards had cast their lot on the sandy coastal plain and had reached accommodations with the caciques that limited Spanish demands on Indian societies just as fully, perhaps even more fully, than Imperial laws did. These were not prescriptions for rapid colonial growth.

5·　　　　　　　　　　　　　　　　　　　　　　　🐚

THE INLAND FRONTIER,
1609–1650

The baptism of the paramount chief of the Utina at St. Augustine on Easter Sunday 1609 marked the effective creation of the inland frontier. During the next forty years, that frontier successively encompassed the Potano and the Utina, the Yustaga (after 1623), the Acuera (1620s?), and the Apalachee (after 1633). The Mayaca and Ais, on the southern march of the tidewater frontier, continued to have an uncertain relationship with the Spaniards, sometimes friendly, sometimes hostile but always influenced by gifts, trade, and epidemics that seem to have swept outward from the Spanish center, especially in 1613–1617. The same was true of peoples further removed from the areas under Spanish influence, including the Pojoy of the Tampa Bay region, the peoples of the areas later incorporated into the inland frontier, and the peoples behind the coast of Guale and to the north of its mission stations. As before, Native American elites were the usually willing collaborators in the spread of Spanish influence because of the benefits they received. Yet the Indians increasingly may have been drawn to the Spaniards because the epidemics called into question native religious beliefs and at least partially killed off the shamans and other elders who had perpetuated those beliefs. Seeking meaning for their lives, some

Indians turned to the Spaniards and their seemingly more powerful god.

Obedient to their belief that baptism was essential if a soul
were to reach heaven, by 1609 the more enthusiastic friars
wanted to expand their mission work to the tens of thousands of
Indians known to them because of Fr. Martín Prieto's travels in
Potano and Utina, in 1606–1607, and to Apalachee in 1608. That
it took a generation to carry the inland frontier into Apalachee
was the result of caution born of the Guale revolt, the small number of friars prior to 1612, the royal order of 1608 denying military escorts to the friars, and the unwillingness of caciques other
than the paramounts of Potano and Utina to support the missionaries. Gifts and trade goods were not problems until the
1630s, except that the annual costs kept increasing as more and
more elite Native Americans claimed the right to receive gifts.

The development of the inland frontier was checked numerically by the epidemics of 1613–1617 and endemic diseases afterwards, by the changing of Spanish access to trade goods during
the 1630s, by the Apalachee revolt of 1647, and by the shifting of
Spanish attitudes toward the Indians. Yet compared to the prolonged difficulties the Spaniards had in establishing the tidewater frontier, these difficulties hardly caused the expansion to
miss a beat.

Creation of the Inland Frontier, 1609–1650

The creation of the inland frontier began well enough. Utina's
chief followed up his baptism by allowing Fr. Martín Prieto to
burn a dozen idols on the plaza of his town and six more in the
other four major towns of his domain, which also included fifteen
smaller villages dispersed around these main centers in crescent-
like arrangements. Evidently this was the paramount chief's way
of asserting his religious as well as his political authority. The
sources are silent about the reactions of his subjects, but the friars apparently expected hostility. Prieto and his confreres followed up on this victory over Satan, as they would have expressed it, by working a circuit among the towns from a base at
Utina's town (the Fig Springs site?), where the mission San

Martín de Timucua (later San Martín de Ayacuto) was founded. When more Franciscans became available, residences for the friars (*conventos*) were set up in three of these towns and the towns then became *doctrinas:* Santa Fe de Toloco or Teleco (archaeological site 8AL190?), San Juan de Guacara (Baptizing Springs?), and Santa Cruz de Tarihica (or Tarica, founded in 1612 at Indian Pond?). A fifth convent was at Cofa, near the mouth of the Suwannee River.[1] The latter was in existence in 1611; Fr. Luis Gerónimo de Oré visited all but Cofa in 1616.

Critical as the support of the Utina paramount was to this success, it also rested on gift giving and the possibility of armed Spanish support for the missionaries. Governor Juan Fernández de Olivera informed the king in 1611 that "the main foundation [for the growth of the province] is the gift [*sic*] given to the natives and that the friars who teach them receive [military] support."[2] His gift giving that year at St. Augustine included over 300 *varas* (yards) of various kinds of cloth, 64 blankets, 14 hatchets, 148 boxed knives (mostly double-edged), 34 strings of blue and purple glass beads, and 26 "hands" of tobacco, not to mention various other items of clothing and quantities of food. To get around the royal order of 1608 forbidding soldiers to accompany the friars and yet supporting the need to provide them with some protection, governors used soldiers, and some paid Indians, to carry supplies to the missionaries. Since each friar required some 1,800 pounds of rations, wine, and wax per year (including containers), the comings and goings would have been frequent.[3] The gifts and the use of soldiers as bearers were not confined to the Potano and Utina missions, but included the Guale and Mocama missions and, in the case of gifts, pagans who visited St. Augustine.

Not neglecting another method of maintaining Spanish hegemony, in February 1612 Governor Fernández de Olivera visited the provinces of San Pedro (Mocama) and Guale. Among the gifts he took were 41 shirts, 43 pair of scissors, various kinds of cloth, and 960 strings (*sartas*) of beads.[4] We know that Guale and Mocama already were important sources for maize traded to the Spaniards, a fact that may account for renewal of the earlier custom of the governor visiting the caciques in their towns, thus probably enhancing the cacique's status among their peoples as well as displaying Spanish power and superior status.[5] We do not know if the sarsaparilla trade continued or what sort of trade to the interior ran from the coastal towns; a new governor might take a personal interest in both.

Expansion of the frontier to the lower Suwannee River brought the Spaniards into conflict with the Pojoy and Tocobaga, a conflict that gave them a new opportunity to expand their influence by trying to make peace with those peoples and the Calusa. The Pojoy and Tocobaga apparently ranged in their canoes along the west coast of the peninsula from Tampa Bay to at least St. Marks Bay to trade, fish, and on occasion raid the people they encountered. On some unspecified day in 1611, a party of them attacked and killed seventeen baptized Indians carrying supplies to the missionaries at Cofa. A Spanish retaliatory expedition captured the killers and beheaded them and the cacique of Pojoy.[6] Later, probably after 1633, some Tocobaga became Spanish auxiliaries, freighting cargoes by canoe from St. Marks to the Suwannee and other points on the west coast. Villages that included Tocobaga eventually appeared on several rivers in Apalachee.[7] But we anticipate.

Governor Fernández de Olivera's combination of liberality and brutality paid dividends, as similar policies had for his predecessors. Or at least that is how he and the friars understood Indian behavior during 1612. Early in the year, the chief of the Calusa made peace overtures to which the Spaniards responded by sending Ensign Juan Rodríguez de Cartaya from Cofa to "Carlos" (the Calusa) by way of stops at Pojoy and "Tampa" (Charlotte Harbor). At each stop, Rodríguez de Cartaya gave gifts and established peace and friendship. Carlos reciprocated by returning a Black man whose canoe had been blown in a storm from Cuba to Florida, giving two gold objects, and promising to return any Christians who might be wrecked on his coast.[8] In the fall, the paramount of the Apalachee visited St. Augustine seeking missionaries and Spanish military support against unrest among his subjects. Apparently the friars had maintained at least occasional contact with him since 1608. After consultation, the Franciscans and the governor agreed that they would pass up the opportunity because missionaries would only be secure if a small garrison were placed in Apalachee and supplied by sea. The twenty-one new Franciscans who had recently arrived were needed for other missions closer to St. Augustine, even though men working in Utina were eager to learn Apalachee in anticipation of royal authorization (and troops and support!) for mission work there. Other (unnamed) caciques also visited that fall from as far away as one hundred leagues and a distance that took as long as two and a half months of travel time. Like the paramount of Apalachee, all were fed, entertained, given gifts, and encouraged to live in peace with their neighbors and to tell them of the Spaniards' desire that those neighbors become friends and subjects of Philip III.[9] It appeared that the *pax hispanica* extended throughout the peninsula and that Spanish influence was reaching well into the areas beyond Utina, Mocama, and Guale.

The Franciscans rejoiced that the "Day of the Lord" had arrived and that the Indians no longer tried to remove every trace of the Spaniards, and even their cattle, as they had done in 1597. As one wrote, "Although this land in no way attends to the temporal increase of Your Majesty's kingdoms, Your Majesty's great service to God in attending to these poor and forsaken souls, who are encouraged and preserved so much in Your Majesty's shadow, will provide very great increases in the crown of glory that Your Majesty is to enjoy in the heavens."[10] To further their work, the friars called for more soldiers, a total of fifty-five missionaries, and even Spanish settlers. Missionaries, they noted, were cheaper and more effective in subjugating the natives than a war in which the Indians would "do more damage to us than we to them; besides, they are like deer. . . ." The Indians, the Franciscans claimed, were even asking for Spanish colonists to teach them to farm because the Indians lived on only maize, acorns, roots, fish, and occasional game. Wheat, evidently sown in Utina province, had done well. The woods of evergreen oaks (*encinas*), deciduous oaks (*robles*), and hickories were so open that horses could be raced in them. There were great pine forests, white mulberries for silk cultivation, good soils for wheat, and rivers for mills. Spanish settlers, the friars suggested, would give alms to the friars and thus free the king of the need to pay for the missions.[11] The Crown, however, did not recruit settlers.

Other causes for Franciscan pleasure existed in the fall of 1612. In Mexico City, Fr. Francisco Pareja's various books in Timucuan, including his grammar, began to come off the press. Although based on the Mocama dialect, these publications provided the friars with a basic grounding in the language and gave their Timucuan-speaking charges literacy, a gift many took up eagerly.[12] In Rome, the general chapter of the order created a Province of Santa Elena to embrace Cuba and Florida, freeing the Franciscans there from the supervision of the Mexican province.[13] And the missionaries had thirteen new bells, each with a name of a saint.[14] Only a few of the names inscribed on the bells were already in use, suggesting that more missions were to be built.

Reality rather quickly set in. The first problem was that there were not enough vestments or vessels for saying Mass, although that situation was overcome in time.[15] Far more demoralizing were the epidemic diseases that killed half of the mission Indians between 1613 and 1617. The number of converts fell from about 16,000 to approximately 8,000, essentially wiping out the equivalent of the numerical population gains made with the extension of the frontier into Potano and Utina (with additional baptisms in Guale?).[16] The friars consoled themselves that at least the baptized would go to heaven. The more zealous probably redoubled their efforts to baptize even more Indians before disease could sweep them away.

The natures of these diseases are not clearly stated. Bubonic plague (*peste*), possibly even in pneumonic form, was noted by the friars. Typhus or some other adult (rather than childhood) viruses have been suggested as well.[17] Whatever the diseases were, they and their mortality spread slowly and did not discourage caciques from continuing to visit St. Augustine, the governor from visiting Mocama and Guale, and the friars from continuing to expand their missions, especially in Guale where new missions were created at San Diego de Chatoache (Satuache) on the Ogeechee River north of St. Catherines Island and Santa Isabel de Utinahica on the Ocmulgee River (the dates and locations are uncertain).[18]

These epidemics, unlike previous ones, had documentable re-
verberations far beyond the human grief that accompanied the
deaths. The population decline in parts of the tidewater frontier
was so serious that the friars used it as a reason to ask permission
to consolidate villages consisting of ten or fewer households. Evidently permission was granted, because by 1630 "congregated"
villages were noted as among those served by the missionaries.[19]
This fact suggests that native sociopolitical structures in the
Spanish sphere were affected but where and to what degree we
do not know. This fact also alerts us that mission lists hide continuing population decline because of endemic diseases or migration. The listmakers did not include towns subject to the cacique's town that housed the *doctrina* because they were only
interested in maintaining or expanding the number of friars, not
in how many or few persons they served.

The effects of these pandemics on non-mission peoples are
suggested by archaeological evidence. In the Georgia, North Carolina, and eastern Tennessee piedmonts these years mark a period (1600–1630) of apparent demographic decline and population movements away from old chiefly centers such as Coosa.
The gradual disappearance of status-indicating grave goods suggests that the decline of the chiefdoms was in full swing, although there were probably multiple causes for this, not just the
epidemics of 1613–1617. Additional evidence of this change comes
from the upper Oconee (i.e., Tama?). There, as elsewhere in the
piedmont, people dispersed from the old nucleated towns to rural
farmsteads clustered around springheads. This phenomenon has
been interpreted as a sign of the *pax hispanica*, but it may also
have had adaptive value in the face of diseases that spread easily
through nucleated populations.[20] Whatever the truth of these
hypotheses, such dispersal of the population signaled the weak-
ening or even collapse of the chiefly authority formerly associated with the nucleated, often palisaded towns De Soto had seen.
This change is obscured in the few records we have because the
Spaniards continued to call village headmen, as well as tribal
chiefs, "caciques" and continued to support "chiefly" lineages in
the Christian villages.[21]

Far less clear is whether these epidemics facilitated the expansion of the mission frontiers by undermining native faith in their own religious traditions. Scholars generally believe that the deaths of older persons, common in the epidemics that devastated Native American populations after 1492, meant the loss of religious leaders and related knowledge, especially in chiefdoms where such leadership and knowledge were more likely to be confined to one lineage than in the "segmented tribe" where the more egalitarian social structure spread religious and other critical cultural knowledge more widely. In addition, widespread death that traditional religious leaders and healers could not contain is thought to have undercut Indian faith in their previous worldview, opening up the possibility that they might embrace another, such as that offered by Christian missionaries.[22] The 50 percent death rate in the period from 1613 to 1617 likely did have this effect among pagan Guale, Timucuan, and other southeastern peoples, although perhaps to a lesser degree among the latter because the effects of the epidemics may have been lessened by distance and by decreased frequency of contact with the Spaniards. If these supposed religious-psychological effects did occur in La Florida after 1613, then they help to explain the rapid expansion of the inland frontier in Yustaga, Acuera, and the Alapaha River basin after 1617, and the Apalachee and other groups' insistent demand for friars prior to 1633.

Although the governor and friars decided in 1612 to confine the initial expansion of the inland frontier to Potano and Utina provinces—that is, east of the Suwannee River—by 1616 the friars at Santa Cruz de Tarihica were visiting the pagan town of Tarraco, which was on the path that ran from Tarihica across the Alapaha River (a tributary of the Suwannee River) and then across the Tifton uplands to the Ocmulgee River and Santa Isabel de Utinahica. When Fr. Luis Gerónimo de Oré passed that way in late 1616, he noted those visits and the presence of three or four other Timucuan towns nearby. A *doctrina* (mission), Santa María de los Angles de Arapaja, was eventually created in the area.[23] Oré does not indicate how many converts had been won by 1616. Nor do we know when Santa María was founded, but a date in the early 1620s is likely.

The expansion of the inland frontier entered a second phase

in 1623 when Frs. Alonso de Pesquera and Gregorio de Mobilla entered Yustaga province west of the Suwannee River. Rather like Elijah, these prophets were fed at first by a pious woman because the chief refused to do so, in addition to forbidding them to baptize anyone. But shortly the chief received baptism and a rapid missionization began. San Pedro y San Pablo de Potohiriba became the center and a total of four *doctrinas* eventually flourished, although we have no details of when or how. Besides San Pedro, they were Santa Elena de Machaba, San Miguel de Asile, and San Matheo de Tolapatafi. In 1635, a friar claimed that more than 13,000 Yustaga had been converted.[24]

Expansion to the south also occurred in these years. At an unknown date, friars set up missions in Acuera on the Oklawaha River, south of the Aguadulce towns on the St. Johns River. Mission Santa Lucía de Acuera may have existed by 1627. By 1655, San Luis de Acuera also existed.[25]

The expansion into Yustaga seems to account for many of the 12,000 newly baptized Indians claimed around the year 1630 (making a total of 20,000; another 50,000 were instructed but not baptized), and for four of the twelve new *doctrinas* created between Ore's visit of 1616–1617 and 1630. Because Santa María de los Angeles de Arapaja and, apparently, the two Acuera *doctrinas* were extant by 1630, the remaining five additional *doctrinas* were in the other provinces, especially in Utina, where four new names appear on the list of 1655.[26] This rapid expansion was the work of the thirty-five friars in the province in 1617, although that number seems to have declined to twenty-seven by 1630, prior to the arrival of ten additional brothers.[27]

Still other prospects beckoned during the 1620s but could not be taken up immediately because of a lack of manpower. Oré reported around 1617 that Indians from Apalachee (where a few churches had already been built), La Tama, Machagua [Machaba?], and Santa Elena had requested clergy. In January 1617 the friars asked for twenty additional men to meet this and existing needs.[28] But only a dozen were authorized in 1627, of whom ten reached La Florida in 1630. Petitions for an additional twenty-four in 1630 (adding Cayagua—Charleston—to the list of areas requesting clergy) and 1631 were met with authorization for an additional eleven in 1633. However, these eleven were barely sufficient to replace men who had died, left La Florida, or were worn out and had to be replaced.[29] According to one friar, Indians who wanted to live in the missions were migrating into them from areas not served. This may explain the appearance of Leon–Jefferson ceramics in mission sites of this and later dates, well before the forced resettlements of the 1660s.[30]

Even in the face of insufficient manpower, a third major expansion of the inland frontier began in October 1633. At the conclusion that fall of Fr. Lorenzo Martínez's general visitation of the missions, he and Governor Luis de Horruytiner agreed to send two friars who knew the language, and who had volunteered, to begin the long-delayed conversion of the Apalachee. In explaining this to the Crown, the governor highlighted his economic before spiritual motives. He noted that in the province's dozen leagues (measured in an east–west distance) there were as many as 16,000 "indios"—probably men are meant rather than the entire population—and that the land was "of much abundance and fertility," a fact of importance in a year when the spring rainfall may have been so low that the maize crops failed around St. Augustine.[31] This manpower represented potential for the future economic development of Spanish enterprises.

From this beginning, the Apalachee mission grew steadily, although how rapidly is unclear. In 1639, Governor Damián de Vega Castro y Pardo wrote to the king that two friars were working in the province and had made 1,000 converts. However, in 1635 the Franciscan *custodio* of Florida claimed that more than 5,000 of 34,000 Apalachee had been baptized *in anticipation of more friars* (emphasis added) while in 1676 a Franciscan claimed to have seen a listing (*matrícula*) of 1638 showing more than 16,000 Christians in Apalachee![32] The figures from 1635 and the governor's figure from 1639 can be reconciled if it is assumed that the governor was only counting men, with an implied ratio to the total population of one to five. More likely, however, the Franciscan numbers, especially for 1638, are inflated because they are part of arguments for sending them many more friars. How inflated this number may be is suggested by the report that on the eve of the revolt of 1647, only eight of forty Apalachee caciques had been baptized.[33] Assuming that the population was still about 34,000, and that on average each cacique had the same number of subjects (i.e., dividing total population by the number of caciques, then multiplying by eight), the Christian population may be estimated to have been 6,800 in 1647. On the other hand, in 1643 the governor wrote that the evangelization of Apalachee was progressing rapidly, although that fact is not inconsistent with the number just proposed.[34]

The total number of baptized Indians in the various mission provinces in 1647 is not known but may have approached 35,000. This estimate is based on a claim from the year 1635 and the net addition of 5,000 others (including at least 1,800 Apalachee) over the next twelve years in the face of continued but not dramatic demographic decline. In 1635, more than 30,000 converts were said to exist in forty-four *doctrinas* being administered by thirty-nine friars, most of whom worked alone and sometimes had to travel barefoot up to fifty miles (round trip) to administer last rites.[35] Assuming that *doctrinas* embracing perhaps 5,000 baptized Indians had been established by 1635 in all eight of the Apalachee villages listed as Christian in 1647, this statement of 1635 indicates that an additional four *doctrinas* had been established elsewhere in the Spanish realm since 1630, when there were thirty-two, and an additional 5,000 converts made. At least some of those converts were persons who had moved into the missions when it became clear that an expansion of the missions to their (unidentified) towns would be slow in coming, or so a Franciscan claimed in about 1630.[36] The ongoing consolidation of satellite villages probably also brought new persons into the mission towns. Thirty-five thousand baptized Indians and forty-four missions are possible numbers, but what we know about persistent disease mortality suggests caution in accepting the first sum uncritically. As Governor Andrés Rodríguez Villegas wrote to the Crown in 1630, no other Indians in the empire were "less worked or better treated" but "with all of that, they die and are ended, just as in the other parts of the Indies."[37] He seems to have been commenting on events of his time, not just the previous history of the colony. So far as is known, there were no major epidemics from 1617 to 1650.

Events on the Peripheries

On the peripheries of the Spanish frontiers of La Florida, the years 1617 to 1647 saw the last Spanish explorations of the northern Georgia piedmont, a continuation of the previous pattern of alternating mutual hostility and alliance with Indians south of the mission areas, a few instances of raids by hostile Indians along the northern marches, and episodic concern about European raids. We will consider each in turn.

The final four Spanish expeditions into the northern Georgia piedmont were motivated by an Indian report that white men on horseback were in the interior and, we may surmise, by new governors' interest in the reported wealth to be found there. That the Spaniards should receive such a report suggests some degree of trade, perhaps reinforced by occasional visits to St. Augustine by caciques or ordinary Indians from "La Tama." That they acted on it indicates a degree of concern that the English might have penetrated the back country from Virginia. The first expedition, in 1624, got an estimated 150 leagues (at least 375 miles) before a lack of supplies caused it to turn back without obtaining certain news of the strangers. The second attempt did not get even that far. The third and fourth expeditions, in 1628, were in obedience to an order to run the report to ground by going further into the interior. Eleven soldiers and sixty Indians reached Cofitachequi, some 200 leagues from St. Augustine, on the second attempt. The report these men gave of Cofitachequi included a tale of fishing pearls from some lakes near it and the opinion that the rumor of white men on horseback was an Indian tall tale that arose from their "talking every day with the Devil and seeing many witches and sorcerers."[38] The discoverer of the alleged pearl fishery was eventually given permission to exploit it with as many as four soldiers and a few paid Indian helpers. Apparently this license was never used.[39] If nothing else, the report from the second expedition, in 1628, indicates that knowledge of Pardo's discoveries in the interior had not disappeared among soldiers in St. Augustine.

The Spanish relationship with the Indians of the lower west and east coasts of the peninsula continued to follow the general pattern established in earlier periods. On the lower west coast (the domains of the Calusa, Pojoy, and Tocobaga), the Spaniards had little contact and no new conflicts. Indeed, during the initial salvage work on the wrecks of the *Margarita* and *Atocha* in 1621, the Calusa and Matacumbe seem to have been friendly enough that the Franciscans could believe that they wished to receive missionaries.[40] But again, nothing was done.

On the lower east coast, the old pattern of episodic hostility and alliance through gift giving and trade continued into the 1620s but may have diminished afterwards since little seems to be said about it in the documentation. Apparently driving the hostilities were disagreements arising from Spanish failures to respect Indians and their property, the ongoing trade in ambergris and salvaged precious metals, and, after 1620, Indian trade with the Dutch, English, and other non-Spaniards who occasionally landed seeking water, wood, and food. Thus in 1620 or 1621, Governor Salinas tried the leaders of the Ais for killing the sergeant major and three soldiers who had landed among them for water while sailing to Havana. He acquitted all but the *capitanejo*, who was hanged and quartered in front of the others to make the point that the Spaniards were not to be molested when they landed on that part of the coast. Salinas's successor, Luis de Rojas y Borja, used gift giving and trade to draw the Ais and other lower east coast peoples into alliance and a promise that they would not allow non-Hispanic Europeans to land in their territories.[41] This arrangement probably lasted as long as the Spaniards were able to provide trade goods, that is, into the late 1630s. And as in earlier periods, the Spaniards showed no interest in setting up missions or otherwise developing a more permanent presence among these peoples. Considering their strategic location on the Bahama Channel, this lack of interest is surprising. Around 1630, a Franciscan complained that the indifference was due to the fact that the governors were interested only in the ambergis that came from the area, not in the eight thousand souls of the Indians who lived there. His proposal to congregate them, and the archaeological indications that they lived by gathering arrowroot and other plant foods and by hunting and fishing, suggest more fundamental obstacles.[42]

In contrast to this sometime hostility along the southern side of the tidewater frontier, the northern and western rims of the inland and tidewater frontiers remained quiet between 1617 and 1647, although there were two notable exceptions. Evidently the threat of Spanish power and the inducement of gifts and trade normally served to keep the pagan neighbors of the mission provinces on peaceful terms. In Apalachee, this peace was organized by the Spaniards in 1639, coincident with the initiation of regular contact by sea with Havana and St. Augustine (the route was pioneered in 1636).[43] In 1639, the Chacatos, Apalachocolos (Lower Creek), and Amacenos were induced to take up trade in place of their former hostilities with the Apalachee. The Chactos (Choctaw) would not make peace, having "never been at peace with anyone," according to the governor. Archaeological evidence suggests that the tribes of the middle Chattahoochee River Valley were soon enmeshed in a trade involving deerskins and possibly other goods.[44] Indeed, the Amacenos/Amacanos and possibly the others (except the Choctaw) may have been drawn toward Apalachee province by the possibility of trade, a trade apparently established by Timucuans before 1633, on the basis of old networks.[45] Archaeology also shows that remnant populations from throughout the Georgia piedmont were moving into the Chattahoochee and Coosa–Tallapoosa River Valleys in these decades, beginning the formation of the parts of the later Creek confederacy.[46]

The exceptions to this general rule of peace along the northern marches both come from the early 1620s. In 1620, some of the Christian Guale and pagan Indians from around Port Royal Sound renewed the mutual raiding that the Spaniards first had stopped in 1566. Outnumbered, the Christians appealed for Spanish help, which was sent in the form of Captain Alonso Díaz and thirty soldiers. Díaz apparently negotiated a settlement. Impressed, the Guale (or perhaps the friars acting through them) asked for a permanent garrison. However, the soldiers were needed at St. Augustine.[47] A few years later, the first Ysicas or "Chisca" appeared, evidently in the northern areas of Utina where they robbed missionized Indians before apparently retreating in the face of a Spanish patrol. Another group of

"Chisca" returned to the inland frontier in the 1630s. In 1639, the
governor reported that he had given them land ten leagues from
St. Augustine to farm and hunt; he expected to use them to round
up baptized Indians who had fled the *doctrinas.* This people's
identity is unclear aside from the fact that they came from the
west. Nor is it likely that they gave up their nomadic ways to
settle at the site the governor had selected.[48]

The near absence of conflict with Indians before 1647 was not
matched by an absence of military threats from the Dutch, English, and French fleets that sailed the Gulf Stream past Florida.
Thus in 1620 and again in 1626 the presidio lost a *fragata* when
crews ran it aground to escape enemy fleets. In the first case, the
enemy had three large ships, in the second ten large and three
small. In the 1626 case as well, a Dutch fleet landed 200 men at
Ais to get wood and water, causing the Spaniards to muster 150
soldiers and 300 Indians to march against them, although they
did not do so, because the Dutch left. In both years, crewmen
from enemy ships were captured ashore.[49] Research failed to dis-
close if this danger continued into the early 1640s, but it probably
did because shipping from all nations used the Bahama Channel
to exit the Caribbean.

The English colony in Virginia was a recurring concern for
governors into the 1620s. Note has been made of Spanish unease
in 1624 that the mounted white men reported to be in the piedmont might be Englishmen. But the concern about Virginia
dated from the founding of Jamestown in 1607. From their diplomatic sources in Europe, via Madrid, and from Indians, the
Spaniards at St. Augustine kept a close watch. At least initially,
they considered expelling the English. In 1609 and again in 1611,
they sent scouting parties to Chesapeake Bay but did not attack
even though the Council of War at Madrid concluded that the
English were a danger to the Spanish empire because of their
Protestantism, which the Spaniards thought was similar to the
pagan views of the Indians.[50] Father Oré added his own propaganda in favor of an attack on Virginia and Bermuda by reporting on the earlier Jesuit mission to Jacán that had taken
place between 1570 and 1571. He showed a prior Spanish claim to
Virginia and demonstrated what Philip III's father would have

done by reporting the supposed expeditionary force that was to have driven the English from Roanoke in 1590 but did not. He also detailed the force needed to destroy Jamestown and Bermuda: 3 galleons, 2 galleys, three auxiliary craft, and 1,000 well-armed men. His call for strong actions was backed by the governor of Florida.[51] But Anglo–Spanish peace and friendship in Europe were more important as the twelve-years truce (1609–1621) with the Dutch drew toward its close and the possibility of war was again under discussion. Too, the English presence in Virginia had not had any palpable effect on La Florida and any details that the Spaniards could learn about the settlement must have suggested that it was not likely to survive. Incompetent management, summer dysentery, and the Powhatan attacks of 1622 nearly did destroy English settlement although it revived in the late 1620s and continued to grow thereafter.[52] Perhaps confident that Virginia could be destroyed if necessary, the imperial government left it alone.

In sum, while willing enough temporarily to adopt an aggressive posture against enemy landing parties and to expand the mission frontier, the Spaniards normally stood on the defensive in La Florida. They had little choice. Governors typically claimed to find no more than 150 fit men in the nominal garrison of 300. That was a number judged barely adequate for the defense of St. Augustine. As Governor Salinas put it in 1620: "We are so few that we cannot make a clamor."[53] In addition, the wooden fort that had been built after 1586 required approximately bi-annual replacement of major parts of its palisade and artillery platforms. This was done with the labor of soldiers and Indians, the latter mostly recruited from Mocama and paid a real a day for their labor, and by Black slaves.[54] Although the Crown had authorized stone construction in 1595 using the coquina aggregate discovered on Anastasia Island in the 1580s, and although it had sent skilled slaves from the fortification work at Havana and 10,000 pesos from Mexico for that purpose, only a little rock was quarried and some of the foundations opened by 1600. Work stopped because no engineer was sent to direct it. The remaining money was used to rebuild St. Augustine after the hurricane of 22 September 1599. The slaves were put to other tasks.[55] Consequently, governors continued to request the rebuilding of the fort in stone, but it was to no avail until the 1670s. St. Augustine's major defense continued to consist of a partially rotten sand and wood fort.

Events within the Spanish Frontier

As the expansion of the frontiers continued from 1609–1647, the Spaniards made little progress on the other facets of creating a self-reproducing, economically attractive colony. Population grew, but slowly. A few Black slaves were brought from Havana to relieve the soldiers and Indians of the brutal work of hauling timbers for the fort's reconstruction. Replacement soldiers and friars arrived from time to time. Fragmentary church records for St. Augustine show a population pattern typical of a "dependent community," that is, one that maintained its numbers by immigration more than through natural reproduction. On average, there were 6.85 marriages per year (1628–1647), producing 3.6–3.7 children with a slight trend in favor of females. Deaths, which ran two-to-one male because of the garrison, were four for every five births, with a trend that fell slightly over the course of the seventeenth century.[56] We do not know how many Indians, brought to the town for work in the fields or on the fort, remained or died. A guess would put St. Augustine's population at over 1,000 with a growing percentage of locally born persons. Indian women may have been becoming less common as wives.

The search for commercially viable products continued. Proposals were made during the 1620s that Indians from Campeche and Honduras be brought in to teach the Timucua how to cultivate indigo and even cochineal (an insect that grows on a particular type of cactus). Another proposal requested Spaniards to help develop a hemp industry on the Altamaha and lower Suwannee River flood plains. Yet other proposals added cotton, pitch, and the old perennial, silk, to the list of products that could be produced if the Timucua and Guale were instructed.[57] As before, nothing came of these ideas even though the Crown did follow up on the idea of cultivating indigo; it requested knowledgeable Indians be sent from Central America. On the other hand, trade with the Indians north and west of Apalachee for deerskins, with the lower east coast groups for ambergris, and with the Guale for sarsaparilla developed or continued, but went largely unrecorded in official records. As monopolies of the governors and treasury officials and their merchant associates, such trades could not attract civilian immigrants. Without such immigrants, the Spaniards remained in a limbo between being an occupying army and being a growing colony of settlement.

The final of the four problems of settlement—a stable food supply—showed some progress during these years as the Spaniards largely solved the problem of supplying themselves with meat. Governor Salinas imported enough cattle so that he was able to establish viable herds after 1618.[58] Although the anticipated hide exports probably did not develop, by 1627 the herds were large enough and making enough meat available to St. Augustine that Salinas's successor, Luis de Rojas y Borja, could impose a tax of one real per head on cows delivered to the St. Augustine slaughterhouse. At an uncertain date during these years, the royal treasurer, Francisco Menéndez Marqués, began his own ranch, La Chua, using old Indian fields and the natural savannah of Paynes Prairie in Potano province.[59] A few other ranches probably existed between St. Augustine and the St. Johns River, where cattle grazed on the grasses of savannahs created by burning and selectively lumbering the long-leaf pine forests.

Difficulties

This generally positive set of developments after 1609 began to be undermined in the late 1630s. First the *situado* and then the spring rainfall became unstable. Without regular, annual shipments of gift and trade goods to maintain the status system of the Indian caciques, the Spaniards found their hold on the Guale, Timucua, and Apalachee slipping. With unstable spring rainfall patterns, the Spaniards found that the maize crops grown in the fields around St. Augustine with Indian labor were not adequate for their needs. In search of maize or alternatives such as wheat, the governors put more and more economic pressure on the western Timucuans and on the Apalachee. That pressure, too, translated into unintended attacks on native status systems. And since the friars in Apalachee were beginning to move against yet other aspects of the native status system there, as they had earlier in Mocama, Guale, and western Timucua, the stage was being set for the Apalachee rebellion that burst forth in February 1647. We will briefly explore each of these matters in turn.

At the most general level, there were three major difficulties with the *situado*. The Crown tried to end abuses that defrauded it and the soldiers. The wars in Europe caused a diversion of funds. And governors and the proprietary treasury officials continued to try to reap private profits from collecting and dispensing the funds, goods, and credits that were involved. Suffice it to say, none of the "reforms" changed the system. Governors still controlled the retail trade of St. Augustine either directly (Salinas had a store in his house) or indirectly (Rojas y Borja brought in a Portuguese merchant, Martín Freyle de Andrade, made him a captain, and used him to collect the *situado*), and the soldiers still experienced deprivation.[60] So lucrative was this system that Ruiz de Salazar openly bought his governorship in exchange for the finished hull of a 500-ton galleon delivered at Campeche, and some years later reported to a patron at court that he had reduced his debts from 460,000 to less than 40,000 pesos. His bondsmen, creditors, and *situado* agents were Basque merchants from Veracruz.[61] The treasury officials were no better. When they nominally controlled collection from 1629 to 1646, fraud and collection problems were so great that in some years no funds or *situado* goods reached St. Augustine even though they had been procured in Mexico.

The Crown's need for money in the late 1630s affected the *situado* in two ways. The major effect was non-payment in 1637 and less than full payment in the years 1639–1643.[62] A secondary effect was an attempt to bring expenses of the Indian gift fund back within the 2,068 pesos (1500 ducats) authorized in 1615. In 1625, expenses were 3,400 pesos, rising in fits and starts toward an eventual peak of 9,271 pesos in 1650.[63] Most of this increase apparently was not due to price inflation but to the increasing number of caciques who claimed annual gifts. As the treasury officials noted in 1627 with evident disgust, the Christian caciques of Guale came for clothing "as for tribute, and they call it that."[64] By then it was an article of faith among La Florida's officials that, as Governor Vega Castro bluntly wrote to the king in 1636, the gifts were "the foundation and head of the conversion. . . ."[65] Since it was also true that "this presidio cannot be preserved except with the service of these natives," no one in La Florida dared to enforce the parts of the decree of 1615 that indicated gifts were to be given only to pagans (to induce them to accept baptism and friars) or to Indians who actually performed some service for the Spaniards.[66] In Mexico City, however, the treasury officials were prepared to cut back. In 1635, 1637, 1638, 1642, 1643 and 1645 no monies were released for Indian gifts and in 1636, 1639, 1641, and 1644 less than the 2,068 pesos were provided, and some of those payments were for prior years.[67] Indian caciques found themselves without the European clothing they wore to display their rank and without the exotic goods such as axes whose control was a means of building unequal reciprocal relationships with their subjects and maintaining their political–religious authority. Discontent with the Spaniards began to brew. Meanwhile, Spaniards of rank found that they did not have wheat flour bread nor the other imported foods that helped to mark their status within St. Augustine's society.

Benito Ruiz de Salazar Ballecilla, governor from 10 April 1645, chose a unique response to the general problems of the *situado* in the late 1630s and early 1640s. It too played into the rising discontent of Indians in western Timucua and in Apalachee. Keenly interested in making money, he approached the irregular deliveries from Mexico as an opportunity. During an inspection tour, he negotiated the use of land near the village of Asile for a wheat-growing farm and for a cattle and horse ranch. Successful production of those products would, he claimed, free Florida from some of its dependence on Mexico. The cacique of Asile agreed to the lease and helped organize labor to clear the ground on a promise of annual payments of axes, hoes, and clothing and the governor's help in forcing some of his people to return from Apalachee. He apparently did not receive the payments he expected. In addition, after the death of Ruiz de Salazar in 1651 and the successive sale of the hacienda to the Crown and then the sale

of the animals and implements to private parties, the friars—
who had opposed the hacienda from the beginning—claimed
that the governor's agents at the hacienda had coerced unpaid
labor from the Indians, angering them.[68] Ruiz de Salazar also
installed a lieutenant governor in Apalachee, over Franciscan
objections, to monitor (as he said) and to run (as they said) the
province's developing trade with Havana (and his hacienda).[69]

Ruiz de Salazar's hacienda was an unprecedented Spanish intrusion into the Indians' world,[70] but it was not the only sign of
an intensifying Spanish presence at a time when Spanish gifts
were scarce. The other signs arose because of the highly variable
spring rainfalls that began in 1638 and lasted until 1646; these
caused the Spaniards to demand more maize and porters from
the Indians of the inland frontier. Reconstructed ten- and thirty-
year running average rainfall patterns from March to June for
Georgia suggest that the years 1610 to 1660 were generally drier
than normal. A finer-grained reconstruction that assumes crop
losses at March–June rainfall levels 15 percent below or above the
mean shows very unsettled weather (very dry and very wet) from
1638 to 1646, and the possibility of a number of crop failures.[71]
And indeed, the years 1642 and 1643 were noted for a "sterility
of maize" at St. Augustine that got so bad that Spaniards and
Indians had to go to the woods to seek out edible roots. This
drought continued into 1644.[72] In Guale, many baptized Indians
left their coastal and island villages and went to live with their
inland pagan relatives. In Mocama and Timucua, some baptized
Indians dispersed to gather and hunt in the forests as early as
1639. At least in Guale, the refugees began to return only in 1646,
when spring rains returned to normal.[73]

Exactly how the Spaniards counteracted this sudden shortage
of maize is unclear, but apparently they tried to get more maize
from the western Timucuans and especially from Apalachee,
which was less affected, if at all.[74] In doing so, the Spaniards,
probably unthinkingly, violated implicit parts of their accommodation with the Indians.

Evidence taken after the Apalachee revolt of 1647 claimed that
heavy use of Indian porters developed in the late 1630s and early
1640s as the governors had maize brought to St. Augustine. Trade

goods (for a private trade up the Flint and Chattahoochee Rivers) and the friars' supplies were then shipped west with the returning porters. Not only was this labor exacted during a time when the Indians may have been malnourished and thus more likely to die from exposure during the winter months (when much of the maize was transported), but apparently porter service was also demanded of *all* adult men (except caciques) rather than, as was Indian custom, of women, hermaphrodites, and men not admitted to warrior status. Evidently population decline had so decreased the numbers of men in the western Timucuan (non-Mocama) villages that caciques were forced to assign porter duty to men whose status or rank in society had exempted them during the early phases of the expansion of the inland frontier. For the western Timucuans, this service was in addition to their role of providing gangs to cultivate St. Augustine's fields.

Adding injury to insult, at some point in the 1620s (?) the friars, and increasingly other Spaniards, stopped paying the porters who carried their supplies or paid them trivial amounts, such as an axe worth a peso for carrying up to seventy-five pounds more than one hundred miles.[75] In short, the increased demand for porters regardless of social rank and without adequate compensation in trade goods, like the decreased giving of gifts during the same period, was a blow to the male status systems of Indian societies. Some men (temporarily?) absented themselves from their villages rather than endure the underpaid humiliation of being porters. The mission of Santiago de Ocone (east of the Okefenokee Swamp?) seems to have become a center for such refugees.[76]

During roughly the same period, 1620–1645, the Spaniards began to detain for longer and longer periods the Indians sent to cultivate the fields at St. Augustine. They sometimes arbitrarily increased the number of workers, using the "extras" for private purposes. As will be recalled, this supplying of agricultural laborers had started in 1601 as a part of the Spanish–Guale accommodation that ended the Juanillo revolt. The custom was extended into Potano, Utina, and Ustaga after each was brought into the mission system. By the 1640s, the friars, and presumably their caciques, were complaining about the abuses just noted.

The friars also complained about the continuing custom of the unpaid quartering of soldiers who passed through the villages.[77] Both complaints not only looked to the economic well-being of the villagers but also to keeping bad moral examples out of the villages, because soldiers, and Indians who returned from St. Augustine after long residence, were likely to be less pious and respectful of the friars.

To sum up, a combination of events that neither the Spaniards nor the Indians of La Florida could control had created shortages in gifts, trade goods, and maize by the mid-1640s. The results of the Spaniards' efforts to solve the latter problem to their own benefit and of long-standing abuses in the agricultural labor system and the quartering of itinerant soldiers were increasing strains on the mutual accommodations that the Spaniards and the caciques had worked out at the turn of the century. The caciques and Indians would have been right had they concluded that the Spaniards were unilaterally changing the terms of the relationship in ways unfavorable to the Native Americans. Among the Mocama, Guale, and most western Timucuans, the Indians' unrest likely was tempered by their already long histories of living with the Spaniards and the rise of a generation of elite leaders who had been schooled to obedience by the friars.[78] But in Apalachee, the majority of the Indians and caciques were still not even baptized.

The Apalachee Revolt, 1647

On 19 February 1647, pagan Apalachee killed three of the friars gathered at the new mission of San Antonio de Bacuqua. The mission was celebrating that patron saint's day. All nine members of the lieutenant governor's household were killed as well. Baptized Indians helped the province's other five friars escape. Five or six other Spaniards resident on Governor Ruiz de Salazar's hacienda also escaped. The Apalachee burned seven of the eight mission churches.[79]

The Spanish response was predictable. Captain Martín de Cuevas and thirty soldiers were quickly dispatched from St. Augustine to apprehend the leaders of the "riot." Ruiz de Salazar, who happened to be in western Timucua at the time, joined the force with the ten men of his household and helped Cuevas recruit five hundred Timucuan warriors. As this new force moved into Apalachee territory, it was attacked by a large party of warriors (Salazar claimed it numbered more than eight thousand). The fight went on all day and consumed all of the Spaniards' ammunition. The Apalachee left them in command of the field, but the Spaniards retired to St. Augustine to refit and prepare for what they thought might have to be a long campaign.[80]

In fact, the coming of spring planting and low rebel morale because of leadership casualties suffered in the first battle provided the opportunity for Francisco Menéndez Marqués, the royal treasurer, to end the rebellion. He took twenty-one soldiers and sixty Timucuan warriors—the only men who could be spared from the western Timucuan villages during planting season—and captured and executed the dozen principal leaders. An additional twenty-six men were taken to St. Augustine for hard labor. The rest of the Apalachee pledged obedience, rebuilt the churches, and welcomed the friars back. Baptized Apalachee had aided Menéndez Marqués. These actions took a month.[81]

Investigation of why the rebellion had occurred produced much heat but only limited light. The Indians and friars blamed the Spaniards' demand for porters and other economic abuses of the Indians. Ruiz de Salazar (who was suspended from office at the time) blamed the Indians' "natural evil," in effect dismissing economic abuse as a cause. Indian testimony prompted by the next governor suggested that the friars had caused the economic abuse.[82] In short, friars and governors once again blamed each other in the hope of scoring political points in their ongoing struggle over power and ignored the more general causes: the Spanish presence and assaults on the status system of native society.[83]

The Apalachee rebellion shook Spanish confidence only slightly and business as usual only briefly. The Asile hacienda was reoccupied. Wheat was sown and harvested from 1648 to 1651 to build up a store of seed grain. A miller and millstones were sent for but arrived after Ruiz de Salazar's death and the breakup of the hacienda. A new lieutenant governor, Captain Juan Fernández de Florencia, and a small garrison took up residence once more in Apalachee, as did Franciscans. So far as can be determined, commerce carried on Indian backs continued across north Florida. Apalachee's trade in deerskins continued to develop. In Guale and western Timucua, and now also in Apalachee as a price for failure in the rebellion, chiefs had to supply quotas of laborers for the fields of St. Augustine.[84] Ruiz de Salazar resumed office as governor and pressed ahead in his exploitation of La Florida's economy. The only sign to reveal that the Spaniards had learned anything from the rebellion was in their return to gift giving. In four years, 1648–1651, the treasury spent 21,424 pesos for gifts, with 9,271 of them in 1650 (see below), suggesting that there were gifts valued at over 4,000 pesos in each of the other three years.[85] Whether this largesse mollified the caciques' egos that had been bruised by the years of comparative neglect is not known.

New Chisca raids on some of the Timucuan missions in 1650 or early 1651 also failed to interrupt business as usual. Governor Ruiz de Salazar sent seven soldiers to the Timucuan villages on a successful search-and-destroy mission. A second Spanish force was sent to Guale in case any Chisca were there, but apparently it saw no action and returned to St. Augustine.[86]

Although the Apalachee Revolt of 1647 passed into history with little immediate impact on business as usual, we can see that it signaled the beginning of a dozen years of rebellion and disease that hollowed out the Spanish frontiers and transformed the Spanish–Indian relationship. The almost undocumented demographic decline, consolidation of villages, and changing Spanish attitudes toward their Indian subjects (as they increasingly became) during the late 1630s and 1640s had prepared the way for much of what followed after 1647. These developments are explored in the next chapter.

6.

Death, Rebellion, a New Accommodation, and New Defenses: La Florida's Frontiers, 1650–1680

The return of domestic peace to Apalachee in the summer of 1647 and the resumption of many of the same Spanish practices that had brought that people to rebellion and their neighbors to a high degree of restiveness turned out to mark a lull in a dozen-year-long general crisis that began with the rebellion of 1647. That rebellion was followed by three waves of epidemic disease that carried off a major part of the remaining baptized Indian population; by drought; a military threat; and an unsuccessful rebellion by the western Timucuans. The results were changes in the Spanish–Indian accommodation that subordinated the Indians within the frontiers as never before. The Spaniards had hardly begun to enjoy the fruits of this victory when Westo raids on the Guale missions and then buccaneer attacks challenged the security of La Florida. Aided in the 1670s by a slightly revived Spanish imperial government, the friars tried to expand the missions and the soldiers built new defenses and improved the food supply of St. Augustine. But Madrid did not give permission for the destruction of Charleston, founded in 1670, thereby sowing a seed whose fruit proved to be the annihilation of La Florida's missions.

The General Crisis of the 1650s

Three years after the Apalachee rebellion, in the spring of 1650, yellow fever (which appeared in the Caribbean in 1648) or possibly typhus, arrived at St. Augustine.[1] Within the year, Governor Ruiz de Salazar, at least two captains, and several friars were dead. So were other Spaniards by early 1652, including accountant Nicolás Ponce de León, who had assumed the governorship until a new governor could be appointed. The documents are silent as to the toll taken among the Indians, but it must have been at least as severe.[2] Spanish demands for labor now fell on many fewer shoulders, especially in the eastern parts of La Florida where swamps bred the yellow fever–spreading Aedes mosquitoes in abundance.

This epidemic had barely abated when spring rains (as measured in Georgia) again entered what proved to be an eight-year period, 1652–1659, of mostly well below average amounts. Some indication of what happened to maize production in northeastern Florida during this drought comes from the tithe records, which appear to record the maize crop with a one-year lag. After production of about 14,700 arrobas of maize in 1649 and 1650 and almost 14,000 arrobas in 1651, production fell to 10,000 arrobas in 1652, the first year of the drought. The rate held at that level during the more normal rainfall level of the spring of 1653, and then plunged again in 1654 and 1655 to a low of some 7,400 arrobas before recovering in 1656 to 10,000 arrobas.[3] The Spaniards' extension of their trade in foods as far north as Escamacu (the area around St. Helena Sound, South Carolina) during this decade probably provided only marginal relief because the drought extended over the entire region. However, this trade may have resulted in the creation of a *visita* at Santa Elena (Parris Island).[4] Once again, the Spaniards increased their demands on the Indians of the inland frontier, whose own crops must have suffered as well. And once again, short harvests probably reduced the population's biological resistance to disease.

To these natural disasters, the Spaniards added a governmental one of their own creation. When Nicolás Ponce de León died in October 1651, the surviving officers of the garrison elected one

of their own, Pedro Benedit Horruytiner, as interim governor. A
native of St. Augustine, he ruled for eighteen months by currying
favor with all the major interests in the colony. To win the good
will of the creole families and many other soldiers, he created
twenty-three new captains, four *alcaides* (fort wardens), three
sergeant majors, ten *ayudantes*, three accountants, and one treasurer, for a total of forty-four titles. To secure the favor of the
Franciscans, he agreed to sell off the assets of the Asile hacienda
that Ponce de León had purchased for the Crown (for 4,259 pesos
payable in Mexico) from Ruiz de Salazar's son and heir. Creoles,
caciques, and probably a few friars snapped up the eleven yoke
of oxen, the plows and other tools, the eight stallions and mares,
and all of the cattle at bargain prices. The friars and caciques
agreed to continue to produce wheat but only for their own use.[5]
To win over the caciques, Horruytiner may have been exception-
ally liberal with gifts when they came to render homage in 1650,
ballooning those costs to their all-time high, as has been noted.

This orgy of self-serving was interrupted by the arrival of Governor Diego de Rebolledo on 18 April 1654. Like his predecessors,
Rebolledo aimed to make money by using the customary means.
He arrived already connected to Ponce de León's faction and to
the financial interests that had backed Ruiz de Salazar. Not surprisingly, therefore, within eighteen months Rebolledo was being
denounced anonymously for nearly monopolizing the St. Augustine market through various agents, who as usual added mark-
ups of up to 400 percent to the prices of goods sold, on credit, to
the soldiers.[6] Rebolledo also openly favored some soldiers over
the rest and interfered with the authority of the captains over
their men.[7] His public quarrels with the Franciscans seem to
have begun only in 1657, perhaps because in the first years of his
governorship there were as few as two dozen friars in the province, mostly in the missions.[8]

Rebolledo's Indian policies undid whatever repairs Horruytiner's liberality had made to the Spanish–cacique accommodation and did nothing to end the economic abuses complained of
by the Indians and their Franciscan defenders. He began by taking the letter of the decree of 1615 seriously. He did not give the
customary gifts to the Christian caciques, especially to the west-

ern Timucuan caciques, when they came to swear fealty. Instead, he limited his gifts to pagans and, as signs of special favor, to Christian caciques such as those of Apalachee who had something of value to offer such as Indian labor and deerskins.[9] When asked to forbid the use of Indian porters, or at least to see that they were paid a wage proportionate to their labors, as was done in New Spain, he demurred. He did the same thing with a request that caciques be paid for lodging and foods they supplied to soldiers traveling on official business.[10] In both cases, of course, his own profits were at stake. Porters carried goods for the deerskin trade he and his allies ran. Soldier-agents conducted that trade and also traveled to the lower east coast of the peninsula to trade for ambergris for the governor.[11]

And on top of all of that, in January 1655 Pedro Beltrán de Santa Cruz and a staff of clerks arrived to audit the treasury records dating back to 1630. By the time they finished, most of the prominent men in St. Augustine owed money to the Crown because of misappropriation while they had served as *situado* collectors or because they were bondsmen for men who had so served.[12]

In short, the social, financial, and emotional turmoil in St. Augustine society during 1654 and 1655 must have been considerable, and it was all the more pronounced because of the "liberty" of the previous eighteen months.

In the midst of this turmoil, smallpox struck. In the winter of 1654–1655, it swept outward from St. Augustine through the Timucuan provinces and into Apalachee. During 1655 and 1656, smallpox and "plague" devastated Guale. Some Spaniards, all of the king's Black slaves, and an unknown fraction (25–50 percent, possibly even higher) of the baptized Indians perished. Indian villages and tribes suddenly disintegrated after over a generation (1617–1649) of slow decline.[13]

Hints of the devastation can be found in Governor Rebolledo's orders of late 1655 that the population of Santiago de Oconi be removed to repopulate Nombre de Dios and that an agent recruit pagan Acuera and any mission fugitives to cultivate St. Augustine's fields.[14] The latter order specifically said that the Apalachee and western Timucuans could not supply the usual quotas

DEATH,
REBELLION,
A NEW
ACCOMMODATION,
AND NEW
DEFENSES

because of epidemic deaths and lingering illness among survivors. In short, this epidemic, even more than the one of 1649–1651, spelled the end of an era for Native American societies in contact with the Spaniards at St. Augustine.

And in the Caribbean, the Penn-Venables fleet, after failing to capture Santo Domingo, captured Jamaica for England in May 1655. From London that fall came word that the British were planning to take St. Augustine in 1656 in order to gain control of the Bahama Channel, the jugular vein of Spain's imperial commerce and finance.[15]

A warning of a probable English attack, reinforced by stories from Spanish seamen who had been prisoners of English corsairs operating off Cuba, arrived in St. Augustine in the middle of April 1656 on the heels of news that an "English" corsair had visited the St. Marks River south of Apalachee to trade iron tools for food.[16] Rebolledo immediately began to shore up the fort, once again in dilapidated condition, and, with no apparent appreciation of what the recent epidemic had done to Indian society, issued orders affecting the Indians.

Rebolledo ordered the Guale, Timucuan, and Apalachee caciques to come to St. Augustine with all their warriors (but not commoners engaged in planting) with any muskets held in the villages, and with food. The agent who carried this order to Guale was told to purchase on credit as much maize as was available. The Timucuans and Apalachee were each told to bring three arrobas of maize (about seventy-five pounds) when they came. One was for each man's own sustenance; the other two were to increase the reserves at St. Augustine, which were low because of the poor harvest of the previous year. In addition, the Timucuan labor quota was raised to fifty or sixty from the previous year's thirty-two, which had been filled, if at all, only late and probably with a good deal of Spanish coercion since we know that as of March 1655 the Apalachee and western Timucuans were claiming an inability to supply agricultural laborers because of the smallpox epidemic.[17]

Rebolledo's order that the western Timucuan chiefs bring their own food and additional reserves to St. Augustine touched off a rebellion. For Indian leaders like Lucas Menéndez, the nominal great chief of the Utina, and Diego, the leader of the Yustaga and cacique of Potohiriba, the thought that they might personally have to carry seventy-five-pound loads was too great an indignity to swallow because it amounted to their reduction to the status of commoners or even slaves. Already suffering the status loss of having few subjects because of the epidemics, the caciques who rebelled had reached a breaking point. Rebolledo—first by not giving them the customary gifts in 1654 and slighting them in other ways and now by issuing this order with the implication that he would not feed them at royal expense once in St. Augustine—seemed to be saying that he did not accept them as natural lords of the land who were entitled to honors. This violated the caciques' understanding of the imperial relationship that came from their own cultural tradition. They probably had also learned from the Franciscans the Spaniards' ideas of the natural law rights of Indians.[18] The caciques gave Rebolledo a chance to back down by writing to him, explaining why they would not obey his order with respect to the maize, but John Worth is probably correct in observing that this was a maneuver to buy time while they organized other caciques and leading men. They had already decided to rebel. Rebolledo did not relent.[19]

The Timucuan rebels' plan was to remove all Spaniards except the friars from their territories and, if possible, induce the Apalachee to do the same. This would restore a pristine form of the "republic of Indians" while an appeal against abuses was sent to Madrid. The rebels did not question the "rightness" of Spanish rule, only its abuses. In this respect, they were like other seventeenth-century rebels elsewhere in the empire.[20]

The rebels eventually killed four Spaniards, two African slaves, and a Tabascan Indian, all of the latter and two of the Spaniards being hands on the ranch of Juan Menéndez Marqués, La Chua. Menéndez Marqués himself was spared because he and his father (Francisco) had been kind to the Indians, especially to cacique Lucas Menéndez, who organized the attack on La Chua. In Apalachee, the unrest stirred up by the rebels frightened the Franciscans so badly that five of them took a ship, sailed for Cuba, and then were lost at sea. Meanwhile, the rebels built a fort near Machaba.[21]

The Spaniards made no response to the rebellion until the fall
of 1656 when the danger of an English attack had passed. Then
sixty soldiers and a party of Apalachee armed with muskets
taken from the Guale warriors who had come to defend St. Augustine were sent west in early September under the command
of Sergeant-Major Adrián de Canizares y Osorio. Yustagan and
Utinan caciques, whose villages were not directly on the road
to Apalachee, quickly rallied to the Spanish standard. Canizares
eventually lured most of the rebel leaders out of their stronghold
for a conference, arrested them, and then executed one Indian
who confessed to one of the murders. The remaining prisoners
were taken to Ivitachuco in Apalachee to await the governor. Rebolledo left St. Augustine in late November. Once he was in Ivitachuco, he tried the prisoners and ordered the garroting of four
men who had killed and six caciques, in each case near the villages where their "crimes" had been committed or where they
had ruled. Ten lesser figures were sentenced to forced labor at St.
Augustine.[22] New caciques were appointed to govern the villages.
Among the executed were men who had been trained by the
friars.

The epidemic of 1654–1655 and flight after the revolt of 1656
(out of fear of punishment) nearly depopulated several Timucuan missions, prompting Rebolledo to take steps that further
increased the disorder in Timucua. San Juan de Guacara relocated to where the St. Augustine–Apalachee road crossed the Suwannee River. San Martín de Ayacuto (the erstwhile "capital" of
Utina, later replaced by mission Santa Catalina), Santa Fe de
Toloco (or Teleco), and San Francisco de Potano were critical
way stations on the southern branch of that road. To ensure that
travelers could continue to be serviced with food, shelter, and
porters at reasonable intervals along the way, Rebolledo ordered
the northern Timucuan villages of Chamile, Cachipile, and Chuaquin to move to San Martín and San Francisco; Arapaha and its
satellites to move to a relocated Santa Fe; and the Yustagans to
move to the relocated San Juan de Guacara. In each case, a relocated cacique was promoted to replace a cacique who had been
executed for rebellion. The Indians were slow to move and it is
unclear from the documents how much of Rebolledo's plan was

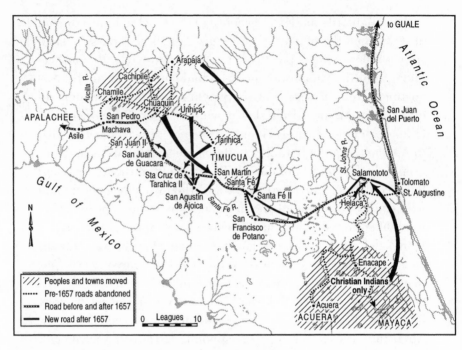

Figure 6.1. Mission consolidations, 1657–ca. 1662. BASED ON JOHN E. WORTH, *The Timucuan Chiefdoms of Spanish Florida* (GAINESVILLE: UNIVERSITY PRESS OF FLORIDA, 1998), FIGURES 5.1 AND 10.2. BY PERMISSION OF THE UNIVERSITY PRESS OF FLORIDA.

achieved before he was arrested in May 1658 by order of the Council of the Indies[23] (Figure 6.1).

Disorder descended into demographic chaos not long after Governor Alonso de Aranguiz y Cotés took office on 20 February 1659. Measles seems to have arrived with his party. He reported on 1 November 1659 that in the eight months since his arrival, 10,000 Indians had died from this disease.[24] Judging from population figures from 1675, this epidemic, in combination with smallpox in 1655 and the apparently less severe (for the Indians) epidemic of 1649–1651, destroyed most of the Christian populations of the Guale, Mocama, Aguadulce, Potano, and Utina and seriously damaged the demographic base in Yustaga and Apalachee. The tidewater frontier and the inland frontier east of the

133

Death,
Rebellion,
a New
Accommodation,
and New
Defenses

Suwannee were reduced to mere shells. For example, the Guale were left with only six towns (all *doctrinas*), the largest of which had approximately twenty-two families as of 1663.[25] That La Florida's eastern frontiers did not collapse at the time was due to Spanish actions and the absence of significant external threats as well as to the resiliency of the survivors and the continued commitment of the majority to living in communities.

Finding the same need to maintain Indian settlements on the road to Apalachee but having fewer means, Aranguiz took up his predecessor's policy of forced resettlement, in this case ordering Yustagans to the four critical way-station missions and consolidating the surviving fragments of satellite villages into the *doctrina* villages. He also relocated all of the other Timucuan settlements to the southern loop of the road to complete the reorganization of "a geographically dispersed and demographically imbalanced aboriginal society into a more or less linear series of populated way stations along the camino real between St. Augustine and Apalache."[26] When the friars asked permission for Indians who had fled Rebolledo's orders to return to their old village sites (such as Arapaha), this permission was denied. In any case, their request seems to have been part of an unsuccessful attempt to continue to play the dominant role in the civil government of the Indians that Rebolledo's disgrace briefly had opened up.[27]

A New Accommodation

The relocation against their will of so many of the surviving western Timucuans during the late 1650s and early 1660s was the principal but not the only sign that the Spaniards permanently had changed the Spanish–Indian accommodation first worked out at the beginning of the century and extended in turn as each new part as the inland frontier opened. The new arrangements appeared to differ in degree more than in kind, but behind them was the assumption that the Indians were absolutely subordinate and would do whatever they were told to do. As John Worth first observed, the Timucuan revolt of 1656 was an attempt to prevent that change in the Spanish–Indian relationship.

But in La Florida—as had occurred elsewhere in the empire in the previous century and beyond—as soon as epidemic diseases destroyed the population base native rulers used to maintain power, the Spaniards were free to rewrite the rules to suit their needs and prejudices.[28] Rebolledo imported this new attitude from his previous service at Cartagena. As we have observed, the beginning of this process can be detected in the Florida documents at least as early as the late 1630s in the first complaints about the misuse of porters and the withholding of gifts. The demographic disaster of the 1650s removed the last obstacles everywhere in La Florida except Apalachee, and even there appearances that the old order continued were deceptive.[29]

Continuation and reform began with Rebolledo. With the western Timucua again under control, Rebolledo attempted to address some Indian complaints, thereby rewarding his Apalachee allies while also discomforting his Franciscan critics, who were as guilty as the officers and soldiers were of abusing the Indians. Meeting various groups of Apalachee and Yustagan caciques during January and early February 1657, Rebolledo inquired about the good order of their towns and about abuses they might have suffered at the hands of Spaniards, especially soldiers, and whether they approved of his posting a dozen-man garrison in Apalachee for its defense. The answers he received suggested that the soldiers were angels but that at least some friars offended and oppressed the Indians by interfering with chiefly authority; by whipping elite Indians, often for trivial offenses; by making Indians carry goods to St. Augustine, the port at St. Marks, and to their pagan neighbors on the Chattahoochee River without payment; by monopolizing trade with Spaniards who came to St. Marks; by forbidding Indians to offer the soldiers hospitality and carriage of their packs; by prohibiting dances and the Indians' traditional ball game; and by using the product of the field(s) (*sabana*) communally cultivated for the friars to purchase church ornaments or for personal gain rather than for subsistence. Rebolledo issued rules that reversed all of these practices, putting the friars on the defensive and apparently upholding Indian rights.[30] Anticipating a royal order dated 18 September 1656 that he would receive in the spring of 1657, the governor forbade all involuntary, uncompensated carriage of

goods ("what they resent the most") except the packs of soldiers
on official business or when the governor ordered goods carried,
both practices of long standing.[31] The Franciscans would have
to pay their porters, but first they got their revenge by forcing
Rebolledo from office with their reports on the rebellion and his
repression of it.[32] For the Indians, the exceptions amounted to
a continuation of the abuse, especially when coupled with their
forceful resettling along the road. And they continued to carry
supplies to the friars, although the government provided at least
some of the food for the journey. Proposals that mules or pack
horses be imported to relieve the Indians got nowhere.[33] In practice, the reforms produced little if any change.

In another indication that the continuation of the old arrangements now had new meanings, Rebolledo and his successors arbitrarily changed the quantities of the annual gifts and the numbers of agricultural laborers for St. Augustine's fields (two key
parts of the accommodation of 1601 with the Guale and of later,
similar arrangements with the Timucua and Apalachee). The
gifts were scaled back so that they cost less than the 2,078 pesos
allowed by the decree of 1615, in spite of protests such as those
of the caciques of Guale (1657).[34] The numbers of laborers demanded remained at pre-revolt levels for a decade, but around
the year 1670 were increased to fifty from both Guale and Timucua (from twenty-five and perhaps thirty-two, respectively) and
by an unknown amount to two hundred from Apalachee as the
Spaniards tried to increase maize production in order to feed the
men who were building Castillo de San Marcos. An additional
eighty to one hundred paid Indian day laborers were recruited,
and frequently replaced, as injury and death thinned their ranks.[35]
But far from growing so as to have men to supply these increased
demands, the populations of all the Indian provinces remained
near their lows of 1660. Nor is there any indication from the
1660s or later that the Spaniards endeavored to restrict the agricultural laborers to spring planting season; they may, in fact,
have extended the time the laborers spent in St. Augustine. Nor
did governors heed orders forbidding the other labors demanded
of St. Augustine's neighbors such as the Tolomato (removed from
Guale in the 1620s), who were compelled to supply stevedores on
demand.[36] In short, the Spaniards unilaterally changed the gift

rules and demanded and mostly got Indian labor to use however they pleased. The caciques were powerless to prevent abuses.

Additional evidence of how the relationship had changed to one of disguised but unequivocal Spanish dominance is found in the apparently increased frequency of Spanish intervention in settling not only disputes in the Indians villages but also in determining successions to office as death disrupted Indian lineages and succession patterns. Examples, probably representing only the tip of an iceberg, are known from 1665, 1668, and 1673.[37]

A new element in the Spanish–Indian relationship, and again a sign of Spanish dominance, was the expansion of Spanish ranching. Probably beginning during the depopulation of the 1650s, caciques, claiming an absolute right over the land even though Spanish law vested authority in such matters in the king, rented or even sold land to private individuals as a way of maintaining incomes. Contradicting the claims of the caciques, governors, especially Pablo de Hita Salazar in the late 1670s, regularly granted the use of unfarmed land as pasturage to encourage ranching. The Crown's order of 1680 that no land be granted except by itself was ignored.[38] The result was a boom in ranching that reached from St. Augustine to Apalachee as Spanish cattle and ranch hands replaced hunting grounds, maize fields no longer being used, and Indians. As in other parts of the Spanish Empire, the Indians had little recourse when cattle invaded their fields.[39] Some Indians, nonetheless, took up cattle herding on a small scale, to judge by the fact that in 1704 the Apalachee fleeing English raids drove their cattle westward to Pensacola.[40]

But the Spaniards did not have everything their way. During the late 1670s, they again tried to prohibit the ball game in Apalachee and western Timucua. Friars unsuccessfully had attempted abolition of this activity in the 1650s. Bishop Calderón forbade it again in 1675, and inspector Domingo de Leturiondo obtained what he thought was Apalachee agreement to end it in 1677. Yet it endured into the 1680s, and possibly to the end of the mission system.[41]

Another arena in which the Spaniards did not get their way involved fugitive Indians who lived in the forests away from the mission villages. As in earlier times, some Indians had temporar-

137

DEATH,
REBELLION,
A NEW
ACCOMMODATION,
AND NEW
DEFENSES

ily fled from demeaning service as porters or agricultural laborers at St. Augustine. Such slender evidence as we have suggests
that some families and small groups of Indian maroons were persons whose attachment to community life had dissolved during
the epidemics. Thus María Jacoba, captured in 1678, had lived
since the 1650s (except for one period in the late 1660s) with men
who hunted while she gathered. A Christian, she claimed that
she had been careful to return to her village to make her yearly
confession each Easter. In Potano, small groups of Indian maroons lived near the Mission San Francisco in the mid-1660s.
Bands of Acuera (noted in 1678 and 1697 but probably wandering since 1660), and probably other peoples as well, regularly
moved about west of the St. Johns River, pursuing a semi-
nomadic life. Spanish efforts largely failed to round up Indian
maroons or to prevent vagabondage and migration, even though
a decree told caciques not to allow individuals to move between
villages without written permission from the lieutenant governor
and the migrant's original cacique.[42] Indian maroonage was
probably not as common as some recent scholarship suggests.
Still, it should not be surprising that some Indians chose this alternative to the missions, given how much even the missionized
Indians still depended on an annual round that included gathering and hunting to supplement their dependence on maize.

In sum, out of the revolts and due to the deaths caused by
epidemics and droughts from 1647 to 1659, there emerged a new
relationship between Spaniards and Indians and a new geography of settlement in both the tidewater and inland frontiers.
Never based on Indian populations as large as those in the piedmont before the 1560s, La Florida after 1660 rested on extremely
slender demographic foundations east of the Aucilla River and
along the Atlantic coast. So fragile was it that its survival depended on the absence of serious military challenges. Almost prov-
identially, none presented itself during the next twenty years.

The Missions' Indian Summer, 1660–1680

The English attack on St. Augustine that Rebolledo had spent
the spring of 1656 preparing to repel did not happen for another

twelve years. In addition, the collapse of La Florida's frontiers under English pressure did not begin until a dozen years after that. Meanwhile, life in the missions went on and, in the 1670s, attempts were made to carry them into new areas. Only a few, seemingly unconnected attacks, like the scattered squalls in the outermost feeder bands of a tropical storm, gave any hint of what was to come. These attacks took place early in the years under consideration and then faded.

The first squall was the raid on one or more of the Guale missions (Talaje at the mouth of the Altamaha River is mentioned) in June 1661 by "Chichimecs" said to be from Jacán (Virginia) but probably Erie Indians driven south by the Iroquois Wars. After taking casualties in a fight with the Guale and losing other men when a crude boat sank as its crew attempted to cross the bay to attack San Joseph de Sapala (Sapelo Island), the Chichimeca retired to La Tama and Catufa. A Spanish force pursuing them apparently inflicted some casualties but did not engage the main force. In the fall of 1662, Chichimecas attacked Huyache (probably on the lower Savannah River), killing everyone they could. Shortly after that, the Chichimecas divided and went north. There they settled in "Yamassee" territory north and west of Port Royal to practice agriculture. Talaje moved to Guadalquini Island (St. Simons).[43]

The friars who reported the latter movements of the Chichimeca mistakenly were confident that the Yamassee, from Escamacu (the area immediately north and west of Port Royal) and Colón (location uncertain) southward would resist any new raid by the Chichimecas, making a Spanish garrison in Guale unnecessary.[44] They were right to the extent that skirmishing seems to have developed, but wrong in thinking that the Yamassee would be a barrier. In 1667, the caciques of Santa Elena and Abaya (Ahoya?) and their people appeared at St. Catherines Island, the first Yamassee refugees from one too many "Chichimeca" attacks, evidently delivered from new "Westo" settlements on the middle Savannah River (above modern Augusta). During the next eight years, Westo raids caused not only Yamassee but also residents of Altamaha, Ocute and two other interior towns (from "La Tama") to flee to the coast, to the Apalachee missions, and to towns of the Creek confederacy. By 1675, there were six pagan vil-

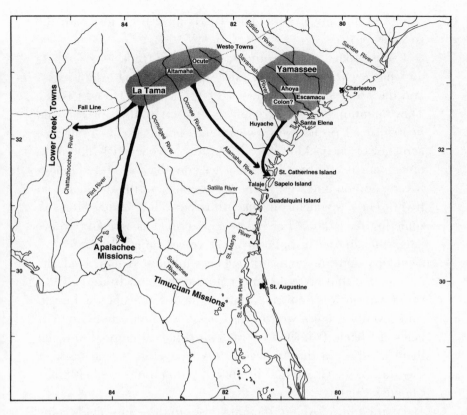

Figure 6.2. Effects of "Chichimec" raids, 1661–1675.

lages on the coastal islands, one of them a Yamassee town of sixty persons. Another was "La Tama" (Altamaha?, with fifty persons) and a second was "Ocotoque" (Ocute) (with forty)[45] (Figure 6.2).

Other signs of the coming storm were the visits of William Hilton and Robert Sandford (respectively) to Port Royal Sound and points northward along the coast, in September 1663 and July 1666. In addition, there was English trade with the Ocaneechee, Tuscarora, and coastal peoples of North Carolina.[46] But what these things meant was unclear aside from the need of the Spaniards to think about consolidating the Guale missions on the islands out of easy reach of the Chichimeca/Westo raiders.

These incidents aside, the long-established peace and small-scale giving of gifts and trade that centered on St. Augustine continued. Delegations of pagan peoples still visited St. Augustine to be fed and given gifts. The details have been lost with the treasury records.

The Spaniards also continued to develop trade for deerskins and maize with the Chacatos, the "Apalachicoli" (Lower Creek), and the peoples of the "province of Toassa" (the Upper Creek). They maintained mostly friendly contacts with the Chiscas, who in 1675 lived respectively two leagues northwest of Apalachee across or on the Ocklochonee River, forty-two leagues (about 110 miles) north on the Chattahoochee, on the Coosa-Tallapoosa Rivers, and on and west of the lower course of the Apalachicola River. The "Apalachicoli" had thirteen villages, the "Toassa" some fourteen. The "Toassa" were described as "pagan barbarians," the same term applied to the slave-catching "Chichimecas." Evidently some mission work had been attempted at an Apalachicolan town that lay a dozen leagues up the Flint from the Chacato towns; it was known as Santa Cruz de Sabacola, the Lesser. And seventy leagues west of the Toassa were reportedly 107 villages of Chacto (Choctaw).[47] Spaniards had attempted to reach them in 1661 via the Apalachicola villages but turned back at Casista (on the Chattahoochee River?) after a meeting with four Choctaw caciques.[48]

An attempt to expand the missions into these new fields coincided with the visit of Bishop Gabriel Díaz Vara Calderón to Apalachee in 1675. He formally inaugurated what proved to be two short-lived missions, one (San Nicolás) among the Chacatos when he confirmed a total of 130 baptized Chacato (in a population estimated to number 600 or more) and the other at Sabacola the Lesser, where he dedicated a church in the presence of the great chief of Sabacola the Greater and many other Indians of note from among the Apalachicola. In both cases, the bishop confidently predicted that conversions would be rapid and would reach the thirteen Apalachicola villages within a short period.[49] However, by the end of the year, the non-Christian Chacato had revolted because the friar at San Nicolás had interfered with the status system by rebuking two pagan warriors, one for adultery and one for polygamy. The Christian Chacato then founded a village, San Carlos de los Chacatos, half a league from San Luis, the headquarters of the garrison.[50] Nothing is known of the fate of the church at Sabacola the Lesser.

🐚 141

DEATH,
REBELLION,
A NEW
ACCOMMODATION,
AND NEW
DEFENSES

Talk of expanding on the southern rim of La Florida seems to have been another fruit of Bishop Calderón's visit and of the arrival of a new group of Franciscans around the year 1678. Indians from the lower west coast of the peninsula had been visiting Cuba for some time to trade fish, manatee fat, and ambergris for tools and other items.[51] Moved by piety or perhaps by a desire to seem zealous, in 1680 Governor Hita Salazar used a report on the small force he had sent to the Calusa to free Spaniards reportedly enslaved there (the force turned back in the face of Calusa hostility) to lobby for mission work in southern Florida. In an indirect criticism of the Franciscans, he reported that Fr. Sebastian Pérez de la Cerda, the secular parish priest at St. Augustine, knew that secular priests at Santiago de Cuba had a long-standing interest in such a project. The Crown approved this new mission. Cuban clerical volunteers were indeed forthcoming in 1681, but no money was made available by officials in Cuba or in Florida. For the time being, this was how the situation remained.[52]

The Spanish Arena

For the Spaniards in La Florida, the years 1660–1680 saw a hint of an important change in demographic patterns, an improvement in their supply of beef and maize (the latter thanks to a growing dependence on Apalachee for maize), and the building of Castillo de San Marcos and a fort at St. Marks in response to corsair attacks. The fort construction temporarily brought new human and economic resources to the province and, together with the attempted expansion of the missions, marked a small revival of Spanish imperialism in La Florida.

Corbett has characterized the years 1658–1670 as a time of "precarious existence" for the small population of St. Augustine. The known pattern of marriages and births per marriage was the same as for the period from 1628 to 1657: fewer than a dozen marriages per year and about three and a half births per marriage. The death records of the parish have not survived, but deaths probably continued to be nearly as high as, and in epidemic years higher than births. The population remained overwhelmingly male although increasingly creole (35.9 percent of grooms) and dominated by creole families that had been established in the sixteenth century. Mexicans accounted for 20 percent of the grooms, ahead of Andalucia's 18.9 percent and both far ahead of Cantabrian Spain's total of 6.3 percent.[53]

The demographic picture improved slightly in the 1670s. Mexican troops arrived to beef up the garrison, and improved food supplies seem to have increased the fertility of married couples. The stage was being set for the near breakthrough to a "self-contained community" that was to take place in the 1680s.

The Spaniards' food supply improved thanks to the expansion of ranching noted earlier, but difficulties continued with the supply of maize and imported goods. Rebolledo opened new fields for himself and a favored few in 1656,[54] and additional ones may have been opened by 1670. Drafted Indians supplied the labor. However, St. Augustine's maize production seems to have continued to fall due to soil exhaustion, a return of abnormal spring rainfalls (1672–1680), and damage by the storm surges of hurricanes on 17 August 1674 and 20 October 1675. Again, Apalachee was the answer. Governor Manuel de Cendoya (1671–1673) monopolized the Apalachee supply for his personal profit, but after his death in July 1673, private parties took over. This private trade was important enough that one of Hita Salazar's first acts was to seize the Apalachee shipments of 1675 because he found only one hundred arrobas of maize in the royal storehouses.[55] Thereafter, the governor sent ships with agents to purchase maize from the friars and caciques of Apalachee for the royal account and to allow private parties (mostly the Fernández de Florencia family) to ship maize on a space-available basis.[56] Hita Salazar and his predecessors also continued to send ships to Guale to buy maize and other foods. Such local initiatives were beneficial because the supply of food and other goods from Mexico collapsed during the 1660s, to be revived only in 1669 with the renewed realization that the English might covet La Florida.[57]

The problem with making Apalachee the bread basket of St. Augustine was the vulnerable sea route via Havana. As the seizure at St. Marks in 1677 showed (see below), that route was subject to interruptions. This may explain why in 1677 Domingo de Leturiondo founded a new mission, Santa Rosa de Ivitanayo, between the St. Johns River and Mission Santa Fe on the site of

an abandoned ranch on the St. Augustine–Apalachee road. Santa
Rosa was peopled (circa 1681) with Yustaga and, later, with anyone else the Spaniards could persuade to move there or wished
to punish. After an initial year of exemption, the residents were
expected to become porters.[58] Hita Salazar was looking toward
using the overland route once again.

On the military front, the early 1660s saw discussion of the need for a fort at St. Marks (Apalachee's port), the actual installation of a small garrison at San Luis (in Apalachee) over the friars' continued objections, and the usual complaints by each new governor about how few able-bodied men he had and how badly the fort at St. Augustine had deteriorated.[59] These concerns received some sympathy in Madrid, but lingering financial troubles and an apparent bureaucratic inertia prevented action on the complaints of a demographically declining mission colony of uncertain military value in a period when the once rich annual convoys to and from the Caribbean had ceased to operate on any schedule and brought back less and less royal revenue when they did sail.[60]

The shouts of Robert Searles's buccaneers in the streets of St. Augustine in the early morning hours of 29 May 1668 awoke not only the sleeping population but also the imperial government. He had captured the presidio's supply ships and used them and their crews to deceive the Spaniards while he waited for the high tide that allowed him to bring those ships and his own across the bar into the bay. The buccaneers gained control of the town but failed to get to the fort before its defenders did. After looting the houses, churches, and royal storehouses, and sounding the bar, Searles's men sailed away. With them went Dr. John Henry Woodward, an English surgeon whom Stanford had left at his own request with the Indians at Port Royal and who had then surrendered to the Spaniards. He had spent more than a year in St. Augustine.[61] We will meet him later.

In assessments of the attack, blame was placed on the governor and, especially, on the sergeant major, the creole Nicolás Ponce de León. He had led a general flight of the soldiers to the forests and had not counterattacked while the buccaneers looted the town. Fearing an English return—why else had they not burned the houses?—the officials reported that they needed three hundred effectives at St. Augustine, not the two hundred or so that they actually had, and a stone fort.[62]

When news of the attack reached Mexico City late that fall, the viceroy and his advisors responded with money, supplies, seventy-five or so soldiers, and authorization to begin construction of a stone fort, the present Castillo de San Marcos. This assistance reached St. Augustine the next spring. By October 1672, an engineer was on hand and a groundbreaking of sorts occurred. Meanwhile, the civilian men of St. Augustine were organized into two companies of militia, one of horse, the other on foot.[63] Construction of the fort lasted until 1687. It brought about a mild boom both economically and in terms of Hispanic population growth. But it also consumed an unknown number of Indian laborers. To man the new defenses and make up for the continued lack of able-bodied men, the nominal size of the garrison was raised to 393 men (including 43 places for friars) in 1673. The new soldiers came from Mexico.[64]

The timeliness of the Spanish response to Searles's raid became evident in 1670, when English nobles moved to make good on Charles II's grant of title to the Southeast from twenty-nine degrees to thirty-six degrees North by founding Charleston in April. Three months later, English and Spanish diplomats signed the Treaty of Madrid (18 July). By article seven of the treaty, Spain recognized English possessions in the Americas, unintentionally including Charleston.[65]

News of the new English settlement reached St. Augustine from the Indians at St. Catherines Island. In late May or the first days of June 1670, an English ship landed a party of a dozen persons seeking food. The Indians attacked, killing seven men and capturing four men, a woman, and a girl. Sent to St. Augustine, they revealed that their ship and two others had been going to settle "the port of Santa Elena." Later that month, their ship returned to St. Catherines in an unsuccessful effort to obtain the prisoners. Still later, a ship visited St. Catherines and traded peacefully for food, deerskins, and ceramics.[66]

The officials at St. Augustine reacted promptly. Antonio de

DEATH,
REBELLION,
A NEW
ACCOMMODATION,
AND NEW
DEFENSES

Argüelles was sent north to Santa Elena with a small party to find out what he could. He quickly discovered that the English were further north and had only a bark and a launch. A committee at St. Augustine then agreed to fit out three ships for an attack on the English colony, but in the end adverse weather caused Juan Menéndez Marqués, the commander, to turn back before the ships reached Charleston. Over the winter and into the following fall, the Spaniards contented themselves with sending Captain Matheo Pacheco and twenty-five men to garrison Mission St. Catherines and with gathering information from Indians who had visited Charleston. They got a remarkably accurate picture.[67] They also got orders from Madrid not to molest the English. For the moment, there appeared no danger to the missions that the garrisons in Guale and Apalachee could not handle. Nonetheless, the residents of San Felipe de Alave and Santa Clara de Tupiqui took the precaution of moving off the mainland to Cumberland and Sapelo Islands, respectively. Outside of the villages, all was not entirely secure. Individuals occasionally disappeared or were killed, victims of the Westo and Chisca, the Spaniards thought.[68] Not surprisingly, given this insecure condition, Bishop Díaz Vara Calderón took a company of Spanish soldiers and two of Indians when he made his episcopal inspection of the Timucuan and Apalachee missions in 1674–1675.[69]

Spanish suspicions that Westo were raiding the back country and the fringes of the missions for Indian slaves were not wrong. In 1674, the Westo visited Charleston to offer a trade in deerskins and slaves in return for munitions and other European goods that they apparently had been getting from the Occaneechee (Susquehannocks), who had a fortified trading town on an island in the Roanoke River, and from Virginia traders like John Lederer, who had first visited the Carolina Piedmont around the year 1670. In October 1674, Dr. Henry Woodward visited the Westo town to work out the arrangements for trade and alliance.[70] By May 1675, the Spaniards had learned from a Chisca woman (who had escaped from Charleston where she had been sold as a slave by Chicimecas) that Englishmen were in the Westo village repairing firearms and concerting a plan for the destruction of the

missions in Apalachee and Timucua.[71] Later reports told of
Westo raids on Indians between their town and Charleston. The
Spaniards also learned about the rapid growth of that town.[72]

Just as Searles's raid on St. Augustine led to the building of a
new fort, so too a buccaneer raid on St. Marks in June 1677 led
to the building of a fort there. The Spaniards' fear of an English
seizure of Apalachee, first aroused by the trading incident of 1655
and strengthened by a report of 1659, was reinforced by this incident during which buccaneers seized two ships at Saint Marks,
fought off two Indian–Spanish attacks, and held three friars until
paid a ransom of thirty pigs. To prevent such losses in the future,
Governor Hita Salazar began the construction of a small fortification with a claim that an order of 30 October 1666 had authorized such work. The labor was provided by Indians, paid in trade
goods such as large and small bells, knives, blue and other colored glass beads, blankets, and brass sheets. The structure was
finished in 1680.[73]

The building of new defenses at St. Augustine and St. Marks;
the establishment of small garrisons at San Luis (Apalachee) and
St. Catherines (Guale); the monitoring of English and Westo activities; the development of an intensified supplying of St. Augustine; and the attempt to expand the inland frontier toward
the populations later known as the Creek were all timely measures, as we will see in the next chapter. The center of the storm
that would sweep the missions and their peoples from the face of
the land was drawing nearer.

Postscript

Bishop Calderón's inspection tour and reports prepared by the
provincial lieutenants during the same year (1675) provide a
comprehensive overview of the mission system and populations,
and allow some evaluation of what had happened since 1647. In
1675, the old tidewater frontier had fifteen Christian and pagan
towns in Guale and Mocama and a total population of more than
750 persons, of whom about half were in eight missions. The
largest was Santa Catalina de Guale (120 persons), which was
also the seat of the garrison and lieutenant governor. Both Ya-

147

DEATH,
REBELLION,
A NEW
ACCOMMODATION,
AND NEW
DEFENSES

massee and Tama had villages on Amelia Island. Yamassee refugees were probably the other "pagans" noted on the Georgia barrier islands.[74] No missions are listed south of St. Augustine or on the upper St. Johns River, but the peoples of the lower east coast still existed, as did those along the west coast, although the populations were small.[75] West of the St. Johns River, the first of nine villages on the road to Apalachee was San Francisco, at sixteen leagues. These nine had a total population of about 1,600 persons. The five missions east of the Suwannee had 60 to 80 persons each except for Santa Fe, which claimed 110. The four missions west of the Suwannee in Yustaga each had 300 inhabitants[76] (Ivitanayo would later have no more than 100 inhabitants). The crown jewel was Apalachee with sixteen missions (including the three newly established ones) and more than 8,600 souls. Here too, Yamassee and Tama had taken refuge at a new mission, known variously as Candelaria and La Purificación. Not counted in this list were three Tocobaga settlements of unknown size.[77] In all, thirty-three missions were listed, with populations totaling 13,152 baptized persons (over age five, most likely). Two-thirds of these people were in Apalachee.[78]

The mission list of 1655, the only previous comprehensive list (and it omits some details), claimed thirty-eight missions and some 26,000 baptized Indians.[79] The major losses by 1675 were the two Acuera missions, the four or more missions on the tributaries of the Suwannee River (Arapaha, Cachipile, Chuaquin, Chamile) that had been relocated in 1656–1659, Oconi, and Chatuache (Guale). Gains had been made in the form of more missions in Apalachee and the soon to be ephemeral missions among the Chacato. The population losses were mostly in Guale, Mocama, and the Timucuan areas east of the Suwannee River. That is, the baptized Indians were consolidated in two lines of settlement, one running north along the barrier islands of modern Georgia and the other west-northwest across north-central Florida into Apalachee, where settlement was not entirely linear. But for all of that, there had been only a slight southward retreat, the abandonment of Satuache in the early 1660s. The frontier districts still stood, if with a scant population, east of the Aucilla River.

7.

The First Contests with the English, 1680–1702

The storm whose outermost squalls had struck La Florida in the 1660s drew nearer in the early 1680s and probably would have struck during the 1690s had not Louis XIV's European ambitions provoked formation of the League of Augsburg, an alliance that brought the Spaniards, English, and Dutch together in 1689 to fight a war against France that lasted until 1697. That uneasy alliance prevented open war in the Southeast, but not trade rivalries, slave raiding or the threat of buccaneer attacks. Once Europe was again at peace, an intense, initially three-sided struggle for control of the American Southeast began that merged into the War of Spanish Succession (1702–1714).

In the two decades leading up to the War of Spanish Succession, the Spaniards again tried but failed to extend their missions to the Apalachicola, the peoples of the upper St. Johns River basin, and among the Calusa of southwestern Florida. As in earlier periods, so in these decades the governors and friars fought over status, power, and the accompanying economic benefits. The Spaniards also removed any doubt that their redefinition of the accommodation with the Indians within La Florida's frontiers meant Indian subordination, a subordination that intensified in part because the Spanish population suffered erosion of its economic base during the 1690s.

☙ 149

THE FIRST
CONTESTS
WITH THE
ENGLISH,
1680–1702

The Retreat of the Guale

In the spring of 1680, two events occurred that signaled the ferocity of the decades to come. In January 1680, a band of Ya-massee Indians fleeing Westo slave raids arrived at the site of Mission San Antonio de Anacape on the St. Johns River, twenty-six leagues south of St. Augustine.[1] Yamassee had sought refuge in the mission system before (notably in Guale), but never so far from their ancestral homes on the coastal plain of South Car-olina. Then in early May 1680, three hundred "Chichimecos" (Westo), Yuchi (later part of the Creek confederacy), and Chi-luque (the latter a Yamassee group) attacked Mission San Bue-naventura de Guadalquini, the Yamassee town of San Simón, and Mission Santiago de Ocone (still on the mainland), looting them and killing some of their residents. Counterattacked by the Spanish garrison based at Mission Santa Catalina, the invaders left Guadalquini Island (St. Simons Island), only to reappear a few days later at St. Catherines itself. Attacking just before dawn, they killed five of the six sentinels. The sixth escaped to warn the town. Lt. Governor Francisco de Fuentes, his six Span-ish soldiers, sixteen Indians armed with muskets, and two dozen other Indian warriors stood off the attackers in a firefight that lasted until four in the afternoon.[2] The defenders used the wall around the mission buildings as cover, while the attackers used the village's houses, keeping up just enough pressure so that the defenders could not prevent the looting of the town. Afterwards, the residents of St. Catherines moved en mass to Sapelo Island, believing that it offered better security.

The Spaniards rushed munitions and men to Guale, deter-mined to make war on the raiders, who were said to have a fort at Cofunufo on the north end of St. Catherines Island. However, by the time the reinforcements arrived the raiders had retired deep into Georgia.[3]

Governor Hita Salazar reported to his superiors that En-glishmen had been with the raiders, a claim made to elicit a prompt, favorable response to his renewed calls for additional men and munitions for his garrison. Officials at Havana rose to the bait, immediately sending fifty soldiers, three blacksmiths, a variety of small arms, and the materials that Hita Salazar had ordered for use in paying Indians who were to build the new fort at San Marcos de Apalachee. The Crown responded with an order of October 1683 to maintain peace with the English while confining them to Charleston. The soldiers improved the fitness of the garrison at St. Augustine but increased its size only slightly because invalids were replaced. Hita Salazar's successor claimed he had only 140 fit soldiers at St. Augustine. Sixteen more were within a short distance, at Matanzas and at the port's bar. Apalachee's garrison stood at thirty men; Guale's at a dozen; Timucua's at half a dozen.[4] These were barely adequate numbers should the buccaneers operating off Cuba decide to unite and attack or should the English at Charleston instigate a major frontier war. The slow construction of Castillo de San Marcos continued.

Hita Salazar next turned to getting the Guale to reoccupy St. Catherines and tend its maize fields—an important source of St. Augustine's supply—and to organizing the Timucua to raid the "Chichimecas" in their home territory.[5] The maize fields may have been tended and harvested, but the Guale did not resume residence on the island, perhaps because Hita Salazar did not meet their condition of increasing the garrison to sixteen men. By staying on Sapelo Island and building a stockaded fort, the adult males of St. Catherines became part of a larger population that stood a proportionately better chance of defending itself than they could do alone[6] (Table 7.1). There is no record that the Timucua sent war parties north. They did not need to. The English, finally exasperated at renewed Westo attacks on the peaceful Indians around Charleston, induced the Savannahs to attack and destroy the Westo in 1681. Some of the Westo ended up in the Apalachicola village of Coweta.[7] For a time slave raiding in La Florida became uncommon.

During the years 1681–1686, buccaneer raids replaced Westo slave raids as the governor's primary military concern. Some of those raids, such as the meat-gathering attacks on La Chua ranch in 1681, June 1682, and 1684, were very small scale and not successful.[8] Others were merely destructive, including an English attack on Indians at Mosquito Inlet that killed ten and enslaved fifteen; the capture of the presidio's supply ship on its way to

151

THE FIRST
CONTESTS
WITH THE
ENGLISH,
1680-1702

TABLE 7.1 Labor Pool, Sapelo Island, 1681

Place	Total Men	Caciques and *Principales*	Married Men	Single Women	Total Labor Pool	Total Population
Tupique	23	6	19	6	4	48
Sapala	15	5	10	8	5	34
Satuache	21	1	18	8	3	47
St. Catherines	30	6	21	8	7	57
Total Mission	89	18	68	30	19	186
Yamassee, 3 villages ?	41	3	Not stated	23	38	>64
Totals	130	21	>68	53	57	>250

Source: AGI, SD 2584, Enclosure No. 7. Worth, *Georgia Coast*, 100–103, with Tables 4 and 5.

New Spain for the *situado;* and an attack on St. Marks that destroyed the fort, all in March 1682.[9] But buccaneer raids in 1683 and 1684 along the Atlantic coast had significant consequences for the extent of the tidewater frontier.

The buccaneer attack on St. Augustine in 1683 was not entirely a surprise. In 1681, captured raiders of La Chua ranch had revealed a plan for seven ships of French, Dutch, and English buccaneers (264 men in all) then operating in the Caribbean and Gulf of Mexico to rendezvous at Key West for an attack on St. Augustine as a side venture to going to the Bahamas to fish for treasure from the wreck of *Nuestra Señora de Las Maravillas*. More concretely, in February 1683, a New York Dutchman named Philip Frederic (?) entered St. Augustine's harbor with his seventeen-ton sloop *Mayflower*, to report that the French buccaneer Michel, Sieur de Grammont (*Agramont* to the Spaniards), was planning to attack the east coast of La Florida with some part of the seven ships reported earlier. This was not a large force but one that experience elsewhere in the Caribbean had taught might be clever and ruthless enough to seize an ill-prepared city.[10]

Forewarned, Governor Marquez Cabrera put out additional sentinels, but Captain Braha (i.e., Abraham?), who directed the buccaneer attack, would have surprised the city had not troops in the guardhouse at the foot of the plaza noticed the approach of several canoeloads of the pirates in the early hours of 5 April. The buccaneers landed on Anastasia Island during the day but did not try to cross the bay to attack the town. That night they reboarded their ships and sailed for Mocama, leaving the governor, the treasury officials, and others to engage in recriminations over the way that the defense had been handled.[11]

In Mocama, the pirates easily seized and sacked San Juan del Puerto, San Felipe, and perhaps the pagan villages on Amelia Island. They then careened their ships at San Pedro bar. A twenty-five man Spanish patrol led by Captain Enrique de Ribera arrived from St. Augustine too late to prevent this theft and apparently retired to St. Augustine before it was known that the pirates were careening their ships at San Pedro bar. The garrison at Sapelo, numbering at most a dozen men, did not challenge the careening even though it left the buccaneer crews vulnerable.[12] Spanish prisoners released before the buccaneers left Mocama reported that the buccaneers had spoken of returning with enough men to seize Guale.[13]

The buccaneers' success in Mocama caused Governor Marquez Cabrera to decide that the eight villages of Christian Indians scattered along the coast from San Juan del Puerto to Sapelo should be consolidated into three at the sites of Santa María (on Amelia Island), San Juan del Puerto (Ft. King George Island) and San Pablo (on the south side of the St. Johns River). This would place them within fourteen leagues of St. Augustine and no more than five leagues distant from each other, allowing for a rapid dispatch of aid and saving money since only three friars would be needed instead of the five then serving. He also asked the Crown for the previously ordered Canary Islanders, in this case to settle halfway between the new towns and St. Augustine.[14]

When Captain Francisco de Barbosa asked the Guale to move in May 1683, Indian opposition was immediate and supported by the Franciscans. The villages on Sapelo refused to relocate to San Pablo because it had a bad landing, was near ranches whose animals might damage their crops, and might have been a place that would subject them to labor demands like those imposed on Tolomato. They did agree to move to the abandoned Santa María

■ 153

THE FIRST
CONTESTS
WITH THE
ENGLISH,
1680–1702

site instead. Other villages said they were willing to move, but only after the crop that had just been planted had been harvested. Frustrated, Marquez Cabrera had a map of the far-flung frontiers of his captaincy drawn up by Alonso Solana (Figure 7.1), reported his ideas to the Crown, and asked for orders that would force the Indians to move and cause the bishop-elect of Cuba to come to Florida to discipline the Franciscans. The Crown replied on 28 March 1684 that no one could force the Indians to move, but that Marquez Cabrera could assist them if they asked for help in moving.[15]

By the time the Crown's wishes were known, two of the four towns consolidated at Sapelo were already moving to the Santa María site, but at least some of the leaders of the other two and of Asao, San Felipe, and San Buenaventura de Guadalquini had changed their minds about moving. Unwilling to accept this situation, and backed by his officers, on 21–22 August 1684 Marquez Cabrera pressured the leaders of Sapala, Tupiqui, Colón, and San Felipe into accepting his plan. In September, the remaining Christian villagers began to move to their new homes but at a leisurely pace that suggests reluctance as well as a planned withdrawal.

A new buccaneer raid in early October 1684 changed the Indians' minds about relocating in a way that Marquez Cabrera's pressure tactics of August had not.[16] San Juan del Puerto, Sapelo, and Asao were sacked and burned. The Sapelo garrison, the remaining residents of Asao, and the townspeople from Guadalquini Island all took refuge on the mainland. The Spaniards made no move to engage the buccaneers, although the cacique of Guadalquini and a scouting party watching the mission did capture a sloop and eleven persons bound for Charleston. By the time reinforcements arrived from St. Augustine about 23 October, the buccaneers were on the verge of leaving and did so within two more days.[17] After these events, the evacuations sped up. By spring planting of 1685, the Guale were resettled.[18] The tidewater frontier had contracted into Mocama.

The mission Indians were not the only peoples living on the coastal islands. Yamassee and La Tamans seem to have remained on the islands, though those who had been at Santa María and

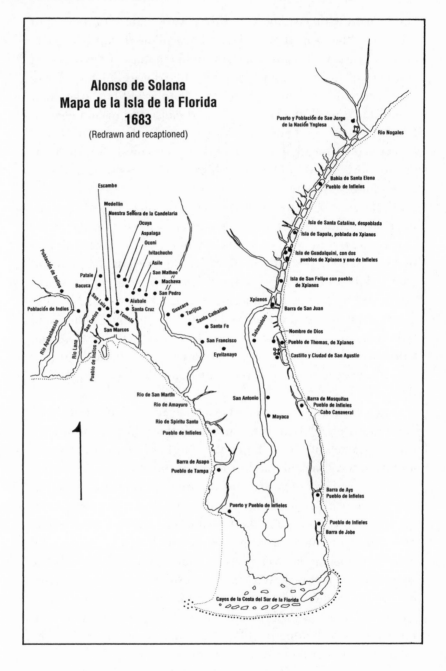

Alonso de Solana
Mapa de la Isla de la Florida
1683
(Redrawn and recaptioned)

Escambe

Medellin

Nuestra Señora de la Candelaria

Ocuya

Aspalaga

Oconi

Ivitachucho

Asile

San Matheo

Población de Indios

Patale

Bacuca

Machava

San Pedro

San Luis

Aiubale

Santa Cruz

Guacara

Tarijica

Santa Cathalina

Santa Fe

San Francisco

Eyvitanayo

San Carlos

Tomole

San Marcos

Pueblo de Indios

Población de Indios

Río Apalachecolo

Río Lana

Rio de San Martin

Rio de Amayuro

Rio de Spiritu Santo

Pueblo de Infieles

Barra de Asapo

Pueblo de Tampa

San Antonio

Mayaca

Puerto y Pueblo de Infieles

Puerto y Población de San Jorge
de la Nación Ynglesa

Rio Nogales

Bahia de Santa Elena

Pueblo de Infieles

Isla de Santa Catalina, despoblada

Isla de Sapala, poblada de Xpianos

Isla de Guadalquini, con dos
pueblos de Xpianos y uno de Infieles

Isla de San Felipe con pueblo
de Xpianos

Xpianos

Barra de San Juan

Salamototo

Nombre de Dios

Pueblo de Thomas, de Xpianos

Castillo y Ciudad de San Agustin

Barra de Mosquitos

Pueblo de Infieles

Cabo Canaveral

Barra de Ays

Pueblo de Infieles

Pueblo de Infieles

Barra de Jobe

Cayos de la Costa del Sur de la Florida

San Pablo left after the raid of 1683. Some of those who remained soon showed displeasure over the withdrawal of Spanish protection and commerce by moving in the fall of 1684 to the Port Royal Sound area in response to an invitation from Lord Cardross's agents at the newly founded Stuartstown. The Scots had decided to use the "Yamassee" as a buffer for Stuartstown against raids by Indians from the interior. By February 1685, perhaps one thousand La Tamans and Yamassee had gathered there from all over eastern and central Georgia, including the Apalachicola villages where they had taken refuge from the Westo. (This new confederation of peoples has been misleadingly called the "Yamassee" but will hereafter be called the *confederated* Yamassee to distinguish them from the Yamassee [Cusabo?] proper.) The Scots reported that the confederated Yamassee were promising to bring in former mission Indians from the "Sapella, Soho, and Sapickays"—San Joseph de Sapala, Asao, and Tupique—by then all relocated on Amelia Island.[19] We do not know if the individuals anticipated were missionized Guale or Yamassee who had married them (likely for Sapala and Tupique). Barcía, writing some thirty years later, claimed that there was a general movement of mission Indians to join the emerging Yamassee confederation, but this information is not supported by known primary documents.[20] Other "Yamassee" either remained on or returned to the Georgia coastal islands.

Even as the Yamassee confederation was forming at Stuartstown, cacique Altamaha led a band of fifty of them in a raid on the Utina/Timucuan mission of Santa Catalina de Ahoica, located near the midpoint of the St. Augustine–Apalachee road. Eighteen Timucua were killed, twenty-two women and three men were enslaved, and the church's ornaments and manuscripts

Figure 7.1. La Florida's missions, 1683. REDRAWN AND SELECTIVELY RECAPTIONED FROM [ALONSO DE SOLANA], "MAPA DE LA YSLA DE LA FLORIDA," REMITIDO POR EL GOBERNADOR MARQUEZ DE CABRERA, 1683. BASED ON A COPY IN THE LIBRARY OF CONGRESS, GEOGRAPHY AND MAP DIVISION. ORIGINAL HELD BY THE SERVICIO GEOGRÁFICO DEL EJÉRCITO, SPAIN.

written in Timucuan were carried back to the Savannah River. A warning sent from Stuartstown by Niquisalla, cacique of the Iguaja and Colona (i.e., Colón), who had been on St. Simons Island in 1681, reached St. Augustine too late to avert the raid. A Spanish-organized force of 150 men sent in pursuit was misled by its guides so that the raiders got away.[21] Although anti-Spanish like the Scots, perceptive persons at Charleston such as Dr. Henry Woodward recognized this raid as a dangerous provocation of the Spaniards. And indeed it was one of the reasons for their attack on Stuartstown in 1686.[22]

Once they were assembled in their new communities, the removed Guale and allied Indians were visited by Sergeant Major Domingo de Leturiondo, the newly appointed Defender of the Indians, who recorded information about the caciques found in each and issued instructions requiring the men to be prepared for war and to cultivate fields to support a friar, if present. He also issued instructions for communities to support the ill and infirm, and to deal with war parties and soldiers traveling through the area. Leturiondo again, as in the 1677–1678 visits, outlawed unpaid burden bearing and the punishment of caciques and *principales* without the governor's approval. The census showed that except for Tupiqui, each town was a consolidation of at least four previously separate towns, many not mentioned in earlier mission lists. At least two towns, Aeste [Aluste] and Talapo, were Cusabo (Yamassee) and two others, Lisocojolata [Ispow Olata?] and Zamomo [Sampa?] may have been so as well (see Table 7.2).[23] A report of 1689 gives the population of these five *doctrinas* as 185 families or about 925 persons.[24]

Spanish Retaliatory Raids, 1686–1687

Spanish officials in Cuba and Florida retaliated for the buccaneer raids of 1683 and 1684 by attacking the English at Charleston and their "Yamassee" allies.[25] Their justification was the decree of 1683 that the English be confined to Charleston and the fact that Grammont used Charleston as a port of call. The agent of this revenge was the privateer captain Alejandro Thomás de León. He sailed out of Havana in July 1686 with two galliots

157

THE FIRST
CONTESTS
WITH THE
ENGLISH,
1680–1702

TABLE 7.2 Caciques and Cacicas, Mocama Towns, December 1685

Sta. Cruz y San Buenaventura	Santa María	San Felipe	Tupiqui	San Juan Del Puerto
Lorenzo Santiago, Sta. Cruz	María, Sta. Catalina	Lucas, San Felipe	D. Joseph de la Cruz, Tunaque of Tupiqui	Juan Luis, San Juan del Puerto
Marcos, Utista*	Juan Chicaste, Sta. María	Diego, Aeste [Aluste?]†		Alonso, Sta. Lucía
Santiago, Lisocojolata* [Ishpow olata?]†	Phelipe, Sapala	Benito, Talapo†		Clemente, Nebalara*
Manuel, Zamomo* [Sampa?]†	Elena, Satuache	Antonio, Ospogue [Espogue]		Domingo, Chololo*
Clara, Utinajica*		Marcos, Oascule* [Fasque?]		
Francisca, Hapofaye*				

* Unique to this list.

† Cusabo town according to Swanton, *Early History of the Creeks*, 67. See also Worth, *Georgia Coast*, 201.

(small, oared ships) and enough munitions not only to meet St. Augustine's continued need (only partially met in 1683) but also to attack Stuartstown and possibly even Charleston. He had earlier pursued Grammont with some success, as had Spanish forces from St. Augustine that had captured one of Grammont's galliots in May 1686.[26] After taking aboard volunteers at St. Augustine and Guale warriors at Amelia Island, de León attacked and burned a deserted Stuartstown. On a claim of following its fleeing residents, the Spaniards went to Edisto Island and the Edisto River. There, in violation of the royal order of 1683 but consistent with their economic interests as privateers, they attacked the rural estates of the governor and provincial secretary of Carolina, among other properties. They found and freed enslaved Christian Indians (later settled at Tolomato near St. Augustine) and recovered religious paraphernalia taken from Campeche and Santa Catalina de Ahoica. The Spaniards also carried away eleven African slaves, probably the major part of the loot that its former owners valued at more than £3,000 sterling. An attempt to attack Charleston failed when a storm wrecked one of the ships, drowning Captain de León among others. The surviving ships returned to St. Augustine. Subsequently, a party of Guale on their way home overland met and killed English traders who had been with Dr. Woodward among the Apalachicola but who were taking a different route to Charleston; the Guale carried off their deerskins and furs.[27]

In a follow-up raid in December 1686, Captain Francisco de Fuentes and a party that included 350 Apalachee and Timucuan warriors attacked the Yamassee confederation and cleared from the Georgia coast those "Yamassee" who had either never left or had returned to the islands (probably in 1685). Thereafter, the "Yamassee" were found only north of the Savannah River.[28] After threatening revenge in 1687, the confederated Yamassee took it in 1690 when some of them joined Englishmen and Yuchi in raiding Mission San Juan de Guacara at the Suwannee River crossing.[29] Individuals also seem to have assisted Creek raiders.

The Carolinians sent a force from Charleston to the Edisto River to counter the incursion of 1686. In the summer of 1687,

☙ 159
THE FIRST
CONTESTS
WITH THE
ENGLISH,
1680–1702

they sent William Dunlop to scout the coast as far south as Sapelo Island in anticipation of an attack on La Florida. However, Governor James Colleton prevented the execution of this plan, thus enforcing the Proprietors' policy of peace. The Spaniards, too, opted for peace, sending agents to Charleston to excuse the de León raid.[30]

Meanwhile, diplomatic conditions in Europe were moving the Dutch and most other European powers to form the League of Augsburg (1687) in an effort to contain Louis XIV's imperialism. England joined in 1688 after the Glorious Revolution brought William of Orange to the English throne. During the next year, war spread from the Franco–German border to involve all of the parties to the League, including Spain. This combination postponed an open Anglo–Spanish clash in the Southeast.

For fifteen years after 1686, Anglo–Spanish relations in the Southeast were limited to mutual spying, mutual return of shipwreck victims, the ongoing contest to control the Creek, and tensions over Indians enslaved by the English and run-away Africans who made it to St. Augustine. The first need not concern us; the second is also unremarkable.[31] Of the fourth it can be said that neither side returned slaves. The Spanish effort to recover their former subjects included diplomatic representations in Europe and a policy of reprisals aimed at taking as many English as the English took baptized Indians. African slave fugitives from Charleston were welcomed at St. Augustine. At first Governor Torres y Ayala promised to pay their value to their owners, but in 1697 he decided to discontinue that policy and return fugitive slaves because of a concern that the English might make a business of encouraging slaves to flee so that they could get the money.[32]

As a military solution, the consolidation of the remnant Guale Christian populations south of the St. Marys River and the clearing of the "Yamassee" from the coast north of it made good tactical sense. Strategically, however, these actions voided the occupational basis for Spanish territorial claims as far as the Edisto River and opened the way for unrestrained English trading to penetrate the Georgia back country.[33]

Struggle for the Chattahoochee Valley

Even as the Guale extension of the tidewater frontier was suffering these attacks and consolidations, the Spaniards again attempted to expand the inland frontier to embrace the Apalachicola (lower Creek). Early in 1680, Fr. Alonso del Moral visited their villages and found the cacique of Sabacola (the Greater?) interested in receiving friars. Fr. Moral also found that the "Chichimecas" living among them were arguing for an attack on Apalachee province. When Fr. Juan Ocón and two assistants went to Sabacola later that year, the cacique of the Coweta drove them out within three days of their arrival. Regrouping, in March 1681 Frs. Pedro Gutiérrez and Miguel Abengojar returned to Sabacola with a military escort of eleven soldiers. By mid-May, they had baptized the cacique, various of his relatives, and several *principales* and their families, a total of fifty-three persons. Seeing that the Indians went about armed, the friars suggested Spanish garrisons at the northernmost end of the Apalachicola villages and at Sabacola. They also suggest a visit by the governor. These suggestions may not have reached St. Augustine before Apalachicola demonstrations of hostility toward the Spaniards caused them to flee back to Apalachee. The hot-headed lieutenant governor there then threatened a war if the caciques failed to come to San Luis and render homage. First the cacique of the Apalachicola and then the cacique of Coweta and eleven subordinates responded. All were given gifts, fed, and sent home apparently content and apparently as vassals of Charles II. But they had refused to a man to allow the friars into their villages. The most they would do was promise to allow any baptized Indians or those who wanted baptism to move to the new mission, Santa Cruz de Sabacola, just below the confluence of the Chattahoochee and Flint Rivers.[34] The trade in deerskins and Spanish manufactures continued.

The English challenge to Spain's trade with the Creek began in the summer of 1685 when cacique Altamaha, newly returned from the raid on Santa Catalina de Ahoica, led Dr. Henry Woodward to the Apalachicola towns, opening up direct trade with Charleston. Lord Cardross's attempt of the spring to keep the

📯 **161**

THE FIRST
CONTESTS
WITH THE
ENGLISH,
1680–1702

Charleston traders from using the Savannah River had failed. Once among the Apalachicola, Woodward obtained permission and began construction of a fortified trading post just above the falls on the Chattahoochee River.[35]

The Spaniards at San Luis de Apalachee heard about Woodward's arrival from their own trade network and responded militarily. In August and December 1685 and almost annually until 1690, the Spaniards sent Spanish–Apalachee forces to the Apalachicola towns to expel the English and to demand that they not be admitted. In 1686, the Lieutenant Governor at Apalachee reported what he thought was success in this venture, but Woodward and other traders always eluded his forces thanks to the help of their hosts.[36]

Maintaining their independence, the Apalachicola refused to exclude anyone who wanted to trade with them, including the Spaniards. The Spaniards decided that only a military presence would prevent trade with the English. So in late 1689 Captain Enrique Primo de Rivera, twenty soldiers, twenty warriors, and twenty carpenters from Apalachee built a small fort near Coweta. They soon obtained Apalachicola promises not to trade with the English. But that summer (1690), the garrison was withdrawn because the soldiers were needed for the defense of St. Augustine against a rumored buccaneer attack. By then, too, many but not all of the Apalachicola had abandoned the Chattahoochee for the upper Ocmulgee River, known to the English as Ochese Creek, whence the English name for the people: Creek.[37]

The Apalachicola who remained on the Chattahoochee, and other peoples further west, continued to trade with Apalachee although probably in a declining volume as more and more trade shifted to the English.[38] As discriminating consumers, the Creek gravitated to the cheaper and more abundant English goods and, as sellers, to merchants who wanted Indian slaves, not just deerskins and maize. In addition, the Spaniards' reluctance to sell firearms had turned into an outright refusal in 1687, to be followed shortly by a prohibition on the Apalachee selling horses, making trade with Apalachee even less appealing to the Apalachicola.[39]

In addition to this English threat to Spanish interests in the

Southeast, in the spring of 1686 Governor Marquez Cabrera received the news that the Sieur de la Salle had established a French colony somewhere on the Gulf Coast west of St. Marks. As part of a multi-pronged search conducted mostly by Mexican naval and land units, he ordered Marcos Delgado (who owned a ranch in Apalachee) from St. Augustine to San Luis, there to organize a party of soldiers and Indians to march westward via Pensacola Bay to seek out the French. Advised by Pensacola Indians, who were visiting San Luis to trade for munitions for a matchlock musket (*arcabuz*) they owned, that no food would be found at Pensacola Bay because of a drought, Delgado shaped his course north and northwest, opening a trading path to the Alabama Indians on the middle course of the Alabama River. They and the Choctaw further west did not have surplus food either. Even so, Delgado lingered among the Alabama River peoples until at least early November, giving gifts in the governor's name and, no doubt, trading for deerskins.[40] The search for La Salle was conveniently forgotten. It may have been a pretext in any case.

In short, by the end of the 1680s, the effort to incorporate the Apalachicola into the inland frontier had failed, although the Spaniards did not give up their pretensions to dominate this confederation of the remnants of the once large populations of the piedmont. From a Spanish perspective, the English had won the contest for the Apalachicola/Creek. But in fact, the Apalachicola had acted in their own interest, just as for the previous half century their caciques and great men had found it advantageous to visit the Spanish governor at St. Augustine and his lieutenant in Apalachee to exchange gifts, to acknowledge the Spaniards' presence and apparent military superiority, and to trade for "exotic" European manufactured goods. Spanish use of military means to try to prevent the Apalachicola from pursuing their economic self-interest did nothing but provoke hostility and cause deaths at the hands of Apalachee and Spaniards, deaths that needed to be avenged.

These events of the 1680s amounted to a resumption of the hostility between the Apalachee and the Apalachicola that the Spaniards had ended in 1635. In response, Creek warriors initi-

⚑ 163

THE FIRST
CONTESTS
WITH THE
ENGLISH,
1680–1702

ated slave raiding, directed toward Apalachee and Timucua provinces from their new homes in central Georgia. Vengeance and profit provided powerful motives.

Two events of the 1690s illustrate this new state of affairs on the northern frontier of Apalachee. In August 1694, a force of seven Spaniards and 400 Apalachee warriors attacked the Apalachicola towns of Coweta, Oconi, Cassista and Tiquipachei in retaliation for a Creek raid on San Carlos de los Chacatos that had carried off forty-two baptized Indians and the church's treasures. Fifty Creek were captured, but the rest of the populations escaped after burning their own towns.[41] The other was the construction in 1694–1696 of a massive blockhouse at San Luis. First ordered in 1688, this structure was two stories tall and built so that it could mount small pieces of artillery on the upper works. It crowned one of the province's higher hills and provided unobstructed views across Apalachee territory. A palisade was eventually added. The garrison numbered thirty-six men in April 1695.[42] Insecurity had become a fact of life on the northwestern side of the inland frontier.

During the 1690s, the governor of Charleston refused to take action against traders in Indian slaves and declared that the Apalachicola were under his protection.[43] The Spanish governors rejected this pretension, but the English continued to assert it and to send traders to both the Creek and to the Apalachicola still resident on the Chattahoochee. Spanish orders that the Indians turn the traders over were ignored.[44] And sometimes Spaniards and their Indian followers committed atrocities such as the 1698 murder of sixteen out of twenty-four Taisquique traders by Francisco de Florencia and forty Chacato.[45] The stage was being set for the war of 1702–1714.

Expansion into Southern Florida

While these dramatic events had been unfolding on La Florida's northern and northwestern frontiers, the Spaniards were once again trying to expand their control over peoples in the southern half of the peninsula. As early as 1680, missionaries had returned to the southeastern frontier among the Yamassee refugees and the Mayaca speakers in a province earlier called Jororo and now known as Mayaca. Friars also had visited the Calusa. However, missions in both areas did not survive beyond 1704.

The details of the missions in Mayaca are few. We know only that in the late 1680s the Mission Concepción y San Joseph de Jororo existed and that in 1693 the friars asked for a large number of iron farming tools. By 1696, missions existed in the villages of San Salvador de Mayaca (thirty-six leagues from St. Augustine), Concepción y San Joseph de Jororo (sixteen leagues from Mayaca), Atissime (nine leagues from Jororo), and Atoyquime (nine leagues from Atissime); Aypala (Ayapaja) may have been a *visita*.[46] These villages were successively further south and southeast in the area between the St. Johns River basin and the coast. In each village, the friars taught these former hunters and gatherers to farm as well as be Christian. A ranch belonging to Juan Alonso Esquivel was nearby.

Suddenly and for no known reason in late October 1696, the Indians of the Mayaca mission rebelled. The leading men of Atoyquime killed Fr. Luis Sánchez and two Indian boys. The entire village of forty persons then fled to the back country. The people of Atissime, Aypala, and Jororo also fled, the latter after desecrating the church and killing two Indian sacristans and a sick Spanish soldier who had been left by a patrol that was searching for the Atoyquime rebels. Eventually, except for the Atoyquime, all of these peoples returned. The returnees were resettled at Los Cofes (one hundred persons) and the woods of Afata (sixty persons) where the friars stationed at Mayaca and San Antonio de Anacape (each two days distant from the new settlements) visited them pending the sending of new missionaries. The Aypala moved into San Antonio de Anacape but then joined the last of the Acuera at Ivitanayo, a Timucuan town.[47] The subsequent fates of these settlements are not known but it is likely that they received missionaries in 1696 and continued to exist until the Creek began their sweeps of the peninsula in 1704. The settlements represent a qualified success as an extension of the inland frontier because the territory had, in fact, been occupied earlier in the century, and then was abandoned due to depopulation.

🏛 **165**

THE FIRST
CONTESTS
WITH THE
ENGLISH,
1680–1702

On the Atlantic coast itself, the Spaniards had no mission presence south of St. Augustine. They continued, however, to give gifts to, to trade with, and, as necessary, to terrorize the Mosquitos, Ais, and other peoples so that they would report shipwrecks and treat any survivors well.[48] Jonathan Dickinson, an Englishman wrecked at Mosquito Inlet in 1696, recorded that the Ais feared the Spaniards.[49]

The history of the mission to the Calusa is better documented. A friar visited them over the winter of 1679–1680.[50] But there was no follow-up. The Calusa continued to trade with Cuba and may have requested missionaries from the Cuban authorities. Then in 1688 their new, young cacique traveled to Apalachee to see Governor Quiroga and ask for missionaries. When asked to send them, the Cuban secular clergy and the Franciscans found reasons to refuse this request. Exasperated that souls were being lost, in 1695 the Crown demanded that four out of six members of a new group of fourteen Franciscans go to the Calusa, with the balance of the group earmarked to resume work in Mayaca province. In due course, six Franciscans departed Havana. All went well until the Calusa realized that the friars would not supply unlimited quantities of gifts. Threatened with death and unable to stop the continuation of pagan worship, the friars pulled out barely two months after their September 1697 arrival.[51]

Friars and Governors Quarrel

The Franciscans' failure to take up the Calusa mission until explicitly ordered to do so was of a piece with their general flaunting of secular authority during the 1680s and 1690s. What was different this time was the determination by the governors to regain the upper hand and enforce the *Patronato Real.* As before, the quarrel turned on the status and authority of the friars in native and Spanish societies and involved the governors' usual charges that the friars whipped Indians without regard for status or the prerogatives of civil authorities; that they exploited the Indians' obligation to cultivate fields and provide game and servants for friars in ways that expressed the high status (in Indian

terms) that the friars claimed; and that they came and went from
La Florida without regard for the *Patronato*'s requirement that
they obtain the authorization of the governor. In a new note, governors stressed how such abuses caused Indians to flee the missions.[52] That such abusive behaviors continued and apparently
were indulged in by a greater number of friars (although still a
minority) probably reflects their recognition of how little status
and power even caciques had after the events of the 1650s. Their
behavior also shows the order's well-defined positions on the dis-
ciplining of Indian converts and its relationship with governors.
For their part, the friars again charged the soldiers with exacting
unpaid services from the Indians.

The most notable events in the struggle came in 1686–1687
when the friars excommunicated Governor Marquez Cabrera
and in 1692 when Governor Quiroga's complaints of Franciscan
misbehavior caught the attention of the Council of the Indies,
the empire's highest governing body. Marquez Cabrera's troubles
with the friars began when he inspected the Apalachee missions
in 1680 and made it clear to the caciques that they were to answer to him, not the Franciscans. Quiroga's quarrels with the
order mostly involved the refusal of the provincial to keep friars
sent to Florida in Florida.[53] They also disliked him because he
allowed Fr. Juan Ferro Machado, an agent for the newly appointed bishop of Cuba, to visit the missions in 1688 and take
testimony about how the friars punished the Indians without regard to status, did not pay them for carrying burdens, and had
been moved by "passion" in denying Marquez Cabrera the sacra-
ments. The final straw was his refusal in 1692 to allow the Franciscan Commissary Jacinto de la Barreda's designated inspector
to visit the missions. Quiroga thought the man was poorly qualified to discipline the Indians because he had been abusive.[54]

When the Council of the Indies took up these matters in 1692
and again in 1695, it seemed to agree with Franciscan Commissary General Fr. Julián Chumillas's observation that the conflict
came down to "favoring the friars less and giving greater freedom to the Indians." However, the Council apparently disagreed
that the evils he alleged ("[the Indians] totally neglect and omit
to go to festivals (*fiestas*), to hear mass and the sermon and in-

📖 167

THE FIRST
CONTESTS
WITH THE
ENGLISH,
1680–1702

struction and even to comply with the annual precept of confession") were real and serious enough to reverse royal policy, which was to enforce the governor's rights as vice-patron.[55] Accordingly, the Council acted on various secondary issues in 1695 and 1697. For example, it found that Fr. Machado's secret inquiry of 1688 into Franciscan abuses of the Indians should not have been allowed, but ordered not only the sending of friars to Calusa (as noted) but also a justification of the number of Franciscans.[56] The Franciscans continued to defend their use of punishment as necessary for the good government, proper raising (*crianza*), and education of the natives. An inquiry at St. Augustine justified the employment of forty-one friars: thirteen for Apalachee, eight for Timucua, five for Guale, six for the missions on the St. Johns River, and nine at St. Augustine.[57] In the end, abusive friars were moved, but the Franciscans continued to resist and governors to assert secular supremacy.

And, as before, at the same time that the Franciscans defended their methods and claims, they also were careful to replace men who caused too much trouble. For example, when Fr. Juan de Uzeda at Sapelo refused to allow the garrison to attend mass while armed (in May 1681), he was quickly replaced by Fr. Simón Martínez de Salas. Similarly, after a decent interval, the order sent Fr. Blas de Robles to inspect the Apalachee missions and discipline Fr. Santos and Fr. Bartolomé de Ayala, the abusive cleric at Ivitachuco (1683).[58]

A final comment on the missions during these last decades: Loucks, Bushnell, Milanich, and Worth, among others, have interpreted the reported incidence of individual, familial, and occasionally group flight from the missions to be the results of increasing demands for labor and increased abuses by friars and soldiers alike.[59] While not wishing to deny that some Indians did leave their villages in response to these problems, and sometimes did so permanently (rather than taking temporary maroonage), it seems to me that what the documents of the 1680s and 1690s record may well be *more reporting* of such flights *for partisan purposes*, not an absolute increase in absenteeism. In this connection, it is of note that most of the increased demand for laborers and porters, for example, came in the 1670s, a period for which reports of flight are not abundant. Such population figures as we have from the 1680s and 1690s suggest fairly stable populations, although that information is difficult to judge because of Yamassee and La Tama (and other peoples') movement in and out of the missions and a lack of knowledge of birth and death rates.[60] We do have more recorded instances of individuals moving to and from, for example, Charleston and the Apalachicola villages, but such migration may say more about kinship, relative opportunity, the degree of interchange that the *pax hispanica* fostered among southeastern Indian groups, and (above all) the Spaniards' improved knowledge of events in the Apalachicola villages than it does about the degree of alleged oppression in the mission system. And as I observed in the previous chapter, it seems evident that the epidemics of the 1650s (not direct Spanish oppression) disrupted some societies to the point of dissolving the ties of individuals to them, creating a new class of Indians who had to wander. In sum, while it seems to be true that the Spanish population of La Florida increasingly treated the Indian population harshly in the decades after 1660 and especially during the 1690s, we need to be skeptical of accepting the increased reports of flight (and the threat of flight) as indicating that ordinary Indians finally were abandoning a system that, it is alleged, no longer served them.

The Hispanic Population and Economy

St. Augustine's population may have nearly achieved the breakthrough to being a "self-contained community" in the 1680s, only to lose that achievement during the economic troubles of the 1690s. The women born in earlier periods came of age and found husbands. Births per marriage rose to an average of four and four-tenths children during the period 1683–1702. As before, more girls than boys were born. This birth-per-marriage figure suggests that a "self-contained" population (one that reproduced itself) was possible, but because we lack data on deaths and total population, except for the report from the 1689 census that there were 1.444 persons in approximately five hundred households, the true story cannot be determined. Still, it seems

🕮 169

THE FIRST
CONTESTS
WITH THE
ENGLISH,
1680–1702

likely that by the late 1690s the population was again in the "dependent community" pattern, expanding only when new levies of soldiers arrived.[61] Proposals to bring Canary Islanders and Gallicians to settle abandoned Indian lands went nowhere.[62]

Sociologically, the community continued to evolve in a pattern similar to that found in some other parts of the Spanish empire. Creoles dominated the town and, after 1691, were freely allowed to enter the garrison, cutting down the need for the immigration of new soldiers. A report from 1696 showed 128 native sons among the 393 places, including the three company captains, many of their officers, and all of the artillerymen.[63] Mexicans and other colonials remained a minor part of the population, and were generally disliked because they were of mixed racial ancestry. Free pardos (mulattos or lighter-skinned persons of African descent) and morenos (Africans or any dark-skinned person) were numerous enough to be organized into a militia company of forty-eight men in 1683. Seven confraternities provided fellowship, services such as the burial of the destitute, and very limited support for particular churches.[64]

On the economic front, the 1680s and 1690s presented a mixed picture but one indicating deteriorating supplies of food. Meat continued to be available thanks to a law that ranchers had to send five head of cattle to the municipal slaughterhouse on an assigned day each month from August to February. The ranchers complained of the low price paid (six pesos per head less tithe, fees, and expenses), the land tax of fifty pesos per square league of range, and the custom that gave the governor the valuable tongues and loins of all cattle slaughtered. Indians roaming the peninsula both rustled and shot cattle on the claim that the animals were wild and thus fair game. These problems aside, ranchers seem to have made money until Governor Joseph de Zúñiga y Cerda increased the delivery requirements and strictly began to collect the tithe in the late 1690s.[65]

Maize presented an ongoing problem because St. Augustine seems to have required as many as fifty thousand arrobas a year in the 1680s, although the figure dropped by at least seven thousand arrobas once laborers on the fort no longer had to be paid following its completion in 1695. Obtaining this supply was a challenge because the years 1684–1687 were marked by spring drought[66] and the collapse of Guale as a supplier because of re-settlements early in the decade. During the 1690s, the friars and caciques of Apalachee seem to have found the trade with Havana more profitable than that with St. Augustine.

Direct information on the supply of maize during the 1680s has not been found, but information on the rations given to the Indians and European convicts working on the fort is available as an indication of the supply. The daily maize rations of the fort's laborers were reduced in 1679 from three to two-and-a-half pounds and in 1684 to two pounds (twenty-nine arrobas a year). The ration remained at that level until work was suspended on 21 August 1687 because there was no food for the workmen nor money to pay them. A shipment of maize from Apalachee in 1688 allowed a resumption of work but likely at the two-pounds-per-day level of ration. To avoid further shortages, the cleared ground around the fort was planted in maize right to the edge of the moat until a royal order in the early 1690s forbade the practice.[67]

The scope of the supply problem came into focus in the 1690s when Governor Torres y Ayala sent the Crown a report on maize receipts for the years 1694–1696 (Table 7.3). It reveals that all Florida sources combined supplied no more than three months' worth of maize (3,000 arrobas) toward the garrison's require-ment of 11,580 arrobas a year. Two-thirds of La Florida's produc-tion came from Apalachee, usually by sea or, as in 1696, by sea and by canoe up the Suwannee River and then overland by horseback.[68] New Spain and Havana (and probably the English colonies as well) had to supply the balance. When they did not, rations were reduced. Thus, in December 1692 the soldiers were put on half rations; in December 1693 on one-third rations; in May 1696 on two arrobas a month, and in December (?) of that year on one arroba per month (probably one-third ration). By the spring of 1697, soldiers were foraging for roots and wild foods.[69] An unsigned note was found in the church threatening to surrender the town to the French, should they attack as re-ported, if the governor did not send to Carolina for food.[70]

Shortages led to expedients. In September 1683 and May 1684, the governor and treasury officials agreed to purchase flour and

171

THE FIRST
CONTESTS
WITH THE
ENGLISH,
1680–1702

TABLE 7.3 Maize Purchases for Garrison, 1694–1696 (Amounts in Arrobas)

Year	Tithe	Apalachee	Other Florida	Total Florida	Havana	New Spain	Total
1694	270	1,673.88	→ᵃ	2,189	1886.5	3,477.6	7,308
1695	484.44	1,957.48		2,441.92		10,985	13,427
1696	>328.6ᵇ	1,884	1,033ᶜ	3,894.6			3,895
			649ᵈ				

Source: AGI, SD 228, fols. 378v–380.

ᵃPart of 946 arr. 23 lbs. of maize and beans was from Apalachee; other parts were from Guale, Timucua, and San Mateo. Guale supplied at least 617 arrobas of this total. A private seller of 109 arr. 13 lbs. obtained his maize from unstated but possibly local sources.

ᵇReported to be a year of a poor harvest. Some tithe included in the 649 arrobas listed as "Other Florida."

ᶜOf this, 833 arrobas was bought from a private supplier. Origin of this maize is unknown but was either local or Havana.

ᵈIncludes some tithe and maize lent by Nombre de Dios natives or supplied on credit.

other foods from the *Mayflower*, the Dutch ship whose captain had warned of the impending attack in the spring of 1683.[71] This trade, strictly illegal, may have continued. In 1687 and again in 1689, supplies were so short that bear, pig, and other animal fats had to be used in place of olive oil in the lamp that illuminated the sanctuary in the city's church.[72] The shortages continued into the 1690s because goods purchased on the *situado* account were lost at sea in 1691 and 1693. Moreover, payment of the *situado* became irregular in the 1690s. The payment for 1690 reached St. Augustine only in 1695; and in 1697, six years of payments were owed.[73] In an effort to get the *situado* back on a regular footing, its funding was switched in 1702 to the sales tax (*alcabala*) of Puebla, Mexico. Half was to be paid in cash; limits were set on the pay and on the period allowed for the men sent from Florida to collect it.[74]

As before, shortfalls in goods supplied locally or via the *situado* meant that favored merchants provided goods at ruinously high prices. Havana merchants remained dominant in supplying the town between receipts of the *situado*. Their primary agent was Juan de Ayala. A native of Havana who migrated to St. Augustine and eventually became the garrison's sergeant major,

Ayala emerged during the 1680s as the key figure in the then current variant on the traditional system. Governors Juan Marquez Cabrera (1680–1687) and Diego de Quiroga y Losada (1687–1693) both used him as a *situado* agent, sending him not only to New Spain and Havana but also to the Canary Islands (1685) and Seville (1687). They were undoubtedly his silent partners.[75]

And as before, there were proposals for reforms to end the abuses. For example, ex-governor Hita Salazar, who was from Veracruz, in 1684 unsuccessfully lobbied the Crown to return to the use of merchants from Veracruz under arrangements like those Ruiz de Salazar had used in the 1650s! This would, he thought, end the abuses he had discovered while auditing the treasury accounts.[76] Needless to say, the abuses were too profitable for governors and their political patrons to change. On the other hand, the Crown tried to cut off royal accountant Tomás Menéndez Marqués's untaxed, small-scale import trade in *aguardiente* (a form of brandy) via the Suwannee River and his ranch at La Chua. In 1691, 1696, and 1700, it ordered the river blocked; floods swept away the pine trees and other means used in attempts to do so.[77]

In short, St. Augustine continued to rely on imported maize and flour. Shortages of these commodities during the 1690s destroyed any possibility that the town's population could expand as rapidly as the births-per-marriage figures for the 1680s suggest might have been possible. Starvation remained a possibility for humble settlers and soldiers up to the eve of the English attack in 1702.[78]

Nor did the Spaniards make any progress in finding resources whose exploitation might attract immigrants aside from soldiers and merchants exploiting the *situado*. The Spaniards did continue to experiment with crops and to seek exploitable economic resources. Thus, around the year 1682 both rice and wheat were planted at St. Augustine with some success; wheat continued to be grown for local consumption in Apalachee.[79] Indian tanning of hides and deerskins, the manufacturing of shoes for the soldiers, and Indian cotton weaving were noted in 1683 and 1688 as productions that might benefit if Spanish or Meso-American craftsmen gave instruction. Naval stores were produced in small amounts from the pines at San Nicolás, a site to the north of St. Augustine. And a few small smithies were repairing tools or making new ones.[80] But as before, none of these possibilities was developed, either because powerful local interests tried to, or did, monopolize them or because development depended on immigrants and royal support for them. Neither was sent. There was no positive change in the Hispanic economy of La Florida nor reason for immigrants to seek it out. If anything, conditions in St. Augustine gradually worsened during the 1680s and 1690s.

Worse was coming.

8.

THE MILITARY FRONTIER, AT LAST, 1702–1763

The storms that swept over Spanish Florida in the years 1702 to 1728 destroyed its mission populations, rolled back its frontiers to the gates of St. Augustine, and converted the colony into a purely military outpost. With a revived military and navy in the 1730s, Spanish Florida stood off James Oglethorpe's attack of 1740 and launched an unsuccessful counterattack against the English settlement of Frederica on St. Simons Island in 1742. Subsequently, Spanish and English forces in the Southeast settled into an armed standoff that evolved into the Neutral Ground agreement of 1748. Peace and Spanish neutrality in the Seven Years War until 1762 prevented further conflict on La Florida's northern frontiers. And even war elsewhere in 1762–1763 had little effect on La Florida. La Florida's first true period as a military frontier ended with its transfer to British sovereignty at the Peace of Paris of 1763. By then, the first of the Seminole had moved into north central Florida, beginning the repopulation of the peninsula and a new frontier period.

The Contest for the Southeast, 1699–1715

The slow deterioration of the Spanish position in La Florida and the low-level Anglo-Spanish hostilities via Indian surrogates

📜 175

THE
MILITARY
FRONTIER,
AT LAST,
1702–1763

on the Apalachee and Timucuan frontiers might have continued for some decades had the French not appeared on the Gulf coast on 26 January 1699. The Spaniards prevented them from occupying Pensacola Bay by putting their own garrison there in November 1698,[1] but that did not change the fact that the French presence at the first Biloxi (modern Ocean Springs) until 1702 and at Mobile thereafter profoundly altered the strategic stakes in the Southeast. And regardless of Spanish intent, in both French and English eyes, La Florida became an integral part of the French grand strategy following the succession of Louis XIV's grandson to the throne of Spain as Philip V in 1701. Pierre LeMoyne, Sieur d'Iberville, the leader of French Louisiana, intended nothing less than to confine the English to the Atlantic seaboard. La Florida occupied a flanking position on the English trade routes to the west and on Carolina itself.

Joseph Blake and James Moore, successive governors of Carolina, soon saw this French design. Traders returned to Charleston with the news that the French were rapidly expanding their alliances and trade with the Indians of the Gulf coast, including the Choctaw, whose lands were just to the west and southwest of the trade path running northwest from the Alabama River to Chickasaw country in southwestern Tennessee. Moore determined to strike at the French by first destroying La Florida so that it could not threaten Carolina or its trade.[2] Over the course of the thirteen years of the War of Spanish Succession (1702–1714), at least three waves of violence rolled out of Charleston to sweep over La Florida and wash at the gates of St. Augustine, Pensacola, and Mobile.

The opening blow in this great war for empire was struck on 20 May 1702 by a party of Creek. Earlier in the spring, Creek had killed three of four Apalachee visiting their villages to discuss again trading horses for firearms, an exchange the Creek angrily refused. Now in May, a party of Creek attacked Mission Santa Fe, a strategic link in the communications between St. Augustine and Apalachee, burning it and taking captives. Lt. Juan Ruiz de Canizares and a small party went in pursuit but the raiders spread into a crescent formation and enveloped and nearly destroyed them.[3]

Fearing more such raids, the Apalachee pressured their Spanish lords for permission to attack the Lower Creek, a policy that

Iberville was also urging as part of his strategic design. The result was another disaster. Forewarned, the Creek ambushed Captain Francisco Romo Uriza, some Spanish soldiers, and as many as eight hundred Apalachee, Timucuan, and Chacato warriors while they were still on the trail from San Luis to the Chattahoochee River. The Creek killed or captured roughly half of the Florida force. Most of the survivors left their weapons on the field of battle in their haste to flee. The balance of power between the two peoples, which had been slowly changing as the Creek gained more and more firearms, shifted decisively against the Apalachee.[4] Spanish leadership, soldiers, and weapons had not made any difference. An important, if largely implicit, part of the Spanish–Apalachee accommodation, and of the Spaniards' obligations as the paramount power of the area, had failed. It was the middle of October 1702.

On 10 September, Governor Moore finally obtained the agreement of the Carolina assembly for an amphibious attack on St. Augustine. His agents urged the Lower Creek towns to join in the attack. A Christian Chacato woman who happened to be in the Lower Creek towns overheard the discussion and hurried to Apalachee to warn the Spaniards. She reached San Luis on 21 October, and the news reached St. Augustine on 27 October. Governor Zúñiga promptly put the town on a war footing, dispatched pleas for help to Havana and Spain, and ordered defenses prepared at Apalachee and Pensacola.[5]

Even with this advance warning, the English caught the Spaniards at San Pedro Bar's blockhouse by surprise when they attacked at midnight on 3 November 1702. The blockhouse and then Mission San Pedro de Tupiqui were overrun. Panic seized the mission Indians and friars as the news spread to Santa María, San Felipe, and San Juan del Puerto. When twenty soldiers arrived from St. Augustine on 5 November, they found that the English had taken and destroyed San Juan del Puerto and Piritiriba (on the south side of the river). Lt. Governor Francisco Fuente de Galarza, his family, soldiers, and most of the mission Indians were hiding in the forests. At St. Augustine, some 1,500 persons, livestock, and supplies crowded into the fort as the English advanced southward by land and sea.[6]

☙ 177

THE
MILITARY
FRONTIER,
AT LAST,
1702–1763

The English arrived at St. Augustine on 8 November. By then, the Spaniards had decided not to attempt to stop them in open battle but hoped that they could wait out a siege until help came from Havana. English prisoners taken during the previous two days disclosed that the English did not have mortars (they had been ordered from Jamaica), meaning that the people crowded into the fort would be relatively safe from artillery fire. Too, the English reportedly had 1,000 men (in actuality less than 800, exclusive of the crews of the fourteen small ships that carried the expedition) whereas the men and boys gathered in Castillo San Marcos numbered but 412, of whom only 174 were trained soldiers.[7]

The siege lasted until 30 December, two days after a Spanish relief force arrived from Cuba and one day after it landed over two hundred soldiers on Anastasia Island. In the end, Moore had to burn the eight small ships he had brought into the bay and march overland to the St. Johns River, where his other ships had remained. His casualties had been few, but the expedition cost over £8,000 and Moore's position as governor.[8] During the siege and as the English left, houses that were later valued at 62,570 pesos were destroyed along with the Franciscan convent and the parish church. Only twenty or so houses made of board and thatch and the hospital of Nuestra Señora de la Soledad remained standing.[9]

After the English left, the Spaniards began to prepare for new assaults. A defensive line was constructed from Mission Nombre de Dios to the San Sebastian River. Some of the Mocama mission inhabitants assembled in new settlements south of the St. Johns River and built stockades and a small fort at Piritiriba. In Timucua, San Francisco de Potano, the seat of the Spanish garrison, was stockaded and Santa Fe's remaining population consolidated there (1703).[10]

Having failed to take St. Augustine, the Carolinians and Creeks turned their attentions westward. Early in 1703, an Anglo-Creek party attacked Mission San José de Ocuia (Ocuya) and possibly either Patali or Piritiriba (both on the St. Johns River) and San Francisco de Potano in Timucua. As many as five hundred mission Indians may have been enslaved. On 7 September, the

Carolina Assembly approved sending Moore and the Creek to attack Apalachee, with the contradictory provisos that the raid pay for itself and that the men try to bring the Apalachee to the English side by peaceful means.[11] As with the attack on St. Augustine, this was preliminary to advancing against Pensacola and Mobile.

Moore's second Florida expedition left Charleston in November 1703. The march was via the Creek settlements on the Ocmulgee River. When Moore appeared outside of Ayubale's palisade on 25 January 1704, he led some 50 Englishmen and 1,000 Creek and confederated Yamassee warriors. Led by their priest, Fr. Angel de Miranda, the 175 or so residents (including about 75 men) of Ayubale held off the attack for nine hours, until they ran out of ammunition and the English thought to burn the church, whose walled courtyard and bell tower sheltered the defenders.[12] A 430-man relief force from San Luis led by Lt. Governor Juan Ruíz de Mexía arrived the next day but was defeated in a half-hour long battle. The survivors retreated to San Luis. In these two days of fighting, Apalachee losses numbered at least 39 killed or burned alive by the Creek in vengeance for their 15 men killed, and 325 men, women, and children captured. The Spaniards lost 14 men killed or wounded, the English 18 killed or wounded.[13] But as in October 1702, the Spaniards had failed to successfully defend the Apalachee against their enemies. Nor were Spanish reinforcements or even munitions on the way from St. Augustine.

Over the next ten days or so, Moore secured a ransom from Ivitachuco and the unconditional surrender of four towns west of Ayubale. Moore does not specify the towns that surrendered but they were likely San Martín de Tomole, Santa Cruz de Capoli (also known as Ychutafún), Nuestra Señora de la Candelaria de la Tama, and the "Ocatoses" (unknown but possibly the Tocobaga village on the Wacissa River and San Pedro de los Chines).[14] Faced with a large number of prisoners, Moore offered freedom of person and property to all Apalachee who would agree to go to Carolina to settle. The caciques and all of the people from at least three towns and many persons from four other towns accepted this offer.[15] Because some of them (especially from Tama) may have had confederated Yamassee kinsmen both in Carolina

🐚 **179**

THE
MILITARY
FRONTIER,
AT LAST,
1702–1763

and with the attacking force, the decision to relocate was probably easier. When Moore wrote to Carolina about his success, he was expecting the people of Ivitachucho to join the exodus, already several days on the road. The migrants numbered some 300 men and 1,000 women and children. Another 325 Apalachee went as slaves because they had been captured at Ayubale and in the countryside before Moore had offered freedom to those who volunteered to go to Carolina.[16]

Apalachee who escaped the Anglo–Creek assault reacted in three ways. Many of the people of Ivitachucho followed their cacique, Patricio de Hinachuba, in a forced march to the southeast, to Potano. There they, some of the Spaniards who left Apalachee with them, and the small Spanish garrison hoped to make a new start out of reach of the Creek. They also wished to be close enough to St. Augustine so that help could be sent if the Creek did attack.[17] Another group of eight hundred abandoned the San Luis area for French protection at Mobile.[18] And yet others angrily told the Spaniards that they would not stay in Apalachee unless it was to join the English and Creek in destroying the Spaniards.[19]

Recent historiography has suggested that the collapse of the Apalachee missions and the recorded expressions of Apalachee anger were long in the making, and that they were reactions to the ways in which the missions and labor demands of the Spaniards and caciques exploited and abused ordinary Apalachee. In this telling of the story, the military defeats were the final straw.[20] Certainly there were abuses, as has been shown. But what seems more likely is that the Spanish failed to uphold an important *implied* bargain in their accommodation with the Apalachee; that is, successful defense against Apalachee enemies in return for accepting Spanish paramountcy. A paramount's success in war was part of the accommodation that made the "subjects" willing to accept the tribute, labor services, and religion that went with the relationship.[21] The Spaniards' protection failed in October 1702 and again in the spring of 1704, with devastating results for Apalachee society. No wonder some Apalachee were angry and left the missions both in response to Moore's offer of settlement near their kin and to abandon rulers who could not,

perhaps would not, protect them. That Spaniards had died disproportionately to their numbers in the fighting in Apalachee
counted less than that they had failed to lead a victorious counterattack. And the silence from St. Augustine may have been
equally telling to men desperately fighting to defend families,
land, and possessions.

Moore's force retired to Carolina, but the Creek did not abandon their raids. In August 1704 they overran the Yustagan missions of San Pedro and San Mateo, capturing and burning alive
their caciques. Other parties raided the La Chua ranch. The following August (1705), raiders laid a twenty-day siege on Abosaya, the town that the Ivitachuco refugees had built. Other raiders harassed San Francisco de Potano and La Chua. Relief forces
sent from St. Augustine were diverted to drive off an attack on
Salamototo (on the St. Johns River) and then split so that the
Chiluque Indians in the force could respond to an attack on their
village near St. Augustine. Pursuing these raiders, the Chiluque
lost as many as twenty-five men in a fight in a marsh five leagues
north of St. Augustine. The other part of the force continued on
to Abosaya, perhaps lifting that siege. In September, a Creek
force again attacked La Chua's blockhouse and so harassed the
refugees at Abosaya (by then weakened by disease) that they
abandoned it for St. Augustine.[22]

The attacks continued in the spring of 1706. San Francisco de
Potano was put under siege in April. The La Chua blockhouse
was attacked so strongly that the survivors of the seven-man garrison fled to San Francisco. The lieutenant governor of Timucua
and the caciques of Santa Fe and San Francisco, with the
agreement of Governor Francisco de Córcoles y Martínez, withdrew their forces to Salamatoto and then St. Augustine. Worth
observes that by 23 May 1706 (the date the San Francisco group
reached St. Augustine), "the Timucuan interior had effectively
become an uninhabited war zone" although Bushnell notes that
several groups of Timucuans, led by their friars, remained wandering in the area until early 1707.[23] North of St. Augustine,
Creek attacked the Afafa hacienda and its Jororo residents, killing twenty. A guard detachment at the mouth of the St. Johns
River was also overrun. A Spanish patrol of eighty men in boats

181

THE
MILITARY
FRONTIER,
AT LAST,
1702–1763

failed to find the raiders but did establish contact with San Francisco prior to its abandonment.[24] At Mobile, Tawasa and Chatot refugees appeared in 1705, followed by more Chatot in 1706 after a Creek raid on the outskirts of Pensacola.[25] Compounding these defeats of 1706, a Havana-based Franco-Spanish raid on Carolina in August ended in defeat and the loss of more than three hundred of the men while doing very little damage. The only good that came of it was a reinforcement of forty-three soldiers for St. Augustine.[26]

With La Florida out of the way, the Anglo–Creek campaign moved west. Creek–English forces attacked Pensacola on two occasions during 1707. On the first, they plundered and burned the town but were driven out of the fort. On the second, in November, the attackers quarreled among themselves and withdrew well before the Sieur d'Bienville arrived with French forces from Mobile. In 1708, Thomas Nairne launched an attack intended to separate the French from their Indian allies (especially the Choctaws) but the internal politics of Carolina and French countermoves stopped him and it.[27]

Looking back in January 1708 over the previous five years, Governor Córcoles y Martínez reported the loss of ten to twelve thousand Indians.[28] The number may be exaggerated, but the fact of the total devastation of what had been left of the Indian societies of the tidewater and inland frontiers is not.

The War of Spanish Succession ended in Europe in 1714, but its real end in the Southeast came only with the failure of the confederated Yamassees' revolt of 1715. Until then, Creek and "Yamassee" parties raided ever deeper in the peninsula, capturing the remnants of the "pagan" peoples beyond the Spanish frontiers and making life insecure even around St. Augustine. For example, in 1709 they may have reached Tampa Bay, destroying Tocobaga.[29] At St. Augustine, the refugee villages had a turbulent but little understood history. A census of 1711 shows nine villages with perhaps 432 Indians of all ages and several tribes. Of these, about three fourths were listed as Christian. Only with the return of more security after 1715 did some of the Indians move their settlements as far as fifteen miles from St. Augustine's protecting fortifications.[30]

Throughout these fifteen years, St. Augustine was militarily and economically insecure. Cultivation of fields beyond gunshot range of Castillo de San Marcos largely ceased; at times even hunters, fishermen, and shellfish gatherers ventured out only at night out of fear of raiders. Thus largely cut off from producing any of its own food and having lost its hinterland of Indian producers, the town had to rely on the never certain delivery of the *situado* from Puebla and trade conducted by Juan de Ayala, the garrison's sergeant major and a man with ties to the merchants of Havana. They also relied on English Flag of Truce ships during the long intervals between the arrivals of the *situado* funds and goods. The usual abuses resulted, compounded by the diversion to salaries and payments for supplies of monies sent for the rebuilding of the town. The worst year was 1712 when no supplies came. Cats, dogs, horses, and roots were eaten while Ayala made record profits. Even after the Yamassee War made local conditions more secure, this exploitation of the garrison and the *situado* continued, ceasing only in 1718 with the arrival of Governor Antonio de Benavides, who jailed Ayala and the royal treasurer, Joseph Pedrosos, in a bid to establish his own power.[31]

The Yamassee and Other Wars, 1715–1729

On Good Friday morning, 15 April 1715, the Yamassee of Pocotaligo Town suddenly killed John Wright and John Cochran. Thomas Nairne, Carolina's principal agent to the Indians, was seized and then burned to death over three days. The three had been trying to resolve disagreements with the confederated Yamassee over debts and trade.[32] So began the Yamassee War, an event that reshaped the political geography of the Southeast and offered the Spaniards an opportunity to resettle Apalachee and regain the influence they had lost with the Creek. They failed to fully realize the potentials of the historical moment.

It will be recalled that the confederated Yamassee had gathered near Stuart's Town, Port Royal Sound in the 1680s. By 1715, they were one of five Indian peoples living along the Savannah River as a sort of frontier guard for Carolina against the Spaniards and the Creek. The war was triggered by many factors:

📯 183

The
Military
Frontier,
at Last,
1702–1763

white settlement on the coast and the building of a road to Port Royal through the Yamassee "reservation" created in 1707; the dishonest trading practices of the Carolina traders; their abuse of Indian women and contempt for the men; their use of men as porters who were paid little or nothing for their labor; a collective debt that amounted to at least a year's deerskin production; and a census taken early in 1715 that convinced the confederated Yamassee that they were about to be enslaved because of their debt and English greed for their land.[33] Because the other peoples of the Savannah suffered some of the same abuses, many joined the attacks, as did the Santee and Congaree, who lived north of Charleston. At least four hundred English men and women died and the Port Royal Sound area was temporarily deserted by them. To their shock and horror, the English found that Indians who had lived with them for a generation aided or even joined the rebels. Yet in the end, the Carolinians mustered enough men, including Indians such as the Tuscaroras, Corees, and Cherokees with scores to settle, and received enough help from other English colonies to devastatingly defeat any rebels foolish enough not to flee after their initial successes.[34]

By the time the war was over in March 1716, the five peoples of the Savannah, and the Ogeechee Creeks on the Oconee and Ocmulgee Rivers, had retreated to Spanish and Creek protection. In a strategy with deep historical roots, these descendants of the Mississippian chiefdoms created a "vacant quarter" to separate themselves from the power of their former paramount rulers, the English, and allied themselves with the only other peoples who might offer protection. Five hundred of the confederated Yamassee (out of twelve hundred) went to St. Augustine, where the Tama chief (once a resident of the Apalachee missions) arranged refuge in May 1715. The other four groups—the Apalachicolas, Apalachees, Savannahs, and Yuchi—joined the Lower Creek on the Chattahoochee.[35]

Among the Creek, the economic and possibly the moral and status abuses of the English traders had also angered some villages. Hearing of the Yamassee War, they killed one or two English traders and decided to expel the English (and encourage the Cherokee to do likewise or even make war on the English) and seek the friendship and trade of the Spaniards and French. For the French, that meant permission at long last to build Fort Toulouse, at the junction of the Cossa and Tallapoosa Rivers (near modern Montgomery). For the Spaniards, it meant visits to Pensacola by large Creek delegations in July and September 1715, with gifting, feasting, and Indian pledges of allegiance to Philip V.[36] To further these ties, a Creek delegation visited Mexico City at the invitation of the viceroy, from February to September 1717. That same July (1717), the French began to build their fort. In August, they welcomed Creek visitors to Mobile and sent them home with gunpowder and shot.[37]

Whatever the unity among the Creek that the crisis and the diplomacy of Coweta's "Emperor Brims" created, it lasted only until the spring of 1717. The more northern Creek welcomed English peace and trade feelers; the southern Tequipaches, Talespuches, Sabacolas, and Apalachicolas—the latter, at least, villages of mostly Hichiti speakers with extensive prior contact with Spanish Apalachee—led by Chipacasi, or Seepey Coffee as the English called him, seem to have argued for a continuation of the Spanish connection. Chipacasi went to St. Augustine in the spring of 1717, perhaps hoping to get the trade goods and gifts that the commander at Pensacola lacked, goods that would support his claim to be Brims's heir. Chipacasi returned to the Chattahoochee with Lt. Diego Peña and a dozen soldiers intent on delivering alliance gifts and buying horses from the Creek as well as preparing the way for a reoccupation of Apalachee or a fort on the Apalachicola. But at Coweta in September, the division of the Creeks became obvious. A party of English traders was there, with a dozen pack horses of goods to sell. Peña was able to purchase ten horses but the Tascayas had to escort his party to the safety of Sabacola.[38] When Juan Fernández a few weeks later escorted the caciques who had been to Mexico to their villages, the Creek ratified the agreements made in Mexico City, but Fernández found it prudent to retreat to Pensacola. In November, Creek representatives set off for Charleston, where in December they renewed their trade agreements. Brims's policy of trade with all three European powers had triumphed, for the moment.[39]

Meanwhile from Sabacola, Peña wrote that the Tasquique,

🎺 185

THE
MILITARY
FRONTIER,
AT LAST,
1702–1763

Apalachicolas, Sabacolas, Chisla [Chisca?], Caliche, Bacuqua (a former Apalachee mission village), and the Yuchi were willing to move to the area of the proposed Spanish post if they were given gifts and trade. In St. Augustine, this news fit with yet another version of the long-running hope that Spanish colonists could be found to occupy and cultivate Apalachee. Canary Island settlers had been suggested earlier (see above), but by June 1715 the Council of the Indies had decided that Indians, perhaps the newly reconciled Yamassee, would be better settlers. In Florida, acting governor Juan de Ayala hoped to send fifty veteran soldiers, but they would be directed to the Apalachicola River or perhaps to St. Marks for the purpose of trading with the Creek in order to keep them allied and to secure the road from St. Augustine to Pensacola.[40]

Peña's news that southern towns of the Lower Creek might move to the area of a Spanish post led, in March 1718, to Captain Joseph Primo de Rivera's rebuilding of the St. Marks fort. That expedition in turn led to the discovery of the short-lived French post on St. Joseph Bay, a post they had created to flank Pensacola to the east but soon abandoned because food could not be raised locally. The Spaniards then moved in but also abandoned the post within the year. St. Marks was reinforced and the Spaniards waited for the Lower Creek to appear to make good on their promises to rally to the Spaniards.[41]

While the Spaniards and French jockeyed, the English not only renewed their trading ties with the Creek but also began to build a defensive perimeter for Carolina against continuing "Yamassee" raids. A fort that became Beaufort, South Carolina, was built in 1716 as a base for small boat patrols along the inland waterway and as one of several posts along the line of the Savannah River that would reestablish the trade route west and guard the frontier with ranger patrols.[42] More ambitious schemes for British posts on the Gulf Coast or the Mississippi River, including negotiations with the Huspaw "King" who led one group of "Yamassee" living on the Altamaha, were unsuccessful. More realistic was Sir Robert Montgomery's proposed Margravate of Azilia between the Savannah and Altamaha Rivers. His propaganda and proposals seem to have influenced Oglethorpe's scheme; his own collapsed with the South Sea Bubble and the refusal of the Lord Proprietors of Carolina to meet government terms for the project.[43]

The War of the Quadruple Alliance (1719–1723) brought this early phase of the four-sided struggle for power in the Southeast to a head and a conclusion. Alerted by his government, Bienville captured Pensacola before the Spaniards could prepare their defense. A Spanish expedition preparing in Havana to attack Carolina was quickly diverted to retake Pensacola, only to have it again lost to a French fleet from the Caribbean. Occupied elsewhere and still militarily weak, Spain did not again try either to take Pensacola or to attack Charleston. The English heard at least two versions of the proposed Spanish plan to attack Carolina during the summer of 1719 and thought about attacking St. Augustine and occupying Apalachee, but concentrated their energies instead in setting up more of the defensive posts to guard Carolina while various agents tried to draw the Yamassee at St. Augustine into an alliance. When that failed, in early October approximately fifty English and Creek attacked three Yamassee villages within a three-league radius of St. Augustine, killing half a dozen, taking twenty-four prisoners and burning Yoa's church. A fifty-man Spanish counterattack suffered a defeat in which fourteen were killed and ten captured. Afterwards, sixteen Creek who had moved to St. Augustine with their Yamassee and Apalachee kin left and tried to induce their kin to do likewise.[44]

After the bursts of fighting in 1719, the sides settled down to wait out events in Europe, while building defenses locally. At St. Augustine, Governor Antonio de Benavides took the last of the monies for the rebuilding of the town and pledges of ten thousand pesos from local residents and used them to begin rebuilding the Cubo Line in coquina stone (running west from Castillo de San Marcos) and extending the town's defenses by building a stockade and ditch along its western side, the so-called Rosario Line. This work took from 1721 to 1724.[45] In Carolina, the Assembly overthrew the Proprietor's government in December 1719 on a claim that it was not providing for the defense of the colony against the Spanish plans to attack. Extending this claim, John Barnwell, a Carolina planter and Indian agent, told the Board of

187

THE
MILITARY
FRONTIER,
AT LAST,
1702–1763

Trade that the French claim to the "River of May" referred to the Altamaha, a prime spot for an English settlement that would improve English control of that waterway to the west. The result of the rebellion in Carolina and of Barnwell's and others' lobbying was the sending from England of Governor Francis Nicholson and a company of one hundred "invalid" troops to build and man a fort on the Altamaha (Fort King George). Construction of Fort King George occurred during 1721.[46]

The arrival of Governor Nicholson at Charleston set in motion a more aggressive Indian policy aimed at tying the Creek, especially those on the Chattahoochee (the Lower Creek), firmly and finally to the English and ending the "Yamassee" raids. A new attempt was created to make peace with the confederated Yamassee. When that failed, a war was waged on them (1723–1725) that soon became entangled in the question of who would succeed Emperor Brims.[47] Chipacasi, who became a leading candidate after "Yamassee" murdered Ouletta, changed allegiances in 1725 and lead an attack on the "Yamassee" among the Lower Creek and in Apalachee as a way of showing the English that he, if made heir, would be a faithful ally. The "Yamassee" among the Creek escaped, thanks to warnings from their Lower Creek kin and hosts. Those at Apalachee fled to St. Augustine (about one hundred) or took refuge under the walls of Fort St. Marcos in Mission San Juan de Guacara.[48] But no warning came to the Tama village north of St. Augustine before thirty Yuchi surprised it on All Saints Day 1725 as the residents were at Mass. Eight residents were killed; another nine and a good deal of loot were taken to Carolina.[49]

Once begun, this (second) Yamassee War was extended deep into peninsular Florida. Refugees flocked to the dubious safety of St. Augustine. A census of 1 December 1726 listed sixteen villages containing 421 men, 338 women, and 252 children. "Yamassees," Iguaja (Guale?), Chiluca, Timucuan, Pojoy, Apalachee, Cosapuya, peoples from the east coast below St. Augustine, and Macapira and Piaja peoples from the Carlos Bay area are identified.[50]

These episodes of Creek hostility toward the "Yamassee" among the Lower Creek, in Apalachee, and near St. Augustine served the temporary interests of some Creek, but did not denote complete English domination of them. Thus in February 1726 and again in March and April, delegations of "Yuchi," again including Chipacasi, visited St. Augustine to make peace and promise to abandon their trade with the English if the Spaniards would provide the same muskets, powder, clothing, and other goods. The Spaniards were interested but unable to match the English.[51] For their part, the English in January 1727 arranged a Creek-Cherokee peace, only to see it dissolve during the summer when a party of Lower Creeks and Yamassee killed five of eight traders ascending the Altamaha toward Matthew Smallwood's new store at its fork. In September, the English withdrew their traders from the Lower Creek villages and their garrison from Fort King George (which had burned in 1726). They prepared to enter the War of the League of Hanover (1727–1729), and their first targets were the "Yamassee" living near St. Augustine.[52]

The end of the confederated Yamassee in La Florida came in the years 1727–1728. An epidemic struck St. Augustine and the mission populations in 1727, dropping the latter total from nine hundred or so to below four hundred. Continued "Yamassee" raids against Carolina likely resulted in other deaths. A nearly fatal blow came on 9 March 1728, when Col. John Palmer led fifty Carolina militiamen and one hundred Indians in an attack on Nombre de Dios. Thirty "Yamassee" were killed, another fifteen captured. Palmer chose not to attempt the other "Yamassee" villages, which may have been stockaded. Nor did the Spaniards sally to challenge him, a failure that had consequences among the Creek for whom Palmer's raid had been intended as a warning. Writing afterward, Governor Benavides suggested that perhaps only one in five "Yamassee" refugees from the 1715 group survived in the summer of 1728.[53] Other groups of "Yamassee" had better luck, but as a people the confederated Yamassee had ceased to exist.

English Encroachment in Guale, 1730–1748

Woven through this thirteen-year-long confederated Yamassee tribulation and in part explaining why the Spaniards did not do

189

THE
MILITARY
FRONTIER,
AT LAST,
1702–1763

much to discourage them from raiding Carolina was the Spanish
effort to get the English to abandon Fort King George. The first
Spanish protest to this encroachment into their territory (as they
understood it to be from the Treaty of Madrid of 1670) was
lodged in April 1721 in London. Over the next eight years, there
were three rounds of diplomatic activity in London and four visits by Florida delegations to Charleston (1721, 1722, 1724, and
1725). No resolution of the fundamental issue occurred because
the Carolina authorities claimed not to have the authority to
agree on a boundary, authority that their Spanish visitors thought
had been conferred (as it had been on them) by the diplomatic
agreements made in Europe. Moreover, the Carolinians claimed
that their charter granted them all lands to 29 degrees North; that
the Spanish had not occupied the Guale coast since 1665; that
the British were in occupation; and that they had traded with
Indians on the Altamaha for forty years. Resolution of other
problems such as the return of fugitive and captured slaves also
foundered because the Spaniards' offer to pay for them did not
satisfy the English. When the subject of territorial claims came
up for the fifth time during negotiations to end the War of the
League of Hanover (1727–1729), the English claimed that the
treaty of 1670 had included Spanish recognition of the entire
Carolina grant, an interpretation the Spanish rejected out of
hand. Since by then Fort King George had been abandoned, the
issue was moot. The Treaty of Seville that ended the war failed to
mention Guale or the other territorial issues outstanding between
Spain and England in the Americas.[54] As Lanning observed,
"The English [beat] . . . the Spaniards with the extensive use of
the Spanish weapons—shirking and delaying."[55]

The English claim that the Spaniards had not occupied the
coast since 1665 provoked a Spanish reaction. In September 1726,
three long-serving soldiers were deposed at St. Augustine about
Spanish occupation of the coast north of the Altamaha.[56] But
such evidence counted for little against actual occupation. Spain
was not prepared to occupy the coast; the English were.

Left free by the Treaty of Seville to make what they would of
Guale, the English began to formulate plans to occupy it. In June
1730, the Board of Trade ordered the laying out of two townships

on the Altamaha and two others on the Savannah. This idea was incorporated into the design for "Georgia" during the next two years. Once on the ground, James Oglethorpe obtained a Creek cession of all land not in use along the Altamaha and Savannah, up to the end of the tidal flow, but not including Ossabaw, St. Catherines, and Sapelo Islands (21 May 1733 OS).[57] Going well beyond earlier projects, Oglethorpe built Fort Frederica on St. Simons Island to protect his colony against Spanish attack. In August 1736, he sent a small force to garrison San Juan Island on the north side of the St. Johns River as a way of validating his claim that Georgia's southern boundary was at least that far south.[58]

The Spaniards reacted with diplomacy, more fact finding, and the preparation of a military force to attack and expel the English. Diplomatic discussions in London and Madrid made little progress until March 1737. Meanwhile, the Spaniards began to gather men, material, and ships at Havana and eventually fell in with John Savy, whom they knew as Miguel Wall. Savy claimed to know a lot about Georgia and Carolina and became the nominal leader of the expeditionary force. In La Florida, Governor Moral Sánchez conducted military censuses of the Indian towns near St. Augustine in 1734 (finding 417 men, [sic! 147?]) and 1736 (124 men). He tried to win Creek loyalty by selling them firearms and munitions, although on at least one occasion he was unpleasant to Creeks whom he suspected of killing a Spanish soldier.[59] He also gathered yet more evidence of the Spanish occupation of the Georgia coast and engaged in shuttle diplomacy that prevented fighting after Oglethorpe's occupation of San Juan Island. Although Madrid repudiated the agreement he worked out, its existence offered an opportunity for diplomacy in Europe to prevent war. As Antonio de Arredondo observed in a letter to the governor of Cuba in January 1737, a diplomatic solution would be easier and less expensive than a war in which success would require garrisons to secure the areas taken and the conquest of more than just Georgia.[60] Evidently thinking along similar lines, in March 1737 the Crown ordered military preparations at Havana suspended; the Governor there had already done so after concluding that Wall was unreliable and that he would not have adequate forces for a campaign and Havana's defense. For his

191

THE
MILITARY
FRONTIER,
AT LAST,
1702–1763

part, Oglethorpe took reports of a Havana force of seven warships and seven thousand men at face value and went to England
in the fall of 1736 to seek a thousand-man regiment to bolster his
colony's defenses.[61]

The true state of Spanish military preparations in La Florida
was described in Arredondo's report of January 1737. An engineer, he had been sent to La Florida both to participate in the
shuttle diplomacy of 1736 and to use the occasion as a cover for
observing the state of English defenses and to inspect Spanish
defenses. On the basis of what he found, he suggested not only
seeking a diplomatic solution but also building extensive new defenses to guard the waterways and land approaches to St. Augustine; new inner defenses for that town; and an increased garrison. He also estimated that at least eight hundred soldiers, four
hundred seamen, eighty small boats, and ample supplies of rum,
tobacco, cloth and muskets (these for Indian auxiliary troops)
would be needed for an invasion of Georgia. The Crown ordered
the garrison increased to four hundred men.[62]

The suspension of preparations for a Spanish attack on Georgia lasted less than a year. The revised plan called for sending
four hundred additional soldiers to St. Augustine and obtaining
as many as a thousand more and 150,000 pesos from Mexico.
Havana was to supply three or four dozen small ships. However,
the Mexican authorities could not supply troops or funds, St. Augustine itself was so short on food reserves that it sought supplies
from the English at Port Royal Sound, and a royal order of
28 November 1737 suspending the attack so that diplomacy could
do its work, all resulted in the project being called off just two
days before a much reduced force was to sail. The only positive
benefit for La Florida was the arrival of four hundred reinforcements with a dozen iron cannons, and eighty-two prisoners for
construction work, several engineers, and some money to work
on fortifications.[63]

The Spaniards prepared along other lines as well. They again
surveyed Indian manpower in and around St. Augustine, finding
at most 109 warriors in populations totaling 350 persons. They
also continued to court the Lower Creek, receiving ten chiefs at
Havana. They may have sent agents to incite slave rebellions in

Carolina.[64] They, and the British, engaged in espionage so that both sides knew the general outlines of the other's offensive strategy.[65] Arredondo and a small force were sent to St. Marks to improve the fort and to scout Apalachee in anticipation of its settlement by Gallicians or Canary Islanders. Often advocated in the past, this settlement was again pursued, although in the end the Isleños (Canary Islanders) did not get any further than St. Augustine.[66] In August, a new blockhouse (Fort Pupo) was built on the west side of the St. Johns River at the St. Augustine-to-Apalachee crossing after an attack by Yuchi (Creek) raiders in July. Supplies were sought from New York to counter English refusals to send food from Carolina. And not least, in November 1738 the Spaniards founded Santa Teresa de Mose, a fort and settlement about three miles north of St. Augustine. It was inhabited by thirty-eight families of former slaves who had fled from Carolina during the previous decade. The men formed a militia company.[67]

Diplomacy postponed war until the fall of 1739. The Convention of El Pardo of 14 January 1739 committed both sides to negotiate the questions of English claims against Spanish coast guard ships and "English rights" in the Americas. The Spaniards demanded that English claims, especially on the border issue, be backed up with documentary evidence. To support their own, the Spaniards gathered fifteen old and new documents at St. Augustine, providing a treasure trove for later historians. The English House of Commons, however, forced the government to uphold "English possessions." Since the English occupied the northern two-thirds of coastal Georgia, that change of wording prevented any compromise with Spain, although the government suggested creating an unoccupied "neutral ground" south of the Altamaha. In the end, the English mercantile war party got its war with Spain to force open the trade of the Spanish Empire.[68]

The run-up to the War of Jenkins Ear (1740–1748) in the Southeast began in August 1739 when Oglethorpe attended a congress with the Creeks and some Chickasaw and Choctaw. The agenda included correcting trade abuses, ratification of the Creek land cessions to Georgia in 1733, Indian recognition of English claims as far south as the St. Johns, and countering Spanish

influence among the Lower Creek. Oglethorpe got most of what
he wanted and the Indians received rich gifts and promises of
more honest trade in the future.[69] When Oglethorpe returned to
Savannah, he found orders to cut off trade with the Spaniards
and to authorize privateers to attack their commerce. On 3 October (OS) he proclaimed war.[70]

Oglethorpe was the first to take aggressive action. The Spaniards were preoccupied with British fleet movements in the Caribbean and so kept the troops and ships at Havana that might
have been used to attack Georgia. Oglethorpe's initial move in
January 1740 was to seize and garrison Forts Picolata and Pupo
(on each side of the St. Johns River where the road west crossed
it). In May, the English successively seized the blockhouse at
Diego Plains, Fort Mose (abandoned by the Spaniards in the face
of the English advance) and on 5 June began a siege of St. Augustine. The plan was to attack St. Augustine both from the
north on land and by amphibious assault from Anastasia Island.
Spanish gunboats anchored under Castillo de San Marcos's guns.
The shallow bar that kept the larger English warships out of the
bay blocked the amphibious assault. English carelessness allowed a successful Spanish night attack on Fort Mose and then
the introduction of seven hundred men and supplies from Havana via Matanzas Inlet. Seeing the odds thus become more favorable to the Spaniards, who now had about thirteen hundred
soldiers compared to his two thousand or so, Oglethorpe withdrew to Frederica early in July. Casualties on both sides were less
than 10 percent[71] (Figure 8.1).

For the next two years, the sides engaged in a war of Indian
raids and privateering, the latter important for providing St. Augustine with food. The main theater of operations was the Caribbean. Only when the English fleet under Admiral Edward Vernon ceased to be a threat to Cuba did the Spaniards take the
offensive against Georgia, where Oglethorpe had been perfecting
his defenses.[72]

Spanish preparations for an attack on Georgia began in May
1741 when eight hundred soldiers were sent to St. Augustine. The
Crown wanted an attack on Carolina because it was the center
of English activity in the Southeast, but an officers' committee

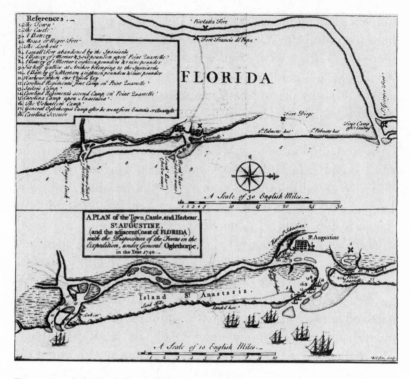

Figure 8.1. Oglethorpe's attack on St. Augustine, 1740.
"A Plan of the Town, Castle, and Harbour, of St. Augustine
(and the adjacent Coast of Florida) with the Disposition of
the Forces in the Expedition, under General Oglethorpe, in
the Year 1740." Published with *An Impartial Account of the
Late Expedition Against St. Augustine under General
Oglethorpe, Occasioned by the Suppression of the Report,
Made by the Committee of the General Assembly in South
Carolina. . . .* (London: Printed for J. Huggonson, 1742).
Courtesy of the Hargrett Rare Book and Manuscript Library,
University of Georgia Libraries.

(junta) at Havana concluded they did not have enough transport
and they did not dare strip the city of all of its defenders even if
Vernon's forces had left the Caribbean. An attack on Frederica
(on St. Simons Island) was planned instead.

Using four hundred men from St. Augustine and thirteen hundred from Havana and at least thirty small boats, but without
major naval units as escorts, the Spaniards forced their way over
St. Simon's bar on 16 July 1742 in the face of artillery fire from

⧂ 195

THE
MILITARY
FRONTIER,
AT LAST,
1702–1763

small British outposts. The Spaniards landed on the southwestern end of the island and began seeking both land and water
routes to Frederica. On 18 July, a scouting party working north
along a path on the edge of a marsh was fired upon. When a
larger party tried to force a passage later in the day, it too was
ambushed in what Anglo-American historiography calls the
"Battle of Bloody Marsh." Pulling back, the Spaniards looked for
other lines of attack but did not immediately find any. Then on
20 July, they received word that English warships were coming
to Oglethorpe's rescue. Having no major warships to protect their
own ships, the officers agreed to withdraw to avoid becoming
trapped in the bay by superior naval forces.[73]

The final five and a half years of the war were relatively peaceful along the Florida–Georgia frontier. The English renewed
their Indian agreements in the fall of 1742 with generous gifts,
which meant that Indian raiding parties continued to prowl the
hinterland of St. Augustine. Oglethorpe again invaded northeast
Florida with a small force but failed to draw the Spaniards outside of their walls and had to be content with occupying posts
on Cumberland and Jekyl Islands and the occasional ambush of
Spanish patrols sent to check on the Anglo–Creek presence at the
mouth of the St. Johns River.[74]

For the people of St. Augustine these were hard years, dominated by an effort to feed themselves from the loot of privateers
and the efforts of the new Havana Company, which had been
given the job of supplying the colony. The population numbers
fell, then recovered to their pre-war level but did not begin to
rise until the 1750s. The only important counter to English activity was Arredondo's compilation of a map (in 1742) and his
"proof" of the Spanish ownership of Georgia.[75]

The difficulty in feeding St. Augustine during a war with the
Anglo-American colonies was that the town had come to depend
on those colonies for a significant part of its food and merchan-
dise supply. From the occasional ship of the 1660s and flag of
truce vessels of the War of Spanish Succession, Spaniards and
Anglo-Americans had developed commerce in foods and mer-
chandise coming from Carolina and then New York. Oranges and
Spanish coins flowed north in payment, especially after the mid-

1720s. For example, first Cornelius Sanford and then Charles Hicks served as New York merchant William Walton's resident agent at St. Augustine.[76] Governor Francisco del Moral Sánchez (1734–1737) may even have used English merchants, just as his predecessors had used Cuban and Mexican merchants—as quasi-monopoly agents. One witness against Moral Sánchez claimed that the English walked about St. Augustine as if they were in London![77]

The War of Jenkins Ear interrupted but did not end this commerce. British Flag of Truce ships appeared and Spanish privateers brought a dozen or more small English prizes into St. Augustine harbor. Trade with the French West Indies was also authorized, although St. Augustine is not known to have done so. The Anglo-American supply was thus disrupted but probably not ended.

The Crown's effort to supply the town using the new Havana Company as the *situado* agent was frustrated. Governor Montiano demanded supplies on credit, claiming that Article 29 of the company's charter allowed such sales in cases of "dire necessity." The Company refused but finally in July 1743 it agreed that if the Florida officials would furnish a list of what was needed, the company would find it wherever it could at the lowest price available (i.e., in the British colonies). Further, the company agreed to attempt to collect the quarter million or so pesos owed to the Florida *situado* account.[78] This agreement failed. In 1746, Governor Montiano wrote to the Crown, stating the case for free trade with the Anglo-Americans as the best solution to the colony's needs. To avoid the danger of their spreading religious heresy, he suggested that exchanges be made on Anastasia Island. Unlike his suggestion for a coinage good only in La Florida, this idea and its evident opportunities for fraud and private gain did not find favor in Madrid.[79]

Not surprisingly, such demographic evidence as we have shows a drop in population during the 1740s. The numbers of deaths were higher than births after a period when births per marriage had been above average (4.3 compared to 3.5), producing an increase in population from 1,509 in 1736 to 2,062 in May 1740. The

◗ 197

THE
MILITARY
FRONTIER,
AT LAST,
1702–1763

death rate seems to have been higher than normal among infants and children. At best, the population held its own due to an average of 16.6 immigrants a year (1733–1756) until after 1753, when the death rate dropped to one for every three births, setting off an upward spiral in population that increased after the arrival of the Canary Islanders (1757–1760). Widows predominated among those remarrying in the late 1740s, as might be expected after a period of military activity.[80]

The war years also coincided with a final crisis for the mission system. There were three main contributors to the crisis: the largely successful effort of the Florida-born friars during the 1720s and 1730s to maintain control over the Franciscan Order in La Florida in the face of occasional groups of newly arrived Spaniards; the only moderately successful reforms of Auxiliary Bishop Francisco de San Buenaventura y Tejada (1735–1745); and renewed royal determination to enforce the laws mandating secularization of mission areas that were not on a remote frontier. Having turned inward, the friars had neglected their duties with the result that in the mid-1730s the four hundred or so inhabitants of the half dozen missions were frequently drunk, uninstructed in Christian fundamentals, and in fact more likely to frequent the Franciscan convent in St. Augustine than the churches in their villages, which were all within a league of the town.[81] When the auxiliary bishop's reforms failed, the Crown ended Franciscan control over Indians living in St. Augustine (1745). The Franciscans were told to minister to Nombre de Dios, Tolomato, and Mose.[82] By then the population of the Indian mission towns had declined to perhaps two hundred (1742). A count of 1752 showed just 158 persons.[83]

Beyond St. Augustine and its tiny security zone, the peninsula lay open and largely unoccupied save for the camps of an occasional Creek raiding or hunting party. But the first winds of change were stirring thanks to the war's raiding activities. Very uncertain evidence suggests that a few Creek settled for a time near the site of La Chua ranch and the wild cattle of the area. Lower Creek continued to use St. Marks as a place for limited trade and for refuge during the group's internal disputes.[84]

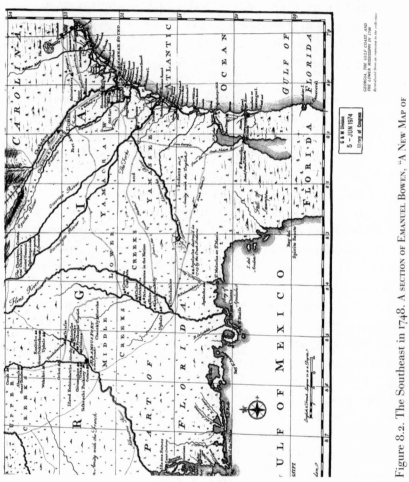

Figure 8.2. The Southeast in 1748. A section of Emanuel Bowen, "A New Map of Georgia . . . ," in John Harris, *Navigatium atque Itinerantium Bibliotheca; or, A Complete Collection of Voyages and Travels* (2 vols.; London, 1744–48). 2: opposite 323. Courtesy of the Library of Congress, Geography and Map Division.

☙ **199**

THE
MILITARY
FRONTIER,
AT LAST,
1702–1763

Peace, 1748–1762

The return of peace in 1748 led to the reorganization of La Florida's defenses, a renewal and intensification of economic dependence on the English colonies, and a final effort to get Spanish settlers to La Florida. Forts Mose, St. Marks, and Picolata were rebuilt, in the latter two cases with stone, although St. Marks was never finished.[85] The reinforcements sent to St. Augustine for the Georgia campaigns and to protect it against new English raids were withdrawn, leaving St. Augustine with 329 military men, of whom 34 were mariners. Since this small garrison was clearly not sufficient, a decree of 9 February 1749 directed that St. Augustine should have three companies (with 102 men each, including 6 officers), an artillery company (with 55 men and officers), a cavalry company (with 54 men and officers), and a five-man training cadre for the militias. In all, 420 men were to be assigned and governed by the rules decreed for Havana in 1719. Of these, five soldiers and two artillerymen were assigned to Fort Mose in support of its thirty-five-man Black militia.

Because the garrison strength decreed in 1749 proved unsatisfactory, the Crown experimented with other arrangements. In 1753, the Florida garrison was merged into that of Havana so that half of the men would rotate each April or May to and from Havana, producing a complete turnover every two years. This system lasted barely eight years, until 1761, when St. Augustine was again given four non-rotating ("fixed") companies, two of infantry (with 100 men each) and one each of 40 artillerymen and 50 cavalry. A 110-man company was to rotate from Havana for a year's duty. This change allowed Florida natives to serve in the garrison (they had refused to rotate to Cuba) and still provided help from Cuba in time of need.[86] Thus reinforced, St. Augustine entered the Seven Years War (1762–1763 for the Spaniards) with approximately double the number of men it had had in 1702. But Great Britain's ability to put armies into the Caribbean theater had more than doubled, as the siege of Havana in the summer of 1762 showed.

The resumption and intensification of St. Augustine's eco-

nomic dependence on the Anglo-American colonies was a natural outgrowth of (relative) peace on the high seas and the practices of the Havana Company, which contracted for supplies with
merchants from New York and Charleston and had them deliver
the goods to St. Augustine. The Charleston merchants in particular quickly resumed their Florida trade, with four ships after the
peace of 1748, eleven in 1749, nine in 1750, and then from two to
seven a year until 1762. In addition, Georgia ranchers drove cattle overland to satisfy St. Augustine's demand, evidently selling
their beef through an Englishman who held the monopoly contract for the slaughterhouse.[87] Sketchy records suggest that by
the early 1750s St. Augustine enjoyed a flourishing commerce
with the British colonies in British ships, even though under
Spanish law, reiterated in 1751, the only lawful trade was that of
Spanish ships or those contracted by the Havana Company. So
attractive were the offerings of both the Company's contractors
and smugglers (sometimes the same persons) that in 1756 the
Treasury Officials broke the Company's legal monopoly of supply
by entering into a contract of their own with William Walton of
New York. Faced with an embargo at the outbreak of the Seven
Years War in 1756, Walton obtained an exemption (for basic
foodstuffs) from the governor of New York and the King in
Council.[88] St. Augustine thus continued to be supplied down to
the eve of Spain's entry into the Seven Years War (1762).

The solidification of this Anglo-American "hinterland" for St.
Augustine kept the town fed, if vulnerable to English embargoes
such as the ones of 1756 and 1762–1763, but it did not change the
fact that most of the soldiers and townspeople may not have had
adequate diets and continued to depend on a variety of local,
mostly seasonal and wild food resources. On the other hand, a
small elite of families that had been founded by officials and officers did very well, enjoying fine foods, clothing, and the growing variety of manufactured goods available in the North Atlantic market.[89]

St. Augustine's virtual annexation into the Anglo-American
market did not lessen the territorial and other bases for potential
hostilities across the neutral ground set up during the 1740s.
Slaves continued to flee Carolina and find a qualified freedom in

᠍ **201**

THE
MILITARY
FRONTIER,
AT LAST,
1702–1763

St. Augustine, to the irritation of their former masters. Georgia's population continued to grow from under three thousand to over eleven thousand (1748–1763) and the Georgians increasingly eyed the neutral ground as an area for expansion. The population of St. Augustine remained almost unchanged at about three thousand. Creeks, consulting their own interests, stole horses from Englishmen and Spaniards alike, although each of the latter blamed the other.[90] And then, in 1755, a group of discontented Englishmen from Georgia led by Edmund Gray moved into the "Neutral Ground" and founded New Hanover thirty miles up the Satilla River. The Spaniards visited them in October 1756, ordering them to leave, but also trading! The English government, too, ordered the settlement demolished, but its residents simply moved to Cumberland Island, among other places. Because neither Spain nor Great Britain wanted war, nothing further was done.[91]

Actual hostilities seemed about to break out in May and June 1759 when a Creek hunting party raided Picolata and ranches near St. Augustine, making work outside St. Augustine's walls unsafe. The blame for this hostility was laid at the feet of the governor of La Florida for forbidding the Creek to cross the St. Johns River. He even forbade the mostly baptized Indians from St. Marks from coming into town with deerskins to sell. But again, nothing further developed. The incident did show that Creek—proto-Seminoles—were regularly hunting in the Alachua area and may even have been served (seasonally?) by English merchants.[92]

Aware that the key to La Florida's economic independence from the Anglo-Americans and its ability to defend itself was settlement with farmers, the Spaniards renewed earlier projects to bring Canary Islanders (Isleños) to the province. The first 363 arrived in October 1757 to find that no planning had been done for their settlement. They were given lands between St. Augustine and Fort Mose. A second group in 1758 was settled south of the town (at La Punta) on land Indians had abandoned as infertile. Later arrivals found shelter, charity, and work as they could even though suggestions had been made to settle them at Santa Fe or San Luis. In all, some 664 of the 711 persons who left the Canary Islands reached St. Augustine, but not all lived long or stayed.[93] English fears of new Spanish settlements along the frontier thus proved groundless. The unfortunate Isleños served only to augment St. Augustine's population.[94]

The End of the Military Frontier

War finally came in 1762 when Spain decided to try to turn the tide of French defeat in the Americas in order to protect its own empire from the British menace. But the British struck first. In the spring of 1763, they laid siege to Havana, taking it in August. St. Augustine again was menaced by roving Indian war and hunting parties and by the cutoff of supplies from the Anglo-American colonies. Spanish privateers joined French ones in using St. Augustine as a point of sale for prizes. The British responded by stationing HMS *Epreuve* off St. Augustine in January 1763 but did not attack the town.[95] The Spaniards, meanwhile, negotiated treaties with the Lower Creek in the hope that the Canary Islanders could be settled away from St. Augustine. The result was a firmer Spanish–Creek alliance.[96]

During the peace negotiations of the fall of 1762 and the spring of 1763, France agreed to give Great Britain all of French North America east of the Mississippi River as far south as the Gulf of Mexico. Spanish protests were ignored. And in the end, Spain had to choose between Havana and the Floridas. The Floridas were sacrificed. By the terms of the Treaty of Paris of 1763, La Florida's residents were given eighteen months to sell and leave if they wished to do so. The first British troops arrived on 20 July 1763 under the command of Capt. John Hodges.[97]

Spanish Florida, 1763

The St. Augustine that Hodges occupied had 3,100 Spanish, mestizo, African, African-descended, and Indian inhabitants occupying 325 houses, patronizing about 50 shops and taverns, and frequenting three churches, including the Franciscan convent's chapel. At least 60 percent of the population and 55 percent of the landowners were in or were directly dependent on the garrison. Of

203

THE
MILITARY
FRONTIER,
AT LAST,
1702–1763

the residents, 350, or about 11 percent were Black slaves and at least another eighty were free persons of African ancestry. Only eighty-three residents were Native Americans. Women made up half of the adult population and 26 percent of the landowners. Free persons of African ancestry holding thirteen properties constituted just 3.3 percent of their racial group (including slaves); by contrast, over 10 percent the Hispanic population owned property.[98]

Housing reflected the marked differences in wealth. Twenty-three houses were of stone with flat roofs. Another twenty-six were of stone (some with two stories) with shingle or board roofs. These were the homes of the almost entirely Floridano (native-born) elite, an elite that claimed vast areas of land, with six extended families each holding more than 10,000 square varas (about two acres) of land in the town and another seven families not far behind.[99] The less fortunate lived in 190 one-story structures of unstated construction and thatch roofs on lots that mostly measured fifty by one hundred feet (about 1/10th of an acre), and the balance (perhaps 90) suffered in board or palm thatch huts, which were drafty and likely to leak during the long winter rainy season. The Indian towns of Tolomato and Nombre de Dios and the homes of many of the Isleños were of these latter types of construction. St. Augustine did boast a newly rebuilt stone governor's house, a stone barracks on the south side of the plaza, and the walls of what would in time become the cathedral church on the north side.[100]

Relatively little food was grown except in some gardens. There were grape arbors and door-yard plantings of figs, peaches, quince, plums, and sweet and sour oranges. Hostile Indians kept the Spaniards close to their town and, in wartime, even out of the fields north and immediately west of the inner defenses. As has been indicated, trade with New York, South Carolina, Georgia, and Spanish and (during the recent war) French privateers provided flour, fresh and salted meat, and most manufactured goods. Fish and shellfish were taken from the waters off the town.[101]

Aside from St. Augustine, the Spaniards had only a very slight presence in the peninsula. Eighty leagues west of St. Augustine, San Marcos had a fifty-man garrison, supplemented by twenty-three prisoners sent to work on the new fortifications. The Lower Creek who lived around San Marcos were not counted in 1763 because they did not leave with the soldiers. But some eighty families of Indians from extreme south Florida—probably the last of the Calusa and nearby groups—did go to Cuba when the Spaniards pulled out. The hundred or so Christian Apalachee and confederated Yamassee who had taken refuge at Pensacola also left, for Veracruz, the destination of the garrison.[102]

Slight though the Spanish presence and influence were at this point, the peninsula was no longer devoid of other human inhabitants. A small village of "Seminole" had appeared on the St. Johns River near the site of modern Palatka. Near modern Micanopy, Chief Cowkeeper led a village, Cuscowilla, of thirty wooden houses sheltering several hundred persons. They ran cattle and pigs, worked maize fields, and gathered and hunted. Further northwest, on the west side of the Suwannee, the chief called The White King had a village of equal size, whose residents traded with Cuba by canoe. In the Brooksville Hills, the town of Chukuchatta was flourishing. And in Apalachee (modern Tallahassee), Tonaby's town consisted of three dozen houses. Nearby, Mikasuki (i.e., Hichiti) speakers had a settlement of sixty houses and seventy warriors on the shore of Lake Miccosukee. Other towns that were part of the emerging Seminole confederation were near the confluence of the Flint and Chattahoochee Rivers.[103]

After over half a century as a no-man's land, the good lands of the Tallahassee, Madison Hills, and the Central Ridge were again being populated. These proto-Seminoles were the first of several waves of immigrants to create their own frontiers in the peninsula during the next century. It remained to be seen if they would prevail or lose out to the Anglo-Americans who were replacing the Spaniards.

The Spaniards' situation in La Florida in 1763 was in large measure the direct consequence of the failure of their sixteenth-century predecessors to seize control of the piedmont's natural resources and peoples and of Spain's long-term lack of capital and "surplus" population with which to carry out large-scale colonization. Now, two centuries later, the descendants of the pied-

205

THE
MILITARY
FRONTIER,
AT LAST,
1702–1763

mont's peoples who had gathered in the Creek Confederacy were taking over the better soils of northern and north-central Florida, areas that their grandfathers had won with British help at the beginning of the eighteenth century because in the peninsula, too, the Spaniards had failed to seize direct control of the better natural and human resources. Instead, except for a few families in Apalachee and Pensacola and the few soldiers there and at St. Marks, most of the Hispanic population of La Florida had remained in a coastal garrison town whose civilian population never seems to have achieved a self-sustaining birth-to-death ratio, much less expansion that might have forced people to seek homes in the interior. Only in a very few years, if any, had that population and its drafted Indian and African laborers locally produced enough food (maize) fully to meet its needs. More commonly, local production barely reached 50 percent of need, even when the commercial productions of the Guale, Timucua, and Apalachee peoples were added in. Having little capital, and that largely obtained by exploiting the *situado* and the commoners, the local elite invested nothing, so far as we know, in improved farming technologies and little in economic enterprises aside from low-cost cattle ranching and minor "collecting" trades such as those in ambergris and sarsaparilla roots. Hammock soils, drainable swamps, and stands of pine trees capable of yielding naval stores were all left unused. All would have drawn Hispanics into the interior and given the area a basis for economic and population expansion.

Having failed to seize the piedmont or even the central Florida ridge and the northern hills, and being unable to expand their own population, the Spaniards had to settle for a colonial relationship with Native Americans that was largely defined by accommodations within Native American ideas of paramountcy. The peoples of the tidewater and inland frontiers who became Spain's "subjects" in La Florida were never numerous and after the epidemics of the 1650s were unable to hold their own demographically during a time when the remnants of the piedmont peoples were assembling into the Creek confederation and beginning to increase in numbers. The Spaniards took advantage of this demographic disaster to remake the local accommodations to more closely resemble the hierarchical arrangements else-where in their American empire. But in doing this, the Spaniards increased the dependence of the Indians, especially on their military protection. Military security was a key but implicit part of Indian recognition of Spanish paramountcy both before and after 1650. When that protection failed, the bonds of the par-amount–subordinate relationship dissolved except with a few groups. Much the same thing had happened whenever the Span-iards breached the limits of what the Indians understood were the accommodations they had reached with the new local para-mount people, the Spaniards. Thus the Floridanos, blinded by their own cultural assumptions about the colonial relationship, probably never understood Apalachee anger in 1704 and cer-tainly never understood Indian resistance to the friars as arising from anything other than the work of the Devil.

And so in the end, after two hundred years and a very large investment by the Crown, Spain's La Florida was little more than what it had been in 1565, a garrison precariously perched on a sand spit by the Atlantic Ocean.[104] Indians, whose ancestors should have been incorporated into the Spanish empire but were not, were the immediate heirs and the proximate agents of the collapse of La Florida's tidewater and inland frontiers. Yet a larger drama was at play, one also tied, we may imagine, to the Spaniards' failure to seize and expansively colonize Ayllón's land "more appropriate for Spaniards." The English, already well es-tablished in Ayllón's Chicora (the Carolinas and Virginia), and their demographically and economically dynamic empire were taking control of the peninsula with consequences that proved far-reaching.

9.

NEW TIDEWATER FRONTIERS, 1763–1790

When Bernard Romans wrote out *A Concise Natural History of East and West Florida*[1] in the early 1770s, he described a colony that had already seen a speculative land boom go bust, leaving in its wake Anglo-American farms and "plantations" promiscuously scattered along the tidal rivers and streams of northeast Florida and a pile of land grants that were preventing new settlement. In the interior, a few hundred Seminoles farmed and herded in Alachua and Apalachee and roamed the peninsula in search of game (as they had since the 1740s). Fifty years after Romans, Charles Vignoles penned his *Observations upon the Floridas*.[2] He described a new American territory with a more extensive, if recently attacked, Seminole presence and a modestly thicker overlay of farms and plantations still largely concentrated along the tidewater streams of northeast Florida, although they could also be found scattered down the east coast on the banks of tidal steams and on limestone ridges as far as Biscayne Bay. On the west coast, Cuban fishermen had a few seasonal fishing stations or *ranchos* from Charlotte Harbor to Tampa Bay.

Neither man told his readers much about the recent history of the place. Had they done so, the readers would have seen how first the Spaniards and then the English had pulled up stakes, leaving what land they had occupied empty, thereby forcing their successors—respectively the English and the Spaniards—to begin again the European peopling of the land. And in the end, for both imperial powers, Anglo-Americans provided the shock troops who, with their African and African-American slaves, cleared and plowed forests and the Indian old fields, ran cattle, drained swamps for rice cultivation, and characteristically sought to strip the land of its natural, timbered wealth while driving off the Native Americans they found while moving out of the tidewater toward the better soils of the central ridge ("Alachua") and the southern extensions of the Tifton Uplands known as the Tallahassee and Madison Hills (i.e., "Apalachee"). Most of the details of that latter conflict fall into a later chapter. This chapter examines the British frontier period and population cycle in East Florida (1763–1784) and the beginnings of the subsequent Spanish cycle. It ends on the eve of the American push to control the peninsula.

Great Britain's prospective acquisition of La Florida (a result of Spain's ill-prepared, ill-timed, and thus disastrous entry into the Seven Years War in 1762) touched off a public debate in England over the wisdom of adding the territory to English North America rather than retaining Havana. The military argument— that possession of Florida would end the Spanish threat to Georgia and provide well-placed bases for privateering in the next war with France—was little contested.[3] The economic argument, on the other hand, pitted writers like Alderman Beckford, who described Florida as nothing but "pine barrens or sandy deserts," against pro-acquisition writers who resurrected the Ptolemaic notion of similar flora and fauna at similar latitudes to suggest that lying on the same latitude as Persia, Florida could produce silk, coffee, and other exotic goods. Once the province was in English hands, the optimists carried the day because of the Board of Trade and Plantation's call for proposals for the settlement of townships, Governor Grant's proclamation in the Americas, William Robert's and especially Dr. William Stork's books and propaganda, and, above all, private letters from Florida. The favorable prospects of indigo, rice, cotton, and silk were especially featured in these latter writings.[4]

In private, a related debate was afoot that involved not just accurate and fanciful geographic knowledge of the peninsula but also Florida's economic future. The government's initial discussion of a Florida–Georgia border favored Georgia's claims from the time of Olgethorpe that the St. Johns River should separate the two colonies. A line was to be drawn from the confluence of the Chattahoochee and Flint Rivers to the mouth of the St. Johns River, bisecting the good land at Apalachee and giving Georgia all of the supposedly good soils along the St. Marys and Nassau Rivers. On the other hand, the Altamaha had been Georgia's de facto southern limit since 1748, with the area between that river and the St. Johns regarded as a neutral ground. At Governor James Grant's insistence, the government decided to split the difference and drew the border from the confluence of the Chattahoochee and Flint Rivers eastward to the St. Marys and down it to the sea.[5]

That final definition of Florida did not come until a general proclamation of 7 October 1763 created a government for East Florida, as well as for the other provinces that Great Britain had acquired in the peace of Paris. East Florida was given the usual governor-and-council form of government for a royal colony, with the possibility of having an elected assembly when population levels warranted it. Meanwhile, the exchange of the ratifications of the Treaty of Paris on 10 March 1763 began the eighteen-month period during which the Spaniards could sell out and leave or elect to stay with a promise of freedom of religion and respect for their property rights. Captain John Hedges (or Hodges) and the first companies of the British occupation force arrived at St. Augustine on 20 July 1763. The province formally came under British rule on 30 July when Major Francis Ogilvie arrived.[6]

The Spaniards began to organize a total withdrawal early in April. Juan Elixio de la Puente was sent from Havana to take charge of removing royal property and to assist Governor Melchor Feliú and his officials in the evacuation of the population. Families sailed as groups in an order determined by their social status, beginning in August 1763 and ending on 22 January 1764. In all, 3,063 individuals from some 542 households left. Table 9.1 shows the breakdown by ethnicity, gender, and age. An additional 65

TABLE 9.1 Evacuees, East Florida, 1763

Households	No. of Families	Men	Women	Boys	Girls	Total
Florida Creoles	364	561	466	442	447	1,916
Catalan Fusiliers	36	98	36	16	11	161
Isleños (1757–61)	96	89	118	119	99	425
German Catholics	6	6	10	5	5	26
Christian Indians	19	20	32	18	19	89
Free Negros	5	10	7	2	4	23
Free Pardos	16	35	27	6	8	76
Slaves		83	96	64	57	300
Convict Laborers		38				38
Crown Slaves		9				9
Totals	542	949	792	672	650	3,063

Source: Gold, *Borderlands Empires*, Table 4, p. 67. Figures do not include evacuees from Apalachee. For a table including them, see his Table 7, p. 76.

persons left St. Marks in February 1764. Except for 77 individuals who ended up in Campeche, the evacuees went to Havana, whence they were resettled in nearby areas.[7] Only one Spaniard stayed, Francisco Xavier Sánchez.

The evacuation went smoothly, with only a few incidents. Among the latter: British officers were quartered with families who did not want them and a few soldiers pulled down empty wooden houses for use as firewood. Two larger disputes appeared but did not disrupt the general tranquility. First, the Floridanos were disappointed that few of the British moving in were interested in purchasing houses or other property, and the few who did buy paid only a fraction of what the Spaniards asked and often made only a small down payment. In the end, many of the property owners entrusted their assets to Elixio de la Puente, who in turn "sold" them in trust to Jessie Fish, the long-term resident agent for the Walton Company of New York, and to John Gordon of Charleston, South Carolina against later payment when the properties might be sold for higher prices. Second, Major Ogilvie asserted a claim to the Florida Keys, but Elixio de la Puente refused to be drawn into a discussion on that topic, which had not been explicitly resolved in the treaty.[8] Disagreement over ownership of the Keys continued without resolution until Spain regained control of Florida in 1783.

As the British settled in St. Augustine, in London the Board of Trade and Plantations issued land grant regulations as part of the decree of 7 October 1763. The governor was allowed to grant lands by headright, subject to quitrents of half a penny per acre, payable after two years. Each head of a household and retired soldier could request headrights of one hundred acres, plus fifty acres per additional person, free or slave, in the household. Individuals willing to promise to pay an additional quitrent of half a penny per acre after two years could gain an additional thousand acres at a cost of a shilling per ten acres. Ex-soldiers did not have to pay quitrents for ten years. Holders of mandamus grants (Orders in Council) for townships of twenty thousand acres (some were for less) did not pay quitrents on their acreage for five years, and then on only half until ten years after the grant. They were supposed to achieve an occupancy rate of one person per hundred acres within ten years and have a third of the grant settled within three. No one ever paid any quitrent during the British period, and until the 1780s no effort was made to enforce other conditions attached to land grants, large or small.[9]

To avoid the sort of unrest that had provoked Pontiac's recent rebellion, the decree ordered Governor Grant to negotiate a treaty with the Indians that would demarcate their lands. Thus, unlike Spanish incorporative imperialism, British imperialism aimed to exclude (non-slave) Indians from English frontier areas while economically exploiting them in their own territories via the deerskin trade. The Creek and proto-Seminole, at least, found this more acceptable than some of their ancestors had found the Spanish brand of imperialism.

The general terms for granting lands were supplemented by an order of April 1764 that required all Spanish land claims other than those for lots and buildings in St. Augustine to be confirmed in London. Although not technically a violation of the Treaty of 1763's promise of property rights for the Floridanos, this requirement amounted to a repudiation of the sense of the article in question. Some Floridanos, the early British purchasers of Florida property, and agent/speculators like John Gordon of South Carolina all lost.[10] The reason for this British action is evident. Fish and Gordon filed a map that showed twenty-two Spanish claims, twelve with named owners, for 4.6 million acres between

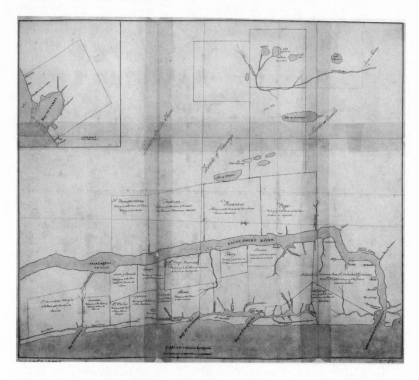

Figure 9.1. Spanish land claims in Florida, ca. 1764.
GREAT BRITAIN, PUBLIC RECORD OFFICE, COLONIAL OFFICE 700,
FLORIDA 7. COURTESY OF THE PUBLIC RECORD OFFICE.

the St. Johns River and the Atlantic Ocean as far south as Ponce
de Leon Inlet and in a wide band reaching through Alachua to
near the Suwannee River. A claim to Tampa Bay was also included[11] (see Figure 9.1). Acceptance of such extensive claims
would have left no land for British grants along the middle
course of the St. Johns River and, with respect to the Alachua
claims, would have violated the royal intention to restrict settlement to the tidewater (including the St. Johns as far as Lake
George) of northeastern Florida. As the Commissioners for Trade
and Plantations told Fish and Gordon's agents in November
1765, "their pretended purchase was not only inconsistent with
the spirit of the Treaty, but did also operate to the prejudice of
the national rights and interests."[12]

Settling the Indian boundary was the first order of business, even as both Governor Grant and the Privy Council in London began to issue land grants. John Stuart, the British Indian agent for the Southern Department, arrived in St. Augustine in the spring of 1764 and in July met with Cowkeeper, the chief of the Alachua band of the proto-Seminoles. During the next year, Stuart went to St. Marks, Mobile, and Pensacola to meet, respectively, with members of five Miccosukee and proto-Seminole towns in the Apalachee–Appalachicola area, the Choctaw and the Chickasaw, and finally the Creek. Upon his return to St. Augustine, he called a general meeting with the Creek Indians, including the proto-Seminole. The delegations met at Picolata 15–18 November 1765 because the Creek would not cross the St. Johns with their horses. They agreed that the British would continue to supply the Indians and that both sides would use blood-for-blood punishment for murders. The boundary between Indian and British areas was fixed approximately thirty-five miles from the coast from the St. Marys River in the north to the Oklawaha River just south of Spalding's Lower Store on the St. Johns River, thence due east to the coast (see Figure 9.2). Elsewhere along the coast of the peninsula, the boundary ran at the distance inland that the tide affected the rivers (up to ten miles). This more than two-million-acre grant was a larger concession than the Creek had been willing to make at a previous conference held at Augusta (Georgia), but they made it because of British gifts and promises of trade and, probably, because the Lower Creek chiefs who made it recognized that the best hunting lands were not included. Too, *they* did not really control Florida. The absence of Cowkeeper, the one chief who *did* live in Florida, underscored the Lower Creek chiefs' relative lack of authority in the peninsula. Cowkeeper agreed to the same terms during an eight-day conference with Grant and Stuart in December.[13] A second Picolata conference of 21–23 November 1767 ironed out minor problems and reinforced the rule on how murders were to be handled. On that occasion, an old Indian man was executed by the Indians to expiate the deaths of two Englishmen at the hand of two young Indians.[14]

The Picolata conferences were part of a larger British initiative that defined Indian country and in so doing sought to protect

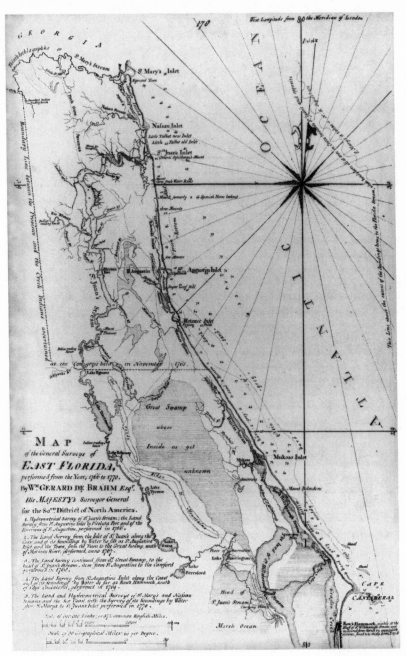

Figure 9.2. British East Florida, 1770. William Gerard de Brahm, "Map of the General Surveys of East Florida . . . 1770." British Library, King's Manuscript 211, fol. 3 (1). By permission of the British Library.

both the deerskin trade and to restrict Anglo-American settlement east of the famous "Proclamation Line" running along the tops of the Appalachian Mountains and now extended into tidewater Florida. For the Creek and their offshoot, the proto-Seminole, this new situation further enhanced their position as the dominant Native American power in the Southeast and increased their sense of being an independent, sovereign nation, even if in alliance with a protective British Crown. But this new situation also furthered their economic dependence on European manufactures that were exchanged for deerskins harvested from an area that ran from what became Tennessee to southern Florida; the area included most of modern Georgia as well as Alabama. Horses made hunting this vast game preserve easy; economic dependence made defending it essential.

The British had their trading posts in place by the date of the Picolata agreement. Saunder's Store on a tributary of the St. Marys River and James Spalding's "lower store" on the St. Johns River at Stoke's landing just north of the Oklawaha River (an important Indian route into central Florida) served as cornerposts for the newly designated English settlement area.[15] Spalding had a second or "upper" store five miles further south on the St. Johns, in Seminole territory (Figure 9.2). Other stores were beginning to open in St. Augustine, and a trading post was planned for St. Marks. In addition, the British soon created a one-village, one-trader system, a move that over time may have encouraged the creation of new towns as Seminole populations grew. All that remained was for the British to keep a store of gifts on hand at St. Augustine and St. Marks to satisfy visiting chiefs and important men.[16] The principal items of commerce were deerskins, European goods, and foods such as rum and coffee.

As the distribution of these stores suggests, the proto-Seminole occupied more than one part of Florida. Best known to history were the central ridge group. Cowkeeper's Cuscowilla, located on high ground south of modern Payne's Prairie, was the head town for a group that by 1775 included Alachua II, Santa Fe, Whachitokha, Talahasochte, and possibly others. These towns became occasional suppliers of maize, rice, watermelons, peaches, potatoes, pumpkins, and cattle to St. Augustine. The Miccosukee villages of Ocklockonee, Mikasuki, and Tallahassee formed another group more or less in the old Apalachee area. A third group of mostly Yuchi (lower Creek) lived along the Chattahoochee and Flint Rivers and included Ekanachatte, Tamathli, Hyhappo, Osochi, and Pokanaweethly towns. All of these groups used Cuban fishing boats or their own multi-person canoes to trade with Havana in pelts, beeswax, honey, and bear grease (among other products) and to collect gifts from the governor. They and the Seminole further south, who also traded with Cuba, told the Spaniards that they were their friends. At the same time, the Indians traded with the English and told them much the same story. Still other small Indian towns were along the lower St. Johns River near modern Jacksonville, near modern Brooksville (Chukuchatta), on the Caloosahatchee River (by the town of the same name), and between Spalding's two stores on the upper St. Johns[17] (see Figure 9.3).

In all, at least nine proto-Seminole towns existed by the time of William Bartram's travels in the peninsula in 1774, double the number present in 1763. Bartram thought that this influx was in response to the relatively more abundant deer and bear populations of the peninsula.[18] The attractions of trade with both Cuba and British trading posts closer than Savannah and Charleston may have been additional factors. All the towns of which we know anything had squares, a council house, and varying numbers of residences. Horses, cattle, swine, and some European plants provided transport and food.[19] In their own way and at their own pace, the partially Europeanized lower Creek/proto-Seminole were repopulating the better soils from which their grandfathers had driven the remnants of the Spanish missions' populations. Because of British imperial policy, this Indian reoccupation of the peninsula could proceed without disturbing English efforts to occupy their own part of the peninsula.

The Creek cession of all of the tidewater areas of coastal Florida solved several of the problems that the peninsula's geography (as they understood it) presented to the British. First, it gave them the river and creekside hammocks, whose oaks and other hardwoods denoted better, more moist soils than the neighboring sands, and swamps that could be drained to reclaim their better

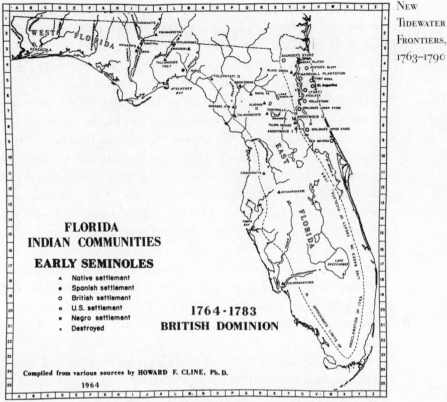

Figure 9.3. Florida Indian communities, 1764–1783. FROM
HOWARD F. CLINE, *Florida Indians II: Provisional Historical
Gazetteer with Locational Notes on Florida Colonial
Communities* (NEW YORK: GARLAND PUBLISHERS, 1974), MAP
No. 5. BY PERMISSION OF SARAH CLINE.

alluvial soils. Second, this tidewater frontier also allowed the
British to continue their well-established pattern of using the
economies of water transport in the early stages of colonial development.

Governor Grant pointed to these facts and to the province's
legendary healthfulness in trying to recruit Anglo-American
settlers and their slaves. He acknowledged that the coastal soils
were "in general sandy, but productive with proper cultivation,"
while the interior areas and those along rivers were "rich and
fertile." Fruits and grains grew easily, almost spontaneously; in-

digo could be cut four times a year; West Indian "fruits and productions" could probably be grown in the southern part of the
peninsula; and timber resources awaited the ax and saw.[20] These
twin themes of healthfulness and natural fertility have been
standards in pro-settlement propaganda ever since.

The advantages obtained in the Treaty of Picolata notwith-
standing, the British failed to develop East Florida in the way its
proponents had envisioned. Among the known reasons for this
failure is the difficulty in clearing some types of land, especially
the more desirable hammock land which had heavy growths of
hardwoods and, sometimes, saw palmettos. A lack of hands was
a reason for some failures. Too, experience showed that even the
best-cleared land planted in indigo and maize "became so foul
with weeds" after four years that it could only be used for pasture and maize thereafter.[21] And there was disillusionment arising from exaggerated expectations based on the propaganda. But
by far the most important reason for the failure was the large
acreages granted to absentees during the first decade of British
rule.

Between 1765 and 1775, Governor Grant and his Council issued
114 warrants for the surveying of Orders in Council grants totaling 1,443,000 acres. The peak years were 1768 to 1771 when
1,025,000 acres were granted, representing 71 percent of the total
of mandamus grants during the first decade.[22] In 1776, Georgia
refugees who wanted land covered by those warrants for survey
claimed that only 16 of 108 mandamus grantees even tried to
settle their grants.[23]

Many grants, whether secured in London or St. Augustine,
were really speculations. For example, in 1769 George Laidler,
Sr.'s family obtained a 5,000-acre grant for him in London for
the area of the Cowford on the St. Johns River (modern Jacksonville). He immediately sold it to Fraser and Richardson, shop-
keepers at St. Augustine, for £50. They held it until 6 May 1772
when they sold it to William Wilson for £15 10/-; Wilson resold it
to Alexander Gray on 11 June for £50. Gray then divided the
grant, selling 2,050 acres to John Read of London on 5 July 1774
for £200, and 2,950 acres to George Rigby of London for the
same sum. Read and Rigby were partners. Gray became their

agent in Florida but failed to develop the property.[24] At the other
end of the scale, James Cameron, a private in the 2nd Battalion
of the Royal Scots regiment, obtained fifty well-timbered acres
on the Nassau River as his King's Bounty when he left the army
(1771) but never did anything with them, preferring instead to
invest in two houses in St. Augustine.[25]

Among the more notable large grants that actually were taken
up were Francis Philip Fatio, Sr.'s three plantations and Denys
Rolle's first grant (20,000 acres) on the St. Johns; Andrew Turnbull, George Grenville, and Sir William Duncan's 101,400 acres
for New Smyrna; Richard Oswald's 20,000 acres on the Tomoka
and Halifax Rivers and three lesser estates elsewhere; and 14,300
acres in three plantations owned by John Moultrie of South Carolina.[26] Promoters such as Dr. Stork obtained large grants on the
promise, never realized, that they would bring German or Swiss
Protestants to settle the land. John Savage's plan to bring poor
farmers from Bermuda to Amelia Island similarly failed. Many
other colonization projects were rejected because they required
government funding.[27]

The eventual beneficiaries of land speculation were men like
John Moultrie, Captain Benjamin Dodd and Denys Rolle. During
the decade of the 1770s, Moultrie acquired grants and made purchases that built up the holdings of his late brother James's
widow and children from James's original 1,000 acres near St.
Augustine to 3,700 acres. He also acquired two major plantations
and some 14,300 acres of land for himself. Dodd, Provost Mar-
shall (head of the military police in the garrison) 1777–1778, was
able to acquire almost 7,000 acres for £110, from which he sold
700 acres for £250 before leaving Florida. Rolle, after a poor initial start with his philanthropic colony, returned to Florida in the
1770s and assembled 3,855 acres twenty-two miles from the St.
Johns Bar, 100 acres forty or so miles further up the river, and
76,085 acres one hundred miles upstream from the bar. He
claimed to own 138 slaves, of whom 96 were able to work.[28]

The Crown's intention in granting 20,000-acre townships to
English proprietors was that white, Protestant settlers would de-
velop them. This policy proved to be a failure. For example, Dr.
Turnbull recruited and transported 1,300 Roman Catholic Mi-

norcans, Italians, and Eastern Orthodox Greeks in 1768 at a cost of £24,000. Rolle, who had idiosyncratic philanthropic purposes, seems to have recruited and indentured 400–500 street people from London, many of whom deserted or died within months of reaching Florida. The Earl of Egmont abandoned his Mount Royal plantation in 1770 after two years of work (mostly by slaves) and a first crop of indigo worth £1,500. His schemes for granting 640-acre homesteads to settlers who would bring eight slaves to work on lands near the Cowford and for bringing Huguenots to Florida also failed.[29] Bernard Romans mocked such efforts, saying, "The late foolish, not to call them cruel attempts of settling East Florida by whites from Europe (I mean as well from England as from the Levant) are likewise a very absolute conviction of the necessity of having Negro slaves" and summed up the result by saying that the St. Johns River's shores "exhibit in a number of places sad monuments of the folly and extravagant idea of the first European adventurers and schemers, and the villainy of their managers."[30]

Settlement by immigrants of lesser means was slightly more successful. A few men came early and claimed land that had already been cleared near St. Augustine, along the North River, and at Diego Plains. Others arrived, or at least obtained grants (orders for survey), in a temporal pattern that matched the mandamus grants, with a plateau of heavy granting in 1769–1771 and another spike in 1775. Many of these grants opened new areas to cultivation or timbering, especially along the Nassau River.[31] In all, some 576 grants totaling 210,672.5 acres were given out to these small holders between 1765 and 1775.[32] Still, in 1771, after over half of the small grants had been given out, Governor Grant reported only 288 white men (excluding the Minorcans and Greeks and the garrison) in the province, of whom 107 were "planters" with about 900 slaves. Judging by a later sample of uncertain representativeness, the largest number would have been Anglo-Americans or British with experience elsewhere in English North America.[33]

Information on the geographic spread of development in Florida prior to the outbreak of the American Revolution is difficult to find. Romans's *Natural History* provides a general idea of

where planting was going on in the early 1770s, and such trade
figures as we have indicate the small economic value of the goods
produced and exported. Romans comments that the banks of the
Nassau River were "almost all very fertile" and that "along its
banks [is] the best body of land in East Florida near the sea."
But he does not indicate any farming. Along especially the eastern side of the St. Johns were a few "fruitful spots," but most of
the peninsula was good only for cattle and tapping pine trees for
naval stores. Exceptions were the area around the headwaters
of San Pablo Creek, the Diego Plains, the "Twelve Mile Swamp"
(eight miles north of St. Augustine), and the Three Mile Swamp
(three miles west of that town), and a few other areas that had
better soils. South of St. Augustine, Lt. Governor Moultrie had a
plantation on St. Nicholas Creek and there was some settlement
at El Peñon, but Romans characterized most of the land as "in
general arid and poor." The plantations on the shores of the
Hillsboro and Halifax Rivers north and south of Mosquito Inlet
produced a "very good indigo." The area was heavily populated
with New Smyrna and other plantations.[34] Land on Biscayne Bay
had been surveyed but remained undeveloped.[35] From Romans's
description, it would appear that relatively little commercial,
export-oriented agriculture had developed except at New Smyrna.

Romans's picture is somewhat confirmed by the few trade statistics we have for 1770–1783. Table 9.2 presents them. Oranges,
harvested from the abundant groves that the Spaniards, Indians,
and avian and other planters had created, were an early and
fairly constant export. Deerskins also seem to have been a stable
export item, running at 3,000–4,000 pounds a year. Indigo, the
colony's commercial hope, rose from nothing to the 20,000–
30,000 pounds per year range in the early 1770s. Much of this
must have come from New Smyrna and half a dozen plantations
in that area. The dye was said to be of good quality if inferior to
Guatemala's better grades. The Crown enumerated it and gave
a four-pence-per-pound bounty.[36] Indigo probably accounts for
the notable rise in the value of Florida's imports into England in
the 1770s (see Table 9.3). Other commercial crops, notably silk
and vines, for which the Crown offered premiums payable at St.
Augustine, were not developed. Rice, a natural for the swamps

TABLE 9.2 Selected East Florida Exports, 1770–1783

Year	Indigo (lbs)	Deer Skins (lbs)	Pine Lumber (ft)	Tar (bbls)	Turpentine (bbls)	Oak Barrel Staves	Oranges	Rice (bbls)
1770	6,189	6,348						
1771	28,143	3,990						
1772		468						
1773							50,000	
1774	22,119							
1775								
1776	58,295 Casks	29,009	>50,000	190	56	87,000	>65,000	860
1777	14,070 Casks	14,813 Casks	553,000	2,241	417	419,000		1,182
1778	29,260 Casks	3,467 Casks	468,800	>8,100	1,980	320,000	5,000	>471
1779								
1780								
1781								
1782	125,533							
1783				20,000 for both				

Source: Mowat, *East Florida,* 77–79; Siebert, *Loyalists,* 1:67–69.

TABLE 9.3 East Florida's English Trade and Subsidy, 1763–1775

Year	Exports to England	Imports from England	Ships from England	Subsidy
1763		£ 9,946		
1764	£ 294	15,004		£ 5,700
1765	684	19,888		5,200
1766	2,113	38,718	1	5,200
1767	12,681	30,963	3	4,750
1768	14,078	32,572	4	4,750
1769	1,744	29,509	8	5,200
1770	3,688	39,857	2	5,300
1771	21,856	66,647	4	5,300
1772	15,722	40,458	3	4,950
1773	7,129	51,502		4,950
1774	22,335	52,149		4,950
1775	21,504	30,628		4,950

Source: Mowat, *East Florida*, Table 1, "Tables of Trade and Shipping Relating to East Florida," and pp. 157, 36 (shipping and subsidy, respectively).

along the St. Marys and other tidal rivers, seems to have had limited development. Lumber, naval stores, sugar and cotton, which would later round out the picture of Florida's exports, do not appear in the figures before 1776.[37] Clearly only planters who had the means to invest in indigo production made any money, and there were few of them.

Cattle and food plants, on the other hand, seem to have flourished, providing a diet not unlike what the Spaniards had enjoyed.[38] Still, we do not know if the plow-using British (as compared to the hoe-cultivating Spaniards and their Indian laborers) attained self-sufficiency in basic foods. Plantations probably did, but St. Augustine seems to have continued to depend on some imported food.

Given this low level of export production and the heavy capital investment needed to get an indigo plantation going, it is not surprising to find that the British colony, like the Spanish one before it, ran a trade deficit and required a subsidy to pay for its government, defense, and Indian gifts (£1,000 a year). Trade figures for England suggest as much as a nineteen-to-one ratio of imports into Florida to exports from it in the initial years, with the ratio dropping to two to one or even less by the middle of the 1770s as indigo production began to redress the imbalance (see Table 9.3). The colony's deficit was probably greater than two to one because of the coastal trade in small sloops and schooners with Charleston, Savannah, and New York that continued the pattern established by Spanish Florida earlier in the eighteenth century. That trade carried to Florida foods both exotic and basic (e.g., hams) and consumers' goods such as saddles, cloth, and furniture. Ships so engaged frequently returned north in ballast.[39] James Adair expressed the frustration of many British citizens, noting that the "sagacious public" had yet to be convinced that the expenses of guarding "a tract of low grave yards" made up for the sugar islands given up to get Florida.[40]

Discouraging as the short-term results of the English colonization policy may have been to London, the British kept on issuing land grants and doing what they could to develop a viable economy. An important aspect of the latter activity was road building. Two contractors were paid to improve the trail from St. Augustine to the St. Marys River, 1773–1776 (north of the St. Johns River it went roughly along the route of modern U.S. 301). Even more notable, the road was extended south to the Timoka River and then to New Smyrna by Robert Bisset, a major landholder in that area. The funding for this and such other works as a new fire engine for St. Augustine came mostly from the silk bounty monies that were never paid out because no silk was produced. Finally, in 1776, Jeffrey Romans was sent to survey the old Spanish road to Apalachee and Pensacola. John Purcell completed the survey and the Stuart-Purcell map (1778). It noted the qualities of the soils along the way, pointed out what might be grown in them, and gave the locations of the ruins of Spanish missions.[41] That is, it was a guide for settlement that did not develop.

This survey of the interior, limited as it was, in part responded to Jonathan Bryan's scheme of 1774–1775 to obtain a "kind of lease" on some five million acres of the "Apalachee" [sic!] old fields around Alachua. Bryan told the Indians he only wanted to run some cattle, but his real intention was to settle the area. When Cowkeeper and others expressed anger at this as well as at earlier trade abuses, Governor Tonyn, Indian agent John Stuart, and others denounced the scheme and took actions to end the trade abuses. Chief Justice William Drayton and Andrew Turnbull, already Tonyn's political enemies, were said to have backed Bryan.[42]

The War Years, 1775–1782

Floridians knew about the discontent in the other British North American colonies as quickly and frequently as the mails arrived. And while some members of the Council had quarrels with Governor Tonyn, and were soon viewed by him as potential rebels, there is no evidence of any interest in rebellion among East Florida's residents, whatever relatives in Georgia or South Carolina might have been doing.

The American Rebellion hit home in the summer of 1775 when an American privateer captured a ship off St. Augustine and the first refugees from the "liberty boys" began to enter Florida. Too, in July Col. John Stuart, Superintendent for Indian Affairs for the Southern District, took up residence in St. Augustine and began to work to keep the Indians neutral in the evolving quarrels further north. On 1 October, slightly less than half of the garrison was sent to Williamsburg, Virginia, leaving St. Augustine with ninety men and smaller groups at New Smyrna, Matanzas, the Cowford on the St. Johns River, and various watchtowers and observation posts along the coast. The *St. Lawrence*, an armed schooner, and a troop of fifty Indian warriors soon arrived to partially make up the gap in defensive forces caused by the halving of the garrison.[43]

Seeing an opportunity in the unrest further north, in November Governor Tonyn caused a proclamation to be printed in Georgia, offering security, fertile land, and a ten-year tax exemption to any Loyalists who moved to Florida.[44] Not long after, Capt. John Baker's seventy-man "patriot" raiding party attacked Jermyn Wright's "fort" and plantations on the north side of the St. Marys River, giving the lie to Tonyn's promise of security.[45]

Governor Tonyn responded to the escalating disturbances in Georgia and South Carolina and to reports of raids along the St. Marys frontier by issuing orders beginning on 2 February 1776 that gradually placed Florida on a war footing. Fixed defenses were repaired and various measures taken to prevent surprise attacks by small groups of raiders. By the middle of the summer, the St. Johns River had become a sort of moat, with all cattle and boats (at night) removed to its eastern side.[46] Militia companies and Lt. Col. Thomas Browne's Florida Rangers were also formed. Mounted and lightly armed, the 130 Rangers included free persons of color and Seminole scouts, as well as a core of poorer Loyalist white refugees from the colonies to the north. A census for the militia companies (taken in March 1776) showed that the St. Marys and Nassau Rivers had forty-two white men fit for military duty (between the ages of sixteen and fifty years), the St. Johns had fifty-three, and New Smyrna had two hundred. From this potential, Tonyn formed two companies of militia on the St. Johns, and one at New Smyrna. At St. Augustine, he organized four white and four Black (pardo, i.e., mulatto) companies, each consisting of twenty-five men and six officers. A report on slaves who could be trusted with firearms was also prepared.[47]

The Americans generally held the military initiative during 1776–1778. In the spring and summer of 1776 and 1777, they launched raids on plantations on the St. Marys River. In May 1777, Col. Samuel Elbert briefly seized Amelia Island. In June 1778, the 900-man vanguard of a 3,000-man force struck into northern Florida, but a mixed Seminole and East Floridian force turned them back at the battle of Alligator Bridge. American privateers occasionally intercepted ships trying to enter St. Augustine harbor. East Florida's principal initiative was to send Browne's Rangers into Georgia to steal cattle, thus continuing by other means a supply pattern of some standing. In their most significant action, in March 1778 the Rangers captured and burned Fort Barrington, thirty miles up the Altamaha.[48]

A cause for unease during these years was the growing number of French and American prisoners housed at St. Augustine. Lacking both space and men to keep them under strict guard, Governor Tonyn allowed them to live on parole in the town. These men rented rooms and survived as best they could, sometimes with charitable help from local residents, including Loyalists in exile. Tonyn exchanged them to the West Indies as quickly as he could.[49]

Florida's military situation changed dramatically with suc-cessful British operations against Savannah in the fall of 1778. Florida mustered some one thousand men (a sign of how many Loyalists had taken refuge in the colony by then) in November. One column looted its way to Midway, while another did the same as far as Sunbury, whose fort was not captured. A force formed from the other two then took the Sunbury fort and moved on to Savannah, which had surrendered in December. With Georgia again under British control, any danger of an American invasion of East Florida ended.

For the rest of the war, St. Augustine underwent the strains, and gains, of being the home base for privateers operating against American, French, and Spanish shipping. Only a Span-ish privateer raid on New Smyrna in the fall of 1779 and rumors of Spanish invasion plans in 1780 and 1781 disturbed the local tranquility.[50]

Further afield, the Creek continued contacts with Cuba. Cu-ban fishermen continued to fish along the west coast and in the Keys. The Cubans told the Creek that a great Spanish fleet would soon attack the Floridas, as indeed Bernardo de Gálvez did at Baton Rouge (1779), Mobile (1780), and Pensacola (1781). Gálvez tried without success to develop an alliance with the Creek both in support of his Gulf Coast operations and in anticipation of an attack on East Florida.[51]

The war's non-military effects on Florida were threefold. Loy-alist refugees swelled its population, defensive considerations caused the population to cluster around St. Augustine, and the principal economic activity shifted from cultivating indigo to the production of naval stores. Cattle raising for hides continued as a secondary economic activity.

The ability of East Florida to field a thousand men in the fall of 1778 was due to the sudden rise in Loyalist refugees in that year and the more gradual increase in the colony's permanent population during the previous two years as propertied Loyalists took refuge there. An influx in the spring of 1778 consisted of 350 Palatines from upland South Carolina, perhaps one hundred "Scopholites" from the 96 District in western South Carolina, and a few men from David Fanning and Ambrose Mill's North Carolina Loyalists. Some of these men had families and were granted lands proportionate to their means, but many ended up in the South Carolina Volunteers and eventually returned north to their homes.[52] Historian Wilbur H. Siebert thought that as many as seven thousand refugees reached Florida in 1778, but that seems doubtful. Whatever the actual numbers, the population of East Florida rose during this part of the war from about three thousand to about five thousand, of whom at least one thousand were whites and three thousand were persons of African descent.[53] Two results followed. Governor Tonyn secured permission for the residents to elect an Assembly (lower house) and, once in session in March 1781, the Assembly and the governor and Council fell into a nasty dispute over provisions of the slave code that ended with the settlers getting the tougher laws they wanted.[54]

The men who settled in East Florida during the war did so under a new land policy. Aware that the old headright and Order in Council system had produced little settlement in East Florida, the British Government attempted in 1774 to install a system of auction sales, but then reversed itself by another decree of 5 July 1775 in anticipation of a Loyalist influx. Quitrents were waved for ten years. This new system came into effect in Florida in November 1775 and was widely reported in Georgia and South Carolina. But since existing grants under Orders in Council were not nullified, the refugees found that much of the better land in the colony was claimed, but not occupied, by the holders of such orders. In response to a petition, Governor Tonyn made limited grants and asked for and eventually got a new order from the Board of Trade and Plantations that grants not taken up within three years of issue would revert to the Crown and could be regranted in blocks of up to five hundred acres, subject to the original grantee's assertion of claim and action to make it good. Although we lack the minutes of the East Florida Council for the years 1776–1780 and thus cannot trace granting activity, we know that the large Order-in-Council grants continued to be a problem in 1781. Still, fragmentary evidence suggests that refugees of means, especially those with slaves, were able to obtain grants proportionate to their means.[55]

A second effect of the war was to concentrate the population

around St. Augustine. Until 1778, the insecurity of the St. Marys
and Nassau River areas discouraged settlement there, as did Tonyn's decrees that cattle be removed. Independent of the war,
discontent with conditions at New Smyrna caused some indentured servants to flee for St. Augustine in the spring of 1777, only
to be returned under court order. However, when most of the
four hundred or so surviving Minorcans moved to St. Augustine
in the late summer, they were allowed to stay. The men took up
military duties; the women and children suffered privation.[56] Additional persons, mostly slaves and their overseers, fled from the
same area in 1779 when a Spanish privateer raided New Smyrna,
William Watson's farm, and Captain Bisset's indigo works. Bisset
resettled his slaves on Pablo Creek, north of St. Augustine.[57]
That same year, former residents of the St. Marys frontier began
to reoccupy their holdings. The town of St. Marys, on the Georgia
side of the river, was founded in 1780.[58]

The third effect of the war was a change in East Florida's principal product. The Spanish raid on the Halifax and Tomoka Rivers in 1779 destroyed most of the flourishing indigo plantations
in Florida. Bisset and other owners removed their slaves to the
area around St. Augustine and made no effort to replace or repair
vats and buildings damaged by the raid. Instead, slaves were put
to tapping long-leaf pines for the sap from which tar, turpentine,
and pitch were created.[59] Stimulated by a rebate, production rose
from 190 barrels of tar and 56 of turpentine in 1776 to 8,100 barrels of tar and 1,980 barrels of turpentine in 1778. By 1783, some
20,000 barrels of both were being exported.[60] By comparison,
other exports did not rise as rapidly, or at all.

The cases of Denys Rolle and Chief Justice James Hume can
serve to illustrate how the richer planters developed their holdings in the midst of these events. After Rolle returned to East
Florida in 1778, he rebuilt his herds, instituted rice cultivation
using slave expertise, and exported both orange juice (from wild
groves on his properties) and turpentine.[61] Mr. Hume bought
William Drayton's Oak Park plantation and soon obtained a
2,500-acre grant (Cypress Grove Plantation) and an additional
1,300 acres in three tracts. He had more than 50,000 pine trees
boxed and producing naval stores by 1783. His second most im-

portant products were citrus fruit and juices from both wild and planted groves. Since his holdings included swamps, he evidently intended to cultivate rice but had not done so by the end of British rule.[62]

Transition

A final phase of the history of British East Florida opened in July 1782 when Loyalist evacuees from Savannah—including 200 Choctaw and 150 Creek—began to reach the colony. They were followed by other Loyalists from across Georgia and, beginning in November, by Charlestonians and other refugees from South Carolina. By the summer of 1783, some 5,090 whites and 8,285 African slaves had flooded in, pushing East Florida's population to 6,090 whites and 11,285 slaves (Table 9.4).[63] The first arrivals received three months' rations, but later ones got as little as six weeks' supply. Food shortages quickly developed, and were made worse in January 1783 by a ten-day Indian conference that brought some 2,000 mostly Creek Indians to St. Augustine in search of information about what would happen to their trade when Great Britain evacuated the province. (Tonyn agreed to Panton, Leslie and Company opening a trading post at St. Marks.)[64] Supplies from New York eventually relieved the food shortage.[65]

The refugees were lured by the reversal of the initial order to prepare East Florida for evacuation and the subsequent pledge

TABLE 9.4   Royalist Refugees and Slaves Entering East Florida, 1782–1783

Dates	Georgia White	Georgia Slave	Carolina White	Carolina Slave	Total White	Total Slave
July–November 1782	782	1,659	1,383	1,681	2,165	3,340
November–December 1782	911	1,786	1,517	1,823	2,428	3,609
December 1782–April 1783					497	1,336
Totals					5,090	8,285

Source: Siebert, *Loyalists,* 2:130–31.

by the local officials to try to get the Crown to agree not to cede the province to Spain. The angry demands of the East Florida Assembly and among refugees on the St. Marys River led by John Cruden forced this local initiative.[66] It was a fruitless quest. The governments of George III and Charles III did not change the terms of the treaty. Still, the illusion that East Florida was a safe haven for Loyalist refugees lasted until 21 April 1783 when Governor Tonyn issued the official proclamation of the cession, together with instructions that everyone who wished to evacuate should register and wind up his affairs. Even so, rumors persisted that Florida might be traded for Gibraltar, giving at least some refugees additional hope, while others reacted with anger at the thought they would again have to start anew elsewhere in the British Empire.[67] Delays in shipping put off the day of departure into the spring and summer of 1784.

Thus lulled with what proved to be false hopes, many of the refugees plunged into securing land, building houses, and pursuing wealth using the labor of their slaves, if they had any. St. Johns Town, built on Hester's Bluff on the St. Johns River, and Hillsborough on the St. Marys River bloomed from one or two houses to three hundred, in the former case. Land grants allowed men like the former Lt. Governor of Georgia, John Graham, to begin the cultivation of rice, indigo, and maize. Other wealthy men like Robert Cunningham, former deputy surveyor general of South Carolina, and his cousin William Cunningham bought land and cleared enough to get a crop to feed their households and slaves. The government placed refugees lacking Graham's two hundred slaves (or comparable resources) as tenants. However, many simply squatted on land already owned but not being worked. According to one account, the tenants were expected to pay one eighth of their maize harvest to the owner, but many were charity cases, who were allowed to live however they could.[68] Almost without exception, the lands occupied by the refugees were along one of the waterways, especially the St. Johns River and its tributaries. The principal products of the newly established Loyalists were naval stores and lumber.[69]

But not all of the refugees took up the hard work of rebuilding their fortunes. Some crowded into the towns and engaged in drinking, gambling, and generally disorderly behavior, so much so that the East Florida Assembly passed new laws regulating the selling of alcohol, gambling, and the price of bread.[70] Still others became thieves and then bandits once the transfer to Spain was announced in April 1783. Notable among the latter were Daniel McGirtt and John Linder, Jr., who were briefly in British custody in the fall of 1783.[71]

Although the order was given in April 1783, the British evacuation of East Florida did not begin until that fall and was not in full swing until the spring and summer of 1784. Meanwhile, Americans claiming slaves tried without success to recover them from British officers who had removed them from Georgia and the Carolinas; a few of the provincial troops who had been brought to St. Augustine mutinied in May; an expedition needlessly captured New Providence, the Bahamas, from the Spaniards (diplomats in Europe already had agreed to give them to Great Britain); and new trade agreements with the Indians were negotiated.[72] Then in the fall most of the regular soldiers were evacuated, to be replaced within a few months by two troops of locally raised cavalry intended to patrol the countryside against the "banditti." And patrol they did because the transports did not begin arriving until April 1784. The Spaniards chose to continue to use these patrols.

The Indians made it clear that they were not happy with the prospective British evacuation. Some Creek demanded to join the evacuation, but the British discouraged that.[73] Cowkeeper and some of his allies took the attitude that the British had no right to give away *their* country and announced that they would assume full title when the British left, and that they would kill any Spaniard who appeared outside of the defenses of St. Augustine.[74] Such bold talk was soon given its opportunity.

Spanish governor Manuel de Zéspedes, five hundred soldiers and officials, and thirteen ships arrived off the St. Augustine bar on 27 June 1784, but required another two weeks to lighter supplies across it. Zéspedes took formal possession of the fort on 12 July amidst a fifteen-gun salute, followed the next day by a *Te Deum* mass and a ball. On 14 and 26 July, the Spaniards issued orders that, among other things, sought to register everyone of African descent, slave as well as free, and informed the English that they had until 19 March 1785 to leave if they wished to do so. Those who wanted to stay were told the terms under which this would be allowed. Zéspedes also announced a safe conduct out of the province for all who had disturbed the peace or committed felonies, if they presented themselves.[75] That order and the orders for those of African descent to register were intended to restore a well-ordered society. The British had freed some slaves because of service in the Loyalist cause, men who had fled to Florida to avoid re-enslavement by the victorious Americans. Others were runaways hoping to take advantage of Spanish laws granting sanctuary on religious grounds, and still others were escaped slaves trying to flee or pass as free persons.[76] Sorting out these claims was essential if free persons and slaves were to be distinguished.

In general, the protracted British evacuation went smoothly thanks to the professionalism of both Spanish and British officials, but there were a few problems. The bandits continued to steal livestock and slaves and to harass the evacuees gathering at Amelia Island in spite of Anglo-Spanish patrols and the arrests of Daniel McGirtt, William Cunningham, Stephen Mayfield, and others said to be their leaders.[77] And a group of Loyalists made one final futile effort to obtain an autonomous province in northeast Florida.[78]

The Indians were brought to accept Spanish rule. Gifts given to Indians who visited St. Augustine and attended two major conferences on 30 September and 8 December 1784 helped to achieve this, but what turned the tide was Zéspedes's decision *temporarily* to allow Panton, Leslie and Company to continue to supply Indian needs from trading posts on the St. Johns, at Apalachee Bay (St. Marks), and at Pensacola. Carlos Howard, Thomas Brown, and John Leslie (of Panton, Leslie) helped bring about this result, which preserved British influence. Panton's supplying of goods for gifting, on credit, also won favor from Zéspedes, who had arrived without any gifts for the Indians![79] For the Creek, this trade was a vital alternative to falling again into dependency on and eventually losing land to traders from Carolina and Georgia. The American Revolution had cut off that former dependence. The Spaniards seem not to have recognized that the eventual fate of their colony depended on the success of the Creek in this matter.

March 19, 1785 came and went without the evacuations being completed. Zéspedes issued a new order allowing the British until 18 July 1785 to sell and leave, but few of the incoming Spanish soldiers and officials were interested in rural properties.[80]

When the final British transport left the St. Marys River on 19 November 1785, it left a province described as in a state of near total desolation, "a desert guarded by Spanish Troops." St. Johns Town, created to house the refugees of 1782–1783, had been completely taken down, its houses shipped in pieces to other places.[81] A report of November 1784 stated that only twenty families lived at Amelia, and another sixty or so ("men without God or King" who ought to be expelled)[82] between the St. Marys and the St. Johns Rivers. Only Francisco Xavier Sánchez's thousand-acre ranch with thirty-four slaves, forty horses, and eight to nine hundred head of cattle, and Francisco Felipe Fatio's plantation still existed on the St. Johns itself, according to another report.[83] Only five "British" holders of large properties remained. They were Francis Philip Fatio, Jesse Fish (with 1,216 acres in five parcels), Carlos Howard, John Leslie (who held some 12,820 acres in nineteen different plots for Panton, Leslie and Company), and John Hudson (who had forty-six slaves). Minorcans, Greeks, and Italians numbering some 460 worked mostly small garden plots near St. Augustine and engaged in shopkeeping, fishing, and a few crafts.[84]

The Second Spanish Tidewater Frontier, 1784–1790

Spanish resumption of control of peninsular Florida occurred in the context of a larger strategic contest with the new United States. Because of its victories on the Gulf Coast and the British cession of West as well as East Florida, Spain claimed most of the Indian territory west of the British proclamation line of 1763. The United States disputed that claim because of its treaty with Great Britain in 1782 (see Figure 9.4).[85] The Creek challenged both claims. Alexander McGillivray, the nominal leader of the Creek Confederation in the 1780s, rather skillfully led Creek

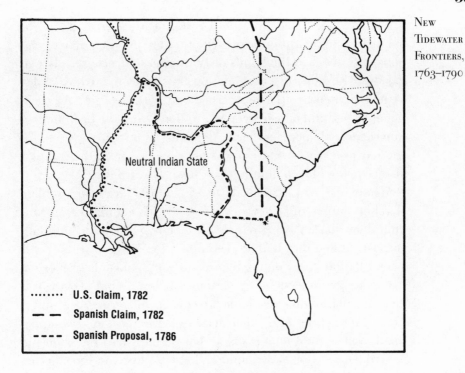

Figure 9.4. Spanish territorial claims, 1783. BASED ON
SAMUEL F. BEMIS, *Pinckney's Treaty* (NEW HAVEN, CONN.: YALE
UNIVERSITY PRESS, 1960), MAP 3.E. BY PERMISSION OF YALE
UNIVERSITY PRESS.

countermoves, some armed and some diplomatic. His maneuvering was complicated by shifting Spanish policy. Spain centralized its relationships with the Creek and other southeastern tribes at New Orleans and, reluctantly, allowed Panton, Leslie and Company to continue to serve the Creek via stores at St. Marks (now placed in the province of West Florida) and Pensacola.[86] This impermanence forced the company to do Spain's bidding and allowed the Spaniards to assist or impede Creek resistance to the Americans according to Spain's needs. The Spanish game was to negotiate in New York and Madrid while keeping American settlement from encroaching on the territory that the Creek and Spaniards claimed. They hoped to do this without involving Spain in a war in defense of Creek boundaries, which were further east than those that Spain claimed.

Seemingly isolated from the Creek and their struggle by the Spanish administrative arrangement that put managing relations with them in the hands of Louisiana's governor, as late as 1795 East Florida's external relationships appeared to be a replay of those of the 1740s (i.e., concerned only with Georgia). An occasional Creek raid on isolated "plantations" and the beginning of American settlement on the St. Marys River in 1788 were reminders that in fact East Florida was not divorced from the complex history being played out on its northwestern frontier.

Meanwhile, in East Florida the Spaniards faced the problem of repopulating the tidewater frontier with enough Europeans (and their Black slaves) to make the colony more than a military outpost. At first they had no clear policy for doing so. Table 9.5 is a compilation of the population records of Spanish East Florida, 1785–1814, as understood by various scholars. What is evident is that the population available to engage in agriculture, naval stores production, and other activities prior to 1790 was quite small, especially if note is made that perhaps half the whites in the 1785–1786 count were children between five and fifteen years of age. A smaller percentage of children probably existed among the slaves. That is, at most perhaps four hundred civilian adults of both races and sexes were available in 1785 for labor outside of the home and the garrison. We know that most of these people lived in St. Augustine and did not venture far from its walls. Only a few owned rural property or slaves. In various ways, the majority depended on the garrison's payroll (*situado*).[87]

This sparse civilian population and its limited economic potential were the principal challenge that the new regime faced. Francis Felipe Fatio (a Swiss) summed the problem up with his observation that "If His Catholic Majesty does not wish to consider this province as anything more than an [North] African presidio, it would be useless to discuss the matter, for population is requisite."[88] Both he and Governor Zéspedes stressed the possibilities of exploiting the colony's forest resources, the abandoned plantation fields' "fertile soil[s]," the pastures, and the marine resources of its rivers and shores. Both hammered the theme that settlers were necessary, and suggested a proportional-to-means land grant policy. The alternative, Zéspedes warned, was a colony dependent on the Crown for income (he asked for fifty thousand pesos!) and its American neighbors for food and other necessities.[89]

As in the Natchez district of Louisiana, so in East Florida religious toleration of a sort and generous land grants were critical to keeping the English Loyalists and their resources in the province. A decree dated 5 April 1786 allowed Anglo-American settlers to remain if they swore an oath of allegiance and agreed to have their children raised as Roman Catholics under the instruction of Irish priests to be sent by the government. Floridanos and the widows and orphans of men who had served in Florida before 1763 were allowed to claim properties once held and were given preferences for new grants sized to provide support for modest households.[90] There were only forty-seven Protestants (among eighty-six foreigners) in Florida at the time, and at least twenty of them were soon baptized into the Roman church, often prior to marriage. Typical was Mary Perry, who became María Dolores Concepción upon her marriage to Ramón de Fuentes, the chief apothecary of the royal hospital. Her widowed mother had property and social standing among the Anglos who remained. The fifty-one Floridanos in fourteen families with eighty-two slaves included a large number of women from old families such as the Mirandas and Averos. These women married the new officials, thus linking the past and future. In sum, the decree did little more than allow the confirmation of some existing titles. Zéspedes and his officials spent the next three years sorting out claims to properties in and around St. Augustine.

Provincial inspection tours in 1784, 1786–1787, and 1788 served to reinforce Spanish opinions that some Anglo-American residents north of the St. Johns River were more of a danger than a benefit to the province because of their undisciplined ways, including smuggling. Totaling 90 percent non-Catholic, with 80 percent or more born in the middle and southern colonies, these mostly English-speaking residents generally held about ten acres and no slaves. They shifted their fields as the soil lost fertility. Some liked being beyond effective Spanish control. But not all were so restless or poor. A petition for confirmation of land holdings dated November 1790 listed ten Anglo-American men living

TABLE 9.5 Population Estimates, St. Augustine and East Florida, ca. 1785–1814

Year	Whites	Garrison	Freed Persons	Total Free including Garrison	Slaves	Total City including Garrison	Country-side	Total Pop.
ca. 1785[1]	781	E 450	?	1,231	461?[22]		(E 300)[3]	E 1,992
1786 City[4]	772?	E 450	?	772 (No garrison)	213	E 1,435	E 257	1,692
1787[5]	451	454[6]	?	905?	490	E 1,395		
1788[7]			63	1,141	588			1,729
1790[8]								2,032
1793[9]	1,607	430[10]	126	[2,163]	1,527		E 2,442[12]	3,690
1797 City[11]	421	430	85	936	312	1,248		3,690
1804 City[13]				947	538	1,485		3,081
1814[14]	801	501[15]	128	1,430	1,651		2,346	
1814 2nd[16]	840	[E 500]			E 540	1,383 (No garrison)		3,729 [4,233 with garrison]
1814[17]	590?	234	E 69	824		1,307 (No garrison)	E 1,774	3,315
1814 City[18]	294	504		867	440	1,307		3,081

[1]Landers, "Black Society," Table 2.2. Garrison figure estimated from Bermudez, "The Situado," 2, for 1787. Dunkle, "Population Change," 14, Table III, gives 616 whites in a total of 881, excluding the garrison. He dates this to ca. 1785.

[2]Persons of African descent; overstates slaves by a small number. Dunkle, "Population Change," 14, Table III, gives 275 slaves.

[3]Miller, *Neponuceno de Quesada*, 7, following Dunkle, "Population Change," 13–17, estimates this number living in rural areas. Her total is 1,703 persons, based on the lower number of whites / free persons that Dunkle uses for the Hassett census.

[4]Johnson, "Spanish St. Augustine Community," 88–91. She revised the Hassett "census" used by Dunkle, "Population Change," 14–15, and Table IV (who gives 660 whites in a total population of 1,703) to add 120 additional persons to the total free population. The "census" was taken to see who might need schooling and so excluded government officials and a few others that she has added back in.

[5]AGI, SD 2668, No. 17, Zéspedes to Marques of Sonora, 12 May 1787, as printed in Whitaker, *Commercial Policy*, 55. Tornero and Romero Cabot used some of this data for an entry for 1786, but that is incorrect. Tornero, *Relaciones*, 32, gives 1,408 as the total.

[6]Bermudez, "The Situado," 2.

[7]Landers, "Black Society," Table 2.2. Tornero, *Relaciones*, 32, gives 1,792, but only 1,729 on p. 35.

[8]Tornero, *Relaciones*, 32.

[9]Landers, "Black Society," Table 2.2. Romero Cabot, "Los Ultimos Años," 15, 25, gives 3,260 total, with 106 free persons of color in a total free population of 1,733, and 1,547 slaves. He is following Tornero, *Relaciones*, 32. Poitrineau, "Demography and Political Destiny," 426, found 1,302 whites, 468 garrison members, 128 free persons of color, and 1,661 slaves, for 3,561 total [*sic!* 3,559].

[10]Landers, "Black Society," Table 2.2. Dunkle, "Population Change," 15, shows 438 soldiers. Poitrineau, "Demography and Political Destiny," 426, gives 468 soldiers.

[11]Dunkle, "Population Change," 17, Table V, sections for St. Augustine only. Tornero, *Relaciones*, 38–40, dates this count to 1793 and shows 2,012 persons in rural areas.

[12]Dunkle, "Population Change," 17, notes 202 persons in the Río del Norte area and 143 in the Río Matanzas, south of the city, as part of this rural total.

[13]Tornero, *Relaciones*, 38–40; Romero Cabot, "Los Ultimos Años," 15, 25. Romero Cabot shows a total for the province of 4,441. Dunkle, "Population Change," 19–20, gives 923 free persons and 424 slaves, for a total of 1,347 in St. Augustine but is not certain of the date of the count he used.

[14]Landers, "Black Society," Table 2.2.

[15]Bermudez, "The Situado," 2–4.

[16]Dunkle, "Population Change," 20–21. His city total is too low because it does not include the garrison.

[17]Marchena, "Guarniciones . . . en Florida Oriental," 111–14.

[18]Tornero, *Relaciones*, 38–40.

on the St. Marys and Nassau Rivers who each claimed two hundred or more acres, and another three who claimed one hundred acres each on the basis of headrights. These thirteen households held sixty-four whites and forty-eight slaves. Another important group of Anglo-Americans lived on the St. Johns near Fatio's "New Switzerland" plantation, with its dock, turpentine still, and trade privileges (Fatio was allowed to trade with the United States in his own bilander, *Condesa de Gálvez*).[91]

Whether men without large households or with many dependents, most Anglo-Americans indicated that they would not improve their holdings until they had secure land titles and free trade. The inspections also showed that the state of religion was poor in spite of the valiant labors of the four priests assigned to the province.[92] Separate reports decried the poor quality and declining effective number of the soldiers stationed at St. Augustine, which was used as a penalty box for troublesome soldiers of the Third Battalion of the Infantry Regiment of Santiago de Cuba and the Hibernia Regiment of Havana.[93]

Schemes for fostering Catholic immigration from Europe and the United States, while not as numerous as those being proposed for Louisiana, were also scouted but came to nothing.[94]

Land grant data show the same thing: almost no new settlement. U.S.-confirmed Spanish land grants dating from 1787 through 1790 number thirteen, totaling just over 10,000 acres. They ranged in size from 10 to 2,600 acres. All were given on a headright basis, so far as can be determined.[95] Examples include John Andrews, Sr, a British-era settler who continued to work land on the North River–Guana Creek neck, married Catalina Pons (a Minorcan) and obtained preliminary recognition of his holdings in 1790; and William Pengree, a British planter who returned in 1787 and obtained 2,600 acres (in four properties on the west side of the St. Johns River at Doctor's Lake) because of his wife, child and forty-eight slaves.[96] But Pengree is the exceptional case in this early period. There were probably other grants.

The other part of the economic development problem concerned trade regulation and volume. A decree of 1783 allowed the export of local products to Havana under what were supposed to be liberal terms expanded by the 1786 decree's ten year tax and

tithe exemptions on the products of new immigrants' labors. In
fact, legal commerce involved two to four American ships a year
trading with Havana under Spanish colors and using St. Augustine as an intermediate stop on one or more legs of the voyage.
Complicating the situation was Panton, Leslie and Company's
monopoly of the pelt trade with the Indians, which soon expanded to include the supply of St. Augustine's slaughterhouse
(a monopoly) with cattle from a ranch at Concepción (south of
modern Palatka) and from the Seminole. The company also enjoyed duty free importation of goods for its trades. Zéspedes was
alleged to favor the company because its agent "was careful to
anticipate the governor's gratitude and to keep it alive as the occasion required."[97] What Zéspedes told the Crown was that free
trade with the United States was needed for at least ten years to
attract and reward colonists.[98] In Spain, the Chamber of Commerce of Barcelona gave its opinion that Florida could be supplied under the *comercio libre* system if the ships were allowed
to carry two-thirds of their outbound cargoes (by tonnage) to
Havana and return from St. Augustine via the United States to
pick up cargoes of rice, flour, and non-manufactured goods. But
José Salcedo suggested that East Florida should be given back to
the British, to save money![99]

That is to say, Zéspedes and the residents slipped back into
old politico-economic patterns of dependence while waiting for
the Crown to authorize free trade with the United States or un-
restricted immigration (or some other panacea) for the province's lack of attractiveness to Spanish-speaking immigrants.

As Madrid was considering what to do about the problem of
the economic and demographic development of East Florida, it
was also confronting a rapidly changing international situation
that amounted to Spain's diplomatic isolation in the face of other
states that coveted the Floridas. The French Revolution began in
July 1789 and quickly lessened the chances that France would
support Spain in its ongoing contest with Great Britain. This became clear when the Nootka Sound incident blew up into a full
crisis in August 1790.[100] At the same time, the United States was
ratifying its new constitution (in 1789) and George Washington
was organizing an effective federal government. Among the Fed-

eral government's early achievements was inducing McGillivray and other Creek leaders to visit New York to sign a treaty settling boundary and trade issues. In this treaty, the Creek finally ceded the disputed Oconee lands to Georgia, but retained hunting rights on the land between the Altamaha and St. Marys rivers. The U.S. government promised them a governmentally sponsored trade. Georgia's land speculators and merchants like Samuel Hammond, who had hoped to have the Creek to themselves, were disappointed by this assertion of the Federal government's authority over Indian affairs.[101] But the Treaty of New York proved stillborn. Neither the Creek nor Georgia's frontiersmen nor the U.S. Congress followed through on its various provisions.

The Treaty of New York, perhaps even more than the immediate effects of the French Revolution, pointed the way to what was to come: Creek subordination to the U.S. government and the erosion and eventual loss of Spain's position in East Florida. Moreover, Americans had begun moving into the old "debatable land" between the Altamaha and St. Marys Rivers in 1788, founding St. Patrick on the latter (St. Marys City after 1792). They looked across the St. Marys River at the higher, more fertile ground and deserted sites of British-era plantations. What they saw excited their cupidity but also alarmed them. Spanish East Florida had a significant minority of free Black persons at St. Augustine, while other Blacks, who appeared to be free, lived with the Seminoles. Both were a danger to the slave system practiced in Georgia. What Spaniards and Americans did about these and other issues that Spanish Florida created are the subject of the next chapter.

10.

The American Frontier Envelops East Florida, 1790–1821

The Nootka Sound crisis of 1790 caused the newly arrived governor of East Florida, Juan Nepomuceno de Quesada y Arrocha, to review his defenses. These defenses were, as he and his engineer Mariano de la Roque said, in terrible shape and not extensive enough. The garrison was too small and dispirited because the *situado* had not come since 1787. The only bright spot was Carlos Howard's small militia among the settlers on the Nassau and St. Marys Rivers.[1] Fortunately the crisis passed, but East Florida's fundamental vulnerability to attack from and absorption into the United States, or less certainly from the British or French Empires, remained. Against long odds, Spain retained its possession during the next thirty-one years in spite of invasions in 1793–1796, 1812–1814, and 1817–1818, and in spite of mounting U.S. diplomatic pressure and Florida's economic dependence on the United States, especially for food. In holding Florida, Spain benefited from the complex international situation created by the French Revolution and its wars. To strengthen its position, Spain somewhat paradoxically allowed an influx of English-speaking settlers and, in 1816–1818, generously rewarded men who served it during the various invasions, in both cases by the granting of the better lands in northeast Florida, along the east coast as far south as Indian River, and in Alachua. This left the rich soils of the Tallahassee and Madison hills for Americans to claim under the terms of the Adams-Onís Treaty of 1819, which became a fact on the ground in July 1821.

New Vigor, 1790–1793

In the aftermath of the Nootka Sound crisis, Spain adopted an increasingly aggressive stance in the Southeast even as its agents in Europe discussed with France the retrocession of Louisiana.[2] This stance involved renewed efforts to populate Louisiana and the Floridas and to organize the Native Americans to resist American advances without, however, drawing Spain into a war with the United States. The population policy was especially problematic because it relied on Americans whose principal interest was in land, not loyal service to the Spanish Crown. The Indian policy, by its very nature, could do little to materially improve Spain's strategic position vis-à-vis the United States. Moreover, it was complicated by continuing unofficial (but never discouraged) British Loyalist designs to seize Louisiana, designs that culminated during the War of 1812 but that well before then had again brought William Augustus Bowles and his merchant backers into Creek country. But as will appear below, the first major threats to Spanish sovereignty arose from Edmond C. E. Genêt's activities on behalf of French imperialism in 1793–1794.

The first sign of the new, more aggressive Spanish attitude was a decree of 20 November 1790 offering land grants under a headright system and the religious terms of 1786 in return for an oath of loyalty to the Spanish Crown. Residents who had not taken the oath were given two months to do so and to select the parcels they wished to claim. They were only required to occupy one in order to claim them all. In effect, this decree confirmed all English land grants that were still being worked. Subsequent decrees allowed importation of goods for personal use under a tariff of 6 percent. Irish priests and two rural hermitages for their use (in effect, new church parishes) were ordered as well. The hermitages seem never to have been built and at least one of the priests, Father Michael Crosby, never left St. Augustine.[3] And a

📖 **245**

The American
Frontier
Envelops
East Florida,
1790–1821

new effort was made in 1791 to get Floridanos in Cuba to return by offering, among other things, compensation for formerly owned properties then held by third parties and, for widows, two reales a day for subsistence and houses built at royal expense, repayable over ten years at 5 percent interest. The Crown also ordered the public auction of all town lots and houses "abandoned" by the English.[4]

The result of the two decrees was that "within months" a spurt of Anglo-American immigration added perhaps 1,200 persons, net (80 percent of them slaves) to the province's census by 1793. The new settlers were not allowed to claim land on the St. Marys River because the Spaniards had suspicions about their loyalty.[5] The United States later confirmed ninety-nine headright grants totaling 55,980 acres issued between 1791 and 1793, mostly from 1791 to 1792. The majority were under 400 acres, although the range varied from 15 to 7,034 acres. They constituted a quarter of all U.S.-confirmed Second Spanish Period headright land grants.[6]

Capping off the new land policy, in 1793 the governor began to issue sawmill grants of a square of land up to twenty-five square leagues (roughly sixteen thousand acres). The grantee had to erect a mill but did not get title to the land except at the site of the mill. Over time, these grants benefited a few already wealthy men like John McQueen and George J. F. Clarke, and increased the colony's exports; apparently, however, the grants did little to bring new settlers, or even more slaves, into the colony.[7]

Among the immigrants of the early 1790s were John McIntosh (the younger), who became a magistrate for the area near his plantation at the Cowford; John McQueen, who amassed as many as ten thousand acres in various grants and purchases; and Spicer Christopher, who owned sixty-four slaves, most of Talbot Island, and property on the St. Marys and St. Johns Rivers by his death in 1806. More typical was Nicolás Sánchez, a returning Floridano, who obtained two hundred headright acres initially but later enlarged his holdings to more than six hundred acres at Diego Plains, where his ancestors had run cattle and maintained a small fort. Also typical was John Simon, with two hundred acres on Potsburg Creek near modern Jacksonville. There were also men fleeing the law or their debts, like John Sanders and

John Peter Wagnon. Whether wealthy or fugitive, some of the Anglo-Americans soon found life under Spanish rule more regulated than they cared for.[8]

On a different front, on 23 June 1791 Spain agreed with Georgia to end the granting of sanctuary to runaway slaves from the United States in exchange for the return of Spanish deserters. This decision was intended to end an important source of friction because the Americans did not like having a slave sanctuary on their border. Both sides soon ignored the agreement and the Seminole, who provided an alternative sanctuary, were not bound by it in any event.[9]

Freer trade, the long-desired complement to generous land grants, did not come until 1793 on the eve of Spain's entry into the war against Revolutionary France for its execution of Louis XVI and then in part to put Panton, Leslie and Company's trade on a permanent footing. Spain and Great Britain became allied against France later that year, making Panton's trade more acceptable. Meanwhile, petitions such as those from Luis Fatio (1790) and John McQueen, Miguel Isnardy, Andrew Atkinson, Jessie Fish, and others (1792) went to Madrid to point out the benefits East Florida, and the empire, would derive from commerce with all comers. The petitioners noted Louisiana's trade rule of 1782 (which allowed trade with France under low tariffs) and Florida's unrealized economic possibilities, which now included cotton as well as indigo, naval stores and timber, rice, citrus, and many lesser crops. They even suggested a free port at Fernandina on the northern tip of Amelia Island to attract American violators of U.S. tariffs. The Crown responded to the agitation for freer trade on 9 June 1793 with a decree that allowed "free trade" (*comercio libre*) subject to a revenue tariff and with the proviso that only locally produced goods could be taken into the Spanish empire. That is, East Florida could try its economic fortunes in the larger Atlantic world, but was not to become an avenue for thinly disguised smuggling *into* the Spanish empire. The result was "a growth without precedents" in the volume of trade and the nearly total absorption of Florida into the U.S. economic system. However, freer trade produced comparatively little growth in population.[10]

If there was any truth to the argument that free trade would stimulate immigration to bolster the colony's potential military manpower, these were timely steps. The U.S. Census of 1790 showed that Georgia already had 82,548 persons, of whom 29,264 were slaves. Tennessee counted 77,202 persons that year. Spanish East Florida had but 3,690 persons, including the garrison but excluding an unknown number of Native Americans and possibly some Anglo-American squatters.[11] This number is probably low, but even if twice as many people lived under Spanish rule (the Indians did not), East Florida still had less than a tenth of the population of Georgia, ominous odds at a time of increasingly aggressive American land hunger.

Further afield, in Louisiana, the Spaniards were backing away from their previous policy of urging the Creek to make and keep the peace with the United States. In 1792, Louisiana's new governor, the Baron Carondolet, instituted a policy of uniting the southeastern Indians against the Americans, of providing them with traders, and of building forts on the four high ground locations that were close to and that could potentially control the Mississippi.[12] He worked with William Panton to obtain Creek non-compliance with the Treaty of New York. For East Florida, the immediate consequence was that Panton had to move his store at Kings Ferry on the St. Marys to the site of Fort Pupo on the west side of the St. Johns. For some time, settlers on the St. Marys had feared the Indians who visited the store. Now rumors from Georgia threatened an attack because Panton allegedly had prevented peace with the Creek.[13] The St. Johns location was somewhat remote from any plantations.

But there was another reason for the Creek troubling the Georgia and Florida frontiers. William Augustus Bowles had returned to the Apalachicola River in August 1791 intent on establishing a trade that would displace Alexander McGillivray and Panton, Leslie and Company with himself and a trade sponsored by Miller, Bonnamy, and Company of New Providence, the Bahamas. He and his sponsors were part of a loosely defined group of Loyalists and imperialists who did not think that the Treaties of Paris of 1783 or the preliminary Anglo-American Treaty of 1782 were the last word on a British presence west of the Appalachian

Mountains. Never sanctioned by Whitehall, they were not discouraged either, a fact that gave their activity a certain boldness.[14]

Bowles reminded the Creek of their former relationship with the British and promised them unlimited trade with the Bahamas if they would throw off the Spaniards and Panton, Leslie and Company. His promises of abundant British goods won over enough Indians that in January 1792 he was able to threaten Panton's store and an invasion of East Florida. But the supplies that he expected did not arrive. Meanwhile, Governor Quesada sent a few soldiers to protect the store, instituted patrols on the St. Johns River, and put the Spanish post at St. Marks on alert. Bowles and a party of Indians duly raided Panton's warehouse at St. Marks and then attacked the Spanish fort. Bowles was then persuaded to visit New Orleans, ostensibly to obtain Spanish agreement to his trade. There he was arrested and eventually sent to Havana, Spain, and finally to exile in the Philippine Islands. One of his associates, George Wellbank, continued to work among the Creek during 1792 and early 1793 to persuade them to abandon Panton and the Spaniards. Other agents of the same New Providence merchants who had supported Bowles appeared in 1793, but were captured by Spanish patrols. In the end, even those Indians who had been Bowles's partisans went to St. Augustine to seek peace and gifts.[15] The whole episode revealed the lack of unity among the Creek and Seminole and thus the difficulty of using them as part of a Spanish strategy to contain U.S. expansion.

The French and American Challenges, 1793–1795

A new outbreak of border troubles in March 1793 turned into a major crisis that lasted into 1795 because Edmond C. E. Genêt, the French Republic's diplomatic representative to the United States, arrived at Charleston that spring and immediately began organizing an attack on Spanish Florida. Merchants like Samuel and Abner Hammond were drawn to it because Genêt's scheme offered an opportunity to strike at Panton, Leslie and Company. Land speculators saw an opportunity to overthrow U.S. protection of Creek lands. Discontented Anglo-American residents in northeast Florida saw an opportunity to throw off Spanish restrictions on their activities.

⊳ **249**

THE AMERICAN
FRONTIER
ENVELOPS
EAST FLORIDA,
1790–1821

The border crisis arose because northern tribes had won a victory over the American army under U.S. General Arthur St. Clair, and also because whites were grazing cattle in southwest Georgia close to Seminole towns. Excited by the news of the northern tribes' victory and angered at the same time by the white encroachments, some of the Seminole (or were they Creek?) attacked James Seagrove's store at Colerain, Georgia, killing two persons. Other Creek entered East Florida and stole horses, cattle, and slaves. Raiders also killed John Houston, a British-era settler on the St. Marys at Lofton's Bluff. But many Creek and James Seagrove, U.S. Indian agent for the area, wanted peace and would have arranged it in May or June had not the Georgia militia, mobilized after the first attacks, raided Indian towns. But Seagrove persisted and in November held a conference that eventually produced a peace agreement in April 1794.[16] Meanwhile, Carondolet and the major tribes signed the Treaty of Nogales (28 October 1793), creating his general alliance. The document pointedly did not allow for a war with the United States should it refuse to recognize Indian land claims.[17]

The Spanish responses to these new Indian raids were to demand restitution and to patrol the St. Marys frontier with mounted militiamen. They also restored Panton, Leslie and Company's store at Kings Ferry under the protection of a small garrison, which served as a warning to the Indians and the Georgians to keep the peace.

The proclamation of the war with France at St. Augustine on 9 June came in the midst of these local activities. Like the Baron Carondolet at New Orleans, Governor Juan Nepomuceno de Quesada at St. Augustine soon professed to see partisans of France among his subjects.[18]

Nepomuceno de Quesada's suspicions of his subjects seemed proven when on 30 December 1793 Ruben Pitcher revealed details of the plan that Genêt had developed with Samuel and Abner Hammond. Arrests on the night of 16 January 1794 and over the next few days brought John McIntosh, magistrate at the Cowford; Richard Lang; John Peter Wagnon; Abner Hammond and his father-in-law, William Jones, into Castillo de San Marcos as prisoners. William Plowden escaped to Georgia. Investigation revealed that the Hammonds planned to move supplies to the Cowford under cover of shipping food into Florida to meet local short-ages. Men enlisted in Georgia were promised French commissions upon entering Florida, a lot in St. Augustine and land in the coun-tryside, half of any prizes taken, and that East Florida would become an independent republic once the war was over. France would supply naval units to blockade harbors and would admin-ister the province until the end of the war. Tories, debtors, and others who had fled to East Florida from Georgia were promised pardons and respect for their properties. In short, the indepen-dent republic that the Loyalists had asked for in 1783–1784 would be created, ironically, under French auspices! As part of the plan, Panton, Leslie and Company stores would be destroyed.[19]

The arrests and other Spanish actions broke up the plot but also made the Anglo-American settlers even less politically reli-able. The conspirators' lengthy confinements in Spanish jails that year embittered most and set the stage for the invasion of Florida in 1795. Other recent immigrants to northeast Florida were angered by an order of 21 January 1794 that they remove themselves and their moveable property south (and east) of the St. Johns River. At least forty families returned to the United States rather than comply. Newly organized pardo (i.e., mulatto) militiamen from St. Augustine enforced this scorched-earth pol-icy, sending about 120 persons to crowd into St. Augustine, where they received government assistance. Rural development was set back and the Anglo stereotype of arbitrary, despotic, yet ineffec-tive Spanish government was confirmed. And the use of free per-sons of color to enforce government orders on white people was an affront to the race norms of many of the more recent immi-grants.[20]

Tensions continued high until June 1795 when decrees by Georgia's governor, George Mathews, seemed to calm the fron-tier. Meanwhile, three companies from the Regiment of Mexico arrived in St. Augustine in March. Col. Henry Gaither, of the U.S. Army, appeared at St. Marys City that same month with a small force and the purpose of enforcing U.S. neutrality. French support disappeared on 6 March 1794 when the new French agent to the United States, Jean Antoine Joseph Fauchet, dis-missed Genêt and forbade any French violations of American

🐚 **251**

THE AMERICAN
FRONTIER
ENVELOPS
EAST FLORIDA,
1790–1821

neutrality. However, French privateers continued to cruise the coast, intercepting Spanish ships.[21] And none of this deterred Elijah Clark from establishing his Trans-Oconee Republic that summer.[22] One way or another, some Georgians intended to push the Creek off the land.

Then in June, Richard Lang, released from prison in December 1794, invaded East Florida with his sons and a small party from Georgia. With help from nominally Spanish militiamen, who included American settlers arrested in 1794, they seized both Fort Juana and Fort St. Nicolas, the posts on either side of the St. Johns at the Cowford. The Spaniards armed the St. Augustine militia, including many free men of color, and with help from a British naval vessel retook Fort St. Nicolas (12 July). Many of the invaders fled to an unoccupied French defensive work on Amelia Island (built by the French early in July) from which they vainly sent messages to Charleston asking the French for help. On 2 August, Spanish troops that had been sent from Havana attacked the island, but most of the invaders were able to escape to Georgia.[23]

Afterwards, the Spaniards held courts-martial for sixty-eight men implicated in these events, of whom thirty-five had fled to Georgia and four had died in jail. Death sentences were handed out to thirty-three but no one was executed and all who remained in Florida were eventually pardoned. Twenty of the indicted lost their property to confiscation and sale.[24] Spain again had successfully defended La Florida. In Europe, the Franco-Spanish war had ended in April.

On 1 October 1795, the French Consul at St. Marys announced the Treaty of Basel (22 July 1795), which ended the Franco-Spanish war. He made it clear that France would no longer support attacks on Spanish Florida. But this news apparently did not reach some of the Georgians. A final invasion was defeated near Mills Ferry. Elijah Clarke, again in Creek territory, this time west of the Satilla River and for a time north of the St. Marys (he invaded Florida), was forced to disband his men when both the United States and Spain sent forces against him.[25] From all appearances, the worst was over. Except for the loss of population, relatively little damage was done to Florida's economy.

The Treaty of Basel contained a secret article requiring Spain to join France in a war against England within two years. This provision, when honored, placed Spain and its colonies squarely in the sights of Great Britain until 1808, when Napoleon's attempt to seize Spain made Great Britain the ally of Spain's Junta Central government. In anticipation of that Anglo-Spanish hostility, Manuel Godoy, Spain's de facto head of government, reversed Spain's long-standing policy and agreed to U.S. claims.[26] On 27 October 1795, he signed the Treaty of San Lorenzo (Pinckney's Treaty), granting the United States the long-coveted right to use the Mississippi River, a deposit at New Orleans for five years, and setting the U.S. boundary on that river and at thirty-one degrees North and on the line of the St. Marys River. With the strokes of the signers' pens, the Creek and other southeastern Indians lost official Spanish interest in their welfare and the border of Georgia was definitively set on the St. Marys, as it had been, de facto, for a generation.

These two treaties, Basel and San Lorenzo, set the stage for the final American assault on East Florida. Yet like many diplomatic instruments, the Treaty of San Lorenzo was intended to buy time in the short run, with the longer run taking care of itself as circumstances changed. And those changing circumstances in the form of British intrigues in the Great Lakes area in 1796–1797 gave the Spaniards excuses to hold up the implementation of the Treaty of San Lorenzo until 1798. Surveying the line and thus the creation of new diplomatic facts on the ground took until 1800. And even after 1800, the situation on the U.S. border with East and West Florida remained fluid because officials on both sides of the line, much less the major Indian groups affected, were not prepared to accept it as anything more than a temporary matter. Until 1810, there was little violence. East Florida once again became a place of immigration and some prosperity.

Peace and Prosperity, More or Less, 1796–1807

The troubles of 1793–1795 receded into memory as East Florida enjoyed demographic growth, a modest prosperity based on cotton, and relative peace until 1807. After a period (1794–1802)

▶ **253**

THE AMERICAN
FRONTIER
ENVELOPS
EAST FLORIDA,
1790–1821

that was drier than normal, the spring rainfall pattern turned favorable (1802–1809), although we do not know how this affected Florida's agriculture. Exactly how many European heads of family entered the colony in these years is also unclear. A set of books recording loyalty oaths from 1797 to 1811 indicates that 210 heads of families took the oath (1797–1807), bringing 1,520 slaves and an unstated number of other dependents into the colony. But records now in the East Florida Papers and covering 1794 to 1811 suggest the number of heads of family was perhaps double the other number, according to one author. Daniel L. Schafer's even more detailed study of the same documents found 750 heads of family, 1790–1804, and shows that 63 owners imported 2,270 slaves in 1803 alone.[27] U.S.-confirmed headright grants, 1794–1811, total 211, with 61 (19,096 acres) from the 1795–1800 period.

While these studies leave some doubt as to the exact number of immigrants who took the oath of loyalty prior to 1807, what seems certain is that immigration peaked in the years 1802–1804 in response to the opening of Fernandina as a port in 1802 and the closing of East Florida to American immigrants in 1805 because of a decree issued at Madrid on 14 November 1804. Headright grants show this pattern quite clearly, with a peak in 1803 of forty-six U.S.-confirmed grants totaling 29,445 acres. Headright grants issued from 1800 to 1805 were 26 percent of the total acreage so granted. The year 1803 alone accounted for 13.6 percent of the total acreage granted, making it second to 1792 (16.3 percent) and just ahead of 1817 (12 percent). The 1803–1805 acreages would have been even higher had not Governor Enrique White responded to earlier abuses by reducing the schedule by 50 percent and imposing age restrictions. His new rules allowed fifty acres for the head of the household, twenty-five acres per person over sixteen, and fifteen acres per person aged eight to sixteen.[28]

At least 60 percent of the white immigrants were Americans, with British subjects (Scots, Irish, English) and French-speakers in second and third place, respectively. The Americans who were not New England merchants pretending to be immigrants so that they could import up to six thousand pesos in goods duty free came mostly from the South and were farmers and artisans. A third claimed to have property in the United States; a sixth claimed no property. Two hundred and seventy heads of family (1790–1804) owned at least one slave. Collectively, they are known to have imported about five thousand slaves, almost all of the slaves imported prior to 1810. The merchant immigrants provided some credit to the colony during the late 1790s when the *situado* was not being paid. They also provided capital to some of the cotton planters.[29]

Examples of the types of immigrants arriving during these years are as follows. General Jorge Biassou, a free Black who had led pro-Spanish armies in the war on Hispaniola, arrived in 1796 with twenty-four of his followers, including his wife. He soon became famous, or infamous to some, for his unwillingness to be subservient. Antonio Suarez, a Protestant, moved to Amelia Island in 1799 with his wife, five children, fifteen slaves, three horses, and twenty head of cattle. James Cashen also immigrated in 1799. His first grant of five hundred acres was on the St. Johns River south of the Cowford. In 1802, he moved to Amelia Island where he bought and was granted a total of over one thousand acres by 1809. By that year, he was a petty judge (*juez pedáneo*) and an important merchant. Zephaniah Kingsley imported seventy-four slaves in 1803 when he was given a land grant of 3,300 acres. A slave merchant who went on to acquire much property and a fortune smuggling slaves into the United States after 1808, he lived on a plantation on Ft. George Island with Anna Madgigene Jai, an African princess and the mother of some of his children. He had other children by other women, most of them his slaves. Jane Landers has found fifteen other "prominent planters, merchants, and government officials with African wives and consorts and mixed-race children."[30] George Atkinson started with ten slaves and 550 acres in 1803. Through growing cotton, importing slaves, buying land, and trading, he accumulated 17,585 acres and six lots in Fernandina by 1821. At the other end of the scale, Isaac Travers, a free Black, obtained 115 acres for himself, a wife, and a daughter in 1803 but never added to them.[31]

These immigrants entered Florida for a variety of reasons. Perhaps a small number were drawn by East Florida's developing reputation as a healthful place.[32] The possibilities of both

255

THE AMERICAN
FRONTIER
ENVELOPS
EAST FLORIDA,
1790–1821

legal and illegal trade also drew immigrants. But the principal motive seems to have been obtaining land for cotton production in response to the high prices of these years. The concentration on cotton reached such intensity that in January 1800 Governor Enrique White vainly ordered that maize and other food crops had to be planted before cotton would be allowed. His aim seems to have been to secure a source of food for St. Augustine so that it, and the plantations, would be less dependent on imported food.[33] But cotton was a fickle thing, if John McQueen's letters to his family are any indication. After a small crop in 1800, he experienced poor harvests in 1801, 1804, and again in 1806, and a smaller than expected harvest in 1803. At one point, he contemplated selling his cotton lands and going into rice production, evidently intending to supplement the harvest of his own land with rice imported from Georgia or South Carolina, which he would then ship to Havana as if it were his own.[34] McQueen's experiences aside, by 1805 cotton production had grown so that Fernandina exported 77,000 pounds, followed by 66,000 and 60,900 pounds in 1806 and 1807, respectively.[35] How much of that was local and how much was brought in from southern Georgia is not known.

Sugar cultivation, restarted in the New Smyrna area by Loyalists induced by the government to return from the Bahamas, seems to have been of minor importance compared to cotton or even oranges and their juice.[36] Further south on the east coast and into the Keys, lumbering, fishing, ship salvaging, and dreams of coffee and sugar estates drew a few immigrants, but most preferred the more developed northeastern part of the colony.[37]

Important as cotton was, the opening of Amelia Island as a port by a decree dated 19 October 1802 proved in the long run to be equally important both as a lure for immigrants and as a source of trouble. Since 1793, Florida officials had requested the establishment of a customs house at Fernandina. They wanted it for two reasons: to handle the growth of lumber and cotton production along the St. Johns, Nassau, and St. Marys Rivers and on the coastal islands; and because the silting of the bar at St. Augustine made it impractical to require all exports and imports to pass through the customs house at St. Augustine. Peace in Europe in 1802 paved the way. The customs house opened in May 1803 with a deputy collector at San Vicente Ferrer on the St. Johns, so that goods produced along that river did not have to go to Fernandina for clearance. The tariffs were those of 1793: 15 percent on imports not from Spain or its colonies and 6 percent on exports to non-Spanish or Spanish colonial ports. Only goods produced in East Florida could be exported to Spain or its colonies. Slave imports immediately increased, but many ended up in the United States. The prohibition of land grants to Americans ordered in 1804–1805 (after the tightening of the rules in 1803) also carried restrictions on merchants and seems to have meant that Fernandina's promise as an entrepôt was postponed until the U.S. Embargo Act of 1807 came into force, followed in 1808 by the end of legal slave importation.[38] Even so, what little we know about trade through the port before 1807 suggests that most cotton, timber, oranges, and other products were sent to the United States, although rice went to Cuba.

Among the Indians too, the 1790s and early years of the nineteenth century saw population growth and immigration into East Florida and a continuing movement toward European-style agriculture. The Seminole and Miccosukee populations continued their natural growths, supplemented by new migrations from the Creek heartland. Cline's careful study of the evidence shows that by 1802, in addition to the Alachua villages and the Suwannee old town, new Seminole settlements existed on the Oklawaha River (just off the St. Johns) and at Tala Apopka and the Mosquito Inlet. In Apalachee, the Wacissa and Welika villages had developed. And two new villages had appeared on the Chattahoochee. Covington thinks that Hichiti or Mikasuki speakers (Kinache's group among others) moved into Apalachee (Tallahassee hills) in the 1790s. As well, he shows that the Seminole had seasonal hunting camps at Tampa Bay by 1793. Seminole also continued contact with the winter-season Cuban fishing camps along the west coast from Tampa Bay to Caloosahatchee Bay. Through them they traded with Cuba and in them they may have begun to provide labor, as was the case in the 1830s.[39]

In addition to this growth in Seminole numbers in the 1790s and early nineteenth century, villages of Black slaves were also

🏳 **257**

THE AMERICAN
FRONTIER
ENVELOPS
EAST FLORIDA,
1790–1821

appearing next to Seminole towns. Some of these persons had been bought by the Seminole, others had been captured in raids on plantations in Florida and Georgia, and yet others had run away. The relationship between the Seminole and these Blacks was more complex than a simple master–slave relationship. Somewhat later descriptions suggest a sort of sharecropping arrangement and a degree of equality not found in American master–slave relationships. The addition of this Black element to Seminole communities augmented their economic base and demographic and hence military strength, but also provided yet another reason that white American frontiersmen looked upon the Seminole as a group to be removed from the land.[40]

Further afield, the Creek began to experience the commercial consequences of Pinckney's Treaty. Even before the ratifications had been exchanged and the survey begun (1798), the U.S. government set up official trading posts for the Creek and Cherokee. The U.S. agents hoped to convert them into farmers, thus freeing hunting grounds for American settlement, and to eliminate British trading influence that flowed via Panton, Leslie and Company and the various Bahamian merchants who were working among the Creek with the accompanying danger of a successful British invasion of the old Southwest. The Blount Conspiracy of 1796–1797 was a reminder of that danger. The Creek store was located at Colerain from the fall of 1795 to the summer of 1797, after which it was moved to near Fort Wilkinson, west of the Oconee River. For their part, shortages of funds because of nonpayment of the *situado* caused the Spaniards to reduce the gifts they gave Indians who visited St. Augustine, Pensacola, and St. Marks. Panton's trade with the Creek initially seems to have been only slightly affected because the U.S. government bought its goods domestically, and thus even selling them at cost had to charge more than Panton did. However, by about 1800 the U.S. stores ("factories") were price competitive with those of Panton.[41]

This fluid situation, which the Indians experienced as uncertainties of supply and price, played to the continuing interest of Governor Dunmore of the Bahamas and of his business associates John Miller, Joseph Hunter, and John DeLacy in displacing Panton, Leslie and Company's trade with the Creek and in seizing West Florida as part of an unsanctioned (but never officially disavowed) effort to contain the United States and create a Loyalist colony. That grand vision, which other British persons shared (especially in Canada), had not diminished after Bowles's arrest and the failure of other agents in the early 1790s and of the Blount Conspiracy. Indeed, Spain's declaration of war on Great Britain in 1796 and rumors that the French would soon get Louisiana back gave these schemers reason to hope for official British support. And as it happened, their ideal agent, a man who claimed chiefly status among the Creek, was available.[42]

The return of William Augustus Bowles to the Creek from November 1799 to May 1803, like his previous activity among them, had only marginal effects on East Florida although his success would have brought serious consequences. Bowles had managed to escape from his exile and returned to the Apalachicola River on a British warship as the self-proclaimed head of the "Free State of Muscogee." Misfortune plagued him, however, from the moment that his ship grounded entering the river, ruining most of its cargo. He then narrowly escaped capture by Spanish forces that were sent to find him. To make good his losses, he again attacked Panton's storehouse at St. Marks and then took the Spanish fort, although Spanish troops from Pensacola retook it the following June. By actively patrolling, the Spaniards largely prevented Bowles's Bahamian associates from sending him trade goods, thus undercutting his influence among the Indians. For his part, he issued letters of marque from the Free State of Muskogee whose use cost the Spaniards some shipping.

Bowles remained at large among the Creek until Spanish agents, gifts, and promises of debt cancellation at a conference at St. Marks in August 1802 persuaded a Creek majority no longer to support him. He was finally seized at the Hickory Ground conference on the Coosa River in late May 1803. By then, a general peace in Europe (The Peace of Amiens, 1802) had ended any unofficial British interest in his project. The Creek handed Bowles over to the Spaniards, who took him to Havana, where he died in jail in December 1805. A new governor in the Bahamas began to hang sailors who used Bowles's letters of marque, effectively ending that part of his scheme.[43]

☙ **259**

The American
Frontier
Envelops
East Florida,
1790–1821

Bowles's presence among the Creek produced a series of Indian raids that touched East Florida. Trouble began when the U.S. survey party running the border according to the terms of the Treaty of San Lorenzo reached the junction of the Flint and Chattahoochee Rivers in 1799. Seminole from Chief Kinache's Lake Miccosukee group stole horses from the surveyors and made it clear that they did not welcome the survey. The following year, and each year until the St. Mark's Conference of 1802, and in 1803, Indian raiders appeared on the St. Johns and North Rivers and as far south as the Mosquitos area in search of slaves, cattle, and horses. They were particularly attentive to properties that they thought were Panton's. The Spaniards responded by sending the free Black militia to the more exposed locations while posting the white militia in "safer posts" closer to St. Augustine. The Black militia were Biassou's men from Santo Domingo and men who had fled slavery in the United States. They turned in a credible record in a number of skirmishes, especially in 1802.[44]

The extent of economic losses that these raids caused in East Florida is not known and in any event proved but temporary setbacks in the colony's general development.[45] The losses were probably soon overcome by the influx of new settlers and slaves in the years up to 1805.

The Euro-African occupation of Florida west of St. Marks (and east of Pensacola) took a preliminary step forward in 1804. On 22 August of that year, John Forbes and James Innerarity, doing business as John Forbes and Company, successors of Panton, Leslie and Company, acquired a major land cession (1,427,289 acres) between the Apalachicola River and the St. Marks and Wakulla Rivers in payment of Seminole debts to the firm of 66,533 pesos. A condition of the grant was that the company had to set up a store at Prospect Bluff. At the time, the only settlers in the land cession were at Hannahchela, on the Little River, and on the Kennaird's farm on the Wakulla River.[46] Forbes and company hoped to attract settlers and sell the land, but those hopes were dashed in the short term because the validity of this cession was challenged by the Upper Creeks in 1806. They refused to pay damages that Bowles had done (most of the claim) and because the cession had been made without the consent of the whole Creek nation.[47] The Seminole, too, repudiated the cession during the War of 1812, but eventually agreed that it was valid. Still, the result was that no land sales or settlement occurred until after 1814.

Thus ever so slowly during the 1790s and early 1800s, the peninsula was being repopulated by Europeans, Blacks, and Seminoles in spite of the Creek raids associated with Bowles's activities and Spain's wars elsewhere in the world. In the panhandle, most of the land was still used only for hunting, but that too was on the eve of change as settlers continued to move north along the waterways entering Perdido and Pensacola Bays.

Entanglements, 1807–1814

Although La Florida maintained a relative non-involvement in the war of 1796–1802, this was not the case with the war that began in 1804 when Napoleon broke the Peace of Amien. Spain once again joined France. Great Britain now saw an opportunity to seize Mexico, especially once Spain lost most of its navy at the Battle of Trafalgar (1805). General Arthur Wellesley, later the Duke of Wellington, was set to work preparing an invasion force to attack Mexico. It was on the point of sailing when Napoleon invaded Portugal in 1807. Wellesley and his army were diverted there. For its part, the United States tried to stay out of the war and imposed upon itself the Embargo and Non-Intercourse Act of 1807 as a way of punishing Great Britain for the impressment of American seamen and for failing to honor the terms of Jay's Treaty.

The renewal of war in Europe in 1804 produced multiple but at first mostly economic effects in the Floridas. Trade interruptions showed up as a drop in St. Augustine's imports from the United States from an annual average value for customs purposes of about 59,000 pesos (1802 and 1803) to an annual average of about 21,800 pesos (1804–1807), while exports to all destinations fell from an annual average of 15,633 pesos (1802 and 1803) to about 9,600 pesos (1804–1807).[48] Land grants to Americans legally stopped in 1805, supposedly cutting off new population and capital. The garrison, reduced by 1801 to under three

☙ **261**

THE AMERICAN
FRONTIER
ENVELOPS
EAST FLORIDA,
1790–1821

hundred men, remained at that low level. Receipt of the *situado* remained irregular.[49]

Napoleon's attack on Spain in the spring of 1808 and the full force of the U.S. Embargo Act marked the beginning of a decade of threats to the rebuilding gains that Spain had achieved in East Florida after the events of 1793–1795 and the Creek raids. Coincidentally, the area experienced a decade of drier than normal spring weather, with as yet unexplored consequences for subsistence and staple agriculture.[50] Moreover, Great Britain suddenly became an ally of Spain instead of an enemy, an ally some of whose subjects still dreamed of a colony in West Florida and the Mississippi Valley. Aaron Burr's conspiracy of 1805–1806 may have marked the resumption of this scheming.[51] And Indians again took to raiding. Ever vigilant for its opportunities and fearful of a British seizure of the mouth of the Mississippi River, the U.S. government saw in the apparent collapse of the Spanish government in 1808–1810 the possibility of seizing West Florida, and perhaps East Florida as well. Events were thus set in motion that in time resulted in two U.S. invasions of the Floridas. We will begin with what the United States attempted, 1808–1812.

When premature news of the collapse of the Spanish government in 1808 reached Washington, President James Madison immediately began to encourage Americans living in both East and West Florida to rebel and seek U.S. protection.[52] When the Spanish government did collapse in 1810, Americans in the Baton Rouge district acted before Madison had his forces ready. The rebels created the Republic of West Florida, whose leaders contracted debts they expected the United States to assume but which Madison refused to acknowledge. Consequently, Major General James Wilkinson had to take control of the Baton Rouge district without the agreement of the Republic's leaders. For East Florida, the story was more complex.

Madison's agent for East Florida was seventy-two-year-old George Mathews, Revolutionary War hero, former governor of Georgia, and one-time Yazoo land speculator. Madison's authority was a secret Congressional resolution of 15 January 1811 authorizing him to spend up to $100,000 and to take such actions as might be needed to prevent a foreign government (Great Britain) from seizing the Floridas or as might be requested by local authorities. Madison suggested to Mathews that U.S. forces would lend him aid and he could draw on the customs houses at New Orleans and Savannah for his expenses.[53]

Mathews went first to Mobile, where he secured a letter from Governor Vicente Folch y Juan saying that if Cuba did not send him reinforcements he would agree to a U.S. occupation (U.S. forces were just outside of the town). Mathews then journeyed to northeast Florida where he found that none of the leading American residents wanted to risk his property by taking part in a rebellion, although Georgia resident John Houston McIntosh,[54] who owned land in Florida, did agree to lead an invasion force. Mathews promised five hundred acres of land to men who would join, and he convinced seventy Georgians and nine residents of Florida to sign up. He also tried, but failed, to get U.S. troops to spearhead a rapid march to seize Castillo San Marcos on a Monday morning, when he supposed the hundred or so men of the garrison would be recovering from the weekend. In the end, he had to settle for an invasion that proclaimed the "Republic of Florida" at Rose's Bluff on 15 March 1812. Backed by U.S. Navy ships, the attackers then secured the surrender of the ten-man garrison at Fernandina. U.S. Army troops then crossed the St. Marys to occupy the town.[55] The Spaniards mobilized their militias on 16–19 March as the invaders advanced on St. Augustine and eventually put it under a loose siege.[56]

By the time Mathews pulled off his invasion and began the so-called "Patriot War," the Madison administration had published the Henry letters purporting to show British efforts to foment rebellion in New England using similar techniques to those that Mathews was employing. Revelation of the administration's hand in Mathews's actions would have been a political embarrassment. Consequently, Secretary of State James Monroe repudiated Mathews's actions as soon as he learned of them. Mathews did not get the news for some time and meanwhile moved on to besiege St. Augustine with U.S. Army forces commanded by Lt. Colonel Thomas A. Smith and Georgia militiamen. Governor Mitchel of Georgia, given control of the situation by Madison, chose to continue the campaign, as Madison knew he would.

☙ **263**

THE AMERICAN
FRONTIER
ENVELOPS
EAST FLORIDA,
1790–1821

The Spanish response was to send pardo militiamen on deep patrols behind the "Patriot" lines, with orders to seize slaves and certain other goods for the Crown and food for themselves. In June, the Seminoles under Chief Payne were brought into the fight with promises of loot. Slaves who fled to St. Augustine for protection were cared for by Bernardo Segui.[57]

Then on 16 June 1812, the United States declared war on Great Britain, adding a new player to the drama. Mathews's "Republic of Florida" was left to its own devices, although Smith's U.S. forces remained in the field. Spanish harassment did not at first break the siege of St. Augustine, but on 12 September a pardo and Indian force ambushed and destroyed a supply train at Twelve Mile Swamp northwest of St. Augustine.[58] Smith withdrew his forces to the St. Johns River, effectively ending the siege. Smith's withdrawal signaled that the war was about to shift its focus.

Seminole participation in harassing "Patriot" lines drew a response. Frustrated at St. Augustine, Georgians led by militia Major Daniel Newman turned on the Indians, incited especially by the Blacks who fought alongside them and by greed for Seminole slaves, cattle, and land in Alachua, long reputed to be the best land in north central Florida. In late September 1812, Newman took 116 men and four days' worth of supplies and marched on Payne's town. In a running battle that began on 27 September, he was stopped, put under siege, and finally forced to retreat when reinforcements failed to arrive. According to some accounts, Chief Payne was mortally wounded.[59] Afterwards, the Seminole asked for peace but the Madison administration delayed a settlement. It and firebrands in Georgia intended that the war should continue.

In East Tennessee, word of the invasion of Florida led to the creation of a volunteer force that arrived on the Georgia–Florida frontier in late 1812. Uniting with Georgians into a force some four hundred strong, the Tennesseans invaded the Alachua district (3–17 February), and fought at least two indecisive skirmishes with the two hundred or so Indian and Black defenders, killing twenty or so Seminole, and capturing another nine (of whom four escaped). They then destroyed all three villages and their maize stores, while seizing deerskins, horses, and cattle.[60] The Seminole scattered to other parts of the peninsula.

Meanwhile, Spain mobilized diplomatic resources and offered an amnesty (on 15 December 1812) to all of its subjects (such as Zephaniah Kingsley) who had joined the invasion. That, complementing the public outcry against a U.S. attack on a Spain that was fighting Napoleon and Congressional refusal to sanction U.S. troops in Florida, allowed the Madison administration to withdraw U.S. forces without seeming completely to abandon the East Florida "Patriots." The U.S. Army and Navy left Florida in early May 1813. Thus abandoned by the United States, some "Patriots" fled to Georgia.

Hostilities continued. In the fall of 1813, Buchner Harris raised a troop led by Samuel Alexander that raided in North Florida. Then in January 1814, Harris himself set up Fort Mitchell in Alachua with seventy settlers. He asked for but failed to get U.S. recognition. He then offered to cease raiding if his men received a complete amnesty, the Cuban pardo troops were sent home, and the "Patriots" were granted lands in Alachua. Florida's officials ignored the proposal. When Harris was killed in an ambush in early May, the settlement broke up and its residents retreated to Georgia.[61]

The losses from the "Patriot War" and related events were substantial. Most of the crops of 1812 were destroyed and many planters did not plant commercial crops in 1813. Many farms lost buildings, cattle, and other movables, especially slaves. In ruling on claims arising from the war, U.S. District Judge Isaac Bronson declared in 1851 that by the spring of 1813 "the whole inhabited part of the province was in a state of utter desolation and ruin" outside of the walls of St. Augustine.[62] This is almost certainly an exaggeration. Still, the losses were high. Among the claims filed against the United States was that of the estate of John Fraser of Greenfields Plantation. His executors claimed $111,000 for crops not planted, as many as 211 of 370 slaves run away or stolen, and other property stolen or destroyed. Several other claims in that range were also filed. More typical were those of twenty-six free Blacks, who filed claims ranging from $320 to $3,062, with an average of about $2,000.[63] James Cashen of Amelia Is-

🏴 **265**

THE AMERICAN
FRONTIER
ENVELOPS
EAST FLORIDA,
1790–1821

land, who had tried to remain neutral during the invasion, lost thirty-eight slaves, horses, cattle, and all of his crops. He also spent a period of time as a rebel prisoner. The value of his losses is not known.[64] William Harvey, Father Miguel Crosby, Manuel Romero, Roque Leonardi's sons, José Peso de Burgo, Nicholás Sánchez, William Carney, Joseph Summerall, John E. Tate, William and Abner Williams, and Luis Mattair all later claimed that they had been driven from their land grants by the invasion, although they did not state the value of their losses. John Underwood saw Indians burn his sawmill on Black Creek just off the St. Marys River before he fled into Georgia. Most of these men returned to their properties, often within the year.[65]

As the "Patriot War" was developing in East Florida, West Florida was drawn into the Red Stick War (1811–1814) and the War of 1812 (1812–1815). The Red Stick War originated in October 1811 in the efforts of Tecumseh, a Shawnee Chief, to organize an Indian confederacy to resist American occupation of Indian lands. New British plans to seize the Mississippi Valley and the Gulf Coast were in the background, although how well they were known to the Indians is unclear. It is also unclear whether the drier than normal spring weather of those years had produced distress among the Creek. These matters aside, some Upper Creek warriors and medicine men took up the cause in spite of the American victory at the Battle of Tippecanoe on 7 November 1811, especially once they saw the "Patriot War" underway in East Florida in 1812. A party of warriors went to Pensacola in the summer of 1813, seeking arms and munitions. Although they did not get all that they wanted, they were able to defeat a U.S. force at Burnt Corn Creek near Mobile on 27 July and then take Fort Mims (on 30 August). The American response was swift. On 12 October 1813, General Andrew Jackson and 3,500 Tennessee militiamen invaded Alabama, followed on 24 November by Georgia militiamen. The Red Sticks, as the insurgents were known, were defeated at the battles of Holy Ground (23 December 1813) and Horseshoe Bend (6 March 1814). Many survivors fled to Spanish Florida. Jackson wrapped up the war by imposing a Creek cession of a strip of land sixty miles wide and running along the West Florida border from the Chattahoochee River westward

(Treaty of Fort Jackson, August 1814). The American intention was to cut the Creek off from Spanish supplies at Pensacola.[66]

The Red Stick attacks on American settlements and defeat at Jackson's hands took place before the British could organize their expedition to the Gulf coast as part of the War of 1812. Nonetheless, the British pressed ahead. In May 1814, brevet Captain George Woodbine, of the Royal Marines, brought to the mouth of the Apalachicola River two ships loaded with guns, munitions, and other items that the Creek wanted. He took over Forbes and Company's warehouses at Prospect Bluff and began to recruit Indians and runaway African slaves. On 24 August, brevet Lt. Col. Edward Nicholls, Royal Marines, reached Pensacola with a small force, which occupied it without Spanish permission. He too began to recruit, with special emphasis on slaves, who were promised freedom, land, and transportation to a British colony. His objective was to keep major parts of the U.S. Army tied down on the West Florida border while the main British expeditionary force moved against Louisiana. But his plan failed. Jackson and his troops marched on Pensacola, which the British abandoned without a fight. Nicholls and the freedmen and Indians he had recruited retired to Prospect Bluff, where they erected the "Negro Fort" and prepared to continue the fight. After a brief occupation of Pensacola, Jackson too left, for the Battle of New Orleans where the American victory ended British plans to recreate a British West Florida.[67] The combatants there did not know that the war had already ended.

While these British actions of 1814 took place in West Florida, East Florida also experienced some effects from the last stages of the War of 1812. A few Americans again took the opportunity to raid, and the British under Admiral Sir George Cockburn seized Cumberland Island and raided St. Marys City in January 1815. Not much is known about the American marauders, which suggests that they were not a major problem to what was left of the plantations clustered on the lower St. Johns River. The British presence on Cumberland Island, on the other hand, did create difficulties because they tried to recruit the Americans' slaves and, less likely because of the location, Indians for the British cause with the same promises that Nicholls had used at Pen-

☙ 267

THE AMERICAN
FRONTIER
ENVELOPS
EAST FLORIDA,
1790–1821

sacola. When some Spanish slaves chose to flee to the British (Spain's ally), Cockburn refused to return them but did give permission for owners to visit their former chattels to try to persuade them to return. Few, if any, did. When Cockburn evacuated the island at the end of the war, he took the fugitives with him to Bermuda. John Forbes, and probably other owners as well, sued in the British courts for compensation but had no success.[68]

Until the "Patriot" invasion of 1812 temporarily removed Fernandina and St. Augustine's hinterland from the Spanish trading sphere, East Florida as a whole enjoyed a small but unevenly distributed commercial boom after 1808, thanks to use of Amelia Island's port (named Fernandina in 1811 when the town was formally laid out) to evade the U.S. embargo and a general surge in demand for East Florida's exports. St. Augustine, however, suffered as its bar continued to silt up and its relative remoteness from the plantations on the lower St. Johns, Nassau, and St. Marys Rivers cost it business that went to Fernandina. Thus in 1808, its imports from the United States dropped further from pre-1804 levels to 9,466 pesos (customs value) while exports to the United States fell to 4,666 pesos (out of 5,383 total exports for the province). The drop experienced in 1804–1808 reversed during the years 1809–1811, with average annual imports more than tripling to 35,395 pesos. But that was still only 60 percent of the pre-war (1802–1803) average. St. Augustine's exports followed a similar pattern, although the swings were not so dramatic.[69]

Amelia Island's port, on the other hand, sprang to life as American cotton planters and British shippers converted it into an entrepôt through which they evaded the Embargo Act. Trade data for Amelia Island is not available for 1807 and 1808. When they begin, they do so with a two-year high (1809–1810) in both imports and exports, each averaging over half a million pesos (customs values). The U.S. decision to again allow the direct export of cotton to Europe, beginning in 1810, and Spanish requirements that ships have consular certificates produced a 90 percent decline during the next two years in the pounds of cotton imported from the United States and exported to Great Britain. Imports and exports of rice and flour show similar temporal patterns, if less notable changes.[70] Exports of forest products, especially staves and lumber, increased sharply in 1809. Exports of lumber, for example, shot up almost tenfold in 1809 as compared to 1808, to one million board feet. Unlike most of the cotton (in 1809–1810, East Florida produced 75,000 pounds at most of the 653,000 pounds exported, with 73 percent of them sent to Great Britain), these forest products were produced in the colony.[71]

Recognizing the decline in Fernandina's commerce (aside from that caused by the "Patriot" occupation), in December 1813 the Spaniards allowed goods to be deposited for transshipment for up to two months provided a 3 percent transshipment tax was paid along with the 1.5 percent war tax.[72] This measure did little to halt the slide.

This commerce aside, Fernandina also served as a major port for the importation of slaves into Georgia in defiance of the U.S. ban on the slave trade that took effect on New Year's Day 1808. Jane Landers's careful compilation of known slave ships from incomplete records shows seven in 1810, one each in 1812 and 1814, six in 1817, four in 1818, one each in 1819 and 1820, and two in 1821, although in most cases the number of slaves landed is not known. Planter-slave traders Zephaniah Kingsley and John Fraser, merchants Joseph Hibberson and Henry and Philip Robert Yonge (doing business as Hibberson and Yonge), and Fernando de la Maza Arredondo, Sr., and his son of the same name were major players in this trade.[73]

Planters in Florida are known to have purchased a part of many cargoes and to have kept at least some of them for use on their own plantations. The census of 1814 shows that the rural population was 53 percent Black. Along the lower St. Johns River, where most of the plantations clustered, Blacks outnumbered whites by four to one.[74]

The Final Years of Spanish Florida, 1815–1821

Improvement in the general economic situation came slowly after the return of peace. Zephaniah Kingsley claimed in 1816 that the province was still in a "deplorable state" because agriculture and commerce were in "total decay." As proof, he cited

☞ 269

THE AMERICAN
FRONTIER
ENVELOPS
EAST FLORIDA,
1790–1821

the condition of the late John Fraser's idled properties, which had but 159 of the original 370 slaves. Samuel Betts could also have attested to the difficulties that some planters were experiencing. In 1815, he had assigned his 1,800 acres of land to his creditors, Joseph M. Arredondo, Philip R. Yonge, and George Fleming, as security for debts he owed ten men.[75]

Demographically, these years of war after 1804 were marked by a flattening out of growth. Births recorded at St. Augustine declined from an average of sixty-five per annum (1800–1804) to 48.8 (1812–1822). Curiously enough, recorded marriages actually rose until 1810, although their levels fell afterwards. A famine in 1808 and an epidemic in October 1809 were the only major disruptions aside from the events of 1812–1813.[76]

The census of 1814 revealed that the civilian population had hardly grown at all since 1793, or rather had peaked and then fallen. About 7 percent of the province's population were soldiers in the garrison (N = 234), about 53 percent were living outside of St. Augustine and Fernandina (the only towns), and the rest, slightly over 39 percent, were in the two towns, mostly at St. Augustine. The total was about 4,200 persons, including the garrison[77] (see Table 9.5).

Nor had East Florida's economic dependence on the United States been changed in spite of the wartime trade with Great Britain. Once the War of 1812 ended, St. Augustine returned to importing 90 percent or more of its goods from the United States. Fernandina's imports averaged about 80 percent from the United States. For both ports, exports to the United States fell to about 60 percent of all exports. Great Britain and its colonies' share of the trade of both ports proved highly variable, with a falloff at Fernandina to under 20 percent. Spain and its colonies continued to be major export markets for St. Augustine, especially for rice, but were otherwise marginal to the economy of the colony.[78]

Some officials in East Florida believed that the land law was a key cause of this general stagnation after 1804, a stagnation made worse by the destruction of the "Patriot" war and the British presence on Cumberland Island. As early as 1811, Juan José Estrada, temporary successor to Governor Enrique White, proposed that land be sold outright rather than granted with the then required ten-year occupancy to validate the title. He seems to have been afraid that residents might lose their land if the much-rumored transfer of Florida to another power were to take place. The Captain General of Cuba rejected this idea and reminded Estrada of the decree of 1804 that forbade grants to U.S. citizens. The next year, newly arrived governor Sebastián Kindelán proposed that most of the Spaniards in the province, but especially those who had served against the invaders of 1793–1795, be *given* land, an idea later elaborated as six *caballerias* (about two hundred acres) for each head of family and three *caballerias* for each member of his household, including slaves. Instead, the Constitutional government of Spain (1810–1814) ordered the sale of municipal lands in fee simple. Half of the proceeds were to be used to pay government debts locally, if there were any, and then the national debt. A quarter of the land in each municipal district was reserved for distribution to the poor by lot, with a four-year occupancy requirement before title was given. It is unclear if these provisions applied to or were applied in East Florida.[79]

Ferdinand VII's restored government took up Kindelán's suggested policy. In 1815, it authorized land grants to veterans.[80] Rumors that Florida would be sold to the United States caused the governor to make numerous grants under this and other laws. Headright grants with the usual conditions rose sharply, totaling seventy-eight U.S.-confirmed grants and 47,496 acres, 1815–1818, or 22 percent of all U.S.-confirmed headright grants. They remained relatively modest in size (see median sizes in Table 10.1). Service grants, on the other hand, conveyed immediate, absolute title to more land (322,884 acres) in four years, 1815–1818, than all the headright grants did during the entire second Spanish period (215,990 acres; see Table 10.2). Most of the land went to eighteen individuals, eleven of whom (Joseph M. Arredondo, his brother Fernando de la Maza Arredondo, Jr., their father, Fernando de la Maza Arredondo, Sr., Andrew Atkinson, Charles W. Clarke, Joseph Delespine, Domingo Fernández, George Fleming, José Fontane, Eusebio María Gómez, and Henry Yonge) were given more than 10,000 acres each. Some grantees had served in 1812–1813, but others gained their grants for service in 1817, in events to be noted. With the cession of Florida clearly in the

271

THE AMERICAN
FRONTIER
ENVELOPS
EAST FLORIDA,
1790–1821

TABLE 10.1   Headright Grants, 1815–1818

Year	Number	Total Acres	Mean Size	Median Size
1815	19	7,746	407.68	250
1816	16	7,717	482.31	285
1817	32	25,812	806.64	300
1818	11	6,221	565.55	400

Source: SLGF data base.

TABLE 10.2   Service Grants, 1790–1819

Year	Number	Total Acres	Mean Size	Median Size
1790	1	300		
1791	1	1 town lot		
1804	1	1,000		
1806	1	500		
1811	1	1,000		
1814	3	6,297	2,099.0	1,000
1815	23	42,925	1,866.3	815
1816	41	61,021	1,488.3	449
1817	56	208,154	3,717.0	2,000
1818	10	10,784	1,078.4	805
1819	3	1,915	638.3	400
Sum	141	333,897	2,368.1	640

Source: SLGF database.

works, Governor José Coppinger was generous indeed to men already in Florida!

But the largest grant of all was to the firm of Arredondo and Sons. Citing a royal order of 3 September 1817 that he encourage the settlement of the Floridas, in December of that year the Cuban Intendant, Alexander Ramírez, gave the Arredondos 289,645 acres "for settlement" in a square defined as four leagues in each of the cardinal directions from the site of an old Indian village, Payne's Town (i.e., eight Spanish leagues on a side). This "Arredondo Grant" embraced most of Alachua, long the most coveted piece of north central Florida real estate. To gain title, the firm only had to settle two hundred families, beginning within three years of the date of the grant.[81] While not a service grant as such, this grant was justified in part by the firm's role in supplying Florida with slaves and other supplies before, during, and after the war of 1812–1814. Arredondo and Sons was almost certainly the economic partner for the last Spanish governors' exploitation of the office.

And not to be outdone, on 17 December 1817 and 6 February 1818, Ferdinand VII issued grants to the Duke of Alagón (Captain of the Bodyguards), the Conde de Puñoenrostro (a king's chamberlain), and D. Pedro de Vargas (Treasure of the Household), supposedly for colonization projects but in fact as land speculations anticipating the American takeover. The grantees were given all the remaining, ungranted lands in the province! Alagón sent an agent, Nicolás Garrido, to Florida and actually had the man begin a review of titles in the fall of 1818. But unknown to Ferdinand and his favorites, on 24 January 1818 the Spanish Minister to the United States, Luis de Onís, announced that Spain was agreeing to cede the Floridas. That date eventually became the last one on which any Spanish land grant would be valid (if its terms were later met). The last of the three grants was thus invalid. But to be certain that the other two did not alienate most of the peninsula, Adams eventually got Onís to agree that the Alagón and other grants were void, thus preserving most of Florida for the U.S. government.[82]

By the time the granting frenzy was over, Acting Governor Juan José de Estrada, Governor José Coppinger, and Cuban Intendant Ramírez had granted (between 1815 and 1818) some 781,494 acres. This totaled about 58 percent of the 1,359,548 acres (excluding the 1,427,289 acres of the Forbes's Cession) in grants that the United States confirmed. Included in the 781,494 were 97,030 acres in ten sawmill grants. Several tens of thousands of acres in other grants dating to these years were not confirmed. The service grants were almost entirely speculative (see Figure 10.1).

A temporary change that took place during the war years was the wholesale reorganization of East Florida under the terms of the Spanish constitution of 1812. (St. Augustine still has its monument from 1813 celebrating the local promulgation of that docu-

273

THE AMERICAN
FRONTIER
ENVELOPS
EAST FLORIDA,
1790–1821

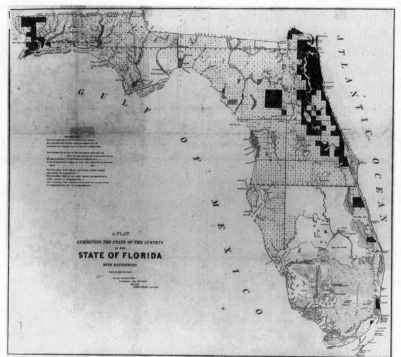

Figure 10.1. Townships with one or more Spanish land
grants, 1821, per SLGF database. SUPERIMPOSED ON UNITED
STATES, 30TH CONGRESS, 2ND SESSION, *Senate Executive
Documents*, No. 2, ANNUAL REPORT OF THE COMMISSIONER OF THE
GENERAL LAND OFFICE, "A PLAT EXHIBITING THE STATE OF THE
SURVEYS IN FLORIDA, 1848." MAP COURTESY OF P. K. YONGE LIBRARY
OF FLORIDA HISTORY, UNIVERSITY OF FLORIDA.

ment on 17 October 1812.) East and West Florida became parishes
of the city of Havana for electoral purposes because they lacked
the five thousand persons needed for district (*partido*) status.
Through an as yet undescribed process, Fernando de la Maza
Arredondo, Sr. and Bernardo Segui were elected as delegates to
the Provincial Deputation of Havana (local legislature). They
served at their own expense, as they reminded the governor when
they applied for service grants.[83] Three districts were created
within East Florida (St. Augustine, Upper and Lower St. Johns,
and Fernandina), but they were kept under military control both

because of the invasion of 1812 and out of a desire to prevent ex-rebels from controlling the city government at Fernandina. In place of elected officials, the governor ("political chief") imposed a system of appointed roving judges, styled *capitanes de partido*. Philip Robert Yonge was placed in charge of the Amelia and St. Marys district, Francisco Fatio was given the upper St. Johns, and Farquahar Bethune the lower St. Johns. This system lasted until 1815 and the receipt of an order from Ferdinand VII's restored absolutist government abolishing the partidos. But the idea of using the *capitanes de partido* endured. Indeed, in 1816 at the request of prominent residents of northeast Florida, Governor Coppinger subdivided the old Amelia district into the districts of Nassau River, Upper and Lower St. Marys, and Fernandina (Amelia). The residents of all except Fernandina were allowed to elect magistrates and militia officers.[84]

The First Seminole War and U.S. Annexation

Seemingly not destined to know peace for more than a year or two, in 1816–1818 Florida experienced new invasions, although the effects were mostly felt by the Seminole and town of Fernandina. The immediate cause of these new hostilities was the Negro Fort on the Apalachicola. Not only did it continue to attract fugitive slaves, but it also became a center for raiding parties into American Territory. Both the Americans and the Spaniards (in response to U.S. pressure) determined to destroy it (July 1816). The Americans got there first and, thanks to a lucky hot shot that fell into an open powder magazine on 27 July, had cleaned out the fort by the time Captain Benigno García Calderón and his forty Spanish soldiers arrived on 2 August. Of the 334 Blacks in the place, 270 were killed outright by the explosion and many others were wounded. But a few slipped away to join the Seminole at Bowleg's town on the Suwannee, where they resumed occasional raiding.[85]

The following summer, Gregor McGregor led a small force of Americans from Baltimore, Charleston, and Savannah in an attack that took Amelia Island on 29 June 1817 in the face of a hastily mustered militia. He then proclaimed the Green Flag Re-

275

THE AMERICAN
FRONTIER
ENVELOPS
EAST FLORIDA,
1790–1821

public of Florida. The Spaniards initially retreated from St. Nicolas on the St. Johns but later engaged in aggressive mounted patrols. Besides the filibusters, they had to worry about parties of Indians raiding farms on the St. Johns River. Then on 10 September, they gathered to defend Luber's and Waterman's plantations near Fernandina and conducted an unsuccessful attack on that town. Now unwilling to tolerate such activities in territory it was certain it would acquire, the United States sent troops who in December 1817 occupied the island. McGregor fled and threatened to return in 1818, but never did.[86] As in previous invasions, some landowners lost property, or claimed they did. William Garvin said he lost $2,500 in the form of a house and his half interest in a tannery near Fernandina. Francis Pellicer claimed he lost cattle. Gabriel W. Perpall claimed he had horses stolen by the rebels and forty-four slaves who ran off to the Indians. Each asked for and received land in compensation.[87]

Meanwhile, a confrontation developed between the United States and some of the Seminole. The U.S. Army built Fort Scott on the west side of the Flint River in the area that the Creek had been forced to cede at Fort Jackson. It was north of the Seminole town of Fowltown, which was on the east side and north of the Florida border (see Figure 10.2). However, Chief Neamathla and other Seminoles refused to recognize that cession. When Col. Edmund P. Gaines demanded (through subordinates) the right to hunt "runaway slaves" among the Miccosukee villages and to pass into Florida as far as the Suwannee River, Neamathla told the Colonel to keep himself and his men west of the river. Incensed by this demand, Gaines ordered an attack that struck on 21 November 1817, killing five Indians and burning the town. Shortly afterwards, the Indians retaliated by killing thirty-seven of forty soldiers, as well as six women and four children on a boat making its way up the Apalachicola River. They also raided the Forbes and Company trading post on Prospect Bluff (13 December). Indian and Black raiders struck elsewhere as well.[88]

The First Seminole War had begun. The U.S. War Department issued orders that allowed pursuit of hostile Indians into Spanish Florida. Gaines, meanwhile, was ordered to Amelia Island to direct U.S. operations there against McGregor.

Figure 10.2. Florida Indian communities, 1816–1819.
From Howard F. Cline, *Florida Indians II: Provisional
Historical Gazetteer with Locational Notes on Florida Colonial
Communities* (New York: Garland Publishers, 1974), Map No. 9.
By permission of Sarah Cline.

To fill Gaines's place, the United States sent General Jackson
to Fort Scott to prosecute the war. His well-known personal aims
were to remove all Indians from U.S. territory, destroy the Black
villages associated with the Seminole, and drive the Spaniards
from East Florida. All, in his mind, were dangers to the integrity
of the United States. Jackson's biographer, Robert Remini, concludes that President James Monroe intended Jackson to act on
these views, although the president carefully created deniability,
an action that later infuriated Jackson.[89]

Jackson assembled some 4,800 men, including 1,500 Creek

☙ **277**

THE AMERICAN
FRONTIER
ENVELOPS
EAST FLORIDA,
1790–1821

warriors, for his sweep into Florida. Roughly 1,000 "Seminole" and 300 "Black Indian" warriors were his targets. In need of supplies from ships reported at the mouth of the Apalachicola River, Jackson marched south, destroying Miccosukee towns along his route. He rebuilt the Negro Fort as Fort Gadsden and then moved eastward to St. Marks. He also ordered a U.S. naval siege of Spanish St. Marks. By a deception, the naval forces engaged for this action captured Hillis Hago (the Prophet Francis) and another Seminole leader. Jackson took the Spanish fort on 6 April. Hillis and his companion were promptly hanged. The Spanish commander was told that the diplomats could sort out the legal details; Jackson wanted the fort as a base for his future operations. He installed a two-hundred-man garrison.[90]

At St. Marks Jackson found and arrested Alexander Arbuthnot, a seventy-year-old Scots trader from Nassau who had been supplying the Indians since August 1817 and who had been serving as Bowlegs's "speaker" (i.e., writer of letters). Arbuthnot believed that the Indians had been ill-treated by the United States and that under Article 9 of the Treaty of Ghent (ending the War of 1812) the Creek should have been given back their lands ceded at Fort Jackson. His aim was to get British and Spanish support for this claim. Perhaps correctly, Jackson believed Arbuthnot's ideas had encouraged Seminole resistance the previous fall. The U.S. position was that the Treaty of Ghent came after the Treaty of Fort Jackson and so did not abrogate it.[91]

Jackson next advanced on the Suwannee, defeating a Red Stick party and a Black and Indian rear guard. He destroyed Bowlegs's town and captured Robert C. Ambrister, a British soldier of fortune who had been training the Blacks and Indians. Ambrister entered the town unaware of the U.S. presence.

Returning to St. Marks, Jackson promptly tried Arbuthnot and Ambrister as outlaws and pirates because as British subjects they were making war on the United States when Great Britain and the United States were at peace. Legal scholars have concluded this was a dubious argument. Whatever its merits, Jackson found enough documents in his support so that he and, later, Secretary of State John Adams were able to argue that Arbuthnot was working with Nicholls of Negro Fort fame. Jackson also claimed that Arbuthnot was associated with George Woodbine, who in turn was working with McGregor. Ambrister was alleged to be McGregor's advance agent for an invasion of Tampa Bay. After a court-martial (later judged to have involved numerous violations of legal procedure), Ambrister was shot and Arbuthnot was hanged from a yard of his ship, the *Last Chance*.[92]

That done, Jackson turned to Pensacola, which he entered on 24 May in an effort, he said, to prevent its being used as a base for Indian raids into U.S. territory that its Spanish governor seemed powerless to prevent. He claimed that hundreds of hostile Indians were gathered there, although none were in evidence when he actually entered the town. The surrender he forced out of José Masot, the governor, amounted to a cession. After setting up a military government and promising to respect Spanish laws and property rights, Jackson returned to Tennessee.[93] The first Seminole War was over, but its consequences were not.

Jackson's raid set the Miccosukee and the Seminole into motion. Fowltown relocated further south on the Apalachicola. The Miccosukee moved closer to the Suwannee. The remaining Red Sticks moved to Tampa Bay. The Alachua, who had been on the Suwannee after 1812, moved to Okihamki, just west of Lake Harris (in Lake County). Still other Indians and their Black associates went to Cape Florida; a few even went to the Bahamas. In each case, satellite villages of Blacks were present.[94]

On the diplomatic front, news of Jackson's seizure of St. Marks and Pensacola, both of which he had left garrisoned, very nearly derailed the Adams–Onís negotiations for settling outstanding issues between Spain and the United States. Formal discussions had resumed in December 1815. At the time, Spain still rejected the U.S. claim that the Louisiana Purchase had included West Florida as far as the Perdido River, wanted satisfaction for American violations of Pensacola's neutrality during the War of 1812, and was especially upset that the United States allowed privateers and filibustering expeditions to use its ports in support of Latin American independence. The United States countered with claims against Spain for American ships and property that had been condemned by French consular agents in Spanish ports during the Quasi-War with France in the 1790s, for financial

🏺 **279**

THE AMERICAN
FRONTIER
ENVELOPS
EAST FLORIDA,
1790–1821

losses when the deposit at New Orleans was closed in 1802, and for Spain's failure to ratify an agreement of 1802 that dealt with the first and various issues connected with seamen. The United States was interested in exchanging East Florida for its settlement of the claims of U.S. citizens, but it declined to discuss the areas in West Florida that it had annexed in 1812.[95]

In March 1816, Onís was allowed to suggest that a general treaty might produce agreement on the western border of Louisiana and on the cession of all remaining Spanish territory east of the Mississippi. But nearly two more years passed before 24 January 1818, when Onís announced that his government might cede the Floridas and settle all remaining differences.[96] He and Adams were making progress on those differences when news of Jackson's actions arrived in Washington and Madrid. Indeed, on 25 April 1818 Madrid had ordered Onís to agree to the cession of the Floridas in return for considerations west of the Mississippi and a U.S. promise not to aid or recognize the Latin American rebels.

Onís rightly protested Jackson's acts, which amounted to an act of war. The Cabinet and U.S. Congress took up the issue both for its various constitutional implications and because Jackson was widely regarded as a presidential contender in 1824. Monroe dodged the issue during June but then began to blame Jackson for exceeding orders while lawfully engaging in the defense of the country. Spain's failure to keep the Indians at peace with the United States was also alleged, in effect justifying Jackson's action. Over the summer, the controversy simmered, but Great Britain decided to take no action to avenge its citizens, Arbuthnot and Ambrister.

The final stage of diplomacy began in the fall of 1818 under the good offices of the French ambassador, Hyde de Neuville. Knowing it would get no help from any European country, Spain reluctantly returned to the bargaining table. The United States withdrew its forces from Pensacola, although with a warning that it would act if the Spaniards failed to keep the Indians under control. Congress strengthened U.S. neutrality laws, which met part of Spain's desire regarding Latin America. Negotiation over the western boundary of the Louisiana Purchase was the critical issue, one resolved when Spain agreed to the U.S. position in

January 1819. Because the other issues from before 1808 had largely been resolved, conclusion of the treaty quickly followed. On 22 February 1819, Adams and Onís signed the treaty that has since carried their names. The U.S. Senate unanimously ratified the treaty two days later.[97]

And then matters came to a halt for two more years. The treaty provided that ratifications would be exchanged in six months. But that deadline came and went. In Madrid, the king and some of his ministers decided to hold up the ratification in the hope that the United States would agree to stop aiding the Latin Americans and would accept the three major land grants noted above. Confronted with this delay, some Americans, mostly Southerners, demanded that Congress authorize an immediate seizure of the Floridas and Texas, but sectional politics defeated that possibility. To prevent U.S. action, in April 1818 Ferdinand VII appointed D. Francisco Dionisio Vivés as his new representative to the United States. Vivés took his time traveling to Washington, arriving only in April 1820. He made it clear that the sticking point was Spanish concern that the United States would recognize the rebel governments in Latin America, a topic it had raised with various European states during the previous year.

Vivés's arrival coincided with the Spanish Revolution of 1820, which resulted in further delays in the Spanish ratification. Under the newly reinstated Constitution of 1812, Ferdinand VII had to submit the Adams–Onís Treaty to the Cortés (the Spanish parliament). Submitted in July, it was finally acted upon in early October. The Cortés nullified the land grants, as the United States demanded, and advised the king to ratify the treaty. On 24 October 1820, Ferdinand did so, including the express annulment of the three land grants. Since the treaty had expired for want of ratification within the original six-month period, Monroe resubmitted it to the Senate on 19 February 1821. It was ratified on 22 February, two years to the day after it had first been signed.[98]

Acting quickly, the United States named Andrew Jackson governor, to reside at Pensacola, with Lt. Robert Butler to represent him at St. Augustine. These agents took control on 17 and 10 July 1821, respectively. La Florida was at last in U.S. hands. The

Anglo-Spanish conflict over it that had begun in the sixteenth century had been won by English speakers, even if not by Great Britain. Anglo-Americans already constituted a majority of Florida's white inhabitants and had been important, even controlling, in its trade since the 1670s. Territorial annexation was an anticlimax.

II.

THE AMERICAN FRONTIERS, 1821–1860

Although this book has already shown that East Florida was economically and demographically part of the United States by 1821 and thus already an "American frontier" in many senses of the term, the nineteenth-century historiographic tradition of subordinating all other events to constitutional and political changes connected to national, territorial states dictates that the year 1821 serve as the beginning of a new chapter in the story of Florida's frontiers. However, using 1821 as a division reflects important facts aside from those of a political nature. Once Americans gained a legal claim to all of the territory, they set about rapidly, and in characteristic ways, grasping actual control of the land and exploiting its resources. The speed and scale of those actions was unlike anything that had happened before. By 1860, the American frontier had engulfed almost the entire peninsula.

In 1821 there were two old centers of Euro-African populations at Pensacola and in Northeast Florida. There were also several tiny, mostly detached beginnings of additional settlements at Spring Creek (modern Jackson County), Mosquitos, Alachua, the Cuban fishing camps from Tampa Bay southward along the west coast, and at Key West.[1] The Americans quickly added a third major center that eclipsed the others: Middle Florida. At the same time, they got the Native American population that had occupied Middle Florida to agree to a reserve south of Alachua and inland from both coasts. Americans thus gained access to the better soils of the Tallahassee, Madison, Marianna, and Quincy hills (Middle Florida), to the better part of the central ridge, and to the hammocks and drainable swamps that existed in the extensive pine woods of the coastal terraces.

By 1835, both the Indians and the Americans found this situation unsatisfactory. For the Indians, it meant confinement to areas where their traditional crops and hunts were less productive, although we may infer that they were beginning to adapt to the new environment and its resources. For the Americans, who were rapidly filling Middle and East Florida with farms and plantations, and cattle where the soils would not support farming, having the Indians as neighbors was increasingly less desirable because of cultural hostility and a desire to take and use as much land as they wished. The resulting Second Seminole War, 1835–1842, interrupted the expansion of American settlement into the spaces between the major and minor centers. The outcome was the removal to Oklahoma of a major part of the Native American population. A remnant of several hundred remained, farming hammocks deep in southern Florida and trying hard to remain at peace with their aggressive neighbors.

When American frontier expansion resumed after the Second Seminole War, it did so primarily down the east and west coasts and spilled southward from Alachua toward Lake Okeechobee and eastward from Tampa into the Peace River Valley, formerly a major center for Creek and Seminole populations removed from Middle Florida. A third war with the remaining Seminoles, 1856–1858, ended in further but not complete removals. The way was cleared for settlers, most of whom were cattlemen, to move into the remaining part of southern Florida. Only the Everglades remained unsurveyed and unoccupied save for a few very small groups of Indians.

By 1860, population density measured over the entire peninsula was 2.6 persons per square mile, slightly above the minimum of two persons per square mile that defined what the U.S.

Census Bureau later (1890) labeled the frontier of "occupance," the first of the five densities of frontier population that it recognized.[2] By that date as well, contracts for the survey of the range and township division of the peninsula had reached the northern, western, and eastern edges of the Everglades, effectively taking in all of the land that could be used prior to twentieth-century drainage works.[3] A few of those surveys were not completed until after the Civil War and many parts of the rest of Florida remained frontiers long after 1860 (one thinks of the conditions described in Marjorie Kinnan Rawlings's *The Yearling* [1938] as evidence). Still, the control over the land that these surveying contracts aimed to impose marks the end of the "wilderness" in Florida—that is of land unsurveyed or otherwise reduced to a "civilized" order (for example by towns or rectilinear farms), and hardly occupied (by Americans). Finally, by 1860 Indian removal had ended. Even though a few hundred Seminole and Miccosukee remained deep in the Everglades and a few Tallahassees (Creek) lived in the Peace River Valley, the peninsula was effectively empty of the Native American peoples who had occupied it after 1704. Completion of Indian removal was a key marker of the advance of the U.S. frontier (however defined) through and beyond any given region. For all these reasons, this study ends with 1860. Florida's frontiers had not vanished, but what remained of them were very localized.

Preparing the Way

The arriving American authorities faced several problems. Removal of the Spanish troops and such Spanish subjects as wished to emigrate was one of them. Another was that Spanish land grants in northeast Florida and around Pensacola needed sorting into those that were valid and those that were fraudulent. This was important because the United States wanted as much of the territory in public lands as possible because their sale was to be the source of the money to pay the American claims against Spaniards that the U.S. government had assumed under the treaty of 1819. Surveying the public lands so that they could be offered for sale was a related, if separate problem. For most of the peninsula, Indian occupation was the main impediment to this task. Indian removal thus also was a problem as well as a matter of policy. And finally, the Americans needed to connect the two Euro-African population centers both by road and with a common government.

The Spanish evacuation of St. Augustine and Pensacola took place generally without difficulty and was achieved by the end of 1821. There were arguments over public records, first at Pensacola in the infamous widow Vidal case and somewhat later at St. Augustine when American officials seized the public archives after their Spanish keepers indicated that they might not surrender them, as the treaty required.[4] Notable among the persons leaving Florida for resettlement at royal expense in Cuba were 145 free persons of color who had resided in or near St. Augustine. Other individuals of this description remained at Pensacola and in northeast Florida. Among the latter were Zephania Kingsley's families.[5]

Setting up an effective, unified government for the two parts of Florida was the next order of business. Governor Andrew Jackson arrived with two secretaries, one for each part of the territory. But on 30 March 1822, Congress passed an act providing for a government consisting of a governor, one secretary, and a thirteen-member Legislative Council. All were initially presidential appointees. The governor, in turn, appointed the judges who controlled the counties (to 1829). William P. Duval, an associate of Jackson's, was named governor. Other Jacksonians also obtained appointed offices.[6]

The new Legislative Council met at Pensacola in late July 1822 and then at St. Augustine in May 1823. Travel difficulties made it clear that such alternation was unsatisfactory. The St. Augustine meeting agreed that a place between the two old towns should be found for a permanent capital city. In other business, these two sessions created Duval County from "east Florida" (St. Johns County) and Jackson County from "west Florida" (Escambia County) in 1822, and Gadsden and Monroe Counties in 1823.[7] Each new county contained a population that wished to be ruled locally rather than from distant St. Augustine or Pensacola.

The decision to find a site for a capital midway between St.

Augustine and Pensacola coincided with the efforts of the U.S. government to remove the Indians living in "Middle Florida" (defined by the Suwannee and Apalachicola Rivers) so that Apalachee and Alachua could be opened for settlement. Jackson's 1818 campaign through Apalachee had revealed the agricultural potential of the hill country, a fact attested by its rather large Indian population, which had grown in the years after 1818 as more and more Creek moved away from American settlements in Alabama and Georgia. Alachua had been known and coveted since the late eighteenth century. Recognizing that both were prime real estate, over the summer of 1821 American officials gathered information on Indian numbers and land titles (and Spanish land grants), convincing themselves that the Spanish government had never recognized Indian ownership of any land, except possibly individual holdings, and that there were less than two thousand Indians in the whole peninsula.[8] Next Jackson met with Neamathla, a Red Stick leader of the Seminole in Apalachee, and two other chiefs at Pensacola, 18–19 September 1821. They described the fifteen towns that made up the Seminole nation, stretching from Tampa Bay and Mosquitos to the Apalachicola River. Jackson in turn told them that the coasts were to be white territory. To Secretary of War John C. Calhoun, he wrote that he favored removal of these Indians to the Creek areas of Alabama and the separation of fugitive Blacks from among them.[9]

By early 1822, U.S. officials understood that the Seminole (Muskogee speakers) were only one of three groups. Red Stick Creek, and other Upper Creek who had been expelled from their towns for bad conduct, were a second group. The Miccosukee (Hitichi speakers) were also present, if poorly differentiated by the officials from the Seminole as such. All three groups were being raided by Cowetas, encouraged by whites who purchased Blacks captured in the raids.[10]

Organization of the territorial government under the Act of 1822 soon led to new calls by Americans for Indian removal. Governor William P. Duval and Joseph M. White, Secretary of the Land Commissioners at Pensacola, both wrote to Secretary of War John C. Calhoun, asking for removal from this "fairest portion of Florida" (Middle Florida). Florida's territorial delegate,

Joseph M. Hernández, lobbied Congress for the same thing. But removal involved expense and thus required Congressional action. The House Committee on Indian Affairs asked for and received a report from Calhoun. In the meanwhile, Duval undertook to assist the Indians because heavy rains had ruined their summer maize crop, producing potential famine, which in the past had meant Indian raids on settlers' cattle. A meeting he arranged for St. Marks in November 1822 failed because the U.S. Indian agents did not arrive on time. In any case, they had little money with which to assist the Indians.[11]

The report of the Committee on Indian Affairs, dated 21 February 1823, began to move the matter off dead center. Observing that the Indians were "dependent upon our will, and yet without the pale of our laws," the Committee recommended land grants to individual families (the Seminole had told Jackson that they were rumored to get 640 acres) within a defined, more compact area "so as to promote the interest and prosperity of the white citizens" who would move into Florida. No other government aid should be given.[12]

Duval, Bernard Segui, and Col. James Gadsden (a Jackson crony) were named commissioners to negotiate with the Indians for their removal to southern Florida (7 April 1823). After preliminary meetings at St. Augustine in June, on 6 September 1823 they met at Moultrie Creek south of St. Augustine with seventy chiefs and leading men. Neamathla, John Blunt, Tuski Hago, Econchatiomico, the Mulatto King, and other leaders were present. Some would be prominent in the Second Seminole War. The American "talk" was fairly blunt, reminding the Indians that the whites were like the fruit and leaves of trees, which increased annually, whereas they were like deer, that "might be hunted to their destruction." Under pressure, the Seminole agreed to accept the Red Stick Creek onto their land and to remove, but not so far south as Charlotte Harbor and the Peace River. That far south, there were no hickory nuts, acorns, persimmons, or other familiar forest foods that the Indians used to supplement their agricultural production. Content to keep the Indians fifteen miles from the Gulf and twenty from the Atlantic and thus from munitions and arms smuggled in by Cubans and others—and south

of the area of immediate interest to U.S. settlers—the Commissioners agreed to a reserve that included the Brooksville Hills and
other southern extensions of the central Florida ridge. They also
agreed that six of the chiefs from the Apalachee area should have
private reserves of two to four square miles along the lower
course of the Apalachicola River. The Indians gave up 24 million
acres (of 37.9 million in the territory) and any fugitive slaves
they held in exchange for a twenty-year annuity of $5,000 annu-
ally, moving expenses, a year's food, payment for improvements
being abandoned, a school, a blacksmith, a gunsmith, farm
tools, and livestock. The Treaty of Moultrie Creek was signed by
thirty-one chiefs on 18 September 1823. Afterwards, gifts were
given by the commissioners.[13]

As these developments were unfolding, the capital site selec-
tion committee was traversing north Florida. On 20 November
1823, they selected the site of Tallahassee, an area of Indian old
fields almost exactly halfway between Pensacola and St. Augustine. The U.S. government gave a quarter section of land for the
town and also helped develop the road from St. Augustine to
Pensacola that passed through Tallahassee. On 9 April 1824, the
first settlers arrived with "wagons, teams, hogs and cattle, to
build upon the capital site." The Indians still there were allowed
to remain until the fall harvest. The first session of the Legislative Council was held in a log structure on 8 November 1824.[14]
By then, the Seminole and Miccosukee had begun to leave the
area for their reserves.

Removal had been postponed until the late fall of 1824 because
of Indian resistance and delays in U.S. preparations to assist
them. The resistance came mostly in the winter of 1823–1824 and
was blamed on Neamathla's leadership, which likely reflected a
widespread Indian unwillingness to give up what they knew was
the better part of Florida. A mark of this resistance was the killing of cattle belonging to white settlers. Governor Duval had to
use the threat of force and to engineer Neamathla's replacement
by "John Hicks" (Tuskalmathla), a more compliant Miccosukee
chief, in July 1824 before an agreement on the date of removal
(after the fall harvest) could be obtained.[15]

On the U.S. side, the delay was due to waiting for Congress to appropriate $65,700 for general expenses and $24,500 for such things as compensation for improvements ($4,500), farm implements and animals ($6,000), and the survey of the reservation boundaries ($5,000). American officials were also looking for a contractor(s) who could deliver the foods promised at the lowest possible price. They anticipated delivering six hundred rations at Cantonment Brooke, newly opened (January 1824) at Tampa, and four hundred at the mouth of the Oklawaha River. Each was to be 1.25 pounds of fresh beef or 0.75 pounds of salt pork, one quart of maize or one pound of good wheat flour, and one quart of salt per hundred rations, the whole to cost no more than 11.5 cents per ration at Tampa, or 14 cents at the Oklawaha.[16]

The exodus got underway in November 1824. John Bellamy evaluated the towns and distributed $3,570 in silver coins to the departing Indians. Liquor merchants were at hand to relieve the Indians of even that small payment. A few wagons and even canoes were provided, but most Indians seem to have walked. As the Indians arrived on the main, southern reservation, they experienced problems finding soils suitable for maize and other crops, locating coontie (also known as arrowroot, a source of edible starch), and clearing the land. They had already demanded that the Big Swamp area be included in the reservation that James Gadsden had laid out, a demand that Congress agreed to in 1826. Big Swamp contained, by one estimate, five to six thousand acres of "pretty good land," whereas most of the rest of the northern part of the reservation (the only part really known to white officials, and then poorly) was "the poorest part of Florida" that flooded during the winter rainy season or consisted of sandy hills of low fertility (the Brooksville and Hernando Hills area).[17]

Some Seminole villages existed within the area of the reserve, one reason Gadsden had extended the reserve north of where some whites wanted it (i.e., below Charlotte Harbor). Yet these earlier migrants were not much better off than those who had been forced into the area in 1824. As William Duval discovered in February 1826 when he examined the towns near the military road from the Indian agency at Silver Springs to Cantonment Brooke (Tampa) during a dreary, thirteen-day trip with cold, almost constant rain falling from a stalled front, most were on poor

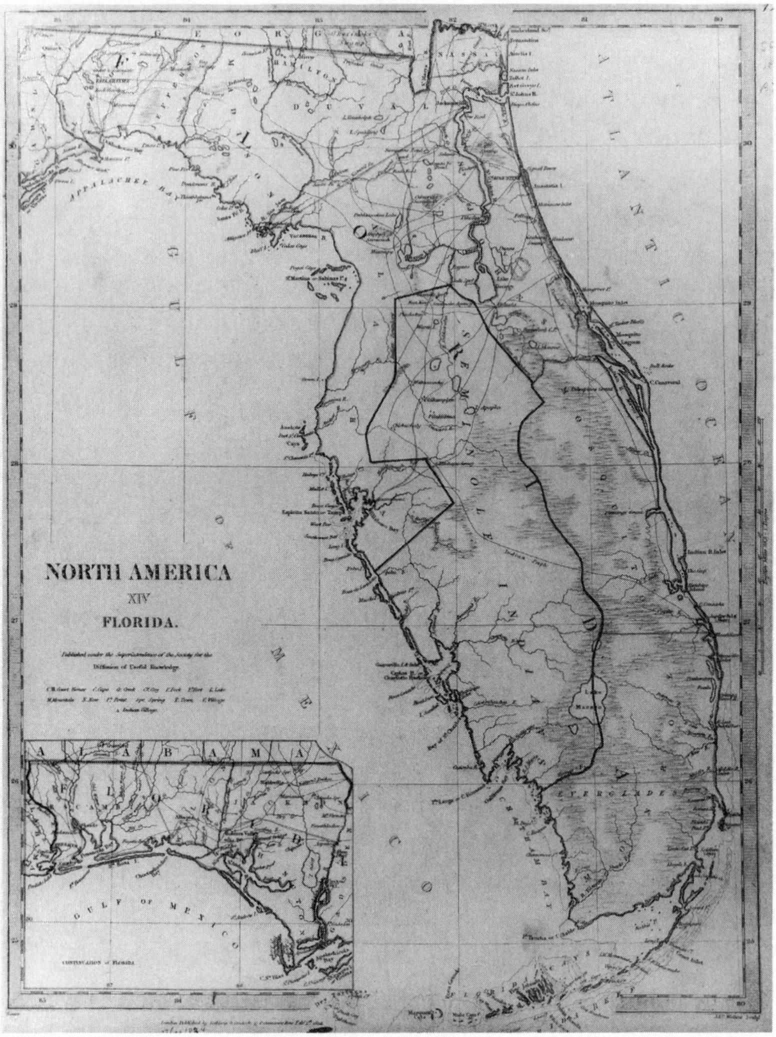

Figure 11.1. The First Seminole Reservation. "NORTH
AMERICA, XIV, FLORIDA" (LONDON: BALDWIN AND CRADOCK, 1834).
COURTESY OF THE P. K. YONGE LIBRARY OF FLORIDA HISTORY,
UNIVERSITY OF FLORIDA. RESERVATION BOUNDARY ENHANCED.

ground. However, he missed the settlements in the Cove of the
Withlacoochee River, which were more favorably situated. Nor
did he get far enough south to visit Oponney's plantation at Lake
Hancock. That chief had a two-story board house and many out-
buildings, a peach orchard, a herd of three hundred cattle, and

some twenty slaves. He produced rice, maize, and potatoes for St. Augustine's market. But his case seems to have been exceptional. For most of the Seminole, Miccosukee, and Red Stick Creeks in the reserve, whether long resident or recently arrived, conditions were poor.[18] This was due not just to the poor quality of the land but also to the fact that some 1,600 Indians had removed, but only 1,000 rations were provided. U.S. officials had refused to believe Indian estimates that there were 4,900 Indians and Blacks in thirty-seven towns, including those within the southern reservation area. Of the 4,900, roughly 1,000 persons (255 men with their families) remained in the Apalachicola reserves, or moved to the Creek areas in Alabama.[19]

These poor environments and ignorance of local resources, late arrival in the spring of 1825, disease, problems with delivering the rations, drought, and white fears produced reports in the spring of 1825 that the Indians were in desperate condition. It was said that the Indians acted to redress their condition by murdering a farmer in Alachua, killing cattle belonging to whites, and preventing the survey of lands not in the reserve. Recriminations among the U.S. officials charged with supplying the Indians filled the mails and eventually secured additional monies for rations in the early summer. But on 10 October, those rations stopped. As many as three hundred of the immigrants, faced with no rations, no game, and no harvest, returned across the Suwannee River to an area southeast of Tallahassee. There they killed cattle and seemed threatening to settlers who had purchased land. Duval secured additional rations and sent them to the reserve.[20]

The hard times for the Indians continued until 1827. Drought returned in 1826. While some ration monies were voted by Congress in 1826 in response to the starvation reported among the Seminole in late 1825, the distributions under that provision were minimal. Bands of men, more often Miccosukee than not, continued to roam beyond the reservation in search of food. Settlers complained that they and their cattle were not safe. The Legislative Council responded with a law of 1827 that punished Indians found outside of the reserves with thirty-nine strokes of a whip on the bare back. Better weather that spring and greater familiarity with the resources of their reserve and a desire to avoid removal to west of the Mississippi—a growing theme among whites from Washington to Tallahassee—led the Indians to begin to police themselves. The immediate crisis of removal passed. But white determination remained not to tolerate a separate society within their own or even to have Indian neighbors.[21]

Once the Indians had been removed from Middle Florida, the surveyors moved in, beginning the range and township survey of the peninsula. They ran their zero meridian just east of Tallahassee (modern Meridian Road) and their east–west base line just south of the town. Their instructions (in 1824) were to run only the township lines on poor quality lands, reserving section marking for good land that would sell. The first presidential proclamation announcing the Tallahassee Land Office sales of lands so surveyed was issued on 26 January 1825, with the sale taking place on 16 May 1825. At the St. Augustine Land Office (established 1826), sales were not proclaimed until February 1828 and not held until 1831 because of the complications of sorting out Spanish land grants. And finally, the Alachua Land Office (opened in 1842) had a sale in 1844. The terms were always the same: cash; first come, first served; and purchase of at least a quarter section (160 acres) at $1.25 per acre.[22] Large maps were issued almost yearly to show the progress of the surveys. By December 1831, some 5,487,658 acres had been surveyed, of which only 424,618, or about 1 percent of the potential public lands, had been sold. By 1835, all of West Florida (except the Forbes property) had been surveyed and much of it had been offered for sale.[23] Land sales totaled about 972,534 acres by 1850 and about three million acres by 1860.

As noted, the principal delay in surveying and selling land in East Florida and around Pensacola came from the need to settle Spanish land grants. Congress set up a claims commission for both areas in 1822, expecting that the job would take a year. In 1823, the law was amended to provide for two commissions, with power to confirm suitably documented grants of up to 3,500 acres. The West Florida Commission, based at Pensacola, finished its work in 1825. The East Florida Commission, at St. Augustine, was finally abolished in 1827. Most of the small Spanish grants had been determined in spite of various complications arising from the complexity of many claims and the politically motivated turnover of the officials doing the work. Congress ordered all remaining claims transferred to the Register and Receiver of the Land Office (at St. Augustine) for determining remaining claims under 3,500 acres. These were to be settled within one year because the surveys were underway in the area. December 1, 1828 was soon fixed as the last day for the Registers and Receivers to decide pending claims of up to one league square (a Spanish league was about 2.5 miles in length). All other claims were referred to the superior court in whose district each fell, with a right of appeal to the U.S. Supreme Court. A further law on 26 May 1830 provided that certain claims confirmed by the Spanish government after 24 January 1818 and accepted by the commissions were to be reexamined by the next session of the Congress. That ended legislation on the land claims. However, court battles over titles continued as late as the 1880s, shifting from the superior court to the state circuit courts (1845) and new Federal District Courts (1847).[24] In all some 1,359,548 acres were confirmed in East Florida and some 952,952 acres in West Florida, exclusive of the "Forbes Purchase."[25]

It is worth noting that on-the-ground resistance to some of the large, disputed Spanish grants could be substantial. A particularly notable case was Moses E. Levy's claim to 38,000 acres on "Alligator Creek" in the Alachua district. This land had been given to Fernando de la Maza Arredondo, Sr. as a service grant on 24 March 1817. Levy's claim arose out of a settlement of a debt by Arredondo, his sometime business partner. The claim was litigated from approximately 1826 to 1850, when the district court ruled it was valid, but allowed Levy to claim it in "floats," that is, in surveyed areas not sold to third parties. What is of note is that when it appeared that Levy might gain title to the original area during the 1840s, the deputy surveyor working the case reported that he expected physical harm from local residents if he pressed an inquiry on the "calls" or landmarks of the grant. Too, various witnesses, who claimed to have been in the area in the 1820s when the first attempt was made to locate the "calls," evidently lied about the non-existence of "Alligator town" (one of the calls; modern Lake City) and a group of citizens of Columbia County and their Grand Jury both intervened in the case because residents had purchased the land from the United States.[26] Similar, if less heated, conflicts between purchasers and claimants were usually settled to protect the occupants by granting land elsewhere if the Spanish grant was found to be valid.

An unexpected problem in settling land issues was the large number of American squatters who had moved into Florida once word had spread that Spain was going to give the land up. Those in the Pensacola and Spring Creek (Jackson County) areas may have included veterans of Jackson's 1818 campaign who had seen the possibilities of the land, while others were a spillover from settlement in the area of southern Alabama ceded by the Creek at Fort Jackson in 1814. In East Florida, several dozen squatters, at least, were also present, according to the land grant files.[27] The first U.S. response was the Donation Act of 1824, allowing squatters and holders of doubtful Spanish titles (often purchased) who could prove they had been in the Floridas before 1821 to claim up to 640 acres, free. A preemption law of 1826 allowed persons who had been in Florida before 1 January 1825 to purchase land they were using at $1.25 per acre if it was not "rightfully claimed" by anyone else. The *Pensacola Gazette* of 6 May 1826 called this the "salvation of much of the present population."[28]

The First Boom, to 1840

Attracting immigrants was not just a matter of removing Indians, surveying, and clearing titles to the land and offering it for sale. Propaganda was needed. The prospective settler of Florida did not want for at least limited information. Many older maps of Florida were available, although they told little about where the better soils and forest resources were. The "Geographical, Statistical, and Historical Map of Florida" by F. Lucas, Jr., was published in Carey and Lea's *A Complete Historical, Chronological, and Geographical American Atlas* in 1823; it made an effort to note these factors. Border annotations indicated that the better soils were on river banks, but the publication cautioned that "[t]he country, however, has been imperfectly explored, and few agricultural experiments have been made. Much of the land which, on superficial view, has been supposed to be not worth cultivating, it is believed may be turned to very profitable account." Coffee, sugar, cotton, oranges, olives, cattle, "cured" fish, oak, naval stores, timber, maize, rice, potatoes, hemp, and tropical fruits were listed as possible or actual products. Even more informative was Henry S. Tanner's *New American Atlas*, produced in 1823, 1825, 1827, 1836, and 1850. The Florida map published in it showed land qualities and vegetation (e.g., "pine land") for large areas, roads and trails, Indian towns, and much more (Figure 11.2, NE section). A map by Tanner also accompanied Charles Vignoles's book in 1823. Its legend even specifies the sources for its various parts so that the user could obtain further details. Like other maps by Tanner, it noted the "rich lands" along the Suwannee River, "fertile lands" of the central ridge area north of the Arredondo Grant, and the "flat pine lands" of many other areas.[29]

Maps aside, the promotion of Florida was aided by the publication of three books in the early 1820s: John Grant Forbes, *Sketches, Historical and Topographical, of the Floridas* (1821); William H. Simmons, *Notices of East Florida* (1822); and Charles B. Vignoles, *Observations Upon the Floridas* (1823). Forbes extolled the possibilities in East Florida, from Mosquitos northward. Indigo, cotton, rice, oranges, olives, and oak trees offered prospects. Mosquitos, in particular, had soils among the *"most luxuriant and highly productive"* (italics in original), while St. Augustine was the "Montpelier of North America" in healthfulness.[30] Simmons was a bit more realistic, noting that the Atlantic coastal region had hammocks of excellent soils but was mostly sterile pine forests. He had crossed the lower end of the central ridge and reported that those who knew it thought it was "superior to any body of soil in the United States of similar extent—from its fertility, the nature of its climate, and the adjacency of the greater part of it to convenient navigation" on the Ocklawaha and St. Johns Rivers. Unlike some other promoters, he comments on the political importance of denying the peninsula to enemies, cutting off the Indians from foreign supply, us-

Figure 11.2. Northeast Florida showing details of land qualities and roads. Per H. S. Tanner, *New American Atlas*, 1823. Courtesy of the P. K. Yonge Library of Florida History, University of Florida.

ing Tampa and Pensacola as naval bases (supported by the oak forests), and growing sugar within the United States. Vignoles noted much the same things but also that most of the better areas had already been granted.[31] Curiously, none of these men said much about Middle Florida, yet that was where the first American boom took place.

Whether because of this propaganda or because of private correspondence or word of mouth, immigrants, many of them planters from elsewhere in the South, began to move into Middle Florida. The cotton plantation rapidly became the frontier institution of that region. Unsystematic data suggests that Jackson and Gadsden Counties were occupied by planters from Georgia and North Carolina, among other places. Virginia planters such as Thomas Brown, John and Robert Gamble, and Hector Braden bought land and moved themselves, their families and their slaves to Leon County. Madison County, further east and settled a bit later, came to be dominated by South Carolinians. In 1839, Leon County alone had thirty planters, each with thirty to forty-five slaves.[32]

Men with lesser means from Georgia and perhaps other parts of the upland South moved into the pine flatwoods south and east of the hills and into Columbia, Suwannee, Union, Bradford, and Alachua Counties. Living by subsistence farming and hog and cattle raising, often without the benefit of title to the land they used, these poorer whites became known as "crackers." The origins of the name are disputed, but is most likely to have been in their use of whips to drive cattle. Their houses were one or two "crib" affairs; if the latter, they formed the classic "dogtrot" house.[33] Often restless, they eyed the Indian reserve.

Census and land sales data give a general idea of the boom that began around 1825 and lasted until the collapse of cotton prices in 1840. In 1821, there were perhaps 10,000 persons in Florida (Table 11.1). A special census taken in August 1825 of the three Middle Florida counties (Jackson, Gadsden, and Leon) showed 4,604 inhabitants or about 35 percent of the estimated 13,400 persons in the entire territory. Except for a few thousand persons around Pensacola, the rest resided in northeast Florida.[34] By 1830, the population was triple the level of 1821, thanks largely to the beginning of land sales. Fully 45 percent was in Middle Florida. Growth in the 1830s slowed to a 54 percent increase (to 54,477 in 1840) due to the uncertainties of the Seminole War, but land sales surged. Middle Florida held over 60 percent of the population recorded in 1840, with East Florida coming second at 25 percent. St. Augustine, the largest town in the territory, recorded 1,335 whites, 1,037 slaves, and 172 free persons of color in

TABLE 11.1   General Census Data, Florida, 1830–1860

Year	Total Pop.	% Male	% Female	% White	% Black	% Rural	% <15 years	% 15–44 years
1830	35,000	54	46	51	46	100	26	26[†]
1840	54,000	56	46*	52	50*	100	22	17[†]
1850	87,000	53	48*	54	46	100	45	53
1860	140,000	52	48	56	45*	96	44	51

Source: Historical Statistics of the United States, 29.
*Rounding in raw numbers and percentages exceed 100%.
[†]These percentages seem too low.

1830, numbers that remained steady during the 1830s, dropped during the 1840s, and recovered to about the same level by 1860.[35]

Land sales match the rapid population growth up to 1830 but do not correlate with the demographic slowdown thereafter. Instead, after languishing from 1831 to 1834, they rocketed upward in response to the higher cotton prices of 1833–1839, to a peak of 93,052 acres in 1837, and remained at high levels until a collapse in 1840 (Table 11.2).

Supporting the boom, John Lee Williams published *The Territory of Florida* in 1837, which highlighted the rich lands of the Tallahassee and Madison hills and Alachua, the rich hammocks on the rivers of East and West Florida and even the possibilities of the Everglades. There was hardly a part of Florida that Williams did not find capable of yielding a profit, although he admitted that over a quarter of it was lakes, rivers, and bays and even more was swamps, marshes, and brush (*matorrales*). He also noted that much of the land in northeast Florida was exhausted from long cultivation, and that unless that land and the land then cultivated for cotton were replenished with fertilizers (local sources of which he notes) there would be little profit in the future. His list of actual or potential commercial crops included not only cotton, rice, sugar cane, tobacco, indigo, and citrus, but also sweet potatoes, peaches, cochineal, and silk.[36]

This rise in land sales in the late 1830s was not simply a response to the improved price of cotton. It was also due to a credit balloon made possible by the creation of banks. The Legislative Council approved bank charters as early as 1823, but Governor

TABLE 11.2 Public Land Sales, 1825–1860 (Figures in Acres)

Year	Tallahassee	St. Augustine	Newnansville	Tampa	Total
1825	58,317				58,317
1826	52,433				52,433
1827	138,323				138,323
1828	34,626		80*		34,706
1829	47,186				47,186
1830	57,074				57,074
1831	25,114		935*		26,048
1832	9,086				9,086
1833	12,166		160*		12,326
1834	16,282		836*		17,118
1835	47,869		451*		48,321
1836	77,054	50	689*		77,793
1837	77,340	685	15,028*		93,053
1838	42,528	1,286	21,041*		64,854
1839	32,982	2,030	25,191*		60,202
1840	15,556	2,032	4,570*		22,158
1841	3,424	289	756*		4,469
1842	2,510		2,688		5,198
1843	5,254	536	6,090		11,880
1844	7,149	316	5,087		12,552
1845	6,353	704	8,041		15,098
1846	10,442	1,758	24,639		36,840
1847	17,741	1,203	7,931		26,875
1848	12,673	582	4,798		18,053
1849	17,578	2,002	2,787		22,366
1850	17,391	1,898	8,586		27,874
1851	16,084	1,840	17,084		35,008
1852	5,332	2,488	13,300		21,121
1853	28,832	10,590	51,046		90,468
1854	171,427	3,831	87,993	1,144	264,396
1855	93,944	1,601	70,579	5,772	170,896
1856	11,837	583	13,823	487	34,136
1857	18,447	960	17,054	1,244	37,704
1858	38,793	1,879	37,597	4,408	79,710
1859	44,616	1,990	22,461	1,134	70,201
1860†	23,733	995	3,327	329	28,384

Sources: through 1845, U.S. 30th Congress, Second Session, *Senate Documents*, No. 2, Appendix 3, Florida land sales by year, district and year of offering. After 1845, figures from Annual Reports of the Commissioner of the General Land Office, as published in the *Senate Documents* for a given Congressional session, adjusted beginning in 1849 to fit the calendar year. Figures from 1849 onward reported semi-annually (Jan.–June, July–Dec.) on a fiscal year (July to June) basis. All figures rounded to the whole acre and all should be regarded as approximate because adjustments were sometimes made in later years for lands returned or other causes.

*District created in 1842. Sales before then were actually from the Tallahassee office.
†Half a year only due to secession.

Duval vetoed those charters for many of the same reasons his friend Andrew Jackson opposed the Bank of the United States. A Bank of Florida charter passed over his veto in 1828, followed in quick succession by ten others (to 1836). Of these, the most successful and important for the boom was the Union Bank of Florida, chartered in 1833 (with Duval's approval) with a capital of $3 million and located at Tallahassee. It opened for business in 1835.[37]

Planters could buy stock in the Union Bank with cash and 50 percent mortgages on their slaves and land (often given exaggerated values). Stockholders could, in turn, obtain loans for up to two-thirds of the value of their stock. Most did and immediately bought more land, slaves, and stock. Land sales reflect this activity as does the complaint in 1835 of a Jackson County planter that the best land already had been purchased by speculators.[38] The Territory provided twenty-four to thirty-year "faith bonds" equal to the subscribed stock, bonds that John G. Gamble and other promoters marketed in Europe. The Union Bank then assumed the obligation to pay the principal and 6 percent interest. Bond buyers were led to believe that the Territory's taxing power would back up the bank. Even so, they discounted the bonds when they bought them. The bank also issued its own currency, making additional loans against the value of land and slaves. Because of the rise in cotton prices, those who were optimistic thought that the planters' loans could be paid back in as little as two years.[39] It was a classic American state bank swindle that provoked political opposition because of the "insider" nature of the loans (see below). Still, this maneuver (and other factors) allowed an increase in cotton production from 338 bales in 1827 to 15,870 in 1834, and to 31,620 in 1840.[40] Table 11.3 provides antebellum figures on cotton production.

Nor was cotton the only speculative crop of the late 1830s. Silk cultivation, or more correctly the cultivation of Chinese mulberry trees around St. Augustine to meet a demand in the North, also followed the boom and bust of the late 1830s. Dr. Andrew Anderson of St. Augustine had as many as 150,000 cuttings in the ground in 1839; estimates were that one million were being grown, a replacement for the citrus trees lost in the hard freeze

TABLE 11.3 Florida Cotton Production, 1821–1860

Year	U.S. Crop in Bales	Fla. Crop in Bales	Fla. Crop as % of U.S.	Av. Bale Weight (lbs)	N.Y. Price, Lowest	N.Y. Price, High	N.Y. Price, Av.
1821	647,482	no data		278	$0.11	$0.20	$0.1432
1830	976,845	338*		339	$0.08	$0.125	$0.1004
1840	2,177,835	31,620†	1.45%	383	$0.06	$0.135	$0.0892
1850	2,333,718	45,131†	1.93%	429	$0.10	$0.179	$0.1234
1860	4,861,292	65,153	1.34%	461	$0.105	$0.118	$0.11

Source: Watkins, *Production and Price of Cotton.*
*1827 figure
†400-lb bales

of February 1835. Like the cotton boom, the mulberry tree frenzy collapsed in 1840.[41]

Easy credit and the boom in cotton production also brought about the completion of the first internal improvements, which, like state banks and land speculation, were characteristic developments of the American frontier. Enthusiasm for canals, including one or more across the peninsula, swept Florida in the 1820s but died when surveyors reported various technical difficulties that would have made them prohibitively expensive. Railroads replaced canals in the 1830s as the internal improvement of choice. Cotton planters in Middle Florida, and boosters of St. Joseph (Port St. Joe) and Pensacola built lines to speed the bales to market. The Pensacola railroad (the Alabama, Florida and Georgia Railroad Company) built roadbed but never operated, and the St. Joseph and Iola ran only from 1839 to 1841. But the Tallahassee to St. Marks railroad began operations in 1836 and continued to operate with mule and occasional steam power until 1860. Other projects failed, although at least two received Congressional grants of right-of-way.[42] Successful railroad development had to wait for the 1850s.

Other measures of the boom included the creation of counties and the founding of towns. From two in 1821, the number of counties grew to fourteen in 1828, then twenty-eight in 1844. Besides Tallahassee (1824), Middle Florida saw the incorporation of Quincy (1825), Monticello (1828), Marianna, and St. Marks (1829).[43]

Morton D. Winsberg has used still another gauge: the founding of post offices that lasted at least five years. Cautioning that locations were based only loosely on population (politics was often a factor), he found that thirty-two offices were founded before 1830, mostly in Middle Florida and the lower St. Johns area, twenty-seven in the decade of the 1830s, fifty-two in the 1840s, and seventy-three in the 1850s. His maps show Middle Florida and lower St. Johns River cores, with expansion after 1840 southward along the St. Johns and into the central ridge area, and in the 1850s into the newly opened southwest, mostly the Peace River Valley area. Which is to say that settlement followed the better soils as they were opened for purchase, with the St. Johns River serving as a major avenue to the interior.[44]

The population expansion was sustained by cotton, of course, but also by cattle, two forest products, sugar and, to 1835, citrus. Of cattle, little more can be said than to note that cows, pigs, and horses were the cash crops of the crackers, Indians, and even some planters. The forest products were the various derivatives of pine sap (tar, turpentine) and live oak "knees" reserved for the U.S. Navy's shipbuilding. Sugar cane grew at Mosquitos until the Seminole War, in the Alachua district (including Marion County), and in Middle Florida, although only a few planters there went beyond molasses production. Citrus was a major export from St. Augustine and the St. Johns Valley until the ten-day hard freeze of February 1835 destroyed the trees. Thereafter, groves both wild and planted further south along both coasts gradually replaced what had been lost.[45]

The society of the boom years was described at the time by some of its participants. Reports from St. Augustine, Pensacola, and Tallahassee indicate that balls and banquets were the major forms of elite entertainment. In Pensacola, the king who gave the ball won that right by shooting a wooden duck (*pato* in Spanish) or "patgo" on the top of a pole to which the young women of the town had attached ribbons. The youths were usually drunk by the time they took aim. In St. Augustine (during the days leading up to Lent) and Tallahassee, the custom involved the use of flowers, with the queen of one ball selecting the king of the next from among the revelers by handing him a bouquet. This custom was one of the few Hispanic ones adopted by the Americans, who did not engage in the religious festivals, chivarees, and elaborate wakes and funerals that the Hispanic populations of Pensacola and St. Augustine continued to practice.[46] At Tallahassee, the meeting of the legislature in January and February created a social season. Beyond the balls and banquets, it was enlivened by race week and sometimes a circus and traveling players. To end the season, a "May Party" ball was celebrated in Tallahassee from the late 1830s onward. Heavy drinking by the men, and the occasional (illegal) duel regularly accompanied these activities.[47]

The American planters and the infrequent foreign traveler who visited Florida in these years had little good to say about their social inferiors. White overseers were characterized as "very rough men, but seldom cruel," the majority of Tallahassee's population as "indifferent people," and the Minorcans as "a pleasant, easy going, amiable people" who lacked the energy and intelligence of the Yankees who settled among them and were called by some of the latter "Turnbull's negroes." "Crackers" were disdained as ignorant and sometimes idle but accorded some status because they were white Americans, voters, and welcoming of strangers. Black slaves were recognized as the clearers of the land ("nature's pioneer, preparing an area where the higher genius of the white man can play a part free from obstruction") but were otherwise stereotyped in the usual ways as "benefiting" from slavery. Free Blacks were anathema and subject to increasingly severe restrictive laws.[48]

East and West Florida did not experience as much of a boom as Middle Florida. West Florida grew little cotton and East Florida's production was constrained by the need to fertilize the hammock and island soils that had, in some cases, grown long-staple "sea island" cotton since the 1780s. Moreover, there was little "good" land in the St. Johns Valley that had not already been claimed, making it difficult for the planters to move production when "old" land became exhausted. Even more, East Florida suffered from the outbreak of the Second Seminole War, which coincided almost exactly with the period of the boom, although it lasted longer, and produced the usual insecurity along the frontier even though Seminole raids were few and widely spread except in Mosquitos and parts of the upper St. Johns Valley. The Americans had themselves to blame for the outbreak of the war.

The Second Seminole War

Florida and American officials began to challenge the Indian reserves created in 1823 as early as 1828, but they systematically attacked them once Andrew Jackson became president in 1829. Covetousness, racism, the defense of slavery (the Seminole allegedly provided refuge for fugitives), claims of self-defense against real and imagined Indian raids on cattle and other property, and a resolve to have a single, national society all played parts in white determination to be rid of the Indians once and for all. As Chief Jumper was said to have observed during a conference in April 1828, "It seems that the white people will not rest, or suffer us to do so, till they have got all the property belonging to us, and made us poor."[49]

To achieve removal from the main, southern reserve, Col. James Gadsden met at Paynes Landing on the Ocklawaha with fifteen Seminole[50] chiefs led by Miccanopy. A drought in that spring of 1832 had caused the Indians to seek government rations, which Gadsden refused to supply unless the Indians agreed to go west. In the end, by the Treaty of Payne's Landing of 9 May 1832, the chiefs agreed that a delegation of seven leaders would go to Oklahoma to evaluate the land. The Indians later claimed that this delegation was to report to the nation; U.S. officials claimed that it had full power to sign a treaty of removal, which was coerced from the delegation at Fort Gibson on 28 March 1833. Removal of some of the Apalachicola groups was obtained by treaty (11 October 1832), through payment for lands, and through the threat of force if the Indians did not comply.[51]

When U.S. agents attempted to arrange removal under the Treaty of Fort Gibson in the fall of 1834 and during the spring, summer, and fall of 1835, they found that all but a small group of Indians refused to agree. Nonetheless, Indian Agent Wiley Thompson and Brigadier General Duncan L. Clinch (who had a plantation near Fort King, i.e., modern Ocala) pushed ahead with plans to sell the Seminole cattle and embark the Indians and their slaves for Oklahoma. Additional U.S. Army troops were ordered to Florida to enforce the treaties. Emathla Holata, an older chief, finally gave in to this pressure and took his cattle to Fort Brooke for sale. Osceola, by then a leader of the resistance, killed him on 26 November 1835. Indian raids on frontier farms began at about the same time. In early December, the militia was called to duty.[52]

Thus begun, the Second Seminole War dragged on until 1842 when the United States declared victory (in reality a truce) and ceased to pursue the six hundred or so remaining Seminole, Miccosukee, Creek, and their Black associates who were living south of the headwaters of the Peace River. The Seminole enjoyed early success, notably with the Dade Massacre of 28 December 1835, but were ground down by a combination of scorched-earth tactics like those that the Spaniards had used against the Mocama Timucuans in 1568–1569 and against the Guale in 1598–1600. These tactics were followed by more systematic search-and-capture or destroy tactics from an expanded set of forts, coupled with the arrests of leaders who were negotiating under flags of truce. Still, into the early 1840s the Seminole and their Creek allies were able to raid at will in areas adjacent to their reserve, and even further afield in some cases. Many militiamen seem to have regarded the war as a slave and cattle hunt (in 1837 they were allowed to keep cattle they captured) and to have regarded their government salaries and rations as an entitlement. Indeed, the issue of the slaves living with the Seminole derailed the Fort Dade agreement of 6 March 1837 that might have shortened the war. The Seminole claimed them as property, but General Thomas S. Jesup felt compelled to honor the claims of white slave owners instead[53] (see Figure 11.3).

At the end of the war, the reckoning showed that the United States and Florida had spent $30–40 million, suffered 1,621 white deaths (many from disease), and deported as many as 4,420 Seminole, including some of their Black associates. The Indians had lost several hundred killed, including at least forty of their Black associates. An estimated ninety-five warriors remained under a live-and-let-live agreement that confined them to the least

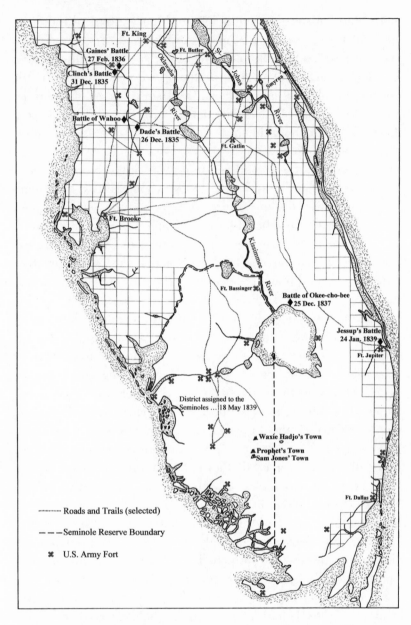

Figure 11.3. Second Seminole War, 1835–1842, fort, trail, and battle locations. BASED ON UNITED STATES, 30TH CONGRESS, 1ST SESSION, *Senate Executive Documents, No. 2*, ANNUAL REPORT OF THE COMMISSIONER OF THE GENERAL LAND OFFICE, "MAP OF THE STATE OF FLORIDA SHOWING THE PROGRESS OF THE SURVEYS, 1847." COURTESY OF THE LIBRARIES, LOUISIANA STATE UNIVERSITY.

desirable parts of South Florida between the Peace and Kissimmee Rivers. Sugar plantations in the Mosquitos area had been destroyed, and many Americans had retreated from the area immediately north of the old reservation line. The Cuban fishing camps at Tampa and Sarasota Bays and at Charlotte Harbor had also ceased to exist.[54] There do not seem to be any estimates of the economic damage done.

New Foundations and Expansion

By the time the Second Seminole War was declared over, the cotton and banking booms had collapsed and Florida was well on its way to becoming a state. Removal of millions of acres from the Indian reserve and the Armed Occupation Act of 1842 prepared the way for the second and third periods of frontier expansion before 1860.

The collapse of the cotton boom is starkly indicated by a few prices. Average New York prices for middling upland cotton dipped in 1838 from $0.133 per pound to $0.101, rebounded in 1839 to $0.134, and then collapsed in 1840 to $0.089. They sank even lower, bottoming out at $0.056, in 1845.[55]

These numbers spelled ruin for planters who had mortgaged their lands, slaves, and cattle to the banks in the boom of the 1830s and for the promoters of St. Joseph and its railroad. In an effort to help, the Legislative Council suspended tax collections on land and slaves in 1840 and indefinitely suspended them in 1841. Even so, some planters, like the Gambles and Bradens, went bankrupt and had to start over, in both cases on the Manatee River where they began to cultivate sugar. St. Joseph was abandoned after windows and doors were removed from the buildings. Apalachicola, its rival for the Apalachicola River cotton trade, survived.[56]

The collapse of cotton prices also brought down the state-chartered banks, which had already been under pressure for political reasons. Opposition to the Union Bank and the "insider" nature of its benefits arose in 1838 and rapidly became a Democratic Party weapon against the Whigs. Limitations on the banks were incorporated in the financial regulations written into the proposed constitution of 1839. Sectionalism partially underlay this division; Democrats were strong in East and West Florida, which had gotten no benefit from the bank, while the Whigs were concentrated among the planters of Middle Florida. Even more importantly, ordinary Floridians discovered that they might be liable for the $3.9 million in "faith bonds" that the territory had issued to support not just the Union Bank ($3 million) but also the bankrupt Pensacola Bank ($500,000) and St. Augustine's Southern Life Insurance and Trust Company ($400,000) which was also a bank in spite of its name.

The first round of political action on the bank issue at the constitutional convention of 1838–1839 was followed by others at the legislative sessions of 1839–1843. Florida House committees, reporting in 1840, lambasted the banks and called for repudiation of the bonds. When the Union Bank failed to make an interest payment on 1 July 1841, the legislature of 1842 repudiated the bonds and imposed harsh conditions on the banks. Then in 1843, the legislature demanded that the banks cease operations until they could redeem their notes in specie, upon demand. That effectively destroyed what was left of the bank boom of the 1830s.[57] Banking legislation of the late 1840s and the 1850s provided for generally sounder institutions.

Politically, the boom and subsequent bust moved Florida closer to statehood. Interest in statehood began with American control and increased as immigration picked up. Some settlers wanted it as their birthright, others to get control of the sixteenth-section school lands (which were to be sold to support schools) if not the rest of the public land as well, and still others, in the 1830s, because they saw statehood as a way to defend slavery. Congressional abolition of slavery in the District of Columbia (a territory like Florida, it was said) in 1835 seems to have brought the latter concern to the fore. Fiscal and tax issues also figured into the mix at various points.

After several earlier proposals had failed, the Legislative Council in 1837 authorized a referendum on statehood that passed in Middle and West Florida but was rejected in East Florida. Governor Richard Keith Call, a member of the so-called "nucleus" of Jacksonians and Virginians who favored statehood, then called for elections to a constitutional convention to be held in December. At the same time, the territory's representative to the U.S. Congress, Charles Downing, secured an act setting up an elected, bi-cameral territorial legislature (to replace the council). When it met (from 3 December 1838 to 11 January 1839), the convention quickly adopted many of Alabama's constitutional provisions and then fell into quarrels between the sectional interests over banking legislation and representation. Middle Florida's Whigs lost on the banking issues but united with West Floridians to have their way on representation at the expense of East Florida. Constitutional articles supporting slavery and granting the legislature the right to limit or forbid manumission and the movement of free Blacks into the state were also adopted. Submitted to a popular vote in August 1839, the proposed constitution passed 2,065 to 1,961.[58]

The issue of statehood was stalled for the next five years. East Florida tried, but failed, to get Congress to separate it from the rest of the territory. The Florida legislative houses repeatedly took different stands on the issue of immediate statehood. In the end, admission depended on the people of Iowa, who finally approved their own statehood in 1844, allowing Iowa and Florida to enter the Union together on 25 January 1845, thus preserving the balance of free and slave states. Congress disallowed the provisions of the 1839 draft constitution allowing a division of the state at some future time, forbidding the abolition of slavery, and forbidding the entrance of free Blacks. The new state's flag had horizontal stripes of blue, orange, red, white, and green, with the motto on the orange, "Let Us Alone."[59]

The Final Waves of American Expansion

The land freed up by the removal of the Seminoles was first opened to settlement under the Armed Occupation Act of 4 August 1842. A new land office at Newnansville (near modern Gainesville) made it somewhat easier to file a claim under the act. The act allowed any man able to bear arms and over the age of eighteen to claim 160 acres provided they were not on a barrier island nor within two miles of a fort. Five years' residence, a house, and at least five acres under cultivation would lead to a title. During the year in which the act had force, some 1,317 permits were issued for slightly less than the 200,000 acres allowed. The new claims were restricted to various blocks of land south of the boundary of Townships 10S and 11S. These included the mouth of the Suwannee River; an inverted "U" of land at the northern end of the former reservation; a block around Lake Tohopekattigo; another on the upper St. Johns River; and from Township 28S, just north of Tampa, to Charlotte Harbor and as far east as Peace River (from Township 34S the boundary was Range 22E). These were all areas selected to enhance the security of adjacent areas. Many of the claimants were former militiamen and cattleraisers who were being forced off land further north as it was bought up for cotton production, but others were men like the Gambles and the Bradens, who had moved south in time to take advantage of the act to start over.[60] The act was extended in 1844 and 1848 to take care of certain classes of claims under it.[61]

The end of the Second Seminole War and the removal of the Seminole to a much reduced reserve of 4,288,000 acres meant that surveying and selling land in the center and down both coasts of the state resumed. The surveying reached Township 27S in 1848 and, on the west coast, the Caloosahatchee River (roughly Township 43S) by 1860. A narrow fringe of townships three- or occasionally four-deep opened up the east coast by 1848 (see Figure 11.4). The result was a steady stream of immigrants, for example, the Georgians who moved into the Indian River and Lake Worth areas in the early 1840s. To prevent incidents, in 1845 a twenty-mile-wide buffer zone was placed around the reservation.[62]

Reports from 1847, 1850, and 1852 tell the story of the surveying and land sales that followed. Of the estimated 36,137,137 acres in public lands (out of 37,931,520 total acres in Florida), 15 million had been surveyed by 1848, 21.5 million by 1850, and 22.5 million by 1852. However, sales continued to be disappointing. Through 1850, only 972,534 acres had been sold, a figure dwarfed by donations to the state for schools and universities (973,442 acres) and internal improvements (500,000 acres). Only 227.49 acres were recorded as reserved for Indians, a clear indication of

Figure 11.4. Twenty-mile buffer zone around the second
(temporary) Seminole reservation, as shown on "A Plat
Exhibiting the State of the Surveys in the State of
Florida, 1852." UNITED STATES, 32ND CONGRESS, 2ND SESSION,
Senate Executive Documents, No 1. REPORT OF THE
COMMISSIONER OF THE GENERAL LAND OFFICE, "A PLAT EXHIBITING
THE STATE OF THE SURVEYS IN THE STATE OF FLORIDA, 1852."
COURTESY OF THE LIBRARIES, LOUISIANA STATE UNIVERSITY.

U.S. policy. Sales had increased by November 1852 to a total of 1,035,416 acres, all of them of land fertile enough that someone would pay $1.25 or more an acre for it. For the four years between 1850 and 1853, sales averaged 15,542 acres per year at Tallahassee, 17,020 at Newnansville, and 3,007 at St. Augustine, or an average of 35,569 acres annually.[63] Then in 1854, Congress decided to sell off less desirable lands at prices ranging from 12.5 cents to $1.00 per acre. Sales during that year and the next leaped by a factor of six, with the Tallahassee Land Office selling 8.4 times its previous average, much of it land priced at $0.25 to $0.50 per acre. Thereafter, sales settled down to an annual average of 60,204 acres (1856–1860), 1.7 times the average of the four years leading up to the new policy. By the end of 1860, total sales had reached roughly 1,825,000 acres.[64]

The few published travelers' accounts from the 1850s uniformly describe vast expanses of seemingly uninhabited land along the banks of the St. Johns River, across central Florida on routes south of modern Interstate 4, and between the small towns (modern Brooksville, Ocala, Newnansville [near modern Gainesville], Alligator [Lake City]) from Tampa to Madison. The luxuriant flora of the St. Johns River Valley was contrasted with the pine-palmetto flatwoods and sandy hills of the center of the state. Visitors generally noted the oranges and various vegetables available in March, months before they would be available back home. Most found abundant food, often including venison and wild turkey. Travelers also note the invalids who flocked to Jacksonville, St. Augustine, Tampa, and Orange Springs in the hope that the milder winter weather would restore lungs congested by a variety of ailments. Even fellow southerners like Clement Claiborne Clay sometimes criticized the locals—most likely poorer whites—as "indolent & inert, & do little for themselves. A more worthless & ignorant & artless population cannot be found in the Union. . . ."[65] What these visitors did not see was how such "cowdrivers" were gradually gaining rudimentary control of the land even as their few, more affluent, and "refined" neighbors were cultivating cotton and sugar on the limited areas of better soils. Both sorts of resident were needed on this frontier, as on most American frontiers in the South.

The advance of the surveyor's frontier to the Caloosahatchee River meant that it had intruded on the Seminole reserve established in 1842. This was part of a general effort to get the remaining bands to remove to Oklahoma even though they were peaceful until 1849. Poor whites who hoped for government rations, wages, and loot from the Indians if a war started circulated rumors of attacks. Government officials conspired, unsuccessfully, to kidnap Billy Bowlegs.[66] A census of 1847 showed that there were about 150 Indians in four groups (see Table 11.4).

Pressure for removal accelerated in 1849. In January, the Florida legislature passed a law forbidding the Seminole from leaving their reserve but also forbidding the sale of alcoholic drinks to them. Then, for reasons unknown, at the spring Green Corn dance Chipco and some twenty other men were "exiled" from the reserve by the others. On 12 July, four of these "outsiders" killed William Barker and wounded James Russell on the latter's farm four miles north of Fort Pierce. This attack provoked a general exodus of settlers from Key Biscayne to New Smyrna. Five days later, these same four attacked the Kennedy and Darling store on the Peace River, killing two and wounding two. Unwilling to start a war, Bowlegs eventually turned over three of the four guilty men to the U.S. Army, but refused to consider removal when Major General David E. Twiggs told him that those were his instructions and offered monetary inducements.[67]

American pressure increased in 1850–1851. Delegations from Oklahoma and money persuaded seventy-four Indians to leave at the end of February 1850. Bowlegs negotiated and might have

Table 11.4 Seminole Census, 1847

Leader	Ethnicity	Males, age 12 or older	Total Number	Location
Chipco	Creek	26		Lake Istokpoga
Billy Bowlegs	Seminole	54	120–130	SW of Okeechobee
Sam Jones (Arepika)	Miccosukee	36	100	Big Cypress
Ismahtee	?	10		10,000 Islands

Sources: James W. Covington, "A Seminole Census: 1847," *Florida Anthropologist*, 21, No. 4 (Dec. 1968), 120–22 and Brown, *Peace River*, 70–71.

been brought to an agreement, but two of his men who had gone
to trade at Ft. Hamer on the Manatee River were swept up with
those who had agreed to depart. Remembering white lack of
good faith during the previous war, he withdrew after a final conference with Indian Agent John Casey on 11 April 1850. Meanwhile, General Twiggs built a series of forts to cordon off more
of the reserve. Passage of the Swamp and Overflowed Lands Act
that same year gave the state of Florida and sugar planters and
cattle ranchers who had been eyeing areas north of the Caloosahatchee River and the Big Cypress Swamp additional incentives
to remove the Seminole. Florida boldly claimed 22,244,541 acres
of public land as swamp and overflowed lands, including all of
South Florida! In January 1851, the legislature passed an act setting up a mechanism to sell these lands and another to force the
final removal of the Indians.[68]

Even more pressure was applied in the years 1852–1855. In
March 1852, mounted militia in state pay captured nineteen Indians in a camp on the St. Johns River, well outside of the reserve.
Bowlegs tried to put off further attacks by negotiating the Treaty
of Washington of 20 September 1852. But neither he nor the U.S.
government was acting in good faith, and the Florida militia patrols continued to hunt Indians. Then in March 1854, President
Franklin Pierce gave in to political pressure and ordered an embargo on trade with the Seminole except where it concerned the
government store. He also ordered the survey and sale of their
reserve. Soldiers could be used, if necessary, to defend settlers.
The surveyor general of Florida had already been surveying on
the reserve as a way of pressuring the Indians. Soon exploring
parties from the army began to move into Big Cypress Swamp
and even into the Everglades. The Indians held one final general
council among themselves in the fall of 1855, expelled Chipco
because he would not fight, and then went to war.[69]

The Third Seminole War began on 7 December 1855 when the
Seminole ambushed Lt. George L. Hartsuff's patrol. Outnumbered four to one when the war began, the Seminole soon faced
fourteen-to-one odds. Nonetheless, they maintained the initiative
for much of 1856, striking, among other places, Miami, the Manatee River, and even north of Tampa. But the tide turned against

them in the fall and into 1857 as the U.S. Army began to use
boats to invade the swamps and visit the hammocks that dotted
them. Little by little, the Seminole hiding places were discovered,

Figure 11.5. "Map of the State of Florida Showing the
Progress of the Surveys, 1857." UNITED STATES, 34TH
CONGRESS, 3RD SESSION, *Senate Executive Documents, No. 5*,
PART III, ILLUSTRATIONS. ACCOMPANIED THE ANNUAL REPORT OF THE
SURVEYOR GENERAL FOR 1856. COURTESY OF THE P. K. YONGE
LIBRARY OF FLORIDA HISTORY, UNIVERSITY OF FLORIDA.

standing crops and huts destroyed, women and children captured. Western Seminoles were again brought to Florida to negotiate with Bowlegs. He finally agreed in March 1858 to leave, and
did so with 163 others on 7 May. The next day, the United States
declared the war at an end, even though about one hundred Indians (men?) remained. Seventy-five went west in February 1859.
Chipco and his Tallahassees remained, as did small groups of
Miccosukee and Seminole.[70]

With the end of the third Seminole War and the removal of
most of the Indians, and with the completion of surveys north of
the line of the Caloosahatchee River, the American Frontier in
Florida finally closed. Lumbermen and cattle ranged the pine
woods and swamps where Indians had once hunted deer. Americans and their slaves farmed the hammocks and the better soils
of the central ridge and the Tallahassee–Madison hills where the
Indian towns had once been. Roads that followed ancient trails
crisscrossed the peninsula. Constrained by the same ecology—
although they were beginning to modify it with their technology—the Americans thus duplicated the pre-Spanish settlement
pattern, but more extensively and with a much larger and ever
growing population. However, this was not simply a repeopling
of the land after three centuries. Railroads reached from Jacksonville to Tallahassee and Cedar Key, and from Tallahassee to
St. Marks. Port towns existed where none had ever been. Plows,
crosscut saws and axes, wagons, draft animals, and steam engines, among other technological inventions, allowed the Americans and their slaves to clear trees and farm far more extensively
and intensively than Native Americans had ever been able to do.
If weakly, the towns were now linked by county and state government, more powerful political institutions than had ever existed
before. Few of the newcomers knew that their ways had been
prepared by many earlier frontiers as Europeans and their Black
associates, slave and free, tried to make the land, and sometimes
its Native American inhabitants, their own.

Notes

1. The Secrets of the Land

1. Gonzalo Fernández de Oviedo y Valdés, *Historia general y natural de las Indias*, 3 vols. (Madrid: Imprenta de la Real Academia de la Historia, 1851–1853), 3:630.

2. Pedro Menéndez de Avilés to Philip II, St. Augustine, 15 Oct. 1565, and Havana, 25 Dec. 1565, in Eugenio Ruidiaz y Caravía, ed., *La Florida; Su conquista y colonización por Pedro Menéndez de Avilés*, 2 vols. (Madrid: Imprenta de los hijos de J. A. Gracia, 1893), 2:94, 131, respectively. Juan López de Velasco, *Geografía y descripción universal de las Indias* (1574; Madrid: Fortanet, 1894), 157. For this cartography see Lawrence C. Wroth, *The Voyages of Giovanni da Verrazzano* (New Haven: Yale University Press, 1970), 186–98 and plates 9–22, 32–36. Menéndez de Avilés seems to have given up his belief in this geography early in 1566. See Paul E. Hoffman, *A New Andalucia and a Way to the Orient: The American Southeast during the Sixteenth Century* (Baton Rouge: Louisiana State University Press, 1990), 232–40.

3. Basil Hall, *Travels in North America in the Years 1827 and 1828*, 2 vols. (Philadelphia: Carey, Lea, & Carey, 1829), 2:248.

4. E[mma] Lucy Braun, *Deciduous Forests of North America* (New York: Macmillan, 1950), 282–84, 260–62, 195–97, for general description. Elise Quarterman, "A Fresh Look at Climax Forests of the Coastal Plain," *Association of Southern Biologists Bulletin* 28:4 (1981), 143–44. Timothy Silver, *A New Face on the Countryside: Indians, Colonists and Slaves in South Atlantic Forests, 1500–1800* (New York: Cambridge University Press, 1990), 14–25.

5. B. W. Wells, "Ecological Problems of the Southeastern United States Coastal Plain," *Botanical Review* 8 (1942), 534; E. V. Komarek, "Lightning and Lightning Fires as Ecological Forces," Tall Timbers Fire Ecology Conference, 8th (1968), *Proceedings* (n.p. [Tallahassee?], 1968), 169–97.

This complexity is reflected in broad classifications such as the twelve ecosystems of Florida (plus three hydric ones—the lakes, rivers, and springs) described in *Ecosystems of Florida*, ed. Ronald L. Myers and John J. Ewen (Orlando: University of Central Florida Press, 1990) (summarized on p. 315), and in Charles H. Wharton, *The Natural Environments of Georgia* (Atlanta: Georgia Department of Natural Resources, 1977) (summary, pp. 5–9), with its twenty-four "natural vegetation associations" plus several hydric ones for the Georgia coastal plain's thirteen physiographic regions. For the Georgia piedmont, he describes thirteen natural vegetation associations and several hydric ones for four physiographic regions. Descriptions of the floral communities in other states in our study area are similarly complex. John M. Barry, *Natural Vegetation of South Carolina* (Columbia: University of South Carolina Press, 1980), includes forty-eight "natural vegetation associations" (when duplications are eliminated) in the state's twenty-seven physiographic "features" [regions]. Arthur W. Cooper, Ralph J. McCracken, and Louis E. Aull, "Vegetation and Soil Resources," in *North Carolina Atlas: Portrait of a Changing Southern State*, ed. James W. Clay, Douglas M. Orr, Jr., and Alfred W. Stuart (Chapel Hill: University of North Carolina Press, 1975), 128–35, indicate more than a dozen plant associations, but their scale, like that in *Ecosystems of Florida*, is not as fine as Wharton's or Barry's. See also Norman L. Christensen, "Vegetation of the Southeastern Coastal Plain," in *North American Terrestrial Vegetation*, ed. Michael G. Barbour and W. D. Billings (New York: Cambridge University Press, 1988), 321–63.

6. A lay person's discussion of the plate tectonics and other geological events that formed the Appalachians, Piedmont, and coastal plains is found in Silver, *A New Face*, 9–13.

7. Donald J. Colquhoun et al., "Quaternary Geology of the Atlantic Coastal Plain," in *Quaternary Nonglacial Geology: Conterminous United States*, ed. Roger B. Morrison (Boulder: Geological Society of America, 1991), 629–30. North of Florida, from the coast inland, the soils of the lower coastal plain are of the Aquept (order: Inceptisols), Aquult, and Udult suborders (order: Ultisols). In Florida, the soils of the lower coastal plain are Aquods (order: Spodsols). On the middle plain terraces, the soils are of the Paleudult (order: Ultisol, suborder: Udult) and Quartzipsamments (order: Entisols, suborder: Psamment) great families. On the upper coastal plain, the soils are of the Hapludults and Paleudults great families (order: Ultisol, suborder: Udult). See Geological Survey (U.S.), *The National Atlas of the United States of America* (Washington, D.C.: U.S. Government Printing Office, 1970), plate 86. For soil types see *Keys to Soil Taxonomy*, 6th ed. (Washington, D.C.: U.S. Department of Agriculture, Natural Resources Conservation Service, 1994), and Amster K. Howard, *Soil Classification Handbook: Unified Soil Classification System* (Denver: Geotechnical

Branch, Division of Research and Laboratory Services, Engineering and Research Center, Bureau of Reclamation, 1986). See also Christensen, "Vegetation," 321–22, for descriptions of soils.

8. Colquhoun et al., "Quaternary Geology," 629–30, 635; Hugh H. Mills and Paul A. Delcourt, "Quaternary Geology of the Appalachian Highlands and Interior Low Plateaus," in *Quaternary Nonglacial Geology: Conterminous United States*, ed. Roger B. Morrison (Boulder: Geological Society of America, 1991), 623–26. The exact reason for some terraces is disputed.

9. The identifications of particular terraces in Florida with the Atlantic coast sequence from further north is uncertain. That is, geologists continue to disagree about if and how given geological formations in Florida fit into the general scheme. Colquhoun et al., "Quaternary Geology," 629–32. Colquhoun et al.'s Table 1, p. 632, attempts to correlate the terraces by state, using standard names derived from Virginia and North Carolina. Their Table 2, p. 637, correlates them in Virginia and North Carolina, using local names. For Florida, see Jules R. Dubar, "Florida Peninsula," in Jules R. Dubar et al., "Quaternary Geology of the Gulf of Mexico Coastal Plain," in *Quaternary Non-Glacial Geology: Conterminous U.S.*, ed. Roger B. Morrison (Boulder: Geological Society of America, 1991), 595; cf. S. David Webb, "Historical Biogeography," in *Ecosystems of Florida*, ed. Ronald L. Myers and John J. Ewel (Orlando: University of Central Florida Press, 1990), 92–94 and Table 4. 1. For the debate see Wells, "Ecological Problems," 533.

10. Braun, *Deciduous Forests*, 280–304, esp. 296–97, for the supposed natural climax forest.

11. Christensen, "Vegetation," 331–34 (a savannah has fewer than 150 pines per hectare and a gramineous understory), 326–31 (for sand hills), 340, 344–47 (for swamp types); E. V. Komarek, "Fire Effects on Temperate Forests and Related Ecosystems: Southeastern United States," in *Fire and Ecosystems*, ed. Clifford E. Ahlgren and Theodore T. Kozlowski (New York: Academic Press, 1974), 256–60; Wharton, *Natural Environments of Georgia*, 194–96 (pine flatwoods), 188–89 (hammocks), 196–99 (long-leaf), 182–91 (sand hill communities), 78–83 (swamps); Warren G. Abrahamson and David C. Harnett, "Pine Flatwoods and Dry Prairies," in *Ecosystems of Florida*, ed. Ronald L. Myers and John J. Ewel (Orlando: University of Central Florida Press, 1990), 104–106.

12. Morgan R. Crook, Jr., *Mississippian Period Archaeology of the Georgia Coastal Zone* (Athens: University of Georgia Laboratory of Archaeology, Series Report no. 23, 1986), 50–51.

13. Lewis H. Larson, Jr., *Aboriginal Subsistence Technology of the Southeastern Coastal Plain during the Late Prehistoric Period* (Gainesville: University Presses of Florida, 1980), 35–65, esp. 56.

14. Hugh H. Mills and Paul A. Delcourt, "Quaternary Geology of the Appalachian Highlands and Interior Low Plateaus," in *Quaternary Nonglacial Geology: Conterminous United States*, ed. Roger B. Morrison (Boulder: Geological Society of America, 1991), 623–26. The soils are classified as Udults, primarily of the Hapludult and secondarily of the Paleudult great groups. Soil descriptions from "Soils of the South: Orders, Suborders, and Great Groups," as found in Geological Survey, *The National Atlas of the United States of America* (Washington, D.C., 1969), plate 86, and in Christensen, "Vegetation," 321. The Hapludults were formerly classified as red-yellow podzolic and gray-brown podzolic soils.

15. T. C. Nelson, "The Original Forests of the Georgia Piedmont," *Ecology* 38 (1957), 391–92, 396; Braun, *Deciduous Forests*, 259–64. She classifies most of the forest as oak-pine.

16. The soils are gray-brown Hapludult soils. Wharton, *Natural Environments of Georgia*, 103, suggests that the Indians may have drained beaver ponds to obtain fertile soils for maize and then allowed the beaver back when the fertility declined. This periodic flooding also killed trees, making clearing easier.

17. Wharton, *Natural Environments of Georgia*, 134–36; Braun, *Deciduous Forests*, 195–207; quotation from 195.

18. The soils are classified as red-yellow Paleudults and gray-brown Quartzipsamments (Paleudults mixed with quartz and other minerals). Marion M. Almy, "The Archaeological Potential of Soil Survey Reports," *Florida Anthropologist* 31 (1978), 75–91; Marion F. Smith, Jr. and John F. Scarry, "Apalachee Settlement Distribution: The View from the Florida Master Site Files," *Florida Anthropologist* 41 (1988), 355–39 tested the association of sites with particular soils, especially near Tallahassee, finding a "mild preference" for the Dothan–Orangeberg association.

19. Wharton, *Natural Environments of Georgia*, 179. Cf. Ronald L. Myers, "Scrub and High Pine," in *Ecosystems of Florida*, ed. Ronald L. Myers and John J. Ewel (Orlando: University of Central Florida Press, 1990), 175–77; William J. Platt and Mark W. Schwartz, "Temperate Hardwood Forests," in ibid., 209–10; and Theodore H. Hubbell, A. N. Laessle, and J. C. Dickinson, Jr., "The Flint-Chattahoochee-Apalachicola Region and Its Environments," Florida State Museum, *Bulletin, Biological Sciences* 1 (1956), 19. For soils see Geological Survey, *National Atlas*, plate 86.

20. The gray-brown soils are Quartzipsamments (order: Entisols); the red-yellow sandy loams are Paleudults and Quartzipsamments (order: Ultisols).

21. They are classified as Aquods (order: Spodosols).

22. Soils of the Histosol order and the Aquent (order: Entisol) and Aquept (order: Inceptisol) suborders.

23. Randall B. Brown, Earl L. Stone, and Victor W. Carlisle, "Soils," in *Ecosystems of Florida*, ed. Ronald L. Myers and John J. Ewel (Orlando: University of Central Florida Press, 1990), 42–53, describe the soils by order and suborder, noting that the larger the scale of a map, the less accurate it is. See also *Atlas of Florida*, ed. Edward A. Fernald (Gainesville: University Presses of Florida, 1992), 64–65, for a map by major soil orders (Figure 1.4, herein). Note: The U.S. Department of Agriculture, Soil Conservation Service, *General Soil Map, Florida* (Gainesville, 1982), does not classify the soil "associations" in quite the same way as does the Geological Survey, *National Atlas*, plate 86.

24. Jerald T. Milanich, *Florida Indians and the Invasion from Europe* (Gainesville: University Press of Florida, 1995), 29. From 400 B.C. to about A.D. 500, maize was cultivated in the area, but apparently sea level change caused a rise in the water table that brought such production to an end.

25. Samuel B. Hilliard, *Atlas of Antebellum Southern Agriculture* (Baton Rouge: Louisiana State University Press, 1984), maps 9 and 10.

26. Generally the Indians used soils classified as Utisols, just as modern farmers would. These ca. 1500 preferences did not necessarily apply during the entire 12,000 or so years human beings have been in the Southeast.

27. Jack T. Wynn, *Mississippi Period Archaeology of the Georgia Blue Ridge Mountains* (Athens: University of Georgia, Laboratory of Archaeology Series, Report no. 27, 1990), 8, notes "at least 120 such valleys" where conditions were right, although not many had been surveyed for sites. Ibid., 57–58, 68, re location of sites in ecotones.

28. David G. Anderson, "Examining Prehistoric Settlement Distribution in Eastern North America," *Archaeology of Eastern North America* 19 (1991), 16 and Figure 5, p. 15 (my thanks to Jerry Milanich for calling this to my attention); Jerald T. Milanich and Charles H. Fairbanks, *Florida Archaeology* (New York: Academic Press, 1980), 17. The "edge of floodplain forests, with mast-producing bottomland hardwoods and proximity to other species in the adjoining mesic forests . . . support perhaps the greatest density and diversity of wildlife in Florida" (Katherine C. Ewel, "Swamps," in *Ecosystems of Florida*, ed. Ronald L. Myers and John J. Ewel [Orlando: University of Central Florida Press, 1990], 315). Kenneth W. Johnson, "The Utina and Potano Peoples of Northern Florida: Changing Settlement Systems in the Spanish Colonial Period" (Ph.D. dissertation, University of Florida, 1991), for the ecology of the Alachua (Potano) (p. 63), the "eastern Utina" (pp. 84–91), and the "Northern Utina" (pp. 94–95). See also Lana Jill Loucks, "Political and Economic Interactions between Spaniards and Indians: Archaeological and Ethnohistorical Perspectives of the Mission System in Florida" (Ph.D. dissertation, University of Florida, 1979), 103–108.

29. A. Sidney Johnson et al., *An Ecological Survey of the Coastal Re-*

gion of Georgia (Washington, D.C.: National Park Service Scientific Monograph Series 3, 1974), 32–64; Clair A. Brown, *Vegetation of the Outer Banks of North Carolina* (Baton Rouge: Louisiana State University Coastal Studies Series, no. 4, 1959), 23–44; Larson, *Aboriginal Subsistence Technology*, 13–22; Alan E. McMichael, "A Model for Barrier Island Settlement Pattern," *Florida Anthropologist* 30:4 (1977), 190–91; Grant D. Jones, "The Ethnohistory of the Guale Coast through 1684," *Anthropological Papers of the American Museum of Natural History* 55, part 2 (1978), 178; David Hurst Thomas, *Historic Indian Period Archaeology of the Georgia Coastal Zone* (Athens: University of Georgia, Laboratory of Archaeology Series, Report no. 31, Georgia Archaeological Research Design Paper no. 8, 1993), 9; Milanich and Fairbanks, *Florida Archaeology*, 24–25.

30. William E. Odum and Carole C. McIvor, "Mangroves," in *Ecosystems of Florida*, ed. Ronald L. Myers and John J. Ewel (Orlando: University of Central Florida Press, 1990), 539–44.

31. Larson, *Aboriginal Subsistence Technology*, 221–24, summarizing data in his chapters 5–10. Charles W. Spellman, "The Agriculture of the Early North Florida Indians," *Florida Anthropologist* 1 (1948), 44; John H. Hann, "Use and Processing of Plants by Indians of Spanish Florida," *Southeastern Archaeology* 5 (1986), 91–102. Elizabeth J. Reitz, "Comparison of Spanish and Aboriginal Subsistence on the Atlantic Coastal Plain," *Southeastern Archaeology* 4 (1985), 42–43.

32. For the models see Larson, *Aboriginal Subsistence Technology*, and Crook, *Mississippian Period Archaeology*, 17–33; cf. Grant Jones, "Ethnohistory of the Guale Coast," 191–94, and Elizabeth J. Reitz, "Evidence for Coastal Adaptations in Georgia and South Carolina," *Archaeology of Eastern North America* 16 (1988), 150, who make the point that the European sources are not reliable in view of archaeological and other documentary material. See also Thomas, *Historic Indian Period Archaeology*, 47–55.

33. Stephen J. Pyne, *Fire in America: A Cultural History of Wildland and Rural Fire* (Princeton: Princeton University Press, 1982), 47; A. Greller, "Deciduous Forest," in *North American Terrestrial Vegetation*, ed. Michael G. Barbour and W. D. Billings (New York: Cambridge University Press, 1988), 292; Henry Dobyns, *Their Number Became Thinned: Native American Population Dynamics in Eastern North America* (Knoxville: University of Tennessee Press, 1983), 214–45.

34. Larson, *Aboriginal Subsistence Technology*; Milanich and Fairbanks, *Florida Archaeology*, 169, for the Alachua tradition; Jones, "Ethnohistory of the Guale Coast," 178.

35. The Guale, for example, ranged from St. Simons Island to Ossabaw Island (if that far), apparently in a pattern reflecting their relatively recent migration down the Altamaha River and out along the coastal zone (including some of the barrier islands). North of St. Cath-

erines Island limited populations could be found on the Edisto River
(Orista and Escamacu), in the depths of Charleston Harbor, and along
the western shores of the North Carolina sounds, but not on the barrier
islands. See Lewis H. Larson, Jr., "Cultural Relationships between the
Northern St. Johns Area and the Georgia Coast," *Florida Anthropologist* 10 (1958), 18; Anderson, "Examining Prehistoric Settlement Distribution," 15–17, especially Figure 5, p. 15 (Figure 1.5, herein).

36. Milanich and Fairbanks, *Florida Archaeology*, 246, 237–39, estimate about 30,000 persons exclusive of the St. Johns and Kissimmee valleys, for which they offer no estimate. Their breakdown is: Calusa, 10–15,000; Lake Okeechobee area, 5–10,000; Keys, 500–1,000; Miami area (Tequesta), 7,500; Jeaga and Ais (farther north on the coast), 2,000.

37. Mark Williams, "Growth and Decline of the Oconee Province," in *The Forgotten Centuries: Indians and Europeans in the American South, 1521–1704*, ed. Charles Hudson and Carmen Chaves Tesser (Athens: University of Georgia Press, 1994), 179–96; Chester B. DePratter, "Cofitachequi: Ethnohistorical and Archaeological Evidence," in *Studies in South Carolina Archaeology; Essays in Honor of Robert L. Stephenson*, ed. Albert C. Goodyear III and Glen T. Hanson (Columbia: South Carolina Institute of Archaeology and Anthropology, 1989), 133–56, and "The Chiefdom of Cofitachequi," in *The Forgotten Centuries: Indians and Europeans in the American South, 1521–1704*, ed. Charles Hudson and Carmen Chaves Tesser (Athens: University of Georgia Press, 1994), 197–226; David Anderson, "Examining Prehistoric Settlement Distribution," and *The Savannah River Chiefdoms: Political Change in the Late Pre-Historic Southeast* (Tuscaloosa: University of Alabama Press, 1994), which is based on his dissertation, "Political Change in Chiefdom Societies: Cycling in the Late Prehistoric Southeastern United States" (University of Michigan, 1990), 193–96, 198–99, 211. See also Jay K. Johnson, "Chiefdom to Tribe in Northeast Mississippi: The Soto Expedition as a Window on a Culture in Transition," in *The Hernando de Soto Expedition, History, Historiography, and "Discovery" in the Southeast*, ed. Patricia K. Galloway (Lincoln: University of Nebraska Press, 1997), 295–312.

38. John D. Daniels, "The Indian Population of North America in 1492," *William and Mary Quarterly*, 3rd Series, 49 (1992), 298–320, reviews the literature and methods used, including by Dobyns.

39. Dean R. Snow and Kim M. Lamphear, "European Contact and Indian Depopulation in the Northeast: The Timing of the First Epidemics," *Ethnohistory* 35:1 (1988), 15–21. For the idea of virgin soil epidemics see Alfred W. Crosby, Jr., "Virgin Soil Epidemics as a Factor in the Aboriginal Depopulation of America," *William and Mary Quarterly*, 3rd Series, 33 (1976), 289–99.

40. George G. Milner, "Epidemic Disease in the Postcontact South-

east: A Reappraisal," *Mid-Continental Journal of Archaeology* 5 (1980), 47. Ann F. Ramenofsky and Patricia Galloway, "Disease and the De Soto Entrada," in *The Hernando de Soto Expedition: History, Historiography and "Discovery" in the Southeast,* ed. Patricia K. Galloway (Lincoln: University of Nebraska Press, 1997), 259–79, examine which of the nineteen common human diseases and parasites might have made it into the Southeast prior to sustained European settlement and conclude that pigs were the most likely carriers on that occasion, and possibly afterwards as feral animals spread.

41. David Henige, "If Pigs Could Fly: Timucuan Population and Native American Historical Demography," *Journal of Interdisciplinary History* 16 (1986), 701–20. Studies of actual village sizes are few, but see Morgan R. Crook, Jr., "Spatial Associations and Distribution of Aggregate Village Sites in the Southeastern Atlantic Coastal Area," *Florida Anthropologist* 31 (1978), 21–34; David J. Hally, "The Chiefdom of Coosa," in *The Forgotten Centuries: Indians and Europeans in the American South, 1521–1704,* ed. Charles Hudson and Carmen Chaves Tesser (Athens: University of Georgia Press, 1994), 228, 239, 241, and Johnson, "Utina and Potano," on the Utina.

2. Discovering the Secrets

1. The poorly recorded voyage of Vincente Yáñez Pinzón and Juan Díaz de Solís into the Gulf of Mexico in 1508–1509 may be the exception to this statement. See Carl O. Sauer, *The Early Spanish Main* (Berkeley: University of California Press, 1966), 166–68; John H. Parry, *The Discovery of South America* (New York: Taplinger Publishing Co., 1979), 114. Cf. Robert S. Weddle, *Spanish Sea: The Gulf of Mexico in North American Discovery, 1500–1685* (College Station: Texas A&M Press, 1985), 20–21, who follows Henry Harrissee in having the Yáñez Pinzón expedition turn east, not north. At issue is whether Yáñez Pinzón or Pedro de Ledesma told the truth in 1513 when testifying in the "Pleitos de Colón."

2. Parry, *Discovery of South America,* 78–79, 104–10, 114. This double strategy was formalized by a committee that met at Burgos in 1508.

3. Parry, *Discovery of South America,* 104 (Waldseemüller map), 128.

4. Sauer, *Early Spanish Main,* 218–37, 247–65, and Pablo Alvarez Rubiano, *Pedrárias Dávila: Contribución al estudio de la figura del "Gran Justador," gobernador de Castilla del Oro y Nicaragua* (Madrid: Consejo Superior de Investigaciones Científicos, Instituto Gonzalo Fernández de Oviedo, 1944) (Central America); Sauer, *Early Spanish Main,* 197–98, 212–14 (Cuba).

5. None of the early-sixteenth-century historians such as Peter Martyr, Bartolomé de las Casas, or Gonzalo Fernández de Oviedo mention

Ponce's voyage, suggesting that it was not well known at the time. The only account of the voyage was published in the 1607 by Antonio de Herrera y Tordesillas, *Historia general de los hechos de los Castellanos en las islas y tierrafirme del mar oceano* (reprint, 10 vols., Asunción: Editorial Guaranía, 1944), 2:207–12. See also Weddle, *Spanish Sea*, 42–48, 51–52, or Samuel Eliot Morison, *The European Discovery of America: The Southern Voyages, 1492–1616* (New York: Oxford University Press, 1974), 506–13, 515. Cf. Jerald T. Milanich and Nara B. Milanich, "Revisiting the Freducci Map: A Description of Juan Ponce de Leon's 1513 Florida Voyage?" *FHQ* 74 (1996), 319–28.

6. Paul E. Hoffman, "New Voyage of North American Discovery: Pedro de Salazar's Voyage to the 'Island of Giants,'" *FHQ* 58 (1980), 415–26. Salazar probably landed on one of the barrier islands of the Georgia–South Carolina coast.

7. Alonso de Chaves, *Alonso de Chaves y el libro IV de su "Espejo de Navegantes,"* ed. Paulino Castañeda, M. Cuesta and P. Hernández (Madrid, 1977), 116–22; Weddle, *Spanish Sea*, 99–103. Weddle identifies the Río del Espíritu Santo as the Mississippi, but a plot of Chaves's materials, which he did not use, shows that prior to 1540 the river has to be the Sabine, although Chaves's description of the entrance and bay gives greatly exaggerated distances (six leagues for its entrance, twenty leagues for the depth of the bay by ten leagues wide), that is ca. eighteen nautical miles entrance, sixty-five nautical miles long and nearly thirty-two nautical miles wide. There is no feature on the Gulf coast with those dimensions. Sabine Lake otherwise fits the description given. According to Chaves, the Río del Espíritu Santo was the northeastern boundary of New Spain, a fact that has been overlooked in considerations of why some of the De Soto materials discuss it. For the history of the cartography and other sources see Jean Delanglez, *El Río del Espíritu Santo: An Essay on the Cartograpy of the Gulf Coast and the Adjacent Territory during the Sixteenth and Seventeenth Centuries,* ed. Thomas J. McMahon (New York: United States Catholic Historical Society, Monograph Series, no. 21, 1945). Father Delanglez concluded that Galveston Bay was the outlet of the Río del Espíritu Santo and shows conclusively that that river and the Mississippi were not the same.

8. Weddle, *Spanish Sea*, 91–92, 95–108. The map is preserved as AGI, Mapas y Planos, Mexico, no. 5; the rutter is incorporated into Chaves, *Espejo de Navegantes*, 116–22; the Cedula of 4 June 1521 summarizing Garay's letter is in Martín Fernández de Navarrete, ed., *Colección de los viages y descubrimientos que hicieron por mar los españoles desde fines del siglo XV . . . ,* 5 vols. (1825–37; Buenos Aires: Editorial Guaranía, 1945–46), 3:147–53.

9. Navarrete, ed., *Colección de los viages*, 3:160. Weddle, *Spanish Sea*, 130–42, gives Garay's unhappy history.

10. He had contact with the Ais and the Abaiós village of the Tequesta on the east coast. Weddle, *Spanish Sea*, 42, 45, 48. For the archaeological culture of all three peoples see Jerald T. Milanich, *Florida Indians and the Invasion From Europe* (Gainesville: University Press of Florida, 1995), 27–29; Jerald T. Milanich and Charles H. Fairbanks, *Florida Archaeology* (New York: Academic Press, 1980), 182, 188–89, 232–41, 246–48.

11. Paul E. Hoffman, *A New Andalucia and a Way to the Orient: The American Southeast during the Sixteenth Century* (Baton Rouge: Louisiana State University Press, 1990), 3–15, is the best modern account of these events. The identification of these Indians is uncertain, although they may have been the Shakori later met in North Carolina.

12. Datha's identify is uncertain, but among the provinces he was said to rule was Hitha, which a Castillian might pronounce in a way similar to the "Isa" that Juan Pardo encountered. A *mandador* of Isa in 1567 was named "Dudca." Charles Hudson, *The Juan Pardo Expeditions: Exploration of the Carolinas and Tennessee, 1566–1568* (Washington, D.C.: Smithsonian Institution Press, 1990), 233–37 (Spanish), 279–83 (English). The nature of this office is unclear, but it may have been the way the Spaniards designated a war leader (red chief) (i.e., "commander"). Thus it is possible that Francisco el Chicorano's report about Datha is actually a report of the extent of Isa's territory, or, if Hudson is correct that Isa was subordinate to the paramount of Cofitachequi, of Cofitachequi's hegemony.

13. Pietro Martiere d'Anghiera, *Décadas del Nuevo Mundo*, trans. Edmundo O'Gorman, 2 vols. continuously paged (Mexico: J. Porrua, 1964–65), 594–607. The province list is in AGI, Justicia 3, no. 3, fols. 9v–17, Asiento, 12 June 1523; printed in a poor transcription in *Colección de documentos inéditos relativos al descubrimiento, conquista, y organización de las antiguas posesiones españoles de América y Oceanía, sacados de los archivos del reino, y muy especialmente del de Indias*, ed. Joaquín F. Pacheco, Francisco de Cardenas, and Luis Torres de Mendoza, 42 vols. (Madrid, 1864–1884), 14:504–15.

14. Hoffman, *New Andalucia*, 10, 35–36; cf Louis De Vorsey, Jr., "Early Maps and the Land of Ayllón," in *Columbus and the Land of Ayllón: The Exploration and Settlement of the Southeast*, ed. Jeannine Cook (Darien, Ga.: Lower Altamaha Historical Society-Ayllón, 1992), 10–13, on the topic of Ayllón's veracity.

15. AGI, Justicia 3, no. 3, fols. 9v–17, Contract, 12 June 1523. Hoffman, *New Andalucia*, 34–40. For the Dominican position and the larger argument about Indian rights, see Lewis U. Hanke, *The Spanish Struggle for Justice in the Conquest of America* (Boston: Little Brown, 1965). For the importance of natural law, see Colin M. MacLachlan,

Spain's Empire in the New World: The Role of Ideas in Institutional and Social Change (Berkeley: University of California Press, 1988), chapters 1–3, but esp. p. 128, and Alfonso García-Gallo, "El Pactismo en el reino de Castilla y su proyección en América," in *El pactismo en la historia de España* (Madrid: Instituto de España, 1980), [145]–68, esp. 158–62, for the evolution of the legal relationship between the Castilian crown and the Indians. Elena Lourie, "A Society Organized for War: Medieval Spain," *Past and Present* 35 (1966), 55, makes the point that the Spanish version of Roman law made any land without a lord the king's. Conquest, by overthrowing the natural lords, left the land to the king; voluntary subordination to the king produced the difficult relationship that MacLachlan and García-Gallo discuss.

16. Hoffman, *New Andalucia*, 48–58, and map 4 therein.

17. Hoffman, *New Andalucia*, 60–80.

18. Gonzalo Fernández de Oviedo y Valdés, *Historia general y natural de las Indias . . .* , 3 vols. (Madrid: Imprenta de la Real Academia de la Historia, 1851–55), 3:630. Alonso de Santa Cruz, *Islario general de todas las islas del mundo . . .* , 2 vols. (Madrid: Imprenta de Huérfanos de Intendencia y Intervención Militares, 1918), 1:441–42.

19. Oviedo, *Historia general*, 3:628, 630–31.

20. Alvar Núñez Cabeza de Vaca, *La Relación o Naufragios de Alvar Núñez Cabeza de Vaca*, ed. Martín A. Favata y José B. Fernández (Potomac, Md.: Scripta Humanistica, 1986), 12–21; see also Paul E. Hoffman, "Narváez and Cabeza de Vaca in Florida," in *The Forgotten Centuries: Indians and Europeans in the American South, 1521–1704*, ed. Charles Hudson and Carmen Chaves Tesser (Athens: University of Georgia Press, 1994), 50–73.

21. Cabeza de Vaca, *Relación*, 21–36, covers the Florida material; for the Texas and Mexican wanderings see Donald Chipman, "In Search of Cabeza de Vaca's Route across Texas: An Historiographical Survey," *Southwestern Historical Quarterly* 91 (1987), 127–48, and works cited therein.

22. Paul E. Hoffman, "Hernando de Soto: A Brief Biography," in *The De Soto Chronicles: The Expedition of Hernando de Soto to North America in 1539–1543*, ed. Lawrence A. Clayton, Vernon J. Knight, Jr., and Edward C. Moore, 2 vols. (Tuscaloosa: University of Alabama Press, 1993), 1:433–50.

23. Fidalgo de Elvas, "The Account by a Gentleman from Elvas," trans. and ed. in *The De Soto Chronicles, The Expediton of Hernando de Soto to North America, 1539–1543*, ed. Lawrence A. Clayton, Vernon J. Knight, Jr., and Edward C. Moore, 2 vols. (Tuscaloosa: University of Alabama Press, 1993), 1:48; Luis Hernández de Viedma, "Relation of the Island of Florida," trans. and ed. John E. Worth, ibid., 231.

24. *De Soto Chronicles*, 1:360, Contract, 20 Apr. 1537.

25. Alvarez Rubiano, *Pedrárias Dávila*, 209–10, 142–68, for the Isthmian practice.

26. Marvin T. Smith and David J. Hally, "Chiefly Behavior: Evidence from Sixteenth-Century Spanish Accounts," in *Lords of the Southeast: Social Inequality and the Native Elites of Southeastern North America*, ed. Alex W. Barker and Timothy R. Pauketat (Washington, D.C.: American Anthropological Association, 1992), 99–110, looks at how the Indians treated De Soto and why he did not always have to resort to capturing caciques.

27. The literature on the route is extensive, and growing. See Jeffrey P. Brain and Charles R. Ewen, "Bibliography of DeSoto Studies" [to 1991], in *De Soto Chronicles: The Expedition of Hernando de Soto to North America, 1539–1543*, ed. Lawrence A. Clayton, Vernon J. Knight, Jr., and Clarence C. Moore, 2 vols. (Tuscaloosa: University of Alabama Press, 1993), 1:515–50. I have followed Charles Hudson's reconstruction as being, on the whole, the best fit between the written accounts and the archaeological and geographical ones. His only weakness is a tendency, in which he is not alone, to rely on Garcilaso de la Vega because of the detail he provides.

28. A mound center had functioned earlier at Lake Jackson, just north of Tallahassee.

29. The classic statement of the redistributional basis for chiefdoms is Elman Service, *Primitive Social Organization: An Evolutionary Perspective* (New York: Random House, 1962), 173–74. This redistributional model has been modified in favor of a stress on ranked lineages and clans in recent studies by David G. Anderson ("Political Change in Chiefdom Societies: Cycling in the Late Prehistoric Southeastern United States" [Ph.D. dissertation, University of Michigan, Ann Arbor, 1990], 15–17, 124–30, 168–71), Vernon J. Knight, Jr. ("Social Organization and the Evolution of Hierarchy in Southeastern Chiefdoms," *Journal of Anthropological Research* 46 [1990], 1–23), and Randolph J. Widmer ("The Structure of Southeastern Chiefdoms," in *The Forgotten Centuries: Indians and Europeans in the American South, 1521–1704*, ed. Charles Hudson and Carmen Chaves Tesser [Athens: University of Georgia Press, 1994], 125–55). Chester DePratter, *Late Pre-historic and Early Historic Chiefdoms in the Southeastern United States* (New York: Garland, 1991), 121–27, 148–50, summarizes the non-mission evidence regarding chiefly power (i.e., right to use violence). There is reason to doubt chiefs used violence often or served as judges in the European sense. Clan vengeance was probably as present in the sixteenth and seventeenth centuries as we know it to have been in the eighteenth. See Patricia Galloway, "The Barthelemy Murders: Bienville's Establishment of the *Lex Talionis* as a Principle of Indian Diplomacy," in *Pro-*

ceedings of the Eight Annual Meeting of the French Colonial Historical Society, ed. E. Fitzgerald (Lanham, Md.: University Press of America, 1985), 92–93.

30. Rodrigo Rangel, "Account of the Northern Conquest and Discovery of Hernando de Soto," trans. and ed. John E. Worth, with footnotes by John E. Worth and Charles Hudson, in *The De Soto Chronicles: The Expedition of Hernando de Soto to North America in 1539–1543,* ed. Lawrence A. Clayton, Vernon J. Knight, Jr., and Clarence C. Moore, 2 vols. (Tuscaloosa: University of Alabama Press, 1993), 1:272 (Ocute); Elvas, "Account," in ibid., 86, 89.

31. Rangel, "Account," in *De Soto Chronicles,* 1:271–73; Elvas, "Account," in ibid., 78 (I have altered the translation).

32. Mark Williams, "Growth and Decline of the Oconee Province," in *The Forgotten Centuries: Indians and Europeans in the American South, 1521–1704,* ed. Charles Hudson and Carmen Chaves Tesser (Athens: University of Georgia Press, 1994), 191–92.

33. Elvas, "Account," *De Soto Chronicles,* 1:84.

34. Viedma, "Account," *De Soto Chronicles,* 1:231; Elvas, "Account," in ibid., 84.

35. David J. Hally, "The Chiefdom of Coosa," in *The Forgotten Centuries: Indians and Europeans in the American South, 1521–1704,* ed. Charles Hudson and Carmen Chaves Tesser (Athens: University of Georgia Press, 1994), 227–28, 246–48; Rangel, "Account," *De Soto Chronicles,* 1:284; Elvas, "Account," in ibid., 93.

36. Elvas, "Account," in *De Soto Chronicles,* 1:83. None of the other sixteenth-century accounts mention this alleged epidemic. Chester B. De Pratter, "The Chiefdom of Cofitachequi," in *The Forgotten Centuries: Indians and Europeans in the American South, 1521–1704,* ed. Charles Hudson and Carmen Chaves Tesser (Athens: University of Georgia Press, 1994), 215–17, is a useful corrective to the pandemic theorists.

37. George F. Kunz, "History of Gems Found in North Carolina," North Carolina Geological Survey, *Bulletin,* no. 12 (1907), 29–35. Alexander, Burke, Catawba, Iredell, and Lincoln Counties report finds. All are clustered northwest of modern Charlotte. Edwin C. Eckel, "Gold and Pyrite Deposits of the Dahlonega District, Georgia," U.S. Geological Survey, *Bulletin,* no. 213 (1902), 57–63.

38. Elvas, "Account," *De Soto Chronicles,* 1:89, 91.

39. Rangel, "Account," in *De Soto Chronicles,* 1:257. Elvas's judgment is not so stark but suggests the same evaluation (Elvas, "Account," ibid., 58, 63). For the current thinking about Ocita's location see Jerald T. Milanich and Charles Hudson, *Hernando de Soto and the Indians of Florida* (Gainesville: University Press of Florida, 1993), 39–70.

40. George M. Luer and Marion M. Almy, "Temple Mounds of the Tampa Bay Area," *Florida Anthropologist* 34 (1981), 127–55; Jeffrey M. Mitchem and Brent R. Weisman, "Changing Settlement Patterns and Pottery Types in the Withlacoochee Cove," *Florida Anthropologist* 40 (1987), 154–66.

41. Elvas, "Account," in *De Soto Chronicles*, 1:62 (Paracoxi); Viedma, "Account," ibid., 225–26 (Paracoxi and Ocale); Rangel, "Account," ibid., 261 (Ocale). Viedma and Elvas disagree on the amount of food at Ocale. For locations see Milanich and Hudson, *Hernando de Soto*, 73–76, 91–96.

42. I have stripped these names of the term "chief" that is attached to Itara*holata* (i.e., orata, a Muscogian term) and *Utina*mocharra (the Timucuan term). Elvas, "Account," in *De Soto Chronicles*, 1:66–67; cf. ibid., 78, where he suggests that the Indians had hidden their foods after De Soto's advance party passed through; Rangel, "Account," ibid., 263; Elvas, "Account," ibid., 66. Viedma, "Account," ibid. 226, dismisses them as "some towns" passed through in five to six days' travel. Evidently all three chroniclers were with De Soto's advance party, which did not spend any time in them.

43. Elvas, "Account," ibid., 1:66–69; Rangel, "Account," ibid., 263–66. This evidence, and less certainly the Narváez material, suggests that contrary to Worth and some other writers, the division of the Suwannee Valley people into the "Utina" (or Northern Utina) east of the river and the Yustaga to the west arose after De Soto. Cf. John E. Worth, "The Timucuan Missions of Spanish Florida and the Rebellion of 1656" (Ph.D. dissertation, University of Florida, 1992), 23.

44. Milanich and Hudson, *Hernando de Soto*, 154–63. The battle at Napituca is described in Elvas, "Account," in *De Soto Chronicles*, 1:67–69, and Rangel, "Account," in ibid., 264–66.

45. Worth, "Timucuan Missions," 17; Viedma, "Account," in *De Soto Chronicles*, 1:226–27; Rangel, "Account," in ibid., 266–67; Elvas, "Account," in ibid., 69–71. See also Milanich and Hudson, *Hernando De Soto*, 164–67.

46. Elvas, "Account," in *De Soto Chronicles*, 1:72; Viedma, "Account," in ibid., 227. Rangel, "Account," in ibid., 267, devotes a paragraph to Apalachee, and most of that is taken up commenting on Indian resistance and the evidence of Narváez's camp. See also Charles R. Ewen and John H. Hann, *Hernando de Soto among the Apalachee: The Archaeology of the First Winter Encampment* (Gainesville: University Press of Florida, 1998).

47. Elvas, "Account," in *De Soto Chronicles*, 1:78.

48. Francisco López de Gómara, *Historia general de las Indias* (1552), 2 vols. (Barcelona: Editorial Iberia, 1954), 1:72; Andrés Gonzalez

de Barcía Carballido y Zúñiga, *Chronological History of the Continent of Florida*, trans. Anthony Kerrigen (Gainesville: University of Florida Press, 1951), 25; Hoffman, *New Andalucia*, 98–99.

49. Agustín Dávila Padilla, *Historia de la Fundación y discurso de la provincia de Santiago de Mexico de la orden de Predicadores . . .* (Madrid: En Casa de Pedro Madrigal, 1596), 215–31. See also Woodbury Lowery, *Spanish Settlements within the Present Limits of the United States*, 2 vols. (New York: G. P. Putnam's Sons, 1901–1911), 1:411–27, and Hoffman, *New Andalucia*, 99–101.

50. *Documentary Sources for the Wreck of the New Spain Fleet of 1554*, trans. David R. McDonald, prepared by David R. McDonald and J. Barto Arnold III (Austin: Texas Antiquities Committee, 1979); AGI, Mexico 280, Fr. Andrés de Olmos to Council of the Indies, and Same to King, Mexico City, 25 Nov. 1556; Hoffman, *New Andalucia*, 145–49.

51. Francisco López de Gómara, *Historia General de las Indias. . . .* Zaragoza: Agustín Millan, 1552. [Gentleman of Elvas], *Relaçam verdadeira dos trabalhos q[ue] ho governador dõ Fernãdo de Souto e certos fidalgos portugueses passarom no descubrimẽto da provincia da Frolida, Agora nouamẽte feita per hũ fidalgo Deluas*. Evora: A. de Burgos, 1557. Giovanni Battista Ramusio, *Navigationi et Viaggi: Venice 1565–1606*, 3 vols. (reprint, Amsterdam: Theatrum Orbis Terrarum, 1967–1970), 3:350v–358; Hoffman, *New Andalucia*, 126–43.

52. The actual text of this decree has not been found, but it is quoted in Audiencia to Tristan de Luna, Mexico City, 30 Mar. 1559. Herbert I. Priestley, ed. and trans., *The Luna Papers: Documents Relating to the Expedition of don Tristan de Luna y Arellano for the Conquest of La Florida in 1559–1561*, 2 vols. (Deland: Florida State Historical Society, 1928) (cited hereafter as *Luna Papers*). Hoffman, *New Andalucia*, 152. An encomienda was legally a trusteeship that required its holder to instruct the Indians so held in Christianity and "Christian" living and to protect them. In return they provided unpaid labor. The Crown issued laws in 1542 that sought to prevent the arrangement from being slavery under another name and to eventually abolish it altogether. It had been the principal means by which the conquistadors created wealth in a society that did not use European-style money.

53. Francisco Cervantes de Salazar, *Life in the Imperial and Loyal City of Mexico in New Spain . . .* , trans. Mimia Lee Barrett Shepard (Austin: University of Texas Press, 1953), 79.

54. *Luna Papers*, 2:285, 287, 289, Deposition of Alonso de Montalván, Ocoa, Española, 11 Aug. 1561. The most recent study of the expedition in light of archaeological knowledge is Charles Hudson, Marvin Smith, Chester B. DePratter, and Emilia Kelley, "The Tristán de Luna Expedition, 1559–1561," *Southeastern Archaeology* 8 (1989), 31–45. Cf. Patricia

Galloway, *Choctaw Genesis 1500–1700* (Lincoln: University of Nebraska Press, 1995), 143–60; Hoffman, *New Andalucia*, 169–70; and Lowery, *Spanish Settlements*, 1:362–68.

55. *Luna papers*, 1:222–33, Letters from Friars, Coosa, 1 Aug. 1560; cf ibid., 218–23, Mateo del Sanz to Luna, Apica, 6 Jul. 1560; the chronology comes from ibid., 237, 239, Joint Letter to the Viceroy, Coosa, 1 Aug. 1560, and the dates of the letters.

56. *Luna Papers*, 1:218–43, Mateo del Sanz to Luna, Apica, 6 Jul. 1560; Friars to Luna, Coosa, 1 Aug. 1560; Joint letter to Viceroy, Coosa, 1 Aug. 1560; cf. John R. Swanton, *Early History of the Creek Indians and Their Neighbors* (Washington, D.C.: Bureau of American Ethnology Bulletin 73, 1922), 230–31. Many archaeologists have been misled by Swanton and his source (see below regarding later reports).

57. For the case against Luna see *Luna Papers*, 1:198–253, and 2:2–129. The quotation is from ibid., 2:120.

58. Paul E. Hoffman, "Legend, Religious Idealism, and Colonies: The Point of Santa Elena in History, 1552–1566," *South Carolina Magazine of History* 84 (1983), 59–71.

59. Hoffman, *New Andalucia*, 172–80. See also *Luna Papers*, 2:281–319, Depositions of Alonso de Montalvan, Cristobal Velazquez, and Miguel Sánchez Serrano, all at Ocoa, Española, Aug. 1560.

60. Hoffman, *New Andalucia*, 181–201; AGI, SD 11, no. 43bis, Interrogatories for Lucas Vázquez de Ayllón, Madrid and Seville, 1553 and 1561; AGI, CT 3309, Florida Book, fols. 143–49, Contract, 28 Feb. 1562.

61. Hoffman, *New Andalucia*, 172–81, esp. 176–77, for evidence that Villafañe and his men lied, with one exception whose deposition we do not have. *Luna Papers*, 1:192–93.

62. AGI, PAT 19, no. 11, fol. 2; Hoffman, *New Andalucia*, 180–81.

63. Dávila Padilla, *Historia*, as quoted in translation in Swanton, *Early History*, 231. The origins of Dávila Padilla's version of events can be found in statements in the *Luna Papers*, 2:51 ("the [former] account of this land and these provinces was false and not true, judging by what has been seen in the province of Coosa, which was declared the most fertile, best disposed, and provisioned part for Spaniards to live and settle in, whereas it seems to be quite the opposite, being of such an undesirable nature that everyone asserts that there is no place where one may remain or erect a town."), and 2:291 (where Coosa is said to have only 6–7 little places in a two-league radius around it). These statements are contradicted by the letters written from Coosa and cited above.

64. The paramount chiefdom may have had 24,000 Indians, of whom 2,850 to 5,400 lived at Coosa (the Little Egypt site and its six associated sites) (Hally, "Chiefdom of Coosa," in *Forgotten Centuries*, 239–41, 248). The letters from Coosa and the Pardo reports do not indicate a

polity that had been fatally damaged by the deus ex machina of old world diseases, at least not yet. Cf. George G. Milner, "Epidemic Disease in the Postcontact Southeast: A Reappraisal," *Mid-continental Journal of Archaeology* 5 (1980), 39–56; Marvin T. Smith, *Archaeology of Aboriginal Culture Change in the Interior Southeast: Depopulation during the Early Historic Period* (Gainesville: University Presses of Florida, 1987), 4–6, 12, 58; Hally, "The Chiefdom of Coosa," 248–50, all of whom rely on Dávila Padilla. Galloway, *Choctaw Genesis*, 157, 159, and Paul E. Hoffman, "Did Coosa Decline between 1541 and 1560?" *Florida Anthropologist* 50 (1997), 25–29, are skeptical of the demographic decline of Coosa.

65. AGI, PAT 19, no. 11, fol. 2; Hoffman, *New Andalucia*, 180–81.

66. Diplomatic reports in Spain, Sovereigns, etc., 1556–1598 (Philip II), *Negociaciones con Francia, 1559–[1568]*, 11 vols. to 1960 (Madrid: Real Academia de la Historia, 1950–[1960?]), 3:172, 270, 294, and 5:18–19, 51–52.

67. Hoffman, *New Andalucia*, 185–87.

68. Hoffman, *New Andalucia*, 193–201.

69. Lucy L. Wenhold, "Manrique de Rojas' Report on French Settlement in Florida, 1564," *Florida Historical Quarterly* 38 (1959), 45–62.

70. Hoffman, *New Andalucia*, 215–17.

71. AGI, PAT 19, "Memorial de Pero Menéndez de Avilés respecto a las medidas que sería conveniente tomar para la segura posesión de la Florida y evitar que los franceses e ingleses pudieran causar perturbación en aquellos dominios," [Feb. 1565?]. Also in Eugenio Ruidiaz y Caravía, *La Florida: Su conquista y colonización por Pedro Menéndez de Avilés*, 2 vols. (Madrid: Imprenta de los hijos de J. A. Garcia, 1893), 2:320–26.

72. Hoffman, *New Andalucia*, 224–27.

73. Eugene Lyon, "The Cañete Fragment: Another Narrative of Hernando de Soto," in *The De Soto Chronicles: The Expedition of Hernando de Soto to North America in 1539–1543*, ed. Lawrence A. Clayton, Vernon J. Knight, Jr., and Edward C. Moore, 2 vols. (Tuscaloosa: University of Alabama Press, 1993), 1:307–10.

74. Eugene Lyon, *The Enterprise of Florida: Pedro Menéndez de Avilés and the Spanish Conquest of 1565–1568* (Gainesville: University Presses of Florida, 1976), 52–55.

75. Hoffman, *New Andalucia*, 229–30, 222; Lyon, *Enterprise*, 97, 101–106, 110–14.

76. Lyon, *Enterprise*, 125–30, 140–41, 150. AGI, SD 115 (Stetson), Menéndez de Avilés to Crown, Matanzas, Cuba, 5 Dec. 1565; Archivo de Protocolos (Madrid), Protocolo 646 (1569), fol. 258v, Title as Gov. of Río de Socorro for Captain Juan Velez de Medrano, 10 Nov. 1565 (Note courtesy of Eugene Lyon).

3. The Spanish Tidewater Frontier, First Phase, 1562–1586

1. David G. Anderson, David W. Stahle, and Malcolm K. Cleaveland, "Paleoclimate, and the Potential Food Reserves of Mississippian Societies: A Case Study from the Savannah River Valley," *American Antiquity* 60 (1995), 266–68, found that 1565 was the only year of normal rain between 1559 and 1569 but in David W. Stahle, Malcolm K. Cleaveland, Dennis B. Blanton, M. D. Therrell, and D. A. Gray, "The Lost Colony: Jamestown Droughts," *Science* 280 (1998), 564–67, they shifted the drought to 1562–71, with its worst years 1565–69 (Rebecca Saunders called this to my attention).

2. René Goulaime de Laudonnière, *L'Histoire notable de la Florida situee es Indes Occidentales contenant les Trois voyages . . .* (1586) (reprint, Lyon: Audin, 1946), fols. 22–31v (pp. 67–80). Also in René Goulaime de Laudonnière, *Three Voyages*, trans. with introduction by Charles E. Bennett (Gainesville: University of Florida Press, 1975), 38–51.

3. Timucua—the name we use for the people of this area and their language—is derived from "thimegona" ("enemy"), Saturiwa's name for the people of Outina, a chiefdom further up the St. Johns River. He and they spoke the same language. We do not know what the people of this language group called themselves.

4. Laudonnière, *L'Histoire notable*, fols. 43–44 (pp. 95–96), or *Three Voyages*, 68–69. John T. McGrath, *The French in Early Florida: In the Eye of the Hurricane* (Gainesville: University Press of Florida, 2000), is a modern retelling of these events.

5. Laudonnière, *Three Voyages*, 121, 114. Hioacaia identification is from John H. Hann, *A History of Timucua Indians and Missions* (Gainesville: University Press of Florida, 1996), 11.

6. Laudonnière, *Three Voyages*, 121–42, passim, esp. 130–31. Although there is no reliable dendroclimatalogical data for northeastern Florida, spring rainfall may have been more normal there in 1565, as it was further north, with a resulting better harvest. See n. 1, above.

7. Laudonnière, *Three Voyages*, 127, 135; Gonzalo Solís de Merás, *Pedro Menéndez de Avilés*, trans. Jeannette T. Connor (1923; facsimile ed., Gainesville: University of Florida Press, 1964), 202–204.

8. This polity has no agreed-upon name. Aguacalecuem is Viedma's name for this cacique in the De Soto materials. Luis Hernández de Viedma, "Relation of the Island of Florida," in *The De Soto Chronicles: The Expedition of Hernando de Soto to North America in 1539–1543*, ed. Lawrence A. Clayton, Vernon J. Knight, Jr., and Edward C. Moore, 2 vols. (Tuscaloosa: University of Alabama Press, 1993), 1:499. Modern scholars call these people the Utina, Northern Utina, or Timucua (the seventeenth-century name). See Jerald T. Milanich, "The Western Ti-

mucua," in *Tacachale: Essays on the Indians of Florida and Southeastern Georgia during the Historic Period*, ed. Jerald T. Milanich and Samuel Proctor (Gainesville: University Presses of Florida, 1978), 60–63, 69–75, where he conflates the St. Johns River people with the western group. Kenneth W. Johnson, "The Utina and Potano Peoples of Northern Florida: Changing Settlement Systems in the Spanish Colonial Period" (Ph.D. dissertation, University of Florida, 1991), 110–28, has identified these people, his "Northern Utina," with the Indian Pond ceramic complex.

9. Laudonnière, *Three Voyages*.

10. Eugenio Ruidiaz y Caravía, *La Florida, Su conquista y colonización por Pedro Menéndez de Avilés*, 2 vols. (Madrid: Imprenta de loa hijos de J. A. Garcia, 1893), 2:84–105, 127–41, 142–54, as Pedro Menéndez de Avilés to Crown, St. Augustine, 15 Oct. 1565, and Havana, 25 Dec. 1565 and 30 Jan. 1566. Paul E. Hoffman, *A New Andalucia and a Way to the Orient* (Baton Rouge: Louisiana State University Press, 1990), 232–42.

11. Solís de Merás, *Menéndez de Avilés*, 124–29, 138–53, 164–81; Eugene Lyon, *The Enterprise of Florida: Pedro Menéndez de Avilés and the Spanish Conquest of 1565–1568* (Gainesville: University Presses of Florida, 1976), 147–50, 153–58.

12. Lyon, *Enterprise*, 162–69, 171–73; Charles Hudson, *The Juan Pardo Expeditions, Exploration of the Carolinas and Tennessee, 1566–1568* (Washington, D.C.: Smithsonian Institution Press, 1990), 23–46, 146–53, and "Long" and "Short" Bandera Relations, 205–304 (Spanish and English texts).

13. Eugene Lyon, *Enterprise*, 174–81; Solís de Merás, *Menéndez Avilés*, 228.

14. Solís de Merás, *Menéndez de Avilés*, 221, 223, 228–29.

15. AGI, CT 5012 (Stetson), Menéndez de Avilés to Philip II, Havana, 10 Feb. 1567. Nine hundred may be an exaggeration.

16. Lyon, *Enterprise*, passim, is the best modern account of these transitory garrisons.

17. AGI, SD 115 (Stetson), Menéndez Marqués to Menéndez de Avilés, Havana, 28 Mar. 1568.

18. Hudson, *Pardo Expeditions*, 175–77. The timing suggests that food shortages just before the summer harvest were a major source of Spanish–Indian conflict. The women may have been another.

19. Lyon, *Enterprise*, 189–94, 197, 207. An example of the benefits that flowed from the governorship is the Cabildo of Havana's grant of the use of "las sabanas nuevas" west of the city for raising hogs and cattle to supply La Florida. Havana. Ayuntamiento, *Actas capitulares del Ayuntamiento de la Havana*, preface and preliminary study by Emilio Roig de Leuchsenring, 3 vols. (Havana, 1937–40), 3:141, 17 June 1569.

20. Part of their suffering was the exploitation of the soldiers by Menéndez's lieutenants, especially Esteban de las Alas. The men were made to cut lumber and create iron goods for las Alas's private trade. AGI, JU 1001, no. 2, R. 1, declarations of Pedro Baez, Pedro de Torano, Martín de Lezcano, Juanes de Leyca and Martín de Leyca, St. Augustine, Dec. 1569.

21. AGI, JU 1001, no. 2, R. 1, Pedro Menéndez de Avilés to Esteban de las Alas, Havana, 15 June 1570, ordering the reduction to 150 men in the three forts and AGI, SD 115 (Stetson), García Osorio to SM, Havana, 1571, reporting the removal. Las Alas had 110 men with him when he reached Seville.

22. Louis-André Vigneras, "A Spanish Discovery of North Carolina in 1566," *North Carolina Historical Review* 46 (1969), 398–414, and Hoffman, *New Andalucia*, 244–46. For Verrazano's geographical ideas and their influence see Lawrence Wroth, *The Voyages of Giovanni da Verrazano* (New Haven: Yale University Press, 1970), and Hoffman, *New Andalucia*, 107–14, 137–39, 224–27, 233–34.

23. Clifford M. Lewis and Albert J. Loomie, *The Spanish Jesuit Mission in Virginia, 1570–1572* (Chapel Hill: University of North Carolina Press, 1953), is the definitive study. J. Leich Wright, Jr., *The Only Land They Knew: The Tragic Story of the American Indians in the Old South* (New York: Free Press, 1981), 52, notes a tradition among the seventeenth-century Powhatans of a member of that chief's family having lived among and grown to hate the Spaniards.

24. Solís de Merás, *Menéndez de Avilés*, 159; for fragmentary evidence on gifts see AGI, JU 1001, no. 2, R. 1, and no. 4, R. 2.

25. Lyon, *Enterprise*, 170, 180; Solís de Merás, *Menéndez de Avilés*, 182–83 (burning), 233–35 (peace negotiation), 182–84 (Indian tactics), 236 (first raid); AGI, JU 1001, no. 2, R. 1, Pieza 1, fol. 11, entries 1 and 3 of report on extraordinary rations authorized by Esteban de las Alas; AGI, IG 1093 (Stetson), Menéndez de Avilés to Crown, 24 Nov. 1569; AGI, JU 1001, no. 2, R. 1, Pieza 4, fol. 4, Testimony of Gerónimo de Sobrador, 1570, regarding cattle killed by Indians and their threat to fishermen; Hann, *History of Timucua*, 59–68, covers the war. See also James W. Covington, "Relations between the Eastern Timucuan Indians and the French and Spanish, 1564–1567," in *Four Centuries of Southern Indians*, ed. Charles Hudson (Athens: University of Georgia Press, 1975), 23–24 (a summary of Solís de Merás).

26. AGI, JU 1001, no. 2, R. 1, Pieza 1, fols. 58v–59 (no. 10), 14v (no. 16); Pieza 2, fols. 15v–16v (no. 14), for supplies issued to these troops. *Colección de documentos inéditos relativos al descubrimiento, conquista, y organización de las antiguas posesiones españoles de América y Oceanía, sacados de los archivos del reino, y muy especialmente del de Indias*, ed. Joaquín F. Pacheco, Francisco de Cardenas, and Luis

Torres de Mendoza, 42 vols. (Madrid, 1864–1884), 13:307–309, "Disposición de quatro fuertes que havia de haber en la Florida, año 1569"; Hann, *History of Timucua*, 66–67.

27. AGI, SD 124 (Stetson), Menéndez Marqués to Treasury Officials, Havana, 9 Dec. 1570. See also Woodbury Lowery, *Spanish Settlements within the Present Limits of the United States*, 2 vols. (New York: G. P. Putnam's Sons, 1901–1911), 2:289; Jerald T. Milanich, "Tacatacuru and the San Pedro de Mocamo Mission," *FHQ* 50 (1972), 285.

28. AGI, SD 115 (Stetson), García Osorio to SM, Havana, 1571; AGI, PAT 19, R. 33, "Discurso sobre la población de la costa de la Florida y inconvenientes que se ofrecieron para su fortificación y defensa," n.d. [ca. 1574]. A general peace, however temporary, may have been patched up because seventeen jackets (*ropillas*) were given to "Moloa, Guale, Soloy, and other" caciques at some point between 1565 and 1569. See AGI, JU 1001, no. 4, R. 2, fol. 16v.

29. Anderson, Stahle, and Cleaveland, "Paleoclimate," 266–68. The drought is suggested by evidence from the Jesuits at Chesapeake Bay noted in Felix Zubillaga, *La Florida: Misión Jesuítica y la colonización Española* (Rome: Institutum Historicum S. I., 1941), 371–73, and by Solís de Merás's stories of how the Indians of Guale (1566) and Utina (1566) wanted Menéndez de Avilés to bring rain which they had not had for eight and six months, respectively. Since the winter months (the eight months preceding the Guale event) are always rainy along the Georgia and Florida coasts, the six to eight "month"–long drought was probably a Spanish misunderstanding of some other, probably shorter period of time or a more general reference to the long period of unusually dry weather then underway. Solís de Merás, *Menéndez de Avilés*, 177, 178, 202. Henry Dobyns, *Their Number Became Thinned: Native American Population Dynamics in Eastern North America* (Knoxville: University of Tennessee Press, 1983), 275–76, reads the 1570 Jesuit report from Chesapeake Bay, the memory of a 1568 epidemic and earthquake among the Narragansett, and one of Le Moyne's engravings as evidence of a pandemic in the years 1564–70, but the Jesuit materials, at least, seem to refer to drought-produced famine mortality, not epidemic disease.

30. AGI, SD 115 (Stetson), Pedro Menéndez Marqués to Pedro Menéndez de Avilés, Havana, 28 Mar. 1568. The Spaniards did not follow through because of a lack of supplies and a storm that wrecked the ship they had planned to use. The Guale were rewarded with axes and knives. The Tacatacuru lived on Cumberland Island and probably were not under Saturiwa's paramountcy, but may have been influenced by him.

31. Solís de Merás, *Menéndez de Avilés*, 202–204 (quotation on 203), 206–207. Lyon, *Enterprise*, 168–69, sees this as the beginning of an alli-

ance intended to put pressure on Saturiwa. A subordinate of Outina, Calabay, an Indian cacique whose villages were further upstream on the St. Johns, entered into alliance with the Spaniards on this same trip.

32. The name implies the villages were located above the tidal flow, which is consistent with their location about sixty miles (twenty Spanish or forty–fifty French leagues) up the St. Johns River from its mouth.

33. AGI, JU 1001, no. 4, R. 2, fols. 16v, 18; JU 1001, no. 2, R. 1, Pieza 1, fols. 11v, 12, entries 9, 10; John E. Worth, "The Timucuan Missions of Spanish Florida and the Rebellion of 1656" (Ph.D. dissertation, University of Florida, 1992), 27, gives 20 Spanish deaths; see his p. 33 for the likely location of Outina's village.

34. AGI, CD 941, entries in muster rolls, 1566 (for garrison); Solís de Merás, *Menéndez de Avilés*, 171, and Archivo del Instituto de D. Juan de Valencia, Envio 25, H, no. 162, Menéndez de Avilés to Council of Indies [Madrid, Nov. 1569], on potential (citation courtesy of Eugene Lyon); on Jesuit Missions: Felix Zubillaga, *Monumenta Antiquae Floridae (1566–1572)* (Rome: Apud Momumenta Historica Soc. Jesu, 1946), esp. Father Rogel to Juan de Hinestrosa, St. Elena, 11 Dec. 1569 (pp. 401, 403), Fr. Sedeño to Francisco Borja, Guale, 14 May 1570 (pp. 430–31), and Fr. Francisco Villareal to Borja, Tupiqui, 5 Mar. 1570 (pp. 419–20); AGI, JU 1001, no. 4, R. 2, fols. 15, 16v, 17, 25, for undated gifts to the caciques around Santa Elena: Guale, Escamacu, and Oya [Ahoya?] are mentioned as well. Cloth, jackets (*ropillas*), pants, hose (*medias calcas*), blankets, autajia buttons, mirrors, hawksbells, and knives figure in the list. Much of this was given in 1566; see AGI, JU 1001, no. 2, R. 1, entry of 18 Aug. 1566 for purchases of 5,113 reales' worth of goods. Fr. Sedeño said that there were thirty Guale villages of not more than twenty households each, or about six hundred in all; we may infer a population of ca. three thousand.

35. On the annual cycle of the coastal peoples, see above, chapter 1; re Ahoya Orata, see Hudson, *Pardo Expeditions*, 294.

36. Pardo had found quartz crystals believed by many to be diamonds. He had not found silver (which does not exist in the Appalachian Mountains) but had come close to the gold placers of Dahlongia, Ga.

37. AGI, EC 154A, fols. 1203–37, 1318–24, declarations of Juan de Junco and related documents, 17 May 1567 and 10 Dec. 1569. He claimed 650 hogs, 132 goats and sheep, and 22 calves had been imported by May 1567.

38. For the problems of European domestic breeds in hot climates see F. N. Andrews, "Adaptation to the Environment," in *Introduction to Livestock Production*, ed. H. H. Cole (San Francisco: Freeman, 1966), 475, 481. For specific problems during this period see Charles W. Arnade, "Cattle Raising in Spanish Florida, 1513–1763," *Agricultural History* 35,

no. 3 (Jul. 1961), 117–18; AGI, SD 232 (per Maynard J. Geiger, *The Franciscan Conquest of Florida (1573–1618)* [Washington, D.C.: Catholic University of America, 1937], 242), Friars to SM, 16 Oct. 1612 (re Indian hostility toward cattle). Reports: *1567:* AGI, CD 1174, fols. 13, 14v; AGI, EC 154A, fols. 1203–1237v, 1318–1324; *1570:* AGI JU 1001, no. 2, R. 1, Pieza 4, fol. 4; *1574,* AGI, PAT 19, R. 33, "St. Agustín, lo que es. . . ."

39. AGI, CD 548, no. 8, Item 3, fol. 17 (1572 sale of maize, hams, pumpkins, kidney beans); AGI, CD 944, no. ?, Tanteo de Pedro Menéndez de Avilés El Mozo, no. 54, Cargos de Laurel, Nos. 5, 14 (purchases of locally produced maize, 1575, 1576); Archivo del Instituto de D. Juan de Valencia, Envio 25, H, no. 162, Menéndez de Avilés to Council of Indies, [Madrid, Nov. 1569] (farmers, sugar); AGI, JU 1001, no. 2, R. 1, pieza 1 (Alas's trade).

40. AGI, EC 154A, fols. 1311v–1315v, report on ships sent for supplies, ca. 1569, and AGI, CD 299, no. 2, pliego 107, for supplies sent from Spain in 1568.

41. Archivo del Instituto de D. Juan de Valencia, Envio 25, H, no. 162, Menéndez de Avilés to Council of Indies, n.d. [Nov. 1569], quotation and justification.

42. Eugene Lyon, *Santa Elena: A Brief History of the Colony, 1566–1587* (Columbia: Institute of Archaeology and Anthropology, University of South Carolina, 1984), 9–10. His power of attorney to his brother, Gutierre, and six other men was dated at St. Augustine, 11 Apr. 1576, AGI, CD 944, Castresana accounts, [fols. 1vto-5].

43. Lyon, *Santa Elena,* 7, 9, and AGI, EC 154A, fols. 980–81, Testimony of Bartolomé Martínez, Havana, 25 June 1577; AGI, CD 944, no. ?, Delgado's accounts, Item 37, fol. 15.

44. AGI, IG 1373, Menéndez de Avilés to SM, Madrid, 5 Mar. 1571, requesting permission to take up to 100 farmers, with decrees so ordering as AGI, SD 2528 (Stetson), King to Casa, Madrid, 5 Mar. 1571. In Aug. 1572 there were 179 settlers of all ages and both sexes, and 76 officers and soldiers at Santa Elena (48 married residents). In Apr. 1571 St. Augustine's garrison was 79, with 8 married residents. See Lyon, *Santa Elena,* 6; AGI, CD 548, no. 8, no. 5, *Datas* for St. Augustine; married men from Solís de Merás, *Menéndez de Avilés,* 246.

45. AGI, CD 548, no. 8, Item 3, fol. 17 (Payment to Alonso de Olmos, Juan Gómez, Pedro Hernández de Ribadeo); AGI, CD 944, no.? Tanteo de Pedro Menéndez de Avilés (el Mozo), no. 54 and also Cargos de Laurel, no. 5, both records of a purchase from four residents of Santa Elena, 23 Oct. 1575; AGI, JU 817, no. 5, Pieza 2 (libro mayor), fols. 13v–15, entries of 8 Feb. and 6 Mar. 1575 (sales at St. Augustine). Compare with AGI, CD 548, no. 8, Item 3, fols. 14v–16v, entry of 18 Jul. 1572; AGI, JU 817, no. 5, Pieza 2, fols. 9v–10, entry of 22 Dec. 1573.

46. AGI, JU 817, no. 5, Pieza 2, fols. 2v–4v, entry of 27 Aug. 1573, and

fols. 9v–10, entry of 22 Dec. 1573. AGI, PAT 19, R. 33, "San Agustín, Lo que es."

47. Lyon, *Santa Elena*, 7, citing AGI, EC 154A, fol. 993v (Question 12); Luis Gerónimo de Oré, *The Martyrs of Florida (1513–1616)*, trans. Maynard Geiger (New York: J. F. Wagner, 1936), 34, says that Indians "in Spanish service" had fled Santa Elena in 1576, on the eve of the Guale-Cusabo uprising; Amy Turner Bushnell, *Situado and Sabana: Spain's Support System for the Presidio and Mission Provinces of Florida* (New York: American Museum of Natural History; Athens: distributed by the University of Georgia Press, 1994), 60.

48. Paramountcy in Indian terms was not the same thing as the Spaniards' notion of the Indians as subjects of their king. Paramountcy involved a one up/one down relationship between potential equals based on reciprocity and kinship as well as force. The Spanish notion of "subject" did not imply any possibility of equality.

49. Lyon, *Santa Elena*, 9, citing AGI, EC 154A, fols. 110v, 125; AGI, JU 817, no. 5, pieza 2 (libro mayor), fols. 27v–28v, entry of 17 Sept. 1576 and AGI, CD 944, no. ?, Cuenta of Pedro Menéndez de Avilés (el Mozo), fragments, entries 81, 90.

50. Oré, *Martyrs*, 33; Geiger, *Franciscan Conquest*, 34–41; Gregory J. Keegan and Leandro Tormo Sanz, *Experiencia misionera en la Florida (Siglos XVI y XVII)* (Madrid: Consejo Superior de Investigaciones Científicas, 1957), 263–64; Lyon, *Santa Elena*, 8–9; Bushnell, *Situado and Sabana*, 42–43.

51. Son, according to Velasco. See Bushnell, *Situado and Sabana*, 61–62.

52. Lyon, *Santa Elena*, 10, using documents from 1577; Oré, *Martyrs*, 33–34; Bushnell, *Situado and Sabana*, 61–62.

53. Lyon, *Santa Elena*, 10.

54. Lyon, *Santa Elena*, 10–11; Oré, *Martyrs*, 33–36. AGI, PAT 75, no. 1, R. 4, fol. 3v, Testimony of Cristobal Gordillo, Mexico City, Mar. 1577, says that the town was looted and burned the day after the last patrol was ambushed. See also AGI, SD 125 (Stetson), Bartolomé Martínez to SM, Havana, 17 Feb. 1577. Bushnell, *Situado and Sabana*, 62. Anderson et al., "Paleoclimate," 268, notes that 1576 was a year of unusually heavy spring rains, which probably damaged crops, causing the Spaniards to confiscate maize from the Guale, who naturally resisted because their own reserves would have been low.

55. Lyon, *Santa Elena*, 11–12; AGI, SD 125 (Stetson), Menéndez Marqués to SM, Havana, 30 Jun. 1577; AGI, JU 1002, no. 5, Información de parte de Gutierre de Miranda, questions 12, 15, with answers, 13 Jul. 1577.

56. AGI, SD 118 (Stetson), Diego de la Ribera to Crown, Havana, 9 Oct. 1578, commenting on Indian relations; Lyon, *Santa Elena*, 13. For

the French see Mary Ross, "French Intrusions and Indian Uprisings in Georgia and South Carolina, 1577–1580," *Georgia Historical Quarterly* 7 (1923), 251–81, and AGI, SD 229 (Stetson), Treasury Officials to Crown, 12 Oct. 1580.

57. María Teresa de Rojas, ed., *Indice y extractos del archivo de Protocolos de la Habana, 1578–1595,* 3 vols. (Habana, 1947–), 1:330, Entry 562, "Transacción concertada entre Bernaldo de Valdés . . . y Pero Sánchez . . . , 9 Aug. 1585." Information courtesy of Eugene Lyon.

58. This suggests that the rebel against cacique Guale in 1576 was the cacique of Tupique and that his nephew, who killed Guale, was the cacique of Guano, replaced by 1580 by another nephew. The killer was executed by the Spaniards. However, documents from 1577 say the assassin was Perico from Sapelo Island, the *son* of an unnamed cacique (Bushnell, *Situado and Sabana,* 61–62). Guano, which means either "palm tree" or "sea bird droppings," does not appear in the mission lists of the seventeenth century.

59. AGI, SD 125, no. 150-D, Certification by Juan Miel, Notary, Merits and Services of Captain Tomás Bernaldo de Quirós, 1579–80, fols. 5v–11 (citation courtesy of Eugene Lyon). A cedula of 10 Jun. 1580 authorized the treasury officials to collect tributes and other forms of local income (AGI, SD 2528 (Stetson), pp. 253–55). Name corrections in brackets from Grant Jones, "The Ethnohistory of the Guale Coast through 1684," *Anthropological Papers of the American Museum of Natural History* 55, pt. 2 (1978), 205, 207. The last three names on this list of Tolomato's subordinates include towns that Jones believed belonged to the Asao–Talaxe chiefdom, not Guale–Tolomato, although some names appear on both of his lists.

60. AGI, SD 231 (Stetson), Gutierre de Miranda to SM, 14 Oct. 1580; AGI, SD 229 (Stetson), Juan Cevadilla to Crown, Havana, 22 Jan. 1582 (reporting the "pestilence" at Santa Elena); AGI, SD 231 (Stetson), Pedro Menéndez Marqués to SM, 19 Jul. 1582; AGI, SD 146, Gabriel de Luxán to SM, Havana, Jan. 1582. Jones, "Ethnohistory," 182–83. The destruction of the town and people of Agoza [Yagoa?] is mentioned in Capt. Alonso Diaz de Badajoz's account of his service against the rebel Indians of Santa Elena. AGI, SD 232 (Stetson), question 2. The spring rainfall pattern favored the production of surpluses of maize (Anderson et al., "Paleoclimate," 269).

61. AGI, SD 224, fols. 85–86, Menéndez Marqués to SM, 27 Dec. 1583. The dendroclimatilogical data do not record unusually dry years prior to 1583, but do for the 1583–87 period (Anderson et al., "Paleoclimate," 268–69).

62. AGI, SD 224, fol. 85, Menéndez Marqués to SM, St. Augustine, 27 Dec. 1583; Geiger, *Franciscan Conquest,* 43. The treasury officials complained to the Crown about the construction of the first of these

new Indian settlements in a letter of 6 Mar. 1580, saying it was built with soldiers' labor and was next to the cornfield of Menéndez Marqués (AGI, SD 229 (Stetson)).

63. AGI, SD 229 (Stetson), Treasury Officials to SM, 10 Oct. 1580, noting rebellion in "Timucua." Worth, "Timucuan Missions," 28–29. San Sebastian and Tocoy were a single village governed by Pedro Marqués, a convert; Nombre de Dios was governed by Doña María, wife of Clemente Vernal, a Spanish soldier. These seem to have been the two villages within half a league of St. Augustine. See Bushnell, *Situado and Sabana*, 120.

64. AGI, IG 739, Consulta, 15 Feb., 12 Mar. 1578, and Menéndez Marqués to SM, 12 Oct. 1577; AGI, PAT 255, *Visita* of Alvaro Flores de Quiñones, Santa Elena and St. Augustine, 1 Nov. and 19 Nov. 1578.

65. AGI, SD 2528 (Stetson), fols. 225, 238–39, Cedulas of 24 and 31 Jan and 9 Feb. 1580; AGI, SD 229 (Stetson), Treasury Officials to SM, 12 Oct. 1580 reporting the arrival of Miranda; for the Indian wives see AGI, EC 154-A, fols. 65–68v, Decree freeing nine Indian women slaves (including the 3 wives), St. Augustine, 17 Dec. 1576.

66. AGI, SD 229 (Stetson), Juan Cevadilla to SM, 22 Jan. 1582. They were twenty-three men and seven women; AGI, SD 231 (Stetson), Treasury Officials to SM, 20 Dec. 1583.

67. Geiger, *Franciscan Conquest*, 46–50.

68. AGI, SD 224 (Stetson), Menéndez Marqués to SM, 27 Dec. 1583.

69. AGI, SD 168 (Stetson), Menéndez Marqués to SM, 2 Apr. 1579. C. Margaret Scarry, "The Use of Plant Foods in Sixteenth Century St. Augustine," *Florida Anthropologist* 38 (1985), 74–79.

70. The Library of Congress, Jeannette T. Connor Papers Box 11, Microfilm Roll 4, AGI, no signature shown, Claims for compensation totaling 1,391 ducats for houses and thirty-five "gardens," in Decrees, St. Aug., 19 Oct. 1588; AGI, SD 2528 (Stetson), Crown to Fla Gov., Madrid, n.d. [1588], and 21 Feb. 1590 ordering payment. Not all homeowners claimed to own gardens; five owned two gardens, three owned only a house. Materials from the Connor Collection are referred to hereafter as JTC#4, indicting the fourth roll of microfilm, or third, as the case may be.

71. Elizabeth J. Reitz, "Faunal Evidence for Sixteenth Century Spanish Subsistence at St. Augustine, Florida," *Florida Anthropologist* 38 (1985), 62–64; Scarry, "Use of Plant Foods," 77–79. See also Elizabeth J. Reitz, "Dieta y alimentación hispano-americana en el Caribe y la Florida en el siglo XVI," *Revista de Indias* 51 (1991), 11–24.

72. AGI, SD 2528 (Stetson), Crown to Governor of Florida, 6 Jul. 1579, 24 Jan. 1580, 25 May 1585; AGI, SD 229 (Stetson), Treasury Officials to SM, 6 Mar. 1580 (courtesy of Eugene Lyon); AGI, SD 2528 (Stetson) Crown to Treasury Officials of Florida, Badajoz, 30 Sept. 1580

(granting a four-year license to import livestock); AGI, SD 231 (Stetson), Information for Gutierre de Miranda, Havana, 17 Feb. 1588, Question 13 and replies.

73. The Crown's effort to divorce the governing of Florida from its support failed. An independent treasurer, Juan Cevadilla, was co-opted through marriage by the Asturians and quickly took up the exploitation of the situado for private gain (AGI, SD 229, no. 44). Menéndez Marqués also took a hand in the situado collection (AGI, SD 99, no. 2, doc. 95 (Stetson), Gov. Luxán to SM, Havana, [Jul. 1583]; AGI, SD 231 (Stetson), Juan Cevadilla to SM, 24 Dec. 1582; AGI, SD 224, fol. 89, Menéndez Marqués to SM, 27 Dec. 1583). For imported ceramics see Kathleen A. Deagan, "Archaeology of Sixteenth Century St. Augustine," *Florida Anthropologist* 38 (1985), 18–22.

74. AGI, SD 99, R. 3, no. 86, Gov. Francisco Carreño to SM, Havana, 12 Feb. 1578; AGI, SD 229 (Stetson), Treasury Officials to SM, 12 Oct. 1580; AGI, IG 1887 (Stetson), Gov. Diego Menéndez de Valdés to Crown, Puerto Rico, 5 Jan. 1584.

75. Paul E. Hoffman, *Spain and the Roanoke Voyages* (Raleigh: North Carolina Department of Cultural Resources, 1987), 22–26.

76. The Spaniards had had warning of his activities in the Caribbean since January of that year and had built a new artillery platform and fort—San Juan de Pinillo—opposite the end of the channel into the bay. Concerned for the safety of their families, who had been removed to the forests west of town when the English appeared off St. Augustine bar, and outnumbered, the soldiers manning the new fort had put up a perfunctory resistance, spiked the guns, and decamped to the woods. Drake's men not only burned the town, they also cut down fruit trees and maize fields and tore up gardens and took building hardware. Irene A. Wright, ed., *Further English Voyages to Spanish America, 1583–1594* (London: Haklyut Society, 1951), 163–64, 180–84, 198–202. For the entire West Indian raid see Harry Kelsey, *Sir Francis Drake: The Queen's Pirate* (New Haven: Yale University Press, 1998), 257–77.

77. Dobyns, *Their Number Became Thinned*, 276–78; earlier the English had spread disease at Roanoke, but it is unlikely it traveled down the coast.

4. The Tidewater Frontier, Second Phase, 1586–1608

1. Luis Gerónimo de Oré, *The Martyrs of Florida*, trans. Maynard Geiger (New York: J. F. Wagner, 1936), 42, for Indian threat. A consolidated garrison also would allow the simultaneous guarding of the fort and the sending of large forces to march about the countryside keeping the Indians "llanos y quietos" (AGI, SD 224, fol. 93v, Juan de Posadas to SM, 2 Sept. 1586).

2. AGI, SD 2528 (Stetson), Cedulas of 17 Oct. 1584 (Juan Mordazo de Rivera and wife and children), 8 Jun. 1588 (Diego López and wife and son), 29 Jun. 1588 (Pablos Juan and family), 9 Mar. 1592 (Petronilla de Junco, widow), 18 Mar. 1592 (Juan Núñez de los Ríos and family), 29 Apr. 1592 (Pedro de Rueda and family).

3. The governors were Pedro Menéndez Marqués, Gutierre de Miranda, Francisco de Salazar (elected by the mutineers), Rodrigo de Junco (who drowned in a shipwreck at the St. Johns Bar on his way to assume office) and Avendaño. For the rebellion see: AGI, SD 99 (Stetson), Juan de Tejada to SM, Havana, 22 Mar. 1593.

4. Account of Father Andrés de San Miguel, 1595, as summarized in Albert Manucy, "The Physical Setting of Sixteenth Century St. Augustine," *Florida Anthropologist* 38 (1985), 41–42.

5. AGI, SD 224, fols. 155-vto, Mendez de Canzo to SM, paragraph 37, 24 Feb. 1598; AGI, SD 229 (Lockey), Bartolomé de Argüelles to SM, 18 Mar. 1599 (re fire) and 20 Feb. 1600 (re flood); AGI, SD 224 (Stetson), Mendez de Canzo to SM, 28 Feb. 1600 (re hurricane). AGI, CD 956, Accounts of Juan López de Avilés, items questioned (at end of the account), showing 391 arrobas, 7.5 lbs of maize burned and various other supplies said to have been destroyed in the hurricane.

6. AGI, SD 224, fol. 156v, Mendez de Canzo to SM, 24 Feb. 1598 (also in Manuel Serrano y Sanz, ed., *Documentos históricos de la Florida y la Luisiana, Siglos XVI al XVIII* (Madrid: V. Suarez, 1912), 137). We do not know if the number of married couples had been increased by the dozen single women Canzo was authorized to take to the colony (AGI, SD 2528 (Stetson), Cedula, 25 May 1596).

7. Manucy, "Physical Setting," 46, using AGI, SD 231, no. 119, Jul. 1600; AGI, SD 224, fols. 4–5v, Mendez de Canzo to SM, 28 Feb. 1600; AGI, SD 224 (Stetson), Gov. Ibarra to SM, 15 Aug. 1607 (for forty-two non-Spanish wives in the garrison). A typical early modern European population had approximately equal numbers of men and women and at least 36 percent children under the age of fifteen, and at that barely managed to maintain a stable total, or grow slightly. See Peter Laslett, *The World We Have Lost: England before the Industrial Age*, 2nd ed. (New York: Charles Scribner's Sons, 1973), 108–109.

8. Irene A. Wright, ed., *Further English Voyages to Spanish America, 1583–1594* (London: Hakluyt Society, 1951), 187. Paul E. Hoffman, *Spain and the Roanoke Voyages* (Raleigh: America's Four Hundredth Anniversary Committee, North Carolina Department of Cultural Resources, 1987), 34–36.

9. Eugene Lyon, *Santa Elena: A Brief History of the Colony, 1566–1587* (Columbia, S.C.: Institute of Archaeology and Anthropology, 1984), 14–15. AGI, SD 231, no. 64.

10. Oré, *Martyrs*, 43; Robert A. Matter, *Pre-Seminole Florida: Spanish Soldiers, Friars, and Indian Missions, 1513–1763* (New York: Garland,

1990), 40; AGI, SD 224, fol. 96, Menéndez Marqués to SM, Havana, 17 Jul. 1588. Cf. Gregory J. Keegan and Leandro Tormo-Sanz, *Experiencia Misionera en la Florida (Siglos XVI y XVII)* (Madrid: Consejo Superior de Investigaciones Científicos, 1957), 342, who erroneously include missions in Guale and Potano. For the location and archaeology of San Pedro, see Jerald T. Milanich, "Tacatacuru and the San Pedro de Mocamo Mission," *FHQ* 50 (1972), 283–91. According to Juan Menéndez ("Relación," in Eugenio Ruidiaz y Caravía, ed., *La Florida, Su conquista y colonización por Pedro Menéndez de Avilés*, 2 vols. (Madrid: Imprenta de los hijos de J. A. García, 1893), 2:495–509), the Christian cacique of San Pedro, D. Pedro Marqués, had emerged as the leader of the Timucua not only on his island and the adjacent mainland but also along the St. Johns River, where his authority had replaced the late Saturiba's.

11. Matter, *Pre-Seminole Florida*, 41; Maynard J. Geiger, *The Franciscan Conquest of Florida (1573–1618)* (Wasington, D.C.: Caltholic University of America, 1937), 58–59; AGI, SD 127 (Stetson), Bartolomé de Argüelles to SM, Havana, 12 Dec. 1592. The *Patronato Real* was the name for the Crown's rights to control the Catholic Church and to receive certain benefits from it.

12. Amy Turner Bushnell, *The King's Coffer: Proprietors of the Spanish Florida Treasury, 1565–1702* (Gainesville: University Presses of Florida, 1981), 13; AGI, SD 224, fol. 95, Menéndez Marqués to SM, Havana, 17 Jul. 1588, complaining that not a grain of maize could be sown because of the dryness; David G. Anderson, David W. Stahle, Malcolm K. Cleaveland, "Paleoclimate and the Potential Food Reserves of Mississippian Societies: A Case Study from the Savannah River Valley," *American Antiquity* 60 (1995), Figs. 2, 3, for rainfall patterns in coastal South Carolina, which may be similar to those in northeast Florida. Henry Dobyns, *Their Number Became Thinned: Native American Population Dynamics in Eastern North America* (Knoxville: University of Tennessee Press, 1983), 278, has another epidemic in the summer of 1596, but his source suggests the problem was summer diarrhea among the population at St. Augustine, not a measles (or smallpox) epidemic such as he postulates.

13. Engel Sluiter, *The Florida Situado: Quantifying the First Eighty Years, 1571–1651* (Gainesville: P. K. Yonge Library of Florida History, 1985), Table, entries for 1587–97; AGI, SD 224, fol. 153v, Gov. Mendez de Canzo to SM, St. Augustine, 24 Feb. 1598; loc. cit., fols. 109–38, Expediente re need to employ Francisco Diaz Pimienta, 6 May 1591; AGI, SD 2528 (Stetson), Crown to Pedro Menéndez Marqués, San Lorenzo, 2 Oct. 1593, ordering report on complaints about high prices.

14. AGI, SD 231 (JTC#4), Avendaño to SM, Jul. 1595; AGI, SD 224, fol. 144, Avendaño to SM, 15 Sept. 1595. Had he lived, he might have begun construction of a coquina stone fort, but with his death the trea-

sury officials found ways to put that off. AGI, SD 2528 (Stetson), Crown to Avendaño, 21 Jun. 1595; AGI, SD 231 (JTC#4), Treasury Officials to SM, 13 Dec. 1595. Coquina had been identified as a building stone as early as 1583. AGI, SD 224, fol. 87, Menéndez Marqués to SM, 27 Dec. 1583.

15. Missions listed from south to north. J[ames] G. Johnson, "The International Contest for the Colonial Southeast, 1566–1763" (Ph.D. dissertation, University of California, 1924), 42; Juan de Torquemada, *Monarchia Indiana*, 3 vols. (Madrid: N. Rodriguez Franco, 1723 [1725]), 3:350; Juan Menéndez Marqués to Fr. Miguel Avengózar, 159?, in Ruidiaz, *La Florida*, 2:495–509. Any Turner Bushnell, *Situado and Sabana: Spain's Support System for the Presidio and Mission Provinces of Florida* (New York: American Museum of Natural History; Athens: distributed by the University of Georgia Press, 1994), 65.

16. AGI, SD 235 (Stetson), Fr. Francisco de Marón to SM, 23 Jan. 1596; Geiger, *Franciscan Conquest*, 63–64, 67–68; Matter, *Pre-Seminole Florida*, 41.

17. AGI, SD 235 (Stetson), Testimony of Alonso Sánchez Saez de Mercado, 23 Jan. 1597, enclosed with Fr. Francisco de Marón to SM, 23 Jan. 1596. See also Geiger, *Franciscan Conquest*, 67–68.

18. Charles Hudson, *The Juan Pardo Expeditions: Exploration of the Carolinas and Tennessee, 1566–1568* (Washington, D.C.: Smithsonian Institution Press, 1990), 259–60 (an example of the tribute), 288–93 (maize to Santa Elena); AGI, SD 231, Treasury Officials to SM, 13 Dec. 1595 (JTC#4), and Avendaño to Sec. Ibarra, 14 Jan. 1595 (Stetson).

19. AGI, SD 231, Treasury Officials to SM, 13 Dec. 1595; Saez de Mercado to Juan de Ibarra, 6 Jan. 1596 (mentioning a summary of the tribute obligations forwarded to the Council of the Indies); AGI, SD 224, fol. 51, Treasury Officials to SM, 8 Oct. 1601. If the baptized Indians totaled 2,900, and all male heads of household paid, this suggests households of 5.47 persons, a credible number.

20. Geiger, *Franciscan Conquest*, 65; Matter, *Pre-Seminole Florida*, 41.

21. Avendaño was noted as the right sort of governor in Friars to SM, 14 Jan. 1617, in Keegan and Tormo Sanz, *Experiencia misionera*, 304. Capilla quotation in Geiger, *Franciscan Conquest*, 222.

22. Torquemada, *Monarquia Indiana* (1725), 3:350.

23. Geiger, *Franciscan Conquest*, 77–78, n. 23, lists twenty-two names. The additional names came from materials cited in n. 20. John E. Worth, "The Timucuan Missions of Spanish Florida and the Rebellion of 1656" (Ph.D. dissertation, University of Florida, 1992), 36–38, suggests the caciques were seeking to obtain clothing and other items of conspicuous display rather than more utilitarian items such as hatchets that could be used to build obligations under the redistribution system. However, the list of gifts given does not entirely support his suggestion.

24. Library of Congress, Jeannette Thurbur Connor Papers, Box 11 (JTC#4), poor photocopy of certified list of what was given Indians at St. Augustine, 10 Jun.–Jul. 1597; AGI, SD 231 (Stetson), Testimonies, 17 Sept. 1597 (for 2 Aug. to 14 Sept.); AGI, CD 956, Account of Factor Juan López de Avilés, *Data* of Cloth, 30 Sept. 1597. Utina's gifts are noted in Worth, "Timucuan Missions," 40.

25. AGI, SD 235 (Lockey), Declaration of Fray Baltasar López, 15 Sept. 1602, per Geiger, *Franciscan Conquest*, 146–51.

26. For the Chozas expedition to La Tama see John E. Worth, "Late Spanish Military Expeditions in the Interior Southeast, 1597–1628," in *The Forgotten Centuries: Indians and Europeans in the American South, 1521–1704*, ed. Charles Hudson and Carmen Chaves Tesser (Athens: University of Georgia Press, 1994), 105–109.

27. Torquemada, *Monarquia Indiana*, 3: 351–54, based on Oré, *Martyrs*, 74–96. The story is retold at length in James G. Johnson, "The Yamasee Revolt of 1597 and the Destruction of the Georgia Mission," *Georgia Historical Quarterly* 7 (1923), 44–53; John T. Lanning, *The Spanish Missions of Georgia* (Chapel Hill: University of North Carolina Press, 1935), 82–93; and Geiger, *Franciscan Conquest*, 91–122.

28. AGI, SD 229 (Lockey), Argüelles to SM, 20 Feb. 1600 (friars' views; Argüelles was their business agent); AGI, SD 224, fol. 51, Treasury Officials to SM, 8 Oct. 1601; AGI, SD 150 (Stetson), Bishop Juan de las Cavezas to SM, 24 Jun. 1606. Fr. Añón was the one who tried to prevent the movement of Indians among the villages. See also Torquemada, *Monarquia Indiana*, 3:350–51; Andrés Gonzales de Barcía Carballido y Zúñiga, *Chronological History of the Continent of Florida*, trans. Anthony Kerrigan (Gainesville: University of Florida Press, 1951), 181–84. Amy Bushnell (personal communication) has suggested that the occasional French trading venture to Guale during this period provided an alternative to Spanish supply and thus emboldened D. Juan to rebel. There is no indication of this as a motive in the sources.

29. Worth, "Late Spanish Military Expeditions," 105–109; AGI, SD 229, Argüelles to SM, 20 Feb. 1600; AGI, SD 224 (Stetson), Mendez de Canzo to SM, 28 Feb. 1600. Torquemada, *Monarquia Indiana*, 3:351, invents a speech for D. Juan in which he sets out grievances against the friars and Spaniards.

30. AGI, SD 224, fols. 302–304, Testimony of obedience of certain caciques of Guale, 18 May 1600.

31. AGI, CT 5112 (Stetson) Mendez de Canzo to SM, 22 Feb. 1598; Matter, *Pre-Seminole Florida*, 43; AGI, CD 956, Accounts of Juan López de Avilés, *Data* of Maize, no. 4 (entry of 12 Jan. 1598); Torquemada, *Monarquia Indiana*, 3:353.

32. Torquemada, *Monarquia Indiana*, 3:354, is a general account. For details see AGI, SD 224, fol. 211, Mendez de Canzo to SM, 8 Aug. 1598; AGI, CD 956, Accounts of Juan López de Avilés, *Data* of Vizco-

cho, 11 Oct. 1597, 11 Feb., 22 May, 23 Jul., 16 Nov., 19 Dec. 1598, and 19 Jan., 25 May, 1599; and his *Data* of Flour, entries 40, 67, 82. For harvests see Georgia rainfall estimates in Table 4.1.

33. AGI, SD 224, fols. 302–304, Testimony of the obedience of certain caciques, 18 May 1600. AGI, CD 956, Accounts of Juan López de Avilés, *Data* of Maize, no. 39, 26 Jan. 1600; *Data* of Vizcocho, 20 Apr., 5 and 14 May 1600; *Data* of Flour, nos. 108–109, 12 and 14 May 1600.

34. AGI, SD 224 (Stetson), Información, 27 Nov. 1601. See also Matter, *Pre-Seminole Florida*, 44–45; Serrano y Sanz, *Documentos*, 161.

35. AGI, SD 231 (JTC#4), Marginal note on Treasury Officials to SM, 13 Dec. 1595; AGI, SD 224, Mendez de Canzo to SM, 24 Feb. 1598 (printed in Serrano y Sanz, *Documentos*, 135–36); AGI, SD 224, fol. 51, Treasury Officials to SM, 8 Oct. 1601; AGI, SD 6 (Stetson), Consulta of Consejo de Indias, 16 Aug. 1598; AGI, SD 224 (Stetson), Mendez de Canzo to SM, 28 Feb. 1600 (noting many Indians did not grow maize but lived on seafood, roots, and fruits). Cf. Alan R. Calmes, "Indian Cultural Traditions and European Conquest of the Georgia-South Carolina Coastal Plain, 3000 BC–1733 AD: A Combined Archaeological and Historical Investigation" (Ph.D. dissertation, University of South Carolina, 1968), 74. The first collections of four ears per tributary were made at San Pedro in 1600, with a yield of ten arrobas.

36. AGI, SD 224, fol. 155, Mendez de Canzo to SM, 24 Feb. 1598 (reporting his goal); AGI, CD 956, Accounts of Juan López de Avilés, *Data* of Maize, no. 13 for 209 arrobas of maize used to feed 148 Indian laborers who helped to repair the fort against the Earl of Cumberland's expected attack; AGI, SD 224, fols. 302–304, Testimony, 11 May 1600 (reporting the laborers and agreement); AGI, SD 231 (Stetson), Pedro Redondo Villegas to SM, 18 Apr. 1600, reporting the clearing of a mosquito-breeding wetland ("el gran mosquitero que solía [h]aver") as well as forested areas. By then the royal fields were twenty years old.

37. AGI, SD 224 (Stetson), Mendez de Canzo to SM, 24 Apr. 1601 (also in Serrano y Sanz, *Documentos*, 161); AGI, CD 956, Accounts of Factor Juan López de Avilés, *Data* of Maize, nos. 52, 62.

38. AGI, SD 2533 (Stetson), fols. 24v–27v, Testimony of Francisco de Ecija, 1602, notes the many plagues and birds that reduce the harvest and the insects that damage the grain in storage. Eugene Lyon kindly provided this information.

39. For a discussion of the magical/religious qualities of exotic goods and their relationship to the powers of the cacique see Mary W. Helms, "Political Lords and Political Ideology in Southeastern Chiefdoms: Comments and Observations," in *Lords of the Southeast: Social Inequality and the Native Elites of Southeastern North America*, ed. Alex W. Barker and Timothy R. Pauketat (Washington, D.C.: American Anthropological Association, 1992), 187–88.

40. The estimate is derived from 1697 ration data for soldiers that worked out to be 34.57 arrobas per man per year or 2.36 lbs. per day. See AGI, SD 228, fols. 281–85, Torres y Ayala to SM, no. 15, 4 Feb. 1697: 6 months rations for 335 men was 5,790 arrobas of maize.

41. AGI, SD 229 (Lockey), Argüelles to SM, 18 Mar. 1599. García's full name is from AGI, CD 956, Account of Juan López de Avilés, *Cargo* of Clothing, no. 1, 15 Nov. 1601.

42. AGI, SD 224, fols. 157v–158, Mendez de Canzo to SM, 23 Feb. 1598, and ibid., fols. 215–217v, Mendez de Canzo to SM, 14 Nov. 1598 and ibid., no folio (Stetson), Mendez de Canzo to SM, 28 Feb. 1600; AGI, SD 229 (Lockey), Bartolomé de Argüelles to SM, 18 Mar. 1599; AGI, SD 224 (Stetson), Mendez de Canzo to SM, 31 Jan. 1600.

43. AGI, SD 224, fol. 216v, Mendez de Canzo to SM, 14 Nov. 1598. AGI, SD 229 (Lockey), Bartolomé de Argüelles to SM, 20 Feb. 1600, expressing the friars' point of view that men are more moved by fear than love.

44. AGI, CD 956, Accounts of Juan López de Avilés, *Data* of Flour, no. 15, 7 Mar. 1598; no. 65, 5 May 1599; no. 116, 25 Aug. 1600; no. 148, 26 Jun. 1601; AGI, SD 224 (Serrano y Sanz, *Documentos*, 161–62), Mendez de Canzo to SM, 24 Apr. 1601.

45. AGI, CD 956, Accounts of Juan López de Avilés, *Data* of Flour, nos. 116 and 117, 28 Aug. 1600; *Data* of Cloth, no. 3. AGI, SD 224 (Serrano y Sanz, *Documentos*, 161–62), Mendez de Canzo to SM, 24 Apr. 1601. Doña Ana's predecessor, D. Juan, was lauded in Mendez de Canzo to SM, 28 Feb. and 26 Jun. 1600, AGI, SD 224, fols. 219–28, with two copies of summario, 230–52.

46. AGI, SD 224 (Serrano y Sanz, *Documentos*, 161–62), Mendez de Canzo to SM, 24 Apr. 1601, and Worth, "Timucuan Missions," 40–43.

47. AGI, SD 232 (JTC#4), Juan Menéndez Marqués to SM, 13 Apr. 1601 and 21 Apr. 1603; AGI, SD 229 (JTC#2), Treasury Officials to SM, 20 Apr. 1603, reporting purchase of 500 arrobas of sarsaparilla root at San Pedro. Mary Ross, "French on the Savannah, 1605," *Georgia Historical Quarterly* 8 (1924), 167–94.

48. AGI, SD 232 (JTC#4), Juan Menéndez Marqués to SM, 21 Apr. 1603, charging the governor with trading in ambergris; AGI, CD 955, Accounts of Factor Las Alas, *Cargas*, no. 56, purchase of 12 *manos* of "tobaco de la cosecha desta tierra." Re Juan García see AGI, SD 229 (Lockey), Bartolomé de Argüelles to SM, 18 Mar. 1599.

49. AGI, SD 224, Mendez de Canzo to SM, 24 Apr. 1601. Also in Serrano y Sanz, *Documentos*, 160.

50. AGI, SD 224, fols. 258–67, "Información," 4–6 Feb. 1600; Mendez de Canzo to SM, 28 Feb. 1600. See also Serrano y Sanz, *Documentos*, 141–59. A poor translation is Katherine Redding, trans., "Letter of Gonzalo Menéndez [*sic*] de Canço, Governor of Florida to Philip II of Spain

of June 28, 1600," *Georgia Historical Quarterly* 8 (1924), 215–28. Geiger, *Franciscan Conquest*, 125–29. For the 1602 entrada see Worth, "Late Spanish Military Expeditions," 109–10. The white men were almost certainly a memory of Tristan de Luna's Coosa party or possibly even De Soto.

51. AGI, SD 224, fols. 156v–157v, Mendez de Canzo to SM, 23 Feb. 1598, and ibid., fols. 258–67, Mendez de Canzo to SM, 28 Feb. 1600; both in Serrano y Sanz, *Documentos*, 138, 141–59. AGI, SD 229 (Lockey), Argüelles to SM, 20 Feb. 1600.

52. AGI, SD 232 (JTC#4), Argüelles to SM, n.d. [May 1593?]; Charles W. Arnade, *Florida on Trial, 1593–1602* (Coral Gables: University of Miami Press, 1959), 11–12; AGI, SD 235 (Stetson), Fr. Baltasar López to SM, 12 Dec. 1599. In a lengthy consulta of 16 Aug. 1598, the Council gives no hint of these questions. See AGI, SD 6 (Stetson), Consulta, 16 Aug. 1598. Interest in the Miami location for a fort/coast guard station dates to the 1570s, according to Juan López de Velasco, *Geografía y descripción universal de las Indias* (1574) (reprint, Madrid: Fortanet, 1894), 166.

53. AGI, SD 224, fols. 280–280v (also Stetson), copy of paragraph of report of General Luis Fajardo, [1600?].

54. AGI, SD 2528 (Stetson).

55. Arnade, *Florida on Trial*, passim, is the only detailed study of this episode. See also Geiger, *Franciscan Conquest*, 141–53, and John H. Hann, *A History of the Timucua Indians and Missions* (Gainesville: University Press of Florida, 1996), 157–63. The Fernando de Valdés file is in AGI, SD 235 (Lockey and Stetson).

56. Geiger, *Franciscan Conquest*, 160–63. Lanning, *Spanish Missions*, 126–45, 152–59, and Mary Ross, "The Restoration of the Spanish Missions in Georgia, 1598–1606," *Georgia Historical Quarterly* 10 (1926), 171–99, cover Mendez de Canzo's inspection of 1603, Ibarra's visitation of 1604, and Bishop Caveza's visitation of 1606.

57. AGI, SD 232 (JTC#4), Pedro de Ibarra to Father Benito Blasco, 7 Dec. 1605. See also AGI, SD 150 (Stetson), Bishop Juan de la Cavezas to SM, 24 Jun. 1606. Geiger, *Franciscan Conquest*, 190–94.

58. AGI, SD 224 (Stetson), Pedro de Ibarra to SM, 8 Jan. 1604; and "Relación del viage que hizo el Señor Pedro de Ibarra, Nov.-Dic. 1604." The latter is also in Serrano y Sanz, *Documentos*, 164–93.

59. AGI, SD 224 (Stetson), "Diligencias," 1605; Geiger, *Franciscan Conquest*, 178–83. AGI, SD 224 (Stetson), Ibarra to SM, 26 Dec. 1605.

60. AGI, SD 224 (Stetson), Ibarra to SM, 16 May 1607. Ibarra had also had the San Mateo River explored and had sent a map of it with a letter of 1 Feb. 1605. During these years the Spaniards were trying to update their maps of La Florida, as was Hondius, the great Dutch mapmaker. See AGI, SD 224 (Stetson), Ibarra to SM, 26 Dec. 1605 and 16 May 1607.

William P. Cummings, "Geographical Misconceptions of the Southeast in the Cartography of the Seventeenth and Eighteenth Centuries," *Journal of Southern History* 4 (1938), 478–79.

61. Worth, "Late Spanish Military Expeditions," 110–11; AGI, SD 150 (Stetson), Cavezas to SM, 24 Jun. 1606. Ibarra's first request for one hundred soldiers was to fill out his garrison. See AGI, SD 224 (Stetson), Ibarra to SM, 8 Jan. 1604.

62. AGI, SD 224 (Stetson), Ibarra to SM, 8 Jan. 1604 and Geiger, *Franciscan Conquest*, 169; Ross, "French on the Savannah," 186–93. The crewmen who would not convert to Catholicism were eventually executed (AGI, SD 224 (Stetson), Ibarra to SM, 4 Jan. 1608).

63. AGI, SD 232 (Stetson), Ibarra to Fray Pedro de Vermejo, 13 Dec. 1605.

64. AGI, SD 235 (Stetson), Bishop to SM, 26 Jun. 1606; Geiger, *Franciscan Conquest*, 186, lists the friars and assignments by name. John Hann, "Summary Guide to Spanish Florida Missions and Visitas, with Churches in the Sixteenth and Seventeenth Centuries," *The Americas* 46 (1990), 441, notes that in this period "Potano" was "among the Freshwater Timucua possibly. . . ." Since it is linked with the other two cacicazgos in AGI, SD 232 (Stetson), Ibarra to Fr. Pedro de Vermejo, 13 Dec. 1605, this is almost certainly correct. Recall that the new, teenaged cacique of Potano requested permission in 1594 to rebuild the town near the St. Johns that Menéndez de Avilés had visited in 1567. Since that had been done, it accounts for the inclusion of "Potano" with the other Freshwater towns, although we do not have evidence the Potano were actually evangelized. Hann notes that as late as 1607 the cacique of the interior Potano was hostile to the Spaniards.

65. Geiger, *Franciscan Conquest*, 223–27 (from Oré) for the spouse problem.

66. Worth, "Timucuan Missions," 97.

67. Keegan and Tormo Sanz, *Experiencia misionera*, 298, for the adoration; AGI, SD 235 (Lockey), Declaration of Fr. Francisco de Pareja, 14 Sept. 1602, regarding cacique authority and the governors. The other friars who testified in 1602 said much the same thing. Geiger, *Franciscan Conquest*, 156, defends clerical authoritarianism as necessary for "continued Christian discipline and example" to counter pagan customs. Friars in Mexico also made this claim of a breakdown in the preconversion social discipline of commoners (Charles Gibson, *The Aztecs under Spanish Rule* (Stanford: Stanford University Press, 1964), 118). The friars do not seem to have noticed the irony that Indian informants they quoted blamed *conversion* for the loss of this discipline.

Other modern apologists for the friars' position are Keegan and Tormo Sanz, *Experiencia misionera*, 334–38, and Cristobal Figuero del Campo, *Missiones Franciscanos en la Florida* (Madrid: Comisión Episcopal del V. Centenario, 1992), 121–25. Given what we know of how the *lex talionis* worked in Indian society, it is doubtful that caciques could execute people at will.

68. Alonso Gregorio de Escobedo, "La Florida," in James W. Covington, ed., *Pirates, Indians, and Spaniards: Father Escobedo's "La Florida,"* trans. A. E. Falcones (St. Petersburg, Fla.: Great Outdoors Publishing Co., 1963), 152: "Responden desta suerte: 'Si admitimos la ley de Dios, la causa fue el vestido. Pero después, señor, que lo rompimos, pusimos vuestros ritos en olvido.'"

69. Geiger, *Franciscan Conquest*, 227–31; Worth, "Timucuan Missions," 50–57; Matter, *Pre-Seminole Florida*, 54. Cf. Oré, *Martyrs of Florida*, 112–18. Geiger's figures of two hundred baptisms at San Miguel and two hundred at San Francisco seem more realistic than Worth's note that over one thousand adults were baptized in all of the towns.

70. Oré, *Martyrs*, 112, 117; John H. Hann, *Apalachee: The Land between the Rivers* (Gainesville: University Presses of Florida, 1988), 10–11.

71. Geiger, *Franciscan Conquest*, 229 (1608); cf. ibid., p. 231 (1609). Oré, *Martyrs*, 114, does not give a date.

72. AGI, SD 224 (Stetson), Mendez de Canzo to SM, Valladolid, 19 Mar. 1605, per Arnade, *Florida on Trial*, 81–85; see also AGI, SD 25 (Stetson), Capt. Pedro Florés de la Coba to SM, Madrid, n.d. [1606?]. AGI, SD 150 (Stetson), Bishop Cavesas to SM, 4 Oct. 1606.

73. I did not find the original decree. It is noted in AGI, Mexico 1065, tomo V, fol. 44, SM to Ibarra, Valladolid, 16 Aug. 1608. For discussion of some of the antecedents, see above and Matter, *Pre-Seminole Florida*, 52–54, who follows Geiger, *Franciscan Conquest*, 208–12, and Zelia Sweett and Mary H. Sheppy, *The Spanish Missions of Florida* (1940) (reprint, New Symrna Beach, Fla.: Luthers, 1993), 39.

74. AGI, SD 224 (Stetson), Fr. Francisco de Pareja and Dr. Alonso de Peñaranda to SM, 6 Nov. 1607; AGI, SD 224 (Stetson), Gov. Ibarra to SM, 4 Jan. 1608 (2 letters) with enclosure: "Recopilación que yo Pedro de Ybarra. . . ."

75. AGI, SD 224 (Stetson), Frs. Francisco de Pareja and Alonso de Peñaranda to SM, 6 Nov. 1607.

76. AGI, SD 224 (JTC#2), Ibarra to SM, 22 Aug. 1608. This news provoked a royal order that the soldiers not be used outside of St. Augustine's immediate area except to defend the Christian Indians. AGI, Mexico 1065 (Stetson), fols. 106–106v, SM to Ibarra, Madrid, 15 Mar. 1609.

77. AGI, Mexico 1065, Tomo V, fols. 44–46v (Stetson), SM to Ibarra, Valladolid, 16 Aug. 1608; ibid., fols. 64v–65v, SM to Ibarra, 8 Nov. 1608.

78. AGI, Mexico 1065, fol. 106 (Stetson), SM to Ibarra, Madrid, 15 Mar. 1609. The 1573 Ordinances of New Discoveries and Population

made the same point. DII, 8:484–537. Also summarized in Jeremy D. Stahl, "An Ethnohistory of South Florida, 1500–1575" (M.A. thesis, University of Florida, 1986), 79–80.

5. The Inland Frontier, 1609–1650

1. Maynard J. Geiger, *The Franciscan Conquest of Florida (1573–1618)* (Washington, D.C.: Catholic University of America, 1937), 229; John E. Worth, "The Timucuan Missions of Spanish Florida and the Rebellion of 1656" (Ph.D. dissertation, University of Florida, 1992), 57–63; Kenneth W. Johnson, "The Utina and Potano Peoples of Northern Florida: Changing Settlement Systems in the Spanish Colonial Period" (Ph.D. dissertation, University of Florida, 1991), 245–303 (for Santa Fe de Toloca).

2. AGI, SD 225, fol. 1, Fernández de Olivera to SM, 15 Dec. 1611.

3. AGI, CD 958, Account of Factor Andrés de Sotomayor, Relación jurada de data, 31 Dec. 1611 (?); AGI, SD 225, fol. 29, Gov. Juan Fernández de Olivera to SM, n.d. [1610–1612], and ibid., fol. 31, Gov. Juan Treviño Gillamas to SM, 20 Nov. 1618 (re use of soldiers and paid Indians). The Crown authorized up to 1,500 ducats (2,068 pesos de ocho) expenses for Indian gifts on 15 Nov. 1615 and again on 20 Nov. 1618 (AGI, SD 225, fol. 31). Amy Turner Bushnell, *Situado and Sabana: Spain's Support System for the Presidio and Mission Provinces of Florida* (New York: American Museum of Natural History; Athens: distributed by the University of Georgia Press, 1994), 113, for the weight of goods carried. If a man could carry fifty lbs., thirty-six porters would be required; at seventy-five lbs. per man, only twenty-four.

4. AGI, SD 232 (Stetson), Fernández de Olivera to SM, 6 Feb. 1612; AGI, CD 958, Account of Andrés de Sotomayor, entry of 4 Feb. 1612 of items governor is taking on his *visita.*

5. AGI, CD 958, Account of Andrés de Sotomayor, 6 Jun. 1613, trade goods given to Francisco Leal for *rescates* of maize on the royal account. Iron tools, knives, glass beads, cloth, and *congas* are listed.

6. Worth, "Timucuan Missions," 151–52, from testimony of Alonso Díaz de Badajoz, Apr. 1630, regarding the raid and retaliation.

7. Brian G. Boniface, "An Historical Geography of Spanish Florida, circa 1700" (M.A. thesis, University of Georgia, 1971), 173–74; John H. Hann, *Apalachee, The Land between the Rivers* (Gainesville: University Presses of Florida, 1988), Figure 2.1 (p. 34), and 41–42.

8. AGI, SD 229 (Lockey), Fernández de Olivera to SM, 13 Oct. 1612 (reporting the peace mission). The Spaniards were also trying to make peace between the caciques of Tequesta and Matacumbe (AGI, SD 232 (Stetson), Fernández de Olivera to SM, 3 Feb. 1612). The results are not known.

9. AGI, SD 225, fols. 10–11, Gov. Juan Fernández de Olivera to SM, 13 Oct. 1612; AGI, SD 232 (Stetson), Friars to SM, 16 Oct. 1612. See also Hann, *Apalachee*, 13, and his "Apalachee in the Historic Era," in *The Forgotten Centuries: Indians and Europeans in the American South, 1521–1704*, ed. Charles Hudson and Carmen Chaves Tesser (Athens: University of Georgia Press, 1994), 335; Bonnie G. McEwan, "San Luis de Talimali: The Archaeology of Spanish-Indian Relations at a Spanish Mission," *Historical Archaeology* 25 (1991), 36–37.

10. AGI, SD 232 (Stetson), Fr. Lorenzo Martínez to SM, 4 Sept. 1612.

11. AGI, SD 232 (Stetson), Friars to SM, 16 Oct. 1612.

12. John H. Hann, *A History of The Timucua Indians and Missions* (Gainesville: University Press of Florida, 1996), 123, for a list of the books and evidence of literacy.

13. Robert A. Matter, *Pre-Seminole Florida: Spanish Soldiers, Friars, and Indian Missions, 1513–1763* (New York: Garland, 1990), 54–55; Robert L. Kapitzke, "The Secular Clergy in St. Augustine during the First Spanish Period, 1565–1763" (M.A. thesis, University of Florida, Gainesville, 1991), 47; Geiger, *Franciscan Conquest*, 237.

14. AGI, CD 958, Account of Factor Andrés de Sotomayor, Relación jurada de data, 31 Dec. 1612. The bells were: Santiago (275 lbs.), San Bartolomé (268 lbs.), San Pedro (256 lbs.), San Buenaventura (254 lbs.), Santa Isabela (182 lbs.), San Diego (176 lbs.), Santa Lucía (166 lbs.), San Pablo (165 lbs.), Santa Ynés (162 lbs.), San Antonio (161 lbs.), Santa Catalina (160 lbs.), Santa María (158 lbs.), and San Francisco (154 lbs.).

15. Geiger, *Franciscan Conquest*, 241.

16. AGI, SD 235 (JTC#4), Friars to SM, 17 Jan. 1617. Hann, *History of Timucua*, 262.

17. John R. Swanton, *Early History of the Creek Indians and Their Neighbors* (Washington, D.C.: Bureau of American Ethnology Bulletin 73, 1922), 338, quoting friars' letter of 1617 mentioning *peste* (plague) and other diseases; Henry Dobyns, *Their Number Became Thinned: Native American Population Dynamics in Eastern North America* (Knoxville: University of Tennessee Press, 1983), 278–79; Alfred W. Crosby, Jr., "Virgin Soil Epidemics as a Factor in the Aboriginal Depopulation of America," *William and Mary Quarterly*, 3rd Series, 33 (1976), 290 (plague, New England, 1616–69); Dean R. Snow and Kim M. Lamphear, "European Contact and Indian Depopulation in the Northeast: The Timing of the First Epidemics," *Ethnohistory* 35 (1988), 15–33, passim (typhus or another virus in New England, 1616–19).

Whatever the diseases and however serious their effects in particular parts of the Southeast, they were *not* preceded by short early summer harvests. Dendroclimatological data for Georgia show March–June rains below average only in 1611, 1616, and 1618 but otherwise normal or above average well into the 1620s. Spanish storehouse records (St. Augustine) show abundant supplies for 1611–13, 1615, and 1616, when maize was used to feed Indians repairing the fort (for one real a day in wages) and visiting chiefs. See David W. Stahle and Malcolm K. Cleaveland, data set, collection of the author; AGI, CD 958, Account of Andrés de Sotomayor, *Datas* of Maize, 1611–1616; AGI, CD 955, Account of Juan Menéndez Marqués, *Data* no. 75, Oct. 1616, noting the wage rate.

18. AGI, CD 958, Accounts of Factor Andrés de Sotomayor, entries for 31 Dec. 1615, 1 Feb., 10 May, 6 Nov. 1616, and *Datas* of Maize, 1611–1616 (entertaining caciques); the missions are from the Oré inspection, Luis Jerónimo de Oré, *The Martyrs of Florida*, trans. Maynard Geiger (New York: J. F. Wagner, 1936), 12. The quantities of goods supposedly used as gifts for the Indians suggest misappropriation for private trade. Worth believes that Santa Isabel de Utinahica was at the junction of the Oconee and Ocmulgee Rivers (Jerald T. Milanich, personal communication, 10 Jul. 1996).

19. AGI, SD 235 (JTC#4), Friars to SM, 17 Jan. 1617; Fr. Francisco Alonso de Jesús, "1630 Memorial of Fray Francisco Alonso de Jesús on Spanish Florida's Missions and Natives," trans. John H. Hann, *The Americas* 50 (1993), 100. In addition to population loss, this request for *congregación* reflected the friars' desires to lessen their travel time among the dispersed settlements characteristic of the Guale and Mocama.

20. Marvin T. Smith, *Archaeology of Aboriginal Culture Change in the Interior Southeast: Depopulation during the Early Historic Period* (Gainesville: University of Florida Press, 1987), 68–112; Charles H. Fairbanks, "Creek and Precreek," in *Archeology of the Eastern United States*, ed. James B. Griffin (Chicago: University of Chicago Press, 1952), 285–300, notes similar loss of traits from archaeological evidence from the Macon Plateau area of central Georgia; Mark Williams, "Growth and Decline of the Oconee Province," in *The Forgotten Centuries: Indians and Europeans in the American South, 1521–1704*, ed. Charles Hudson and Carmen Chaves Tesser (Athens: University of Georgia Press, 1994), 191–93. Equivocal archaeological evidence from Utina suggests that a dispersal to smaller settlements may have taken place after this first documented pandemic. See Johnson, "Utina and Potano," 439–41, 454, Table 10.5. The devolution of chiefdoms into segmented tribes is discussed in Patricia Galloway, *Choctaw Genesis 1500–1700* (Lincoln: University of Nebraska Press, 1995), 67–71.

21. The terminology reflects the Spaniards' political imperative to see their empire as consisting of natural lords ruled by a Spanish king-emperor.

22. Galloway, *Choctaw Genesis*, 140–42, for a discussion.

23. Oré, *Martyrs*, 129. It is listed in 1628: AGI, SD 2584 (Stetson),

Certified copy of a list of officials of the Franciscan Order, 8 Jan. 1628, as enclosure no. 4 with Gov. Montiano to SM, 14 Aug. 1739.

24. Worth, "Timucuan Missions," 63–70; Hann, *History of the Timucua*, 190; Fr. Ocaña, 1635, quoted in Gregory J. Keegan and Leandro Tormo Sanz, *Experiencia misionera en la Florida (Siglos XVI y XVII)* (Madrid: Consejo Superior de Investigaciones Científicas, 1957), 289–90. The Spanish referred to the province as "Cotacochona"—which seems to be "cota" (a rough part of a boar's back) and "cochón," a term for a large pig. If this is what the term meant, it probably referred to the rough terrain of much of the area, which is west of the Suwannee and east of the Aucilla River.

25. For Acuera see Worth, "Timucuan Missions," 184, n. 8.

26. For 1616: Oré, *Martyrs*, 126–130, and AGI, SD 232 (Stetson), Testimony of Franciscans [from Guale] for Capt. Alonso de Pastrana, 16 May 1616 (also in Geiger, *Franciscan Conquest*, 247–48) and Saturiwa and Mocama from 1655 list in Hann, *History of Timucua*, 190; 1630: ibid., 263; 1655: ibid., 190.

27. Geiger, *Franciscan Conquest*, 248 (1617); AGI, SD 225, fols. 143–44, Fr. Francisco Alonso de Jesús to SM, Madrid?, 27 Feb. 1635 (noting 1627 and 1630 situations), and Hann, *History of Timucua*, 263, noting Fr. de Jesús' statement of ca. 1630 as to the number.

28. AGI, SD 25 (Stetson), Luis Gerónimo de Oré to SM, n.d. [1617?]; Geiger, *Franciscan Conquest*, 248.

29. AGI, SD 235, Fr. Juan de Santander (Franciscan Commissary General for the Indies) to SM, 25 Nov. 1630, as noted in John T. Lanning, *The Spanish Missions of Georgia* (Chapel Hill: University of North Carolina Press, 1935), 202; AGI, SD 225, fols. 143–44, Fr. Francisco Alonso de Jesús (*Custodio* of La Florida) to SM, 27 Feb. 1635 (indicating only 8 friars authorized in 1634); Worth, "Timucuan Missions," 167, quoting Fr. Francisco Alonso de Jesús to SM, 12 Jan. 1633.

30. Alonso de Jesús, "1630 Relation," 99. For the Leon–Jefferson problem see Worth, "Timucuan Missions," 173–78, and Jerald T. Milanich, *Florida Indians and the Invasion from Europe* (Gainesville: University Press of Florida, 1995), 214–15, 219–20. Milanich (personal communication 10 Jul. 1996) thinks that Timucuan-speaking potters from east of the Okefenokee Swamp may be part of the explanation for this sudden appearance of Leon–Jefferson ceramics in western Timucua and Yustaga. That fits with the idea that people who knew about Christianity but were not being served by missions were moving into mission areas. See the materials herein presented about early missionary exploration of the mainland west of Cumberland Island, in areas known as "Los Pinales" and Yufera, Ibi, etc.

31. Worth, "Timucuan Missions," 167, noting Fr. Alonso de Jesús to SM, 12 Jan. 1633; AGI, SD 233 (Lockey), Gov. Horruytiner to SM, 15

Nov. 1633; David W. Stahle and Malcolm K. Cleaveland, "Reconstruction and Analysis of Spring Rainfall over the Southeastern U.S.A. for the Past 1000 Years," *Bulletin of the American Meteorological Society* 73 (1992), 1947–61, and their rainfall data for Georgia, collection of the author. 1634 was also 15 percent below the mean in Georgia. The year 1631 had had spring rains 15 percent above the mean, which may have caused some of the crop to fail as well. Hann, "The Apalachee in the Historic Era," 335, notes that Apalachee was listed as a source of supply as early as 1625.

32. AGI, SD 225, fol. 169v, Gov. Vega Castro y Pardo to SM, 22 Aug. 1639; AGI, SD 225, fols. 143v–144, Fr. Francisco Alonso de Jesús to SM, 27 Feb. 1635; AGI, SD 235 (Stetson), *Informe* of Fr. Juan Luengo, 30 Nov. 1676. Lanning, *Spanish Missions*, 166–67, expressed doubts about the population figure of 34,000, saying it was given by a "doubtful authority."

33. AGI, SD 229 (JTC#3), Treasury Officials to SM, 18 Mar. 1647.

34. Hann, *Apalachee*, 16.

35. AGI, SD 225, fols. 143–44, Fr. Francisco Alonso de Jesús to SM, Madrid, 27 Feb. 1635. Also quoted in Matthew Connolly, "The Missions of Florida," in *Exploration and Settlement in the Spanish Borderlands: Their Religious Motivations* (St. Augustine, Fla.: Mission Nombre de Dios, 1967), 29, and in Cristobal Figuero del Campo, *Misiones Franciscanas en la Florida* (Madrid: Comisión Episcopal del V. Centenario, 1992), 134.

36. Alonso de Jesús, "1630 Memorial," 99.

37. AGI, SD 225, fol. 112, Rodriguez Villegas to SM, 27 Dec. 1630. Also noted in Boniface, "Historical Geography," 82. No epidemics were reported in Florida during the 1620s. The outbreak of smallpox in New England during the early 1630s does not seem to have reached La Florida. Voyage times from Mexico, where the disease may have been endemic by 1630, were probably too long to transmit it to St. Augustine. Crew immunity because of childhood exposure in Spain and the Caribbean and small size and the absence of children among the few immigrants to reach La Florida may explain why smallpox did not arrive from Havana or Mexico or Spain at this time. Nonetheless, Indians continued to die at rates that observers thought were not normal, suggesting Old World diseases were endemic with high mortality but did not pass the "tipping point" at which the Spaniards would have perceived an epidemic. Too, we have no way to know if sexually transmitted diseases were changing Indian fertility and infant mortality. For the New England epidemic and problems of smallpox transmission, see Snow and Lamphear, "European Contact," 23–26.

38. John E. Worth, "Late Spanish Military Expeditions in the Interior Southeast, 1597–1628," in *The Forgotten Centuries: Indians and Euro-*

peans in the American South, 1521–1704, ed. Charles Hudson and Carmen Chaves Tesser (Athens: University of Georgia Press, 1994), 112–15; quotation from AGI, SD 225, fols. 106–108, Gov. Luis de Rojas y Borga to ?, 30 Jun. 1628.

39. AGI, SD 225, fol. 109, Memorial of Alferez Pedro de Torres, Madrid, 1 Aug. 1629, with marginal notes for a cedula authorizing the exploitation.

40. AGI, SD 225 (JTC#3), Fr. Francisco Alonso de Jesús to SM, 2 Feb. 1635.

41. AGI, SD 225, fols. 75–76, Gov. Salinas to SM, 15 May 1621; ibid., fols. 106–108, Rojas y Borja to SM, 30 June 1628.

42. Alonso de Jesús, "1630 Memorial," 100.

43. AGI, SD 225, fols. 153–54, Gov. Horruytiner to SM, 24 June 1637.

44. AGI, SD 225, fol. 169v, Gov. Vega Castro y Pardo to SM, 22 Aug. 1639; Hann, "Apalachee in the Historic Era," 335–37; Gregory A. Waselkof, "Seventeenth-Century Trade in the Colonial Southeast," *Southeastern Archaeology* 8 (1989), 117–28. Galloway, *Choctaw Genesis*, 71–72, notes the evidence that some proto-Choctaw were living in the Alabama and Mobile river flood plains at this period (as the Urn burial culture). She missed this earliest of all references to the tribal name. The Apalachicola lived along the middle Chattahoochee or possibly up the Flint River, about thirty leagues (ca. seventy-five miles) from the Apalachee (AGI, SD 229 (JTC#3), Sergeant-major Eugenio de Espinosa to SM, Madrid, 1647). The Chacatos apparently lived west of the Chattahoochee River on the Mariana Red Hills.

45. AGI, SD 233 (Lockey), Gov. Horruytiner to SM, 15 Nov. 1633, noting the Amacanos as a friendly group that had come near to Apalachee, promising to build a church and convent for friars. They are sometimes identified as Yamassee but I believe that name was applied only to the natives of the South Carolina coastal plain, ca. 1662.

46. Smith, *Aboriginal Culture Change*, is a detailed examination of the movement along the Coosa–Tallapoosa drainage.

47. AGI, SD 225, fols. 75–76, Gov. Juan de Salinas to SM, 15 May 1621.

48. Worth, "Timucuan Missions," 152–54, citing the 1635 Merits and Services claims of Adrian de Canizares y Osorio, a document with a number of anachronisms; AGI, SD 225, fol. 169v, Gov. Damián de Vega Castro y Pardo to SM, 22 Aug. 1639. Vega Castro y Pardo thought they had come from New Mexico and the "Río Blanco." Andrés Gonzales de Barcía Carballido y Zúñiga, *Chronological History of the Continent of Florida*, trans. Anthony Kerrigan (Gainesville: University of Florida Press, 1951), 218, misdates the second appearance to ca. 1638. John H. Hann, "Florida's Terra Incognita: West Florida's Natives in the Sixteenth and Seventeenth Century," *Florida Anthropologist* 41 (1988), 75–79, tries to link this group to De Soto's Chisca and to the Chacato, but

his arguments are not convincing. Swanton, *Early History of the Creek,* 286–312, argues that they were Yuchi from the southern Appalachian Mountains. I wonder if the name "Ysica" is a Muskogean term for "other" or in some way categorical, just as was the Spanish use of "Chichimeca" for other groups of migrating Indians who captured slaves.

49. AGI, SD 225, fols. 75–76, Gov. Salinas to SM, 15 May 1621; AGI, SD 225 (JTC#3), Rojas y Borja to SM, 13 Feb. 1627; Worth, "Timucuan Missions," 141–42, picked up a report from 1630 of this use of Indian warriors from Rojas y Borja's *residencia* but misdates it to 1627–1628. See AGI, EC 154B, Certified copy of sentences from *residencia,* 20 Aug. 1630 (copy made 1632), Charge no. 7, indicating three caciques were given soldier's rations.

50. AGI, Mexico 1065, tomo V, fols. 64–65, SM to Gov. Ibarra, El Pardo, 8 Nov. 1608 (ordering Fernández de Ecija north); ibid., fols. 250v–251, Crown to Gov. of Havana, 20 Mar. 1611; Oré, *Martyrs,* 52, for an account of the 1611 voyage.

51. Oré, *Martyrs,* 45–53; AGI, SD 232 (Stetson), Gov. Treviño de Guillamas to SM, 12 Oct. 1617. For the falsity of the story of the supposed fleet to expel the Roanoke colony, see Hoffman, *New Andalucia,* 305–306.

52. Carville V. Earle, "Environment, Disease, and Mortality in Early Virginia," in *The Chesapeake in the Seventeenth Century: Essays on Anglo-American Society,* ed. Thad W. Tate and David L. Ammerman (Chapel Hill: University of North Carolina Press for the Institute of Early American History and Culture, 1979), 99–104; J. Leich Wright, Jr., *The Only Land They Knew: The Tragic Story of the American Indians in the Old South* (New York: Free Press, 1981), 67–68, 73–76.

53. AGI, SD 232 (Stetson), Salinas to ?, 4 June 1620. The word *ruido,* used for "clamor," also means "difference," so that the phrase could be translated "We are so few we cannot make a difference."

54. AGI, SD 225, fol. 29, Gov. Juan Fernández de Oivera to SM, n.d. [1610–12]; ibid., fol. 35, Gov. Salinas to SM, 20 Nov. 1618; ibid., fols. 75–76, Gov. Salinas to SM, 15 May 1621; ibid., fols. 116–17, Gov. Andrés Rodriguez Villegas to SM, 18 Jan. 1631; ibid., fol. 216, Gov. Damián de Castro y Pardo to SM, 29 Aug. 1644.

55. Verne E. Chatelain, *The Defenses of Spanish Florida, 1565 to 1763* (Washington, D.C.: Carnegie Institution of Washington, 1941), 53–55. Luis R. Arana and Albert Manucy, *The Building of Castillo de San Marcos* (St. Augustine, Fla.: Eastern National Park Momument Association for Castillo de San Marcos National Monument, 1977), 12.

56. Theodore Corbitt, "Population Structure in Hispanic St. Augustine, 1629–1763," *FHQ* 54 (1976), 263–84.

57. AGI, SD 225, fol. 77, Gov. Salinas to SM, 15 May 1621, and ibid. (Stetson), Consulta of Consejo de Indias, Madrid, 15 Apr. 1623, and

AGI, Mexico 1065, Tomo 7 (Stetson), Cedula to VR of Mexico, Madrid, 24 May 1623 (re indigo and cochineal); AGI, SD 225 (JTC#3), Gov. Rojas y Borja to SM, 13 Feb. 1627 (re hemp); Alonso de Jesús, "1630 Memorial," 88–89, 105. A request for Campeche Indian cotton weavers to instruct the Apalachee, made in 1673, also failed to produce results in spite of repeated royal orders to the governor of Yucatán. See AGI, SD 226 (Lockey), Domingo de Leturiondo to SM, Madrid, Mar. 1673 (?) and cedulas of 1673 (AGI, SD 834 (Lockey), 1676 (Index of Cedulas, East Florida Papers, 1676, no. 3) and 1681 (Index of Cedulas, East Florida Papers, 1681, no. 30). Also noted by Wright, *The Only Land They Knew*, 163.

58. AGI, SD 232 (Stetson), Gov. Salinas to ?, 4 June 1620; AGI, SD 225, fols. 75–76, Gov. Salinas to ?, 15 May 1621; ibid., fol. 78v., Gov. Salinas to ?, 30 Jan. 1623; The export of hides was authorized by a decree of 1621 noted in William R. Gillaspie, "Juan de Ayala y Escobar, Procurador and Entrepreneur: A Case Study of the Provisioning of Florida, 1683–1716" (Ph.D. dissertation; University of Florida, 1961), 22, and (without date) in AGI, SD 225, fol. 86, Gov. Luis de Rojas y Borja to SM, 27 Aug. 1626.

59. AGI, EC 154–B, Autos of Luis de Rojas y Borja, 1632, certifying copy of *residencia* sentences of 30 Aug. 1630, Charge no. 6 (re tax at slaughterhouse used to build a new church); Amy [Turner] Bushnell, "The Menéndez Marqués Cattle Barony at La Chua and the Determinants of Economic Expansion in Seventeenth-Century Florida," *FHQ* 56 (1978), 417–18; cf. Hann, *History of Timucua*, 102–105. Menéndez Marqués's ranch was said to be worth eight thousand pesos about 1646 and may have had two hundred head of cattle. Boniface, "Historical Geography," 145, locates La Chua at the Zetrower Site, ten miles southeast of Gainesville. Charles Arnade, "Cattle Raising in Spanish Florida: 1513–1763," *Agricultural History* 35 (1961), 121–22, incorrectly dates the beginning of ranching to the 1630s. Deagan, using only archaeological evidence, has argued that beef and its by products bypassed St. Augustine, but this is an error. See Kathleen Deagan, "St. Augustine and the Mission Frontier," in *The Missions of Spanish Florida*, ed. Bonnie G. McEwan (Gainesville: University Presses of Florida, 1993), 90–91.

60. AGI, SD 229 (Stetson), Expediente of Antonio de Herrera, 1619–20, including copy of cedula, 18 Sept. 1618; AGI, SD 225 (JTC#3), Gov. Salinas to SM, 30 Jan. 1623 (re his store); AGI, EC 154B, Autos of Gov. Luis de Rojas y Borja, 1632, including certified copy of sentence of his *residencia*, 20 Aug. 1630, charge 8; AGI, SD 229 (JTC#3), Treasury Officials to SM, 30 Jan. 1627.

61. AGI, SD 225, fols. 190–208, Documents regarding the offer of Benito Ruiz de Salazar Ballecilla, 1642 ff; ibid., fol. 299, Ruiz de Salazar to Sec. Gerónimo de Canenora, 14 Jul. 1650; AGI, SD 230 (JTC#3), Francisco Menéndez Marqués to SM, 8 Feb. 1648.

62. Engel Sluiter, *The Florida Situado: Quantifying the First Eighty Years, 1571–1651* (Gainesville: University of Florida Libraries, 1985), Table; Bushnell, *Situado and Sabana*, 47, Table 3.2.

63. AGI, SD 229 (JTC#3), Treasury Officials to SM, 30 Jan. 1627; AGI, SD 226 (Lockey), Cedula, Madrid, 18 Sept 1656, noting figures for 1648–1651, when the total was 21,424 pesos, or an average of 5,356 pesos per year.

64. AGI, SD 229 (JTC#3), Treasury Officials to SM, 30 Jan. 1627.

65. AGI, SD 225, fol. 170, Vega Castro to SM, 22 Aug. 1639.

66. AGI, SD 229 (JTC#3), Treasury Officials to SM, 18 Mar. 1647; AGI, SD 226 (Lockey), Cedula, Madrid, 18 Sept. 1656 incorporated with Petition of Treasury Officials, 30 May 1679, in copy of Hita de Salazar to SM, 6 Mar. 1680, reviewing the cedulas of 1593 and 1615; Worth, "Timucuan Missions," 188–91. On the other hand, the treasury officials took part of their pay in trade goods, 1619–1623. See AGI, EC 154A, Autos of Factor Juan de la Cueva re his accounts 1619–1623.

67. Bushnell, *Situado and Sabana*, 108, Table 9.1, from Sluiter, *Florida Situado*, Table. Payment made in 1640 of 2,880 p. for 1636 (plus 3,970 p. for 1639); in 1641 for 1637 (partial); in 1644 for 1642 (partial); in 1646 for 1640 (1,137 p.) and 1641 (1,360 p.) I have interpreted Sluiter's data somewhat differently from Bushnell's reading, esp. for 1642, 1643, and 1645.

68. AGI, SD 225, fols. 294–95, Treasury Officials to SM, 10 Jul. 1650; Worth, "Timucuan Missions," 107–11. A brief account is Katherine S. Lawson, "Governor Salazar's Wheat Farm Project, 1645–1657," *FHQ* 24 (1946), 196–200.

69. AGI, SD 229 (JTC#3), Ruiz de Salazar to SM, 22 May 1647; Hann, "Apalachee in the Historic Era," 338.

70. Hann, "Apalachee in the Historic Era," 337–38.

71. Stahle and Cleaveland, "Reconstruction and Analysis," 1954–56: "sustained growing-season rainfall deficits of 10–15 percent below the mean certainly have practical significance in terms of agricultural production" (ibid., 1956).

72. AGI, SD 225, fols. 210–211, Gov. Vega Castro to SM, 9 Jul. 1643, and ibid., fol. 214, Gov. Vega Castro to SM, 29 Aug. 1644.

73. AGI, SD 229 (JTC#3), Treasury Officials to SM, 18 Mar. 1647. They blamed the lack of gifts and what they considered the fickleness of the Indians but the former complaint was in the context of a campaign against the new rules for *situado* collection that had diminished their opportunities for graft. AGI, SD 225, fol. 169v, Gov. Damián de Vega Castro y Pardo to SM, 22 Aug. 1639. This dispersal is usually interpreted as resistance to increasing demands for porters.

74. AGI, SD 225, fols. 210–11, Gov. Vega Castro to SM, 9 Jul. 1643. He says Apalachee was flourishing and exporting.

75. AGI, SD 229 (Stetson), Treas. Joseph de Prado to SM, 30 Dec.

1654. Marvin T. Smith and David J. Hally, "Chiefly Behavior: Evidence from Sixteenth-Century Spanish Accounts," in *Lords of the Southeast: Social Inequality and the Native Elites of Southeastern North America,* ed. Alex W. Barker and Timothy R. Pauketat (Washington, D.C.: American Anthropological Association, 1992), 103, note that the providing of porters was an Indian custom. The abuses were in who had to do it, for whom, and for what compensation.

76. Hann, *Apalachee,* 19–20; Worth, "Timucuan Missions," 137–38; Clifton Paisley, *The Red Hill of Florida, 1528–1865* (Tuscaloosa: University of Alabama Press, 1989), 28. The evidence was supplied by the friars to Joseph de Prado who was sent to investigate the cause of the uprising. Ideas about the status implications of porter service are my own. For Santiago de Ocone see Worth, "Timucuan Missions," 156–59.

77. AGI, SD 834 (Lockey), King to Gov. and Officials of Florida, Madrid, 8 Aug. 1648, reporting complaints from Fr. Pedro Moreno Ponce de León and enjoining adherence to existing laws. For complaints about soldiers see Friars to SM, 14 Jan. 1617, quoted in Keegan and Tormo Sanz, *Experiencia misionera,* 304, and AGI, SD 229 (Stetson), Joseph de Prado to SM, 30 Dec. 1654.

78. Bushnell, *Situado and Sabana,* 106–107.

79. AGI, SD 229 (JTC#3), Ruiz de Salazar to SM, 22 May 1647; ibid., Treasury Officials to SM, 18 Mar. 1647; Hann, *Apalachee,* 16–17.

80. AGI, SD 229 (JTC#3), Treasury Officials to SM, 18 Mar. 1647; ibid., Ruiz de Salazar to SM, 22 May 1647; Hann, *Apalachee,* 17.

81. AGI, SD 229 (JTC#3), Menéndez Marqués to SM, 8 Feb. 1648; Hann, *Apalachee,* 17–18; Lanning, *Spanish Missions,* 168–69, has a number of facts wrong.

82. AGI, SD 229 (Stetson), Treas. Joseph de Prado to SM, 30 Dec. 1654; ibid. (JTC#3), Ruiz de Salazar to SM, 22 May 1647; Hann, *Apalachee,* 16–23.

83. John Hann concluded that the Apalachee rebels feared that the Spanish presence, especially the governor's hacienda at Asile, meant far-reaching changes in their ways of life, ones that they were unwilling to make. In the area of status, the friars expected men who were baptized to cut their hair and keep it clipped like the Spaniards, to give up dances and even the ball game, to kneel, to give up anklets and bracelets, to make oral confession, and to accept corporal punishment. All were male adornments or activities associated with status. We have already noted the status implications of the decrease in gifts and of serving as porters. See Hann, *Apalachee,* 16–18, largely using later evidence; Alonso de Jesús, "1630 Memorial," 97, 99, 101.

84. AGI, SD 225, fols. 294–95, Treasury Officials to SM, 10 Jul. 1650; AGI, SD 233 (JTC#4), Nicolás Ponce de León to SM, 20 Sept. 1651; Lawson, "Salazar's Wheat Farm," 197; Worth, "Timucuan Mission," 94

(re lieutenant); AGI, SD 229 (Stetson), Joseph de Prado to SM, 30 Dec. 1654 (re labor).

85. AGI, SD 229 (Stetson), Treas. Joseph de Prado to SM, 30 Dec. 1654. Some of these expenses were payments to Indians who cultivated the fields at St. Augustine. The 1650 figure may have been due to the loss of the *situado* cargos in 1649 to English corsairs but almost certainly was due to the politics of the time. AGI, SD 225, fols. 283–84, Treasury Officials to SM, 28 May 1649.

86. Worth, "Timucuan Missions," 154. Wright, *The Only Land They Knew*, 87, notes that the late 1600s were a period when western Virginia was invaded by peoples fleeing the Iroquois Wars further north. We do not know if that invasion and the new Chisca raids had anything in common.

6. Death, Rebellion, a New Accommodation, and New Defenses: La Florida's Frontiers, 1650–1680

1. Henry Dobyns, *Their Number Became Thinned: Native American Population Dynamics in Eastern North America* (Knoxville: University of Tennessee Press, 1983), 279–80.

2. Dobyns, *Their Number Became Thinned*, 279–80; AGI, SD 225, fols. 302–302v, Anonymous to SM, 20 Nov. 1655. Ponce de León was interim governor for six months.

3. The rains were more than 15 percent below average in five of the eight years; one of the other three had a rainfall 15 percent above average (Stahle and Cleaveland data set, collection of author); AGI, SD 229 (JTC#3), Gov. and Treasury Officials to SM, 31 May 1658 (tithe figures). The tithe on cattle also dropped sharply beginning in 1652, although this may not reflect effects of the drought.

4. Amy Turner Bushnell, *Situado and Sabana: Spain's Support System for the Presidio and Mission Provinces of Florida* (New York: American Museum of Natural History; Athens: distributed by the University of Georgia Press, 1994), 123.

5. AGI, SD 225, fol. 302, Anonymous to SM, 20 Nov. 1655; AGI, SD 233 (JTC#4), Nicolás Ponce de León to SM, 20 Sept. 1651, listing the assets. AGI, SD 226 (Lockey), Gov. Juan Marquez de Cabrera to SM, 14 June 1681. The sale was made even though the Crown had approved Ponce de León's purchase. Such was the power of local interests!

6. AGI, SD 225, fols. 302–302v, Anonymous to SM, 20 Nov. 1655, and fols. 345–72, Interrogatory, Havana, 10 Jul. 1657 (with details of the price fixing).

7. AGI, SD 225, fols. 302–304, Anonymous to SM, 20 Nov. 1655; ibid., fol. 307, Capt. Juan Ruiz Maroto to SM, 28 Nov. 1655, and fol. 309, Capt. Gregorio Bravo to SM, 5 Dec. 1655.

8. This estimate is based on Fr. Juan Luengo to SM, Madrid, 22 Sept. 1676, in which he notes that thirty friars and three servants went to Florida in 1658, to fill up the forty-three authorized positions. In 1676, a similar number were being requested and he stated that there were then fewer than thirty friars in the province. *Archivo Ibero-americano* 1 (1914), 368, 367.

9. John H. Worth, *Timucuan Chiefdoms of Spanish Florida*, 2 vols. (Gainesville: University Press of Florida, 1998), 2:39–41, presents Rebolledo's policy as self-serving. John E. Worth, "The Timucuan Missions of Spanish Florida and the Rebellion of 1656" (Ph.D. dissertation, University of Florida, 1992), 188–91; John H. Hann, *A History of the Timucua Indians and Missions* (Gainesville: University Press of Florida, 1996), 202–203 (for Rebolledo's favoritism). He did, however, order the continued feeding at royal expense of Indians working in St. Augustine or who came to visit, especially if they fell ill, even though there was no decree authorizing those expenses. See AGI, SD 229 (Stetson), Copy, Rebolledo to Treasurer, 24 Jul. 1654, enclosed with Joseph de Prado to SM, 30 Dec. 1654; cf Hann, *History of Timucua*, 202.

10. AGI, SD 229 (Stetson), Treasurer Joseph de Prado to SM, 30 Dec. 1654, enclosing Prado to Rebolledo, 23 Dec. 1654 (regarding Indian porters and payments to caciques). Rebolledo claimed he was too new to the job to order such changes in customary ways!

11. AGI, SD 225, fols. 302–304, Anonymous to SM, 20 Nov. 1655; AGI, SD 229 (Stetson), Treasury Officials to SM, 3 Sept. 1661.

12. AGI, SD 233 (JTC#4), Beltrán de Santa Cruz to SM, Havana, 20 Nov. 1655. He claimed the finished audits were so voluminous that he did not think it worth the 28,000 pesos it would cost to copy them for forwarding to Spain. The only copy remained at Havana.

13. Dobyns, *Their Number Became Thinned*, 280; Worth, "Timucuan Missions," 167–68. Rebolledo's claim that the slaves died is not supported by a list that Worth published that shows six slaves from 1653 to 1658. Ibid., 287, n. 33. Worth, *Timucuan Chiefdoms*, 2:12–13, 20–25, 38–51, and the general thrust of his argument, which is structuralist and synchronic, does not recognize the interplay of these epidemics and the rebellion in the way that seems appropriate.

14. Hann, *History of Timucua*, 240–41.

15. Worth, "Timucuan Missions," 193; Nancy Lee-Riffe, "The Heavenly Plantation: A Seventeenth-Century Mention of Florida," *FHQ* 56 (1977), 148–49, notes a 1649 mention of Florida in a royalist publication in England. Oliver Cromwell's Puritan government sent Admiral William Penn (1621–1670) and General Robert Venables to seize not only Hispaniola but also the Isthmus of Panama as part of a "Western Design" inspired by the feats of Sir Francis Drake in 1586. The objective was to cripple the Spanish empire by cutting off the flow of money from the Americas.

16. John H. Hann, *Apalachee: The Land between the Rivers* (Gainesville: University of Florida Press, 1988), 198.

17. Worth, "Timucuan Missions," 193–207; AGI, SD 2584 (Stetson), Copy, Rebolledo to Caciques of Guale, 20 Apr. 1656, as enclosure no. 5 with Gov. Montiano to SM, 14 May 1739; Hann, *History of Timucua*, 203 (labor quota). We do not have a copy of the order sent to the Apalachee.

18. Worth, *Timucuan Chiefdoms*, 2:55–59; AGI, SD 225, fol. 313, Fr. Juan Gómez de Ungrava to ? Havana, 13 Mar. 1657: "this creole governor from Cartagena has oppressed and outraged them, obliging them to come 100 leagues from Apalachee loaded as if they were mules or horses, something that when they were pagans was never done with elite Indians. . . ." In another letter, dated 4 Apr. and addressed to Fr. Francisco Martínez, Gómez says that the caciques protested that they were not slaves and had only been conquered by the Word of God, to which they had submitted voluntarily (AGI, SD 225, fol. 315). For natural law rights, see Colin M. MacLachlan, *Spain's Empire in the New World: The Role of Ideas in Institutional and Social Change* (Berkeley, 1988). See also Hann, *History of Timucua*, 200–205, where the slow building up of discontent is stressed. Worth, "Timucuan Missions," 4–5, suggests the revolt was a jurisdictional fight between the caciques and the soldiers, but on p. 219 he embraces the status argument presented here and in Hann's *History of Timucua*.

19. Worth, "Timucuan Missions," 214, and *Timucuan Chiefdoms*, 2:55–56. Rebolledo replied that even Spanish officers bore burdens when it was militarily necessary.

20. William B. Taylor, *Drinking, Homicide, and Rebellion in Colonial Mexican Villages* (Stanford: Stanford University Press, 1979), 114–22, discusses the typical pattern of village revolts.

21. Worth, *Timucuan Chiefdoms*, 2:60–64; Hann, *History of the Timucua*, 205–12; Worth, "Timucuan Missions," chapter 8. Hann, *Apalachee*, 22, notes that the friars' fears were without foundation. The memory of 1647 accounts for their action.

22. Worth, *Timucuan Chiefdoms*, 2:66–87; Worth, "Timucuan Missions," 253–80; Hann, *History of Timucua*, 212–21. John T. Lanning, *The Spanish Missions of Georgia* (Chapel Hill: University of North Carolina Press, 1935), 169–70, gives a brief and inaccurate account.

23. Worth, *Timucuan Chiefdoms*, 2:97–104; Hann, *History of Timucua*, 224–26, comments on Rebolledo's actual accomplishment. Cf Worth, *Timucuan Chiefdoms*, 2:111, 115. The evidence for these years is from Rebolledo's *residencia* and is vague as to what happened and when.

24. Dobyns, *Their Number Became Thinned*, 280–81.

25. AGI, SD 2584 (Stetson), Statements of Friars to Capt. Antonio de Argüelles, Guale, 1663, as Enclosure no. 6 with Gov. Montiano to SM, 14 Aug. 1739. Assuming twenty families of five persons over five years

of age in each town, this meant there were six hundred Guale in the missions.

26. Hann, *History of Timucua*, 227 (Yustagans); Worth, *Timucuan Chiefdoms*, 2:97–104; Kenneth W. Johnson, "The Utina and Potano Peoples of Northern Florida: Changing Settlement Systems in the Spanish Colonial Period" (Ph.D. dissertation, University of Florida, 1991), 435–36 (consolidation, as shown by Baptizing Springs site); Worth, "Timucuan Missions," 295; quotation from Hann, *History of Timucua*, 226–27. Worth attributes this realignment to Rebolledo, but I think Hann's evidence shows that much of the actual achievement of it was Aranguiz's doing.

27. Hann, *History of Timucua*, 227; AGI, SD 225 (JTC#3), Aranguiz to SM, 15 Nov. 1661: "It is known that these religious want to have superior dominion over the said natives without governors being allowed to know [anything about] them, as I at present am experiencing." Discussions about setting up an Abbot to supervise the friars did not produce any result in the late 1650s. See AGI, SD 229 (JTC#3), Treasury Officials to SM, 31 May 1658, reporting tithe and expenses as the Crown tried to find 1,800 pesos for salary, and ibid., Gov. Juan de Salamanca to SM, Havana, 1 Nov. 1658, supporting the idea of an abbot.

28. Worth, *Timucuan Chiefdoms*, vol. 2, sees what happened as a final incorporation of the Indians into the Spanish colonial system. For other examples, see Steve Stern, "The Rise and Fall of Indian-White Alliances: A Regional View of 'Conquest' History," *Hispanic American Historical Review* 61 (1981), 461–91; Susan E. Ramirez, "The 'Dueño de Indios': Thoughts on the Consequences of the Shifting Bases of Power of the 'Curaca de los viejos antiguos' under the Spanish in Sixteenth-Century Peru," *Hispanic American Historical Review* 67 (1987), 575–610; and Charles Gibson, "Caciques in Post Conquest and Colonial Mexico," in *The Caciques: Oligarchical Politics and the System of Caciquismo in the Luso-Hispanic World*, ed. Robert Kern and Robert Dolkart (Albuquerque: University of New Mexico Press, 1972), 18–26.

29. Bonnie G. McEwan, "San Luis de Talimali: The Archaeology of Spanish-Indian Relations at a Spanish Mission," *Historical Archaeology* 25 (1991), 43, 57, notes Apalachee resistance to the Spaniards on the basis of the council house design and activities known to have taken place there.

30. Fred L. Pearson, Jr., *Spanish-Indian Relations in Florida: A Study of Two Visitas, 1657–1678* (New York: Garland, 1990), 69–106, summarizes the *visita* and gives his regulations, pp. 75–77. Lana Jill Loucks, "Political and Economic Interactions between Spaniards and Indians: Archaeological and Ethnohistorical Perspectives of the Mission System in Florida" (Ph.D. dissertation, University of Florida, Gainesville, 1979), 50–56, uses this testimony to paint a negative image of

"many" of the friars, whereas the testimony identifies only three as particularly abusive. For a description of the ball game, see Amy Turner Bushnell, "That Demonic Game: The Campaign to Stop Indian Pelota Playing in Spanish Florida, 1675–1684," *The Americas* 35 (1978), 5–7. The object was to kick a tiny ball against a post, scoring points according to where it hit.

31. AGI, SD 839 (in Manuel Serrano y Sanz, ed., *Documentos históricos de la Florida y la Luisiana, Siglos XVI al XVIII* (Madrid: V. Suarez, 1912), 205), Rebolledo to SM, 18 Sept. 1657; AGI, SD 229 (Stetson), Notes by *Fiscal* of Council of Indies, 3 Jul. 1656 and marginal note of cedula of 9 Sept. 1656; AGI, SD 226 (Lockey), Cedula, Madrid, 18 Sept. 1656, copy with Hita de Salazar to SM, 6 Mar. 1680; Worth, "Timucuan Missions," 289. Hann, *History of Timucua*, 231, notes the reaffirmation of this order in 1658.

32. AGI, SD 225, fols. 316v–320, Notes on Council of Indies review of Florida, Madrid, 10 and 12 June 1657, attached to a file with the anonymous denunciation, letters from two captains, and Fr. Gómez's letters from Havana, 13 Mar. and 4 Apr.

33. AGI, SD 226 (Lockey), Treasury Officials to SM, 1680, noting that maize for Indians who carry Franciscan supplies cost about four hundred pesos per year; AGI, SD 229 (Stetson), Treas. Joseph de Prado to SM, 30 Dec. 1654, and AGI, SD 226 (Lockey), Cedula, 18 Sept. 1656, copied in Hita de Salazar to SM, 6 Mar. 1680 (re fifty mules).

34. AGI, SD 226 (Lockey), Gov. Pedro de Hita Salazar to SM, 6 Mar. 1680, indicating that annual costs for the 1670s had averaged under 1,200 pesos per year, in part because gift monies had not been sent from Mexico since 1677; AGI, SD 235 (Lockey), Caciques of Guale to SM, 16 Oct. 1657.

35. AGI, SD 2584 (Stetson), Copies of orders, 1666–1673, Enclosures no. 5 and no. 1, Gov. Montiano to SM, 14 Aug. 1739 (Guale); Hann, *History of Timucua*, 203, and AGI, SD 235 (Lockey). Opinion of former governor Francisco de la Guerra, Madrid, 20 Oct. 1673 (Timucua); AGI, SD 839, fol. 156, Certification of Treasury Officials of costs, 15 May 1675. The Indians were paid one real a day plus maize. Six Indian carpenters earned eight reales a day (Spanish carpenters earned twelve reales). Replacement of the Indian day laborers with African slaves was suggested in 1674 (AGI, SD 226 (JTC#3), Gov. Nicolás Ponce de León to SM, 1674); one hundred convicts were sent from Mexico in the 1680s (Brian G. Boniface, "An Historical Geography of Spanish Florida, circa 1700" (M.A. thesis, University of Georgia, 1971), 77).

36. AGI, SD 235 (Lockey), Caciques of Guale to SM, 16 Oct. 1657, and AGI, SD 229 (JTC#3), Juan Menéndez Marqués to SM, 25 Jan. 1667, and AGI, SD 235 (Lockey), Fr. Moreno to SM, 1673 (Indians kept beyond planting season); AGI, SD 839, fol. 258, Cedula of 30 Dec. 1675,

noted in Indice, 26 Apr. 1678 (enjoining good treatment); AGI 233 (Lockey), Santiago, Mico of Tolomato to SM, 21 Mar. 1658 and AGI, SD 225 (JTC#3), Crown to Gov. of Florida, 26 Feb. 1660, and AGI, SD 225 (JTC#3), Gov. Aranguiz to SM, 15 Nov. 1661 (re Tolomato).

37. AGI, SD 2584 (Stetson), Copies of orders to agents 17 Jan. 1665, 4 Mar. 1665, 22 Apr. 1668, as Enclosure no. 5, Gov. Montiano to SM, 14 Aug. 1739; AGI, SD 228, fol. 75, Order of Gov. Guerra y Vega, 19 Jul. 1670, incorporated into Merits and Services document of Gerónimo Regidor; AGI, SD 839, fol. 147v, Gov. Nicolás Ponce de León to SM, 8 Jul. 1673.

38. AGI, SD 229 (JTC#3), Treasury Officials to SM, 2 Mar. 1680, with notes by *Fiscal* of Council of Indies; AGI, SD 226 (JTC#3), Gov. Hita de Salazar to SM, 6 Sept. 1677. Salazar also taxed ranches and farms. See Amy [Turner] Bushnell, "The Menéndez Marqués Cattle Barony at La Chua and the Determinants of Economic Expansion in Seventeenth-Century Florida," *FHQ* 56 (1978), 426–28. Other discussions of ranching during this period are Charles W. Arnade, "Cattle Raising in Spanish Florida, 1513–1763," *Agricultural History* 35 (1961), 121–22; Boniface, "Historical Geography," 139–40.

39. The export of hides up to 13,750 pesos in value was authorized in 1673. See William R. Gillespie, "Juan de Ayala y Escobar, Procurador and Entrepreneur: A Case Study of the Provisioning of Florida, 1683–1716" (Ph.D. dissertation, University of Florida, 1961), 22–23; Hann, *Apalachee*, 53, for an example from the 1690s involving a ranch on Bacuqua's old fields, established by 1677. In 1680, the treasury officials reported a recent increase in cattle production (AGI, SD 229 (JTC#3), Treasury Officials to SM, 18 Feb. 1680).

40. Hann, *Apalachee*, 305.

41. Hann, *Apalachee*, 73–92, following Bushnell, "Demonic Game," 1–19. See also, Pearson, *Two Visitas*, 231–33.

42. Hann, *History of Timucua*, 241–44 (María Jacoba and the Acuera in 1678), and 256 (re vagrants); Worth, "Timucuan Missions," 307–309 (Potano).

43. AGI, SD 2584 (Stetson), Depositions of Friars, Guale, Apr. 1663, as Enclosure no. 6 with Gov. Montiano to SM, 14 Aug. 1739. Alan R. Calmes, "Indian Cultural Traditions and European Conquest of the Georgia-South Carolina Coastal Plain, 3000 BC–1733 AD: A Combined Archaeological and Historical Investigation" (Ph.D. dissertation, University of South Carolina, 1968), 76, incorrectly says the missions attacked were "north of the Savannah River" and that they were destroyed. John E. Worth, *The Struggle for the Georgia Coast: An Eighteenth-Century Spanish Retrospective on Guale and Mocama* (New York: American Museum of Natural History; Athens: distributed by the University Press of Georgia, 1995), 15–19, is a good account. Cited hereafter as Worth, *Georgia Coast*.

Verner S. Crane argued that these raiders were the "Westo" of post-
1670 fame and possibly even were the Ricahecrians who defeated the
Virginians in 1656. John R. Swanton suggested that they were Yuchi or
Chisca from the southern Appalachian mountains, although in later
work he suggested that the Ricahecrians, the Chichimecs of 1661, and
the Westo were all Chisca/Yuchi. Identification with the Chisca seems
to be due to a misreading of AGI, SD 225 (JTC#3), Gov. Alonso de
Aranguiz y Cotes to SM, 8 Sept. 1662, where Chisca, captured near
Apalachee, are described as the source of a report on the Chichimeca,
but not, as Swanton thought, as veterans of the raid. See Calmes, "Indian Cultural Traditions," 76 (for the Swanton–Crane dispute), and
John R. Swanton, *Early History of the Creek Indians and Their Neighbors* (Washington, D.C.: Bureau of American Ethnology Bulletin 73,
1922), 286–312. John T. Juricek, "The Westo Indians," *Ethnohistory* 11
(1964), 134–73, suggests the Westo were a combination of Timucuan,
Oustaca, Iroquoian Richohockans [*sic*], and possibly others, but I do
not find his new documentary evidence credible.

See J. Leich Wright, Jr., *The Only Land They Knew: The Tragic
Story of the American Indians in the Old South* (New York: Free Press,
1981), 85–87, and Marvin T. Smith, *Archaeology of Aboriginal Culture
Change in the Interior Southeast: Depopulation during the Early Historic Period* (Gainesville: University Presses of Florida, 1987), 131–32,
for the turmoil in the Virginia piedmont caused by colonial activities
further north. I have followed Smith's interpretation of who the "Chichimecas" were.

If the "Chichimecs" were the later Westo, then they moved south (or
west) to the Savannah River between 1663 and 1674. My Santee River
location fits with William Owen's 1670 statement that the coastal Indians near Charleston feared the Yamassee to the south and the Westo
"behind them." Quoted in Verner W. Crane, *The Southern Frontier,
1670–1732* (Durham: Duke University Press, 1928), 12. It will be recalled
that in 1605 a linguistic frontier lay between St. Helena Sound and
Charleston. The data on the initial location of the Chichimeca settlement given here raises interesting questions about the linguistic distribution in the interior.

44. AGI, SD 2584 (Stetson), Depositions of Friars, Guale, Apr. 1663,
as Enclosure no. 6 with Gov. Montiano to SM, 14 Aug. 1739. This document is the first mention of the Yamassee as the occupants of the coastal
plain of South Carolina. In the 1680s they were identified as those of the
"Yamas" language. They seem to have been both the original Cusabo
inhabitants and other folk forced south and east by the troubles in the
back country.

Scholars working prior to Worth's publication of this document in
Georgia Coast, 92–94, have read the post-1685 English lists of the refugee communities in the Yamassee confederation (especially a 1715 list)

as saying that all of the "Yamassee" who were not Guale or Coosa were from the La Tama towns even though at least two village names cannot be identified. They have ignored Henry Erskine's clear statement (which they usually use to document the gathering in 1685) that the *Yamassee* were *returning* to a place they had once lived (the Port Royal area). Much has also been made of the fact that Cacique Altamaha led the 1685 gathering of the "Yamassee." This is a puzzle, if he was from La Tama, but the 1663 document and the ones usually cited seem to me to show clearly that the Tama people (Altamaha, Ocute, Isichi, etc.) and the Yamassee were distinct groups, each of which fled Westo raids. Cf. William Green, "The Search for Altamaha: The Archaeology and Ethnohistory of an Early 18th Century Yamasee Indian Town" (M.A. thesis, University of South Carolina, 1991), 15–23, and David A. McKivergan, Jr., "Migration and Settlement among the Yamasee in South Carolina" (M.A. thesis, University of South Carolina, 1991), 35, 38. Chester DePratter kindly sent me copies of these works.

Is the name derived from the characteristic "Yaa" greeting that Juan Pardo noted? (Charles Hudson, *The Juan Pardo Expeditions: Exploration of the Carolinas and Tennessee, 1566–1568* (Washington, D.C.: Smithsonian Institution, 1990), 205–54, passim). That is, "Ya más" (meaning "More 'ya'"). Anthropologists refer to them as the Cusabo; they spoke a form of Muskogean. Worth suggests they were "an aggregation of Indian towns of diverse origins," an idea not incompatible with the one presented here. See Worth, *Georgia Coast*, 20.

45. AGI, SD 2584 (Stetson), Copy, Gov. Guerra to Capt. Alonso de Argüelles, 18 Aug. 1667, in Enclosure no. 5 with Montiano to SM, 14 Aug. 1739; Worth, *Georgia Coast*, 200 (Arcos List of 1675). Apparently responding to the same danger of Westo attack, San Diego de Satuache relocated from the mainland to St. Catherines Island between 1663 and 1666 (ibid., 19, 190–91).

46. For Hilton and Sandford, see A. S. Salley, *Narratives of Early Carolina, 1650–1708* (New York: Scribner, 1911), 38–45, 100–106, respectively; Wright, *The Only Land They Knew*, 95–96 (on English trade out of Virginia, 1654 ff.).

47. Bishop Calderón in Lucy L. Wenhold (trans.), "A 17th Century Letter of Gabriel Díaz Vara Calderón, Bishop of Cuba, Describing the Indians and Indian Missions of Florida," *Smithsonian Miscellaneous Collections* 95, no. 16 (1936), 9–10 (cited hereafter as Calderón, "Letter"). The Apalachicola villages were thirty leagues north of Sabacola el menor, which was twelve leagues from the Chacato villages on the Río Agna (Oklockonee). These may be the people that in 1673 a Franciscan claimed he had invited to live on the lower Apalachicola River (i.e., the Flint, not the river with that name today), although the list includes names like Ocmulgui that are recognizable as from central

Georgia; many of the other details of the claim do not match. See Hann, *Apalachee*, 33, for discussion.

48. Hann, *Apalachee*, 183, noting a 1672 report of frequent trade with the Apalachicolas and Nicolás Ramirez's testimony of 1687 regarding his activities with Pedro de Ortes, lieutenant governor of Apalachee. The caciques said there was no food available and told Ortes not to advance further.

49. Calderón, "Letter," 9; Hann, *Apalachee*, 47; John H. Hann, "Summary Guide to Spanish Missions and Visitas, with Churches in the Sixteenth and Seventeenth Centuries," *The Americas* 46 (1990), 492–93, lists the three Chacato missions and gives a brief history. I disagree with his placement of Sabacola at this time on the upper Apalachicola, "just below the confluence of the Flint and the Chattahoochee." That was the location based on 1693 trail references whereas Calderón is quite clear that Sabacola El Menor was a dozen leagues up the "Apalachicoli"—which seems to be the Flint in his account. Cf. Hann, *Apalachee*, 47–48, and Calderón, "Letter," 9. Hann, *Apalachee*, 32, is probably right that expansion of the missions from Apalachee was set back by the deaths of the five friars who fled in 1656.

50. Hann, "Summary Guide," 492–94; Hann, *Apalachee*, 184 (for cause of revolt).

51. Calderón, "Letter," 11–12, lists the South Florida peoples; James W. Covington, "Trade Relations between Southwestern Florida and Cuba, 1600–1840," *FHQ* 38 (1959), 114–16.

52. John H. Hann, ed. and trans., *Missions to the Calusa* (Gainesville: University of Florida Press, 1991), 23–36; Robert L. Kapitzke, "The Secular Clergy in St. Augustine during the First Spanish Period, 1565–1763" (M.A. thesis, University of Florida, 1991), 20. *Archivo Ibero-Americano* 1 (1914), 366–68, Custodio Fr. Juan Luengo to SM, Madrid, 22 Sept. 1676, is a request for twenty-two friars and three servants to complete the class of thirty and four authorized in 1673. Eight friars and one servant had gone out that year. He claimed there were fewer than thirty friars in Florida, not enough for the forty-three existing missions. I do not know if any of the twenty-two actually reached Florida.

53. Theodore G. Corbett, "Population Structure in Hispanic St. Augustine, 1629–1763," *FHQ* 54 (1976), 269, 271, 276; Theodore G. Corbett, "Migration to a Spanish Imperial Frontier in the Seventeenth and Eighteenth Centuries: St. Augustine," *Hispanic American Historical Review* 54 (1974), 418, Table I. Corbett notes that Latin Americans accounted for 29.7 percent of the grooms, just behind Peninsulares with 31.6 percent, but both lagging native sons at 35.9 percent.

54. Hann, *History of Timucua*, 203 (for his private profit, the friars charged).

55. Stahle and Cleaveland, data in collection of author. At ±15 per-

cent, seven of these nine years might have experienced crop failures, four from excessive rain, three, including 1672–1673, from drought. AGI, SD 229 (JTC#3), Treasury Officials to SM, 15 Oct. 1674, and AGI, SD 839, fol. 239, Hita Salazar to SM, 23 Nov. 1675 (storm surges); AGI, SD 229 (JTC#3), Treasury Officials to SM, 21 Mar. 1672 (protesting governor's monopoly and suggesting space not needed for King's maize on shipping be opened to private parties); AGI, SD 839, fol. 214, Hita Salazar to SM, 24 Aug. 1675.

56. AGI, SD 839, fol. 244, Hita Salazar to SM, 6 Sept. 1677, and fol. 308v, for 1679 example. The harvest was short throughout La Florida in 1677 (ibid., fol. 254, Hita Salazar to SM, 26 Apr. 1678). The friars were expected to sell maize grown for the purchase of ornaments (on the *sabana*) against payment from the next *situado*.

57. AGI, SD 225 (JTC#3), Gov. Francisco de la Guerra y Vega to SM, 8 Apr. 1666, noting that the *situado* was seven years in arrears and that Treasurer Joseph de Prado had been in Mexico for two years fruitlessly trying to collect and that Guerra had been bringing in supplies on his own credit to help the garrison [and make his fortune!].

58. Boniface, "Historical Geography," 89–90; Hann, *History of Timucua*, 252–53.

59. Hann, *Apalachee*, 198–200; Verne E. Chatelain, *The Defenses of Spanish Florida, 1565 to 1763* (Washington, D.C.: Carnegie Institution of Washington, 1941), 61–62.

60. John Lynch, *Spain under the Hapsburgs*, 2 vols., 2nd ed. (New York: New York University Press, 1981), 2:207–208, 210–11, for irregular convoys and revenue decline.

61. AGI, SD 229 (JTC#3), Treasury Officials to SM, 30 June 1668; Additional documentation is in AGI, SD 225 (JTC#3); Chatelain, *Defenses*, 62–63. For Woodward see Bushnell, *Situado and Sabana*, 136. Searles was a typical buccaneer, operating more or less without regard to the state of war and peace in Europe, although at the time of his raid France and Spain were engaged in the War of Devolution (May 1667–1668). His crew was mostly French.

62. AGI, SD 229 (JTC#3), Treasury Officials to SM, 30 June 1668, and AGI, SD 225 (JTC#3), Gov. Francisco de Guerra to SM, 8 Aug. 1668 (re Ponce de León); Luis R. Arana, "The Spanish Infantry: The Queen of Battles in Florida, 1671–1702" (M.A. thesis, University of Florida, Gainesville, 1960), 10, discusses how creoles had come to see office as rightly theirs.

63. Chatelain, *Defenses*, 59, 63–64; AGI, SD 839, fol. 73, Gov. Cendoya to SM, 31 Oct. 1671; AGI, SD 839, fols. 459–466, "Relación de lo que se ha proveido y ordenado sobre socorro de las provincias de la Florida . . . ," Madrid, 16 Sept. 1683, lists sending men from Mexico, orders to provide artillery and a series of measures during the 1670s.

All Floridanos who received pay or rations (as royal *merceds*) were enrolled in the new militia, even if physically infirm.

64. Chatelain, *Defenses*, 64–75; Luis R. Arana and Albert C. Manucy, *The Building of Castillo de San Marcos* (St. Augustine, Fla.: Eastern National Parks Monument Association for Castillo de San Marcos National Monument, 1977); Robert A. Matter, "Missions in the Defense of Spanish Florida, 1566–1710," *FHQ* 54 (1975), 30 (re increase in garrison); Corbitt, "Migration," 418, Table 1, showing 26.7 percent of grooms were from New Spain, 1671–91, and p. 427 for general comments.

65. Frances G. Davenport, *European Treaties Bearing on the History of the United States and Its Dependencies*, 4 vols. (Washington, D.C.: Carnegie Institution of Washington, 1917–37), 2:187–96, for text; [Antonio de Arredondo], *Arredondo's Historical Proof of Spain's Title to Georgia*, ed. Herbert E. Bolton (Berkeley: University of California Press, 1925), 151–52, used the treaty to argue in 1740 that the English had implicitly recognized Spanish ownership of North America, including "Georgia," by accepting article seven.

66. AGI, SD 839, fols. 56–70, "Declaraciones de los Ingleses." They are unlikely to have used "Port of Santa Elena." That was a Spanish fixation. Maurice Mathews to Lord Ashley, Charleston, 1670, in Salley, *Narratives of Early Carolina*, 114; See also Abbie M. Brooks, *The Unwritten History of Old St. Augustine* (St. Augustine, Fla.: The Record Company, 1909/1907), 117–20; James G. Johnson, "The International Contest for the Colonial Southeast, 1566–1763" (Ph.D. dissertation, University of California, Berkeley, 1924), 77; Lanning, *Spanish Missions*, 215.

67. AGI, SD 228, fols. 151–52, Francisco de Guerra to SM, Madrid, 12 Jul. 1673, and Lanning, *Spanish Missions*, 215 (re expedition); AGI, SD 839, fols. 50–53, Report on San Jorge (Charleston), including Indian reports and Argüelles's report of his trip of Aug. 1670; Robert A. Matter, *Pre-Seminole Florida: Spanish Soldiers, Friars, and Indian Missions, 1513–1763* (New York: Garland, 1990), 105 (Guale garrison).

68. Worth, *Georgia Coast*, 23, 191–93, 194, suggesting that the Spaniards organized this village movement even though there is no documentation of such an order; Serrano y Sanz, *Documentos*, 207, Gov. Pablo de Hita Salazar to SM, 10 Nov. 1678, noting such losses for "many years."

69. Calderon, "Letter," 5; Matter, "Missions in Defense," 26–27.

70. Wright, *The Only Land They Knew*, 105–107, and John A. Caruso, *The Southern Frontier* (Indianapolis: Bobbs-Merrill, 1963), 127–28 (Westo); William P. Cummings, "Geographical Misconceptions of the Southeast in the Cartography of the Seventeenth and Eighteenth Centuries," *Journal of Southern History* 4 (1938), 479–84 (Lederer).

71. AGI, SD 839, fols. 193–94, Testimony of Andrés de Escobedo, 23

May 1675. Also in "Plans for the Colonization and Defense of Apalachee, 1675," trans. Katherine Redding, *Georgia Historical Quarterly* 9 (1925), 169–75. Noted in Lanning, *Spanish Missions*, 174–75. See also AGI, SD 839, fol. 196, Copy of paragraph of Capt. Juan Fernández de Florencia to Gov. Hita Salazar, Apalachee, 25 May 1675.

72. AGI, SD 839, fols. 273–281, Hita Salazar to SM, 10 Nov. 1678, with attachments. For Westo activities see Wright, *The Only Land They Knew*, 105–107, 138–39. AGI, SD 839, fols. 310–21, Depositions of five Englishmen, Oct. 1679, attached to Hita Salazar to SM, 11 Nov. 1680.

73. Hann, *Apalachee*, 198 (1655); AGI, SD 839 (Lockey), Consulta of Junta de Guerra, Madrid, 14 Jul. 1660, noting the threat against Apalachee from a letter of Gov. Aranguiz dated 5 Jan. 1659; AGI, SD 839, fol. 243, Hita Salazar to SM, 6 Sept. 1677, and Pearson, *Two Visitas*, 237–39 (re the loss of Fernández de Florencia's *fragata* and cargo— including deerskins), and Hann, *Apalachee*, 201. Lucy L. Wenhold, "The First Fort of San Marcos de Apalache," *FHQ* 34 (1956), 301–14. For the trade goods see AGI, SD 839, fol. 259, Memorial by Hita Salazar, 26 Apr. 1678. Gregory A. Waselkov, "Seventeenth-Century Trade in the Colonial Southeast," *Southeastern Archaeology* 8 (1989), 117–133, shows these are the sorts of goods recovered archaeologically in the "Creek" areas.

74. AGI, SD 839, fols. 236–236v, *Relación* of Pedro de Arcos, 1675, enclosed with Gov. Pablo de Hita Salazar to SM, 24 Aug. 1675 (also in Mark F. Boyd, "Enumeration of Florida Spanish Missions in 1675 with Translations," *FHQ* 27 (1948), 182–84), and Calderón, "Letter," 7. Ripley P. Bullen and John W. Griffin, "An Archaeological Survey of Amelia Island, Florida," *Florida Anthropologist* 5 (1952), 37–64. My count includes Nombre de Dios (thirty persons), Tolomato (no figure given), and Salamototo (forty persons) since they fall within the original tidewater frontier.

75. Calderón lists the Surruques, Ais, Santa Lucía, *Geigas*, Jobese, Vizcaynos, Matacumbe, *Bahía Honda*, Cuchiaguas, Pojoy, *Pineros*, Tocobaga, and Carlos (groups not previously noted herein, italicized) (Calderón, "Letter"). A 1679 search for Spaniards reported shipwrecked somewhere on the west coast listed (north to south) the Alcola (three hundred persons), Pojoy (three hundred persons?), Elafay (forty persons), Apajola Negra (twenty persons), and Tiquijagua (three hundred persons) (AGI, SD 226 (JTC#3), Depositions, 20 Aug. 1680). San Diego de Salamatoto, the river crossing town on the St. Johns, was not a mission.

76. AGI, SD 839, fol. 235, Report of Juan Fernández de Florencia, enclosed with Hita Salazar to SM, 24 Aug. 1675; Calderón, "Letter," 8, adds Ajohica three leagues from Santa Catalina. San Miguel de Asile is included in Timucua on both lists. Fernández Florencia admitted that

the population figures were not from a census, and that in any case the
Indians died daily.

77. AGI, SD 839, fol. 234, Report of Fernández de Florencia enclosed
with Hita Salazar to SM, 24 Aug. 1675 (Boyd, "Enumeration," 184–85;
Hann, *Apalachee*, 35, Table 2.3); Hann, *Apalachee*, 34, Figure 2.1; The
Tocobaga settlement on the Wacissa River was visited in 1678 and
found to have 348 persons of various Indian groups (Hann, *Apalachee*, 43).

78. Calderón, "Letter," 12, claimed he had confirmed 13,152 Indians in
Guale, Timucua, Apalachee, and Apalachicola. Cf. Fr. Juan Luengo to
SM, 22 Sept. 1676, claiming that there were forty-three missions (the
number of authorized *plazas!*) served by thirty friars (*Archivo Ibero-
Americano*, 1 (1914), 366–68); AGI, SD 235 (Stetson), Informe de
Luengo sobre el memorial de Fr. Alonso de Moral, 30 Nov. 1676, states
that a "matrícula" of Apalachee during Lent 1676 showed "hardly
5,000" persons, a figure at variance with Fernández de Florencia's and
the bishop's. Boyd, "Enumeration," 182 (for Pedro de Arcos's and Juan
Fernández de Florencia's 1675 counts). Hann, *Apalachee*, 35–40, and
Hann, *History of Timucua*, 245–51. Hann discusses the technical problems and later data.

79. Serrano y Sanz, *Documentos*, 132–33.

7. The First Contests with the English, 1680–1702

1. Preoccupied with other matters, especially the ongoing efforts to
extend the mission frontier into the territories of the lower Creek, Governor Pablo de Hita Salazar and Fray Jacinto de Barreda, the Franciscan's commissary, responded only by sending an order to Fray Bartolomé de Quiñones, at Mayaca, to visit the new arrivals. AGI, SD 226
(JTC#3), Autos of Gov. Hita Salazar and Fray Barreda, Feb. 1680.

2. AGI, SD 839, fols. 333–36 (also in Manuel Serrano y Sanz, ed.,
Documentos históricos de la Florida y la Luisiana, Siglos XVI al XVIII
(Madrid: V. Suarez, 1912), 216–19), Gov. Pablo de Hita Salazar to SM,
14 May 1680. Amy Turner Bushnell, *Situado and Sabana: Spain's Support System for the Presidio and Mission Provinces of Florida* (New
York: American Museum of Natural History; Athens: distributed by the
University of Georgia Press, 1994), 146. Carolina's officials, needing
peaceful relationships with Indian groups close to Charleston and its
outlying plantations, in the spring of 1680 got the Westo to agree, temporarily as it turned out, not to attack the Cusabo. To reinforce the
agreement, the English also armed potential Westo victims. The Westo
turned their attention to Guale.

3. AGI, SD 2584 (Stetson), fols. 43–44v, 39–40, 47–48v (pp. 235–38,
228–30, 243–46 of photostat), Orders of Pablo de Hita Salazar, 17, 23,

26 May 1680 as copied in Enclosure no. 5, Gov. Montiano to SM, 14 Aug. 1739.

4. AGI, SD 839, fols. 333–36 (also in Serrano y Sanz, *Documentos*, 216–19), Gov. Hita Salazar to SM, 14 May 1680 (evidently not sent until early June since it mentions some of the items ordered after 14 May; AGI, SD 2584 (Stetson), King to Gov., Buen Retiro, 26 Oct. 1683, original as enclosure no. 8, Gov. Montiano to SM, 14 Aug. 1739; AGI, SD 226, no. 71 (Lockey), Francisco de la Rocha to SM, 12 Dec. 1680, and AGI, SD 226, no. 69 (JTC#3), Gov. Marquez Cabrera to SM, 8 Dec. 1680 (re supplies and men).

5. AGI, SD 2584 (Stetson), fols. 41–42v, 45–46v (pp. 231–34, 239–42 of photostat), Orders of Gov. Hita Salazar, 18, 22 Jul. 1680, copied in Enclosure no. 5, Gov. Montiano to SM, 14 Aug. 1739. Raid proposal noted in John E. Worth, *The Struggle for the Georgia Coast: An Eighteenth-Century Spanish Retrospective on Guale and Mocama* (New York: American Museum of Natural History; Athens: distributed by the University of Georgia Press, 1995), 33. The next governor tried but failed to obtain one hundred Canary Islanders to settle St. Catherines Island and again make it a "frontier" against the English at Charleston and one of St. Augustine's granaries. See AGI, SD 226, no. 69 (JTC#3), Gov. Marquez Cabrera to SM, 8 Dec. 1680; John T. Lanning, *The Spanish Missions of Georgia* (Chapel Hill: University of North Carolina Press, 1935), 219, citing AGI, SD 616, nos. 5–6, Cedula, 10 Nov. 1681; and Juan Fernández Marchena and Felipe del Pozo Redondo, "La emigración canaria a la Florida oriental Española (1600–1821)," in Coloquio de historia Canario-Americana, 9th Spain, 1990, *Actas* (Las Palmas 1992), 1:529, who laid the failure on the high cost of providing for the immigrants, who were to be sent five families per hundred toneladas of shipping, to Havana.

6. Bushnell, *Situado and Sabana*, 146. A census of the labor pool of the coastal missions carried out in June 1681 reveals why the St. Catherines Indians resisted resettlement. Sapelo Island was home to as many as seven villages containing 130 men and boys over age twelve (Table 7.1). By living together, the Christian and Yamassee Indians on Sapelo had the potential of defeating an attack like that of 1680 because together they would have been outnumbered only about 2.3 to one; if the St. Catherines mission villagers had returned there, they would have faced impossible six-to-one odds, offset to an unknown degree by the help of the Spanish garrison.

7. John R. Swanton, *Early History of the Creek Indians and Their Neighbors* (Washington, D.C.: Bureau of American Ethnology Bulletin 73, 1922), 307, 317. See also Alan R. Calmes, "Indian Cultural Traditions and European Conquest of the Georgia-South Carolina Coastal Plain, 3000 BC–1733 AD: A Combined Archaeological and Historical

Investigation" (M.A. thesis, University of South Carolina, 1968), 64, 76; James G. Johnson, "The International Contest for the Colonial Southeast, 1566–1763" (Ph.D. dissertation, University of California at Berkeley, 1924), 88. Daniel Fornel, who had fled Charleston, noted that a new group of Indians had arrived in March 1679 and fought with the "Chichimecos." If these were the Savannahs, their use against the Westo may have been suggested by this event. AGI, SD 839, fol. 317, Deposition of Daniel Fornel, 25 Oct. 1679, with Hita Salazar to SM, 11 Nov. 1680.

8. AGI, SD 839, fols. 348 ff, "Información," Havana, 22 May 1681; ibid., fols. 354–55, Marqués Cabrera to SM, 16 Jul. 1682; Amy Turner Bushnell, "The Menéndez Marqués Cattle Barony at la Chua and the Determinants of Economic Expansion in Seventeenth-Century Florida," *FHQ* 56 (1978), 428–29. Efforts to block the entrance to the Suwannee were attempted in 1682 but failed because flood currents swept away the barriers.

9. AGI, SD 839, fols. 354–55, Marquez Cabrera to SM, 16 Jul. 1682.

10. AGI, SD 839, fols. 348 ff., "Información," Havana, 22 May 1681; ibid., fols. 354–55, Marquez Cabrera to SM, 16 Jul. 1682; AGI, SD 226, no. 97 (JTC#3), Gov. Marquez Cabrera to SM, 8 Apr. 1683; for buccaneers elsewhere, Peter Earle, *The Sack of Panama: Sir Henry Morgan's Adventures on the Spanish Main* (New York: Viking Press, 1981), passim.

11. AGI, SD 226, no. 97 (JTC#3), Gov. Marquez Cabrera to SM, 8 Apr. 1683, with detailed report dated 20 May 1683; AGI, SD 229, no. 155 (JTC#3), Treasury Officials to SM, 25 May 1683, and a second letter of the same date, AGI, SD 226, no. 100 (JTC#3). Bushnell, *Situado and Sabana*, 162–63, had mixed details of this attack and the raid of 1686 (including its date of 30 Apr.).

12. AGI, SD 839, fols. 424–26, "Nómina del número de yndios que tiene la provincia de Guale . . . ," 27 May 1683; AGI, SD 226, no. 97 (JTC#3), Marquez Cabrera to SM, 8 Apr. 1683. The missions lost six bells and all their ornaments. Worth, *Georgia Coast*, 36–37, makes the case for the attack on the pagans.

13. AGI, SD 226, no. 104 (JTC#3), Depositions of released prisoners, 8 May 1683. Lanning, *Spanish Missions*, 219. The attacking force consisted of four ships from Jamaica and New England; the fifth was French. The attack had been suggested by a disgruntled native of St. Augustine, Alonso de Aveçilla.

14. AGI, SD 839, fol. 418, Marquez Cabrera to SM, 28 June 1683. He had first asked for one hundred Isleños to settle St. Catherines Island (AGI, SD 226 (JTC#3), Marquez Cabrera to SM, 8 Dec. 1680). They were ordered by a decree of 10 Nov. 1681 (AGI, SD 834 and SD 616, Cedula, 10 Nov. 1681), but as Lanning, *Spanish Missions*, 219, observed,

"the project lost itself in a maze of documents." See also Marchena and Pozo Redondo, "Emigración canaria," 29.

15. AGI, SD 839, fols. 424–26, "Nómina del número de indios . . . ," Guale, 27 May 1683, which records their replies; AGI, SD 839, fols. 418–418v, Marquez Cabrera to SM, 28 June 1683, and AGI, SD 226, no. 105 (Lockey), Marquez Cabrera to SM, same date; AGI, SD 226, no. 118 (JTC#3), Marquez Cabrera to SM, 26 Aug. 1684. AGI, SD 839, fols. 433–34 (also Lockey), SM to Governor of Florida, Madrid, 28 Mar. 1684. See also Bushnell, *Situado and Sabana*, 163, 165; Worth, *Georgia Coast*, 38–40. The map is the Solana Map, 1683, "Mapa de la Isla de la Florida," copies in Library of Congress, Cartographic Division and P. K. Yonge Library of Florida History, Maps, no. 32. Discussed by Luis R. Arana, "The Alonso Solana Map of Florida, 1683," *FHQ* 43 (1964), 258–66.

16. Worth, *Georgia Coast*, 38–40. AGI, SD 226, no. 118 (JTC#3), Autos of Marquez Cabrera, 21–25 Aug. 1684, enclosed with Same to SM, 26 Aug. 1684. The governor said that an attack earlier that year led to an agreement to settle on Guadalquini but there seems to be no other record of this; perhaps he misspoke, meaning the raid of 1683.

17. AGI, SD 228, fols. 514v–515, Certification of Services of Sebastian López de Toledo, 20 Aug. 1689 (re the attacks at San Juan); and AGI, SD 2584 (Stetson, pp. 315–65 of photostat), Autos Criminales contra Capt. Juan Saturino, 1684, as Enclosure no. 10, Gov. Montiano to SM, 14 Aug. 1739 (actions at Sapelo). Also covered in Worth, *Georgia Coast*, 40–42; Lanning, *Spanish Missions*, 219. The identify of the corsair leader is in dispute. Lanning says "Kinckley"; Worth gives "Thomas Jingle."

18. Barcía's generally pro-Franciscan and unreliable account of these events says that many Guale refused to move and took to the forests rather than do so. He also says that the Franciscans tried to persuade the "Yamassee," especially cacique Altamaha's group, to move as well but failed because Altamaha had a grievance against the governor. Andrés Gonzales de Barcía Carballido y Zúñiga, *Chronological History of the Continent of Florida*, trans. Anthony Kerrigan (Gainesville: University of Florida Press, 1951), 287. Herbert E. Bolton and Mary Ross, *The Debatable Land* (Berkeley: University of California Press, 1925), 39–41; Verner W. Crane, *The Southern Frontier 1670–1732* (Durham: Duke University Press, 1928), 24–26; Lanning, *Spanish Missions*, 218–21; James W. Covington, "Stuart's Town: The Yamasee Indians and Spanish Florida," *Florida Anthropologist* 21 (1968), 9; and Bushnell, *Situado and Sabana*, 163–67, are variants of this story.

19. Calmes, "Indian Cultural Traditions," 59–60, 90. The Altamaha played a major role by providing transportation. La Tamans—who had been living evidently as refugees among the Coweta and Kussetau

[Kasihta], Creek groups on the Ocheese Creek—constituted the majority of this thousand. Clearly not all the "Yamassee" villages and bands gathered near Port Royal, but probably the majority did. George P. Insh, *Scottish Colonial Schemes, 1620–1686* (Glasgow: Maclehouse Jackson & Co., 1922), 209–10, makes the Yamassee the active agents in these events. See also Covington, "Stuart's Town," 9–10. Worth, *Georgia Coast*, 37, notes that the Solana map of 1683 shows a pagan town on Hilton Head Island. He believes this was Yamassee and that they had all fled from Guale in 1683 because Barbosa's *visita* mentions only sites they had abandoned. I think that Barbosa's charge did not require him to mention Yamassee.

20. Barcía, *Chronological History*, 287. Bolton claimed that "in the turmoil many of the neophytes of Zapala, San Simón, Tupique, and Asao fled with the heathen Yamassees to the Scotch colony at Santa Elena" (*Debatable Land*, 39–40); Bushnell makes this "streams of disaffected Guales" pouring into the area around Stuartstown (*Situado and Sabana*, 166). As has been noted in Chapter 6, previous writers have failed to distinguish the Yamassee proper from the later confederation in which the La Tamans are the major group. Nor has the possibility of intermarriage among the La Tamans, Yamassee, and mission Guale (1661–1684) been considered.

21. Lanning, *Spanish Missions*, 220–21; J. Leich Wright, Jr., *The Only Land They Knew: The Tragic Story of the American Indians in the Old South* (New York: Free Press, 1981), 139; John H. Hann, "Summary Guide to Spanish Florida Missions and Visitas, with Churches in the Sixteenth and Seventeenth Centuries," *The Americas* 46 (1990), 472; Bushnell, *Situado and Sabana*, 166–67. Antonio de Arredondo, *Arredondo's Historical Proof of Spain's Title to Georgia*, ed. Herbert E. Bolton (Berkeley: University of California Press, 1925), 157, makes Altamaha a "Christian Catholic Yamazes chief." For the subsequent history of the Yamassee on the Savannah, see Covington, "Stuart's Town," 10–12, and David A. McKivergan, Jr., "Migration and Settlement among the Yamasee in South Carolina" (M.A. thesis, University of South Carolina, 1991).

22. Crane, *Southern Frontier*, 30–31.

23. AGI, SD 2584 (Stetson), pp. 279–85, 272–76, 308–10 of the photostat, respectively, copy of Auto of Domingo de Leturiondo, Santa Cruz y San Buenaventura, Mocama, 21 Dec. 1685, and "Autos de visita . . . ," 1685, and Leturiondo's rules, 1685, as Enclosure no. 9, with Gov. Montaino to SM, 14 Aug. 1739. For names, see Swanton, *Early History*, 81–83.

24. Charles W. Arnade, *The Siege of St. Augustine in 1702* (Gainesville: University of Florida Press, 1959), 9 (from Bishop Calderon to SM, Havana, 28 Sept. 1689).

25. In a declaration (auto) of 5 Aug. 1686, Governor Marquez Cabrera noted buccaneer raids of 1683, 1684, and 1686 but I have not found evidence for the latter. Worth, *Georgia Coast*, 147. Bushnell, *Situado and Sabana*, 167.

26. Bushnell, *Situado and Sabana*, 167; Lanning, *Spanish Missions*, 223–24; Robert S. Weddle, *The French Thorn: Rival Explorers in the Spanish Sea, 1682–1762* (College Station: Texas A & M Press, 1991), 47–48, are accounts of varying length of the events near St. Augustine. After interrogation, these men were hanged.

27. AGI, SD 2584 (Stetson), "Autos hechas en la entrada en este puerto las galeotas de que era cavo y capitán Alejandro Thomás de León," 5 Aug. 1686, as Enclosure no. 11 with Gov. Mediano to SM, 14 Aug. 1739, also in Worth, *Georgia Coast*, 146–71. Insh, *Scottish Colonial Schemes*, 210–11; Paul Grimball, "Paul Grimball's Losses by the Spanish Invasion in 1686," *South Carolina Historical Magazine* 29 (1928), 231–37; Lanning, *Spanish Missions*, 223–24; Bolton and Ross, *Debatable Land*, 41–43; Crane, *Southern Frontier*, 31; J. Leich Wright, *Anglo-Spanish Rivalry in North America* (Athens: University of Georgia Press, 1971), 58. The commander of the ships seized the Guales' loot. The governor confiscated the African slaves for the fort construction on the grounds that de León had violated the royal order of 1683 when he invaded the area of English settlement around Charleston.

28. Worth, *Georgia Coast*, 162–63. Arredondo, *Historical Proof*, 158–59, conflates the two raids.

29. AGI, SD 228, fols. 181–82, Gov. Quiroga to Ayudante Manuel de Solana, 26 Aug. 1687 (regarding a patrol against the expected attack); Lanning, *Spanish Missions*, 224.

30. Crane, *Southern Frontier*, 32–33; Worth, *Georgia Frontier*, 162. See also J. G. Dunlop, "Spanish Depredations, 1686" and "Captain Dunlop's Voyage to the Southward, 1687," in *South Carolina Historical Magazine* 30 (1929), 81–89, 127–33, respectively.

31. For examples see Jonathan Dickinson, *God's Protecting Providence* (1700; New York: Garland, 1977), and copies of orders by Gov. Laureano Torres y Ayala, 10 Mar. 1699, and Gov. Joseph de Zúñiga y Cerda, 25 Oct. 1700, in Gov. Montiano to SM, 18 Aug. 1739, AGI, SD 2584 (Stetson).

32. AGI, SD 6 (JTC#2), Consulta of Council of Indies, 7 Aug. 1693; AGI, SD 2584 (Stetson), Cedula to Gov. of Florida, Madrid, 12 Aug. 1693, Enclosure no. 13, Gov. Montiano to SM, 14 Aug. 1739; AGI, SD 228, fol. 82, Gov. Torres y Ayala to SM, no. 6, 30 Apr. 1696 (ten fugitive Africans); ibid., fol. 434, Gov. Torres y Ayala to SM, no. 25, 9 Aug. 1697. Wright, *The Only Land They Knew*, 276, does not have the correct reasons for the decision of 1697.

33. Bushnell, *Situado and Sabana*, 177, notes that Jonathan Dickin-

son found Yamassee in the Mocama villages trading for deerskins in fall 1696–spring 1697.

34. Lanning, *Spanish Missions*, 173; AGI, SD 839 (in Serrano y Sanz, *Documentos*, 218), Gov. Hita Salazar to SM, 14 May 1680, and AGI, SD 226 (JTC#3), Gov. Hita Salazar to SM, 14 Mar. 1680, including the note that gifts would have "conquered" their wills; AGI, SD 226 (JTC#3), Fr. Francisco Gutiérrez de Vera to Gov., Sabacola, 19 May 1681, and ibid., Marquez Cabrera to SM, 5 Jan. 1682.

35. Crane, *Southern Frontier*, 29–30. Herbert E. Bolton, "Spanish Resistance to the Carolina Traders in Western Georgia (1680–1704)," *Georgia Historical Quarterly* 9 (1925), 120–23, is an account of Woodward's expedition of 1685–86.

36. Crane, *Southern Frontier*, 34–36; Bolton, "Spanish Resistance," 122–23; Lanning, *Spanish Missions*, 177–81.

37. Crane, *Southern Frontier*, 36; Bolton, "Spanish Resistance," 125; Lanning, *Spanish Missions*, 182–83. The withdrawal was intended to be temporary, pending reinforcement of St. Augustine on a permanent basis.

38. Boniface, "Historical Geography," 186, noting reports from 1700 and 1702, mostly about trade in Apalachee proper.

39. East Florida Papers, Index of Cedulas, 1687, no. 17, Cedula forbidding any increase in the firearms held by the Indians or the sale of those belonging to dead soldiers. Lanning, *Spanish Missions*, 216, 226, mistakenly thinks the Spaniards did not allow any Indians to have firearms. In fact, they had a number, as the events of 1657 showed.

40. Mark F. Boyd, "The Expedition of Marcos Delgado from Apalachee to the Upper Creek Country in 1686," *FHQ* 16 (1937), 3–32. For the Mexican search see Robert Weddle, *The French Thorn*, 41–81.

41. AGI, SD 839 (Serrano y Sanz, *Documentos*, 224–227).

42. AGI, SD 228, fols. 121–22, Torres y Ayala to SM, no. 11, 15 Apr. 1696 (reporting near completion). AGI, SD 228, fol. 573, Certification by Accountant Tomás Menéndez Marqués, 26 Apr. 1696. In 1689, Apalachee had a reported 1,920 families, with perhaps 9,600 persons (Arnade, *Siege of St. Augustine*, 9).

43. Lanning, *Spanish Missions*, 184.

44. Bolton, "Spanish Resistance," 126.

45. John H. Hann, *Apalachee: The Land between the Rivers* (Gainesville: University Presses of Florida, 1988), 233.

46. John H. Hann, ed. and trans., *Missions to the Calusa* (Gainesville: University of Florida Press, 1991), 37–38, citing a letter from the Franciscan chapter to the King, 5 Dec. 1593. See also AGI, SD 230 (JTC#3), "Relación," 15 Apr. 1697, with Treasury Officials to SM, 20 Apr. 1697, which lists the five missions: San Antonio de Anacape, Mayaca, Jororo, Tissimi [*sic*], and Aturquimi [*sic*].

47. AGI, SD 228, fols. 299–300, Torres y Ayala to SM, no. 1, Feb. 3, 1697 (also printed in Hann, *Missions to the Calusa*, 143–55); ibid., fols. 622–23, Torres y Ayala to SM, no. 9, 16 Sept. 1699 (printed in Hann, *Missions to the Calusa*, 213–16); John H. Hann, *A History of Timucua Indians and Missions* (Gainesville: University Press of Florida, 1996), 244. One of the boys killed at Atoyquime was the cacique of Aypala.

48. AGI, SD 228, fols. 516–17, Gov. Quiroga to Ayudante Reformado Sebastian López de Toledo, 18 May 1695, with orders to do all three things for the ends noted. His services on this expedition are ibid., fols. 518v–19, Certification of Services, 1697. The Spaniards wanted ambergris. See Boniface, "Historical Geography," 188.

49. Charles M. Andrews, "The Florida Indians in the Seventeenth Century," *Tequesta* 1 (1943), 42, from Dickinson's Journal.

50. AGI, SD 226 (JTC#3), Gov. Hita Salazar to SM, 6 Mar. 1680.

51. Hann, *Missions to the Calusa*, 36–42, with documents from the 1697 attempt on pp. 155–210.

52. AGI, SD 226 (JTC#3), Marquez Cabrera to SM, 8 Dec. 1680; ibid. (Lockey), Franciscans to Governor of Florida, 1681 (copies); ibid., Marquez Cabrera to SM, 14 June 1681, with enclosures re incidents in Guale; ibid., Capt. Francisco de Fuentes to Gov. of Fla, Sapala, 30 Oct. 1681 (Asao problems); ibid., Testimony re abuses at Nombre de Dios, 2 Sept. 1682; ibid., Marquez Cabrera to SM, 28 June 1683. For Guale see Bushnell, *Situado and Sabana*, 148–60.

By controlling surpluses of grain, eating diets rich in meat, and having households full of women (even if not wives), the friars were displaying the traditional status attributes of caciques. They also used both majolica (tin-glazed, painted pottery) and earthenwares manufactured on European patterns by Indian potters, another way of setting themselves above the Indians. The use of whips fit with the friars' belief that fear was necessary to teaching the Indians correct behavior, including deference to the friars. Marquez Cabrera proposed the use of the *sabana* or dedicated garden or field for the support of the friars and Church as a way to end arbitrary demands for food.

53. AGI, SD 227B, fols. 930–35, Gov. Quiroga to SM, no. 40, 28 Nov. 1692, and ibid., fols. 852–53, Gov. Quiroga to SM, no. 22, 18 Apr. 1692, enclosing complaints against the commissioner by Fr. Manuel de Mendoza to Quiroga, Bacuqua y San Antonio (Apalachee), 10 Sept. 1687; ibid., fols. 874–79, Fr. Blas Martínez de Robles to ?, 12 Apr. 1692 (the new men as place seekers lacking the spiritual qualities needed for the mission work). These materials are part of a 1695 Council of the Indies file on these matters (ibid., fols. 844–910). See also Lanning, *Spanish Missions*, 193–94; Cristobal Figuero del Campo, *Misiones Franciscanas en la Florida* (Madrid: Comisión Episcopal del V. Centenario, 1992), 124. AGI, SD 228 (Stetson), Quiroga to SM, 1690.

54. AGI, SD 228, fols. 110–19, "Extracto de lo que contienen los expedientes . . . ," Madrid, 19 Nov. 1695 (published in a not entirely accurate translation in Hann, *Mission to Calusa*, 133–42). Robert L. Kapitzke, "The Secular Clergy in St. Augustine during the First Spanish Period, 1565–1763" (M.A. thesis, University of Florida, 1991), 48, notes this incident. The burdener incident of 1691 is AGI, SD 227B, fols. 905–910, Informe, 5 Mar. 1691; also noted in Lanning, *Spanish Missions*, 194–95. Lanning also notes a report that 350 of 400 Indians at the Tama mission had fled because of Fr. Domingo Santos's frequent use of the whip on them. AGI, SD 227B, fols. 842–843v, Quiroga to SM, no. 22, 18 Apr. 1692, with related documents fols. 844–51.

55. AGI, SD 227B, fol. 924, Chumillas to Council of Indies, Madrid, 17 Nov. 1692.

56. AGI, SD 227B, fol. 924, Chumillas to Council of Indies, Madrid, 17 Nov. 1692; AGI, SD 228, fols. 110–19, "Extracto de lo que contienen los expedientes . . . ," 1695; AGI, SD 227B, fols. 930–35, Notes of Fiscal, 27 Nov. 1695, and AGI, SD 228, fols. 550–51, 29 Aug. 1697 (recommending ordering governors and bishops of Cuba to use Law 11, Title 13 of Book 1, Nueva Recopilación against friars who punished excessively).

57. AGI, SD 228, fols. 562–63, Commissary General Antonio de Cardona to Martín de Suerralta, Madrid, 22 Sept. 1697 (justifying punishments); AGI, SD 230, Report, 15 Apr. 1697, enclosed with Treasury Officials to SM, 20 Apr. 1697.

58. AGI, SD 226 (JTC#3; Lockey), Francisco de Fuentes to Governor, Sapelo, 4 May 1681, enclosed with Marquez Cabrera to SM, 14 June 1681; AGI, SD 226, no. 105, Expediente re abuse of Indians, where Fr. Robles's inspection is noted.

59. This line of interpretation began with Barcía in the 1740s, as has been noted.

60. AGI, SD 124 (Stetson), Bishop Calderón to SM, Havana, 28 Sept. 1689, reports 2,796 families in the missions. At an average of five persons per family, the population would be 13,980 persons; his count was 13,152. The 1681 and 1683 census of the Guale and Mocama missions show only slight variations (Worth, *Georgia Coast*, Table 1, p. 37).

61. Theodore G. Corbett, "Population Structure in Hispanic St. Augustine, 1629–1763," *FHQ* 54 (1976), 267, 269, 271; Theodore G. Corbett, "Migration to a Spanish Imperial Frontier in the Seventeenth and Eighteenth Centuries: St. Augustine," *Hispanic American Historical Review* 54 (1974), 418, Table 1. The population count of 1689 was reported in Bishop Diego Evelina de Compostela to SM, Santiago de Cuba, 28 Sept. 1689 (Boniface, "Historical Geography," 75, citing a copy from AGI, SD 151 (Stetson)).

62. AGI, SD 2584 (Stetson), Crown to Gov. of Florida, Buen Retiro, 20 May 1689, as enclosure no. 12 with Gov. Montiano to SM, 14 Aug.

1739, citing documents from 1680–81; See also Lanning, *Spanish Missions*, 219 (Canary Islanders). AGI, SD 226 (Serrano y Sanz, *Documentos*, 220–21), Gov. Diego de Quiroga to SM, 1 Apr. 1688 (one hundred Gallicians for St. Augustine and Apalachee).

63. AGI, SD 228, fol. 139, Report of Accountant Tomás Menéndez Marqués, 12 Apr. 1696.

64. Bushnell, "The Menéndez Marqués Cattle Barony," 421, and AGI, SD 839, fol. 147v, Gov. Ponce de León to SM, 8 Jul. 1673 (re Mexicans); Jane Landers, "Black Society in Spanish Florida, 1784–1821" (Ph.D. dissertation, University of Florida, 1988), 12 (Pardos and Morenos); AGI, SD 226 (JTC#3), Marquez Cabrera to SM, 30 Jan. 1682 (Cofradías).

65. Boniface, "Historical Geography," 149–50 (monthly supply, problems and tax); Bushnell, "Cattle Barony," 429 (price paid). The ferrying of cattle across the St. Johns River at Salamatoto damaged the *piraguas* used, costing the government 5,217 reales (including the salaries of the operators) vis income of 1,999 reales, 1689–93 (Boniface, "Historical Geography," 178–80). The tithe records of 1698 and 1699 note payments from twenty-five ranches near St. Augustine, on the St. Johns River, and in central Florida (near modern Gainesville), confirming the five-head-a-month figure. Nine other ranches existed in Apalachee, but it is unlikely they sent cattle to St. Augustine. See Arnade, "Cattle Raising in Spanish Florida," 124, and Boniface, "Historical Geography," 147. On Indian rustling see Bushnell, "Cattle Barony," 430–31. AGI, SD 228, fol. 534, 542–43, Gov. Torres y Ayala to SM, 29 Aug. 1697, enclosing petition of Luisa de los Ángeles, seeking a *plaza* of four reales per day because her late husband's herd (and thus her income) had diminished during the previous ten years because of these heavy demands.

66. David W. Stahle and Malcolm K. Cleaveland, data in collection of author; Marcos Delgado's expedition of 1686 found shortages among the Alabama and Choctaw. Boyd, "Expedition of Marcos Delgado"; AGI, SD 228, fols. 281–85, Torres y Ayala to SM, no. 15, 4 Feb. 1697.

67. Luis R. Arana and Albert Manucy, *The Building of Castillo de San Marcos* (St. Augustine, Fla.: Eastern National Park Monument Association for Castillo de San Marcos National Monument, 1977), 21, 35.

68. AGI, SD 228, fols. 357v, *Informe* of Tomás Menéndez Marqués and Joachím de Florencia, 15 Aug. 1697, describes this overland carriage. There is no mention of Indian bearers.

69. AGI, SD 228, fols. 472–73, Quiroga to Joaquím de Florencia, 14 Dec. 1692, noting ration; ibid., 473–74, Quiroga to Joaquím de Florencia, 17 Dec. 1693; ibid., 382–83, Treasury Officials to SM, 8 Feb. 1697 (re late 1696 reduction; "There is no maize here").

70. AGI, SD 228, fols. 366–67, Torres y Ayala to SM, no. 4, 17 Apr. 1697. He is not known to have sent to Carolina, but the suggestion im-

plies that resort to non-Spanish suppliers had continued after 1683 when the *Mayflower* had brought in flour.

71. AGI, SD 229 (JTC#3), Treasury Officials to SM, 20 Sept. 1683 (purchases totaled 2,427 pesos 5 reales); AGI, SD 226 (JTC#3), Marquez Cabrera to SM, 30 May 1684, enclosing documents justifying the purchase in Sept. 1683. It entered St. Augustine harbor ostensively to return two persons captured by buccaneers in the raid of 1683 and released at New York. No justification was recorded in 1684.

72. Kapitzke, "Secular Clergy," 63.

73. AGI, SD 227B, fols. 832–33v, Gov. Quiroga to SM, 16 Apr. 1692 (loss of 1691); William R. Gillaspie, "Juan de Ayala y Escobar, Procurador and Entrepreneur: A Case Study of the Provisioning of Florida, 1683–1716" (Ph.D. dissertation, University of Florida, 1961), 49 (1693 capture); AGI, SD 228, fols. 281–85, Gov. Torres y Aylla to SM, no. 15, 4 Feb. 1697, and fols. 382–83, Treasury Officials to SM, 8 Feb. 1697 (re *situado*).

74. Gillaspie, "Juan de Ayala," 75–77; John J. TePaske, *The Governorship of Spanish Florida, 1700–1763* (Durham: Duke University Press, 1964), 82–83.

75. Gillaspie, "Juan de Ayala," 15–19, 21, 34–46 (Seville 1687), 53–55 (Quiroga y Losada's protection), and Boniface, "Historical Geography," 195 (re Canary Islands, 1685); AGI, SD 839, fols. 338–42, Hita Salazar to SM, 8 Feb. 1684. AGI, SD 839, fol. 480, Marquez Cabrera to SM, 20 Mar. 1686, said that in his experience as governor of Honduras he had never seen accounts so tangled and puzzling (*tan enmarañadas*) as those of La Florida.

76. AGI, SD 839, fols. 338–42, Hita Salazar to SM, 8 Feb. 1684.

77. AGI, SD 227B, fols. 950–51, Gov. Quiroga to SM, no. 3, 7 Apr. 1693; AGI, SD 228, fols. 351–59, Gov. Torres y Ayala to SM, no. 14, 16 Apr. 1697, with Council of the Indies *Fiscal*'s notes, 1699, and ibid., fols. 356–357v, *Informe* of Tomás Menéndez Marqués and Joachím de Florencia, 15 Apr. 1697. East Florida Papers, Index of Cedulas, 1691, no. 64; 1696, no. 44; 1700, no. 7.

78. TePaske, *Governorship*, 79, citing letters from Gov. Zúñiga to SM, 24 Oct, 28 Oct. 1701, noting starvation prior to the arrival of a supply ship on Christmas Day.

79. AGI, SD 226 (JTC#3), Marquez Cabrera to SM, 8 Dec. 1680 (re abundance of cattle on ranches four or more leagues from Indian villages); East Florida Papers, Index of Cedulas, 1682, no. 57, a cedula approves the sowing of rice; AGI, SD 226 (JTC#3), Marquez Cabrera to SM, 28 June 1683 (wheat); AGI, SD 227 (Serrano y Sanz, *Documentos*, 222–23), Quiroga y Losada to SM, Apr. 1688 (re Apalachee). Lilly Library, Latin American Manuscripts—Mexico (Copy, P. K. Yonge Library of Florida History), King to Bishop Ignacio de Urbina, Barcelona,

8 Mar. 1702, seeking a dozen Tlaxcalan Indians to teach Florida Indians improved methods of wheat cultivation. They were not sent.

80. AGI, SD 226, no. 106 (Lockey), Marquez Cabrera to SM, 28 June 1683; AGI, SD 227 (Serrano y Sanz, *Documentos*, 222–23), Quiroga y Losada to SM, Apr. 1688; Loucks, "Political and Economic Interactions," 306 (noting smithy parts found at the Scott Miller site in Apalachee); Boniface, "Historical Geography," 204, 211.

8. The Military Frontier, at Last, 1702–1763

1. For background, see Robert S. Weddle, *The French Thorn: Rival Explorers in the Spanish Sea, 1682–1762* (College Station: Texas A & M Press, 1991), 41–134.

2. Verner W. Crane, *The Southern Frontier, 1670–1732* (Durham: Duke University Press, 1928), 71–75.

3. Lana Jill Loucks, "Political and Economic Interactions between Spaniards and Indians: Archaeological and Ethnohistorical Perspectives of the Mission System in Florida" (Ph.D. dissertation, University of Florida, 1979), 59; Kenneth W. Johnson, "The Utina and Potano Peoples of Northern Florida: Changing Settlement Systems in the Spanish Colonial Period" (Ph.D. dissertation, University of Florida, 1991), 249–51; John T. Lanning, *The Spanish Missions of Georgia* (Chapel Hill: University of North Carolina Press, 1935), 184.

4. John H. Hann, *A History of the Timucua Indians and Missions* (Gainesville: University Press of Florida, 1996), 293–94; Lanning, *Spanish Missions*, 185; Crane, *Southern Frontier*, 73–74.

5. Charles W. Arnade, *The Siege of St. Augustine in 1702* (Gainesville: University of Florida Press, 1959), 11–13; Hann, *History of Timucua*, 292. Arnade (ibid., 4) says that the Carolina Assembly decided on war on 28 August, two days after the official declaration reached Charleston. Crane, *Southern Frontier*, 76, says the decision was taken on 10 Sept. Lt. Gov. Solana in Apalachee was ordered to build stockades around the towns and seek help from Pensacola.

6. Arnade, *Siege*, 14–15, 21, 25–29.

7. Arnade, *Siege*, 25–37. William R. Gillaspie, "Juan de Ayala y Escobar, Procurador and Entrepreneur: A Case Study of the Provisioning of Florida, 1683–1716" (Ph.D. dissertation, University of Florida, 1961), 90, reports how the 350 places in the garrison broke down; see Juan Marchena Fernández, "Guarniciones y población militar en Florida Oriental (1700–1820)," *Revista de Indias*, nos. 163–64 (1981), 97–98, for the muster of 15 Mar. 1702.

8. Arnade, *Siege*, 37–59, gives a detailed account; see p. 7 for British costs. Amy Turner Bushnell, *Situado and Sabana: Spain's Support System for the Presidio and Mission Provinces of Florida* (New York:

American Museum of Natural History; Athens: distributed by the University of Georgia Press, 1994), 190–92. Crane, *Southern Frontier*, 76–77, for the English side.

9. Arnade, *Siege*, 43, 57–59. The Spaniards destroyed structures within 750 feet of Castillo de San Marcos worth 15,430 pesos and belonging to 31 owners. The balance of the compensation was claimed by 118 owners.

10. Hann, *History of Timucua*, 297. Charles W. Arnade, "Piribiriba on the Salamototo: Spanish Fort on the St. Johns River," *Papers of the Jacksonville Historical Society* 4 (1960), 67–84, is a brief history of this fort.

11. Crane, *Southern Frontier*, 78–79. Crane cites Zúñiga to King, 30 Mar. 1704, for the attacks on Patali and San Francisco, but John H. Hann, *Apalachee: The Land between the Rivers* (Gainesville: University Presses of Florida, 1988), 274, and Hann, *History of Timucua*, 294–95, do not mention them as having been raided prior to the main attack in 1704. Ibid., 297, does note a raid on Piritiriba and San Francisco, from the same source. As many as five hundred Indians were enslaved.

12. Extract of Colonel Moore's Letter to the Lords Proprietors, 16 Apr. [*sic*] 1704 (hereafter as Moore to Proprietors), in Hann, *Apalachee*, 386, and "Colonel Moore's Letter to Sir Nathaniel Johnson (hereafter as Moore to Johnson)," 16 Apr. [*sic*] 1704, in ibid., 387. Ibid., 265–78, is an extended discussion of the difficulties of these texts and their various copies. He does not comment on the misdating. The letters were written after 23 Feb. (OS) because in Moore to Johnson (p. 388) he states he had left Apalachee on the 23rd of the month (OS, i.e., 6 Mar.) and expected to be in Carolina in the middle of March. Moore to Johnson suggests that the English troops did most of the attacking, which evened out the odds for the defenders. J. Leich Wright, Jr., *The Only Land They Knew: The Tragic Story of the American Indians in the Old South* (New York: Free Press, 1981), 140–41, notes that obtaining a share of the captives likely motivated the English militiamen.

13. Sources as in previous note. Amy Turner Bushnell, "Patricio de Hinachuba: Defender of the Word of God, the Crown of the King, and the Little Children of Ivitachuco," *American Indian Culture and Research Journal* 3 (1979), 8–9. The relief force was thirty Spaniards and four hundred Apalachee. It suffered 50 percent casualties (killed, wounded, captured) but we do not have exact figures for the Apalachee.

14. Hann, *Apalachee*, 274, 282, noting Governor Zúñiga's list of Ayubale, Tomole, Capoli, Tama, and "Ocatoses" as places from which persons were carried off. Moore's letters indicate he marched through five towns besides Ayubale, of which all surrendered without condition (Moore to Johnson, p. 388) or four did and one did not (Moore to Proprietors, p. 386). The one that surrendered with conditions evidently

was Ivitachucho. Hann found later Spanish evidence for Tomole (p. 274) and Tama (p. 282) as two of the four unconditional towns. His discussion on this topic lacks clarity.

15. Hann, *Apalachee*, 274, argues for four towns on the basis of the four settlements the emigres founded in Carolina, but I think Moore's letters mean that three complete towns migrated, and a fourth cacique and some of his people did also. The fourth settlement in Carolina also could have been made up of the peoples from the other four towns he mentions as suppliers of some emigres. Moore to Johnson (Hann, *Apalachee*, 388), noting "I now have in my company all the whole people of three Towns" but in Moore to Proprietors (ibid., 386) he says "four kings and all their people came away with me. . . ." The letters agree that parts of the population of four other towns, including some people from San Luís, were also among the migrants accompanying Moore back to Carolina. Spanish sources said two towns went voluntarily, which points to the lower of the two numbers Moore gives.

16. Hann, *Apalachee*, 269–70, 387–89, shows that Moore's claim of four thousand enslaved women and children cannot be correct. Kathleen A. Deagan, "Spanish-Indian Interactions in Sixteenth-Century Florida and Hispaniola," in *Cultures in Contact: The Impact of European Contacts on Native American Cultural Institutions, AD 1000–1800*, ed. William W. Fitzhugh (Washington, D.C.: Smithsonian Institution Press, 1985), 291, notes 1,168 Apalachee killed and 4,325 captured or enslaved, figures that exaggerate the number of deaths.

17. Bushnell, "Patricio de Hinachuba," 11–14.

18. Hann, *Apalachee*, 280. The French commented on the religious knowledge and nature of these refugees and how they dressed and, for the women, wore their hair in the Spanish style, details that suggest their abandonment of the Spaniards was not because of cultural rejection. See James W. Covington, "Apalachee Indians, 1704–1763," *FHQ* 50 (1972), 223. Beside the Apalachee, some Escambe, Chacato, and Yamassee went west, perhaps in part at Bienville's invitation.

19. Hann, *Apalachee*, 280. This declaration was made before the decision to abandon San Luís for Mobile.

20. This line of thought seems to have begun with Lanning, *Spanish Missions*, 226 and 281, n. 72, and was elaborated by Charles W. Arnade, "The Failure of Spanish Florida," *The Americas* 16 (1980), 277–81. Both suggest the attractions of English materialism and freedom seduced the Indians away from the discipline and labor demands of the missions. Loucks, "Political and Economic Interactions," 8–9, 11, 72, argues that ordinary Indians (but not the caciques) found the system contrary to their expectations and needs to the point that "the political and economic 'license' simply expired, there was no longer a strong interest in *both* [her stress] parties to continue the system, nor were they able to do so" (p. 72). Bushnell, *Situado and Sabana*, 145, 150, 161, elaborates

on these ideas. Hann, *Apalachee*, 280, stresses that by 1704 the majority of the Apalachee were "demoralized and disillusioned" with the Spaniards because of the military disasters and Spanish failure to provide help. Matter, "Missions in Defense," 36, takes a structuralist approach and blames the friars for opposing Spanish settlement and the military development of the Indians.

21. I thus disagree with Loucks that the Spanish–Indian relationship was one of equals, except possibly at the very beginning, while following her ideas about Indian expectations of the relationship. Cf. Loucks, "Political and Economic Interactions," 8–9.

22. For 1704, see John E. Worth, *The Timucuan Chiefdoms of Spanish Florida*, 2 vols. (Gainesville: University Press of Florida, 1998), 2:145–46; for 1705, Hann, *History of Timucua*, 298–300, and Bushnell, "Patricio de Hinachuba," 15–16.

23. Hann, *History of Timucuans*, 300–302; Worth, *Timucuan Chiefdoms*, 2:146; Bushnell, *Situado and Sabana*, 193. See also John M. Goggin, "Fort Pupo: A Spanish Frontier Outpost," *FHQ* 30 (1951), 145. The Caciques had wanted to stay at Santa Fe and San Francisco until after the maize harvest.

24. Hann, *History of Timucuan*, 301.

25. James G. Johnson, "The International Contest for the Colonial Southeast, 1566–1763" (Ph.D. dissertation, University of California at Berkeley, 1924), 136–38.

26. J. Leitch Wright, Jr., *Anglo-Spanish Rivalry in North America* (Athens: University of Georgia Press, 1971), 66–67; Crane, *Southern Frontier*, 86–87; John J. TePaske, *The Governorship of Spanish Florida, 1700–1763* (Durham: Duke University Press, 1964), 117–120; Bushnell, *Situado and Sabana*, 194; Marchena, "Guarniciones," 98.

27. Crane, *Southern Frontier*, 88–89 (1707) and 89–94 (1708). Nairne also proposed English settlement in Apalachee, which he said was the best land in the Southeast and had herds of wild horses and cattle left behind when the missions were destroyed.

28. Wright, *The Only Land They Knew*, 147, from Corcoles to SM, 14 Jan. 1708.

29. Crane, *Southern Frontier*, 81 (raid of 1708); Wilfred T. Neill, "An Indian and Spanish Site on Tampa Bay, Florida," *Florida Anthropologist* 21 (1968), 112, and Crane, *Southern Frontier* 81 (Tocobaga); Gillespe, "Juan de Ayala," 99–100.

30. Hann, *History of Timucuans*, 305–306.

31. Gillaspie, "Juan de Ayala," 99–100, 103–105; TePaske, *Governorship*, 82–93. A hurricane in 1707 flooded the town and destroyed the houses that had been rebuilt (Hann, *History of Timucua*, 304). Some 40,000 pesos of reconstruction money was misappropriated (TePaske, *Governorship*, 92–93).

32. Wright, *The Only Land They Knew*, 123.

33. The five peoples were the Yamassee in ten villages, the Apalatchi-colas (Appalachicolas) in two, the Apalachee in four, the Savanna in three, and the Yuchi in two villages. Alan R. Calmes, "Indian Cultural Traditions and European Conquest of the Georgia–South Carolina Coastal Plain, 3000 BC–1733 AD: A Combined Archaeological and His-torical Investigation" (Ph.D. dissertation, University of South Carolina, 1968), 86–87; Crane, *Southern Frontier*, 162–67, and Timothy Silver, *A New Face on the Countryside: Indians, Colonists, and Slaves in South Atlantic Forests, 1500–1800* (New York: Cambridge University Press, 1990), 92, and Wright, *The Only Land They Knew*, 122–25.

34. Wright, *The Only Land They Knew*, 123–25; Johnson, "Interna-tional Contest," 150–153.

35. For the Yamassee: James W. Covington, "The Yamassee Indians in Florida, 1715–1763," *Florida Anthropologist* 23 (1970), 121; Wright, *The Only Land They Knew*, 122, and Bushnell, *Situado and Sabana*, 195; for the others: Johnson, "International Context," 150–54, and Calmes, "Indian Cultural Traditions," 99, noting names on the 1722 Barnwell Map. The Santee and Congaree were enslaved or killed.

36. Manuel Serrano y Sanz, ed., *Documentos históricos de la Florida y la Luisiana, Siglos XVI al XVIII* (Madrid: V. Suarez, 1912), 238–40, Gregorio de Salinas Barona to Sergeant Major Juan de Ayala, Pensa-cola, 24 Jul. 1717; Herbert E. Bolton and Mary Ross, *The Debatable Land* (Berkeley: University of California Press, 1925), 64–65; Crane, *Southern Frontier*, 180–85.

37. Serrano y Sanz, *Documentos*, 239, 240–41, Salinas Varona to Ay-ala, Pensacola, 24 Jul. 1717 and 9 Sept. 1717 (respectively), naming chiefs of the Talesis, Tequipaches, Aleposes, and a son of the cacique of Talesis among the seven who went; see also Bolton and Ross, *Debatable Land*, 65; Crane, *Southern Frontier*, 256 (Fort Toulouse).

38. Serrano y Sanz, *Documentos*, 238, Salinas de Barona to Ayala, Pensacola, 24 Jul. 1717 (a St. Augustine report of the first visit?); John T. Lanning, *The Diplomatic History of Georgia: A Study of the Epoch of Jenkins Ear* (Chapel Hill: University of North Carolina Press, 1936), 30–31, and *Spanish Missions*, 188–89; Crane, *Southern Frontier*, 256–58.

39. Herbert E. Bolton, "Spanish Resistance to Carolina Traders in Western Georgia (1680–1704)," *Georgia Historical Quarterly* 9 (1925), 129, and Bolton and Ross, *Debatable Land*, 66; Crane, *Southern Fron-tier*, 259.

40. Serrano y Sanz, *Documentos*, 227–35, Peña to Ayala, Sabacola, 20 Sept. 1717; Juan Marchena Fernández and Felipe del Pozo Redondo, "La emigración canaria a la Florida oriental Española (1600–1621), in Coloquio de Historia Canario-Americana, 9th Spain, 1990, *Actas*, 2 vols. (Las Palmas: Ediciones del Excelentísimo Cabildo Insular de Gran Canaria, 1992), 1:540; Serrano y Sanz, *Documentos*, 242, Salinas

Varona to Ayala, Pensacola, 9 Sept. 1717, endorsing the 50 old soldiers
for the province of "Apalachicola"; Peña said the fort would be at St.
Marks. Ibid., 235–36, Peña to Ayala, Sabacola, 20 Sept. 1717. See also
Clifton Paisley, *The Red Hills of Florida, 1528–1865* (Tuscaloosa: University of Alabama Press, 1989), 35. As Sergeant Major, Ayala became
acting governor in 1716 when Pedro de Olivera y Fullana died in office.
He held the office for nearly two years.

41. Mark F. Boyd, "The Fortifications of San Marcos de Apalache,"
FHQ 15 (1936), 8–9; Paisley, *Red Hills*, 35.

42. Covington, "Yamasee Indians," 122 (raids; by 1721 over two hundred Black slaves had been seized from the English); Crane, *Southern Frontier*, 172, 189; Calmes, "Indian Cultural Traditions," 146–51; Johnson, "International Context," 154 (for Savannah Town, one of the up-country forts).

43. Kenneth Coleman, "The Southern Frontier: Georgia's Founding
and the Expansion of South Carolina," *Georgia Historical Quarterly*
56 (1972), 165, for proposals; Crane, *Southern Frontier*, 264, n. 26, re
the Huspaw; for Azilia see Kenneth Coleman, *Colonial Georgia: A History* (New York: Scribner & Son, 1976), 8–9, and Lanning, *Diplomatic
History*, 8–10, and Crane, *Southern Frontier*, 210–14. Montgomery's father had been a supporter of Lord Cardross's Santa Elena colony.

44. Crane, *Southern Frontier*, 264; James W. Covington, "Some Observations Concerning the Florida Carolina Indian Slave Trade," *Florida Anthropologist* 20 (1967), 15–16, somewhat expanded in his "Yamasee Indians," 122–23. Wright, *The Only Land They Knew*, 144, gives
different details.

45. Verne E. Chatelain, *The Defenses of Spanish Florida, 1565 to 1763*
(Washington, D.C.: Carnegie Institution of Washington, 1941), 85–86.
The Crown authorized the expenditure by decree of 8 Apr. 1721, *on condition* that the church and convent had been rebuilt, a condition Benavides ignored because his officers' junta agreed that defense was more
important. See TePaske, *Governorship*, 92–93, for a history of these
funds.

46. Coleman, *Colonial Georgia*, 9–10; Crane, *Southern Frontier*,
229–33; Lanning, *Diplomatic History*, 10–11.

47. Crane, *Southern Frontier*, 264–66; Bushnell, *Situado and Sabana*, 195–96. English-supported Cherokee hostility toward the Upper
Creek kept them firmly allied to the Carolinians (Crane, *Southern Frontier*, 268).

48. Bolton and Ross, *Debatable Land*, 67–68; Calmes, "Indian Cultural Traditions," 114; Crane, *Southern Frontier*, 267; Covington, "Yamasee Indians," 122; Lanning, *Spanish Missions*, 190.

49. Bushnell, *Situado and Sabana*, 196; Covington, "Yamasee Indians," 123.

50. Cristobal Figuero del Campo, *Misiones franciscanas en la Florida* (Madrid: Comisión Episcopal del V. Centenario, 1992), 165–66; see also Hann, *History of Timucua*, 314–15; Bushnell, *Situado and Sabana*, 196–98, lists the pagan peoples more specifically.

51. Bushnell, *Situado and Sabana*, 196; Crane, *Southern Frontier*, 245, 269.

52. Crane, *Southern Frontier*, 269–72, 248.

53. Henry Dobyns, *Their Number Became Thinned: Native American Population Dynamics in Eastern North America* (Knoxville: University of Tennessee Press, 1983), 283–84, and Robert L. Kapitzke, "The Secular Clergy in St. Augustine during the First Spanish Period, 1565–1763" (M.A. thesis, University of Florida, 1991), 37, noting that the governor said 166 of 1,101 mission Indians died. Cf. Hann, *History of Timucua*, 308–17, passim, and Covington, "Yamasee Indians," 124–25, which suggest a much higher death rate; Crane, *Southern Frontier*, 247, and Covington, "Yamasee Indians," 124 (raids); Crane, *Southern Frontier*, 249–51, and Lanning, *Diplomatic History*, 31 (Palmer raid and consequences). On the western frontier, at least one English trader attempted to win over the Yamassee among the Lower Creek in 1727 (Crane, *Southern Frontier*, 264, n. 26). Benavides is noted in Covington, "Yamasee Indians," 124–25.

54. Crane, *Southern Frontier*, 239–46. Serrano y Sanz, *Documentos*, 243–60, is the text of various documents from the 1725 Spanish visit to Charleston. Lanning, *Diplomatic History*, 12–27, follows Crane's account.

55. Lanning, *Diplomatic History*, 27.

56. AGI, SD 2584 (Stetson), Enclosure no. 14 with Gov. Montiano to SM, 14 Aug. 1739.

57. Crane, *Southern Frontier*, 294; Louis DeVorsey, Jr., "Indian Boundaries in Colonial Georgia," *Georgia Historical Quarterly* 54 (1970), 65. Crane, *Southern Frontier*, 282–95, discusses the background of this proposed use of townships, as does Coleman, "The Southern Frontier," 163–74. Old Style (OS) or the English date according to the Julian Calendar was then eleven days behind the Gregorian Calendar used by the Spaniards and ourselves.

58. Bolton and Ross, *Debatable Land*, 72–74.

59. Lanning, *Diplomatic History*, 50, 59–64, 221, and "Don Miguel Wall and the Spanish Attempt against the Existence of Carolina and Georgia," *North Carolina Historical Review* 10 (1933), 186–213; Johnson, "International Contest," 195 (census of 1734); Hann, *History of Timucua*, 321 (1736); Bushnell, *Situado and Sabana*, 203; Goggin, "Fort Pupo," 149. See also Trevor R. Reese, "Georgia in Anglo-Spanish Diplomacy, 1736–1739," *William and Mary Quarterly*, 3rd Series, 15 (1958), 168–90.

60. Arredondo to Governor of Cuba, 22 Jan. 1737, quoted in Chatelain, *Defenses*, 89.

61. AGI, SD 2584 (Stetson), Certification by Capt. Luis Rodrigo de
Ortega, 27 Nov. 1736, as enclosure no. 15, Gov. Montiano to King, 14
Aug. 1739; Lanning, *Diplomatic History*, 45–49, 50, 59–64; Wright,
Anglo-Spanish Rivalry, 81–82. Johnson, "International Contest," 194–
96, notes the report that one Thomas Bacon served as a Spanish spy in
the Georgia expedition and the information the Spanish ambassador at
London gathered on it.

62. Chatelain, *Defenses*, 82–90; AGI, Mapas y Planos, Florida y Luisiana, no. 40, Antonio de Arredondo, "Plan de la Ciudad de San Agustín
de la Florida . . . ," plate 10 in Chatelain, *Defenses;* Wright, *Anglo-
Spanish Rivalry*, 82–83. Bushnell, *Situado and Sabana*, 202, 204.

63. Lanning, *Diplomatic History*, 75–77, and Joyce E. Harmon, *Trade
and Privateering in Spanish Florida, 1732–1763* (St. Augustine, Fla.: St.
Augustine Historical Society, 1969), 11, on the plan; *Collections of the
Georgia Historical Society*, 7, pt. 1 (Savannah: Georgia Historical Society (Savannah Morning News), 1909), 12, 13, Governor of Florida to
Governor of Cuba, no. 17, no. 18, 3 and 4 Feb. 1738, regarding supply;
Marchena, "Guarniciones," 98–99, and TePaske, *Governorship*, 95,
135–38, on reinforcement. Juan Ignacio Arnaud Rabinal et al., "Estructura, composición y comportamentos de la familia rural en Florida,
1600–1763" (MS del Equipo Florida, Universidad de Sevilla, 1992; Copy
at P. K. Yonge Library of Florida History, University of Florida) 14,
notes the effects on St. Augustine's female population.

64. Hann, *History of Timucuans*, 316 (census); William C. Sturtevant,
"Spanish-Indian Relations in Southeastern North America," *Ethnohistory* 9 (1962), 71 (Creeks); Chatelain, *Defenses*, 161, n. 24 (slaves).
The Spanish did free fugitive slaves at St. Augustine that spring,
using a decree of 29 Oct. 1733. This replaced a policy of "selling"
them to local residents. Jane Landers, "Spanish Sanctuary: Fugitives in Florida," *FHQ* 62 (1984), 300–301, and Wilbur H. Siebert,
"Slavery and White Servitude in East Florida, 1726–1776," *FHQ* 10
(1931), 3.

65. *Collections of Georgia Historical Society*, 7, pt. 1 (1909), 12–13, 19,
29–30, 30–31, respectively, Gov. of Fla. to Gov. of Cuba, nos. 17–18, 3–4
Feb. 1738 (mission of Juan Jacinto Rodriguez); no. 4, 3 June 1738 (Edward Bullard visit to St. Augustine); no. 133, 2 Apr. 1739, and no. 151,
date? 1739 (exchange of delegations regarding fugitive slaves), Serrano
y Sanz, *Documentos*, 260–64, "Relación del yndio Juan Ignacio de los
Reyes," 30 Aug. 1738 (British forts, knowledge of St. Augustine, and
plan of attack, as used in 1740).

66. *Collections of the Georgia Historical Society*, 7, pt. 1 (1909), 20,
Gov. of Fla. to Gov. of Cuba, no. 57, 17 June 1738; Boyd, "Fortifications
of San Marcos," 9–11. This revival began in 1732, when one Carlos
Blondeau (evidently a Frenchman) proposed to set up a town to be
called "La Tama." Governor Benavides suggested that two fifty-man

infantry companies and two one-hundred-man dragoon companies be posted to San Marcos and the proposed new settlement. Gov. Moral Sánchez endorsed using Canary Islanders. Offered free passage and start-up support, Gallicians refused to go. The Havana Company, created in 1740, was then given the task of transporting volunteers from the Canary Islands but only a few arrived at St. Augustine during the 1740s. TePaske, *Governorship*, 87–88; Marchena and Pozo Redondo, "Emigración canaria," 1:140.

67. Goggin, "Fort Pupo," 147–50; *Collections of Georgia Historical Society* 7, pt. 1 (1909), 27, Gov. of Fla. to Gov. of Cuba, no. 76, 31 Aug. 1738 (re supply); Landers, *Black Society in Spanish Florida* (Urbana: University of Illinois Press, 1999), 28–30; Bushnell, *Situado and Sabana*, 204; Siebert, "Slavery," 3–4.

68. Lanning, *Diplomatic History*, 147–49, 161–68; AGI, SD 2593 (Stetson), Gov. Montiano to SM, 20 Aug. 1739, with enclosures. This has recently been published in translation as John E. Worth, ed., *The Struggle for the Georgia Coast: An Eighteenth-Century Spanish Retrospective on Guale and Mocama* (New York: American Museum of Natural History; Athens: distributed by the University of Georgia Press, 1995). Bolton and Ross, *Debatable Land*, 81, for the "neutral ground" proposal.

69. H. B. Fant, "The Indian Trade Policy of the Trustees for Establishing the Colony of Georgia in America," *Georgia Historical Quarterly* 15 (1931), 218–19; Lanning, *Diplomatic History*, 221–22; Johnson, "International Contest," 189.

70. Harmon, "Trade and Privateering," 34; Johnson, "International Contest," 209; Lanning, *Diplomatic History*, 221–22.

71. Goggin, "Fort Pupo," 151–55; *Collections of the Georgia Historical Society* 7, pt. 1 (1909), 32–62, are the Spanish governor's reports on the attack and siege while John T. Lanning, *The St. Augustine Expedition of 1740: A Report to the South Carolina General Assembly* (Columbia: South Carolina Archives Department, 1954), gives one of several British reports; See also Lanning, *Diplomatic History*, 222–26, and Wright, *Anglo-Spanish Rivalry*, 90. In March a review found 613 soldiers at St. Augustine, including fifty armed Indians and the forty free persons of color. Of these only 356 were considered fit for duty.

72. Harmon, "Trade and Privateering," 34–36; Wright, *Anglo-Spanish Rivalry*, 93–94.

73. *Collections of the Georgia Historical Society* 7, pt. 3 (Savannah: Savannah Morning News, 1913), 8–14, 21–28, 50–51, 59, 65–67, 73, 75, 89, 93–94; Bolton and Ross, *Debatable Land*, 92–96, and Wright, *Anglo-Spanish Rivalry*, 95–97, are brief accounts. Jane Landers, *Black Society*, 38, notes that about one-third of the troops were of African ancestry. For a map, see Spain, Ejército, Servicio Geográfico, *Carto-*

grafía de Ultramar, 4 vols. in 8 (Madrid: Imprenta de Servicio Geográfico del Ejército, 1949–57), vol. 2, plate 63, "Demonstración de la gloriosa entrada de los navíos y tropas de SM en el puerto de Gualquini, que los Yngleses llamavan Federico." In further justification of this decision, Governor Montiano noted that he had supplies to last only to 30 August, the growing danger of tropical storms, and the anxiety of the governor of Cuba to have his troops back. The Spaniards had destroyed some English property, had attained the "gallant" forcing of the entrance to the bay, and had shown the English that they could bring significant if not decisive force to bear on Georgia.

74. Lanning, *Diplomatic History,* 185–87; Chatelain, *Defenses,* 92; Bolton and Ross, *Debatable Land,* 90–91, 98; *Colonial Records of the State of Georgia,* 32+ vols. (Atlanta: C. P. Byrd and others, 1904–), 27:7–8, William Horton to Rev. Thomas Bosomworth, Frederica, 15 Sept. 1744 (a fight on the St. Johns).

75. Arredondo's "Mapa de la costa de la Florida . . ." is AGI, Mapas y Planos, Florida y Luisiana, no. 45, reproduced in William P. Cummings, *The Southeast in Early Maps,* 3rd ed., Revised and Enlarged by Louis de Vorsey, Jr. (Chapel Hill: University of North Carolina Press, 1998), plate 56, and in Spain, Ejército, Servicio Geográfico, *Cartografía de Ultramar,* vol. 2, plate 50. His work is *Arredondo's Historical Proof of Spain's Title to Georgia,* ed. Herbert E. Bolton (Berkeley: University of California Press, 1925).

76. Harmon, *Trade and Privateering,* 22–24; J. Carver Harris, ed., "The Memorial of William Walton of the City of New York, Merchant," *El Escribano* 3 (1966), 14, 19–20. Harmon (p. 21) shows that the focus of this trade shifted from Charleston to New York in 1736.

77. TePaske, *Governorship,* 88–89; Bushnell, *Situado and Sabana,* 202–203, summarizing depositions taken by Arredondo, in particular that of Fr. Juan de la Via. Gov. Moral Sánchez wanted the *situado* paid in cash, which would have cut out all Spanish merchants except the few foolish enough to carry goods to St. Augustine.

78. Harmon, "Trade and Privateering," 34–43; *Collections of the Georgia Historical Society* 7, pt. 1 (1909), 63, Gov. of Fla. to Gov. of Cuba, 28 Jul. 1740 (re trade restrictions); TePaske, *Governorship,* 97–103. An overview of the Havana Company's activities in Florida is José Ventura Reja, "Abastecimiento y poblamiento de la Florida por la Real Compañía de Comercio de la Habana," in Congreso de la Historia de los Estados Unidos, Universidad de la Rabida, 5–9 Julio 1976, *Actas* (Madrid: 1978), 111–29.

79. AGI, SD 848, Gov. Montiano to SM, 15 Apr. 1746, noted in TePaske, *Governorship,* 90, and in Harmon, *Trade and Privateering,* 21; AGI, SD 849, Montiano to SM, 8 Feb. 1744, noted in TePaske, *Governorship,* 89. The coins were to contain silver equal to one-fourth their

face value but be used at full face value in St. Augustine. Montiano was also interested in developing the pitch and tar industries (TePaske, *Governorship*, 106).

80. Juan Ignacio Arnaud Rabinal et al., "Estructura de la población de una sociedad de frontera, La Florida Española, 1600–1763," *Revista Compultense de Historia de América* 17 (1991), 99–100, 105–108, 112, and Theodore G. Corbett, "Population Structure in Hispanic St. Augustine, 1629–1763," *FHQ* 54 (1976), 269, 275–76, 282.

81. Bushnell, *Situado and Sabana*, 200–201; Hann, *History of Timucua*, 321–22; Kapiztke, "Secular Clergy in St. Augustine," 52–53; TePaske, *Governorship*, 167, from Bishop to Crown, 1 Oct. 1735 and 29 Apr. 1736, AGI, SD 2584 and SD 864, respectively.

82. Kapitzke, "Secular Clergy," 112; cf. Bushnell, *Situado and Sabana*, 205.

83. Bushnell, *Situado and Sabana*, 205, for 1736; Covington, "Yamasee Indians in Florida," 125, for 1742; Hann, *History of Timucua*, 322–23, for 1752.

84. James W. Covington, *The Seminoles of Florida* (Gainesville: University Press of Florida, 1993), 10–12; Sturtevant, "Spanish-Indian Relations," 71–72.

85. Chatelain, *Defenses*, 93 (Mosa); Mary B. Graff, "Fort Picolata," *Papers of the Jacksonville Historical Society* 1 (1947), 54, 56–57; Boyd, "Fortifications of San Marcos," 1–13.

86. Marchena, "Guarniciones," 99, 100–102.

87. Harmon, *Trade and Privateering*, 52; TePaske, *Governorship*, 105–107; Susan L. Pickman, "Life on the Spanish-American Colonial Frontier: A Study in the Social and Economic History of Mid-Eighteenth-Century St. Augustine, Florida" (Ph.D.dissertation, University of New York at Stoney Brook, 1980), 69–70, lists some of the merchants who billed the government for supplies in 1750–54.

88. Harris, "Memorial of William Walton," 14–19; Pickman, "Life," 56–57, 76–77, 130–34; Harmon, *Trade and Privateering*, 46–47, 56–57.

89. Pickman, "Life," 139–45. Pickman's study shows that the official cost of food rose about 28 percent, 1754–1758.

90. Siebert, "Slavery," 4–5; DeVorsey, "Indian Boundaries," 71 (population of Georgia); *Colonial Records of Georgia*, 27:48–49, "Memorial and representation . . . from some freeholders," Darien, 18 Apr. 1752.

91. Bolton and Ross, *Debatable Land*, 101–105; Charles L. Mowat, *East Florida as a British Province, 1763–1784* (Berkeley: University of California, 1943), 4–5; Lanning, *Diplomatic History*, 234.

92. Juan Joseph Solana Report on the Condition of St. Augustine, 1760, trans. Staff of Historic St. Augustine Preservation Board in *America's Ancient City, Spanish St. Augustine, 1565–1763*, ed. Kathleen A. Deagan (New York: Garland Publishing, 1991), 545–56. Solana's evidence was intended to paint the governor, Lucas Fernando de Palacio

y Valenzuela, in the worst possible light. Cited hereafter as "Solana Report."

93. Marchena and Pozo Redondo, "Emigración," 36–59; Arnaud Rabinal et al., "Estructura, composición, y comportamento . . . ," 11, 16–17; "Solana Report," 575–76.

94. *Colonial Records of Georgia* 28, pt. 1, 100, Henry Ellis to William Pitt, Georgia, 10 Dec. 1757.

95. Harmon, *Trade and Privateering*, 72–74.

96. Robert L. Gold, *Borderlands Empires in Transition: The Triple-Nation Transfer of Florida* (Carbondale: University of Southern Illinois Press, 1969), 156–57.

97. Treaty of Paris, Article 20, in Frances G. Davenport, ed., *European Treaties Bearing on the History of the United States and Its Dependencies*, 4 vols. (Washington, D.C.: Carnegie Institution of Washington, 1917–37), 4:96; Mowat, *East Florida*, 6–7.

98. Wilbur H. Siebert, "The Departure of the Spaniards and Other Groups from East Florida, 1763–64," *FHQ* 19 (1940), 146; Arnaud Rabinal et al., "Estructura, composición, etc.," 10; Jane Landers, "Black Society in Spanish St. Augustine, 1784–1821" (Ph.D. dissertation, University of Florida, 1988), 33–34. For ownership, see Pickman, "Life," 164–76.

99. Pickman, "Life," 184–88, from an analysis of the De La Puente maps.

100. For the housing and taverns, "Solana Report," 544–59, 564, 566–67, 570.

101. "Solana Report," 545–69. *Colonial Records of Georgia,* 28, pt. 2:191, Copy of James Wright's answers to question 14 from the Board of Trade, 15 Feb. 1763.

102. "Solana Report," 564–65; Sturtevant, "Spanish-Indian Relations," 70; see also Robert L. Gold, "The Settlement of the East Florida Spaniards in Cuba, 1763–1766," *FHQ* 42 (1964), 216–31, and "The Settlement of the Pensacola Indians in New Spain, 1763–1770," *Hispanic American Historical Review* 45 (1965), 657–76. There is some uncertainty as to how many Indians were evacuated from St. Augustine. Eighty-three is the most commonly given figure, but I have seen seventy-nine, eighty-six, and eighty-nine.

103. Covington, *Seminoles*, 13–17; Howard F. Cline, *Florida Indians II: Provisional Historical Gazeteer with Locational Notes on Florida Colonial Communities* (New York: Garland Publishing, 1974), map 4 and Table 2. Spain, Ejército, Servicio Geográfico, *Cartografía de Ultramar,* vol 2, plate 53, Juan Joseph Elixio de la Puente, "Nueva descripción de la costa oriental y septentrional de las Provincias de la Florida," 1768, shows areas of cultivation at the Flint–Chattahoochee junction but no settlement in the interior of the peninsula.

104. If the theological assumptions of the Spaniards were correct, sev-

eral tens of thousands of Indian souls had been saved and the kings of Spain had earned good deeds to help offset the sins they committed. For some Spaniards of the time these were not unimportant achievements and fully justified the expense.

9. New Tidewater Frontiers, 1763–1790

1. Published in 1775. Facsimile Reproduction of the 1775 Edition with Introduction by Rembert W. Patrick (Gainesville: University of Florida Press, 1962).

2. Facsimile Reproduction of the 1823 Edition with an Introduction and Index by John H. Moore (Gainesville: University Presses of Florida, 1977).

3. Maps published in 1763 showed extensive waterways, especially in the southern half of the peninsula. Thomas Jeffreys, "Florida from the Latest Authorities," in William Roberts, *An Account of the First Discovery and Natural History of Florida* (London: Printed for T. Jeffreys, 1763); J. Gibson, "A Map of the New Governments of East and West Florida," *The Gentleman's Magazine and Historical Chronicle* 33 (Nov. 1763).

4. Charles L. Mowat, "The First Campaign of Publicity for Florida," *Mississippi Valley Historical Review* 30, no. 3 (Dec. 1943), 359–76, is a detailed review of this literature. See also Charles L. Mowat, *East Florida as a British Province, 1763–1784* (Berkeley: University of California Press, 1943), 6–7; Robert L. Gold, *Borderland Empires in Transition: The Triple-Nation Transfer of Florida* (Carbondale: University of Southern Illinois Press, 1969), 16–17.

5. Mowat, *East Florida*, 11–12; Gold, *Borderland Empires*, 118, 126–27. Oglethorpe based his claim on the original Carolina charter of 1660, that set 29 degrees North as its southern boundary. For the agreements of the 1740s see Herbert E. Bolton and Mary Ross, *The Debatable Land* (Berkeley: University of California Press, 1925).

6. Gold, *Borderland Empires*, 18, 20, 87; Mowat, *East Florida*, 7. Gold has Hedges arriving on the 21st. Major Francis Ogilvie and the 9th Regiment arrived on 30 Jul. 1763 and assumed command.

7. Gold, *Borderland Empires*, 66–76 and Table 4, p. 67. Twenty percent of the evacuees had died within two years and most ended up in poverty because the government failed to provide resettlement help. A detailed study of the Floridano communities in Cuba is Jane Landers, "An Eighteenth-Century Community in Exile: The *Floridanos* in Cuba," *New West Indian Guide* [Netherlands] 70 (1996), 39–58. For the Apalachee evacuations see Gold, *Borderland Empires*, 93–99. See also Maynard Geiger, "The Settlement of East Florida Spaniards in Cuba, 1763–1766," *FHQ* 42 (1964), 216–31.

8. Gold, *Borderland Empires*, 23–28, 90–93.

9. Gold, *Borderland Empires*, 118–22; Mowat, *East Florida*, 54–56. The grantees had to clear or otherwise develop three of every fifty acres within three years. If they did so and documented the fact in court, they could obtain a permanent title.

10. Great Britain, Public Record Office, *Journal of the Commissioners for Trade and Plantations*, 14 vols. (London: H. M. Stationery Office, 1920–1938), 12:38–39; Gold, *Borderland Empires*, 27–28, 36–54. Fish, who held 204 properties in St. Augustine, may have lost 1,969 pesos on his investment there. The value of his other holdings is not known. Gordon lobbied in London for £15,000 in compensation for his claims. He even proposed a method for collecting the quitrents (to be used to pay his claim), but died without receiving a penny. Charles L. Mowat, "The Land Policy in British East Florida," *Agricultural History* 14 (1940), 75.

11. Great Britain, Public Record Office, *Crown Collection of Maps of North America*, Series III, Colonial Office 700: North American Colonies, Florida, no. 7, which is based on no. 57 and no. 58, Spanish originals. The Spanish original (no. 58) names the heirs of Tomás Menéndez Marqués and his son, the Contador Francisco Menéndez Marqués, as owners of the three interior grants, shown on no. 7 without owners. The other Spanish map (no. 57) lists three other properties with owners, but evidently Gordon was not their agent. *Journal of Commissioners* 12:23–24, says there were one thousand square leagues, while ibid., 218, lists the total claimed at nearly six million acres. On 21 Nov. 1765, the Commissioners told agents for Fish and Gordon that this was an extravagant claim; the agents then asked for the actual costs of their principals and for 100,000 acres within the areas claimed. Eventually the matter went to trial in 1767. Ibid., 225, 228, 333, 336, 373.

12. *Journal of Commissioners*, 12:225.

13. Mowat, *East Florida*, 21–23; James W. Covington, *The Seminoles of Florida* (Gainesville: University Press of Florida, 1993), 15–17; Gold, *Borderland Empires*, 178–82. Grant reported expenses with this congress of £380 16 sh 8.5 pence (*Journal of Commissioners*, 12:268).

14. The murders took place on 18 Sept., apparently in revenge for a whipping some Indians had received from Englishmen who thought they had stolen a horse. See *Colonial Records of the State of Georgia*, 32 vols. (Atlanta: C. P. Byrd and others, 1904–1989), 28, pt. 2:243–44, James Wright to the Board of Trade, Savannah, 24 Oct. 1767, and Mowat, *East Florida*, 22–24. In Dec. 1768, Governor Grant executed two Anglo frontiersmen for the murder of an Indian youth. The boy's father and other Indians were witnesses.

15. Excavations of the site have revealed twenty-four types of ceramics, including five oriental ones, mute evidence of the reach of En-

gland's trade. Kenneth E. Lewis, Jr., "History and Archaeology of Spalding's Lower Store (Pu-23), Putnam County, Florida" (M.A. thesis, University of Florida, 1969), passim, and esp. 146–85.

16. Governor Grant summarized his Indian policy (1764–1771) as kindly treatment, reliance on the Indians' honesty and sense of justice, negotiation rather than threats or force, and gift giving, preferably at a conference where the gifts could reinforce status distinctions among the Indians. Mowat, *East Florida*, 21.

17. John K. Mahon and Brent R. Weisman, "Florida's Seminole and Miccosukee Peoples," in *The New History of Florida*, ed. Michael Gannon (Gainesville: University Press of Florida, 1996), 188–89; James W. Covington, "Trade Relations between Southwestern Florida and Cuba, 1600–1840," *FHQ* 38 (1959), 116–17, and Angel Sanz Tapiá, "Relaciones entre Cuba y los Indios de la Florida oriental durante el dominio Inglés (1763–1783)," in *La Influencia de España en el Caribe, La Florida, y la Luisiana, 1500–1800* (Madrid: Instituto de Cooperación IberoAmericana, 1983), 286–87, 292–97; Howard Cline, *Florida Indians II: Provisional Historical Gazeteer with Locational Notes on Florida Colonial Communities* (New York: Garland Publishing, 1974), Map 5 and Table 2. I have followed Cline's spellings, but the reader should be aware that there are many variants for most of the names. For St. Marks, see Mark F. Boyd, "The Fortifications of San Marcos de Apalachee," *FHQ* 15 (1936), 13–15, and Clifton Paisley, *The Red Hills of Florida, 1528–1865* (Tuscaloosa: University of Alabama Press, 1989), 36. For the Apalachee group, see Paisley, ibid., 36–40.

18. Mahon and Weisman, "Florida's Seminole and Miccosukee," 188–89; Joel W. Martin, "Indians and the English Trade," 319, and n. 58.

19. Romans, *Concise History*, 16, describes their technique of burning the wire grass.

20. James Grant Forbes, *Sketches, Historical and Topographical of the Floridas*, facsimile ed. (Gainesville: University of Florida Press, 1964), 186–87, "Extract from Governor Grant's Proclamation, dated St. Augustine, 7th Oct., 1763 [*sic*, 1764]." See Daniel L. Schafer, "'Yellow Silk Ferret Tied Round Their Wrists': African Americans in British East Florida, 1763–1784," in *The African American Heritage of Florida*, ed. David R. Colburn and Jane L. Landers (Gainesville: University Press of Florida, 1995), 71–76, for more on Grant's advice to prospective planters.

21. Wilbur H. Siebert, *Loyalists in East Florida, 1774–1785: The Most Important Documents Pertaining Thereto . . .* , 2 vols. (Deland: Florida State Historical Society, 1929), 2:100, testimony of Col. James Moncrief regarding hammock lands cleared on the Tomoka River near New Smyrna.

22. Mowat, *East Florida*, 61: Table, "Land Grants in East Florida,

1765–1775." The Privy Council issued 242 grants for about 2.9 million acres, but only 114 were presented at St. Augustine (Gold, *Borderland Empires*, 120).

23. Siebert, *Loyalists*, 1:49.

24. Siebert, *Loyalists*, 2:164–68.

25. Siebert, *Loyalists*, 2:150–53.

26. Marion F. Shambaugh, "The Development of Agriculture in Florida during the Second Spanish Period" (M.A. thesis, University of Florida, 1953), 10.

27. Daniel L. Schafer, "Plantation Development in British East Florida: A Case Study of the Earl of Egmont," *FHQ* 63 (1984), 175; Mowat, *East Florida*, 61, 63–64, notes eight promoters by name and suggests there were many others. All wanted government subsidies; not all received land grants. Stork, for example, wanted the government to supply a ship.

28. Siebert, *Loyalists*, 2:97–99, 237–50; 191–95; 288–91 respectively. Moultrie was Lieutenant Governor, 1771–1774. Rolle purchased most of the lower plantation from James Penman, who had assembled the land by purchase. Of the upper tract, Rolle purchased 53,000 acres in four blocks; the rest were grants to him.

29. Siebert, *Loyalists*, 2:298–300; 287–97, respectively; the casualty figures are from Romans, *Natural History*, 270. Robin A. Fabel, "British Rule in the Floridas," in *The New History of Florida*, ed. Michael Gannon (Gainesville: University Press of Florida, 1996), 141, says Rolle's people included "London vagrants, beggars, debtors, and prostitutes." Turnbull's Greeks were supposed to know how to cultivate silk and cotton. Schafer, "Plantation Development," 46–49, for Egmont.

30. Romans, *Natural History*, 104, 34.

31. For examples see Siebert, *Loyalists*, 2:112–14, 117 (Dorothy Moore); 2:254–55 (Captain Robert Bisset).

32. Mowat, *East Florida*, 63, "Land Grants in East Florida, 1765–1775."

33. Mowat, *East Florida*, 64, following DeBrahm; and 66, where he tries to estimate the place of origin using 26 pre-1775 grantees who elected to remain under Spanish rule. Fable, "British Rule," 136, notes a report by Governor Grant in a letter of 1771.

34. Romans, *Natural History*, 258–60, 264, 266, 268, 273; see pp. 274–75 for his description of the Alachua–Santa Fe area and its fertile soils and Indian settlements.

35. Daniel L. Schafer, "Everything Carried the Face of Spring: Biscayne Bay in the 1770s," *Tequesta* 44 (1984), 23–31. Lord Dartmouth claimed 100,000 acres; Samuel Touchett and John Augustus Ernest each claimed 20,000 acres.

36. Mowat, *East Florida*, 77–79. Orange exports rose from 21 barrels

in 1764 to 46 barrels, 5.25 casks of juice, and 3 hogsheads of peel in 1768. Francis Philip Fatio, "Description of East Florida," St. Augustine, ca. 18 Mar. 1785, in Joseph B. Lockey, *East Florida, 1783–1785: A File of Documents Assembled, and many of them Translated by Joseph Byrne Lockey*, ed. John W. Caughey (Berkeley: University of California Press, 1949), 479, claims the indigo was close to the best grades from Guatemala but notes the exhaustion of the soils in three to four years. John Ferdinand Smyth Stuart, *A Tour of the United States of America . . .* , 2 vols. (London: Printed for G. Robinson, 1784), 2:35–38, says that Chief Justice Drayton found three plantations south of New Smyrna and five others "deserving of notice" between there and St. Augustine.

37. Mowat, *East Florida*, 76–79; Romans, *Natural History*, 149–53 (naval stores).

38. Elizabeth J. Reitz, "Spanish and British Subsistence Strategies at St. Augustine, Florida, and Frederica, Georgia, between 1565 and 1783" (Ph.D. dissertation, University of Florida, 1979), 156.

39. Mowat, *East Florida*, 157, Table 7, "Place of Departure or Destination of Ships Entering or Clearing St. Augustine, 1764–1772," shows the pattern. Charleston sent an average of 18.875 ships per year and received 21.625, with the surplus north-bound coming mostly from ships arriving at St. Augustine from New York and Pennsylvania. New York and Savannah were poor seconds, with 20 percent or less of Charleston's numbers. For a verbal summary of the trade see ibid., 76–79.

40. James Adair, *The History of the American Indians, Particularly Those Adjoining to the Mississippi, East and West Florida, Georgia, South and North Carolina and Virginia* (1775; reprint, Johnson City, Tenn.: Watauga Press, 1930), 490.

41. Mowat, *East Florida*, 68, 40; Siebert, *Loyalists*, 1:19. Mark F. Boyd, "A Map of a Road from Pensacola . . . to St. Augustine, 1778," *Florida Historical Quarterly* 17 (1938), 15–23; Great Britain, Public Records Office, *Crown Collection*, Catalog no. 54, Series III, plate III–12.

42. Siebert, *Loyalists*, 1:14–15; Mowat, *East Florida*, 88–91, 93–94; J. Leich Wright, Jr., *Florida in the American Revolution* (Gainesville: University of Florida Press, 1975), 24–25. The Indians had raided Spalding's upper store but the differences were patched up at a conference at St. Augustine. Creek, upset by changing trading policies in Georgia, harassed farms along the St. Marys river.

43. Mowat, *East Florida*, 119; Siebert, *Loyalists*, 1:24–30.

44. Wright, *Florida in the American Revolution*, 22.

45. Siebert, *Loyalists*, 1:26, 37. This "fort" was a few miles from the mouth, on the north side.

46. Siebert, *Loyalists*, 1:37, 39. This was similar to the policy the Spaniards had used earlier.

47. Siebert, *Loyalists*, 1:33; Mowat, *East Florida*, 109. For the Rangers see Siebert, 1:38 and Mowat, 110, and Wright, *Florida in the American Revolution*, 108–109. Carole W. Troxler, "Allegiance without Community: East Florida as the Symbol of Loyalist Contract in the South," in *Loyalists and Community in North America*, ed. Robert M. Calhoon, Timothy M. Barnes, and George A. Rawlyk (Westport, Conn.: Greenwood Press, 1994), 125–26, uses them as an example of a group with high internal loyalty but no identification with East Florida. For Ft. Mose, see Wright, *Florida in the American Revolution*, 28.

48. Mowat, *East Florida*, 119–21; Siebert, *Loyalists*, 1:38, 50. See also Wright, *Florida in American Revolution*, 31–44. Elbert's raid caused some men to suggest offering the Americans the province's neutrality in exchange for no future raids (Siebert, *Loyalists*, 1:45–47, and Mowat, *East Florida*, 107, 110). Chief Justice Drayton was the most outspoken in favor of offering neutrality. James Penman, Capt. Robert Bisset, Robert Payne, Andrew Turnbull, Jr., Spencer Man, and Alexander Gray also expressed concern about the adequacy of local defenses. They were among the men consistently critical of Governor Tonyn.

49. Wright, *Florida in the American Revolution*, 106–108, 52–54 (regarding the prisoners). There were 400 Frenchmen in town in Aug. 1778.

50. Sibert, *Loyalists*, 1:51, 57–59, 71–73, 81, 99; Wright, *Florida in the American Revolution*, 54–59, 83, 129–30. The principal effect of the invasion scare of 1781 was that slaves were turned out to work on the town's walls on three occasions.

51. Sanz Tapiá, "Cuba y los Indios de la Florida," 296–98, 302–307; Wright, *Florida in the American Revolution*, 83. The Creek seem to have been mostly interested in trade; their contacts with Savannah and Charleston were disrupted by the war.

52. Troxler, "Allegiance without Community," 124; Siebert, *Loyalists*, 1:52, 61, 67; Wright, *Florida in the American Revolution*, 54–55. The "Scopholites" were named for their leader, Joseph Scophol.

53. Siebert, *Loyalists*, 1:61 (re 7,000) and 1:131 (re 5,000); John R. Dunkle, "Population Change as an Element in the Historical Geography of St. Augustine," *FHQ* 37 (1958), 11 (reported composition of population).

54. Mowat, *East Florida*, 127; Siebert, *Loyalists*, 1:62, 88–89, 96–100 (detailed discussion); Troxler, "Allegiance without Community," 129–30; Fabel, "British Rule," 147. The assembly, made up of many refugees, wanted to follow the custom in Georgia of trying capital cases involving slaves with local juries presided over by Justices of the Peace; the Council wanted such cases tried in the Court of General Sessions, which tried white men. In the end, the lower house prevailed.

55. Mowat, "Land Policy," 76–77, and his *East Florida*, 55–56; Sie-

bert, *Loyalists*, 1:13, 23–24, 49–50, 94–95. Most of the grants made in the early 1780s carried only a two-year exemption from quitrents of ½ pence per acre.

56. Siebert, *Loyalists*, 1:36–37; Wright, *Florida in the American Revolution*, 57. Gold, *Borderland Empires*, 151; Dunkle, "Population Change," 11.

57. Siebert, *Loyalists*, 2:155, 250–59.

58. Wright, *Florida in the American Revolution*, 82; Siebert, *Loyalists*, 2:380 (a payment to Wilkinson and Gordon for establishing St. Marys City). Governor Tonyn unsuccessfully proposed to annex Georgia south of the Altamaha to Florida, citing pre-1740 precedents and Brown's Florida Rangers' "conquest" of the area during the war (Wright, *Florida in the American Revolution*, 82).

59. William M. Jones, "A Late Eighteenth Century Work Camp, St. Johns Bluff, Duval County," *Florida Anthropologist* 26 (1973), 139–42, describes a British era turpentine work camp southeast of the St. Johns Town site.

60. Stanley C. Bond, Jr., "The Development of the Naval Stores Industry in St. Johns County, Florida," *Florida Anthropologist* 40 (1987), 189, from Siebert, *Loyalists*, 1:67–68, 150.

61. Siebert, *Loyalists*, 2:287–97, 367–71.

62. Siebert, *Loyalists*, 1:80–81 and 2:37–45.

63. Mowat, *East Florida*, 136; Siebert, *Loyalists*, 1:106–107, 124, 130–31.

64. William S. Coker and Thomas D. Watson, *Indian Traders of the Southeastern Spanish Borderlands: Panton, Leslie & Company and John Forbes & Company, 1783–1847* (Pensacola: University of West Florida Press, 1986), 50–54.

65. Siebert, *Loyalists*, 1:119.

66. Siebert, *Loyalists*, 1:101–109. The order to evacuate was read to East Florida's assembly on 18 June 1782, but by the end of July had been revoked because of shipping problems. Cruden's activities included a scheme to take Charleston Loyalists to the Gulf Coast to secure it for Great Britain (1782) and overtures to the Spaniards in 1783 for the creation of an autonomous loyalist enclave in northeast Florida. J. Leich Wright, Jr., *Anglo-Spanish Rivalry in North America* (Athens: University of Georgia Press, 1971), 137; *Florida in the American Revolution*, 137.

67. Siebert, *Loyalists*, 1:131 (first report of definitive cession, Dec. 1782); Mowat, *East Florida*, 14. Troxler, "Allegiance without Community," 129–31 (re anger).

68. "St. Johns Town," Jacksonville Historical Society *Papers* 4 (1960), 85–89 (based on Siebert, *Loyalists*, 1:117–18); Mowat, *East Florida*, 126; Siebert, *Loyalists*, 1:110–11 (Graham), 127–28 (Cunningham), 2:16 (the nominal rent), 87, 241–42, 248 (refugees as tenants).

69. José del Rió Cossa, *Descripción de la Florida oriental hecha in 1787*, ed. P. Agustín Barreiro (Madrid: Soc. Geográfica Nacional, 1935), 12, 16.

70. Siebert, *Loyalists*, 1:132–33.

71. Joseph B. Lockey, "Florida Banditti," *FHQ* 24 (1945), 87.

72. Siebert, *Loyalists*, 1:122–24, 137–47; Wright, *Florida in the American Revolution*, 132–33 (mutiny); Covington, *Seminoles*, 20.

73. Covington, *Seminoles*, 19; Wright, *Florida in the American Revolution*, 133–35. See Mark F. Boyd, "Events at Prospect Bluff on the Apalachicola River, 1808–1818: An Introduction with Twelve Letters of Edmund Doyle, Trader," *FHQ* 16 (1937), 57.

74. Lewis, "Spalding's Lower Store," 23, Thomas Nixon's report from St. Augustine, spring 1784.

75. Lockey, *East Florida*, 7–8, 272; Wright, *Florida in the American Revolution*, 135–36; Mowat, *East Florida*, 145 (Proclamations; for their texts see Lockey, *East Florida* 233–35); Lockey, "Florida Banditti," 88–89 (safe conduct). A general overview is Shambaugh, "Development," 46–47.

76. Lockey, *East Florida*, 21–24; Siebert, *Loyalists*, 1:162–64; Jane Landers, *Black Society in Spanish Florida* (Urbana: University of Illinois Press, 1999), 76, and "Spanish Sanctuary, Fugitives in Spanish Florida, 1687–1790," *FHQ* 63 (1984), 296–313. She found 251 declarations of former slaves for 1784–90.

77. Lockey, "Florida Banditti," 88–98; Siebert, *Loyalists*, 1:164–67, 174. The prisoners were in jail by 4 Apr. 1785. For examples of complaints about this lawlessness see Lockey, *East Florida*, 399–410.

78. Petition of Loyalists to Spanish Crown, St. Marys, 28 Oct. 1784, in Lockey, *East Florida*, 301–302, 134 (for discussion of this idea in England in 1783).

79. Covington, *Seminoles*, 20–21; Helen H. Tanner, "The Second Spanish Period Begins," *El Escribano* 25 (1988), 34–35; Wright, *Florida in the American Revolution*, 149–50; Lockey, *East Florida*, 278, Zéspedes to Juan Ignacio de Urriza, 16 Sept. 1784.

80. Siebert, *Loyalists*, 1:170, 175.

81. Paraphrase of Tonyn to Lord Sydney, 10 Aug. 1785 in Siebert, *Loyalists*, 1:175–76; Francis Philip Fatio, "Description of East Florida," St. Augustine, 18 Mar. 1785, in Lockey, *East Florida*, 479–82 (quotation, 481); Zéspedes to Bernardo de Gálvez, 29 Jul. 1785, Lockey, *East Florida*, 571, describes "the state of extreme decadence of this province . . . and a general desolation reigning over the whole province up to the gates of the town and even within. . . ."

82. Lockey, *East Florida*, 306–308 (quotation from 307), Nicolás Grenier's report of 10 Nov. 1784. Zéspedes likened them to nomadic Arabs "distinguished from savages only by their color, language, and the

superiority of their depraved cunning and untrustworthiness." Quotation in Marianne Sherry Johnson, "The Spanish St. Augustine Community, 1784–1795: A Re-evaluation" (M.A. thesis, University of Florida, 1989), 115.

83. Sánchez's widow, María del Carmen Hill, and children claimed at least 3,925 acres in nine grants on the St. Johns River and at Diego Plains. Most dated from 1791–1793, although the original, British-era ranch was confirmed in 1786. At the time of his death he had ten legitimate and eight "natural" children and fifty-two slaves (*SLGF* 5:25–41; see also Landers, *Black Society*, 73, 151–52, 164). Thomas Dunnage, Fatio, and Rivaz and Naville had bought "New Castle" from Robert Harris in 1770. He had obtained 350 acres on a governor's order of 1767. Fatio arrived in 1771 to develop it for the partnership. At the change of flags, Fatio bought out his associates and became a Spanish subject (*SLGF* 3:67–68).

84. Lockey, *East Florida*, 12; ibid., 285–86, Zéspedes to José de Gálvez, no. 25, 20 Oct. 1784 (re Minorcans); Zéspedes to Gálvez, 20 Oct. 1784 enclosed a detailed census of the families then in St. Augustine who had decided to stay or were thinking of doing so (not printed in Lockey, *East Florida*). See Ramón Romero Cabot, "Los últimos años de la soberanía española en la Florida, 1783–1821" (Ph.D. dissertation, Universidad de Sevilla, 1983), 20–22, for details (copy in P. K. Yonge Library of Florida History, University of Florida). It should be noted that these various reports fall during the period of evacuation. They are probably inaccurate. For Leslie see Coker and Watson, *Indian Traders*, 34–36, and Abel Poitrineau, "Demography and the Political Destiny of Florida during the Second Spanish Period," *FHQ* 66 (1988), 425; Poitrineau (p. 423) gives the figures for Xavier Sánchez and mentions a few other owners of slaves such as Joseph Terris who had seventeen on two farms and Brian Langley who had fifteen. Jesse Fish's holdings are based on Siebert, *Loyalists*, 2:276.

85. Iñigo Abad y La Sierra, *Relación de el Descubrimiento, conquista y población de las Provincias y costa de la Florida* (1785), in Manuel Serrano y Sanz, ed., *Documentos históricos de la Florida y La Luisiana, Siglos XVI al XVIII* (Madrid: V. Suárez, 1912), 1–133, laid out Spain's right to this area. It also repeated the usual description of the salubrity and fecundity of Florida and the Southeast. See also Samuel Fagg Bemis, *Pinckney's Treaty: A Study of America's Advantage from Europe's Distress, 1783–1800* (Baltimore: Johns Hopkins University Press, 1926).

86. Coker and Watson, *Indian Traders*, chapters 1–7, cover this story in detail. Spanish officials kept hoping they could substitute one or more Spanish companies for Panton et al. but until 1789 did not undertake to find prototypes of Indian trade goods for Spanish factories to copy.

87. Romero Cabot, "Últimos años," 24.

88. Fatio, "Description of East Florida," St. Augustine, ca. 18 Mar. 1785, in Lockey, *East Florida*, 479–82.

89. Ibid., and Zéspedes to Bernardo de Gálvez, St. Augustine, 29 Jul. 1785, in Lockey, *East Florida*, 570–73.

90. Grants were to contain enough land to produce one hundred fanegas (about 1.6 bushels each) of wheat and ten of maize (or what twenty oxen could plow in a day) plus pasture for twenty cows, five mares, one hundred sheep, twenty goats, and eight breeding sows and a town lot 50 × 100 feet.

91. Susan R. Parker, "Men without God or King: Rural Settlers of East Florida, 1784–1790," *FHQ* 69 (1990), 135–55; James A. Lewis, "Cracker—Florida Style," *FHQ* 63 (1984), 191. Fatio was allowed to ship local products directly from his plantation (Susan R. Parker, "I Am Neither Your Subject nor Your Subordinate," *El Escribano* 25 (1988), 47). *SLGF* 3:30–32 (petition of 1790; the claims were based on the head-right law that had been announced but whose details were still not known to Governor Quesada).

92. Lockey, *East Florida*, 306–12, Report of Nicolás Grenier, 10 Nov. 1784, and his "Brief Description of the Coasts of East Florida" (smuggling and geography); Río Cossa, "Descripción," 16–18 (naval stores); Arthur P. Whitaker, trans. and ed., *Documents Relating to the Commercial Policy of Spain in the Floridas, with Incidental Reference to Louisiana* (Deland: Florida State Historical Society, 1931), 49–61; Zéspedes to Marqués de Sonora, 12 May 1787 (hereafter as Whitaker, *Commercial Policy*); Landers, *Black Society*, 117–18 (Auxiliary Bishop of Cuba Cyril de Barcelona's visitation of 1788).

93. Romero Cabot, "Últimos años," 117–136; Landers, *Black Society*, 204. The decline in numbers was mostly after 1790.

94. The decree is in AGI, SD 2587. For its terms see Johnson, "Spanish St. Augustine," 104 (who also covers the sorting out process), and Shambaugh, "Development," 33, and Pablo Tornero Tinajero, *Relaciones de dependencia entre Florida y Estados Unidos (1783–1820)* (Madrid: Ministerio de Asuntos Exteriores, 1979), 59. For the conversions, see Richard Murdock, "Governor Céspedes and the Religious Problem in East Florida, 1786–1787," *FHQ* 26 (1947), 325–44; Dunkle, "Population Change," p. 15, Table IV, for the Floridano population in 1786; Johnson, "Spanish St. Augustine," 101–103. A similar decree was issued for Spanish Louisiana, to accommodate the Anglo planters at Natchez. In both cases, the instruction of the young was occasional because the Crown did not send enough Irish priests. Charles E. Bennett, *Florida's "French" Revolution, 1793–1795* (Gainesville: University of Florida Press, 1982), 8 (Dr. James O'Fallon's scheme of 1788).

95. *SLGF* database.

96. *SLGF* 2:26–30; 4:8–11.

97. Tornero, *Relaciones*, 71; "Representation with regard to the commerce of East Florida by various inhabitants of St. Augustine," 27 Nov. 1794, in Whitaker, *Commercial Policy*, 184–87 (quotation, 187). Fatio was given a trade privilege for his bilander, *Condesa de Gálvez* (Parker, "Neither Your Subject," 47).

98. AGI, SD 2668 (Whitaker, *Commercial Policy*, 57, 59), Zéspedes to Marqués de Sonora, 12 May 1787.

99. Bennett, *Florida's "French" Revolution*, 8 (O'Fallon's settlement proposal); Whitaker, *Commercial Policy*, 69–71, Report of the Junta de Comercio, Barcelona, 19 June 1788; ibid., 75–99, Discourse of José Salcedo, San Ildefonso, 20 Aug. 1788.

100. Spain and Great Britain both claimed this site on Vancouver Island. The Spaniards took over a British sea otter hunting camp, setting off the confrontation in which the British threatened war. Because the French National Assembly refused to honor the Family Compact, Spain had to back down. In spite of major improvements in its military and naval forces since 1762, it was not a match for Great Britain's power. For details see Warren L. Cook, *Flood Tide of Empire: Spain and the Pacific Northwest, 1543–1819* (New Haven: Yale University Press, 1973).

101. Richard K. Murdock, *The Georgia-Florida Frontier, 1793–1796: Spanish Reaction to French Intrigue and American Designs* (Berkeley: University of California Press, 1951), 4, 7; Bennett, *Florida's French Revolution*, 10; Coker and Watson, *Indian Traders*, 143–48.

10. The American Frontier Envelops East Florida, 1790–1821

1. Janice B. Miller, *Juan Nepomuceno de Quesada: Spanish Governor of East Florida, 1790–1795* (Washington, D.C.: University Press of America, 1981), 7–10, 14; "Plano general de la plaza de San Agustín de la Florida de 1791," *Revista de Historia Militar* (Madrid), no. 63 (1987), 218–20.

2. See Elijah W. Lyon, *Louisiana in French Diplomacy, 1759–1804* (Norman: University of Oklahoma Press, 1934), passim.

3. For decree see Joseph M. White, comp., *A New Collection of Laws, Charters, and Local Ordinances of the Governments of Great Britain, France, and Spain, Relating to the Concession of Land in Their Respective Collonies . . .* , 2 vols. (Philadelphia, 1939), 245–46; Robert E. Rutherford, "Spain's Immigration Policy for the Floridas, 1780–1806" (M.A. thesis, University of Florida, 1952), 37; and Miller, *Nepomuceno de Quesada*, 47–48. Crosby was named curate for the St. Marys district in 1791 but the church was never built. Fr. Michael O'Reilly was St. Augustine's parish priest to 1812. Crosby claimed 2,500 acres in two properties at Mt. Tucker on the upper St. Johns for his services in 1818

(*SLGF* 2:347–49). The United States eventually recognized 36,955 acres in British-era land grants held by various parties during the second Spanish period (*SLGF* database).

4. Robert L. Gold, *Borderlands Empires in Transition: The Triple-Nation Transfer of Florida* (Carbondale: University of Southern Illinois Press, 1969), 86; *SLGF* 3:59, citing law of 18 Mar. 1791; United States, Laws, Statues, etc., *Laws of the United States . . . Spanish Regulations and Other Documents Respecting the Public Lands*, 2 vols. (Washington, D.C.: 1828–1836), 1:999–1000.

5. Pablo Tornero Tinajero, *Relaciones de dependencia entre Florida y Estados Unidos (1783–1820)* (Madrid: Ministerio de Asuntos Exteriores, 1979), 33–34 (1,079 immigrants, 1790–1793); Jane Landers, *Black Society in Spanish Florida* (Urbana: University of Illinois Press, 1999), 75 (1,000 slaves, 300 whites); quotation from Daniel L. Schafer, "A Class of People Neither Freemen nor Slaves: From Spanish to American Race Relations in Florida, 1821–1861," *Journal of Social History* 26 (1993), 588; Miller, *Nepomuceno de Quesada*, 121 (re where settled). Help with immigration should have come when Jedidiah Morse published his *The American Geography* in 1789 and 1792 (1789, 1792; reprint, New York: Arno Press, 1970) with the usual claims for Florida. See esp. pp. 445, 450, 476–77. Thomas Jeffreys, "The Peninsula and Gulf of Florida: The Coast of West Florida and Louisiana," 1792, was a map common at the time (copy in the P. K. Yonge Library, no. 123).

6. Statistics on Confirmed Land Grants, 1791–1793, from *SLGF* database.

YEAR	NUMBER	MEAN	MEDIAN	STANDARD DEVIATION	RANGE
1791	28	500	379	117–883	104–1,800
1792	48	734	375	1–1,814	92–7,034
1793	23	292	220	81–503	15–1,000

7. *SLGF* 1:xxvi–xxvii; ibid., 5:64–67, is Sept. 1827 testimony about title by Joseph M. Hernández and Gabriel W. Perpall (timber only) and George G. F. Clarke, Charles W. Clarke, and Antonio Álvarez (title if mill built); the U.S. confirmed parts of 5 sawmill grants for the 1790–1806 period. One was for 1,000 acres (1793), two for 3,000 acres (1790, 1799), and the others for 9,470 acres (1805) and 5,460 acres (1806) (*SLGF* database). John McQueen, *Letters of D. Juan McQueen to His Family Written from Spanish East Florida 1791–1807* (Columbia, S.C.: Bostick and Thornely, 1943), 30, John McQueen to Eliza Anne McQueen, Hermitage [E. Fla.], 21 Feb. 1796; and p. 32, Same to John McQueen, Jr., St. Augustine, 9 Mar. 1796.

8. Charles E. Bennett, *Florida's French Revolution, 1793–1795* (Gainesville: University of Florida Press, 1982), 12–14; *McQueen Letters*, 81–82, "Memoranda, lands granted by the Spanish government of East Florida to Jno McQueen"; *SLGF* 2:284–93 (Spicer Christopher), 5:43–45 (Sánchez), 3:229–30 (Simon). Bennett, *Florida's French Revolution*, 165, deposition of Daniel McMurphy, 8 Apr. 1794 (Sanders and Wagnon were both alleged to be forgers); Richard K. Murdoch, *The Georgia-Florida Frontier, 1793–1796: Spanish Reaction to French Intrigue and American Designs* (Berkeley: University of California Press, 1951), 6 and Bennett, *Florida's French Revolution*, 82, 87, 88, 132 for examples of Spanish restrictive rules.

9. Jane Landers, "Free and Slave," in *The New History of Florida*, ed. Michael Gannon (Gainesville: University Press of Florida, 1996), 179; Miller, *Nepomuceno de Quesada*, 30.

10. William S. Coker and Thomas D. Watson, *Indian Traders of the Southeastern Spanish Borderlands: Panton, Leslie & Company and John Forbes & Company, 1783–1847* (Pensacola: University of West Florida Press, 1986), 187–88; Miller, *Nepomuceno de Quesada*, 63–69, 77–84; Arthur P. Whitaker, trans. and ed., *Documents Relating to the Commercial Policy of Spain in the Floridas, with Incidental Reference to Louisiana* (Deland: Florida State Historical Society, 1931), 124–39; Luis Fatio, "Description of the Commerce of East Florida," Havana, 17 Nov. 1790 (hereafter Whitaker, *Commercial Policy*); Bennett, *Florida's French Revolution*, 21–22; Tornero, *Relaciones*, 77–78, quotation from 80. There were other provisions restricting trade to nations with which Spain was at peace and had commercial treaties and requiring ships returning from Europe to stop at Corcubión (in Galicia) or Alicante (this restriction was removed in 1794). Other laws issued in 1791 and 1792 aimed to stop smuggling into East Florida under cover of immigration or from it with goods not locally produced. See Miller, *Nepomuceno de Quesada*, 80, and Rutherford, "Spain's Immigration Policy," 52–53.

11. Ramón Romero Cabot, "Los últimos años de la soberanía española en la Florida, 1783–1821" (Ph.D. dissertation, Universidad de Sevilla, 1983), 213; Table 9.1 (copy in P. K. Yonge Library of Florida History, University of Florida).

12. These were Baton Rouge, Nogales (Vicksburg), New Madrid, and Chickasaw Bluffs (Memphis).

13. Coker and Watson, *Indian Traders*, 158–59, 161–65.

14. J. Leitch Wright, Jr., *Anglo-Spanish Rivalry in North America* (Athens: University of Georgia Press, 1971), 146–48.

15. Miller, *Nepomuceno de Quesada*, 98–110; Wright, *Anglo-Spanish Rivalry*, 146–48; Coker and Watson, *Indian Traders*, 148–56.

16. James W. Covington, *The Seminoles of Florida* (Gainesville: Uni-

versity Press of Florida, 1993), 22; Coker and Watson, *Indian Traders*, 189–92; Miller, *Nepomuceno de Quesada*, 32. For Houston, see *SLGF* 4:201–205. These negotiations were in part with Payne, Cowkeeper's successor. Covington, *The Seminoles of Florida*, interprets this as an indication of the further emergence of an independent Seminole identity.

17. Coker and Watson, *Indian Traders*, 180–81.

18. Miller, *Nepomuceno de Quesada*, 115–22. U.S. privateers were also off the coast during the spring and into the summer.

19. Bennett, *Florida's French Revolution*, 32–171, is mostly documents from the Spanish investigation. For details see pp. 39–48, 57–64, 75, 94–97, 150–69.

20. Romero Cabot, "Últimos años," 218; Bennett, *Florida's French Revolution*, 75–78 for text; Miller, *Nepomuceno de Quesada*, 134–35. John Leslie of Panton, Leslie and Company was the commander of the Pardo (free mulatto) company of fifty men. He had a Black consort and mulatto children by her (Landers, *Black Society*, 207). There were three white militia companies. For American racial attitudes see Landers, *Black Society*, 199–200.

A few of the displaced can be identified. Artemas E. Ferguson (settled 1791 with twenty slaves) lost his improvements on Doctor's Creek; he moved to the North River but had to seek work in St. Augustine. He was dead by 1796 (*SLGF* 3:78). William Pengree (1787 with forty-eight slaves) lost four properties at Doctor's Lake and crops he claimed were worth 7,000 pesos. The stress of relocating killed him. His widow was unable to make crops in 1795 and 1796 and had to sell slaves to pay debts to Panton, Leslie & Company. She finally sold out to Zephaniah Kingsley in 1803 (*SLGF* 4:8–11). Timothy Hollingsworth (1787, 9 slaves) lost "almost everything he had, all his houses being burned." He managed to start over and obtained title to his land in 1805 (*SLGF* 4:107). Andrew Pleyn (1789) also lost properties at Doctor's Lake in what he recalled was "Wagner's War," a possible corruption of Wagnon (*SLGF* 4:210). William Carney lost buildings on the St. Marys River; Joseph Summerall was forced off his Nassau River stock farm; and Thomas Travers lost buildings west of the St. Johns River (*SLGF* 5:69–70, 137, 155–56).

21. Miller, *Nepomuceno de Quesada*, 141–47. Mathews made it clear that the state did not support the filibusters, including Elijah Clark.

22. Murdoch, *Georgia-Florida Frontier*, 51–61.

23. Janice B. Miller, "Rebellion in East Florida in 1795," *FHQ* 57 (1978), 173–86, and Miller, *Nepomuceno de Quesada*, 153–66; Bennett, *Florida's French Revolution*, 172–203. He notes the prominent later careers of some of the leaders of the 1794–95 events on pp. 199–203. Georgia's drier than normal spring rainfall in 1794 and 1795 may have made

some frontiersmen there more inclined to gain wealth by raiding Florida because their maize crops may have done poorly (David W. Stahle and Malcolm K. Cleaveland, Rainfall Tables A.D. 933–1985, collection of author).

24. Miller, *Nepomuceno de Quesada*, 161–64; Murdoch, *Georgia-Florida Frontier*, 105–13. Landers, *Black Society*, 173, notes the ninety-one slaves initially confiscated, of whom sixty-seven were auctioned off in 1799.

25. Murdoch, *Georgia-Florida Frontier*, 114–33.

26. The reasons he did this are debated. It was once thought that he did not know the terms of Jay's Treaty between the U.S. and Great Britain and feared an alliance, but it has been shown that he knew its general provisions and could have guessed it would not resolve U.S.–British disputes (Arthur P. Whitaker, "New Light on the Treaty of San Lorenzo: An Essay in Historical Criticism," *Mississippi Valley Historical Review* 15 (1928–29), 435–54). More likely, Pinckney's Treaty reflected his general disinterest in Spain's larger claims in North America, a disinterest already signaled by Franco–Spanish negotiations for the retrocession of Louisiana if Spain could exact a suitable European price. See also Raymond A. Young, "Pinckney's Treaty—A New Perspective," *Hispanic American Historical Review* 43 (1963), 526–35.

27. Tornero, *Relaciones*, 54, using books in AGI, PC 473; Abel Poitrineau, "Demography and the Political Destiny of Florida during the Second Spanish Period," *FHQ* 66 (1988), 438–40, using Bundle 350U4 of the East Florida Papers (reels 163–64 of the microfilm); Schafer, "A Class of People," 589. Schafer also used East Florida Papers Bundle 350U4, Reel 163. Landers, *Black Society*, 160, notes that the Spanish government granted tax moratoriums in 1789–91 and 1793–96 in a effort to stimulate slave imports. She concludes that the 1,185 slaves found in the census of 1793 showed the government's program was working.

28. Decree of 14 Nov. 1804: Robert E. Rutherford, "Settlers from Connecticut in Spanish Florida," *FHQ* 31 (1952), 54; White's rules: *SLGF* 1:xxii–xxiii. The 1804 decree was repeated over date of 31 Mar. 1806 (Rutherford, "Settlers," 56–57).

29. Tornero, *Relaciones*, 54, provides an annual table. His percentages over the entire 1797–1811 period are 73 percent Americans, 15 percent British (including Irish), 9.4 percent French, and the balance from other countries (p. 56). Poitrineau's analysis over the 1794–1811 period indicates 61 percent Americans, 24 percent British, 15 percent Francophones ("Second Spanish Period," 438–40). Schafer, "A Class of People," 589, suggests that more than 80 percent of these immigrants, 1790–1804, were of American or British origins. About 10 percent were French. Poitrineau's article identifies the U.S. places of origin and suggests professions and property holding; Tornero, *Relaciones*, 124, notes that many were merchants.

30. Landers, *Black Society*, 209–16 (Biassou); Poitrineau, "Second Spanish Period," 426–27; *SLGF* 2:259–71; J. Leitch Wright, Jr., *Florida in the American Revolution* (Gainesville: University of Florida Press, 1975), 146–47, and Joseph B. Smith, *The Plot to Steal Florida: James Madison's Phoney War* (New York: Arbor House, 1983), 135–37; Landers, *Black Society*, 150.

31. *SLGF* 2:118–31; 134–37.

32. *Letters of D. Juan McQueen*, 24, 26, 38.

33. Romero Cabot, "Últimos años," 316. The average New York price for middling upland cotton hovered above $0.20 per pound (*Historical Statistics of the United States, Colonial Times to 1970* (Washington, D.C.: U.S. Bureau of the Census, 1975), Series E26).

34. *Letters of D. Juan McQueen*, 56, 59, 64–65, 67, 73.

35. Christopher Ward, "East Florida during the Embargo, 1806–1812: The Quantities of Semi-Illicit Commerce," typescript on file, P. K. Yonge Library of Florida History, University of Florida, p. 13.

36. Wright, *Florida in the American Revolution*, 146. Ambrose Hull allowed some of the Bahamians to use his land near New Smyrna in 1803 but Indian troubles of that year caused most to desert the area. William Williams, a Bahamian planter who immigrated with forty-five slaves in 1803, got 180 acres on the Halifax River and 2,020 at Spring Garden near the St. Johns River when the balance of his 2,200-acre grant could not be laid out on the Halifax because of land-granting policies. *SLGF* 3:292; 5:216–20.

37. *Letters of D. Juan McQueen*, 71, McQueen to Robert MacKay, St. Augustine, 6 May 1806. McQueen had gotten an exclusive ship rescue-and-salvage license for the Keys. He notes a few persons "among the Keys" and his hope to grow coffee and sugar and obtain fish oil and salt fish. When Juan Ponce visited Key Biscayne in 1804, he recalled twenty years later, one Vincent lived there and he saw Guinea corn and coffee growing. Pedro Fornells obtained a land grant for the key in 1805; there were three residents. In 1824, 175 acres (Fornell's head rights?) were sold by Rafael Andreu and his wife to Mary Ann Davies for $100, beginning a chain of events that finally ended in 1896 when a descendant sought a U.S. patent for the land (*SLGF* 3:2–13). George Sibbald obtained land on Drayton's Island in Lake George in 1804 with a scheme to raise coffee (*SLGF* 4:14–18).

38. Tornero, *Relaciones*, 80–83; *Letters of D. Juan McQueen*, 71. Merchants were only allowed to stay for the period needed to transact their business; they were forbidden to apply for immigrant status, thus forcing them to pay tariffs on the first 6,000 pesos worth of goods imported. For the decrees of 1803, 1804, and 1806, see Rutherford, "Settlers," 54, 55–57.

39. Howard Cline, *Florida Indians II: Provisional Historical Gazeteer with Locational Notes on Florida Colonial Communities* (New York:

Garland Publishing, 1974), Map 7, Table 2, and Maps 14 & 15, and text, pp. 229–230; Covington, *Seminoles*, 26–27.

40. Landers, *Black Society*, 68, 229; see also Kenneth W. Porter, *The Negro on the American Frontier* (New York: Arno Pres, 1971), 205–93, passim, for the later history of these Blacks and the Seminole.

41. Coker and Watson, *Indian Traders*, 195–96, 201, 229; Wright, *Anglo-Spanish Rivalry*, 156–58, on the Blount Conspiracy; Covington, *Seminoles*, 21. Romero Cabot, "Últimos años," 103–106, gives these figures for the gift fund: 1799: 731 pesos; 1805: 2,170 pesos. William Blount, U.S. Senator from Tennessee, conspired with other westerners and the British to drive the Spaniards out of Louisiana and Florida. Publication of one of his letters in July 1797 exposed the plan and led to his expulsion from the Senate.

42. *Letters of D. Juan McQueen*, 37, John McQueen, Jr., to Eliza Anne McQueen, Pensacola, 5 Feb. 1797. Wright, *Anglo-Spanish Rivalry*, 146–47, 156–58, 160–61, 165–66.

43. Coker and Watson, *Indian Traders*, 232–33, 235–42; Wright, *Anglo-Spanish Rivalry*, 161–63; Cline, *Florida Indians II*, 118–23. Bowles was active among the Creek during the last years of the dry spell of 1794–1802, but what effect that had on their food supply and interest in trade is not known (Stahle and Cleaveland, Rainfall Tables, collection of the author).

44. *SLGF* 4:51–52 (1800), 3:38 (1802), 5:150–52 (1803); Covington, *Seminoles*, 1–22; Jane G. Landers, "Black Society in Spanish St. Augustine, 1784–1821" (Ph.D. dissertation, University of Florida, 1988), 190–95, quotation on p. 192; see also Landers, *Black Society*, 217–20 (where the quotation does not appear); Coker and Watson, *Indian Traders*, 237.

45. E.g., James Cashen moved his family to Amelia Island and went on to prosper (*SLGF* 2:261, 263, 266); Roque Leonardi's widow, sons, and slaves temporarily abandoned their properties on the North River, fifteen miles or so above St. Augustine (ibid., 4:51–52); Thomas Travers lost his San Patricio plantation on the St. Johns in 1803 but rebuilt the next year (ibid., 5:150–52).

46. Mark F. Boyd, "Events at Prospect Bluff on the Apalachicola River, 1808–1818: An Introduction to Twelve Letters of Edmund Doyle, Trader," *FHQ* 16 (1937), 63.

47. Coker and Watson, *Indian Traders*, 251–53; for the company's efforts to settle its debts and how that fit with U.S. policy, see their pp. 243–272. See also *SLGF* 3:133–38, for the U.S. confirmation of the 1,427,289 acres in question and lists of supporting documentation. The debt is listed as $66,536.50 in silver.

48. Tornero, *Relaciones*, 162, 163 (Tables 10 and 11).

49. *SLGF* database shows six grants in 1806; Juan Marchena Fernández, "Guarniciones y población militar en Florida Oriental (1700–

1820)," *Revista de Indias*, nos. 163–64 (1981), 108. He shows (pp. 130–31, 122–23, 125–26, respectively) that the officer corps was like that elsewhere in the empire in composition—40 percent of noble origins with relatively few sons of soldiers—but unlike it in that 71 percent were peninsulares, with only 23 percent creoles. The rest of the American army had 60 percent creole (locally born) officers. The soldiers too were disproportionately peninsular (74 percent) compared to the 90 percent creole norm for other garrisons in the Americas.

50. Stahle and Cleaveland, Rainfall Data, collection of author. Eight of the eleven years 1809–1819 had spring rainfalls 15 percent or more below normal in Georgia, a range at which effects should have been felt on crops. The other years fell within the normal range.

51. Former Vice President Aaron Burr, like Blount before him, conspired with westerners to seize land, most likely in Spanish Texas although the Floridas and even Louisiana were also possibilities. (He never disclosed his true intentions.) He unsuccessfully attempted to enlist British and then French and Spanish help. General James Wilkinson, a friend and initial co-conspirator, arrested Burr and his followers, ending the conspiracy.

52. Rembert W. Patrick, *Florida Fiasco; Rampant Rebels on the Georgia-Florida Border, 1810–1815* (Athens: University of Georgia, 1954), and Joseph B. Smith, *The Plot to Steal Florida: James Madison's Phoney War* (New York: Arbor House, 1983), are two detailed accounts of the events in the Floridas in 1810–1814. The discussion that follows is drawn from them except as noted.

53. Smith, *The Plot to Steal Florida*, 113–116.

54. *Letters of John McQueen*, 63, n. 107, clarifies his identify as not the same John McIntosh of Bellevue involved in the 1793–95 troubles.

55. Smith, *The Plot to Steal Florida*, 147–51, 158–83. See also Covington, *Seminoles*, 28–33, Thomas Graham, "Spain's Two Floridas, East and West," *El Escribano*, 25 (1988), 10–11, and Romero Cabot, "Últimos años," 447–55. Romero Cabot makes the common mistake of confusing this John H. McIntosh with the John McIntosh who was involved in the troubles of 1793–95.

56. *SLGF* 4:1–3, 5:172.

57. Landers, *Black Society*, 221–28; *SLGF* 5:52. The Spanish situation was so desperate that they had to trade an absolute title to land for John Russell's schooner (ibid., 2:225–35).

58. Landers, *Black Society*, 223–27, is the best account of the actions of the Black militia under Captain Jorge Jacobo and Lt. Juan Bautista Witten in carrying out these raids. See also Porter, *Negro on the American Frontier*, 194–198.

59. Porter, *Negro on the American Frontier*, 194–98; Smith, *The Plot to Steal Florida*, 267–69.

60. Patrick, *Florida Fiasco*, 231–34; Smith, *The Plot to Steal Florida*,

274–80; Smith says a few Indians and Blacks were killed. Patrick, *Florida Fiasco*, 234, and Covington, *Seminoles*, 32, specify twenty; Porter, *Negro on the American Frontier*, 201, claims fifty–sixty were killed. All such numbers are guesses. All sources agree on the number of houses destroyed and quantities of other objects destroyed or stolen.

61. Smith, *The Plot to Steal Florida*, 287–88; Porter, *Negro on the American Frontier*, 201–202. Alexander's raid *SLGF* 4:6–8. Kingsley claimed he had been coerced into joining the invaders.

62. Quoted in Patrick, *Florida Fiasco*, 302.

63. William S. Coker and Susan R. Parker, "The Second Spanish Period in the Two Floridas," in *The New History of Florida*, ed. Michael Gannon (Gainesville: University Presses of Florida, 1996), 163. Patrick, *Florida Fiasco*, 302–303; Schafer, "A Class of People," 590 (Zephaniah Kingsley cited Fraser as an example, but did not claim all 211 were lost during the war); Landers, *Black Society*, 102–106. I have not found a total for the claims or payments.

64. *SLGF* 2:262.

65. *SLGF* 4:32–34, 51–52, 78–80, 5:43–45, 70, 131–34, 216–20; 3:162–64; 5:180–81.

66. Joel W. Martin, *Sacred Revolt, The Muskogee Struggle for a New World* (Boston: Beacon Press, 1991), sees the Red Stick uprising as a nativist effort to purge the Creek of European influences. Porter, *Negro on the American Frontier*, 213–25; Wright, *Anglo-Spanish Rivalry*, 168–79; Coker and Watson, *Indian Traders*, 279–81; William W. Rogers, *Antebellum Thomas County, 1825–1861* (Tallahassee: Florida State University Studies, no. 39, 1963), 3–4. Romero Cabot, "Últimos años," 287, notes that Jackson and his Tennessee officers and others grabbed the best of these lands, leading him to conclude that "the acquisition of Florida was a private enterprise carried out under official protection, from which both [private and official interests] obtained benefits."

67. Coker and Watson, *Indian Traders*, 281–91.

68. Wright, *Anglo-Spanish Rivalry*, 172, discusses requests from various parties in 1811 that Great Britain seize East Florida and make it "another Canada"; Coker and Watson, *Indian Traders*, 292–97; Landers, *Black Society*, 230–31. The largest flight from Florida involved thirty-four slaves from one of the Forbes Company properties on the lower St. Johns River.

69. Smith, *The Plot to Steal Florida*, 139–40 (Fernandina); Tornero, *Relaciones*, 162, 163 (Tables 10 and 11).

70. Based on Tornero, *Relaciones*, Tables 6–27; Romero Cabot, "Últimos años," 58, notes the Spanish decree of 24 Mar. 1810; Ligia María Bermudez, "The Situado: A Study in the Dynamics of East Florida's Economy during the Second Spanish Period, 1785–1820" (M.A. thesis, University of Florida, 1989), 17, notes the lesser dependence of East Florida on the United States during the period of the Embargo.

71. Ward, "East Florida During the Embargo," 13–17.

72. Tornero, *Relaciones*, 78, 84–88.

73. Landers, *Black Society*, 276–77 (for slave ships), 176–77 (for merchants and planters).

74. Landers, *Black Society*, 161. She found that the sex ratios were even for both Blacks and whites, an unusual situation for a frontier society.

75. Kingsley to Governor, noted in Schafer, "A Class of Citizens," 590, n. 13; *SLGF* 2:183–85. Joseph Mariano Hernández tried to prevent a decline in his own fortunes by anticipating the exhaustion of the land he was farming and getting replacement grants. He claimed he was getting $8,000–10,000 a year from the 1,890 acres he cultivated in 1817 (ibid., 3:235–38).

76. Poitrineau, "Second Spanish Period," 429–30, 434; 432 (epidemic); Romero Cabot, "Últimos años," 24. *SLGF* 5:80–81 notes the "cruel famine" of 1808 and an epidemic in 1809. Perhaps the explanation for the fall in births was out migration of young men and their brides to Cuba in search of economic opportunities they did not have in Florida because so many were the children of officials who had no capital or slaves to invest in rural development.

77. Marchena, "Guarniciones," 111–15.

78. Tornero, *Relaciones*, Tables 10, 11, 26, 27, and (for Rice) 9, 21. At St. Augustine, the record of imports ceased in 1815, although exports continued to be recorded.

79. *SLGF* 1:xxiv (1811); Tornero, *Relaciones*, 60 (1812); U.S. *Laws of the United States.* . . . , 1006 (decree of 14 Jan. 1813).

80. *SLGF* 1:xxiv–xxv.

81. *SLGF* 2:90–91.

82. Romero Cabot, "Últimos años," 33–37; *SLGF* 1:xxviii; 3:16; Hubert B. Fuller, *The Purchase of Florida, Its History and Diplomacy* (Cleveland: Burrows, 1906), 309.

83. Duvon C. Corbitt, "The Administrative System of Floridas, 1783–1821," *Tequesta*, 1, no. 2 (Aug. 1942), 45, 61–63; *SLGF* 2:42–44 and 5:52.

84. Corbett, "Administrative System," 1:45–46, 61–63.

85. Coker and Watson, *Indian Traders*, 307–309; John K. Mahon and Brent R. Weisman, "Florida's Seminole and Miccosukee Peoples," in *The New History of Florida*, ed. Michael Gannon (Gainesville: University Press of Florida, 1996), 191; Wright, *Anglo-Spanish Rivalry*, 184.

86. T. Frederick Davis, "MacGregor's Invasion of Florida, 1817," *FHQ* 7 (1928), 2–71; David Bushnell (Comp.), *La República de las Floridas: Text and Documents* (Mexico City: Pan American Institute of History and Geography, 1986); T. Graham, "Spain's Two Floridas," 12–13; Coker and Parker, "Second Spanish Period," 164. See also *SLGF* 5: 32 and 42; 3:224–25; 5:172, for individual service claims; ibid., 2:118, 174, and 5:80 for men who claimed to be at the battle of Waterman's house;

ibid., 5:91–92, 138, for Indian troubles. Witnesses in Ezekiel Hudnell's land claim case of 1827 stated that hostile Indians and free Negroes had prevented the locating of his grant near Lake George in 1817–1818, but this is not otherwise reported (ibid., 3:277).

87. *SLGF* 3:156–58; 4:173; 4:181–83.

88. Mahon and Weisman, "Florida's Seminole and Miccosukee Peoples," 191–92; Porter, *Negro on the American Frontier*, 215–224.

89. Robert V. Remini, *Andrew Jackson and the Course of American Empire, 1767–1821* (New York: Harper and Row, 1977), 332–36, 346–49; Porter, *Negro on the American Frontier*, 235–36; Fuller, *Purchase of Florida*, 239–240. Romero Cabot, "Últimos años," 392, suggests that as commander of the southern region by 1818 Jackson had positioned regular army troops on the Florida frontier with the aim of seizing the province when the time was right, but Remini and others show that he raised most of his men in Tennessee and among the Creek.

90. Remini, *Course of American Empire*, 351–54; Coker and Watson, *Indian Traders*, 318–19. An American ship entered St. Marks under the British flag. Thinking British help had arrived, Hillis Hago and his companion went aboard.

91. Remini, *Course of American Empire*, 354; Coker and Watson, *Indian Traders*, 314–19; Fuller, *Purchase of Florida*, 247, 342.

92. Remini, *Course of American Empire*, 357–59; Fuller, *Purchase of Florida*, 350–54, for part of the text of U.S. Note to Spain dated 28 Nov. 1818 that deals with these men, and pp. 252–67, 335–39 (later condemnation); Porter, *Negro on the American Frontier*, 223, 227, 232.

93. Remini, *Course of American Empire*, 359–65; Porter, *Negro on the American Frontier*, 221–232; Mahon and Weisman, "Florida's Seminole and Miccosukee Peoples," 191–92. See also Herbert J. Doherty, Jr., "The Governorship of Andrew Jackson," *FHQ* 33:1 (Jul. 1954), 4–5.

94. Porter, *Negro on the American Frontier*, 233–34; Cline, *Florida Indians II*, 239–40, and Maps 14 and 15.

95. Fuller, *Purchase of Florida*, 217–23.

96. Fuller, *Purchase of Florida*, 224, 300–301. Spain's position on the Louisiana–West Florida issue was that Spain had received West Florida from Great Britain in 1783, not France in 1762 as the United States claimed, and had not ceded it to France under the ambiguous language of the treaty of 1800 repeated in the Purchase treaty of 1803: "The colony or province of Louisiana, with the same extent that it now has in the hands of Spain, and that it had when France possessed it; and such as it should be after the treaties subsequently entered into between Spain and other states." (Samuel Fagg Bemis, *Diplomatic History of the United States* (New York: Henry Holt, 1942), 180–82).

97. Bemis, *Diplomatic History*, 189–95; Fuller, *Purchase of Florida*, 296–310. For a more extensive treatment see Philip C. Brooks, *Diplo-*

macy and the Borderlands, The Adams-Onís Treaty of 1819 (Berkeley: University of California Press, 1939).

98. Bemis, *Diplomatic History*, 195; Fuller, *Purchase of Florida*, 310–22; 374 for Article 8, which nullified the land grants.

11. The American Frontiers, 1821–1860

1. *SLGF* database; Charles B. Vignoles, *Observations upon the Floridas* (1823; facsimile ed., Gainesville: University of Florida Press, 1977), 25–39, 96–97, and William H. Simmons, *Notices of East Florida* (1822; facsimile ed., Gainesville: University of Florida Press, 1977), to p. 50 (northeast Florida, St. Augustine, and Mosquitos); Daniel L. Schafer, "U.S. Territory and State," in *The New History of Florida*, ed. Michael Gannon (Gainesville: University Press of Florida, 1996), 212 (450 or so Americans in the area around Pensacola; *SLGF* database indicates most were on the upper reaches of the Escambia and Perdido River drainages); Clifton Paisley, *The Red Hills of Florida, 1528–1865* (Tuscaloosa: University of Alabama Press, 1989), 57 (Jackson Co., with 31 families and about 150 persons); *SLGF* 2:88–103 and Simmons, *Notices*, 49–50 (Alachua where settlement had just begun in 1820 under terms of the Arredondo Grant); Covington, "Trade Relations," 119–23 (fishing Ranchos on west coast) and Janet S. Matthews, *Edge of Wilderness: A Settlement History of Manatee River and Sarasota Bay* (Tulsa: Caprine Press, 1983), 71–72 (seven Spanish fishermen/settlers on Sarasota Bay); James R. Snyder, Alan Herndon, and William B. Robertson, Jr., "South Florida Rockland," in *Ecosystems of Florida*, ed. Ronald L. Myers and John J. Ewel (Orlando: University of Central Florida Press, 1990), 271 (for settlement at Key West, also in Vignoles, *Observations*, 121–22); and Sidney W. Martin, *Florida during the Territorial Days* (Athens: University of Georgia Press, 1944), 186, 190 (Jacksonville, Mandarin, Palatka) (cited hereafter as Martin, *Territorial Days*).

2. John Solomon Otto, *The Southern Frontiers, 1607–1860: The Agricultural Evolution of the Colonial and Antebellum South* (Westport, Conn.: Greenwood Press, 1989), 1, from the writings of Frederick Jackson Turner. Density figure from *Historical Statistics of the United States, Colonial Times to 1970* (Washington, D.C.: U.S. Bureau of the Census, 1975), 29.

3. The Interior Department, which controlled the surveys, decided by 1860 that it would not extend them into swamp and overflow lands south of the Caloosahatchee River because the few "islands" of ground that could be farmed were not worth the costs of survey using boats and other special equipment. See U.S. 36th Congress, Second Session, *Senate Documents no. 1*, pp. 151–52, Report of Surveyor General of Florida, 1 Oct. 1860.

4. Delays and the transfer ceremony at St. Augustine are described in Rogers W. Young, "The Transfer of Fort San Marcos and East Florida to the United States," *FHQ* 14 (Apr. 1936), 231–43 (what was agreed upon), and in Thomas Graham, *The Awakening of St. Augustine: The Anderson Family and the Oldest City, 1821–1924* (St. Augustine, Fla.: St. Augustine Historical Society, 1978), 6–9, using an eyewitness account. Martin, *Territorial Days*, 19, 21–22, describes events at Pensacola. For the Jackson–Callava dispute over the Widow Vidal's demand for certain documents relating to her late husband's estate, see Herbert J. Doherty, Jr., "The Governorship of Andrew Jackson," *FHQ* 33 (Jul. 1954), 14–19; for the seizure of the East Florida archives see Martin, *Territorial Days*, 25 and others.

5. Vignoles, *Observations*, 112–16, and Williams, *Territory*, 15–16, and Graham, *Awakening*, 11–12, note yellow fever outbreaks accompanied these evacuations, probably because of mosquitos brought from Havana by evacuation ships; for the free people, see Jane G. Landers, "Black Society in Spanish St. Augustine, 1784–1821" (Ph.D. dissertation, University of Florida, 1988), 206; Daniel L. Schafer, "A Class of People Neither Freemen nor Slaves: From Spanish to American Race Relations in Florida, 1821–1861," *Journal of Social History* 26 (1993), 590, copies this; Jane Landers, *Black Society in Spanish Florida* (Urbana: University of Illinois Press, 1999), 247–48, gives an account of the evacuation but without this number. For Kingsley, see Landers, *Black Society*, 99–100, 168–71. Simmons, *Notices*, 42, also notes the flight of free persons because of fears about U.S. laws.

6. Martin, *Territorial Days*, 32–35; Herbert J. Doherty, Jr., "Andrew Jackson's Cronies in Florida Territorial Politics, with Three Unpublished Letters to His Cronies," *FHQ* 34 (1955), 3–29.

7. Martin, *Territorial Days*, 35–36. Monroe County embraced most of South Florida, with a seat at Key West.

8. *The New American State Papers: Indian Affairs*, ed. Thomas C. Cochran, 13 vols. (Wilmington, Del.: Scholarly Resources, 1972), 6:230–36, extracts of Jean A. Peniere to General Jackson, 15 Jul., 21 Jul. (five thousand Indians), 27 Aug., and to Secretary of War, 19 Jul. 1821, and ibid., 238–41, George G. F. Clark to Capt. John R. Bell, St. Marys, 15 Aug. 1821 (estimating eight hundred Indians "humbled to the dust") (hereafter as *NASP, Indian Affairs*). Simmons, *Notices*, 41–42, 58, 75–76 (1,200–1,500 Seminole and four hundred Blacks with them).

9. *NASP, Indian Affairs*, 6: 234–37: Report on Conference, and Jackson to Calhoun, 2 and 17 Sept. 1821, also noted in Doherty, "Governorship of Andrew Jackson," 19–21.

10. *NASP, Indian Affairs*, 6:241–42, extract, Capt. Bell to Sec. of War, St. Augustine, 22 Jan. 1822; Simmons, *Notices*, 54–96, passim, and Cantor Brown, Jr., *Florida's Peace River Frontier* (Gainesville: Univer-

sity Press of Florida, 1991), 20–22, discuss the raids which Brown found began in May 1821, before the United States had taken control.

11. James W. Covington, *The Seminoles of Florida* (Gainesville: University Press of Florida, 1993), 50–51; *NASP: Indian Affairs*, 6:229–30, White to Calhoun (quotation is from this); ibid., 227–43, are the documents Calhoun sent to the Committee.

12. *NASP, Indian Affairs*, 6:250–57, quotations from 251, 256.

13. *NASP, Indian Affairs*, 6:350–454 (report on the Conference), and Covington, *Seminoles*, 52–54; *NASP, Indian Affairs*, 6:368 (U.S. talk), 370 (Neomathla's famous reply about the hickory nut, acorn, and persimmon).

14. Paisley, *Red Hills*, 71–75; Martin, *Territorial Days*, 61–62; Mark F. Boyd, "The First American Road in Florida: Pensacola–St. Augustine Highway, 1824," *FHQ* 14 (1935), 73–106 and 138–92. Quotation from Ellen Call Long, *Florida Breezes; or Florida New and Old* (1883; facsimile ed., Gainesville: University of Florida Press, 1962), 46.

15. *NASP, Indian Affairs* 6:380–81, 383, 388–89, 393, Duval to Calhoun, Pensacola, 12 Jan. 1824; Duval to Calhoun, Pensacola, 7 Apr. 1824; Duval to Calhoun, 12 Jul. 1824; Duval to Calhoun, St. Marks, 29 Jul. 1824, respectively. See also Covington, *Seminoles*, 54–56. Neamathla eventually moved back among the Creek rather than occupy his personal reserve near modern Quincy.

16. *NASP, Indian Affairs*, 6:385–86, John C. Calhoun to Gov. Duval, Washington, D.C., 2 June 1824.

17. Covington, *Seminoles*, 56–58; *NASP, Indian Affairs*, 6:414–15, Benjamin Chaires to William P. Duval, Tallahassee, 13 Jan. 1825 (quotations and land qualities). Covington, *Seminoles*, 57, notes that Gadsden thought that the reserve, extended northward to the Big Swamp area, would provide adequate food both cultivated and hunted and gathered.

18. Covington, *Seminoles*, 56, 58, 60; *NASP, Indian Affairs*, 6:457–58, William Duval to Col. Thomas L. McKenney (General Superintendent of Indians Affairs, Florida Agency), 22 Feb. 1826.

19. *NASP, Indian Affairs*, 6:370 (Indian estimate of 4,883 persons in twenty-seven towns); 379 (U.S. official discounting of same); 406, Duval to Calhoun, 2 Oct. 1824 (re 249 men under the six chiefs of the western reserves); 429 (1,600 removed vis 1,000 rations).

20. *NASP, Indians Affairs*, 6: 420, George Walton to Col. G. Humphreys, Tallahassee, 14 Apr. 1825, with reply by Humphreys, p. 424; ibid., 431, Humphreys to Acting Governor George Walton, Camp near Tampa, 13 June 1825; ibid., 434–35, Walton to Col. Thomas L. McKenney, Tallahassee, 6 Oct. 1825; ibid., 449, Duval to Calhoun, 16 Dec. 1825.

21. *NASP, Indian Affairs*, 6: 477–78, Oren Marsh to William P. Duval, Florida Agency (Silver Springs), 1 Jan. 1825 [*sic*, 1827] (reporting the drought; Stahle and Cleaveland data for 1826 show a low year as well);

Covington, *Seminoles*, 59–61. For a clear example of the white attitude see *NASP, Indian Affairs* 6: 313–16, Duncan Campbell and James Merriweather, U.S. Commissioners, talk to the Creeks, 9 Dec. 1824, declaring that the Indians had lost their land rights when they and the British were defeated ("conquered") during the American Revolutionary War and that removal was necessary to end Indian hunting and teach them to become farmers and Christians. John C. Calhoun was quoted as saying that a "distinct society or nation" within any state was "incompatible with our system, and must yield to it." (p. 324). Campbell and Merriweather concluded their talk with the blunt statement: "we want the country you now occupy" (p. 316). Long, *Florida Breezes*, 44–45, records similar sentiments: "The American came to stay, therefore the Indian must go."

22. Martin, *Territorial Days*, 86–87, 89, n. 55.

23. William G. Murray, *Appraisal of Seminole Lands in Florida in 1823 and 1832: Dockets 73 and 151 before Indian Claims Commission* (Ames, Iowa, 1969), 63–65 (copy in P. K. Yonge Library of Florida History, University of Florida). Figures given in U.S. 30th Congress, Second Session, *Senate Documents no. 2*, Appendix 3 of the report of the Commissioner of the General Land Office, add up to 414,084 acres, but these are lower annual figures than those published by that same office for the individual years. U.S. 24th Congress, First Session, *Senate Document, no. 3*, "Annual Report of the Commissioner of the General Land Office," 8 Dec. 1835, p. 7.

24. *SLGF* 1: xxxiii–Lii; see also Martin, *Territorial Days*, 71–77. See also George Whatley and Sylvia Cook, "The East Florida Land Commission: A Study in Frustration," *FHQ* 50 (1951), 39–52. In Dec. 1835, in response to a Congressional inquiry, Richard Keith Call, by then Receiver of Lands at Tallahassee, reported 154 cases in litigation, some of them involving substantial amounts of land such as three sawmill grants each claiming a square sixteen miles on a side.

25. *SLGF* database. This figure does not include the Forbes Purchase of 1,427,289 acres, which falls in Middle Florida, but does include the Arredondo Grant in East Florida.

26. *SLGF* 2:46–86.

27. Schafer, "U.S. Territory and State," 212; Paisley, *Red Hills*, 57–61, 62–68 (story of Henry Yonge); Hugh Young, "A Topographical Memoir of East and West Florida with Itineraries of General Jackson's Army, 1818," Introduction and annotations by Mark F. Boyd and Gerald M. Ponton, *FHQ* 13 (1934), 16–50, 82–104, 129–64, shows what the Jackson men might have observed and gives leads to accounts that were published at the time, as this one was not. *SLGF* database.

28. Schafer, "U.S. Territory and State," 215; *SLGF* 1:xlvi (1824); Martin, *Territorial Days*, 91–92, with quotation p. 92 (1826).

29. An example of an older map is the "Southern Provinces of the United States," 1817 (reproduced, Ithaca, N.Y.: Historic Urban Plans, 1987); Lea and Cary *Atlas*, 1822, Plate 37, copy in P. K. Yonge Library of Florida History; from *A Complete Historical, Chronological, and Geographical American Atlas* (Philadelphia: H. C. Carey and I. Lea, 1823); Henry S. Tanner, *New American Atlas* (Philadelphia: Tanner, Vallance, Kearny, 1823). Issued with various imprints and the additional title *Containing Maps to the Several States of the North American Union;* Vignoles, *Observations,* map inserted before title page (facsimile ed.).

30. John Grant Forbes, *Sketches: Historical and Topographical of the Floridas* (1822; facsimile ed., Gainesville: University of Florida Press, 1964), 59, 67, 72–91, 119–20, quotations from 90 and 59, respectively.

31. Simmons, *Notices,* passim but esp. 10, 51–53; Vignoles, *Observations,* 35–56, 146–48.

32. Bertram H. Groene, ed., "Lizzie Brown's Tallahassee," *FHQ* 48 (Oct. 1969), 155–58 (Brown's story); Schafer, "U.S. Territory and State," 212–13, lists other scions of prominent Virginia families to settle in Leon County; Long, *Florida Breezes,* 128, states that "very much of the old provincial society of Virginia has slipped down here"; Paisley, *Red Hills,* 147, comments on the South Carolinians; Julia Hering, "Plantation Economy in Leon County, 1830–1840," *FHQ* 33 (Jul. 1954), 32.

33. Brown, *Peace River,* 34–35; Otto, *Southern Frontiers,* x–xi; James M. Denham, "The Florida Cracker before the Civil War As Seen through Traveler's Accounts," *FHQ* 72 (Apr. 1994), 456–67 (general characterization); Martin, *Territorial Days,* 109–10. Long, *Florida Breezes,* 52, describes a rural farm in the pine land between St. Marks and Tallahassee, and 170, another; her generally sympathetic description of crackers is on p. 186.

34. Dorothy Dodd, "The Florida Census of 1825," *FHQ* 22 (Jul. 1943), 33–40; Schafer, "U.S. Territory and State," 213, gives the 13,400 estimate. Jackson County had 2,236 persons, Gadsden County had 1,374 persons, and Leon had 996.

35. Schafer, "U.S. Territory and State," 213; Martin, *Territorial Days,* 91, 109 (1840 census data); John R. Dunkle, "Population Change as an Element in the Historical Geography of St. Augustine," *FHQ* 37 (1958), 23–26. The number of free persons of color declined by 1860 to half the level of 1830, a reflection of the pressures put on that segment of the population. See Schafer, "A Class of People," 593.

36. John Lee Williams, *The Territory of Florida; Or Sketches of the Topography, Civil and Natural History of the Country, the Climate, and the Indian Tribes from the First Discovery to the Present Time* (1837; facsimile ed., Gainesville: University of Florida Press, 1962).

37. Kathryn Abby Hanna, *Florida: Land of Change* (Chapel Hill:

University of North Carolina Press, 1941), 193–96; Kathryn T. Abby, "The Union Bank of Tallahassee: An Experiment in Territorial Finance," *FHQ* 15 (Apr. 1937), 207–31; Martin, *Territorial Days*, 145, 148–55; Long, *Florida Breezes*, 84, 209. A similar arrangement for "faith bonds" but for a smaller capital was made for the Bank of Pensacola (really a railroad corporation). The St. Augustine–based Southern Life Insurance and Trust Company, the other big bank of the period, drew its capital from New York City. Cotton prices rose from an average of $0.0971 per pound in 1831 to $0.123 in 1833 to $0.175 in 1835, held at $0.165 in 1836 and $0.133 in 1837, and then fell to $0.101 in 1838. By 1842, they were back to $0.095 per pound.

38. Julia Floyd Smith, *Slavery and Plantation Growth in Antebellum Florida, 1821–1860* (Gainesville: University of Florida Press, 1873), 23, 27.

39. Abby, "Union Bank," 207–31; Long, *Florida Breezes*, 84, 209.

40. James L. Watkins, *Production and Price of Cotton for One Hundred Years* (U.S. Department of Agriculture, Bureau of Statistics, *Bulletin*, no. 9; Washington, D.C.: Government Printing Office, 1895), 6; Hering, "Plantation Economy," 32–43. For biographies of planters in several counties, see Smith, *Slavery and Plantation Growth*, 122–52. According to Long, *Florida Breezes*, 220, a 500 lb. bale of cotton was the result of 1600 pounds of boles with seeds that took ten person-days of slave labor to pick.

41. Graham, *Awakening*, 39–40, 70. Anderson died in early 1840 before the market collapse of April. For the freeze of 1835, see Williams, *Territory*, 18.

42. Dorothy Dodd, "Railroad Projects in Territorial Florida" (M.A. thesis, Florida State University, 1929), passim; Martin, *Territorial Days*, 131–44; for East Florida see Graham, *Awakening*, 33–34.

43. Martin, *Territorial Days*, 35, 38, 65.

44. Morton D. Winsberg, "The Advance of Florida's Frontier As Determined from Post Office Openings," *FHQ* 72 (1993), 191–94, 197 (maps).

45. For sugar see Martin, *Territorial Days*, 114 (Alachua, 1833 where gross income per slave employed in sugar averaged $387 a year); Paisley, *Red Hills*, 89 (Leon and Jackson Cos.), Smith, *Slavery and Plantation Growth*, 129–32; for citrus see Williams, *Territory*, 18. Long, *Florida Breezes*, 85–86, notes that the extensive clearing of the 1820s led to killing frosts in 1828, whereas in 1826 maize was waist high in February.

46. Dinners, dances, and chivarees: Groene, "Lizzy Brown's Tallahassee," 118, 162–63, 167; Long, *Florida Breezes*, 121–22; Graham, *Awakening*, 16–17 (from *A Winter from Home*); Martin, *Territorial Days*, 97–123; wakes and funerals: "Diary of J. N. Glenn," *FHQ* 24 (1945), 152–53, and Edward C. Anderson, *Florida Territory in 1844: The Diary of Master Edward C. Anderson*, ed. W. Stanley Hoole (University: University of

Alabama Press, 1977), 62–64. Elizabeth Duval supposedly ended the custom at Tallahassee because she thought it unfair to the young men, who bore a considerable expense for the food, drink, and musicians (Groene, "Lizzy Brown's Tallahassee," 163).

47. Long, *Florida Breezes*, 94–108 (passim); Groene, "Lizzy Brown's Tallahassee," 167; Clifton Paisley, "Tallahassee through the Storebooks, 1843–1863: Antebellum Cotton Prosperity," *FHQ* 50 (1971), 112–14 (May party).

48. Long, *Florida Breezes*, 186–87; Diary of Judge Robert Raymond Reid, quoted in Martin, *Territorial Days*, 64; Graham, *Awakening*, 14–15, from *A Winter from Home* and other sources; Long, *Florida Breezes*, 170, and Denhan, "Florida Crackers," 461–62; quotation re slaves, Long, *Florida Breezes*, 33. For the pressures put on free blacks see Schafer, "A Class of People," 591–99. He found that to ca. 1840 they were able to evade some of the laws in St. Johns and Duval Counties but free Blacks rapidly lost their legal standing once the development of a large group of white small farmers meant that they no longer were needed to protect property from the Indians and once men like Kingsley and George J. F. Clarke had died.

49. Covington, *Seminoles*, 62, quoting from John T. Sprague, *The Origin, Progress, and Conclusion of the Florida War* (New York: D. Appleton and Company, 1848), 50–51. Throughout the 1820s there were isolated instances of Indians going off the reservations to kill cattle when game and crops failed or when young men wanted to display their bravado. The chiefs tried to prevent this activity, especially after the law of 1827, noted above.

50. The reader will understand that this is a conventional label that disguises the roles of the three different Indian groups and their Black associates.

51. Covington, *Seminoles*, 63–70. John K. Mahon, "Two Seminole Treaties: Payne's Landing, 1832, and Fort Gibson, 1833," *FHQ* 41 (1962), 1–21, is a full discussion of what Mahon concludes were the fraudulent actions of the Americans at Fort Gibson.

52. Covington, *Seminoles*, 73–79.

53. John K. Mahon's *History of the Second Seminole War* (Gainesville: University of Florida Press, 1967) is the best detailed account. I have used Covington's shorter account (largely based on Mahon) in *Seminoles*, 82–109, as my principal narrative source with additional materials derived from Kenneth W. Porter, *The Negro on the American Frontier* (New York: Arno Press, 1971), 64–68; Brown, *Peace River Frontier*, 42–64; Graham, *Awakening*, 44–51; William W. Rogers, *Ante-Bellum Thomas County, 1825–1861* (Tallahassee: Florida State University Studies, no. 39, 1963), 36–39; and Matthews, *Edge of Wilderness*, 80–127. See also George Klos, "Blacks and the Seminole Removal De-

bate, 1821–1835," in *The African American Heritage of Florida*, ed. David R. Colburn and Jane L. Landers (Gainesville: University Press of Florida, 1995), 128–56.

54. Covington, *Seminoles*, 72; Porter, *Negro on the American Frontier*, 68; *NASP, Indian Affairs*, 11:311–21, Report of T. Hartley Crawford to J. M. Potter, Secretary of War, 20 Jan. 1844 (3,824 Indians removed; estimate of 42 Seminole, 33 Miccosuki, 10 Creeks, 10 Tallahassee warriors remaining).

55. *Historical Statistics of the United States*, Series E 126, Raw Cotton, average New York price for middling upland cotton during a year that ran 1 Sept. to the following 31 August.

56. Dorothy Dodd, ed., *Florida Becomes a State* (Tallahassee: Florida Centennial Commission, 1945), 77; Matthews, *Edge of Wilderness*, 151–57; Anderson, *Florida Territory*, 32–33.

57. Abby, "Union Bank," 215–25.

58. Dodd, *Florida Becomes a State*, 32–38, 51–69.

59. Ibid., 72, 75–76, 78, 82–85, 91 (flag); see also Martin, *Territorial Days*, 277.

60. Matthews, *Edge of Wilderness*, 127–34; Brown, *Peace River*, 65–67; Covington, *Seminoles*, 110. See also Michael G. Schene, "Sugar along the Manatee: Major Robert Gamble, Jr., and the Development of Gamble Plantation," *Tequesta* 41 (1981), 69–81. The Newnansville office was to handle land sales and grants for the area East of the Suwannee and west of the division between ranges 24 and 25, except for the area north of the basis parallel and east of the St. Marys (Martin, *Territorial Days*, 88). Claims under the Armed Occupation Act for the areas around Lake Tohopekattigo on the upper St. Johns River had to be filed at St. Augustine.

61. U.S. 31st Congress, First Session, *Senate Document no. 1*, pp. 23–26, "Annual Report of the Commissioner of the General Land Office, 28 Nov. 1849." This report indicates 853 permits were "perfected," 290 had permits approved and patents issued while the rest covering some 27,000 acres had various problems.

62. Martin, *Territorial Days*, 94–96, and Schafer, "U.S. Territory and State," 218 (both on the Georgia migration); Covington, *Seminoles*, 110–11 (buffer zone; see also the map published in U.S. 32nd Congress, First Session, *Senate Documents no. 1*, following the "Annual Report of the Commissioner of the General Land Office").

63. U.S. 30th Congress, Second Session, *Senate Documents no. 2*, p. 7, "Annual Report of the Commissioner of the General Land Office"; U.S. 31st Congress, Second Session, *Senate Documents no. 2*, 37–38, "Annual Report of the Commissioner of the General Land Office"; and U.S. 32nd Congress, Second Session, *Senate Documents no. 1*, 112–13, "Report of the Commissioner of the General Land Office," 29 Nov.

1852. Average sales computed from U.S. 31st Congress, Second Session, *Senate Documents no. 2*, 32; U.S. 32nd Congress, First Session, *Senate Documents no. 1*, 25, 30; U.S. 32nd Congress, Second Session, *Senate Documents no. 2*, 99, 105; 33rd Congress, First Session, *Senate Documents no. 1*, 94, 101; and 33rd Congress, Second Session, *Senate Documents no. 1*, 114. I computed the averages for actual calendar years, not the government's fiscal year. The estimates for public lands and total acres in Florida are both inaccurate.

64. U.S. 33rd Congress, Second Session, *Senate Documents no. 1*, 117; U.S. 34th Congress, First Session, *Senate Documents no. 1*, 168–69, 174–75; U.S. 34th Congress, Third Session, *Senate Documents no. 5*, 222, 228; U.S. 35th Congress, First Session, *Senate Documents no. 11*, 104–105, 110–11; U.S. 35th Congress, Second Session, *Senate Documents no. 1*, 142–43, 150–51; U.S. 36th Congress, First Session, *Senate Documents no. 2*, 202–203, 208–209; U.S. 36th Congress, Second Session, *Senate Documents no. 1*, 90–91, 96–97; U.S. 37th Congress, Second Session, *Senate Documents no. 1*, 504–505.

65. Olin Norwood, ed., "Letters from Florida in 1851," *FHQ* 29 (1951), 261–83, quotation from 275; Patricia Clark, ed., "'A Tale to Tell from Paradise Itself': George Bancroft's Letters from Florida, Mar. 1855," *FHQ* 48 (1970), 264–78. See also Rodney E. Dillion, Jr., "South Florida in 1860," *FHQ* 60 (1982), 440–54.

66. *NASP, Indian Affairs* 11: 442–43; Samuel Reid to General W. J. Worth, St. Augustine, 25 Feb. 1844 (peaceful); Brown, *Peace River*, 72–73. He notes that on 27 Aug. 1848 one McCord beat two Seminole at Tampa for no reason and got off with a $3.00 fine for contempt of court.

67. Brown, *Peace River*, 75–79 (Law of 1849); Covington, *Seminoles*, 111–12, 115–19; Brown, *Peace River*, 80–86 (attack on the Kennedy and Darling store).

68. Covington, *Seminoles*, 118–23; Brown, *Peace River*, 86–93. Figure on Florida's claim to swamps and overflowed lands from Murray, *Appraisal of Seminole Lands*, 128, 133–36. Florida in effect claimed all land not previously sold, confirmed under Spanish and other grants, or given to the state.

69. Covington, *Seminoles*, 123–27; Brown, *Peace River*, 93–108; U.S. 34th Congress, First Session, *Senate Documents no. 1*, 268, "Report of Surveyor General of Florida, 30 Oct. 1855."

70. Covington, *Seminoles*, 128–44, and Brown, *Peace River*, 110–19.

Bibliography

Primary Sources

Archivo General de Indias, Seville (AGI)
    Contaduría (CD) 299, 548, 941, 944, 955, 956, 958, 1174
    Contratación (CT) 3309, 5012
    Escribanía de Cámara (EC) 154A, 154B
    Indiferente General (IG) 739, 1093, 1373, 1887
    Justicia (JU) 3, 817, 1001, 1002
    Mexico (MEX) 280, 1065
    Patronato (PAT) 19, 75, 255
    Santo Domingo (SD) 6, 11, 25, 99, 115, 118, 124, 125, 127, 146, 150, 151,
        168, 224, 225, 226, 227, 228, 229, 230, 231, 232, 233, 616, 848, 849,
        2528, 2533, 2584, 2587, 2668

Materials from these *legajos* were consulted in photostat and microfilm copies held in 1994 at the P. K. Yonge Library of Florida History, University of Florida, Gainesville. They were found in the John B. Stetson, Jr. collection of photostats now housed at Flagler College, St. Augustine, a microfilm copy in four reels of the Jeannette Thurber Connor collection of photostats held by the Library of Congress, a microfilm copy of the the Joseph B. Lockey collection also at the Library of Congress, and in microfilms secured since 1968 directly from the Archivo General de Indias.

Stahle, David W., and Malcolm K. Cleaveland. "Rainfall Tables, AD 933–1985." Computer printout in collection of the author courtesy of Doctors Stahle and Cleaveland.

Atlases and Maps

Atlas of Florida. Edited by Edward A. Fernald. Gainesville: University Presses of Florida, 1992.
A Complete Historical, Chronological, and Geographical American Atlas. Philadelphia: H. C. Carey and I. Lea, 1823.

Cumming, William P. *The Southeast in Early Maps.* 3rd ed., revised and enlarged by Louis De Vorsey, Jr. Chapel Hill: University of North Carolina Press, 1998.

DeBrahm, John Gerard William. "Map of the General Survey of East Florida . . . 1766 to 1770." British Library, King's MS 211, fol 3 (1).

Geological Survey (U.S.). *National Atlas of the United States of America.* Washington, D.C.: U.S. Government Printing Office, 1970.

Gibson, J. "A Map of the New Governments of East and West Florida." *Gentleman's Magazine and Historical Chronicle* 33 (1763).

Great Britain, Public Record Office. Crown Collection of Maps of North America. Series III. Colonial Office 700: North American Colonies, Florida, No. 7.

Hilliard, Samuel Bowers. *Atlas of Antebellum Southern Agriculture.* Baton Rouge: Louisiana State University Press, 1984.

Jeffreys, Thomas. *The Peninsula and Gulf of Florida, the Coast of West Florida and Louisiana.* 1792. Copy in P. K. Yonge Library of Florida History.

"Plano general de la plaza de San Agustín de la Florida de 1791." *Revista de Historia Militar,* no. 63 (1987), 218–20.

Southern Provinces of the United States. 1817. Reprinted, Ithaca, N.Y.: Historic Urban Plans, 1987.

Spain. Ejército, Servicio Geográfico. *Cartografía de Ultramar.* 4 vols. in 8. Madrid: Imprenta de Servicio Geográfico del Ejército, 1949–1957.

Tanner, Henry S. *New American Atlas.* Philadelphia: Tanner, Vallance, Kearny, 1823.

United States Department of Agriculture, Soil Conservation Service. *General Soil Map, Florida.* Gainesville: no publisher, 1982.

Printed Collections of Documents

"Annual Report of the Commissioner of the General Land Office" in U.S. 24th Congress, First Session, *Senate Document, No. 3;* 30th Congress, Second Session, *Senate Document, No. 2,* Appendix 3; 31st Congress, First Session, *Senate Document, No. 1;* 31st Congress, Second Session, *Senate Document, No. 1;* 32nd Congress, First Session, *Senate Document, No. 1;* 32nd Congress, Second Session, *Senate Document, No. 1;* 33rd Congress, First Session, *Senate Document, No. 1;* 33rd Congress, Second Session, *Senate Document, No. 1;* 34th Congress, First Session, *Senate Document, No. 1;* 34th Congress, Third Session, *Senate Document, No. 5;* 35th Congress, First Session, *Senate Document, No. 11;* 35th Congress, Second Session, *Senate Document, No. 1;* 36th Congress, First Session, *Senate Document, No. 2;* 36th Congress, Second Session, *Senate Document, No. 1;* 37th Congress, Second Session, *Senate Document, No. 1.*

Brooks, Abbie M. *The Unwritten History of Old St. Augustine, Copied from the Spanish Archives in Seville, Spain.* Translated by Annie Averette. St. Augustine: The Record Company, 1907.

Bushnell, David (compiler). *La República de las Floridas: Text and Documents.* Mexico City: Pan American Institute of History and Geography, 1986.

Colección de documentos inéditos relativos al descubrimiento, conquista, y organización de las antiguas posesiones españoles de América y Oceanía, sacados de los archivos del reino, y muy especialmente del de Indias, ed. Joaquín F. Pacheco, Francisco de Cardenas, and Luis Torres de Mendoza, 42 vols. Madrid, 1864–1884.

Colonial Records of the State of Georgia. 32 vols. Atlanta: C. P. Byrd and others, 1904–1989.

Davenport, Frances G., ed. *European Treaties Bearing on the History of the United States and Its Dependencies.* 4 vols. Washington, D.C.: Carnegie Institution of Washington, 1917–1937.

Documentary Sources for the Wreck of the New Spain Fleet of 1554. Translated by David R. McDonald, prepared by David R. McDonald and J. Barto Arnold III. Austin: Texas Antiquities Committee, 1979.

Dodd, Dorothy (ed.). *Florida Becomes a State.* Tallahassee: Florida Centennial Commission, 1945.

Georgia Historical Society. *Collections of the Georgia Historical Society,* Vol. 7, part 1, *Letters of Montiano, Siege of St. Augustine.* Savannah: Georgia Historical Society / Savannah Morning News, 1909.

———. Vol. 7, part 3, *The Spanish Official Account of the Attack on the Colony of Georgia, in America, and of its Defeat On St. Simons Island by General James Oglethorpe.* Savannah: Savannah Morning News, 1913.

Great Britain. Public Record Office. *Journal of the Commissioners for Trade and Plantations.* 14 vols. London: His Majesty's Stationery Office, 1920–1938.

Hann, John H., ed. and trans. *Missions to the Calusa.* Gainesville: University of Florida Press, 1991.

Havana. Ayuntamiento. *Actas capitulares del Ayuntamiento de la Havana.* 3 vols. Havana: Municipio de la Habana, 1937–1940.

Lanning, John Tate (ed.). *The St. Augustine Expedition of 1740: A Report to the South Carolina General Assembly.* Columbia: South Carolina Archives Department, 1954.

Lilly Library, Latin American Manuscripts—Mexico. *King to Bishop Ignacio de Urbina,* Barcelona, 8 March 1702. Printed document. Copy at P. K. Yonge Library of Florida History.

Lockey, Joseph Byrne. *East Florida, 1783–1785: A File of Documents Assembled, and Many of Them Translated by Joseph Byrne Lockey,* ed. John W. Caughey. Berkeley: University of California Press, 1949.

Navarrete, Martín Fernández, ed. *Colección de los viages y descubri-*

mientos que hicieron por mar los Españoles desde fines del Siglo XV con varios documentos inéditos concernientes a la historia de la marina Castellana y de los establecimientos españoles en Indias. 5 vols. Madrid: Imprenta Real, 1825–1837. Reprinted, Buenos Aires: Editorial Guaranía, 1945–1946.

The New American State Papers, Indian Affairs, Southeast. Edited by Thomas C. Cochran. 13 vols. Wilmington, Del.: Scholarly Resources, 1972.

Priestley, Herbert I, ed. and trans. *The Luna Papers: Documents Relating to the Expedition of Don Tristan de Luna y Arellano for the Conquest of La Florida in 1559–1561.* 2 vols. Deland: Florida State Historical Society, 1928.

Rojas, María Teresa de. *Indice y extractos del archivo de protocolos de la Habana, 1578–1595.* 3 vols. Havana, 1947–.

Ruidiaz y Caravía, Eugenio, ed. *La Florida: Su conquista y colonización por Pedro Menéndez de Avilés.* 2 vols. Madrid: Imprenta de los Hijos de J. A. García, 1893.

Salley, Alexander Samuel, ed. *Narratives of Early Carolina, 1650–1708.* New York: Scribner, 1911. Reprinted, New York: Barnes and Noble, 1967.

Serrano y Sanz, Manuel, ed. *Documentos históricos de la Florida y la Luisiana, Siglos XVI al XVIII.* Madrid: V. Suarez, 1912.

Siebert, Wilbur H. *Loyalists in East Florida, 1774–1785: The Most Important Documents Pertaining thereto . . . with an Accompanying Narrative.* 2 vols. Deland: The Florida State Historical Society, 1929.

Spain. Sovereigns, etc., 1556–1598 (Philip II). *Negociaciones con Francia, 1559–[1568].* 11 vols. Madrid: Real Academia de la Historia, 1950–[1960?].

Spanish Land Grants in Florida. Prepared by the Historical Records Survey, Division of Professional and Service Projects, Work Projects Administration. 5 vols. Tallahassee, Fla.: State Library Board, 1940.

United States. Laws, Statutes, etc. *Laws of the United States . . . Spanish Regulations and Other Documents Respecting the Public Lands.* Compiled by Matthew St. Claire Clarke. 2 vols. Washington, D.C., 1828–1836.

Whitaker, Arthur Preston, trans. and ed. *Documents Relating to the Commercial Policy of Spain in the Floridas, with Incidental Reference to Louisiana.* Deland: Florida State Historical Society, 1931.

Worth, John E. *The Struggle for the Georgia Coast: An Eighteenth-Century Spanish Retrospective on Guale and Mocama.* New York: American Museum of Natural History; Athens, Ga.: Distributed by the University of Georgia Press, 1995.

Wright, Irene A., ed. *Further English Voyages to Spanish America, 1583–1594.* London: Hakluyt Society, 1951.

Books

Adair, James. *The History of the American Indians: Particularly Those Adjoining to the Mississippi, East and West Florida, Georgia, South and North Carolina and Virginia.* 1775. Reprint, Johnson City, Tenn: Watauga Press, 1930.

Alvarez Rubiano, Pablo. *Pedrárias Dávila; Contribución al estudio de la figura del "Gran Justador."* Madrid: Consejo Superior de Investigaciones Científicos, Instituto Gonzalo Fernández de Oviedo, 1944.

Anderson, Edward C. *Florida Territory in 1844: The Diary of Master Edward C. Anderson.* Edited and Foreword by W. Stanley Hoole. University, Ala.: University of Alabama Press, 1977.

Anghiera, Pietro Martiere d'. *Décadas del nuevo mundo.* Estudio y apéndices por Edmundo O'Gorman. 2 vols. Mexico: J. Porrua, 1964–1965.

Arana, Luis R., and Albert A. Manucy. *The Building of Castillo de San Marcos.* St. Augustine: Eastern National Parks Monument Association for Castillo de San Marcos National Monument, 1977.

Arnade, Charles W. *Florida on Trial, 1593–1602.* Coral Gables: University of Miami Press, 1959.

———. *The Siege of St. Augustine in 1702.* Gainesville: University of Florida Press in cooperation with the St. Augustine Historical Society, 1959.

Arrendono, Antonio. *Arredondo's Historical Proof of Spain's Title to Georgia.* Edited by Herbert E. Bolton. Berkeley: University of California Press, 1925.

Barcía Carballido y Zúñiga, Andés Gonzales de. *Chronological History of the Continent of Florida.* Translated by Anthony Kerrigan. Gainesville: University of Florida Press, 1951.

Barry, John M. *Natural Vegetation of South Carolina.* Columbia: University of South Carolina Press, 1980.

Bemis, Samuel Fagg. *Diplomatic History of the United States.* New York: Henry Holt, 1942.

———. *Pinckney's Treaty: A Study of America's Advantage from Europe's Distress, 1783–1800.* Baltimore: Johns Hopkins University Press, 1926. Reprinted 1960, Yale University Press, New Haven, Conn.

Bennett, Charles E. *Florida's "French" Revolution, 1793–1795.* Gainesville: University of Florida Press, 1982.

Bolton, Herbert E., and Mary Ross. *The Debatable Land.* Berkeley: University of California Press, 1925.

Braun, E[mma] Lucy. *Deciduous Forests of North America.* New York: Macmillan, 1950.

Brooks, Philip C. *Diplomacy and the Borderlands: The Adams-Onís Treaty of 1819.* Berkeley: University of California Press, 1939.

Brown, Canter. *Florida's Peace River Frontier*. Gainesville: University Presses of Florida, 1991.

Brown, Clair A. *Vegetation of the Outer Banks of North Carolina*. Baton Rouge: Louisiana State University Coastal Studies Series, No. 4, 1959.

Bushnell, Amy Turner. *The King's Coffer: Proprietors of the Spanish Florida Treasury, 1565–1702*. Gainesville: University Presses of Florida, 1981.

———. *Situado and Sabana: Spain's Support System for the Presidio and Mission Provinces of Florida*. New York: American Museum of Natural History; Athens: Distributed by the University of Georgia Press, 1994.

Caruso, John A. *The Southern Frontier*. Indianapolis: Bobbs-Merrill, 1963.

Cervantes de Salazar, Francisco. *Life in the Imperial and Loyal City of Mexico in New Spain, and the Royal and Pontifical University of Mexico. . . .* Translated by Minnie Lee Barrett Shepard. Introduction and notes by Carlos E. Castañeda. Austin: University of Texas, 1953.

Chatelain, Verne E. *The Defenses of Spanish Florida, 1565 to 1763*. Washington, D.C.: Carnegie Institution of Washington, 1941.

Chaves, Alonso de. *Alonso de Chaves y el libro IV de su "Espejo de Navegantes."* Edited by Paulino Castaneda, M. Cuesta, and P. Hernández. Madrid: Industrias Gráficas España, 1977.

Clayton, Lawrence A., Vernon James Knight, Jr., and Edward C. Moore, eds. *The De Soto Chronicles: The Expedition of Hernando de Soto to North America in 1539–1543*. 2 vols. Tuscaloosa: University of Alabama Press, 1993.

Cline, Howard F. *Florida Indians II: Provisional Historical Gazetteer with Locational Notes on Florida Colonial Communities*. New York: Garland Publishing, 1974.

Coker, William S., and Thomas D. Watson. *Indian Traders of the Southeastern Spanish Borderlands: Panton, Leslie & Company and John Forbes & Company, 1783–1847*. Pensacola: University of West Florida Press, 1986.

Coleman, Kenneth. *Colonial Georgia: A History*. New York: Scribner and Son, 1976.

Cook, Warren L. *Flood Tide of Empire: Spain and the Pacific Northwest, 1543–1819*. New Haven, Conn.: Yale University Press, 1973.

Covington, James W. *The Seminoles of Florida*. Gainesville: University Press of Florida, 1993.

Crane, Verner W. *The Southern Frontier, 1670–1732*. Durham, N.C.: Duke University Press, 1928.

Crook, Morgan Ray, Jr. *Mississippian Period Archaeology of the Georgia Coastal Zone*. Athens: University of Georgia Laboratory of Archaeology Series, Report no. 23, 1986.

Dávila Padilla, Agustín. *Historia de la fundación y discurso de la provincia de Santiago de Mexico de la orden de Predicadores.* . . . Madrid: Casa de Pedro Madrigal, 1596.

Delanglez, Jean. *El Río del Espíritu Santo: An Essay on the Cartography of the Gulf Coast and the Adjacent Territory During the Sixteenth and Seventeenth Centuries.* Edited by Thomas J. McMahon. New York: United States Catholic Historical Society, 1945.

De Pratter, Chester B. *Prehistoric and Early Historic Chiefdoms in the Southeastern United States.* New York: Garland Publishing, 1991.

Dickinson, Jonathan. *God's Protecting Providence (1700).* New York: Garland Publishing, 1977.

Dobyns, Henry. *Their Number Became Thinned: Native American Population Dynamics in Eastern North America.* Knoxville: University of Tennessee Press, 1983.

Earle, Peter. *The Sack of Panama: Sir Henry Morgan's Adventures on the Spanish Main.* New York: Viking Press, 1981.

Ecosystems of Florida. Edited by Ronald L. Myers and John J. Ewel. Orlando: University of Central Florida Press, 1990.

[Elvas, The Gentleman of]. *Relaçam verdadeira dos trabalhos q[ue] ho Governador dõ Fernãdo de Souto e certos fidalgos portugueses passarom no descubrimēto da provincia da Frolida, Agora nouamēte feita per hũ fidalgo Deluas.* Evora: A. de Burgos, 1557.

Escobedo, Alonso Gregorio de. *Pirates, Indians, and Spaniards: Father Escobedo's "La Florida."* Translated by A. E. Falcones. Edited by James W. Covington. St. Petersburg, Fla.: Great Outdoors Publishing Co., 1963.

Ewen, Charles R., and John H. Hann. *Hernando de Soto Among the Apalachee: The Archaeology of the First Winter Encampment.* Gainesville: University Press of Florida, 1994.

Figuero-del Campo, Cristobal. *Misiones franciscanas en la Florida.* Madrid: Comisión Episcopal del V. Centenario, 1992.

Forbes, John Grant. *Sketches, Historical and Topographical, of the Floridas.* 1821. Fac. ed. Gainesville: University of Florida Press, 1964.

Fuller, Hubert B. *The Purchase of Florida: Its History and Diplomacy.* Cleveland: Burrows, 1906.

Galloway, Patricia K. *Choctaw Genesis, 1500–1700.* Lincoln: University of Nebraska Press, 1995.

Geiger, Maynard J. *The Franciscan Conquest of Florida (1573–1618).* Washington, D.C.: Catholic University of America, 1937.

Gibson, Charles. *The Aztecs Under Spanish Rule.* Stanford, Calif.: Stanford University Press, 1964.

Gold, Robert L. *Borderlands Empires in Transition: The Triple-Nation Transfer of Florida.* Carbondale: University of Southern Illinois Press, 1969.

Graham, Thomas. *The Awakening of St. Augustine: The Anderson Family and the Oldest City, 1821–1924.* St. Augustine, Fla.: St. Augustine Historical Society, 1978.

Hall, Basil. *Travels in North America in the Years 1827 and 1828.* 2 vols. Philadelphia: Carey, Lea, & Carey, 1829.

Hanke, Lewis U. *The Spanish Struggle for Justice in the Conquest of America.* Boston: Little Brown, 1965.

Hann, John H. *Apalachee: The Land Between the Rivers.* Gainesville: University Presses of Florida, 1988.

———. *A History of the Timucua Indians and Missions.* Gainesville: University Press of Florida, 1996.

Hanna, Kathryn Abby. *Florida: Land of Change.* Chapel Hill: University of North Carolina Press, 1941.

Harmon, Joyce E. *Trade and Privateering in Spanish Florida, 1732–1763.* St. Augustine, Fla.: St. Augustine Historical Society, 1969.

Herrera y Tordesillas, Antonio de. *Historia general de los hechos de los castellanos en las islas y Tierrafirme del mar oceano.* 10 vols. Asunción, Paraguay: Editorial Guaranía, 1944.

Historical Statistics of the United States, Colonial Times to 1970. Washington, D.C.: U.S. Bureau of the Census, 1975.

Hoffman, Paul E. *A New Andalucia and a Way to the Orient: The American Southeast during the Sixteenth Century.* Baton Rouge: Louisiana State University Press, 1990.

———. *Spain and the Roanoke Voyages.* Raleigh: America's Four Hundredth Anniversary Committee, North Carolina Department of Cultural Resources, 1987.

Howard, Amster K. *Soil Classification Handbook. Unified Soil Classification System.* Denver: Geotechnical Branch, Division of Research and Laboratory Services, Engineering and Research Center, Bureau of Reclamation, 1986.

Hudson, Charles. *The Juan Pardo Expeditions. Exploration of the Carolinas and Tennessee, 1566–1568.* Washington, D.C.: Smithsonian Institution Press, 1990.

Insh, George P. *Scottish Colonial Schemes, 1620–1686.* Glasgow: Maclehouse Jackson & Co., 1922.

Johnson, A. Sidney, H. O. Hillestad, S. F. Shanholtzer, and G. F. Shanholtzer. *An Ecological Survey of the Coastal Region of Georgia.* Washington, D.C.: National Park Service Scientific Monograph Series, No. 3, 1974.

Keegan, Gregory J., and Leandro Tormo Sanz. *Experiencia misionera en la Florida (Siglos XVI y XVII).* Madrid: Consejo Superior de Investigaciones Científicas, 1957.

Kelsey, Harry. *Sir Francis Drake, The Queen's Pirate.* New Haven, Conn.: Yale University Press, 1998.

Keys to Soil Taxonomy. 6th ed. Washington, D.C.: U.S. Department of Bibliography
Agriculture, Natural Resources Conservation Service, 1994.

Landers, Jane. *Black Society in Spanish Florida.* Urbana: University of
Illinois Press, 1999.

Lanning, John Tate. *The Diplomatic History of Georgia: A Study of
the Epoch of Jenkins' Ear.* Chapel Hill: University of North Carolina
Press, 1936.

———. *The Spanish Missions of Georgia.* Chapel Hill: University of
North Carolina Press, 1935.

Larson, Lewis H., Jr. *Aboriginal Subsistence Technology on the Southeastern Coastal Plain During the Late Prehistoric Period.* Gainesville: University of Florida Press, 1980.

Laslett, Peter. *The World We Have Lost: England Before the Industrial
Age.* 2nd ed. New York: Charles Scribner's Sons, 1973.

Laudonnière, René Goulaine de. *L'histoire notable de la Florida situeé
ès Indes Occidentales.* . . . Edited by Suzanne Lussagnet. Paris:
Presses Universitaires de France, 1958.

———. *Three Voyages.* Translated with introduction by Charles E. Bennett. Gainesville: University Presses of Florida, 1975.

Lewis, Clifford M., and Albert J. Loomie. *The Spanish Jesuit Mission
in Virginia, 1570–1572.* Chapel Hill: University of North Carolina
Press, 1953.

Long, Ellen Call. *Florida Breezes; or Florida New and Old.* 1883. Fac.
ed. Gainesville: University of Florida Press, 1962.

López de Gómara, Francisco. *Historia general de las Indias.* 2 vols.
Barcelona: Editorial Iberia, S. A., 1954.

———. *Historia general de las Indias.* . . . Zaragoça: Agustin Millan,
1552.

López de Velasco, Juan. *Geografía y descripción universal de las Indias.* 1574. Madrid: Fortanet, 1894.

Lowery, Woodbury. *Spanish Settlements Within the Present Limits of
the United States.* 2 vols. New York: G. P. Putnam's Sons, 1901–1911.

Lynch, John. *Spain Under the Hapsburgs.* 2nd ed. 2 vols. New York:
New York University Press, 1981.

Lyon, Elijah W. *Louisiana in French Diplomacy, 1759–1804.* Norman:
University of Oklahoma Press, 1934.

Lyon, Eugene. *The Enterprise of Florida: Pedro Menéndez de Avilés and
the Spanish Conquest of 1565–1568.* Gainesville: University Presses
of Florida, 1976.

———. *Santa Elena: A Brief History of the Colony, 1566–1587.* Columbia, S.C.: Institute of Archaeology and Anthropology, 1984.

MacLachlan, Colin M. *Spain's Empire in the New World: The Role of
Ideas in Institutional and Social Change.* Berkeley: University of
California Press, 1988.

Mahon, John K. *History of the Second Seminole War.* Gainesville: University of Florida Press, 1985.

Martin, Joel W. *Sacred Revolt: The Muskogee Struggle for A New World.* Boston: Beacon Press, 1991.

Martin, Sidney W. *Florida During the Territorial Days.* Athens: University of Georgia Press, 1944.

Matthews, Janet S. *Edge of Wilderness: A Settlement History of Manatee River and Sarasota Bay.* Tulsa: Caprine Press, 1983.

Matter, Robert A. *Pre-Seminole Florida: Spanish Soldiers, Friars, and Indian Missions, 1513–1763.* New York: Garland Publishing, 1990.

McGrath, John T. *The French in Early Florida: In the Eye of the Hurricane.* Gainesville: University Press of Florida, 2000.

McQueen, John. *The Letters of D. Juan McQueen to His Family, Written from Spanish East Florida 1791–1807.* Columbia, S.C.: Bostick and Thornely, 1943.

Milanich, Jerald T. *Florida Indians and the Invasion From Europe.* Gainesville: University Press of Florida, 1995.

———, and Charles H. Fairbanks. *Florida Archaeology.* New York: Academic Press, 1980.

———, and Charles Hudson. *Hernando de Soto and the Indians of Florida.* Gainesville: University Press of Florida, 1993.

Miller, Janice B. *Juan Nepomuceno de Quesada, Spanish Governor of East Florida, 1790–1795.* Washington, D.C.: University Press of America, 1981.

Morison, Samuel E. *The European Discovery of America.* 2 vols. New York: Oxford University Press, 1971–1974.

Morse, Jedidiah. *The American Geography.* 1789. 1792. Reprint, New York: Arno Press, 1970.

Mowat, Charles L. *East Florida as a British Province, 1763–1784.* Berkeley: University of California Press, 1943.

Murdoch, Richard K. *The Georgia-Florida Frontier, 1793–1796: Spanish Reaction to French Intrigue and American Designs.* Berkeley: University of California Press, 1951.

Murray, William G. *Appraisal of Seminole Lands in Florida in 1823 and 1832: Dockets 73 and 151 Before Indian Claims Commission.* Ames, Iowa: Mimeographed, 1969.

Núñez Cabeza de Vaca, Alvar. *La Relación o Naufragios de Alvar Núñez Cabeza de Vaca.* Edited by Martín A Favata and José B. Fernández. Potomac, Md.: Scripta Humanistica, 1986.

Oré, Luis Gerónimo de. *The Martyrs of Florida.* Translated by Maynard Geiger. New York: J. F. Wagner, 1936.

Otto, John S. *The Southern Frontier, 1607–1860: The Agricultural Evolution of the Colonial and Antebellum South.* New York: Greenwood Press, 1989.

Oviedo y Valdés, Gonzalo Fernández de. *Historia general y natural de* BIBLIOGRAPHY
las Indias. 4 vols. Madrid: Imprenta de la Real Academia de la Historia, 1851–1855.

Paisely, Clifton. *The Red Hills of Florida, 1528–1865.* Tuscaloosa: University of Alabama Press, 1989.

Parry, John H. *The Discovery of South America.* New York: Taplinger Publishing Co., 1979.

Patrick, Rembert W. *Florida Fiasco: Rampant Rebels on the Georgia-Florida Border, 1810–1815.* Athens: University of Georgia Press, 1954.

Pearson, Fred Lamar, Jr. *Spanish-Indian Relations in Florida: A Study of Two Visitas, 1657–1678.* New York: Garland Publishing, 1990.

Porter, Kenneth W. *The Negro on the American Frontier.* New York: Arno Press, 1971.

Pyne, Stephen J. *Fire in America: A Cultural History of Wildland and Rural Fire.* Princeton: Princeton University Press, 1982.

Quaternary Non-glacial Geology: Conterminous United States. Edited by Roger B. Morrison. Boulder, Colo.: Geological Society of America, 1991.

Ramusio, Giovanni Battista. *Navigationi et Viaggi.* 1565–1606. 3 vols. Reprint, Amsterdam: Theatrum Orbis Terrarum, 1967–1970.

Rawlings, Majorie Kinnan. *The Yearling.* New York: Scribner, 1938.

Remini, Robert V. *Andrew Jackson and the Course of American Empire, 1767–1821.* New York: Harper and Row, 1977.

Río Cossa, José del. *Descripción de la Florida oriental hecha en 1787.* Editado por P. Agustín Barreiro. Madrid: Sociedad Geográfica Nacional, 1935.

Roberts, William. *An Account of the First Discovery and Natural History of Florida.* London: Printed for T. Jeffreys, 1763.

Rogers, William Warren. *Antebellum Thomas County, 1825–1861.* Tallahassee: Florida State University Studies, No. 39, 1963.

Romans, Bernard. *A Concise Natural History of East and West Florida.* 1775. Fac. ed. Gainesville: University of Florida Press, 1962.

Santa Cruz, Alonso de. *Islario General de todas las islas del mundo.* . . . Madrid: Imprenta del Patronato de Huérfanos de Intendencia y Intervención Militares, 1918.

Sauer, Carl O. *The Early Spanish Main.* Berkeley: University of California Press, 1966.

Service, Elman. *Primitive Social Organization: An Evolutionary Perspective.* New York: Random House, 1962.

Silver, Timothy. *A New Face on the Countryside: Indians, Colonists, and Slaves in the South Atlantic Forests, 1500–1800.* New York: Cambridge University Press, 1990.

Simmons, William H. *Notices of East Florida.* 1822. Fac. ed. Gainesville: University of Florida Press, 1977.

Sluiter, Engel. *The Florida Situado: Quantifying the First Eighty Years, 1571–1651.* Gainesville: P. K. Yonge Library of Florida History, 1985.

Smith, Joseph B. *The Plot to Steal Florida: James Madison's Phoney War.* New York: Arbor House, 1983.

Smith, Julia Floyd. *Slavery and Plantation Growth in Antebellum Florida, 1821–1860.* Gainesville: University of Florida, 1973.

Smith, Marvin T. *Archaeology of Aboriginal Culture Change in the Interior Southeast: Depopulation During the Early Historic Period.* Gainesville: University Presses of Florida, 1987.

Solís de Merás, Gonzalo. *Pedro Menéndez de Avilés.* Translated by Jeannette T. Connor. 1923. Fac. Ed. Gainesville: University of Florida Press, 1964.

Sprague, John T. *The Origin, Progress, and Conclusion of the Florida War.* New York: D. Appleton and Company, 1848.

Stuart, John Ferdinand Smyth. *A Tour of the United States of America. . . .* 2 vols. London: Printed for G. Robinson, 1784.

Swanton, John R. *Early History of the Creek Indians and Their Neighbors.* Washington, D.C.: Bureau of American Ethnology Bulletin No. 73, 1922.

Sweet, Zelia, and Mary H. Sheppy. *The Spanish Missions of Florida.* Compiled by W. P. A. Florida Writers' Project. 1940. Reprint, New Smyrna Beach, Fla.: Luthers, 1993.

Taylor, William B. *Drinking, Homicide, and Rebellion in Colonial Mexican Villages.* Stanford: Stanford University Press, 1979.

TePaske, John J. *The Governorship of Spanish Florida, 1700–1763.* Durham: Duke University Press, 1964.

Thomas, David H. *Historic Indian Period Archaeology of the Georgia Coastal Zone.* Athens: University of Georgia, Laboratory of Archaeology Series, Report No. 31, 1993.

Tornero Tinajero, Pablo. *Relaciones de dependencia entre Florida y Estados Unidos (1783–1820).* Madrid: Ministerio de Asuntos Exteriores, 1979.

Torquemada, Juan de. *Monarquía Indiana.* 3 vols. Madrid: N. Rodríguez Franco, 1725.

Vignoles, Charles B. *Observations Upon the Floridas.* 1823. Fac. ed. Gainesville: University of Florida Press, 1977.

Watkins, James L. *Production and Price of Cotton for One Hundred Years.* Washington, D.C.: Government Printing Office, 1895.

Weddle, Robert S. *The French Thorn, Rival Explorers in the Spanish Sea, 1682–1762.* College Station: Texas A & M Press, 1991.

———. *Spanish Sea: The Gulf of Mexico in North American Discovery, 1500–1685.* College Station: Texas A & M Press, 1985.

Wharton, Charles H. *The Natural Environments of Georgia.* Atlanta: Georgia Department of Natural Resources, 1977.

Williams, John Lee. *The Territory of Florida; or, Sketches of the Topography, Civil and Natural History of the Country, the Climate, and the Indian Tribes from the First Discovery to the Present Time.* 1837. Fac. ed. Gainesville: University of Florida Press, 1962.

Worth, John E. *The Timucuan Chiefdoms of Spanish Florida.* 2 vols. Gainesville: University Press of Florida, 1998.

Wright, J. Leitch, Jr. *Anglo-Spanish Rivalry in North America.* Athens: University of Georgia, 1971.

————. *Florida in the American Revolution.* Gainesville: University of Florida Press, 1975.

————. *The Only Land They Knew: The Tragic Story of the American Indians in the Old South.* New York: Free Press, 1981.

Wroth, Lawrence C. *The Voyages of Giovanni da Verrazzano.* New Haven: Yale University Press, 1970.

Wynn, Jack T. *Mississippi Period Archaeology of the Georgia Blue Ridge Mountains.* Athens: University of Georgia, Laboratory of Archaeology Series, Report no. 27, 1990.

Zubillaga, Felix. *La Florida: La misión jesuítica (1566–1572) y la colonización española.* Roma: Institutum Historicum S. I., 1941.

————. *Monumenta Antiquae Floridae (1566–1572).* Roma: Apud Monumenta Historica Soc. Iesu, 1946.

Articles and Book Chapters

Abbey, Kathryn T. "The Union Bank of Tallahassee: An Experiment in Territorial Finance." *Florida Historical Quarterly* 15 (1937), 207–31.

Abrahamson, Warren G., and David C. Harnett. "Pine Flatwoods and Dry Prairies." In *Ecosystems of Florida,* ed. Ronald L. Myers and John J. Ewel, 104–106. Orlando: University of Central Florida Press, 1990.

Almy, Marion M. "The Archaeological Potential of Soil Survey Reports." *Florida Anthropologist* 31 (1978), 75–91.

Anderson, David G. "Examining Prehistoric Settlement Distribution in Eastern North America." *Archaeology of Eastern North America* 19 (1991), 1–22.

Anderson, David G., David W. Stahle, and Malcolm K. Cleaveland. "Paleoclimate and the Potential Food Reserves of Mississippian Societies: A Case Study from the Savannah River Valley." *American Antiquity* 60 (1995), 258–86.

Andrews, Charles M. "The Florida Indians in the Seventeenth Century." *Tequesta* 1 (1943), 36–48.

Andrews, F. N. "Adaptation to the Environment." In *Introduction to*

Livestock Production, ed. H. H. Cole, 467–84. San Francisco: Freeman, 1966.

Arana, Luis R. "The Alonso Solana Map of Florida, 1683." *Florida Historical Quarterly* 43 (1964), 258–66.

Arnade, Charles W. "Cattle Raising in Spanish Florida, 1513–1763." *Agricultural History* 35 (1961), 116–24.

———. "The Failure of Spanish Florida." *The Americas* 16 (1960), 271–81.

———. "Piribiriba on the Salamototo: Spanish Fort on the St. Johns River." Jacksonville Historical Society *Papers* 4 (1960), 67–84.

Arnaud Rabinal, Juan Ignacio et al. "Estructura de la población de una sociedad de frontera, La Florida Española, 1600–1763." *Revista Compultense de Historia de América* 17 (1991), 93–120.

Bolton, Herbert E. "Spanish Resistance to the Carolina Traders in Western Georgia (1680–1704)." *Georgia Historical Quarterly* 9 (1925), 115–30.

Bond, Stanley C., Jr. "The Development of the Naval Stores Industry in St. Johns County, Florida." *Florida Anthropologist* 40 (1987), 187–202.

Boyd, Mark F. "Enumeration of Florida Spanish Missions in 1675 with Translations." *Florida Historical Quarterly* 27 (1948), 181–88.

———. "Events at Prospect Bluff on the Apalachicola River, 1808–1818: An Introduction to Twelve Letters of Edmund Doyle, Trader." *Florida Historical Quarterly* 16 (1937), 55–96.

———. "Expedition of Marcos Delgado From Apalache to the Upper Creek Country in 1686." *Florida Historical Quarterly* 16 (1937), 3–32.

———. "The First American Road in Florida; Pensacola—St. Augustine Highway, 1824." *Florida Historical Quarterly* 14 (1935–36), 73–106, 138–192.

———. "The Fortifications of San Marcos de Apalache." *Florida Historical Quarterly* 15 (1936), 1–34.

———. "A Map of a Road from Pensacola to St. Augustine, 1778." *Florida Historical Quarterly* 17 (1938), 15–23.

Brain, Jeffrey, and Charles R. Ewen. "Bibliography of De Soto Studies." In *The De Soto Chronicles: The Expedition of Hernando de Soto to North America in 1539–1543*, ed. Lawrence A. Clayton, Vernon James Knight, Jr., and Edward C. Moore, 1: 515–550. 2 vols. Tuscaloosa: University of Alabama Press, 1993.

Brown, Randall B., Earl L. Stone, and Victor W. Carlisle. "Soils." In *Ecosystems of Florida*, ed. Ronald L. Myers and John J. Ewel, 42–53. Orlando: University of Central Florida Press, 1990.

Bullen, Ripley P., and John W. Griffin. "An Archaeological Survey of Amelia Island, Florida." *Florida Anthropologist* 5 (1952), 37–64.

Bushnell, Amy T. "The Menéndez Marqués Cattle Barony at La Chua

and the Determinants of Economic Expansion in Seventeenth- Bibliography
Century Florida." *Florida Historical Quarterly* 56 (1978), 407–31.

———. "Patricio de Hinachuba, Defender of the Word of God, the Crown of the King, and the Little Children of Ivitachuco." *American Indian Culture and Research Journal* 3 (1979), 1–21.

———. "That Demonic Game: The Campaign to Stop Indian Pelota Playing in Spanish Florida, 1675–1684." *The Americas* 35 (1978), 1–19.

Chipman, Donald. "In Search of Cabeza de Vaca's Route Across Texas: An Historiographical Survey." *Southwestern Historical Quarterly* 91 (1987), 127–48.

Christensen, Norman L. "Vegetation of the Southeastern Coastal Plain." In *North American Terrestrial Vegetation*, ed. Michael G. Barbour and W. D. Billings, 317–63. New York: Cambridge University Press, 1988.

Clark, Patricia P. "A Tale to Tell From Paradise Itself: George Bancroft's Letters from Florida, March 1855." *Florida Historical Quarterly* 48 (1970), 264–78.

Coker, William S., and Susan R. Parker. "The Second Spanish Period in the Two Floridas." In *The New History of Florida*, ed. Michael Gannon, 150–66. Gainesville: University Presses of Florida, 1996.

Coleman, Kenneth. "The Southern Frontier: Georgia's Founding and the Expansion of South Carolina." *Georgia Historical Quarterly* 56 (1972), 163–74.

Colquhoun, Donald J., Gerald H. Johnson, Pamela C. Peebles, Paul F. Huddlestun, and Thomas Scott. "Quaternary Geology of the Atlantic Coastal Plain." In *Quaternary Non-glacial Geology, Conterminous United States*, ed. Roger B. Morrison, 629–50. Boulder, Colo.: The Geological Society of America, 1991.

Connolly, Matthew. "The Missions of Florida." In *Explorations and Settlements in the Spanish Borderlands: Their Religious Motivations*, 24–34. St. Augustine: Mission Nombre de Dios, 1967.

Cooper, Arthur W., Ralph J. McCracken, and Louis E. Aull. "Vegetation and Soil Resources." In *North Carolina Atlas: Portrait of a Changing State*, ed. James W. Clay, Douglas M. Orr, Jr., and Alfred W. Stuart, 128–35. Chapel Hill: University of North Carolina Press, 1975.

Corbett, Theodore G. "Migration to a Spanish Imperial Frontier in the Seventeenth and Eighteenth Centuries: St. Augustine." *Hispanic American Historical Review* 54 (1974), 414–30.

———. "Population Structure in Hispanic St. Augustine, 1629–1763." *Florida Historical Quarterly* 54 (1976), 263–84.

Corbitt, Duvon C. "The Administrative System in the Florida, 1783–1821." *Tequesta* 1 (1942–43), 41–62, 57–67.

Covington, James W. "Apalachee Indians, 1704–1763." *Florida Historical Quarterly* 50 (1972), 366–84.

———. "Relations Between the Eastern Timucuan Indians and the French and Spanish, 1564–1567." In *Four Centuries of Southern Indians*, ed. Charles Hudson, 11–27. Athens: University of Georgia Press, 1975.

———. "A Seminole Census: 1847." *Florida Anthropologist* 21 (1968), 120–22.

———. "Some Observations Concerning the Florida–Carolina Indian Slave Trade." *Florida Anthropologist* 20 (1967), 10–18.

———. "Stuart's Town, the Yamasee Indians and Spanish Florida." *Florida Anthropologist* 21 (1968), 8–13.

———. "Trade Relations Between Southwestern Florida and Cuba, 1600–1840." *Florida Historical Quarterly* 38 (1959), 114–16.

———. "The Yamasee Indians in Florida, 1715–1763." *Florida Anthropologist* 23 (1970), 119–28.

Crook, Morgan R., Jr. "Spatial Associations and Distribution of Aggregate Village Sites in a Southeastern Atlantic Coastal Area." *Florida Anthropologist* 31 (1978), 21–34.

Crosby, Alfred W., Jr. "Virgin Soil Epidemics as a Factor in the Aboriginal Depopulation of America." *William and Mary Quarterly*, 3rd Series, 33 (1976), 289–99.

Cumming, William P. "Geographical Misconceptions of the Southeast in the Cartography of the Seventeenth and Eighteenth Centuries." *Journal of Southern History* 4 (1938), 476–92.

Daniels, John D. "The Indian Population of North America in 1492." *William and Mary Quarterly*, 3rd Series, 49 (1992), 298–320.

Davis, T. Frederick. "MacGregor's Invasion of Florida, 1817." *Florida Historical Quarterly* 7 (1928), 2–71.

Deagan, Kathleen A. "Archaeology of Sixteenth Century St. Augustine." *Florida Anthropologist* 38 (1985), 18–22.

———. "St. Augustine and the Mission Frontier." In *Missions of Spanish Florida*, ed. Bonnie G. McEwan, 87–110. Gainesville: University Presses of Florida, 1993.

———. "Spanish–Indian Interactions in Sixteenth-Century Florida and Hispaniola." In *Cultures in Contact: The Impact of European Contacts on Native American Cultural Institutions, AD 1000–1800*, ed. William W. Fitzhugh, 281–318. Washington, D.C.: Smithsonian Institution Press, 1985.

Denham, James M. "The Florida Cracker Before the Civil War as Seen Through Travelers' Accounts." *Florida Historical Quarterly* 72 (1994), 453–68.

Depratter, Chester B. "The Chiefdom of Cofitachequi." In *Forgotten Centuries: Indians and Europeans in The American South, 1521–1704*, ed. Charles Hudson and Carmen Chaves Tesser, 179–96. Athens: University of Georgia Press, 1994.

———. "Cofitachequi: Ethnohistorical and Archaeological Evidence." In *Studies in South Carolina Archaeology, Essays in Honor of Robert L. Stephenson*, ed. Albert C. Goodyear III and Glen T. Hanson, 133–56. Columbia, S.C.: Institute of Archaeological and Anthropology, Occasional Papers, Anthropological Studies, 9, 1989.

De Vorsey, Louis, Jr. "Early Maps and The Land of Ayllón." In *Columbus and the Land of Ayllón: The Exploration and Settlement of the Southeast*, ed. Jeannine Cook, 1–25. Darien, Ga: Lower Altamaha Historical Society–Ayllón, 1992.

———. "Indian Boundaries in Colonial Georgia." *Georgia Historical Quarterly* 54 (1970), 63–78.

Dillon, Rodney E., Jr. "South Florida in 1860." *Florida Historical Quarterly* 60 (1982), 440–54.

Dodd, Dorothy. "The Florida Census of 1825." *Florida Historical Quarterly* 22 (1943), 34–40.

Doherty, Herbert J., Jr. "Andrew Jackson's Cronies in Florida Territorial Politics." *Florida Historical Quarterly* 34 (1955), 3–29.

———. "The Governorship of Andrew Jackson." *Florida Historical Quarterly* 33 (1954), 3–31.

Dubar, Jules R. "Florida Peninsula." In Jules R. Dubar et al., "Quaternary Geology of the Gulf of Mexico Coastal Plain," in *Quaternary Non-glacial Geology: Conterminous United States*, ed. Roger B. Morrison, 595. Boulder, Colo.: The Geological Society of America, 1991.

Dunkle, John R. "Population Change as an Element in the Historical Geography of St. Augustine." *Florida Historical Quarterly* 37 (1958), 3–32.

Dunlop, J. G. "Spanish Depredations, 1686" and "Captain Dunlop's Voyage to the Southward, 1687." *South Carolina Historical Magazine* 30 (1929), 81–89, 127–33.

Earle, Carville V. "Environment, Disease, and Mortality in Early Virginia." In *The Chesapeake in the Seventeenth Century: Essays on Anglo-American Society*, ed. Thad W. Tate and David L. Ammerman, 96–125. Chapel Hill: University of North Carolina Press for the Institute of Early American History and Culture, 1979.

Eckel, Edwin C. "Gold and Pyrite Deposits of the Dahlonega District, GA." *U.S. Geological Survey Bulletin* 213 (1902), 57–63.

Elvas, Fidalgo de. "The Account by a Gentleman from Elvas." Translated and edited by James Alexander Robertson, with footnotes and updates to Robertson's notes by John H. Hann. In *The De Soto Chronicles: The Expedition of Hernando de Soto in North America, 1539–1543*, ed. Lawrence A. Clayton, Vernon J. Knight, Jr., and Clarence C. Moore. 1: 19–219. 2 vols. Tuscaloosa: University of Alabama, 1993.

Ewel, Katherine C. "Swamps." In *Ecosystems of Florida*, ed. Ronald L. Myers and John J. Ewel, 281–323. Orlando: University of Central Florida Press, 1990.

Fabel, Robin A. "British Rule in the Floridas." In *The New History of Florida*, ed. Michael Gannon, 134–49. Gainesville: University Press of Florida, 1996.

Fairbanks, Charles H. "Creek and Precreek." In *Archaeology of the Eastern United States*, ed. James B. Griffin, 285–300. Chicago: University of Chicago Press, 1952.

Fant, H. B. "The Indian Trade Policy of the Trustees for Establishing the Colony of Georgia in America." *Georgia Historical Quarterly* 15 (1931), 207–22.

Galloway, Patricia. "The Barthelemy Murders: Bienville's Establishment of the *Lex Talionis* as a Principle of Indian Diplomacy." In *Proceedings of the Eighth Annual Meeting of the French Colonial Historical Society*, ed. E. P. Fitzgerald, 91–103. Lanham, Md: University Press of America, 1985.

García Gallo, Alfonso. "El pactismo en el reino de Castilla y su proyección en América." In *El pactismo en la historia de España*, 145–68. Madrid: Instituto de España, 1980.

Geiger, Maynard. "The Settlement of East Florida Spaniards in Cuba, 1763–1766." *Florida Historical Quarterly* 42 (1964), 216–31.

Gibson, Charles. "Caciques in Post Conquest and Colonial Mexico." In *The Caciques: Oligarchical Politics and the System of Caciquismo in the Luso-Hispanic World*, ed. Robert Kern and Robert Dolkart, 18–26. Albuquerque: University of New Mexico Press, 1972.

Goggin, John M. "Fort Pupo: A Spanish Frontier Outpost [St. Johns River, Florida, 1716?–1740]." *Florida Historical Quarterly* 30 (1951), 139–92.

Gold, Robert L. "The Settlement of the East Florida Spaniards in Cuba, 1763–1766." *Florida Historical Quarterly* 42 (1964), 216–31.

———. "The Settlement of the Pensacola Indians in New Spain, 1763–1770." *Hispanic American Historical Review* 45 (1965), 657–76.

Graff, Mary B. "Fort Picolata." *Jacksonville Historical Society Papers* 1 (1947), 50–66.

Graham, Thomas. "Spain's Two Floridas, East and West." *El Escribano* 25 (1988), 1–14.

Greller, Andrew M. "Deciduous Forest." In *North American Terrestrial Vegetation*, ed. Michael G. Barbour and W. D. Billings, 287–316. New York: Cambridge University Press, 1988.

Grimball, Paul. "Paul Grimball's Losses by the Spanish Invasion of 1686." *South Carolina Historical Magazine* 29 (1928), 231–37.

Groene, Bertram H., ed. "Lizzie Brown's Tallahassee." *Florida Historical Quarterly* 48 (1969), 155–75.

Hally, David J. "The Chiefdom of Coosa." In *The Forgotten Centuries:*

Indians and Europeans in the American South, 1521–1704, ed. Charles Hudson and Carmen Chaves Tesser, 227–53. Athens: University of Georgia Press, 1994.

Hann, John H. "Apalachee in the Historic Era." In *The Forgotten Centuries: Indians and Europeans in the American South, 1521–1704,* ed. Charles Hudson and Carmen Chaves Tesser, 327–54. Athens: University of Georgia Press, 1994.

———. "Florida's Terra Incognita: West Florida's Natives in the Sixteenth and Seventeenth Centuries." *Florida Anthropologist* 41 (1988), 61–107.

———. "Summary Guide to Spanish Florida Missions and Visitas: With Churches in the Sixteenth and Seventeenth Centuries." *The Americas* 46 (1990), 417–513.

———. "The Use and Processing of Plants by Indians in Spanish Florida." *Southeastern Archaeology* 5 (1986), 91–102.

Harris, J. Carver, ed. "The Memorial of William Walton of the City of New York, Merchant." *El Escribano* 3 (1966), 14–22.

Helms, Mary W. "Political Lords and Political Ideology in Southeastern Chiefdoms: Comments and Observations." In *Lords of the Southeast: Social Inequality and the Native Elites of Southeastern North America,* ed. Alex W. Barker and Timothy R. Pauketat, 185–94. Washington, D.C.: American Anthropological Association, 1992.

Henige, David. "If Pigs Could Fly: Timucuan Population and Native American Historical Demography." *Journal of Interdisciplinary History* 16 (1986), 701–20.

Hering, Julia. "Plantation Economy in Leon County, 1830–1840." *Florida Historical Quarterly* 33 (1954), 32–47.

Hoffman, Paul E. "Did Coosa Decline Between 1541 and 1560?" *Florida Anthropologist* 50 (1997), 25–29.

———. "Hernando de Soto: A Brief Biography." In *The De Soto Chronicles: The Expedition of Hernando de Soto to North America, 1539–1543,* ed. Lawrence A. Clayton, Vernon J. Knight, Jr., and Edward C. Moore, 1: 433–50. 2 vols. Tuscaloosa: University of Alabama Press, 1993.

———. "Legend, Religious Idealism, and Colonies: The Point of Santa Elena in History, 1552–1566." *South Carolina Historical Magazine* 84 (1983), 59–71.

———. "Narváez and Cabeza de Vaca in Florida." In *The Forgotten Centuries: Indians and Europeans in the American South, 1521–1704,* ed. Charles Hudson and Carmen Chaves Tesser, 50–73. Athens: University of Georgia Press, 1994.

Hubbell, Theodore H., A. N. Laessle, and J. C. Dickinson, Jr. "The Flint-Chattahoochee-Apalachicola Region and Its Environments." Florida State Museum *Bulletin of Biological Sciences* 1 (1956).

Hudson, Charles, Marvin Smith, Chester B. DePratter, and Emilia Kelley. "The Tristán de Luna Expedition, 1559–1561." *Southeastern Archaeology* 8 (1989), 31–45.

Jesús, Francisco Alonso de. "1630 Memorial of Fray Francisco Alonso de Jesús on Spanish Florida's Missions and Natives." Translated by John H. Hann. *The Americas* 50 (1993), 85–105.

Johnson, James Guyton. "The Yamassee Revolt of 1597 and the Destruction of the Georgia Mission." *Georgia Historical Quarterly* 7 (1923), 44–53.

Johnson, Jay K. "Chiefdom to Tribe in Northeast Mississippi: The De-Soto Expedition as a Window on a Culture in Transition." In *The Hernando De Soto Expedition, History, Historiography, and "Discovery" in the Southeast*, ed. Patricia K. Galloway, 295–312. Lincoln: University of Nebraska Press, 1997.

Jones, Grant D. "The Ethnohistory of the Guale Coast Through 1684." *Anthropological Papers of the American Museum of Natural History* 55, pt. 2 (1978), 178–210.

Jones, William M. "A Late Eighteenth Century Work Camp, St. Johns Bluff, Duval County." *Florida Anthropologist* 26 (1973), 139–42.

Juricek, John T. "The Westo Indians." *Ethnohistory* 11 (1964), 134–73.

Klos, George. "Blacks and the Seminole Removal Debate, 1821–1835." In *The African American Heritage of Florida*, ed. David R. Colburn and Jane L. Landers, 128–56. Gainesville: University Press of Florida, 1995.

Knight, Vernon J., Jr. "Social Organization and the Evolution of Hierarchy in Southeastern Chiefdoms." *Journal of Anthropological Research* 46 (1990), 1–24.

Komarek, E. V. "Fire Effects on Temperate Forests and Related Ecosystems: Southeastern United States." In *Fire and Ecosystems*, ed. C. E. Ahlgren and Theodore T. Kozlowski, 251–78. New York: Academic Press, 1974.

———. "Lightning and Lightning Fires as Ecological Forces." Tall Timbers Fire Ecology Conference *Proceedings* 8 (1968), 169–97.

Kunz, George F. "History of Gems Found in North Carolina." North Carolina Geological Survey *Bulletin*, no. 12 (1907), 29–35.

Landers, Jane. "An Eighteenth-Century Community in Exile: The *Floridanos* in Cuba." *New West Indian Guide* 70 (1996), 39–58.

———. "Free and Slave." In *The New History of Florida*, ed. Michael Gannon, 167–82. Gainesville: University Press of Florida, 1996.

———. "Gracia Real de Santa Teresa de Mose: A Free Black Town in Spanish Colonial Florida." *American Historical Review* 95 (1990), 9–30.

———. "Spanish Sanctuary: Fugitives in Florida." *Florida Historical Quarterly* 62 (1984), 296–313.

Lanning, John Tate. "Don Miguel Wall and the Spanish Attempt

Against the Existence of Carolina and Georgia." *North Carolina*
Historical Review 10 (1933), 186–213.

Larson, Lewis H., Jr. "Cultural Relationships Between the Northern St. Johns Area and the Georgia Coast." *Florida Anthropologist* 10 (1958), 11–22.

Lawson, Katherine S. "Governor Salazar's Wheat Farm Project, 1645–1657." *Florida Historical Quarterly* 24 (1946), 196–200.

Lee-Riffe, Nancy. "The Heavenly Plantation: A Seventeenth-Century Mention of Florida." *Florida Historical Quarterly* 56 (1977), 148–49.

Lewis, James A. "Cracker: Spanish Florida Style." *Florida Historical Quarterly* 63 (1984), 184–204.

Lockey, Joseph B. "The Florida Banditti, 1783." *Florida Historical Quarterly* 24 (1945), 87–107.

Lourie, Elena. "A Society Organized For War: Medieval Spain." *Past and Present* 35 (1966), 54–76.

Luer, George M., and Marion M. Almy. "Temple Mounds of the Tampa Bay Area." *Florida Anthropologist* 34 (1981), 127–55.

Lyon, Eugene, ed. "The Cañete Fragment: Another Narrative of Hernando de Soto." In *The De Soto Chronicles: The Expedition of Hernando de Soto to North America in 1539–1543*, ed. Lawrence A. Clayton, Vernon J. Knight, Jr., and Edward C. Moore. 1: 307–10. 2 vols. Tuscaloosa: University of Alabama Press, 1993.

Mahon, John K. "Two Seminole Treaties: Payne's Landing, 1832, and Fort Gibson, 1833." *Florida Historical Quarterly* 41 (1962), 1–21.

Mahon, John K., and Brent R. Weisman. "Florida's Seminole and Miccosukee Peoples." In *The New History of Florida*, ed. Michael Gannon, 183–206. Gainesville: University Press of Florida, 1996.

Manucy, Albert A. "The Physical Setting of Sixteenth Century St. Augustine." *Florida Anthropologist* 38 (1985), 34–53.

Marchena Fernández, Juan. "Guarniciones y población militar en Florida Oriental (1700–1820)." *Revista de Indias*, nos. 163–164 (1981), 91–142.

———, and Felipe del Pozo Redondo. "La emigración canaria a la Florida oriental Española (1600–1621)." Coloquio de Historia Canario-Americana, 9th. Spain. 1990, *Actas*, 1: 511–549. 2 vols. Las Palmas: Ediciones del Excelentísimo Cabildo Insular de Gran Canaria, 1977.

Matter, Robert A. "Missions in the Defense of Spanish Florida, 1566–1710." *Florida Historical Quarterly* 54 (1975), 18–38.

McEwan, Bonnie G. "San Luis de Talimali: The Archaeology of Spanish-Indian Relations at a Spanish Mission." *Historical Archaeology* 25 (1991), 36–60.

McMichael, Alan E. "A Model for Barrier Island Settlement Pattern." *Florida Anthropologist* 30 (1977), 179–95.

Milanich, Jerald T. "Tacatacuru and the San Pedro de Mocamo Mission." *Florida Historical Quarterly* 50 (1972), 283–91.

———. "The Western Timucua." In *Tacachale: Essays on the Indians of Florida and Southeastern Georgia During the Historic Period,* ed. Jerald T. Milanich and Samuel Proctor, 59–88. Gainesville: University Presses of Florida, 1978.

———, and Nara B. Milanich. "Revisiting the Freducci Map: A Description of Juan Ponce de Leon's 1513 Florida Voyage?" *Florida Historical Quarterly* 74 (1996), 319–28.

Miller, Janice B. "Rebellion in East Florida in 1795." *Florida Historical Quarterly* 57 (1978), 173–86.

Mills, Hugh H., and Paul A. Delcourt. "Quaternary Geology of the Appalachian Highlands and Interior Low Plateaus." In *Quaternary Nonglacial Geology: Conterminous United States,* ed. Roger B. Morrison, 611–26. Boulder, Colo.: The Geological Society of America, 1991.

Milner, George G. "Epidemic Disease in the Postcontact Southeast, A Reappraisal." *Mid-Continental Journal of Archaeology* 5 (1980), 39–56.

Mitchem, Jeffry M., and Brent R. Weisman. "Changing Settlement Patterns and Pottery Types in the Withlacoochee Cove." *Florida Anthropologist* 40 (1987), 154–66.

Mowat, Charles L. "The First Campaign of Publicity for Florida." *Mississippi Valley Historical Review* 30 (1943), 359–76.

———. "The Land Policy in British East Florida." *Agricultural History* 14 (1940), 75–77.

Murdock, Richard. "Governor Céspedes and the Religious Problem in East Florida, 1786–1787." *Florida Historical Quarterly* 26 (1947), 325–44.

Myers, Ronald L. "Scrub and High Pine." In *Ecosystems of Florida,* ed. Ronald L. Myers and John J. Ewel, 175–77. Orlando: University of Central Florida Press, 1990.

Neill, Wilfred T. "An Indian and Spanish Site on Tampa Bay, Florida." *Florida Anthropologist* 21 (1968), 106–116.

Nelson, T. C. "The Original Forests of the Georgia Piedmont." *Ecology* 38 (1957), 390–97.

Norwood, Olin, ed. "Letters from Florida in 1851." *Florida Historical Quarterly* 29 (1951), 261–83.

Odum, William E., and Carole C. McIvor. "Mangroves." In *Ecosystems of Florida,* ed. Ronald L. Myers and John J. Ewel, 517–48. Orlando: University of Central Florida Press, 1990.

Paisley, Clifton. "Tallahassee Through the Storebooks, 1843–1863: Antebellum Cotton Prosperity." *Florida Historical Quarterly* 50 (1971), 111–127.

Parker, Susan R. "I am Neither Your Subject nor Your Subordinate."
El Escribano 25 (1988), 43–60.

———. "Men Without God or King: Rural Settlers of East Florida,
1787–1790." *Florida Historical Quarterly* 69 (1990), 135–55.

Platt, William J., and Mark W. Schwartz. "Temperate Hardwood Forests." In *Ecosystems of Florida*, ed. Ronald L. Myers and John J.
Ewell, 209–10. Orlando: University of Central Florida Press, 1990.

Poitrineau, Abel. "Demography and the Political Destiny of Florida
During the Second Spanish Period." *Florida Historical Quarterly* 66
(1988), 420–33.

Quarterman, Elise. "A Fresh Look at Climax Forests of the Coastal
Plain." *ASB Bulletin* 28 (1981), 143–48 [Association of Southern Biol-
ogists].

Ramenofsky, Ann F., and Patricia Galloway. "Disease and the De Soto
Entrada." In *The Hernando de Soto Expedition: History, Historiography, and "Discovery" in the Southeast*, ed. Patricia K. Galloway,
259–79. Lincoln: University of Nebraska Press, 1997.

Ramirez, Susan E. "The 'Dueño de Indios': Thoughts on the Consequences of the Shifting Bases of Power of the 'Curaca de los viejos
antiguos' Under the Spanish in Sixteenth-Century Peru." *Hispanic
American Historical Review* 67 (1987), 575–610.

Rangel, Rodrigo. "Account of the Northern Conquest and Discovery of
Hernando de Soto." Translated and edited by John E. Worth with
footnotes by John E. Worth and Charles Hudson. In *The De Soto
Chronicles: The Expedition of Hernando de Soto to North America
in 1539–1543*, ed. Lawrence A. Clayton, Vernon J. Knight, Jr., and
Clarence C. Moore. 1: 247–306. 2 vols. Tuscaloosa: University of Alabama Press, 1993.

Redding, Katherine, trans. "Letter of Gonzalo Menéndez de Canço,
Governor of Florida to Philip II of Spain on June 28, 1600." *Georgia
Historical Quarterly* 8 (1924), 215–28.

———, ed. "Plans for the Colonization and Defense of Apalache,
1675." *Georgia Historical Quarterly* 9 (1925), 169–75.

Reese, Trevor R. "Georgia in Anglo-Spanish Diplomacy, 1736–1739."
William and Mary Quarterly, 3rd series, 15 (1958), 168–90.

Reitz, Elizabeth J. "Comparison of Spanish and Aboriginal Subsistence
on the Atlantic Coastal Plain." *Southeastern Archaeology* 4 (1985),
41–50.

———. "Dieta y alimentación hispano-americana en el Caribe y la
Florida en el siglo XVI." *Revista de Indias* 51 (1991), 11–24.

———. "Evidence for Coastal Adaptations in Georgia and South Carolina." *Archaeology of Eastern North America* 16 (1988), 137–58.

———. "Faunal Evidence for Sixteenth-Century Spanish Subsistence
at St. Augustine, Florida." *Florida Anthropologist* 38 (1985), 62–64.

Ross, Mary. "French Intrusions and Indian Uprisings in Georgia and South Carolina, 1577–1580." *Georgia Historical Quarterly* 7 (1923), 251–81.

———. "French on the Savannah, 1605." *Georgia Historical Quarterly* 8 (1924), 167–94.

———. "The Restoration of the Spanish Missions in Georgia, 1598–1606." *Georgia Historical Quarterly* 10 (1926), 171–99.

Rutherford, Robert E. "Settlers from Connecticut in Spanish Florida." *Florida Historical Quarterly* 31 (1952), 33–48.

Sanz Tapía, Angel. "Relaciones entre Cuba y los Indios de la Florida oriental durante el dominio Inglés (1763–1783)." In *La Influencia de España en el Caribe, La Florida, y la Luisiana, 1500–1800*, 231–308. Madrid: Instituto de Cooperación Ibero Americana, 1983.

Scarry, C. Margaret. "The Use of Plant Foods in Sixteenth-Century St. Augustine." *Florida Anthropologist* 38 (1985), 74–79.

Schafer, Daniel L. "A Class of People Neither Freemen nor Slaves: From Spanish to American Race Relations in Florida, 1821–1861." *Journal of Social History* 26 (1993), 587–609.

———. "'Everything Carried the Face of Spring': Biscayne Bay in the 1770s." *Tequesta* 44 (1984), 23–31.

———. "Plantation Development in British East Florida: A Case Study of the Earl of Egmont." *Florida Historical Quarterly* 63 (1984), 172–83.

———. "U.S. Territory and State." In *The New History of Florida*, ed. Michael Gannon, 207–30. Gainesville: University Press of Florida, 1996.

———. "'Yellow Silk Ferret Tied Round Their Wrists': African Americans in British East Florida, 1763–1784." In *The African American Heritage of Florida*, ed. David R. Colburn and Jane L. Landers, 71–103. Gainesville: University Press of Florida, 1995.

Schene, Michael G. "Sugar Along the Manatee: Major Robert Gamble, Jr. and the Development of Gamble Plantation." *Tequesta* 41 (1981), 69–81.

Siebert, Wilbur H. "The Departure of the Spaniards and Other Groups from East Florida, 1763–1764." *Florida Historical Quarterly* 19 (1940), 145–54.

———. "Slavery and White Servitude in East Florida, 1726–1776." *Florida Historical Quarterly* 10 (1931), 3–23.

Smith, Marion F., Jr., and John F. Scarry. "Apalachee Settlement Distribution: the View from the Florida Master Site File." *Florida Anthropologist* 41 (1988), 351–64.

Smith, Marvin T., and David J. Hally. "Chiefly Behavior: Evidence from Sixteenth-Century Spanish Accounts." In *Lords of the Southeast: Social Inequality and the Native Elites of Southeastern North*

America, ed. Alex W. Barker and Timothy R. Pauketat, 99–110. Washington, D.C.: American Anthropological Association, 1992.

Snow, Dean R., and Kim M. Lanphear. "European Contact and Indian Depopulation in the Northeast: The Timing of the First Epidemics." *Ethnohistory* 35 (1988), 15–33.

Snyder, James R., Alan Herndon, and William B. Robertson, Jr. "South Florida Rockland." In *Ecosystems of Florida*, ed. Ronald L. Myers and John J. Ewel, 230–80. Orlando: University of Central Florida Press, 1990.

Solana, Juan Joseph. "Juan Joseph Solana Report on the Condition of St. Augustine, 1760." Translated by Staff of the Historic St. Augustine Preservation Board, edited by Kathleen A. Deagan. In *America's Ancient City, Spanish St. Augustine, 1565–1763*, 543–76. New York: Garland Publishing, 1991.

Spellman, Charles W. "The Agriculture of the Early North Florida Indians." *Florida Anthropologist* 1 (1948), 37–48.

Stahle, David W., and Malcolm K. Cleaveland. "Reconstruction and Analysis of Spring Rainfall over the Southeastern U.S.A. for the Past 1000 Years." *Bulletin of the American Meteorological Society* 73 (1992), 1947–61.

Stahle, David W., Malcolm K. Cleaveland, Dennis B. Blanton, M. D. Therrell, and D. A. Gray. "The Lost Colony: Jamestown Droughts." *Science* 280 (1998), 564–67.

Stern, Steve. "The Rise and Fall of Indian–White Alliances: A Regional View of 'Conquest History.'" *Hispanic American Historical Review* 61 (1981), 461–91.

"St. Johns Town." Jacksonville Historical Society *Papers* 4 (1960), 85–89.

Sturtevant, William C. "Spanish-Indian Relations in Southeastern North America." *Ethnohistory* 9 (1962), 41–94.

Tanner, Helen H. "The Second Spanish Period Begins." *El Escribano* 25 (1988), 15–42.

Troxler, Carole Watterson. "Allegiance Without Community: East Florida as the Symbol of Loyalist Contract in the South." In *Loyalists and Community in North America*, ed. Robert M. Calhoon, Timothy M. Barnes, and George A. Rawlyk, 121–34. Westport: Conn: Greenwood Press, 1994.

Ventura Reja, José. "Abastecimiento y poblamiento de la Florida por la Real Compañia de Comercio de la Habana." Congreso de Historia de los Estados Unidos, Universidad de La Rabida, 5–9 Julio 1976, *Actas* (Madrid, 1978), 111–29.

Viedma, Luis Hernández de. "Relation of the Island of Florida." Translated and edited by John E. Worth. In *The De Soto Chronicles: The Expedition of Hernando De Soto to North America 1539 to 1543*, ed.

Lawrence A. Clayton, Vernon J. Knight, Jr., and Clarence C. Moore. 1: 221–46. 2 vols. Tuscaloosa: University of Alabama Press, 1993.

Vigneras, Louis-André. "A Spanish Discovery of North Carolina in 1566." *North Carolina Historical Review* 46 (1969), 398–414.

Walker, Lawrence C. "Natural Areas of the Southeast." *Journal of Forestry* 61 (1963), 670–73.

Waselkov, Gregory A. "Seventeenth-Century Trade in the Colonial Southeast." *Southeastern Archaeology* 8 (1989), 117–33.

Webb, S. David. "Historical Biogeography." In *Ecosystems of Florida*, ed. Ronald L. Myers and John J. Ewel, 92–94. Orlando: University of Central Florida Press, 1990.

Wells, B. W. "Ecological Problems of the Southeastern United States Coastal Plain." *Botanical Review* 8 (1942), 533–61.

Wenhold, Lucy L. "The First Fort of San Marcos de Apalache." *Florida Historical Quarterly* 34 (1956), 301–14.

———, trans. "Manrique de Rojas' Report on French Settlement in Florida, 1564." *Florida Historical Quarterly* 38 (1959), 45–62.

———, trans. "A 17th Century Letter of Gabriel Díaz Vara Calderón, Bishop of Cuba, Describing the Indians and Indian Missions of Florida." *Smithsonian Miscellaneous Collections* 95, no. 16 (1936).

Whatley, George, and Sylvia Cook. "The East Florida Land Commission: A Study in Frustration." *Florida Historical Quarterly* 50 (1951), 39–52.

Whitaker, Arthur P. "New Light on the Treaty of San Lorenzo: An Essay in Historical Criticism." *Mississippi Valley Historical Review* 15 (1928), 435–54.

Widmer, Randolph J. "The Structure of Southeastern Chiefdoms." In *The Forgotten Centuries: Indians and Europeans in the American South, 1521–1704*, ed. Charles Hudson and Carmen Chaves Tesser, 125–55. Athens: University of Georgia Press, 1994.

Williams, Mark. "Growth and Decline of the Oconee Province." In *The Forgotten Centuries: Indians and Europeans in the American South, 1521–1704*, ed. Charles Hudson and Carmen Chaves Tesser, 179–96. Athens: University of Georgia Press, 1994.

Winsberg, Morton D. "The Advance of Florida's Frontier as Determined From Post Office Openings." *Florida Historical Quarterly* 77 (1993), 189–99.

Worth, John E. "Late Spanish Military Expeditions in the Interior Southeast, 1597–1628." In *The Forgotten Centuries: Indians and Europeans in the American South, 1521–1704*, ed. Charles Hudson and Carmen Chaves Tesser, 104–22. Athens: University of Georgia Press, 1994.

Young, Hugh. "A Topographical Memoir of East and West Florida with Itineraries of General Jackson's Army, 1818." Introduction and anno-

tation by Mark F. Boyd and Gerald M. Pouton. *Florida Historical* BIBLIOGRAPHY
Quarterly 13 (1934), 16–50.

Young, Raymond A. "Pinckney's Treaty: A New Perspective." *Hispanic American Historical Review* 43 (1963), 526–35.

Young, Rogers W. "The Transfer of Fort San Marcos and East Florida to the United States." *Florida Historical Quarterly* 14 (1936), 231–43.

Dissertations, Theses and Unpublished Papers

Anderson, David G. "Political Change in Chiefdom Societies: Cycling in the Late Prehistoric Southeastern United States." Ph.D. dissertation, University of Michigan, 1990.

Arana, Luis Rafael. "The Spanish Infantry: The Queen of Battles in Florida, 1671–1702." M.A. thesis, University of Florida, 1960.

Arnaud Rabinal, Juan Ignacio, Alberto Bernardez Álvarez, Pedro Miguel Martín Escudero, and Felipe del Pozo Redondo. "Estructura, composición y comportamentos de la familia rural en Florida, 1600–1763." Typescript. Universidad de Sevilla, Equipo Florida, 1992. Copy at P. K. Yonge Library of Florida History, University of Florida.

Bermudez, Ligia María. "The Situado: A Study in the Dynamics of East Florida's Economy During the Second Spanish Period, 1785–1820." M.A. thesis, University of Florida, 1989.

Boniface, Brian George. "A Historical Geography of Spanish Florida, circa 1700." M.A. thesis, University of Georgia, 1971.

Calmes, Alan Royse. "Indian Cultural Traditions and European Conquest of the Georgia–South Carolina Coastal Plain, 3000 BC–1733 AD: A Combined Archaeological and Historical Investigation." Ph.D. dissertation, University of South Carolina, 1968.

Dodd, Dorothy. "Railroad Projects in Territorial Florida." M.A. thesis, Florida State University, 1929.

Gillaspie, William R. "Juan de Ayala y Escobar, Procurador and Entrepreneur: A Case Study of the Provisioning of Florida, 1683–1716." Ph.D. dissertation, University of Florida, 1961.

Green, William. "The Search for Altamaha: The Archaeology and Ethnohistory of an Early 18th-Century Yamasee Town." M.A. thesis, University of South Carolina, 1991.

Johnson, J[ames] G[uyton]. "The International Contest for the Colonial Southeast, 1566–1763." Ph.D. dissertation, University of California, Berkeley, 1924.

Johnson, Kenneth Wynne. "The Utina and Potano Peoples of Northern Florida: Changing Settlement Systems in the Spanish Colonial Period." Ph.D. dissertation, University of Florida, 1991.

Johnson, Marianne Sherry. "The Spanish St. Augustine Community, 1784–1795: A Re-evaluation." M.A. thesis, University of Florida, 1989.

Kapitzke, Robert L. "The Secular Clergy in St. Augustine During the First Spanish Period, 1565–1763." M.A. thesis, University of Florida, 1991.

Landers, Jane G. "Black Society in Spanish St. Augustine, 1784–1821." Ph.D. dissertation, University of Florida, 1988.

Lewis, Kenneth E., Jr. "History and Archaeology of Spalding's Lower Store (Pu-23), Putnam County, Florida." M.A. thesis, University of Florida, 1969.

Loucks, Lana Jill. "Political and Economic Interactions Between Spaniards and Indians: Archaeological and Ethnohistorical Perspectives of the Mission System in Florida." Ph.D. dissertation, University of Florida, 1979.

McKivergan, David A., Jr. "Migration and Settlement Among the Yamasee in South Carolina." M.A. thesis, University of South Carolina, 1991.

Pickman, Susan Lois. "Life on the Spanish-American Colonial Frontier: A Study in the Social and Economic History of Mid-Eighteenth Century St. Augustine, Florida." Ph.D. dissertation, University of New York at Stony Brook, 1980.

Reitz, Elizabeth. "Spanish and British Subsistence Strategies at St. Augustine, Florida, and Frederica, Georgia, Between 1565 and 1783." Ph.D. dissertation, University of Florida, 1979.

Romero Cabot, Ramón. "Los últimos años de la soberanía española en la Florida, 1783–1821." Tesis doctoral, Universidad de Sevilla, 1983.

Rutherford, Robert Erwin. "Spain's Immigration Policy for the Floridas, 1780–1806." M.A. thesis, University of Florida, 1952.

Shambaugh, Marion Francis. "The Development of Agriculture in Florida During the Second Spanish Period." M.A. thesis, University of Florida, 1953.

Stahl, Jeremy D. "An Ethnohistory of South Florida, 1500–1575." M.A. thesis, University of Florida, 1986.

Ward, Christopher. "East Florida During the Embargo, 1806–1812: The Quantities of Semi-Illicit Commerce." Unpublished paper on File, P. K. Yonge Library of Florida History, University of Florida. 1987.

Worth, John Eugene. "The Timucuan Missions of Spanish Florida and the Rebellion of 1656." Ph.D. dissertation, University of Florida, 1992.

Index

Paul E. Hoffman

is Paul W. and Nancy W. Murrill Distinguished Professor, Department of History, Louisiana State University and author of several books, including the prize-winning *A New Andalucia and a Way to the Orient: The American Southeast during the Sixteenth Century.*